BITTER VICTO

Lieutenant Colonel Carlo W. D'Este retired from the US Army in 1978 to write full time. Of his first book, *Decision in Normandy: The Unwritten Story of Montgomery and the Allied Campaign* Max Hastings wrote, 'The superb book establishes him at a stroke as a major military historian.' He is emerging as one of the most exciting and stimulating military historians now writing. He lives with his family in Massachusetts.

BITTER VICTORY

The Battle for Sicily
July–August 1943

Carlo D'Este

 HarperPerennial
A Division of HarperCollins*Publishers*

A hardcover edition of this book was published in 1988 by William Collins Sons
and Co. Ltd. It was first issued in a paperback edition in 1989 by Fontana Paperbacks. It is here reprinted by arrangement with William Collins Sons and Co. Ltd.
and Fontana Paperbacks.

First HarperPerennial edition published 1991.

LIBRARY OF CONGRESS CATALOG CARD NUMBER 90-55978

ISBN 0-06-097313-7 (pbk.)

91 92 93 94 95 MPC 10 9 8 7 6 5 4 3 2 1

For Eleanor
whose remarkable courage
has inspired all who
know her

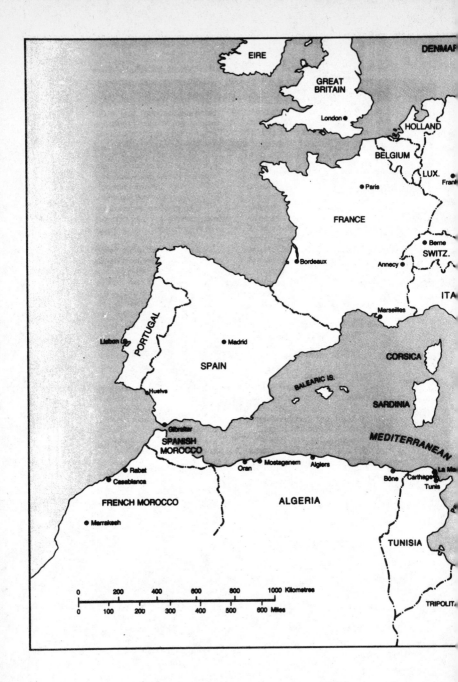

Contents

List of Maps

List of Illustrations

The 30th Corps commander, Lieutenant-General Sir Oliver Leese and
   Montgomery
   (Imperial War Museum)
Major General Lucian K. Truscott, Jr., CG, 3rd Infantry Division
   (Official US Army photograph, National Archives)
82d Airborne paratroopers near Abbio Priolo, 11 July
   (Official US Army photograph, National Archives)

A British officer observing enemy positions on the Plain of Catania
   (Imperial War Museum)
Royal Artillery gunners on the Catania front
   (Imperial War Museum)
Major General Troy H. Middleton, CG, 45th Infantry Division, confers
   with Bradley and Patton
   (Official US Army photograph, National Archives)
Air Vice-Marshal Sir Arthur Coningham, Allied Tactical Air commander
   (Official US Army photograph, National Archives)
The 13th Corps commander, Lieutenant-General Miles Dempsey and
   Major-General Guy G. Simonds, GOC, 1st Canadian Division
   (Imperial War Museum)

The Eighth Army commander, General Sir Bernard Montgomery
   (Imperial War Museum)
Major-General Vivian Evelegh and Colonel 'Paddy' Flint meet outside
   Randazzo
   (Official US Army photograph, National Archives)
US artillery forward observation post directing fire on Troina
   (Official US Army photograph, National Archives)
The 1st Infantry Division entering the ruins of Troina, 6 August
   (Official US Army photograph, National Archives)

Monty explains his strategy for the capture of Messina, 25 July
   (Official US Army photograph, Dwight D. Eisenhower Library)
The British at Sferro, 25 July
   (Imperial War Museum)
The 15th Army Group commander, General Sir Harold Alexander and
   General Dwight D. Eisenhower, Allied C-in-C, Mediterranean
   (Official US Army photograph, Dwight D. Eisenhower Library)
Patton delivers his famous apology to the 1st Infantry Division, 27 August
   (Official US Army photograph, Dwight D. Eisenhower Library)

Major General Geoffrey Keyes accepting the surrender of Palermo, 22 July
   (Official US Army photograph, National Archives)
The captured Italian general Porcinari with his staff
   (Imperial War Museum)
The citizens of Palermo greet the arrival of the 2nd Armored Division, 22
   July
   (Official US Army photograph, National Archives)
Sicilians and US troops celebrating the liberation of Messina, 17 August
   (Official US Army photograph, National Archives)

Acknowledgments

The writing of *Bitter Victory* was undertaken at the suggestion of Nigel Hamilton, Montgomery's official biographer, who became aware of the need for such an account during the research and writing of *Monty: Master of the Battlefield, 1942–1944*, the second volume of his trilogy on the life of Field-Marshal Montgomery. I am exceedingly grateful to both Nigel and his father, the late Sir Denis Hamilton, for permission to use and quote from the Montgomery Papers* which fill what would otherwise have been an enormous void in the story of the Sicily campaign.

The recollections, comments and criticisms of a considerable number of people have been instrumental in the writing of this book. In fact, it is fair to state that it could not have been written without this assistance. Time has largely healed the wounds of the savage war that engulfed the world from 1939 to 1945, even though to recall the Sicily campaign has for many veterans undoubtedly evoked painful memories. Nevertheless, without reservation my many requests for assistance have been met with courtesy and candour. I gratefully take this opportunity to express my gratitude for their contributions: Ralph Bennett; Clay Blair; Martin Blumenson; J. E. Browne; B. Max Corvo; Richard G. Davis; Colonel Bryce F. Denno, USA Ret.; John S. D. Eisenhower; General Sir Victor Fitzgeorge-Balfour; Lieutenant Colonel Burkhardt Franck (*Bundeswehr*); Major-General John D. Frost; Romano Giachetti; J. W. Hunt; Lieutenant-General Sir Ian Jacob; Allen L. Langdon; Sir Harry Llewellyn; Colonel Kenneth P. Lord, USA Ret.; Alfred Otte; Brigadier C. A. Ramsay; David Ramsay; the late Professor Vice Admiral Friedrich Ruge; Colonel Edwin M. Sayre, USA Ret.; the Rt. Hon. the Lord Scarman; Dr John Sweetman; Major-General R. E. Urquhart; the late Colonel Benjamin H. Vandervoort, USA Ret.; Brigadier H. B. C. Watkins; the late General Albert C. Wedemeyer, USA Ret.; Reverend George B. Wood; K. M. White; Brigadier Peter Young; and the Rt. Hon. the Lord Zuckerman, who once again made his personal papers at the University of East Anglia available to the author.

Special thanks to Air Chief Marshal Sir Harry Broadhurst who provided an airman's view of the Sicily campaign, and to Brigadier James A. Oliver, the executor of General Wimberley's estate. Brigadier Oliver, who commanded the 7th Black Watch in Sicily, kindly provided a copy of 'Scottish Soldier' and other documents relating to the operations of the 51st (Highland) Division and commented upon a portion of the manuscript. The

* The Montgomery Papers are now deposited in the Imperial War Museum, Department of Documents.

13

late Lieutenant General James M. Gavin, USA Ret.; the late General I. D. White, USA Ret. and General Robert W. Porter, Jr., USA Ret. all read portions of the manuscript and graciously shared their recollections of the Sicily campaign. General Sir Charles Richardson likewise took time to read and comment on a number of chapters. Georg Schmitz, ably assisted by translator John Hillyer, provided an extremely useful account of the German side of the battle for Primosole bridge. Former parachutist and German historian Helmut Wilhelmsmeyer, who has written two outstanding articles about this battle for the *British Army Review*, offered many important comments, helped track down information about the 1st Parachute Division and generously furnished maps and photographs. Several of the maps in the text are based on these excellent maps.

Lieutenant Colonel Joseph W. A. Whitehorne the historian of the US Army, Office of the Inspector General, kindly supplied the court-martial papers of the 45th Division incident at Biscari. Once again, Sir Edgar Williams graciously took time to read and comment upon the final proofs of the manuscript.

I am indebted to Major General George S. Patton, USA Ret. and Mrs Ruth Ellen Totten, who kindly granted access to their father's important collection of personal papers in the Library of Congress. Brigadier Shelford Bidwell read a portion of the manuscript, offered innumerable suggestions and provided answers to many of my questions from his vast knowledge of the British Army. Official British intelligence historian Edward E. Thomas again proved an invaluable and illuminating guide through the labyrinth of secret intelligence and deception. He also read the intelligence portions of the manuscript and I am sincerely grateful for his important contributions.

I gratefully record my thanks to official Canadian historian Dr William J. McAndrew of the Historical Section, National Defence headquarters, Ottawa for critiquing the entire manuscript and for providing many of the important documents detailing the operations of German forces in Sicily. Bill McAndrew has shared his considerable knowledge of the Sicily campaign and his incisive and thoughtful criticisms have proven an exceptionally important element in the evolution of this book. I hasten to add that sole responsibility for any errors in the book are entirely the author's.

During my travels researching *Bitter Victory* I was able to renew many old acquaintances and to make new ones at the various British and American archives, libraries and other institutions visited. Others with whom I only had written communication were equally helpful. Each invariably made my task easier and to each I express my sincere appreciation. In the United Kingdom: Air Commodore H. A. Probert and the staff of the Air Historical Branch, Ministry of Defence, London; the staff of the Naval Historical Branch, Ministry of Defence, London; the Keeper and always helpful staff of the Public Record Office, Kew, London; the Manuscript Division of the British Library; the Commonwealth War Graves Commission; Mrs Deirdre Sharp, Lord Zuckerman's archivist at the University of East Anglia, Norwich; Miss Patricia Methven, archivist of the Liddell Hart Centre for Military Archives, King's College, London; Major G. Norton, the Airborne Forces Museum, Aldershot; the Director and staff of the Imperial War Museum: Department of Documents, Department of Printed Books, Department of Photographs, Department of Film, and Department of Sound Records.

In the United States: the American Battle Monuments Commission; the Public Affairs Office, 1st Infantry Division (Mech), Fort Riley, Kansas; the staff of the Falmouth (Massachusetts) Public Library, particularly Cindy Mills and Toni Robertson of the Inter-Library Loan Department who cheerfully and efficiently filled my endless requests for books, documents and microfilm; Dr Dean C. Allard who heads the Operational Archives Branch of the Naval Historical Center, Washington Navy Yard has been especially helpful, as has been archivist Martha Crawley. Also the staffs of the Manuscript Division, Library of Congress; Modern Military Branch, National Archives; the Washington National Records Center (National Archives), Suitland, Maryland; the Hoover Institution on War, Revolution and Peace, Stanford University. Dr John E. Wickman and the archivists of the Dwight D. Eisenhower Library, Abilene, Kansas have again gone out of their way to be helpful. The Italian embassy, Washington, DC, and Thomas F. Burdett, curator of the S. L. A. Marshall Military History Collection, University of Texas at El Paso.

Very special thanks to the Director and staff of the US Army Military History Institute, Carlisle Barracks, Pennsylvania. USAMHI proved the richest source of unpublished material relating to the Sicily campaign. In addition their library is an equally important source of World War II historiography. My time at USAMHI was greatly enhanced by the efficiency and helpfulness of the staff: former director, Colonel Donald P. Shaw; current director, Colonel Rod Paschall; archivist-historian Dr Richard J. Sommers; David A. Keough; John J. Slonaker; Dr Edward J. Drea and visiting professor Dr Claude C. Sturgill. Also at Carlisle Barracks is the US Army War College and several of its faculty members have been especially supportive and helpful. I am grateful to Dr Michael I. Handel; Colonel Henry Gole, who kindly translated several important German documents; Dr Jay Luvaas and Dr Harold C. Deutsch.

Grateful acknowledgement is made to Her Majesty's Stationery Office for permission to quote copyright material in C. J. C. Molony, *The Mediterranean and Middle East*, Vol. V, and S. W. Roskill, *The War at Sea*, Vol. III, Part I; to William Kimber & Co Ltd for permission to quote from Sir David Cole, *Rough Road to Rome*, and Hugh Pond, *Sicily*; to Buchan & Enright, Publishers, Ltd for permission to quote from Major-General John Frost, *A Drop Too Many* (new and enlarged edition); to Hamish Hamilton Ltd and McGraw-Hill Book Company for permission to quote from Nigel Hamilton, *Monty: Master of the Battlefield, 1942–1944*; to E. P. Dutton, Inc., for permission to quote from Lucian K. Truscott, *Command Missions*; to Mica Publishing Co. for permission to quote from Strome Galloway, *The General Who Never*

Was; to William Collins Sons and Co. Ltd for permission to quote from Colonel Dick Malone, *Missing From the Record*; to Henry Holt & Co. permission to quote from Omar N. Bradley, *A Soldier's Story*; to Brigadier James A. Oliver for permission to quote from 'Scottish Soldier', the unpublished memoirs of Major-General Douglas Wimberley; to Field-Marshal Montgomery's son, Viscount Montgomery of Alamein, for permission to quote from his father's personal correspondence; and to the Trustees of King's College, University of London, for permission to quote from the Liddell Hart and Alanbrooke Papers in the Liddell Hart Centre for Military Archives; to Helmut Wilhelmsmeyer and the *British Army Review* for permission to reproduce the maps appearing in 'The Battle for Primosole Bridge', Part I, April 1985, and Part II, August 1985.

I am especially grateful to Stuart Proffitt of Collins who painstakingly guided the manuscript into its final form and to Gillian Gibbins for her perceptive guidance and encouragement during the early stages of the book's development, and to my dear friend, Harry Brack, for his warm hospitality during an extended research trip to London in 1984. Lastly, to my wife, Shirley Ann, my indebtedness for her help, devotion and endurance during the four years of research and writing of *Bitter Victory*.

CARLO D'ESTE
Cape Cod, Massachusetts
July 1987

Introduction

As 1942 drew to a close, the first serious cracks began to appear in the great Nazi war machine which had vanquished Europe and was now attempting to dismember Russia. On the Eastern Front the Wehrmacht now found itself engaged in a life and death struggle against the Red Army. The onset of the harsh Russian winter had left the German Army severely overextended and vulnerable to the great Red Army counteroffensive which, by February 1943, saw the annihilation of Field Marshal Friedrich von Paulus' Sixth German Army in the frozen hell of Stalingrad.

In the West a dramatic turnabout in the fortunes of the Allies took place near a wind-blown and fly-infested railroad siding on the Egyptian border with Libya. There, a little known British general led a revitalized Eighth Army to a dramatic victory over Field Marshal Erwin Rommel's celebrated Panzer Army Afrika. Thereafter, the names of both El Alamein and Bernard Montgomery were forever immortalized in the annals of military history, and an exultant Churchill later proclaimed that: 'Before Alamein we never had a victory. After Alamein we never had a defeat.'[1]

The British victory at Alamein had strategic results far beyond its immediate significance as the first major setback suffered by Rommel, who was the first senior German commander to foresee Alamein's long-term implications. As a result, he urged Hitler to withdraw German forces from North Africa while there was still time. By late 1942, Rommel considered further Axis presence in North Africa a futile gesture and at the Fuehrer's headquarters complex near Rastenburg, deep in the forests of East Prussia, he told Hitler that there was no hope of victory and 'the abandonment of the African theatre of war should be accepted as a long term policy. There should be no illusions about the situation and all planning should be directed towards what was attainable. If the Army remained in North Africa, it would be destroyed.'[2]

---

[1] Winston S. Churchill, *The Hinge of Fate*, Boston, 1950, p. 603.
[2] B. H. Liddell Hart (Ed.), *The Rommel Papers*, London, 1953, p. 365.

Rommel's warning was not welcomed and Hitler, who failed repeatedly to comprehend the peril of reinforcing failure, flew into a rage and refused to hear of the plight of his forces in North Africa who were desperately short of manpower, weapons, equipment and fuel. This advice was spurned and despite mounting evidence that the tide had turned in favour of the British, Hitler, who never considered North Africa anything more than a side-show, almost gleefully snubbed Rommel by creating Fifth Panzer Army under General Jurgen von Arnim. Thus he ensured the needless sacrifice of some of the Wehrmacht's finest units at a time when on the Eastern Front German forces were being annihilated with shocking rapidity. Hitler's decision to reinforce North Africa with some 100,000 additional troops came far too late, and ultimately meant only that they were to help prolong the war there until the spring of 1943.

Operation TORCH, the Anglo-American invasion of Morocco and Algeria in November 1942, sealed the fate of Axis forces in North Africa. As Montgomery pursued Rommel's retreating army toward Tripoli, the Allied task force commanded by General Dwight D. Eisenhower moved into Tunisia where the two sides would eventually fight it out in the early months of 1943. When Rommel and his men arrived after an odyssey of over 1,200 miles, Axis forces in Tunisia were over 200,000 strong and fully determined to resist to the bitter end. Although the Allies soon found themselves mired in the mud of the Tunisian winter, it was evident to those responsible for implementing Hitler's strategy that the days of the Axis in North Africa were numbered.

It was equally obvious to both the German and Italian high commands that with the massive air, sea and ground forces at their disposal the Allies would soon strike elsewhere in the Mediterranean once the Tunisian campaign ended. When this reality was finally driven home to Hitler, not even he was in any doubt that the Allies would quickly invade somewhere in southern Europe. The only unanswered question was *where*? Sicily, barely eighty miles off the Tunisian coast, was the gateway to Italy and an obvious target. What Hitler did not know was that the Allies had become greatly divided over future strategy and it was not until the secret Casablanca Conference in January 1943 that agreement was reached to invade Sicily once Axis forces in North Africa were defeated.

For some time Allied planners had been pondering various options for future operations. Churchill and the British Chiefs of Staff were firmly committed to a Mediterranean strategy which would not only exert pressure on the Axis but which would support the Red Army by drawing German reinforcements away from their beleaguered Eastern Front. Moreover, Churchill was anxious to knock Mussolini and the Italians out of the war for good, and by nibbling away at the 'soft underbelly' of Germany the Prime Minister was buying time for the planning and preparation of a cross-Channel invasion of Northern France.

General George C. Marshall, the architect of American strategy, strongly disagreed, arguing for direct action against Germany by means of a cross-Channel invasion in 1943. Although some historians later advanced the notion that an invasion of Europe in 1943 was feasible, we can now see that militarily this was simply not so. Although the bold Anglo-Canadian hit and run raid against Dieppe in August 1942 demonstrated an heroic defiance of Nazi hegemony of Europe, its tragic results explicitly affirmed once and for all that the Allies had yet to master the problems of joint amphibious operations and that a successful invasion of Europe in the near future was out of the question.

When Churchill and Roosevelt met at Casablanca there was considerable uncertainty over the outcome and what strategy the Allies would adopt. After considerable wrangling between the British and US Chiefs of Staff, a compromise strategy eventually was reached. The United States conceded to the British demand for further military operations in the Mediterranean in return for renewed planning action for the inevitable cross-Channel operation, soon to be code-named OVERLORD. The Allies would exploit their Mediterranean success by invading the island of Sicily. Although the composition of the Allied force and the details of the invasion had yet to be fully determined, Eisenhower was given command of what was to be known as Operation HUSKY.

Ever since man first began to wage war, Sicily has been a battleground of immense strategic importance. Yet, in the years since the Second World War, the brutal battles fought in Sicily in 1943 have become all but forgotten. In the memoirs of the principal military and political figures, Sicily has become a brief and unpleasant interlude between the North African and the later campaigns in Italy and Northwest Europe. Despite lacking the mystique now accorded other, better known battles – El Alamein, Normandy and Arnhem, for example – Sicily was nevertheless one of the most important campaigns fought by Anglo-American forces during the war.

The first Allied operation – TORCH – owed its success more to a lack of enemy resistance than as the result of brilliant planning and flawless execution. HUSKY marked the first assault on 'Fortress Europa' by any Allied force, and the first *real* test of the military compatibility of two nations with very different philosophies of war. TORCH had been planned in London and Washington; HUSKY would be the first major operation planned in the field by its participants.

Sicily laid the foundations and set the trend for the decisive battles which followed in 1944. Not all of the fruits of the Allied victory in Sicily were sweet, for the campaign generated controversial divisions of opinion over military strategy and generalship. The campaign brought together the dominant military commanders whose leadership ultimately decided the outcome of the war: Eisenhower, Tedder, Montgomery, Patton, Bradley and (in Italy) Alexander. Although the broad outline of the Sicilian campaign is generally well known, several key phases have never been fully documented, including a little publicized blunder that was to haunt the Allies during the Italian campaign.

Despite the enormous wealth of literature about the Second World War, little has been written about Sicily. Other than the official British, American and Canadian campaign histories,[1] this is the first study of the campaign based upon the full range of official and unofficial primary sources now available.

The official histories focus mainly on the role of their own forces in the campaign. *Bitter Victory* is intended to fill this void. Fortunately, the wealth of unpublished material about Sicily permits the undertaking of an in-depth examination of the second largest amphibious operation ever mounted, those who masterminded it and the ordinary soldiers of both sides who fought there.

For thirty-eight days during the summer of 1943 the attention of

---

[1] C. J. C. Molony, 'History of the Second World War', *The Mediterranean and Middle East*, Volume V, London, 1973; Albert N. Garland and Howard McGaw Smyth, 'U.S. Army in World War II: Mediterranean Theater of Operations', *Sicily and the Surrender of Italy*, Washington, 1965; and G. W. L. Nicholson, 'Official History of the Canadian Army in the Second World War', Volume II, *The Canadians in Italy, 1943–1945*, Ottawa, 1956.

the world centred upon Sicily where yet another chapter in the island's violent history was written by modern warriors. This is the story – much of it never previously written – of how the battle for Sicily was conceived, planned and carried out by the Allies, and how the Germans and their reluctant Italian ally succeeded in turning what ought to have been a great triumph into a bitter victory.

Prologue

By mid-1943 most Italians were thoroughly sick of the war and the misery it had brought them. Beginning with the 1936 invasion of Ethiopia, they had been involved in one campaign or another for seven years as their dictator Benito Mussolini attempted to ape the glory days of the great Roman empires which had dazzled the world with feats of military victory and cultural achievement. Mussolini 'never tired of telling Italians that he had worked selflessly for them; he had tried to give them backbone and make them into a great power that would inspire fear and admiration; under his guidance they had for the first time in history given the rest of humanity a doctrine and style of life, for which Italians would one day be grateful ... History would prove him correct ...'[1]

Instead, Mussolini brought his people an old form of dictatorship wrapped in new cloth. In public, Il Duce's actions were designed to support the claim that he was a great Italian patriot; in private he boasted of being the Duce of Fascism first and the leader of Italy second.[2] The empty sham of what Mussolini had actually brought the Italian people was glaringly evident, and most wanted an end to the war by any means. Nowhere was there greater despair and less hope than on the island of Sicily where invasion and war had become the twin curses of a harsh existence that was as ancient as its civilization.

Ever since Man had discovered the means of conveying himself from one place to another by boat, the island of Sicily has been a beacon beckoning the explorers and conquerors of every major race inhabiting the Mediterranean. From the earliest period of recorded history Sicily has become one of the great racial melting pots of the world. A nineteenth-century account describes the great racial diversity of Sicily where barons, Arab villagers, Saracens, Jews, Franks, Amalfitans and Pisans might all be found within a few miles of one another. Cities contained Greek, Roman

---

[1] Denis Mack Smith, *Mussolini*, London, 1981, pp. 364–5.
[2] Ibid., p. 364.

or Lombard influence where one might find the Latin Mass modified according to Gallican liturgy alongside Greek rites and ceremonies, and rules and discipline of Mosaic law. Streets teemed with a vast array of costumes ranging from Arab robes to the iron mail of Norman knights.[1]

Sicily is the largest island in the Mediterranean, roughly the size of Switzerland, and is named for a Mediterranean tribe called the *Sicels* who lived on the island during the Bronze Age. The earliest traces of human habitation date from around 20,000 BC. Throughout its history Sicily has been a land of migrating peoples, starting, it is believed, with the Neolithic period (4000–3000 BC) through the Copper Age (c. 3000–2000 BC) and the Bronze Age (c. 2000–1000 BC), with one tribe or race often displacing another.

The first of the great empires in Sicily came about 757 BC when the first Greek settlement appeared at Naxos, located at the mouth of the strategically important Strait of Messina which divides Sicily from the toe of the Italian boot around what is today the province of Calabria. The Greeks called the 9,926 square mile island *Trinacria*, for its triangular shape. During the following centuries most of eastern and southern Sicily was colonized by the Greeks and western Sicily by the Carthaginians and Phoenicians. The most famous Greek settlement was the independent city-state of Syracuse which became for more than 500 years the focal point of Greek authority and the power of Greek tyrants. The Peloponnesian Wars brought about the inevitable clash between Athens and Syracuse. The Athenians invaded in 415 BC in what proved an ill-fated venture. Their rival Sparta sent Syracuse a soldier called Gylippus, 'an officer who proved as implacable and crafty as a Prussian junker.'[2] The siege was broken by the generalship of Gylippus who sealed the fate of the Athenians in the harbour of Syracuse. Their celebrated clash was vividly recorded by the first and possibly the best war correspondent who ever lived, Thucydides,[3] who described how the 7,000 Athenian survivors were sold into slavery, where most died.

The fabled Greek empire in Sicily was crushed during the Sec-

---

[1] I. La Lumia, *History of Sicily under William the Good, 1867*, in John Julius Norwich, *The Kingdom in the Sun*, London, 1976, p. xi.

[2] E. V. R. Wyatt, 'Sicilian Lands: The Past of a Checkered Isle', *Commonweal*, August 1943.

[3] *The Peloponnesian Wars*, New York, Modern Library edition, 1951.

ond Punic War (218–201 BC) by the Romans who subjected the island to the most dismal period of cruelty, tyranny and neglect in its history. The land was plundered; many of the native Sicilians were added to the already large slave populace and the wealth of the land wantonly pillaged by corrupt Roman officials. Dislike and distrust of later Italian governments may well have had its origins during these years.

The centuries following the Roman period saw conquest after conquest as races from Europe and Africa succeeded one another in the occupation of Sicily: Vandals, Goths, the Byzantines under their famous general Belisarius and the Lombards who overran northern Sicily. The Saracens invaded in 827 and fought for fifty years before forcing the capitulation of Syracuse and ousting the Byzantines. Sicily then fell under Moslem rule until the coming of the Norman knights in 1061 brought an unprecedented period of revival and culture called 'The Kingdom in the Sun'. The Normans were followed by Swabians, Angevins, Aragonese, British, Spanish and Bourbons, all of whom ruled Sicily at one time or another until 1860 when Garibaldi, the father of modern Italy, led the Sicilians to victory over 3,000 Neapolitans near Palermo which began the process of Italian unification.

Perhaps no other place on earth has been subject to more war, invasion and foreign domination than Sicily. Most towns and cities were situated on mountain tops which even today still show evidence of a long history of fortification. Its people have evolved into a hardy breed of iron-willed, independent-minded people who mistrust outsiders and the outside world. The tormented legacy of Sicily is that the island not only became a breeding ground for poverty over the centuries but it also spawned the growth of crime on a large scale and led to the emergence of a criminal organization known throughout the rest of the world as the Mafia.

There is uncertainty over the origin of this term and how it was coined.* We do know that Sicily's centuries of continuous occupation and the need by the feudal land barons to protect their property and their authority resulted in the creation of small mercenary armies called *compagnie d'armi*. In the beginning these

---

* It is thought to have come from either the word *machfil*, which is the Arab word for union used by the Saracen conquerors of the ninth century, or *maffa*, the Tuscan word for poverty or misery.

served only the interests of the landowners and meted out their own form of 'justice'. Gradually, the leaders of the *compagnie* made accommodations with the outlaws they were paid to destroy. These primitive armies eventually became virtually a law unto themselves and the landowners hostages to their own creation. By playing both sides these groups committed outrages with impunity. Landowners, other bandits — anyone in fact who stood in their way was ruthlessly killed.[1] Rules for the behaviour of all parties emerged, among them the code known as *omertà* which demanded that members take a blood oath never to break a code of silence. Those who did soon died a hideous death that included removal of their tongues. In Sicily the term *omertà* meant more than merely a code of bandits and thieves: it applied equally to the individual family where it was a matter of honour for a victim or anyone in his family to remain silent, not to protect the offender but because it was believed that the responsibility for avenging a wrong lay with the victim or his family.

It was not until the nineteenth century that the word 'Mafia' began to be heard and even then it had two meanings. As Luigi Barzini points out, the term 'mafia' [with a small 'm'] was and still is:

> a state of mind, a philosophy of life, a conception of society, a moral code, a particular susceptibility, prevailing among all Sicilians. They are taught in the cradle, or are born already knowing, that they must aid each other, side with their friends and fight the common enemies even when the friends are wrong and the enemies are right; each must defend his dignity at all costs and never allow the smallest slights and insults to go unavenged; they must keep secrets, and always beware of official authorities and laws.[2]

The second and commonly known 'Mafia' was spawned in part from the first. These secret organizations, loosely aligned as families, were wedded together by marriage, blood and the code of *omertà*. Since then, western Sicily has become the virtual fiefdom of the Mafia where the code of *omertà* and mistrust of the mainland Italian government administered in Sicily by outsiders led to two levels of government and law, with the Mafia in *de facto* control of most of Sicily. The notion that the largely autonomous

[1] Luigi Barzini, *The Italians*, New York, 1964, pp. 258–9.
[2] Ibid., pp. 253–4.

groups which controlled their own local districts were protectors of the peasants is a cruel myth. The peasant was – and indeed continues to be to this day – terrorized, blackmailed into paying tribute, and ruthlessly killed if he dared to seek the assistance of the government or the courts. The dismal result has been a tyranny far worse than that imposed by Sicily's foreign conquerors.

In spite of their oppression, the Sicilians have become a proud people in an impoverished land where the middle class was largely non-existent and the chasm between the enormous wealth of the Mafia dons and the absentee landlords was in stark contrast with the abject poverty of the peasants. Left with little to sustain him but his honour,* the Sicilian is suspicious of outsiders, is notoriously touchy and takes offence – sometimes mortal – over the slightest provocation. Vendettas have been known to occur over the ownership of a lemon tree, a goat, or a real or imagined slight to one's wife or daughter. Quarrels were settled not by the law but by the knife, the garotte or the gun. Sometimes such problems were settled by the local Mafia leader, at other times with his implicit consent. The hostility with which outsiders were viewed was so powerful that it is still not unheard of for a Sicilian to refuse to give even the simplest directions to a stranger.

Mussolini attempted to stamp out the Mafia and its influence in Sicily in the mid-1920s with only modest success. Extraordinary methods such as the suspension of elections and the jury system, torture and summary execution were all used to deal a crippling but not mortal blow to the Mafia's pervasive hold on Sicily. The year 1943 signalled the beginning of a resurrection that, more than forty years later, has left the Mafia as powerful as ever and, until

---

* Honour to the Sicilian and Italian assumes an importance not always understood elsewhere. Sir David Hunt relates the story in the Western Desert in 1941 when the British captured 130,000 Italians of Marshal Graziani's Tenth Army at Beda Fomm. 'Arriving in front of one of the smaller camps [the 7th Armoured Division Support Group commander] sent in an Italian prisoner under a flag of truce to call on the commander to surrender. The prisoner was not long in coming back with the Italian General's reply, which was to the effect that, having been entrusted with the command of this fortified camp, he considered it his duty, for the honour of the Italian Army, to defend it to the last round and the last drop of blood.' As the British commander prepared to lay siege to the camp the emissary proceeded to explain the meaning of the Italian commander's message. 'The General wishes you to understand that he cannot surrender the fort until you have at least opened fire. If however you will be good enough to fire one round he will then be only too pleased to comply with your request.' After the ceremonial round was duly fired, the white flag was raised and the garrison trooped out with their personal effects neatly packed. (David Hunt, *A Don at War*, London, 1966, p. 53.)

recently, the central government powerless to curb their activities.

Sicilians had long since grown accustomed to Mussolini's broken promises. Shortly after bringing the Fascist revolution to Italy he decreed that he would soon solve the problem of poverty-stricken southern Italy. Arriving at Messina in a battleship, escorted by submarines and aircraft, Il Duce assured the Sicilians that their poverty would be turned into riches within the next ten years. He claimed awareness of the dreadful effects of the sulphur mines and expressed shock that more than fifteen years after the Messina earthquake* thousands were still living in poverty in shanty towns under conditions that 'dishonoured the human race'. 'He said that he would not sleep until he had tackled it, adding that he would not make such a promise unless he knew he could keep his word.'[1] In 1943, twenty years later, the shanty towns still existed and the plight of its occupants – indeed, of the populace as a whole – was even grimmer as a result of the war.

If the average Sicilian was stoical about the war and his place in it he could be forgiven, for if Sicily was once again to become the object of an invasion by a foreign force, it was merely a repetition of history. His patriotism was less to Italy than it was to his own land, and the presence of yet more outsiders – this time the Italian Army and units of Hitler's Wehrmacht – was simply another form of unwelcome occupation. While many undoubtedly feared the consequences of an Allied invasion, others saw it as a means of ending the wretched war which had only exacerbated their privation.

In addition to Sicily's strategic importance in the Mediterranean, the island's resources were crucial to the Axis war effort. Before the war, Sicily was the world's largest producer of sulphur outside the United States. In 1940, Sicily produced about 500,000 tons and since then had supplied two-thirds of all this vital resource used by the Axis. Otherwise, Sicily remained a largely ignored outpost of the Fascist empire. No longer: in 1943, war came once again to the troubled island.

---

[1] *Mussolini*, op. cit., pp. 106–7.

* On 28 December 1908, a catastrophic earthquake destroyed 90 per cent of Messina and took 83,000 lives. At an estimated 7.5 on the Richter scale, Messina ranks in the top ten worst earthquakes of history. (Source: *The World Almanac*, 1985 edition.)

PART I

The Road to Sicily

The main lines of offensive action in the Mediterranean
will be the occupation of Sicily.

'The Conduct of the War in 1943'
(Final report of the Casablanca Conference)

CHAPTER 1

Casablanca

The US regarded the Mediterranean as a kind of dark hole, into which one entered at one's peril.

JACOB[1]

The first step along the road which carried the Allies across North Africa and into Sicily commenced with the TORCH landings in Algeria and Morocco by an Anglo-American invasion force the morning of 8 November 1942.

Eleven months earlier the Japanese attack on Pearl Harbor on 7 December 1941 brought the United States into the war. When Hitler was informed that the Japanese raid had brought about a state of war with the United States, he slapped his thighs with joy and exulted that this was 'the turning point'. 'Now it is impossible', he boasted, 'for us to lose the war: we now have an ally who has never been vanquished in three thousand years.'[2]

Germany and Italy issued declarations of war on 11 December 1941. Mussolini's pronouncement from the balcony of the Palazzo Venezia was received with gloom by the Italian people, most of whom did not want war with America. Il Duce regarded the United States with ill-concealed derision and Americans as a stupid and uncultured people in a land of Jews and Negroes. Mussolini's arrogance and naïveté were manifest in his dismissal of the United States as a second-rate power whose industrial capacity was nothing more than a journalistic hoax, and whose military importance was so negligible that its involvement in the war would be of little consequence. Well before Pearl Harbor he had contemplated severing diplomatic relations.[3]

---

[1] Operation 'Symbol', the unpublished Diary of Brigadier Ian Jacob.
[2] David Irving, *Hitler's War 1939–1942*, London, 1983, p. 352.
[3] Denis Mack Smith, *Mussolini*, pp. 317–18.

From the outset of their grand alliance Britain and the United States held sharply divergent strategic views over how the war against the Axis and Japan should proceed. For the British the war had been a calamitous series of reversals ever since April 1940. Norway, Dunkirk, Greece, Crete, Burma, Hong Kong, Dieppe and Tobruk all entered the lexicon of British military disasters. In Malaya the single worst defeat in British military history ended with the surrender of the 85,000 men of Lieutenant-General Percival's army in Singapore in February 1942. Less visible was the Battle of the Atlantic where the Allies were losing the battle with German U-boats which were sinking Allied shipping faster than it could be replaced. When Hitler unleashed Operation BARBAROSSA – the surprise attack against Russia in June 1941 – more than three million German ground troops supported by three thousand tanks and two thousand aircraft swarmed over a front extending from the Black Sea to the Arctic, catching the Russians flatfooted.[1] The Allies were now on the defensive both in the Pacific and in Europe.

Any action to restore the balance in the Far East was clearly out of the question for the foreseeable future, as was Churchill's vision of a return to Nazi-held Europe where the decisive campaign would have to be fought. Only in the Mediterranean was there any immediate possibility of reversing the tide of German success.

In early 1941 Hitler had sent an expeditionary force to North Africa to bolster the sagging fortunes of the Italians whose Tenth Army had suffered a crushing defeat in Cyrenaica at the hands of a British force under the command of Lieutenant-General Sir Richard O'Connor whose brilliant leadership produced the first tangible British victory of the war. For the next eighteen months the British had little else to sustain their morale as the Eighth Army fought a series of losing battles against the Afrika Korps across the vastness of the North African Desert. By July 1942 the Eighth Army was defending the final German obstacle to Egypt: Alam Halfa.

Churchill had already removed General Sir Archibald Wavell as Commander-in-Chief, Middle East, in 1941, and in early August 1942 did the same to General Sir Claude Auchinleck. The arrival of General Sir Harold Alexander and Lieutenant-General Bernard

---

[1] *Hitler's War 1939–1942*, op. cit., pp. 272–3.

Montgomery began a new era of British fortune and a reversal of the humiliating defeats of 1941 and 1942.*

American focus had always been to defeat Germany by the most direct means possible irrespective of political considerations. At the ARCADIA Conference in December 1941 and January 1942 the Allies had agreed to 'tighten the ring' by placing priority on the defeat of Germany over operations in the Pacific against Japan. US Army Chief of Staff, General George C. Marshall, relentlessly pursued the development of sufficient forces and equipment to mount a cross-Channel invasion of northern France. Marshall wanted no part of any Allied operations in the Mediterranean but by the summer of 1942 there was no agreement as to what the Allies would do and where they would do it. As the alliance began to take shape so too did the proposals put forward by each partner. Operation SLEDGEHAMMER was, for example, a plan conceived by the British for an emergency cross-Channel invasion if the situation on the Eastern front deteriorated so badly that the Red Army verged on collapse or in the unlikely event of the German position in Western Europe becoming weakened. This plan was created to compel Hitler to shift Wehrmacht units to France and was attractive to Marshall as a means of implementing direct American involvement.

At Marshall's instigation the Army planning staff modified SLEDGEHAMMER into a joint Anglo-American cross-Channel offensive to be carried out in the summer of 1942. The chief architect of what became known as the Marshall Memorandum was an obscure brigadier general named Dwight Eisenhower. In practice, however, SLEDGEHAMMER was never even remotely feasible, as neither participant in 1942 could organize, equip and train a force of sufficient size complete with the necessary amphibious craft.† The plan devised by Eisenhower called for a large build-up of US forces in the United Kingdom preparatory to a cross-Channel operation in 1943 (Operation BOLERO). ROUNDUP was a British

---

* In the final months of his command Auchinleck had been both C-in-C, Middle East, and GOC, Eighth Army. Alexander became the new C-in-C on 15 August 1942.

† According to General Albert C. Wedemeyer's insider's account, Marshall and his planners were never naïve enough to believe that SLEDGEHAMMER was anything more than a sacrificial diversion to be carried out 'only under extreme emergency conditions . . . Actually Americans continued to advance the idea of SLEDGEHAMMER simply to restrain wild diversionary efforts proposed by the British Prime Minister . . .' (Cf. General Albert C. Wedemeyer, *Wedemeyer Reports!*, New York, 1958, p. 135.)

plan for a massive operation against the continent of Europe in 1943. Churchill strongly opposed SLEDGEHAMMER and at a conference held in Washington in June 1942 succeeded in obtaining American agreement for an entirely new plan called GYMNAST – a joint Anglo-American operation to seize French North Africa as a basis for further action against Axis forces elsewhere in the region.

Taken together, both BOLERO and ROUNDUP were exactly what Marshall desired and in return for American acceptance of GYMNAST the British agreed to these two operations. Moreover, GYMNAST greatly pleased Roosevelt who was anxious to find a suitable role for American combat forces as soon as possible. With no realistic possibility of a joint invasion of Europe before the spring or summer of 1943, he was unwilling to tolerate American inactivity; GYMNAST solved the dilemma to his satisfaction. Marshall was displeased but forced to accede to Roosevelt's wishes. Since the possibility of an invasion of northwest Europe in 1942 no longer existed, Marshall was compelled to accept the reality of an American commitment to military operations in the Mediterranean.

The result was agreement to mount Operation TORCH in November 1942. Separate invasion forces from the United States and Britain were to rendezvous off North Africa where three task forces landed simultaneously. The Western Task Force, commanded by Major General George S. Patton, Jr, sailed directly from the eastern United States and seized Casablanca, Safi and Port Lyautey on the Atlantic side of French Morocco. The other two task forces landed at Oran and Algiers. Afterwards the new Anglo-American command – christened Allied Force Headquarters (AFHQ) – carried the battle to the Axis forces in Tunisia where it was hoped eventually to trap the Afrika Korps between the Allied invasion force* and Montgomery's Eighth Army.

TORCH was the first of many compromises between the Allies. Although the respective Chiefs of Staff had been unable to agree upon a joint strategy, both Churchill and Roosevelt were in firm agreement that the Allies must launch an attack against the Axis in 1942.[1] This decision delighted the British and well illustrates the

---

[1] Michael Howard, *Grand Strategy*, Vol. IV, London, 1972, pp. xx.

* The combat elements of the new Allied force were designated 18th Army Group in February 1943, under the command of Alexander. The primary units consisted of Lieutenant-General Kenneth Anderson's First British Army and II US Corps under the command of Major General Lloyd R. Fredendall.

opportunistic nature of Britain's Mediterranean strategy. At a stroke Churchill had committed the United States to support of the joint policy of 'tightening the noose' his way – that is, by means of operations in the Mediterranean where the British were in serious trouble. Like the fox set loose amongst the chickens, Churchill knew that, once committed, it was unlikely the United States could avoid further military action elsewhere in the Mediterranean. Moreover, Churchill's concession to BOLERO and ROUNDUP was merely a bowing to the inevitable at no cost whatsoever to British grand strategy. Conversely, the American commitment to TORCH left the British with a major bargaining chip in future negotiations, as they were to prove in January 1943 at Casablanca.

In retrospect, it now seems that the obvious choice for the Allies after the conclusion of operations in North Africa was to reinforce their initial success in the Mediterranean by an invasion of Sicily. However, as 1943 began it was very far from obvious to the participants, for the question of future strategy deeply divided the Allied leadership.

The grave position of the Russians in 1941 and 1942 led Stalin to press his new-found western allies for material assistance in the form of tanks, guns, ammunition and aircraft which, in turn, led to the Lend-Lease programme and its shipments to Russia via Murmansk. Stalin also insisted that the only way to relieve the pressure on the Red Army was for the Allies to open a second front in the west. When Churchill met Stalin in Moscow in August 1942 he proposed a meeting between the Big Three allies in December 1942 or January 1943 but Stalin refused, making it clear that without a firm commitment to a second front he saw no reason to meet the Prime Minister and Roosevelt.

Not only was it urgent for the United States and Britain to resolve their strategy for a second front, but there were equally pressing reasons to arrive at agreement for joint action following the North African campaign. Clearly, the western leaders could not face Stalin without first arriving at answers to these questions. In a cable to Roosevelt in early December, Churchill had responded to Roosevelt's suggestion for a meeting with the Prime Minister at either Algiers or Khartoum, saying that 'I will meet you anywhere'. Churchill was especially pleased because 'at present we have no plan for 1943 which is on the scale or up to the level of events'. Moreover, Churchill knew that Stalin 'will greet us with the question "Have you then no plan for the second front in Europe you promised me for 1943?" [1] The Casablanca Conference – code-named Operation SYMBOL – was organized to provide answers to this question.

Churchill had previously suggested Iceland or Alaska as possible meeting sites, but Roosevelt preferred a North African site. The Prime Minister had spent a delightful month in 1936 at Marrakesh located at the base of the Atlas Mountains of Morocco and when it proved impossible to establish the necessary communications at Marrakesh a compromise was soon arrived at: the two Allied leaders would meet at Casablanca in mid-January 1943.

Churchill sent Brigadier Ian Jacob* to North Africa to locate a suitable site at Casablanca and he found a small hotel in the peaceful suburb of Anfa, overlooking the Atlantic. Anfa was an ideal site with many nearby villas able to cope with the large number of visitors who attended the conference. As Jacob noted, 'the amazing thing was that it didn't seem to matter how many more people arrived, the hotel and villas managed to cope. They appeared to be made of elastic, and the food and drink never ran short.' [2]

The British contingent was headed by Churchill and the Chief of the Imperial General Staff, General Sir Alan Brooke, the brilliant and reserved spokesman for the Chiefs of Staff. Also present were the Air and Naval chiefs, Air Chief Marshal (later Marshal of the Royal Air Force) Sir Charles Portal, and Admiral Sir Dudley Pound, the quiet and courtly First Sea Lord whose health was deteriorating, notably from a brain tumour which was to result in his untimely death in October 1943.

The principals arrived at Casablanca backed by a large and

---

[1] Cable, Churchill–Roosevelt, 2 December 1943, quoted in Warren F. Kimball (ed.), *Churchill & Roosevelt, The Complete Correspondence*, Princeton, 1984, Volume II, pp. 55–6.

[2] Jacob Diary, loc. cit.

* Jacob was one of the two military assistants to General Sir Hastings Ismay, the Chief of Staff to Churchill in his capacity as Minister of Defence. When he became Prime Minister in 1940 Churchill elected to keep the Defence portfolio for himself, believing he could not effectively prosecute the war effort unless he kept firm control of the war machinery. In turn a military staff, including a group known as the Joint Planning Staff (JPS), was created to fulfil Churchill's requirements. It was headed by Ismay, a charming and competent officer who was esteemed by British and Americans alike and who, after the war, became the first Secretary-General of NATO. A description of the Joint Planning Staff appears in Chapter 3.

well-organized support staff, many of whom were concealed aboard a small liner converted for use as a headquarters ship for combined operations. The British intended that the support normally provided the Chiefs of Staff in Whitehall be duplicated at Casablanca, believing that 'the best policy would be to take a full bag of clubs, leaving some of them concealed as it were in the locker, i.e., the ship'.[1]

British preparation was equally thorough. Before departing from London, the Chiefs of Staff hammered out a series of position papers and generally agreed upon a joint approach which Brooke, as their spokesman, would elucidate. 'The British were greatly helped by preparation – both practical in terms of staff work and intellectual in terms of earlier dispute between themselves and with the Prime Minister. There was much to be said for the British Chiefs of Staff system of committee debate, and for the vigorous and often exhausting probes and intervention of their political head. It meant that minds were thoroughly prepared, and few counter-arguments were new.'[2]

The British possessed a priceless advantage in the presence of Field-Marshal Sir John Dill, the former CIGS. Now the senior representative of the British Chiefs of Staff in Washington, Dill was one of the unsung heroes of the Allied side and a man who gave his life in the service of furthering Anglo-American co-operation. He had succeeded Field-Marshal Sir Edmund Ironside as the CIGS in May 1940 but did not prosper against the combative personality of Churchill with whom he was frequently at odds. Replaced as CIGS by Brooke, Dill was exiled to Washington as the head of the British Staff Mission where he was enormously successful in dealing with the US military chiefs. He became a great friend and close confidant of Marshall who unburdened himself to Dill as he did with few other men. The American Chiefs of Staff treated him as one of themselves. 'Nothing he said or did gave offence, and when he died [in November 1944], worn out by care and over-work, the American armed forces displayed their feelings by burying him in Arlington Cemetery with their own heroes.'[3]

Brooke had immense respect for Dill and valued his counsel. At

[1] Ibid.
[2] David Fraser, *Alanbrooke*, London/New York, 1982, p. 313.
[3] John Colville, *The Churchillians*, London, 1981, p. 94.

Casablanca he was to be a pivotal figure for both sides: an ambassador to the Americans as well as a counsellor to the British through his knowledge of how the Americans viewed the various issues.

On the first afternoon, the British Chiefs huddled with Dill who warned them of the American aversion to further commitments in the Mediterranean and their apprehension that the British failed to understand their problems in the Pacific against Japan and might renege on the promise to support operations there once Germany was defeated. Adding to the problem, said Dill, was the division of opinion between the Army and Navy – with the Navy concerned almost exclusively with operations and the allocation of resources in the Pacific.[1]

That evening Dill and the Chiefs of Staff met with Churchill who outlined the British approach to the conference. Time was not important; there was to be full discussion of the issues without impatience, like 'the dripping of water on a stone'. While the Combined Chiefs of Staff* sought agreement in conference, Churchill would quietly work on Roosevelt, and in about ten days things would fall into place. The Prime Minister's goals for the conference were ambitious: the 'cleansing of North Africa to be followed by the capture of Sicily, the reconquest of Burma and perhaps even an invasion of northern France on a modest scale'.[2]

The American delegation was small and by comparison woefully unprepared to face the organized British, a mistake they would never make again. Marshall was preoccupied with the war in Europe, while the Chief of Naval Operations, the outspoken Admiral Ernest J. King, was primarily concerned with US naval operations in the Pacific. The British were extremely wary of Admiral King who controlled the production and allocation of all US landing craft. While they respected King as a sound navy man, they were concerned that his habit of speaking his mind in a blunt

---

[1] Jacob Diary. US forces had finally won the long and bloody campaign for Guadalcanal which was the turning point of the war in the Pacific. Henceforth, the United States would go on the offensive against Japan. Dill's observation was not entirely correct; Marshall backed Admiral Ernest J. King's argument that the US must raise the allocation of resources in the Pacific so that the hard-won initiative would not permit Japanese forces time to regroup.

[2] Ibid.

* The term Combined Chiefs of Staff (CCOS) was given to the US and British Chiefs of Staff operating together to formulate strategic policy and command guidance. The Casablanca Conference was in reality a series of informal discussions of the CCOS.

manner might prove a disruptive influence. Not surprisingly, Brooke and the British Chiefs of Staff argued that the allocation of landing craft proposed by King for European operations was wholly inadequate and that if the Allies were to live up to the terms of the ARCADIA Conference, then priority must go to the defeat of Germany. The third member of the American delegation was General H. H. 'Hap' Arnold who headed the Army Air Forces. As the junior US chief, Arnold tended to leave matters of global strategy to Marshall.*

With considerable justification one American historian asserts that 'the blame for this American disarray must be laid at the feet of President Franklin D. Roosevelt, who seemed to have no strategy of his own. Before leaving for Casablanca Roosevelt held only one meeting on 7 January, the result of which could be summed up as "no conclusions". His "policy" was "wait and see".'[1] The failure to come to Casablanca prepared to deal with the British placed the full burden of American argument squarely on to the shoulders of George Marshall.

Marshall has been called 'the organizer of victory', and his official biographer has written that he was 'the perfect blend of soldier and civilian'.[2] No single American was more responsible for organizing and guiding the United States' war effort to victory than this modest man who was the heart and conscience of the United States Army. Marshall commanded universal respect for his leadership and vision which guided the Army through an immensely complex transition from a pathetically ill-equipped, inadequate peacetime force to the mighty war machine that eventually numbered nearly eight million men in the Army and Army

[1] John S. D. Eisenhower, *Allies*, New York, 1982, p. 220.

[2] Forrest C. Pogue, *George C. Marshall: Organizer of Victory, 1943–1945*, New York, 1973; Volume III of Pogue's four-volume biography of Marshall. One of the most endearing tributes to Marshall's leadership is by Air Force Major General Elwood Quesada: 'I think that Marshall was the aristocrat of our time . . . the most selfless man that has reached public office in the last century in this country.' (Oral history transcript of 23 May 1975, USAMHI). President Harry S. Truman later wrote: 'The more I see and talk to him the more certain I am he's the great one of the age.' (Quoted in Roy Jenkins, *Truman*, London, 1986, p. 97.) An example of Marshall's selflessness was the case of General Arnold, the senior airman of the US Army Air Forces, which were under the control of the Army which was represented on the Joint Chiefs of Staff by Marshall. At Marshall's instigation Arnold was made a full member of the JCS in recognition of the important role of airpower in the war.

* Arnold's principal concern at Casablanca was to overcome Churchill's opposition to the American proposal to commence daylight strategic bombing of Germany by the US Eighth Air Force in England. Although obtaining new airfields in Sicily and Italy was attractive, HUSKY ranked fairly low in Arnold's priorities.

Air Forces.* Both as Army Chief of Staff and as Brooke's counter-part as chairman of the US Chiefs of Staff, Marshall was at one and the same time no less than the most powerful and most modest military figure in American military history. Roosevelt relied heav-ily upon his counsel and although the British considered him somewhat less than brilliant as a strategist, they nevertheless deeply respected him.

The American contingent had left most of its experts and prin-cipal staff officers back in Washington; it was only after arriving in Casablanca that they learned the extent of the British organization and preparations. There was a wild scramble as they 'went out into the highways and byways of North Africa and scraped together some sort of staff . . . but both they and we were handi-capped all the way through by their lack of staff and nearly every paper produced during the conference had to be produced by our people with little or no help from the Americans'.[1]

One of Marshall's chief advisers was Brigadier General Albert C. Wedemeyer, a member of the War Plans Division of the War Department. A 1919 graduate of West Point, Wedemeyer was an infantry officer who had attended the German War College (*Kriegsakademie*) in Berlin from 1936 to 1938. As one of the few American officers able to think and plan on a global scale, Wedemeyer conceived American grand strategy with its corner-stone the build-up of a powerful war machine to invade Europe at the earliest possible date.† Wedemeyer later became Marshall's trouble-shooter and his eyes and ears, which included the Sicily campaign.

Wedemeyer was present throughout the Casablanca Confer-ence and recalled with admiration and envy how the British 'swarmed down upon us like locusts, with a plentiful supply of planners and various other assistants to insure that they not only accomplished their purpose but did so in stride and with fair promise of continuing in the role of directing strategy the whole course of this war . . . it was apparent that we were confronted by generations and generations of experience in committee work, in

---

[1] Jacob Diary, loc. cit.

* An indicator of US unpreparedness was that in September 1939 when Hitler invaded Poland and the Second World War broke out, George S. Patton was a colonel in command of a regiment of *horse* cavalry at Fort Myer, Virginia.

† The Marshall Memorandum prepared by Eisenhower in 1942 was the means by which the United States planned to implement the strategy devised by Wedemeyer in 1941.

diplomacy, and in rationalizing points of view. They had us on the defensive practically all the time.'[1]

The British had four major objectives at Casablanca: the exploitation of TORCH to the fullest, beginning with the removal of Italy from the war. This was the foundation of British policy; both Brooke and Churchill reasoned that the loss of Italy, the ineptness of her armed forces notwithstanding, would be a severe blow which would provide Germany no respite, especially when combined with the increased bombing of heartland Germany, continuation of logistical support to Russia, and the ongoing build-up of BOLERO forces in the United Kingdom with a view to carrying out ROUNDUP in August or September 1943 if conditions warranted.[2]

The question of priorities was the first major sticking point between the Combined Chiefs when they met for the first time on 14 January. The US position was a 70%/30% split in the allocation of resources to Europe over the Pacific, while Brooke demanded that nearly everything go to Europe. As expected, King argued for greater priority to the Pacific in the first of a series of stormy sessions that saw the Americans on the defensive without an agreed counterproposal.

In response to Brooke's brusque assertion that the US was failing to emphasize the defeat of Germany, Marshall was equally blunt in his reply that the British appeared content with pursuing a Mediterranean strategy at the expense of BOLERO and ROUNDUP, the operations which would ultimately defeat Germany. British actions in the Mediterranean were doing nothing to solve this problem. After a good deal of frustration and strenuous debate, a compromise was finally arrived at which resolved the question of what would be done in the Pacific.* It now became a matter of finding common ground for a strategy in Europe.

---

[1] *Wedemeyer Reports!*, op. cit., p. 192. Wedemeyer viewed the British and their protestations of friendship with grave suspicion. 'To the British – negotiating, arguing, and fighting in the international arena – the true friend might be the man who could be manipulated or enticed to see things as the British themselves saw them. There was no give and take between British and American planners. It was all "take" on their part, with the pattern established by centuries of negotiation and now symbolized by the voluble Mr Churchill and the sensitive Sir Alan Brooke' (p. 188). Six months earlier Wedemeyer had grown weary of being misquoted by his British counterparts and obtained Marshall's permission to 'bug' his office. Henceforth, all conversations with British officers were secretly recorded (pp. 164–5).

[2] *Allies*, op. cit., p. 221.

* The British agreed to US operations in the South Pacific, and later in 1943 the reconquest of Burma, all of which were to be accomplished within existing resources.

As Brooke's biographer has written, the fundamental difference of opinion between the two Allies was:

> what form the 'strategic offensive in the Western European theatre' should take. True to his original view that the Mediterranean was a blind alley to which American forces had only been committed because of the President's insistence that they should fight the Germans somewhere; and reinforced in that view by the protracted nature which the North African campaign was assuming, Marshall considered that operations in North Africa should be closed down immediately Eisenhower's campaign in Tunisia had achieved victory. Thereafter, all forces should be transferred to the United Kingdom for ROUNDUP as early as possible.[1]

Portal, the able and pragmatic British air chief, recognized the British held the whip hand and proposed a compromise. Despite deep admiration for Brooke who had the unwelcome task of keeping Churchill's feet planted firmly on the ground whenever he put forward one of his wilder schemes, the Prime Minister is reputed to have considered Portal the ablest of the British Chiefs of Staff and the one upon whose judgment he relied most.[2]

In a now famous memorandum Portal outlined the necessity for compromise by reminding his colleagues that some American demands simply could not be ignored. 'We are', he wrote with tongue in cheek, 'in the position of a testator who wishes to leave the bulk of his fortune to his mistress. He must, however, leave something to his wife, and his problem is to decide how little he can in decency leave apart for her'; a problem complicated by the fact that the 'wife' was the US who already owned most of the 'fortune'.[3]

Back and forth went the arguments over four difficult days that left both parties weary. Brooke's diary catalogues the difficulty in reconciling their differences. On the fourth day, disheartened and exhausted, he wrote: 'A desperate day. We are further from agreement than we ever were.' By the following day Brooke was ready to toss in the towel. 'It's no use,' he lamented, 'we shall never get agreement with them.' The astute Dill, who knew Marshall and the Americans far better, disagreed. 'On the contrary,' he told

[1] *Alanbrooke*, op. cit., p. 314.
[2] *The Churchillians*, op. cit., p. 145.
[3] *George C. Marshall: Organizer of Victory, 1943–1945*, op. cit., p. 27.

Brooke, 'you have already got agreement to most of the points and it only remains to settle the rest.'[1]

Portal's paper and Dill's wise counsel were the two most important factors in swaying the reluctant American chiefs into agreement over Anglo-American strategy for Europe. As Dill predicted, the few remaining differences – mainly in the form of assurances that the pressure would be kept on Japan – were resolved in a joint paper that was presented to Churchill and Roosevelt. 'We were congratulated by both of them ... and informed that we had produced the most complete strategic plan for a world-wide war that had ever been conceived, and far exceeding the accomplishments of the last war.'[2] One of its main provisions was the invasion of Sicily.

The idea of invading Sicily first surfaced in London during the summer of 1942 when the War Cabinet's Joint Planning Staff began to examine possible operations in 1943 by British forces. Two important strategic objectives in the Mediterranean emerged: Sicily and Sardinia, and code-names for each were assigned, HUSKY for Sicily and BRIMSTONE for Sardinia.

On 8 July 1942 the British Commanders-in-Chief in the Mediterranean had met to consider the feasibility of capturing Sicily with a British task force consisting of two infantry-divisions, one armoured brigade group plus supporting troops, naval and air cover, with a third infantry division held in reserve in Egypt. But the fall of Tobruk and the retreat of the Eighth Army to the Egyptian frontier near El Alamein quickly ruled out any possibility of an all-British invasion of Sicily in the foreseeable future.

One of the functions of planning is to explore the feasibility of attacking a wide variety of targets of strategic and tactical importance, ranging from targets of opportunity to a full-scale invasion. Since it is impossible in war to predict a course of events it becomes vital that high-level planners prepare for any eventuality so that an opportunity can be seized should the Combined Chiefs of Staff elect to exploit a particular situation. Although there was no

[1] Arthur Bryant, *The Turn of the Tide*, London, 1957, pp. 548–50. Brooke would later write: 'I am certain that the final agreement being reached was due more to Dill than anybody else... I owe him an unbounded debt of gratitude for his help on that occasion and in many other similar ones.'

[2] Ibid., p. 559.

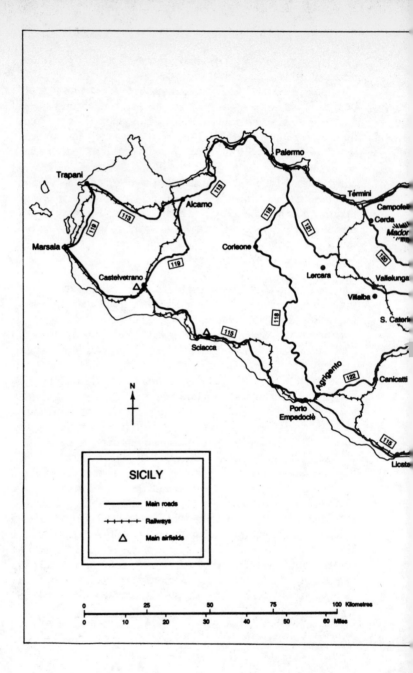

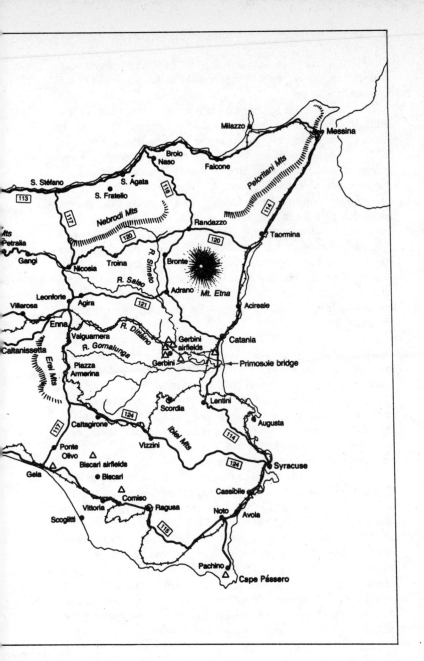

CCOS approval to invade either Sicily or Sardinia, action continued throughout the remainder of 1942 to develop outline plans for both operations.

The joint planners found merit in both HUSKY and BRIMSTONE. Both islands in Allied hands represented a serious threat to the Axis in France and Italy. Sardinia offered the advantage of being far less strongly defended and thus capable of being captured several months earlier than Sicily, where a larger and more complex invasion plan was required. While Sardinia was an excellent base of operations for the air forces, it had far less to offer ground forces other than as a base for commando raids against southern France or the Italian mainland. The main drawback was Sardinia's lack of harbours and beaches suitable for an invasion or for staging amphibious operations against France or Italy. Moreover, with Sicily under Axis control it was evident that if Allied air and naval forces could not close the Strait of Messina – which was not considered feasible by the planners – then the only alternative was an invasion.

The official US naval history incorrectly states that there was a straight division of opinion between the two, with the British in favour of Sardinia and the Americans opting for Sicily. In fact, the British came to Casablanca united in favour of invading Sicily. One of Brooke's highest priorities was to obtain agreement for the invasion of Sicily and, as he later wrote, 'we had many debates on the relative advantages of Sardinia and Sicily before leaving England, and it was only at the end of much hard work that I had obtained general agreement on Sicily'.[1]

Brooke was deeply annoyed when at the last moment the Joint Planning Staff decided to submit a paper which declared that the necessary preparations for Sicily could not possibly be accomplished prior to August 1943, while a Sardinian operation was possible by the end of June even if only British forces were available. Furthermore, the problem facing the naval forces could be solved more easily by an invasion of Sardinia. If the Germans reinforced Sicily prior to an invasion, the planners believed HUSKY would fail. The same, they argued, did not apply to Sardinia. 'Much as we should like to take Sicily, we feel that, against the odds for which we must at present allow, the operation is not

[1] Ibid., p. 557.

practicable. We therefore recommend the capture of Sardinia to be followed by Corsica as soon after as possible.'[1]

This bombshell came as a bitter blow to Brooke who now found his carefully orchestrated plans suddenly undermined by his own planners. He placed much of the blame upon Admiral Louis Mountbatten, the head of Combined Operations and an officer in whom the CIGS was not overly confident. Although Mountbatten was a member of the Chiefs of Staff Committee from March 1942 until he became Supreme Commander in Southeast Asia in October 1943, Brooke was never happy about his presence on the committee, which he considered inappropriate.[2] There were times when Mountbatten exasperated Brooke's patience and Casablanca was certainly one of them. Two weeks earlier the CIGS had recorded in his diary: 'One of the most awful C.O.S. meetings when Mountbatten and Dudley Pound drive me completely to desperation. The former is quite irresponsible, suffers from the most desperate illogical brain and is always producing red herrings; the latter is asleep 90% of the time and the remaining 10% is none too sure what he is arguing about.'[3]

Mountbatten was a favourite of Churchill, a man of intense enthusiasm, unbounded energy and an immense ego whose job it was to produce ideas and plans which could be employed in combined operations. Some of the ideas he and his staff produced were visionary, such as the Mulberry artificial harbours used in the invasion of Normandy in June 1944. Others were of a less practical nature, such as his non-sinkable ship made of huge blocks of ice. At a conference of the Combined Chiefs of Staff in Quebec in August 1943 Mountbatten demonstrated his theory by pulling a revolver out of his pocket and firing several times at ice blocks set up in the conference room. The last bullet ricocheted off the ice and flew about the room, narrowly missing the amazed chiefs. Quebec had begun with another stormy conference and the room

---

[1] War Cabinet Joint Planning Staff Paper J.P. (43) 18 (Final), 'Brimstone' versus 'Husky', 9 January 1943, Public Record Office [hereinafter cited as PRO], London (PREM 3 – 327/1).

[2] *Alanbrooke*, op cit., p. 208.

[3] Alanbrooke Diary. One of the reasons why Brooke supported Mountbatten's appointment as Supreme Commander, Southeast Asia, later in 1943, was his conviction that Mountbatten would be less of a menace out of London. In the event, Brooke undoubtedly lamented his decision, for Mountbatten proved to be more obsessed with his own vision of 'Pomp and Circumstance' than he was with effectively prosecuting the war in Southeast Asia.

had been cleared of all but the principals. Outside one wit was heard to shout, 'Good heavens, they have started shooting now!'[1]

At Casablanca, Mountbatten came out in favour of Sardinia and confided this to Admiral King who recorded that 'Mountbatten cautioned us not to say anything to anybody about his urging the attack on Sardinia instead of Sicily.'[2]

If Mountbatten thought he had an ally in King he was quite mistaken. King scorned the idea of Sardinia as 'merely doing something just for the sake of doing something', noting that eventually Sicily would have to be taken and the time to do it was now.[3] Churchill came to Casablanca fully behind the concept of invading Sicily and on more than one occasion was heard to refer to Sardinia as 'that piddling operation'. Pound favoured Sicily if the US Navy provided the necessary support to augment the Royal Navy, but both Portal and Ismay began to waver as a result of Mountbatten's lobbying tactics and the warning from the joint planners. Churchill fully supported Brooke but for different reasons. As Jacob noted in his diary: 'The Prime Minister had to take account of the size of any projected operation. Whatever we decided to undertake in 1943 would have to be represented to Stalin as something very big. The Prime Minister's nature also favoured large and spectacular events. Taking all these things together, the PM had bounded straight to the conclusion that the only objective in the Mediterranean worth going for was Sicily.'[4]

In the end Brooke won the day by force of argument. Mountbatten's annoying habit of interrupting discussions to make points of detail during consideration of matters of principle destroyed what little influence he might have otherwise enjoyed within the Chiefs of Staff Committee.[5] Brooke was a stubborn man and adamant that his carefully laid plans should not become unravelled at this late stage thanks to Mountbatten and the joint planners. The night of 21 January he recorded that: 'All my arguments with Marshall had been based on the invasion of Sicily and I had obtained his agreement. And now suddenly the Joint Planning Staff reappeared on the scene with a strong preference for Sardinia and expressing

[1] Quoted in *The Turn of the Tide*, op. cit., p. 714.
[2] Papers of Fleet Admiral Ernest J. King, Library of Congress.
[3] Samuel Eliot Morison, *History of United States Naval Operations in World War II*, Vol. IX: *Sicily–Salerno–Anzio*, Boston, 1954, p. 9.
[4] Jacob Diary, loc. cit.
[5] Ibid.

most serious doubts as to our ability to take on the Sicily operation. They had carried with them Mountbatten who never had any
very decided opinions of his own . . . Peter Portal and "Pug" Ismay
were beginning to waver, and dear old Dudley Pound was, as
usual, asleep . . .'[1]

The final hurdle for the British was what Brooke called a three-
hour 'hammer and tongs battle to keep the team together. I told
them that I flatly refused to go back to the American Chiefs of Staff
and tell them that instead of Sicily, we now wanted to invade
Sardinia. I told them frankly that I disagreed with them entirely
and adhered to our original decision to invade Sicily and would
not go back on it.'[2]

Despite his dislike of anything to do with the Mediterranean,
Marshall was never in doubt of the merits of invading Sicily as the
best of the options available and had in fact come to Casablanca
resigned to the fact that Sicily would undoubtedly become the next
Allied target. If his arguments against further operations in the
Mediterranean failed and the Allies were to remain there, then
Marshall accepted Sicily as vitally necessary to shorten the lines of
communication and to open up the entire Mediterranean to Allied
movement. In his opinion, Sardinia was nothing more than a
threat to Italy.[3]

At the CCOS meeting on 22 January 1943 Brooke still had
misgivings that if the question of Sardinia was raised the Americans would not countenance the idea and opt instead to shut down
operations in the Mediterranean altogether. He need not have
worried, for Marshall and the US Chiefs fully backed an invasion
of Sicily and the matter was at last settled to the immense relief of
the CIGS. In order to ensure there would be no unnecessary delay
in the invasion, both Churchill and Roosevelt sent letters to their
respective Chiefs of Staff stating that HUSKY should occur, if
possible, during the June moon.

The other problem that had bothered the CIGS had been settled
several days earlier when he got American agreement to the
appointment of Alexander as the ground Commander-in-Chief
for Tunisia and future operations, including Sicily. Brooke's initial

---

[1] *The Turn of the Tide*, op. cit., p. 557, and Alanbrooke, *Notes on My Life*.
[2] Ibid., pp. 557–8.
[3] George C. Marshall, interview with Howard McGaw Smyth, 25 July 1949, US Army
Military History Institute [hereafter cited as USAMHI], Carlisle Barracks, Pennsylvania.

impression of Eisenhower as a commander and strategist was unfavourable and never changed throughout the remainder of the war. In North Africa it was evident to Brooke that Eisenhower had spread himself too thinly in a losing attempt to be both a field commander and a Supreme Commander at the same time. Brooke did not believe Eisenhower was up to the task of performing this dual role; Eisenhower's physical condition and the general disarray of the new Allied force certainly bore out Brooke's contention. The solution was to appoint Alexander as the commander of all Allied ground forces, soon to be known as 18th Army Group.*

As Brooke saw it: 'Up to now Eisenhower . . . had neither the tactical or strategical experience required for such a task. By bringing Alexander over from the Middle East and appointing him as Deputy to Eisenhower, we were carrying out a move which could not help flattering and pleasing the Americans in so far as we were placing our senior and most experienced commander to function under their commander who had no war experience . . . We were pushing Eisenhower up into the stratosphere and rarefied atmosphere of a Supreme Commander, where he would be free to devote his time to the political and inter-allied problems . . .'[1]

There was, however, one major flaw in the agreement reached at Casablanca. It established Sicily as an end in itself rather than as the first step in an agreed joint strategy for the Mediterranean. Undoubtedly because of American distrust of the Mediterranean the question of what would follow Sicily was left undecided. To have further demanded an invasion of mainland Italy after Sicily would have further stiffened Marshall's determination to detach US forces from the Mediterranean and send them to the United Kingdom for ROUNDUP. If Sicily did indeed knock Italy out of the war there was no guarantee that Hitler would not order the occupation of Italy by German forces. Thus, while an invasion of the Italian mainland was neither a certainty nor a subject of Allied agreement, there is no doubt both parties left Casablanca with the tacit understanding that further operations against Italy were inevitable. Brooke felt it was a mistake not to have resolved the question, but the final communiqué said nothing; officially the course of future Allied action beyond Sicily was uncharted. The

[1] *The Turn of the Tide*, op. cit., p. 556.
* Montgomery's Eighth Army remained independent until it advanced into Tunisia, at which time it would come under Alexander's operational control.

failure to provide Eisenhower with a mandate for further operations was to prove a crucial omission throughout the remainder of 1943.

Another decision taken at Casablanca was to have enormous effects that are still being felt today. This was the announcement that the Allies would only accept an unconditional surrender from Germany, a declaration that has been judged one of the most tragic and disastrous mistakes of the entire Second World War.[1]

The Casablanca agreement was a stunning triumph for British grand strategy. Brigadier Jacob who drafted the final agreement document wrote that 'if I had written down before I came what I hoped [for] . . . I could never have written anything so sweeping, so comprehensive, and so favourable to our ideas . . . [which] prevailed throughout'.[2]

Credit for this success must be given to Brooke, the dour Ulsterman who, until made famous in Arthur Bryant's two postwar accounts, was all but unknown even within Britain.[3] Many believe and few would dispute that Brooke was the best general produced by Britain during the war. He lived in the shadow of the fame of Montgomery, whose public image soared to great heights after the famous victory over Rommel at Alamein, and the immensely popular Alexander. Yet Brooke had proved his mettle both on the battlefield and in the boardrooms of Whitehall where he battled not only the problems of fighting a war on fronts spanning the entire globe but took responsibility for formulating war policy. Though he and Churchill were frequently at odds over policy matters, it was Brooke who kept the impetuous PM on an even keel by his ability to translate the theoretical into the possible. At times Churchill would complain that his generals would not permit him to fight Hitler by their opposition to his plans. But when Brooke said 'No', Churchill would never overrule him.

Casablanca was a masterpiece of the art of compromise. In return for HUSKY, the British committed themselves to ROUNDUP; but, without a specific date set for the cross-Channel invasion, they had merely acknowledged the inevitable. The question of when and where to mount OVERLORD would not be resolved until the

---

[1] Not long afterwards Marshall told Eisenhower that while the idea of unconditional surrender 'sounded well, only time could determine its wisdom'. Quoted in the unpublished manuscript of Dwight D. Eisenhower, furnished courtesy of John S. D. Eisenhower.

[2] Jacob Diary, loc. cit.

[3] *The Turn of the Tide* (1957) and *Triumph in the West* (1959).

Quebec Conference in August. After considerable wrangling, Arnold, aided by the arguments put forth by General Ira Eaker and General Frank Andrews, convinced Churchill to accept the combined bomber offensive.[1] King was temporarily placated by being permitted to retain sufficient naval assets to pursue his immediate goals for the Pacific, and Marshall, while never happy about operations in the Mediterranean, was satisfied that Sicily was the right target and that the conference had taken him one step closer to his goal of an Allied invasion of Europe. Wedemeyer found Casablanca a grave disappointment; he still considered the Mediterranean as a trap which was to prolong the war in Europe by a year. 'It was a side show,' he later wrote, 'and it cost many unnecessary lives.'[2]

Brooke, who had orchestrated the British negotiations so masterfully, came away from Casablanca well satisfied. The Portal paper which was officially ratified by both sides 'specifically committed the Allies to the occupation of Sicily – HUSKY: that was for him the great, the concrete achievement.'[3]

---

[1] See DeWitt S. Copp, *Forged in Fire*, New York, 1982, Chapter Fourteen. The combined bomber offensive called for round-the-clock bombing of Germany: the RAF by night and the USAAF by day.

[2] *Wedemeyer Reports!*, op. cit., p. 168.

[3] *Alanbrooke*, op. cit., p. 320. *Alanbrooke, Allies* and Martin Gilbert's *Road to Victory: Winston S. Churchill, 1941–1945* (London/New York, 1986) contain excellent versions of the Casablanca Conference for those readers interested in a full account.

CHAPTER 2

Tunisia:
The Testing Ground

In Africa we learned to crawl, to walk – then run.

BRADLEY[1]

The commander of Allied forces in North Africa was the former head of the War Plans Division of the US Army General Staff, Dwight D. Eisenhower. During his short tenure in Washington he had so impressed Marshall that he was sent to London in April 1942 to co-ordinate the proposed plan for ROUNDUP, BOLERO and SLEDGEHAMMER with Churchill and the British Chiefs of Staff. Churchill took an instant liking to the personable, outgoing Kansan whose enthusiasm for the Anglo-American alliance was a refreshing change from the attitude of the American contingent stationed in London. In June, Marshall ordered Eisenhower back to England to command US forces in the newly formed European Theater of Operations. Soon afterwards when the decision to launch Operation TORCH called for an American officer to command Allied forces the logical choice was Eisenhower.

The first months of the Allied experience in Northwest Africa following the TORCH landings were a dismal period of intense growing pains for the recently promoted Lieutenant General Eisenhower, for his recently formed Allied Force Headquarters and especially for the untried Anglo-American force engaged in their first serious combat against an experienced and stubborn enemy. To make matters worse was the appalling weather which left the Allies mired in the sticky mud of the cold and wet Tunisian winter, barely able to move and with their lengthy and tenuous logistic lifeline all but closed down. At times it was so dreadful that any vehicle leaving the road and any aircraft that accidentally

---

[1] Omar N. Bradley and Clay Blair, *A General's Life*, New York, 1983, p. 159.

strayed off the pierced-steel planking used for temporary runways sank irretrievably into the mud.

The original aim of Allied operations in Tunisia was to trap the Afrika Korps in Tripolitania between Montgomery's advancing Eighth Army and Lieutenant-General Kenneth Anderson's First British Army. This strategy had to be abandoned after the Allies failed for the second time to capture Tunis in late December 1942.[1]

The less than auspicious start to the Tunisian campaign came at the very moment when Axis forces under von Arnim were being reinforced after Hitler spurned Rommel's advice to withdraw. It doomed the timetable for TORCH to failure and, as the US official history notes, this required a major revision to Allied strategy to ensure that Tunisia was won by early spring so that the invasion of Sicily could take place in June, as both Churchill and Roosevelt had insisted. The problem was that the winter rains prevented the resumption of full-scale offensive action in northern Tunisia until the end of March.[2] As much as anything, it was this stalemate in Tunisia that prompted Brooke to orchestrate the assignment of Alexander to take over the ground campaign and the newly formed 18th Army Group.

At AFHQ Americans and British were having to learn to live with each other's strange customs, differing concepts of war and of how staff work was accomplished. Despite Eisenhower's ruthless insistence that nationality would take a backseat in his command, there were the inevitable misunderstandings, bad feelings and even an occasional resort to fisticuffs.

Behind Eisenhower's infectious grin and sunny outer façade lay a fiery temper that occasionally erupted. One such occasion occurred during a staff meeting when an American colonel made the mistake of telling Eisenhower what his counterpart, 'that British bastard', had done:

---

[1] The dismal weather and repeated setbacks against the Germans led Eisenhower to write candidly to a former War Department colleague that military operations in North Africa 'have violated every recognized principle of war, are in conflict with all operational and logistic methods laid down in text-books and will be condemned, in their entirety, by all Leavenworth and War College classes for the next twenty-five years' (Letter of 7 December 1942 to Major General Thomas T. Handy, Eisenhower Papers).

[2] George F. Howe, *Northwest Africa: Seizing the Initiative in the West*, Washington, 1957, p. 347. The official British history which records this period of the war in North Africa is I. S. O. Playfair and C. J. C. Molony, *The Mediterranean and Middle East*, Volume IV, London, 1966.

Eisenhower's face flushed red. He pounded the table and shouted, 'That will be enough! Don't you ever say that again or I'll bust you down to private. There are no British, American, or French, or any other national bastards at this headquarters. There are certainly bastards aplenty here, and I'm looking at one, but bastardy is NOT a national characteristic. Call a man a bastard, if you must, but don't blame his country for him.'[1]

Early observations of AFHQ were not encouraging. During the preparations for Casablanca, Brigadier Jacob had remarked that there 'was a great deal of restless confusion'.[2] Although there was little overt friction, the commonality of language could not obscure the fundamental differences between the traditions practised in the British Army for centuries and the rawness of the peacetime American Army suddenly thrust into a global war. Harold Macmillan – Churchill's personal representative at AFHQ – described the British as 'the Greeks in this American empire'. He counselled a newly arrived officer that 'you will find the Americans much as the Greeks found the Romans – great big vulgar, bustling people, more vigorous than we are and also more idle, with more unspoiled virtues, but also more corrupt. We must run AFHQ as the Greeks ran the operations of the Emperor Claudius.'[3]

At Casablanca, Marshall had run into unexpected opposition from Roosevelt when he attempted to persuade the President to promote Eisenhower to four-star rank because it was becoming increasingly difficult for the new Allied commander to deal as a lieutenant general with British and French officers senior to him. Roosevelt had complained 'that he would not promote Eisenhower until there was some damn good reason for doing it, that he was going to make it a rule that promotions should go to people who had done some fighting; that while Eisenhower had done a good job, he hadn't knocked the Germans out of Tunisia'.[4]

[1] Quoted in David Schoenbrun, *America Inside Out*, New York, 1984, p. 92. Any American foolish enough to call his counterpart 'a *British* son-of-a-bitch' was guaranteed a trip home via slow boat.

[2] Jacob Diary, loc. cit.

[3] Quoted by Richard Crossman in Nigel Fisher, *Harold Macmillan*, New York, 1982, pp. 100–101. The British blamed much of the early disarray within AFHQ on Lieutenant General Mark Clark who was Eisenhower's deputy pending his eventual assignment as Fifth US Army commander. Clark was considered a hugely disruptive influence who intrigued against the British, caused immense irritation by his habit of issuing direct and sometimes contradictory orders to the staff, terrified the American officers and was considered the 'evil genius' of the force (Jacob Diary).

[4] Witnessed by Admiral King and recorded in his notes for 22 January 1943, King Papers, loc. cit.

Marshall was able to overcome his Commander-in-Chief's objections and Eisenhower was soon thereafter promoted.

En route to Washington, the Chief of Staff stopped in Algiers to confer with Eisenhower and confided that one reason he favoured the invasion of Sicily was his fear that Sardinia might attract a heavy counteroffensive because of its size and strategic location, thus immobilizing large numbers of Allied troops and delaying the cross-Channel invasion. 'This he thought would be a grave mistake ... While the Sardinia idea was a bolder and possibly more valuable operation, the potential danger to OVERLORD* was, in his mind, the controlling factor.'[1]

Eisenhower had more important matters to deal with in Tunisia than the weather and tension between the Allies. Among them were the disorganization and indiscipline in the rear which so discouraged him that Marshall feared for his health. Marshall was equally distressed and heads began to roll as a result. At least one major general was relieved and when he returned to Washington, Marshall blistered his staff and insisted that in the future there be 'no goddamn drugstore cowboys standing around'.[2]

In the months since Alamein, the Afrika Korps had fought a skilful delaying action across North Africa and had demonstrated that, far from being beaten, it was still a deadly foe, as Montgomery learned at Mareth in March 1943. Rommel and his superior, Field Marshal Albert Kesselring, saw an opportunity to strike a blow that could split the Allied lines in two and threaten the overextended lines of communication from Algeria into Tunisia. The attack, to be delivered by all of the panzer strength of the Afrika Korps and Fifth Panzer Army, would be aimed at the inexperienced, fragmented American forces guarding the southern flank of the Allied front.

In the early hours of 14 February the Germans launched their counteroffensive which quickly chewed up units of the US 1st Armored Division at Sidi Bou Zid by superior firepower and the surprise of their attack. American forces were spread too thinly to enable reinforcements to be moved in time, and by 19 February

---

[1] Eisenhower manuscript, loc. cit.

[2] Marshall interview, loc. cit. What the Chief of Staff wanted were troops even better disciplined than combat troops, and what he found instead was a poor state of discipline and training that left him convinced that 'the iron was not in their soul'.

* The new code-name given in the spring of 1943 to the cross-Channel invasion, replacing the old name ROUNDUP.

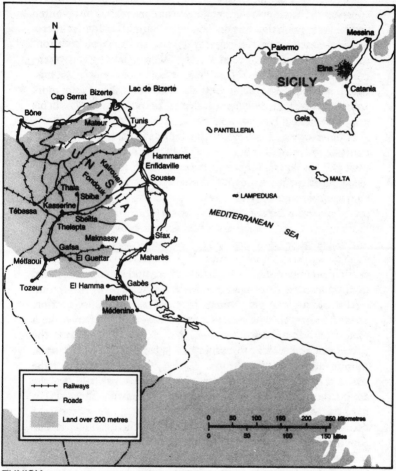

TUNISIA

Rommel's German–Italian task force had advanced over 25 miles and attacked the US forces defending Kasserine Pass, eventually sweeping away all opposition there.

Kasserine was a humiliating defeat for American arms that had results far beyond that of a defeat on the battlefield. Not only were American tactics and dispositions unsound, but once attacked at Sidi Bou Zid some troops abandoned their positions and equipment and fled to the rear. American armour and artillery were no match against the superior German armament and, as the news from the front grew worse by the hour, Eisenhower was forced to assess what had gone wrong. His naval aide wrote in his diary, 'The outstanding fact to me is that the proud and cocky Americans today stand humiliated by one of the greatest defeats in our history.'[1] To Marshall, Eisenhower wrote: 'Our people from the very highest to the very lowest have learned that this is not a child's game and are ready and eager to get down to the business of profiting by the lessons they have learned . . .'[2]

In the United States the news of Kasserine brought about shock and disbelief. 'To the American people, the event was incredible. It shook the foundations of their faith, extinguished the glowing excitement that anticipated quick victory, and, worst of all, raised doubt that the righteous necessarily triumphed.'[3]

The US forces took approximately 6,000 casualties at Kasserine.[4] However, where Kasserine dismayed the American high command was in its stark revelation of deficiencies in American equipment and – more importantly – in the obvious problems of training and leadership. Moreover, as the bad news continued to come in it was evident that unless there was quick and decisive action the possibility of strategic defeat loomed large. Equally harmful was the impact of Kasserine on Anglo-American relations. The British viewed Kasserine as convincing evidence that American fighting ability was more talk than reality.

The failures of American leadership included Eisenhower himself who was exhibiting the uncertainties and inexperience of high

---

[1] Diary of Captain Harry C. Butcher, 23 February 1943, Eisenhower Papers. Butcher also noted that, 'the grimness of war, the casualty lists (when they appear) and the loss of equipment are having a sobering effect upon the wishful thinkers at home who have had us practically storming Rome, some even Berlin by now'.

[2] Cable, Eisenhower–Marshall, 25 February 1943, Eisenhower Papers.

[3] Martin Blumenson, *Kasserine Pass*, Boston, 1967, pp. 3–4. Published in Britain in 1968 under the title *Rommel's Last Victory*.

[4] George F. Howe, *Northwest Africa: Seizing the Initiative in the West*, op. cit., p. 477.

command. Less than a year earlier he had been a brilliant but little known staff officer in Washington whose command experience was limited to the command of an infantry battalion in 1940–41. In the early days of the Tunisian campaign this shortcoming was manifested by his tendency to interfere in the tactical dispositions of small units on the battlefield and in his hesitation in redressing the growing problems within II Corps. 'Eisenhower's willingness to interfere in the affairs of his subordinates,' observed his biographer, 'ill became a man who often waxed eloquent on the subject of the sanctity of unity of command and the chain of command; his violation of his own principles was a reflection of his lack of confidence in [the II Corps commander, Major General] Fredendall, whom he was either unwilling or afraid to remove, as Fredendall was Marshall's handpicked choice.'[1]

The only positive postscript to the Kasserine fiasco came from Rommel who was not deceived by the poor American performance. Writing to his wife on 18 February he noted that: 'Although it was true the American troops could not yet be compared to the veteran troops of the Eighth Army, they made up for their lack of experience by more flexible command. In fact, their armament in anti-tank weapons and armoured vehicles was so enormous that we could look forward with but small hope of success to the coming mobile battles. The tactical conduct of the enemy's defence had been first class. They had recovered very quickly after the first shock and had soon succeeded in damming up our advance by grouping their reserves to defend the passes and other suitable points.'[2]

A good deal of the credit for Rommel's praise goes to Major General Ernest N. Harmon, who at the news of the German offensive was summoned by Eisenhower from Morocco where he was training his 2d Armored Division for Sicily. Realizing that Fredendall had lost control of II Corps, Eisenhower sent the tough, outspoken Harmon to the front to help reverse the situation by whatever means necessary.

Although highly regarded by Marshall and initially by Eisenhower, Fredendall proved a shockingly inept commander

[1] Stephen E. Ambrose, *Eisenhower: Soldier, General of the Army, President-Elect, 1890–1952*, New York, 1983, p. 228.
[2] *The Rommel Papers*, op. cit., p. 407. Full accounts of the battle of Kasserine Pass are contained in the official histories and Martin Blumenson's *Kasserine Pass*, op. cit.

and undoubtedly one of the worst senior command appointments made in the European Theater of Operations. Loud, profane and bitterly anti-British, the fifty-nine-year-old Fredendall was totally out of touch with his command, had stonewalled any attempt at co-operation with General Anderson, and had broken every known principle of leadership in the employment of his corps. He failed to make a positive impact upon his troops or subordinate commanders with whom he feuded constantly. At the time of Kasserine, the corps headquarters was located some sixty-five miles behind the front lines in an enormous underground bunker in a box-canyon. Over 200 combat engineers worked and sweated for weeks constructing this monstrosity when their skills were urgently needed elsewhere. Visitors to Fredendall's bunker came away genuinely embarrassed, including Eisenhower who was appalled by what he observed shortly before the Kasserine battle, but which he did little about other than to counsel Fredendall to get out of his Command Post more often.[1]

Harmon found Fredendall nervous, uninterested and more than willing to wash his hands of all responsibility for his corps. The aggressive Harmon brought common sense and firm leadership to the rapidly deteriorating front at the time it was most needed, and when they were given a taste of determined leadership, American troops responded by blunting the German offensive and convincing Rommel it was time to back-off and regroup.

In his after-action report to Eisenhower after the Kasserine battle, Harmon condemned Fredendall as 'a son-of-a-bitch' who was unfit for command.[2] When he saw Patton several days later he referred to Fredendall as a moral and physical coward.[3] Eisenhower offered the command of II Corps to Harmon who refused, saying he could not accept the position after recommending the relief of its commander.

Fredendall was belatedly dismissed by Eisenhower, and Major General George S. Patton, Jr. was hastily summoned from I Armored Corps, then training in Morocco, as the temporary corps commander. Partly from fear of furthering the embarrassment of American failure in the first ground combat of the war against the

[1] For an account of this episode, see Martin Blumenson and James L. Stokebury, *Masters of the Art of Command*, Boston, 1975, 'Command at Kasserine'.

[2] Major General Ernest N. Harmon, interview with George F. Howe, 15 September 1952, USAMHI.

[3] Martin Blumenson, *The Patton Papers*, Volume II, Boston, 1974, p. 177.

Germans, Fredendall's removal was made to appear as if he were returning home because of his ability to train troops. During the remainder of the war a number of general officers were relieved, reduced in grade and sent home, their careers ruined for relatively minor transgressions. Fredendall, who had sullied American leadership in North Africa at a critical time of the war, returned home to a hero's welcome, the command of a training army and, in the greatest injustice of all, promotion to lieutenant general.

When he arrived to assume command of II Corps, Patton encountered Major General Omar N. Bradley, newly arrived in North Africa and sent by Eisenhower as his 'personal observer'. When Bradley arrived in Tunisia in late February 1943 as an unassigned and very junior major general, untested in combat, he was quickly and rather rudely shocked by what he found there. He was sceptical of the burgeoning size of Eisenhower's headquarters and at Alexander's 18th Army Group he was first exposed to the British with whom Americans allegedly shared a common tongue. 'I had a hell of a time understanding [Lieutenant-General Sir Richard] McCreery [Alexander's Chief of Staff] for the first time.'[1]

Bradley arrived at II Corps about a week before Patton and was greeted by a hostile Fredendall who was not pleased to see his superior's 'personal observer' and banished him to a dingy, windowless, filthy hotel nearby.[2] Like Harmon before him, Bradley was distressed by what he discovered as he toured the II Corps area of operations. The problems Bradley noted went way beyond II Corps: he observed a lack of urgency in Northwest Africa that went clear to Eisenhower who was, he thought, strangely unconcerned by the outcome of the campaign, although he was, of course, deeply worried by the reversal at Kasserine. 'But no one seemed concerned about the ultimate way it would end, nor did they seem frightened that we might be unable to maintain the schedule for the Italian invasion [HUSKY].'[3]

Patton would not countenance having, as he put it, 'one of Ike's goddamn spies' in his command and easily persuaded Eisenhower's Chief of Staff, Major General Walter Bedell Smith to assign Bradley to the position of deputy corps commander. One of Patton's first acts was to relieve the commander of the 1st Armored

[1] Bradley Commentaries, USAMHI.
[2] Ibid.
[3] Ibid.

Division and bring back Harmon as the new commander. From that time on, American forces in North Africa showed marked improvement.

Unfortunately, the significant American recovery made little impression on Alexander. When he arrived to assume command of Allied ground forces on 19 February 1943 Alexander was dismayed by what he discovered. His first inspection of his new command left Alexander dissatisfied with Anderson and pessimistic about American fighting ability.

A confidential six-page handwritten letter to Brooke was a gloomy assessment of the American soldier and his leaders. Calling the poor fighting value of II Corps a very unsatisfactory state of affairs, Alexander observed that American troops were 'soft, green and quite untrained'. 'Is it surprising then that they lack the will to fight ...?'[1] Time and again II Corps missed opportunities and the reason was not hard to find. 'They are not very interested in this North African campaign – the ordinary rank and file, I mean ... There is no doubt that they have little hatred for the Germans and Italians and show no eagerness to get in and kill them. Perhaps these American troops will suddenly get their blood up and find their feet – I say perhaps, because unlike us they are a mercurial people and are either up or down.'

Alexander went on to warn Brooke the problem was 'very serious indeed' and 'unless we can do something about it, the American Army in the European theatre of operations will be quite useless and play no useful part whatsoever.' What really concerned Alexander was HUSKY and the need for a rapid turnabout in American performance, 'because unless we can, they are going to play a very poor part in HUSKY, and in that they shoulder a responsibility as great as our own.'[2]

Alexander reported his findings to Eisenhower in far more diplomatic terms, saying that although American troops were inexperienced in battle, they should soon be the equal of any fighting soldiers in the world. Eisenhower readily accepted Alexander's recommendations and ordered their implementation by Fredendall who was replaced by Patton several days later.

Alexander's claim to Brooke that he would do everything in his power to help reverse the situation was undoubtedly sincere, but

[1] Letter, Alexander–Brooke, 3 April 1943, Alanbrooke Papers.
[2] Ibid.

as subsequent events would demonstrate, he never seemed able to overcome his innate distrust of the American soldier. He told the CIGS '... I have only the American 2d Corps. There are millions of them elsewhere who must be living in a fool's paradise. If this handful of Divisions here are their best, the value of the remainder may be imagined.'[1]

Credit for the dramatic improvement in the combat performance of US forces after Kasserine properly belongs to Patton who assumed command of II Corps on 6 March 1943. He had only ten days to make his presence felt in the Corps before it was to conduct a diversionary attack ordered by Alexander to threaten Rommel's flank while Montgomery launched his long-awaited attack against the Mareth Line. As Bradley later attested, Patton's assignment had come none too soon.

Patton had precious little time to bring about fundamental changes in II Corps and he ruthlessly used shock tactics to cajole, bully, encourage and excite his men into believing that they were capable of defeating their enemy. Patton seemed to be everywhere at once using every leadership stratagem learned during his thirty-three year military career. Uniform regulations were strictly enforced and offenders punished with fines, many nabbed personally by Patton himself. Though seemingly trivial, even nonsensical, what Bradley called Patton's 'spit and polish' reign had a badly needed effect. 'Each time a soldier knotted his necktie, threaded his leggings, and buckled on his heavy steel helmet, he was forcibly reminded that Patton had come to command the II Corps, that the pre-Kasserine days had ended, and that a tough new era had begun ... these Patton reforms promptly stamped his personality upon the corps. And while they did little to increase his popularity, they left no doubt in anyone's mind that Patton was to be the boss.'[2]

Any lingering doubts that the apathy that existed under Fredendall was a thing of the past were erased the night before the II Corps offensive at El Guettar in mid-March when Patton told his staff: 'Gentlemen, tomorrow we attack. If we are not victorious, let no one come back alive.'[3]

The pairing of Patton and Bradley set the stage for one of the

[1] Ibid.
[2] Omar N. Bradley, *A Soldier's Story*, New York, 1951, pp. 44–5.
[3] Ibid., p. 52.

most unusual relationships of military history: the mercurial Patton who might curse one moment and the next get down on his knees to ask for God's help; and the unflappable, pragmatic Bradley. If ever two military men were mismatched it was these two. From the time that circumstance thrust them together in March 1943 it was evident that Patton and Bradley were *not* birds of a feather. They had never before served together and their disparate personalities assured there would be little beyond the formalities of a senior–subordinate relationship. The rather strait-laced Bradley never condoned Patton's use of profanity although he undoubtedly understood Patton's motives. From the time of their earliest association in Tunisia Bradley was privately critical of Patton. After the war he recorded his dismay at Patton's methods:

> Why does he use profanity? Certainly he thinks of himself as a destined war leader. Whenever he addressed men he lapsed into violent, obscene language. He always talked down to his troops. When he went back to visit troops at Oujida, Patton talked to officers and men in the field. His language was studded with profanity and obscenity. I was shocked. He liked to be spectacular, he wanted men to talk about him and to think of him. 'I'd rather be looked at than overlooked'. Yet when Patton was hosting at the dinner table, his conversation was erudite and he was well-read, intellectual and cultured. Patton was two persons: a Jekyll and Hyde. He was living a role he had set for himself twenty or thirty years before. An amazing figure![1]

Bradley criticized Patton's frustration at learning that Rommel, who had returned to Germany an ill man from his two gruelling years in the desert,* was no longer commanding Panzer Army Afrika. El Guettar was Patton's first combat of the war and 'he was possessed of the idea that he, George Patton, was here to do battle with Rommel. "Let me meet Rommel in a tank and I'll shoot it out with the son-of-a-bitch." '[2]

Patton's command of II Corps was only temporary and in mid-April Eisenhower ordered him back to Morocco to hasten

---

[1] Bradley Commentaries, loc. cit.
[2] Ibid.
* General Sir Bernard Freyberg, the gallant and outspoken commander of the New Zealand Division, once called Africa 'the graveyard of generals'. Best known of its victims was Rommel whose years there took a great toll.

planning for HUSKY. Patton had been impressed by Bradley even if this was not reciprocated. The principal combat element of the US invasion force was to have been Major General Ernest J. Dawley's VI Corps but, as Patton told Bradley, 'I've worked with you and I've got confidence in you. On the other hand I don't know what in hell Dawley can do. If you've got no objection, I'm going to ask Ike to fix it up.' At Patton's urging, VI Corps was switched by Eisenhower to Mark Clark's Fifth Army and II Corps slated for Sicily. On 15 April, Bradley was rewarded with his first corps command.

Bradley immediately began to make his own imprint on the corps, first by making the maximum use of his staff as a team. 'My command of II Corps was less flamboyant than had been Patton's. I administered with a firm but more compassionate hand ... I coaxed rather than ordered.'[1]

By the time Bradley had taken over II Corps the battle for Tunisia was nearing completion, but not before American leadership had again been criticized by the British who blamed the US 34th Infantry Division for failing to carry out a mission while assigned to a [British] provisional corps. The criticism was wholly unwarranted and the fault of the corps commander who had decreed the tactics to be used by the division commander, who had a better plan. There was harsh criticism of the division's leadership which was called timid and inexperienced.

Bradley knew that to accept this criticism unchallenged would humiliate a division whose only real weakness was the need of an opportunity to develop self-confidence. The division commander was a West Point classmate of Bradley's who was known to be a sound tactician. Bradley not only challenged an 18th Army Group proposal to withdraw this division to the rear for further training – which would have destroyed its effectiveness and the career of its commander – but went personally to Alexander to plead for its return to II Corps. Despite Bradley's assurance that the division would perform well if given an opportunity, Alexander agreed reluctantly and the incident only deepened American scepticism of Alexander and the British.[2]

---

[1] *A General's Life*, op. cit., p. 155.
[2] Ibid., p. 150. The 34th Division was the first National Guard unit to fight in North Africa and, had it been carried out, Alexander's decision would certainly have had severe consequences.

Ever since Kasserine, American commanders had been seething with frustration over what they considered unfair British criticism, their loose talk to war correspondents and Eisenhower's order that there was to be no criticism of British leadership. Even the mild-mannered Bradley began to question the wisdom of Eisenhower's failure to restrain the British.[1] Similar entries began appearing in Patton's diary, among them: 'Ike is more British than the British and is putty in their hands. Oh, God, for John J. Pershing.'[2]

American distress culminated in the Patton–Coningham incident over air support when Tedder was forced to move quickly to avert what might have been 'a major crisis in Anglo-American relations' after Air Vice-Marshal Arthur Coningham (Commander, Northwest African Tactical Air Force) sent an intemperate signal which suggested that II Corps was not battleworthy. The incident (described more fully in Chapter 6) nearly caused Eisenhower to resign, since it seemed clear to him that if he could not control his own subordinate commanders he had no business being the Allied C-in-C. Fortunately, timely intervention by the pragmatic Bedell Smith prevented Eisenhower from sending such a cable to Marshall.[3]

Alexander's continued distrust of American fighting ability was again demonstrated in his plan for the decisive battle of the Tunisian campaign in which the British were to make the main effort while II Corps was relegated to a minor role of protecting the British flank. The insignificance of the American role did not escape the attention of Marshall who signalled his dissatisfaction to Eisenhower. What disturbed the Chief of Staff was the implication in the US press that the 34th Division had spoiled Montgomery's chances of trapping the Afrika Korps and that American troops were being given menial tasks on the battlefield. With

[1] Ibid., p. 146. In his autobiography Harmon related an example of British disdain for American leadership. Shortly before the final battle in Tunisia, General Anderson visited Harmon who recalled that: 'I was at work in my tent when Anderson arrived ... He looked me over in a rather supercilious manner and inquired what I planned to do with an armored division in that terrain. Pointing out the positions on the map, I explained the plan Bradley and I had worked out for the armored rush on Mateur. Anderson waved his swagger stick vaguely and commented, "Just a childish fantasy, just a childish fantasy." With that he stalked out of the tent ... under my breath I muttered to myself, I'll make that son-of-a-bitch eat those words.' In the event, the plan devised by Bradley and Harmon was a great success. (Ernest N. Harmon, *Combat Commander*, Englewood Cliffs, N.J., 1970, p. 130.)

[2] *The Patton Papers*, Vol. II, op. cit., p. 202.

[3] Lord Tedder, *With Prejudice*, London, 1966, p. 411 and Bradley, *A General's Life*, op. cit., p. 148. See also Chapters 6 and 8.

favourable publicity nearly non-existent, Marshall viewed the problem as a matter of national pride and prestige.[1] He wondered if Eisenhower hadn't given away 'too much to logistical reasons with unfortunate results as to national prestige'.[2] In fact, Marshall's message was a polite but unmistakable directive to Eisenhower to act at once.

A month earlier Bradley had complained personally to Eisenhower about the same problem, insisting that US troops had won the right and that the American people were owed a share of the final victory in Tunisia. Bradley proposed that II Corps be employed in an independent role of driving to Bizerte, thus blocking all further Axis escape.[3] Although Bradley convinced Eisenhower of the need for a greater American combat role, it was Marshall's prodding which finally resulted in Eisenhower's insistence to Alexander that II Corps be employed as Bradley had proposed.

Bradley and II Corps proved equal to the challenge and what had begun as a minor diversionary action turned out to be decisive. The 34th Division was given an important and difficult task and performed brilliantly, as did the rest of II Corps. With the trap sprung and Eighth Army pushing them into the coastal plain around Tunis, von Arnim had no choice except to surrender. About 100,000 of the approximately 250,000 Axis troops bagged near Tunis were German.* With typical modesty Bradley sent Eisenhower a simple two-word message: 'Mission accomplished'. At about the same time Alexander was sending his now famous message to Churchill: 'Sir, it is my duty to report that the Tunisian campaign is over. All enemy resistance has ceased. We are masters of the North African shores.'[4]

With the Tunisian campaign at an end, the excellent perfor-

---

[1] Stephen E. Ambrose, *The Supreme Commander*, London, 1971, p. 183.

[2] Ibid.

[3] In *A General's Life*, Bradley's posthumously published autobiography, Clay Blair wrote (p. 145) that Bradley disputed Eisenhower's taking credit (in *Crusade in Europe*) for the idea of employing II Corps in a stronger role, stating that he was solely responsible for the idea.

[4] Nigel Nicolson, *Alex*, London, 1976, p. 229.

* Figures vary as to the number of German and Italian troops captured near Tunis. The total of 250,000 given by Alexander in his post-war despatch seems excessive. According to Liddell Hart, Army Group Afrika had reported its ration strength for April 1943 at between 170,000–180,000 *before* the final heavy fighting around Tunis. (Cf. *History of the Second World War* [paperback edition], London, 1974, p. 451.) The British official history records a total of 238,243 Axis POWs, the US about 275,000.

mance by II Corps ought to have erased once and for all the previous doubts about American fighting ability. But Alexander's behaviour during the forthcoming Sicily campaign was to suggest very clearly that even the triumph at Bizerte had not erased his impression that American combat troops were still not up to the standard of the Eighth Army. Despite first-class leadership on the part of Patton, Bradley and Harmon, the example of Fredendall and Kasserine still lingered in the minds of the senior British commanders.

Among them was Montgomery who, in mid-February, had organized a study week which was designed to impart the lessons of the battlefield learnt since 1939–40, particularly in North Africa. Senior officers from England and the Middle East assembled at Tripoli. Montgomery's invitation had been extended to US forces in Tunisia and Morocco, but only one senior American officer attended, the commander of an armoured corps whom Montgomery described as 'an old man of about 60'. Montgomery interpreted the poor American representation as a lack of professional interest on the part of the American leadership when, in fact, it was mainly due to the pressures of the Tunisian campaign and training for HUSKY. The Eighth Army commander's impression – however brief – of an 'elderly' American general was distinctly negative. The 'old man' was, of course, George Smith Patton.*

Patton was virtually the only American general who even aroused British curiosity and then only because of his colourful reputation and his appointment to command all American ground forces in Sicily. The British attitude was to carry over into the planning for the invasion of Sicily which was to prove one of the most discordant episodes in the history of the Anglo-American alliance.

---

* With the exception of Montgomery, Freyberg and one or two others, Patton was not impressed with the senior British officers whom he met in Tripoli. Of Montgomery he wrote: 'small, very alert, wonderfully conceited, and the best soldier – or so it seems – I have met in this war'. The remainder, observed Patton, 'are the same non-committal clerical types as our generals'. Patton himself candidly admitted that he was 'certainly the oldest looking general here'. (*The Patton Papers*, Vol. II, op. cit., pp. 171–2.)

PART II

Planning Operation
HUSKY

If we do HUSKY it must succeed . . . I am fighting to get some sanity into the planning. It is hard work; and I am also fighting the Germans – which is much easier.

MONTGOMERY

Operations once decided on in principle must lie in the hands of the commanders chosen, who have to back them with their reputations and their lives.

CHURCHILL [1]

---

[1] Quoted in letter of 30 September 1941 to Admiral Sir Roger Keyes, Chief, Combined Operations Headquarters (COHQ), 1940–41, Bernard Fergusson, *The Watery Maze*, New York, 1961.

CHAPTER 3

'A Dog's Breakfast'

The HUSKY planning is in a hopeless mess ... We are
an amazing race, and it is quite wonderful how we
ever win any wars!!

MONTGOMERY

The decision taken at Casablanca to invade Sicily resulted in the
formal appointment of Eisenhower as the Allied Commander-
in-Chief for HUSKY. Alexander was designated the Deputy C-in-C
and the ground force commander. Command of all Allied naval
forces went to Admiral Sir Andrew Browne Cunningham, the
British naval Commander-in-Chief, Mediterranean. The air
appointment went to Air Chief Marshal Sir Arthur Tedder who
became C-in-C, Mediterranean Allied Air Forces.

One of the most visible results of the British triumph at Casablanca was that they had managed to impose their own committee
system of separate C-in-Cs for air, ground and sea operations into
the Allied force structure, thus ensuring that future military operations in the Mediterranean would be British-dominated. This
decision infuriated Eisenhower who had to be dissuaded by the
cooler head of Bedell Smith from sending a cable of protest to the
Combined Chiefs of Staff demanding the retention of the original
command structure for TORCH. However, at this stage of the war,
Eisenhower had not yet taken a firm grasp of the reins of command
and was in no position to dictate terms to the CCOS. As a result, he
found himself at the head of a committee of four charged with
carrying out the invasion of Sicily.[1]

The committee system of coalition warfare at the formative
stage of the new Allied partnership was wholly ineffective. While a
modified version of this arrangement later functioned exceptionally well for the invasion of Normandy in June 1944, at this time it

[1] Garland and Smyth, *Sicily and the Surrender of Italy* [hereafter cited as *Sicily*], op. cit.,
p. 11.

simply meant that each of the commanders went his own way, leaving the whole less than the sum of its parts. Policy decisions required the approval of each committee member and decisions too often represented the narrower interests of the commander rather than the overall needs of HUSKY. In short, as the Commander-in-Chief, Eisenhower was so far removed from the operational level that he was little more than a chairman of a board, one whose powers were limited to refereeing disputes his board were unable to resolve. If they agreed, 'there was little Eisenhower could do to change the policy unless he was willing to dispense with the board members' services ... Only indirectly could he influence the course of operations once that course had been agreed on by his committee of three.'[1] The defects of this arrangement when combined with the lack of planning direction that was to ensue soon led to one crisis after another.

From the time of its inception as a strategic compromise at Casablanca, the planning of Operation HUSKY was plagued by interminable problems of organization and indecision. The Combined Chiefs had directed Eisenhower to create a separate headquarters to plan HUSKY, and by late January a planning group was formed in Algiers which soon became known as Task Force 141, so named for the room in the St George's Hotel in Algiers where the first meeting took place. Force 141 eventually moved into a nearby French school but until the end of the Tunisian campaign it remained a part of the AFHQ G-3 section,* when it became a separate headquarters under Alexander. After Tunisia the 18th Army Group was deactivated but in fact merely changed its designation to Force 141, the title it retained until D-Day when it was officially activated as the 15th Army Group. Although initially part of AFHQ, Force 141 was an inter-Allied, inter-service force, and as we shall see, it was only one of several planning headquarters for HUSKY.

The Combined Chiefs had left it to Eisenhower to organize the planning for HUSKY but before doing so it was necessary for him to confirm his subordinate command appointments which were announced on 11 February 1943. The CCOS had mandated there be an Eastern and a Western Task Force, each of which would be

---

[1] Ibid., p. 420.
* AFHQ was organized along US general staff lines: G-1: Personnel; G-2: Intelligence; G-3: Operations and training; and G-4: Logistics and supply.

inter-service but *not* inter-Allied; the Eastern Task Force was wholly British, the Western, American. On 13 February the CCOS formally approved Eisenhower's nominations, which were:*

	Eastern Task Force (Br)	*Western Task Force (US)*
GROUND	General Sir Bernard Montgomery	Lieutenant General George S. Patton, Jr.
AIR	Air Vice-Marshal Harry Broadhurst	Colonel L. P. Hickey, USAAF
NAVAL	Admiral Sir Bertram Ramsay†	Vice Admiral H. Kent Hewitt, USN

Inasmuch as the majority of British forces for Sicily would be drawn from those already in the Mediterranean and launched from Mediterranean bases, Alexander's successor as C-in-C, Middle East, General Sir Henry Maitland 'Jumbo' Wilson, was designated by Churchill to assist in the mounting of HUSKY. The Eastern Task Force HQ was therefore established in Cairo under the designation Force 545. Lieutenant-General Miles Dempsey, 13th Corps commander, was Chief of Staff until mid-April when Montgomery sent his own Chief of Staff, Major-General Francis de Guingand, to assume this role. The Western Task Force HQ was initially located in Rabat, Morocco, as Force 343.

London and Washington also became centres of planning since some Anglo-Canadian and American forces were to be staged directly from Britain and the United States. With five separate centres of planning in five widely separated locations there was bound to be considerable confusion – and there was. Added to the mix were the three British C-in-Cs, Middle East, each of whom was to play a role in the forthcoming campaign. As if this were not confusing enough, Cunningham, Tedder and Alexander eventually established *their* operational headquarters in different locations. Despite the enormous distances the wireless and cable net-

* The Allied organization and Order of Battle is detailed in Appendices A–D. Ramsay was then Deputy Naval C-in-C of the Allied Expeditionary Force; Broadhurst commanded the Western Desert Air Force and Hickey commanded the XII Air Support Command.

† Admiral Sir Bertram Home Ramsay was born in 1883 and had already completed a distinguished forty-year career in the Royal Navy when he was recalled from retirement to active duty in 1939 as the Flag Officer, Dover. The following year he masterminded the naval evacuation of the BEF and French forces from Dunkirk. A superb organizer and a brilliant commander, Ramsay planned the naval side of Operation TORCH before assuming duties in the Mediterranean. As the Allied Naval C-in-C for OVERLORD, it was later said of him by Cunningham that 'If Dunkirk was a miracle of improvisation, the naval assault on Normandy was a masterpiece of organisation, and Admiral Ramsay was the architect of both'.

works were excellent, perhaps too good, for as the British official
history remarks, 'good communications often favour debate
instead of hastening decisions'.[1]

The first weeks were critical and urgently required someone to
provide planning guidance from the highest level so that the
planning staffs understood the direction their effort was expected
to take. In theory, the planning of a joint amphibious operation
should centre upon the requirements of the ground forces and
their mission. In practice many factors combined to ensure that
logic was lost in a morass of confusion, disorganization and
disharmony.

As the designated ground force commander, the overall responsibility for developing the invasion plan fell to Alexander and
Force 141, the senior Allied planning headquarters. However,
Alexander was completely preoccupied with the problems in
Tunisia of keeping a tight rein on General Anderson whose leadership he distrusted, and II Corps which was then in chaos and
without a semblance of leadership under the inept Fredendall.
Eisenhower likewise was far removed from the planning and
himself equally absorbed in attempting to deal with the mounting
problems in Tunisia and Algiers to give HUSKY more than token
attention.[2] By default the solution to the numerous problems
requiring rapid resolution were left to Force 141 which proved
ill-equipped for the task. Less than five months remained to mount
what would be the most complex amphibious operation in the
history of warfare: as the British official history later noted, it
seemed a sufficiently wide margin, 'but brute facts were to show
that it was narrow'.[3]

In practical terms Force 141 had no commander until the
Tunisian campaign ended in mid-May. The Chief of Staff was a
British officer, Major-General Charles H. Gairdner, who had been
brought from India where he was a senior staff officer under the
C-in-C, India, Field-Marshal Sir Archibald Wavell. Gairdner had
been Wavell's Deputy Director of Plans in 1941 and had briefly
commanded the 6th and 8th Armoured Divisions before following
his chief to India. His deputy was Brigadier A. A. Richardson,

[1] C. J. C. Molony, *The Mediterranean and Middle East*, Vol. V, op. cit., p. 6.
[2] When the new Chief of Staff of Force 141 met Eisenhower for the first time on 22
February 'he made it abundantly clear that at the moment he did not want to be worried
with HUSKY'. (Diary of General Sir Charles Gairdner, Imperial War Museum.)
[3] *The Mediterranean and Middle East*, Vol. V, op. cit., p. 10.

formerly Commandant of the British Staff College, Haifa, who was later replaced by Major General Clarence Huebner, a tough, outspoken American infantryman whose candour – often in reaction to British criticism of American fighting ability – finally irked Alexander so badly that he was dismissed in July.*

Gairdner was an Irishman with no battle experience during the war who found himself woefully ill-equipped for a senior appointment of such critical importance. He was unfailingly courteous and well-meaning but otherwise out of his depth in the high-powered atmosphere of the Allied high command. The remaining members of the Force 141 staff came from assignments in the Middle East, Britain and the US. Few had experience in planning joint operations on the scale of HUSKY and to make matters more difficult the key commanders of the two task forces – Patton and Montgomery – were also deeply involved in Tunisia and thus far removed from the planning taking place in their respective headquarters.

Trouble began in early February when Force 141 distributed a basic planning document which was a slight modification of the original plan drafted in London by the Joint Planning Staff† and approved in principle by the CCOS at Casablanca. Having been given no other planning guidance, Force 141 began their effort considering only the options presented in this document. However, the JPS outline plan was itself deeply flawed because it only considered two basic options and one variation. These were: single

* With the possible exception of Mark Clark, no officer ever rankled Alexander more than did Huebner whom he called a poor staff officer and 'a square peg in a round hole'. (See Chapters 27 and 28.) Huebner's replacement was Brigadier General Lyman L. Lemnitzer, who served as Alexander's Deputy Chief of Staff throughout the Sicily and Italian campaigns and in the postwar years went on to a distinguished career as US Army Chief of Staff and Supreme Commander of NATO.

† Headed by the Prime Minister, the War Cabinet was the supreme body responsible for directing the British war effort. Within the War Cabinet were a number of permanent civil and military committees which co-ordinated and planned a myriad of functions, such as: manpower, civil defence, production and food. On the defence side, military policy originated within the Chiefs of Staff Committee (US equivalent: the Joint Chiefs of Staff) whose Chairman was Brooke.

Reporting to the Chiefs of Staff Committee was the Joint Planning Staff (JPS), which was composed of the three Directors of Plans of the War Office, Admiralty and the Air Ministry. The JPS functions were carried out by three planning sections, thus enabling it to cut across traditional military boundaries. One of the primary functions of the JPS was to provide the Chiefs of Staff with outline plans for future military operations. The JPS staff was comprised of officers from all three services who brought to the Committee considerable expertise in military matters. (Cf. J. R. M. Butler, *Grand Strategy*, Vol. II, London, 1957, Chapter I and Appendix VII.)

operations against either Palermo or Catania or a dual operation against both ports.[1] This concept of a frontal assault against Sicily required the capture of the island by the ground forces and virtually conceded to Axis forces the possibility of reinforcing the island via the Messina Strait, or to leave it by the same route.

The boldest and most important option was never seriously considered by the Allied planners. Amphibious landings along the Messina and Calabrian coasts along with secondary landings in southern Sicily would have immediately left Axis forces in a hopeless position, with their lifeline – the Messina Strait – sealed off to reinforcement and to escape.*

Throughout the planning for HUSKY the Allied planners accorded their Axis adversary greater respect than circumstances justified. The Allies had created an enormously powerful military machine of air, naval and ground forces that far outnumbered anything the Axis could muster. A Messina/Calabria operation was rejected on grounds that the enemy defences there were too heavy and that an invasion of Calabria constituted an invasion of Italy, which had been implied but never officially approved by the CCOS at Casablanca. Thus, unrealistic planning assumptions, timidity and lack of strategic guidance all combined to rule out the one choice which could have ensured complete military victory in Sicily. The various arguments later advanced for avoiding Messina proved spurious and a sadly accurate reflection of the unwillingness of the Allied high command to act with anything resembling boldness.

After Casablanca, Marshall and the War Department planners urged Eisenhower to consider one other option: a swift strike by a small force in a surprise landing against the weak defences of the Axis garrison in Sicily *before* the inevitable build-up which would follow victory in Tunisia. While such an operation was admittedly *ad hoc* in nature, it offered the priceless advantage of surprise. Intelligence reports confirmed the sorry state of the Italian

---

[1] Operation 'HUSKY', JP (43) 7 (Final), 10 January 1943, PRO (AIR 8/1344).
* The reasons why this option was never given the consideration it deserved are discussed in Chapter 31 and the Epilogue. Had the roles been reversed, this was an alternative the Germans would certainly have employed. The senior German commanders in Italy would later comment with bewilderment at the lack of Allied vision. Kesselring, his chief of staff, General Siegfried Westphal and General Heinrich von Vietinghoff, the Tenth Army commander, all criticized Allied strategy with the latter calling their failure to adopt the Messina option 'incomprehensible'. (Cf. Manuscript D-116, German Report Series, USAMHI.)

defences. Moreover, with most German and Italian troops tied
down fighting in Tunisia, the only reinforcements in Sicily were
those which happened to be in transit there. Prior to April there
were only about 5,000 German troops based on Sicily and none of
these was organized into major fighting units. ULTRA and signal
intelligence (SIGINT) were providing incomplete but nevertheless
useful information about Axis dispositions and intentions. It was
not until mid-April that a German unit of battle group size was
created in Sicily.[1] Had it been possible to mount one at short
notice, an operation against Sicily before mid-May might have
produced the result envisioned by Marshall.

The idea of a lightning strike against Sicily held no appeal to
Eisenhower's conservative nature despite its attractiveness to the
War Department planners. When, at the end of April, Eisenhower
reported that it was impractical, Marshall tried to keep the idea
alive by suggesting that 'your planners and mine may be too
conservative in their analyses'. The element of surprise and Axis
disarray might, argued Marshall, 'justify your accepting calculated risks'. It was Marshall's view that orthodoxy had replaced
the boldness 'which (had) won great victories for Nelson and
Grant and Lee', but his suggestion that Eisenhower's attitude
reflected a lack of adaptability fell on deaf ears and Eisenhower
continued to think it too risky and too difficult to carry out at short
notice.[2] By the time of Eisenhower's final decision on the matter on
10 May the Allies had already committed themselves to a conservative plan for the invasion of Sicily.

The JPS plan* considered by Force 141 had as its primary

---

[1] F. H. Hinsley, et al., British Intelligence in the Second World War, Vol. III, Part I,
London, 1984, p. 74.

[2] Quoted in Sicily, op. cit., p. 66.

* The unhappy tale of the plan produced by the Joint Planning Staff in London and first
presented at the Casablanca Conference is told by Brigadier Sir Bernard Fergusson who has
chronicled the story of Combined Operations in The Watery Maze (New York, 1961). Prior
to Casablanca the planners had put together a rough skeleton plan for an invasion of Sicily,
but, as Fergusson relates: 'It was not really a plan at all. It was a staff study, put together in
some haste by the Joint Planners in London, but decked out so attractively as to give it an
insidious appeal even when read with attention. On a night in Casablanca – a phrase
unhappily reminiscent of the Marx Brothers – the staff [supporting the British contingent]
was told ... to put flesh and blood on it by next morning. With towels round their heads they
worked out perfectly accurate figures of tonnages and loading tables and the like. There was
nothing wrong with their homework, and the result looked convincing; but it was not
founded upon a rock. Unfortunately it was carried with acclamation.' The problem was,
recounts Fergusson, when the Force 141 planners began to examine the plan in depth they
quickly developed grave doubts that 'the plan was a dud'. When they had the temerity to say

invasion objective the seizure of key airfields and ports to be used
in support of the ground forces. The planners considered and then
rejected the idea of two simultaneous US–British assaults against
the southeastern corner of Sicily in the Syracuse–Gela sectors, on
the basis that a force of ten Allied divisions – the total thought
necessary to compete with the estimated Axis strength of eleven
Italian and two German divisions – could not be maintained
through the ports of southeastern Sicily. Instead, the early capture
of the port of Palermo as well as those of Syracuse and Catania was
deemed essential for maintaining Allied invasion forces.[1]

The Force 141 version differed only slightly from the original
JPS plan by adding a reserve force on D-Day and concentrating on
the capture of the important airfields by employing British airborne forces from D-Day through D+3. Their proposed plan was
this: On D-Day three British divisions were to land at widely
separated points on a stretch of coast 100 miles long – from
Syracuse on the east coast to Gela on the southeastern coast. Sixty
miles west of its nearest British neighbour one American division
was to land between Sciacca and Marinella. Two days later
another American landing would take place on the northwest
corner of Sicily against Palermo, and on D+3 another British
landing 140 miles away on the east coast to seize the port city of
Catania. The logic of these widely dispersed landings was that it
would be impossible for the Axis defenders to react simultaneously – and even if one force were heavily attacked or even
defeated, the other was bound to succeed. The plan especially
appealed to Admiral Cunningham who saw it as a means of
diffusing the Axis air and naval threat to his fleet.

Gairdner spent the morning of 28 February with Alexander
whose only action was to emphasize the need for a force reserve
and the avoidance of splitting the airborne troops. Otherwise,
Gairdner noted in his diary, Alexander 'agreed in the main with

---

[1] 'Planning the Invasion of Sicily', prepared in 1943 by the British Historical Section,
Central Mediterranean, PRO (AIR 23/5759).

---

so, a senior British officer on the AFHQ staff told them that 'it was not theirs to reason why;
that was the plan which had been approved on Olympian level at Casablanca, and [it was]
therefore sacrosanct. In vain one of the officers concerned confessed that ... he and his
colleagues had been given only a few hours to put it together; that the inconsistencies now
stuck out a mile. He was told to shut up and get on with the job. Miserably they went on with
a plan they knew to be thoroughly defective' (p. 221).

my conception of the operation'.[1] The plan was formally presented to Eisenhower and his triumvirate who unanimously approved it and ordered that the task force commanders be briefed five days later on 18 March.

During February, while Force 141 was modifying the JPS Plan, Montgomery was deeply involved in battling with Rommel and, as he told Brooke, intent on 'Dunkirking' the Axis on the beaches of Tunis to pay off that old score with respect to 'that other Dunkirk!!' 'Alex wants me to come in on HUSKY, and of course I am delighted. I have told him the British part should be called Eighth Army and that full use must be made of the Eighth Army name and morale', a factor Montgomery considered 'terribly important'. 'I have built up a really good fighting team ... and we must use all that experience, and battle experience, and this will ensure success.'[2]

Montgomery was never in favour of further Allied operations in the Mediterranean after North Africa. He had, in fact, written privately to Brooke his misgivings about the merits of invading Sicily, Sardinia or Italy, believing that North Africa was an unsuitable base from which to support prolonged operations on a large scale: 'It is quite useless to initiate large-scale operations against Italy from North Africa unless you are prepared to see them through.' Instead, Montgomery seems to have favoured a cross-Channel operation and he suggested a feint in the Mediterranean to tie down German forces by the massive bombing of Italy. 'But the real big thing is elsewhere, and suddenly about June 1943 we nip across the Channel.'[3]

Montgomery's first real involvement with HUSKY occurred the afternoon of 13 March when Dempsey and Admiral Ramsay – with whom Monty was on very friendly terms – stopped at his field HQ en route to Algiers to explain the proposed plan. Although he had been furnished a copy earlier by Force 141, Montgomery had been too preoccupied with Eighth Army operations to give it his undivided attention. He was horrified by what he heard and immediately cabled Alexander that 'In my opinion the operation breaks every common-sense rule of practical battle fighting and is

[1] Gairdner Diary.
[2] Letter of 16 February 1943, Montgomery Papers.
[3] Letter, Montgomery–Brooke, 13 December 1942, Montgomery Papers.

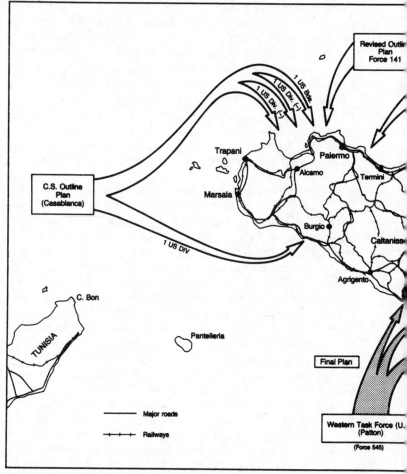

THE EVOLUTION OF OPERATION "HUSKY"

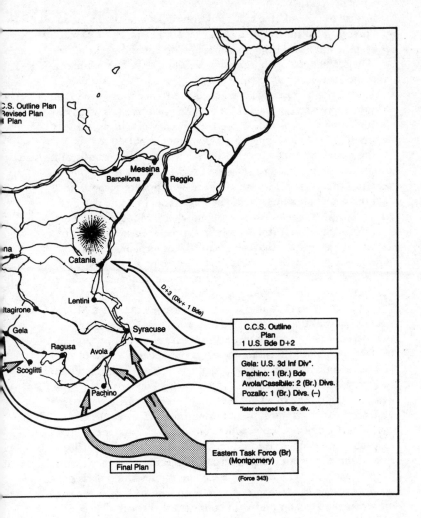

C.S. Outline Plan
Revised Plan
Plan

Messina
Barcellona   Reggio

Catania

na

Lentini   D+3 (Div + 1 Bde)

ltagirone

Gela   Syracuse   **C.C.S. Outline
Plan
1 U.S. Bde D+2**

Ragusa   Avola
Scoglitti
                                                   Gela: U.S. 3d Inf Div*.
                                                   Pachino: 1 (Br.) Bde.
Pachino   Avola/Cassibile: 2 (Br.) Divs.
                                                   Pozallo: 1 (Br.) Divs. (–)

                                                   *later changed to a Br. div.

                                              **Eastern Task Force (Br)
(Montgomery)**

Final Plan

(Force 343)

completely theoretical. It has no hope of success and should be completely recast.'[1]

Brooke too was alerted to his objections: 'I am not happy about the present plan for HUSKY ... I have given my views to Alex ... [but] have not heard from him since and do not know if he agrees ... The real trouble is that neither Alex nor myself have time to bother about HUSKY at the moment.'[2]

Among the planners who manned the trenches at Force 141, Montgomery's broadside was 'one of the rare occasions when the planners were overjoyed to see their homework being torn to tatters: they were being delivered from a nightmare'.[3]

Their chief did not see it as a deliverance but rather as the first of a series of objections and suggested revisions that Montgomery sent to Force 141 in the weeks ahead which were to become a nightmare and ultimately force his resignation. In his diary Gairdner complained that 'to my certain knowledge Monty has had the plan for 4 weeks and this is the first time he rushes into print. Furthermore, he knew that the amended outline plan must by now have been agreed upon by the C's in C ... does he want his Army to think that it was he and he alone that got it changed or what? Anyhow it is a nice baby for me to hold.'[4]

At a meeting on 18 March, Dempsey formally presented Montgomery's opposition to the plan. In the chair was Gairdner who in the absence of Alexander bore the brunt of the Force 545 argument that the mission of capturing the ports of Syracuse, Augusta and Catania would result in a flow of supplies that would be far short of Eighth Army's actual needs. This shortfall could only be compensated for at the expense of the other landing at Gela where the objective was to capture the important airfields of Ponte Olivo, Biscari and Comiso which Tedder considered absolutely essential to protect the troops ashore and Admiral Cunningham's fleet. Both Cunningham and Tedder strongly objected to a cancellation of the Gela landing, but without Alexander present no decisions could be reached and the meeting broke up without any agreement on a course of action and with considerable ill-will all around.

---

[1] Cable, Montgomery–Alexander, 15 March 1943, Alexander Papers, PRO (WO 214/20).
[2] Letter, Montgomery–Brooke, 15 March 1943, Montgomery Papers.
[3] Fergusson, *The Watery Maze*, op. cit., p. 222.
[4] Gairdner Diary, 15 March 1943.

Montgomery had set the cat amongst the pigeons in what was the first of many quarrels over the invasion plan.

Tedder rightly refused to compromise over the requirement to capture the three key airfields around Gela but he did propose an alternative, with which Cunningham concurred, to switch the Western Task Force to Gela and leave Palermo to be dealt with at a later date.[1]

At the centre of the HUSKY debate stood Alexander whose actions throughout this period reflect a less than enthusiastic interest in the problems confronting Force 141. Tedder's postwar memoirs note that 'Alexander and Montgomery had convinced Eisenhower that the (Force 141) plan spread the Allied forces too thinly, and the British force would not be strong enough for the task of capturing rapidly its immediate objectives, the airfields of the south-east, unless it were reinforced by one additional division.'[2] Yet Alexander posed no such objections at the 13 March meeting when the HUSKY outline plan was approved by Eisenhower and the three C-in-Cs. Had not Montgomery raised objections the plan would undoubtedly have been implemented. When he intervened, Montgomery not only succeeded in getting the plan scrapped but also swung Alexander's opinion around to the view that it had been unsound.

Following the 18 March meeting Alexander was briefed by Gairdner and Dempsey and decided that an extra division was required for the Eastern Task Force and that it would *not* be provided from the assets of this force. While still believing in the feasibility of the Palermo assault, Alexander wrote to Eisenhower recommending that Patton's Western Task Force provide one American division for the Gela assault. The remaining US divisions were to be held as a reserve until the opportunity arose to capture Palermo. Despite the fact that this course of action left the Western Task Force with no definite mission, Eisenhower approved the change on 20 March.

Politically and militarily it was an unsound plan that most certainly would have angered Marshall. Yet Eisenhower seemed oblivious to its implications on the ill-defined American role which would have left US forces playing a distant second fiddle to Mont-

[1] Cable, Tedder–Portal, 'Sicily – Diary of Events and Correspondence Relating to the Planning of HUSKY', 18 March 1943, PRO (CAB 106/368).
[2] Tedder, *With Prejudice*, op. cit., p. 427.

gomery and the British. More serious was the fact that the plan left the two task forces – especially the British – vulnerable to Axis counterattack if the planning estimate of generally weak resistance proved false. It also eliminated all possibility of mutual support, thus providing the enemy with the capability to crush either or both invasion forces. Nevertheless, both Tedder and Cunningham pronounced themselves in favour of it and were quite prepared to provide the necessary naval and air support. Montgomery stood alone in his opposition.

Eisenhower's attitude appeared to be ambivalent and he undoubtedly had misgivings about the entire operation, although he later claimed that from the outset he had favoured 'a single concentrated assault on the eastern and southern portions of the island', and that the logisticians had overruled him – thus necessitating the plan for two assaults.[1]

The disparity between Eisenhower who commanded the invasion of Normandy in 1944 and the commander of HUSKY is a study in contrast. The Eisenhower of 1944 demonstrated a confidence and mastery of the situation that were markedly dissimilar to those of the commander who, in early 1943, was tentative in his decisions and unsure of himself in the strange and uncomfortable role as the superior of men with years of battle experience and high command. As a result, Eisenhower failed to play a meaningful role in the planning of HUSKY and his apprehensions greatly alarmed his superiors in Washington and London.

By mid-March, there were indications that Eisenhower was beginning to grasp the perils of the plan. One such example was his cable of 20 March to the Combined Chiefs of Staff in which he voiced his pessimism – not over the liabilities of a plan which split the Allied forces and left no role for Patton – but over the question of Palermo and the probability that the ships of the Western Task Force would be forced to lie fully loaded and vulnerable to air attack in North African ports until at least D+3 or later. But his only conclusion was to express deep gloom over the future of HUSKY as a military operation.

If Montgomery failed to seize the key airfields at Gela 'the whole plan became abortive. It is very doubtful that even partial success

[1] Memo for Personal Record, 1 July 1943, Alfred D. Chandler, Jr. (Editor), *The Papers of Dwight David Eisenhower: The War Years*, Baltimore, 1970 [hereafter cited as *The Eisenhower Papers*], Vol. II, pp. 1230–1.

in the landings in the West could be achieved if the Southeast assault was repulsed.' Moreover, should German ground troops reinforce southeastern Sicily prior to the invasion, 'the chances for success become practically nil and the project should be abandoned'.[1] The entire problem could be resolved, said Eisenhower, if an additional division were made available to Montgomery, thus enabling the restoration of the western invasion which he was now forced to scrap even though he was deeply concerned that the threat it represented to the Axis would be lost and leave them free to counteract, and possibly defeat, the Palermo assault. While the problem was being urgently studied by Force 141 a solution hinged on finding the necessary additional landing craft for the extra division. Every available ship and landing craft had already been allocated. The choice Eisenhower laid out was clear: either additional landing craft had to be found or it would be necessary to resort to the unsatisfactory compromise of using an American division for the Gela assault.[2]

The British Chiefs of Staff reacted swiftly and insisted in a memo for consideration by the entire Combined Chiefs that the extra division must be provided to Eisenhower 'by hook or crook'.[3] As messages began to burn the wires between Algiers, London and Washington it was inevitable that Churchill would intervene, and he did so after another pessimistic cable from Eisenhower on 7 April said that 'the view held by our (Force 141) planners that the operation offers scant promise of success if the region contained substantial well armed and fully organized German troops is concurred in by Admiral Cunningham, General Alexander, and myself. By the term substantial forces is meant more than two German divisions.'[4]

The Prime Minister reacted with outrage at the collective timidity of Eisenhower and the Committee of Three who clearly needed to be shaken from their lethargy. Especially irksome was the suggestion that two or more German divisions were sufficient excuse for cancelling HUSKY. The next day the British Chiefs of Staff received one of the most sharply worded memos ever written by the Prime Minister in which he noted acidly that:

[1] PRO (CAB 106/368).
[2] Ibid.
[3] Paper of 25 March 1943, ibid.
[4] AFHQ Message No. 2274, 7 April 1943, PRO (AIR 23/824).

This statement contrasts oddly with the confidence which General Eisenhower showed about invading the Continent across the Channel, where he would have to meet a great many more than two German divisions. If the presence of two German divisions is held to be decisive against any operations ... open to the million men now in French North Africa, it is difficult to see how the war can be carried on. Months of preparation, sea power and air power in abundance, and yet two German divisions are sufficient to knock it all on the head. I do not think we can rest content with such doctrines.

In the original statement we were told that it was General Alexander and General Montgomery who shared Eisenhower's view. Now, it is only General Alexander. I hope he may be allowed to speak for himself. I cannot believe that he has expressed himself in this crude fashion. It is perfectly clear that the operations must either be entrusted to someone who believes in them, or abandoned.

I trust the Chiefs of Staff will not accept these pusillanimous and defeatist doctrines, from whoever they come. I propose to telegraph shortly to the President, because the adoption of such an attitude by our Commanders would make us the laughing stock of the world ... This is an example of the fatuity of Planning Staffs playing upon each other's fears, each Service presenting its difficulties at the maximum, and Americans and Englishmen vying with each other, in the total absence of one directing mind and commanding willpower. I regard the matter as serious in the last degree. We have told the Russians they cannot have their supplies by the Northern convoy route for the sake of HUSKY, and now HUSKY is to be abandoned if there are two German divisions (strength unspecified) in the neighbourhood. What Stalin would think of this, when he has 185 German divisions on his front, I cannot imagine.[1]

One of the Prime Minister's many roles was to act as the conscience of the Allies. His determination to see the Allies through to victory is now legendary, and never more so than over Sicily. Ever since Casablanca he had continued to insist that the Allies carry out HUSKY during the June moon, noting that 'we shall be the laughing stock if, during the spring and summer, no English and American troops are firing at any German and Italian soldiers'.[2] However disagreeable the contents of his minute may have been, Churchill's words struck at the very heart of the problems develop-

---

[1] Minute D.72/3, 'Most Secret', Churchill–British Chiefs of Staff, 8 April 1943, PRO (CAB 120/368).
[2] Minute D.14/3, 'Most Secret', 13 February 1943, ibid.

ing with HUSKY. The truth was that during April 1943 an almost palpable wave of pessimism seemed to hang over HUSKY. The warnings Montgomery had begun to sound were turning into a troubled reality.

Eisenhower probably never saw Churchill's stinging minute but he was made quickly aware of the indignant reaction he and his commanders had created. First came a chilling message from the British Chiefs of Staff which forcefully reminded Eisenhower that the hazards of the Sicily invasion were not only understood and accepted but with Sicily's relatively undefended coastline manned primarily by Italians these risks were outweighed by the prospects for success. 'The Germans will be limited in numbers and *cannot* defend the entire coast line nor can they counterattack in any strength simultaneously at all points.' Even more stinging was their remark that the Eisenhower view 'really implies that United Nations forces *cannot* take on Germans in combined operations without being able to attack with complete superiority everywhere'.[1]

The Combined Chiefs also rebuked Eisenhower by stating that under no circumstances would they consider abandoning HUSKY. A chastened Eisenhower belatedly realized he had a tiger by the tail and hastily replied that 'HUSKY operation will be prosecuted with all means at our disposal. There is no thought here except to carry out our orders to the ultimate of our ability . . .'[2]

Despite the growing storm, planning continued to drift throughout the month of April while both Eisenhower and Alexander remained essentially oblivious of the urgent need for someone to take charge of HUSKY.

The missing ingredient was Alexander's active involvement. It is difficult to escape the conclusion that, as long as the battle for Tunisia continued, Alexander considered HUSKY a nuisance that — like it or not — would simply have to wait. Part of the problem lay in the inexperience of the Force 141 planners. However, the most serious problem was the same one which was to plague the OVERLORD planners later in 1943: the absence of a full-time commander able to provide guidance and decisions that a chief of staff cannot

[1] Cable, US Chiefs of Staff–Eisenhower, 10 April 1943, PRO (AIR 8/1346). The JCS cable expressed full agreement with their British counterparts and quoted their 8 April signal expressing resolute disagreement with the notion that two or more German divisions could deter the Allies.

[2] Eisenhower–CCOS, 12 April 1943, ibid.

make. During the HUSKY planning the Allies were victims of their own ineptness. Gairdner and his staff were never able to match the experience that Lieutenant-General Sir Frederick Morgan and his planning team brought to COSSAC* a few months later during the initial planning of the cross-Channel invasion.†

The Force 141 planners were in an unenviable and frequently untenable position. Gairdner's diary contains numerous references to his frustration over Alexander's indifference and Montgomery's growing opposition:

> *Tuesday, 30 March:*   I didn't get much out of Alex who I do not think is prepared to stand up to Monty.

> *Thursday, 1 April:*   The day was well-named! ... I can see that Monty is going to be a prima donna who will act as a most unpleasant hair-shirt to me. I can get no decision re the outline plan. Alex won't come to a definite decision because of Monty and he doesn't realise how short time is ... It is the devil.[1]

The unhappy result of all this indecision was a torrent of cables between the various headquarters involved in planning HUSKY which asked a great many questions but could not solve the fundamental deficiencies that continued to plague the operation. Without someone in charge the deadlock had no chance of being broken. Montgomery once attempted to stir Alexander's interest by pointing out that, 'There is some pretty woolly thinking going on – tactically and administratively‡ ... I have no intention of doing some of the things they [Force 141] suggest. We must get the initial stage management right before we go on to details ... Perhaps Charles Gairdner could come and see me before they make a complete mess of the whole thing.'[2] Alexander, however, refused to take more than a cursory interest in HUSKY.

Gairdner, in turn, complained that Monty was far too busy planning the Mareth offensive to see him, with the result that the

---

[1] Gairdner Diary, loc. cit.

[2] Letter, Montgomery–Alexander, 3 April 1943, Alexander Papers, PRO (WO 214/18).

* Chief of Staff to the Supreme Allied Commander, the Anglo-American staff created in March 1943 to plan Operation OVERLORD.

† Montgomery believed Gairdner was an example of the many senior British officers who lacked battle experience, but who were appointed to positions where such experience was vital. A more experienced and stronger-willed officer might have overcome the enormous problems which faced Force 141. Gairdner, while undoubtedly well-intentioned, was too ineffectual to function effectively.

‡ The British term 'administration' equates to 'logistics' in US parlance.

misunderstanding and bad feeling on all sides continued to fester. Montgomery was partly mollified when the British Chiefs of Staff announced they were able to supply the extra division he deemed essential for the Eastern Task Force. Both Alexander and Montgomery approved another revision to the plan assigning this division the landing craft originally set aside for Patton's Western invasion, which meant postponement of the invasion of Palermo until at least D+5. At this point Montgomery appeared satisfied with a plan which now strengthened the landings near Syracuse and fulfilled Tedder's requirement to capture the Gela airfields by using two veteran Eighth Army desert divisions.

Montgomery was not the only senior officer frustrated by Alexander: Admiral Cunningham was equally distressed by the indecision he was encountering daily. In early April he wrote to remind Alexander that 'It has become a matter of great urgency to issue the outline plan for HUSKY if Task Forces are to have a chance to be ready by the end of June.'[1] Alexander was unmoved and replied, 'I am very sorry, but you will have to wait until I have seen Montgomery, which I hope to do tomorrow.'[2]

While Gairdner was in London to secure British approval for the latest version of HUSKY, its architects were beginning to realize they were being tied to a hopelessly unsound plan. The most absurd aspect of the HUSKY venture so far was that Allied headquarters had sanctioned a plan they thoroughly disliked. A signal from Cunningham to the Admiralty on 25 April summarized the problem:

> Eisenhower put forward the plan ... only because this appeared to be the only alternative in view of the demand for an extra division for the Eastern assault. At that time this plan appeared to offer the only solution short of abandoning the operation as impracticable ... The plan is causing grave concern since it is disliked by Eisenhower himself and by almost all those who have had proper time to study the operation. It means the virtual abandonment of the Western assaults and thus pushes the Americans more or less out of the picture and this has caused much heart burning.[3]

At the same time as Cunningham was making these criticisms, Montgomery was beginning again to reassess the plan he had only

[1] Cable, Cunningham–Alexander, 3 April 1943, PRO (CAB 106/368).
[2] Cable, Alexander–Cunningham, 4 April 1943, ibid.
[3] Cable, Cunningham–First Sea Lord, 25 April 1943, PRO (AIR 8/1346).

days earlier pronounced 'about right'. Deciding it was still all wrong, he sent Force 141 another proposed revision. Convinced it was essential that HUSKY be launched with experienced troops, Montgomery argued that the two divisions given the mission of seizing airfields be switched to the eastern coast with the task of capturing the vital port cities of Syracuse, Augusta and Catania. Under this new proposal the Eastern Task Force would be increased from two to *three* corps, one of which would be responsible for securing Tedder's airfields.

This latest signal was received with utter dismay at Force 141, and although it was rejected out of hand on grounds that it interfered with the timetable for HUSKY, it was clear that Montgomery would remain their *bête noire*, and a formidable critic.

The pressures on Montgomery at this time were immense and he was beginning to show definite signs of weariness from the strain of the long campaign against Rommel. Even he was not immune to the toll that the harsh North African environment exacted from the fittest of men. 'I am very fit and well,' he wrote to Brooke in mid-April. Nevertheless, he admitted that 'the pace has been a real cracker since I came out in August last, and I have not had *one single day off*. The next party (Sicily) will be no rest cure!! ... I really believe I would burst into tears if, having come 2,000 miles and got the enemy cold, we mess it up in the end. It would be too frightful.'[1]

As the days ticked away and the date for the invasion of Sicily grew closer there was little progress toward a plan the Allied leadership felt confidence in. In mid-April Montgomery again attempted to arouse Alexander by warning that 'unless Eighth Army is freed from its present battle operations and sent back to get down to HUSKY, the success of that operation will be in grave danger'.[2] Alexander reacted with shock, not that HUSKY might be impaired but that it would be disastrous if Eighth Army were prematurely released to prepare for the invasion.

Even as planning went forward on the assumptions contained in the plan none of the Allied leadership had any confidence in, Montgomery continued to be nagged by doubt. Under the British

---

[1] Letter, Montgomery–Brooke, 15 April 1943, Alanbrooke Papers. In May Montgomery returned to England for his first leave since assuming command of the Eighth Army the previous August.

[2] Cable, Montgomery–Alexander, 17 April 1943, Alexander Papers, PRO (WO 214/18).

military system, dissent is considered acceptable so long as it is offered prior to the execution of an approved plan. Thus, Montgomery did not demur in declaring his continued disapproval of a plan which his experience convinced him was unsound. The HUSKY plan was, he wrote to Brooke in April, 'a dog's breakfast ... it breaks every common-sense rule of practical fighting, and would have no chance of success ... unless someone will face up to this problem and give a decision, there will be a first-class disaster ...'[1]

Montgomery emerged as the central figure during the planning for Sicily but, other than Patton, few Americans had even met General Bernard Montgomery. To the British, however, he was the hero of Alamein and the saviour of the British Army.

[1] Quoted in *With Prejudice*, op. cit., p. 431.

CHAPTER 4

The Hero of Alamein

Indomitable in retreat; invincible in advance; insufferable in victory!

CHURCHILL

At the age of fifty-five, Bernard Law Montgomery had been a
professional soldier for thirty-five years. He had spent all but one
of them in the relative obscurity of the Regular establishment that
comprised the prewar British Army, where he was known as a
loner, and an outspoken, somewhat eccentric officer whose interests revolved solely around his profession. Virtually overnight he
became a hero throughout Britain for his exploits as the new
commander of Eighth Army. However, within the upper echelons
of the American leadership in the Mediterranean little was known
of Montgomery beyond his newly acquired reputation as the
general who bested Rommel at El Alamein. That was soon to
change during the months of planning and preparation for HUSKY
that followed the Tunisian campaign.

The candour which Montgomery brought to all his endeavours
was never more in evidence than during this period which earned
him the enmity of many senior British and American officers who
were involved in the preparations for HUSKY. In the case of Bernard
Montgomery there was rarely a middle ground: he was either
respected and admired or abhorred.

Who was this cocky, diminutive general who was about to lead
the Eighth Army into Sicily? Clearly, the man who became world-
famous simply as 'Monty' was not cut from the same cloth as most
other British officers. He neither acted nor dressed in the manner
of a British officer. When he spoke it was to state with great clarity
exactly what was on his mind, irrespective of the feelings of those
to whom his remarks were directed. His meteoric leap in 1942
from relative obscurity to national hero stirred the passions of
friend and foe as has no other Allied general of World War II,
including Patton. Even his death in 1976 at the age of eighty-seven

has only served to escalate the discussion and differences of opinion about his generalship. To understand what would occur during the Sicily campaign, it is necessary to understand something about the man and his Army during the early months of 1943.

At first sight Montgomery was not impressive. Physically, he stood five feet seven inches tall and during the period of the Sicilian campaign he was thinner than normal, his weight about 147 pounds ($10\frac{1}{2}$ stone). His face was dominated by hawk-like features: a sharply pointed nose and ears that seemed too large for his head. His hair had thinned noticeably on top and his deeply receding hairline was hidden (at least in most contemporary photographs) by his famous black beret. His small, neatly trimmed moustache was speckled with grey. In the heat of the Mediterranean summer his uniform regularly consisted of chukka boots, knee-length tan socks, corduroy trousers or baggy khaki shorts, and a khaki shirt with rolled sleeves, completely devoid of decorations or badges except for the Eighth Army patch sewn at the top of both sleeves. On his shoulders were the cloth epaulettes of a full general. His black beret was adorned with two badges[*] and when he stood to deliver one of his frequent addresses to his troops, his uniform sagged off his thin frame. When he spoke it was in a slightly high-pitched tone and an impeccable English accent, although by birth he was an Ulsterman.

First impressions, particularly physical ones, can be misleading and anyone but a fool soon realized he was in the presence of authority. The first clue was Montgomery's penetrating grey-blue eyes which fastened with thoughtful intensity directly upon a speaker. Undoubtedly they were Montgomery's most striking feature: they literally glittered. 'This was extraordinary,' remembers his long-time subordinate General Sir Charles Richardson.[†] His biographer has described the asceticism and missionary zeal that lay behind the traditional soldier's mask.[1]

Montgomery exuded the air of authority that all great com-

---

[1] Montgomery's life and military career have been recorded in Nigel Hamilton's three-volume official biography: *Monty: The Making of a General, 1887–1942* (1981); *Monty: Master of the Battlefield, 1942–1944* (1983); and *Monty: The Field-Marshal, 1944–1976* (1986).

[*] The General Staff badge and the badge of the Royal Tank Regiment.

[†] General Sir Charles Richardson served in the Eighth Army as GSO 1 (Plans) and later as GSO 1 (Operations). After brief service with Mark Clark's Fifth US Army, he returned to England as BGS (Plans) in 21st Army Group, a post he retained throughout the campaign in Northwest Europe. (Comments in letter to the author, 27 December 1985.)

manders seem to possess. Unable to dominate by his physical presence as did men like Alexander and Auchinleck, Montgomery more than compensated by the magnetism with which he influenced his troops and dominated his Army.

Like every senior British officer – with the possible exception of Alexander – the roots of Montgomery's philosophy of command lay in the desperate battles to halt the great German offensive which opened the Western Front in August 1914. The United States was involved in the 'Great War' for a relatively brief period and the men of the AEF never experienced the prolonged horrors of trench warfare that lasted over four years for the British. Montgomery experienced first-hand as an infantry officer the dreadful butchery that passed for modern warfare. He was severely wounded in the chest during the First Battle of Ypres in 1914, won the DSO, and was shocked by what he saw as a wanton sacrifice of men to outmoded doctrines of war. In 1916 he participated in the Battle of the Somme which he termed 'a perfect shambles', and where in a single day – 1 July 1916 – the British sustained 57,000 casualties, with more than 19,000 killed.* Battalions, regiments, even divisions were consumed as fast as they could be fed into the front lines.

The Somme, Arras and Passchendaele nurtured in Montgomery a revulsion for tactics which used men as cannon fodder. He would undoubtedly have agreed with Ernest Hemingway who described what he saw on the Western Front as the 'most colossal, murderous, mismanaged butchery that has ever taken place on earth'. By war's end he was thirty, had risen to the temporary rank of lieutenant-colonel, and the exalted position of a divisional chief of staff. His later criticism of the war was scathing: 'It was to take the experiences of the 1914–18 war to show me what was wrong in the Army . . . By the time . . . the war was over it had become very clear to me that the profession of arms was a life-study, and that few officers seemed to realise this fact . . . The frightful casualties appalled me. The so-called "good fighting generals" of the war appeared to me to be those who had a complete disregard for human life.'[1]

[1] *Memoirs*, London, 1958, Chapter 2.
* By comparison the British and Canadians lost 16,000 killed and 57,000 wounded during the *entire* battle of Normandy in 1944. Exact figures of British casualties in the First World War are unknown but are estimated to include approximately 1,385,000 dead. (Cf. John Terraine, *The Smoke and the Fire*, London, 1981, Chapter III.)

The gentlemanly approach to the administration of the Army during the inter-war years did nothing to alter Montgomery's belief that the British were ill-equipped, ill-led, and without adequate strategic and tactical doctrine to fight a modern war. His assessment became tragic reality in 1940 at Dunkirk which he recognized as a military disaster despite the eccentric British practice of magically turning military debacles into glorious occasions, as exemplified not only by Dunkirk but later in Burma and at Arnhem.* The so-called 'miracle of Dunkirk' was in reality the result of a German blunder that permitted the escape to England of most of the BEF, among whose commanders was the GOC of the 3rd Division, Major-General B. L. Montgomery.†

The dissolution of the BEF caused Montgomery to thrust himself with an obsessive intensity into the defence of England against what in 1940 was thought to be a certain invasion by the German Army. The real miracle of 1940 was not Dunkirk but the Battle of Britain which dissuaded Hitler from launching Operation *Seeloewe*.‡ During the next eighteen months Montgomery was promoted to lieutenant-general and commanded 5th and 12th Corps and, starting in November 1941, Eastern Command.

Nineteen forty-two marked the nadir of British fortunes in every theatre of their operations. In the east, after the fall of Singapore, came the retreat from Burma by Alexander's army. One setback after another in the Mediterranean was mirrored in the North

* When Churchill addressed the House of Commons on 4 June 1940 he did not mince his words, referring to the events in France as 'this pitiful episode' and reminding MPs that what had just befallen the French Army and the BEF was 'a colossal military disaster'. The Prime Minister went on to deliver perhaps his most famous speech in which he declared that '... we shall fight on the beaches, we shall fight on the landing grounds, we shall fight in the fields and in the streets; we shall fight in the hills; we shall never surrender. . . .' A toned-down version of the same speech was broadcast over the BBC to the British public and nearly forty years later it was revealed that a stand-in had delivered the speech, as indeed he was to do on a number of occasions when Churchill was too occupied with affairs of state to do so himself. (See Sir Winston Churchill, *Great War Speeches* [paperback edition], London, 1978.)

† In the aftermath of military campaigns it is usually possible to identify decisions which, although perhaps insignificant or overlooked at the time, altered irrevocably the outcome of a battle, campaign or even a war. One such example was Dunkirk where Hitler, in a moment of what now appears to have been overcaution, ordered Guderian's XIX Panzer Korps to halt for three crucial days outside Abbeville. This blunder prompted British historian Liddell Hart to write some years later that 'His [Hitler's] action preserved the British forces when nothing else could have saved them. By making it possible for them to escape he enabled them to rally in England, continue the war, and man the coasts to defy the threat of invasion. Thereby, he produced his own ultimate downfall, and Germany's five years later.' (Cf. *History of the Second World War*, London, 1973 [Pan edition], p. 80.)

‡ SEALION was the German code-name for the invasion of Britain.

Atlantic as the Germans demonstrated their mastery of the sea by daring to send the battlecruisers *Gneisenau* and *Scharnhorst* through the English Channel. However, when Churchill moved to end the disastrous setbacks endured at the hands of Rommel and decided to sack General Sir Claude Auchinleck, his first choice was *not* Montgomery. Ignoring the advice of Brooke, Churchill decided to entrust the command of the Eighth Army to an officer of great experience in desert warfare, Lieutenant-General W. H. E. 'Strafer' Gott, then the GOC, 13th Corps. Brooke strongly disagreed, arguing that Gott, who had been involved in the desert war for two full years without a rest, was too physically and mentally worn out to make an effective replacement for Auchinleck. Fate intervened, however, and Gott was killed when his aircraft was shot down and burned on the ground while en route to Cairo. This time, Churchill was forced to listen to his CIGS and agreed that Bernard Montgomery was to be sent at once from England to assume command of the Eighth Army.*

From the time of his premature assumption of command of the Eighth Army from Auchinleck, to his conduct of the two battles which instantly won him fame – Alam Halfa and El Alamein – the name Montgomery continually gained notoriety. Literally within hours of his arrival he instinctively understood that a whole new approach was required to rejuvenate the Eighth Army. His first orders set the tone for the future. Denouncing the defeatist atmosphere he found pervading his new command, Montgomery bluntly told his officers and men:

---

* Churchill first met Montgomery shortly after Dunkirk and their relationship would continue until Churchill's death in 1965. Greatly impressed by the 3rd Division, the Prime Minister invited the austere major-general to dinner, and what ensued was a classic example of one-upmanship between two strong-willed men. Montgomery later wrote that 'Churchill asked me what I would drink at dinner and I replied – water. This astonished him. I added that I neither drank nor smoked and was 100% fit; he replied that he both drank and smoked and was 200% fit' (*Memoirs*, p. 69). The two were good-natured adversaries both during and after the war. Lord Chalfont recounts this anecdote: Monty's 'appalled reaction to the clouds of cigar smoke with which Churchill had filled his tent in the desert was the subject of much amusement, as was Churchill's reply to a questioner in the House of Commons who complained that Montgomery had invited von Thoma, the defeated German general, to dinner in his desert caravan. "Poor von Thoma," said Churchill gravely. "I, too, have dined with Montgomery." ' (Alun Chalfont, *Montgomery of Alamein*, New York, 1976, p. 217.) Although it became more intimate in the postwar years, Monty's wartime relationship with Churchill was businesslike, and founded upon professional admiration and respect. It was, however, devoid of the warmth and intimacy Churchill enjoyed with men like Alexander and Eisenhower and, while Montgomery may have had the Prime Minister's ear, he does not seem to have had his heart.

> *Here* we will stand and fight; there will be no further with-
> drawal. I have ordered that all plans and instructions dealing
> with further withdrawal are to be burnt, and at once. We will
> stand and fight *here*. If we can't stay here alive, then let us stay
> here dead.[1]

To the assembled officers of the Eighth Army he said:

> I understand there has been a good deal of belly-aching out here.
> By belly-aching I mean inventing poor reasons for not doing
> what one has been told to do. All this is to stop at once. I will
> tolerate no belly-aching . . .[2]

As General Richardson recalls, 'We listened with growing
amazement.'[3] During the first days of his command Montgomery
made his presence instantly felt. An officer who was found arranging transportation for the troops to pull back into the Nile Delta
was curtly told that there was *no* transport: 'I have taken it all
away for the attack.' Behind the front lines he discovered some
troops digging a trench. 'You can stop digging,' he told them, 'the
Germans will *not* get this far.' A revitalized Eighth Army won the
defensive battle of Alam Halfa and in late October and early
November defeated Rommel at El Alamein. During the pursuit of
the Afrika Korps into Tunisia, and throughout the spring of 1943,
a new sense of purpose and accomplishment spread throughout
the Eighth Army. British success at Alamein was significant in
strategic terms for it ensured that Axis forces in the Mediterranean
would never again pose a major threat there. Just as important
was the effect of Montgomery's victory for British morale.
Monty's favourable treatment by the British press was in no small
part a result of the mystique with which the campaign was treated
by the war correspondents. His arrival began the process in earnest. Monty's dress, his adoption of an Australian bush hat festooned with the regimental crests of his units, and his many public
remarks, the most famous of which was that he would 'hit Rommel for six', not only impressed his troops but added to his lustre at

---

[1] Quoted in Hamilton, *Monty: The Making of a General, 1887–1942*, p. 623. Not only
has there been considerable contention over Auchinleck's intentions, and whether or not
Monty 'stole' his predecessor's plan and used it for the battle of Alam Halfa, but the
argument presented by Hamilton has created fresh quarrels in the 'Letters' columns of
various British newspapers and journals.

[2] General Sir Charles Richardson, *Flashback*, London, 1985, p. 109.

[3] Ibid.

home. Reporters delighted in faithfully reporting his remarks and in filing stories from the front.

'The war was very heavily reported in romantic terms. The enemy was depicted as brave and, in the case of the Italians, if not brave then chivalrous.' Montgomery's arrival 'added the one factor missing from the romantic vision of the war – a hero-figure.* Montgomery turned out to have many of the qualities of that other amazing character of the desert, Lawrence of Arabia. He had Lawrence's keen sense of publicity, of getting himself a good press while appearing to hate it, of "backing into the limelight".'[1]

Montgomery also possessed other qualities which set him apart from other British military commanders. He gave the men of Eighth Army the prestige and recognition that they craved as soldiers who were daily expected to be prepared to expend their very lives in the name of country and their comrades. As one journalist observed at the time, 'His compact with his troops is a straight business proposition; they gave him their best and in return he gives them victory and its attendant glory . . . Montgomery exploited the Alamein victory to make the world Eighth Army-conscious. One attitude fed upon the other and the reciprocal effort was compounded with each victorious battle until the Eighth Army became in the eyes of the world – more importantly, in the eyes of the enemy – a fabulous fighting organization. Montgomery used the power of publicity to fuse his men with the inspiration his own dour character could never impart.'[2]

---

[1] Phillip Knightley, *The First Casualty*, London, 1975 (Quartet edition, 1982), p. 290. Churchill, perhaps deliberately, aided the process by his public acclaim for Rommel which resulted, as Knightley points out, in 'the British public . . . [treating] "the Desert Fox" as its own hero'. Rommel was less charitable, telling neutral correspondents in Berlin that the British were 'cowards' and their methods of fighting 'dishonourable'. In a December 1942 letter to Brooke, Monty bit the hand that fed him: 'I am quite sick of the press . . . They misinterpret everything you say; in many cases they say what is quite untrue; they play for sensation.' (Quoted in *Monty: Master of the Battlefield, 1942–1944*, op. cit., p. 179.) Needless to say, Monty was not above using the press in the same manner in which he claimed to be used by them.

[2] L. S. B. Shapiro, *They Left the Backdoor Open*, Toronto, 1944, pp. 42–3.

* Unlike any other World War II campaign before or after, the North African battles represented warfare in its purest form. There were few towns or cities to be destroyed by the protagonists, and fewer civilian casualties than in any other theatre of war. In the barren desert the grim conflict was played out as a sort of mythological fable: artillery duels, tank against tank, soldier against soldier, general against general. Even the architects of the action – Rommel and Montgomery – assumed larger-than-life proportions. Forty-two years later the sons of these two famous generals would be honoured on the historic site of this great battle. Rommel's son Manfred, Lord Mayor of Stuttgart, told over 2,000 veterans assembled at El Alamein for the annual reunion that 'I am sure my father would approve of my being here' (*Boston Globe*, 30 October 1984).

One has only to examine the fortunes of Eighth Army after Montgomery's departure to establish the validity of his unique hold upon his men. His successor, General Sir Oliver Leese, tried hard to reflect Monty's style, and for a time in Italy Eighth Army lived on its reputation. But the colourless Leese could not continue to inspire an Army so closely identified with Montgomery.* Under Leese, Eighth Army once again became more ordinary and less charismatic, much like a boxer whose heart is no longer in the fight but who still goes through the motions to salvage professional pride.

What Montgomery accomplished with Eighth Army was to raise their *esprit de corps* to unprecedented levels. The Eighth Army star became not only a badge of honour but a symbol of pride that outlived the war. Monty shrewdly continued to foster his identity with that of his former comrades-in-arms and, for many years, he would appear to a tumultuous reception at the annual Eighth Army reunion.†

Montgomery was fortunate to have in Alan Brooke, the CIGS, a powerful advocate and admirer. Their friendship had been born years earlier when both officers taught at the British Staff College, Camberley, and was cemented during their time in France in 1939–40 when Brooke commanded 2 Corps. One of the most poignant events of either man's life occurred when a distraught Brooke wept in Montgomery's arms after being ordered by Churchill to return to England. Montgomery later remembered 'that

---

* Oliver Leese was a protégé of Montgomery and attempted to emulate him when he took command of Eighth Army at the end of 1943 in Italy. One of the habits of Monty he attempted to copy was the handing out of cigarettes to his troops whenever and wherever he met them. In Italy Leese was reputed to have stopped a Scotsman one day and after a halted conversation thrust a packet of the best John Player cigarettes into his hand. The Scotsman looked up at the towering Leese and disdainfully replied, 'You must be new; there used to be a wee bugger in a black beret before you who did this.'

† Monty was never bashful about exploiting his Eighth Army connection, sometimes with unexpectedly amusing results. Sir Harry Llewellyn recalls one occasion when he arrived for a dinner at which he was to give an address and during the meal his false teeth broke. The old field-marshal did not have a spare set with him and demanded that someone find him a suitable substitute so that his speech could go on as scheduled. Several were quickly offered but none would fit; finally, a gentleman stepped forward with *six* different sets and invited Montgomery to try them out. One set fitted perfectly and a beaming Monty quipped, 'I can always count on one of my Eighth Army chaps to come through in a pinch! What regiment did you serve with?' The somewhat embarrassed gentleman replied, 'I'm afraid I'm a civilian who never served in your Army, sir; I'm the local undertaker.' (Interview of 18 September 1984.)

scene in the sand-dunes on the Belgian coast [as] one which will remain with me all my life'.[1]

With Churchill, Brooke was one of only three people whose authority over Montgomery was absolute.[2] As deeply as Brooke admired his brilliant subordinate he was never loath to rebuke Montgomery whenever he overstepped the mark. Monty, in turn, took his occasional scoldings with uncustomary good grace. 'I always reckoned . . . "Brookie" . . . showed a great wisdom in the way he handled me. I like to be told by my boss what he wants me to do, and then to be left alone to do it – being given all possible support, but without any interference or fuss.'[3]

Not long after he arrived in the desert Montgomery began the practice of sending back-channel communications directly to Brooke in the form of letters, cables and copies of his personal diary in which he recorded his impressions of the events he was masterminding in the desert. It was customary for senior officers in the field to send such communications direct to Brooke in order to keep him informed, and frequently to seek his backing.* For other reasons, Montgomery habitually kept his official superior – Alexander, the C-in-C, Middle East – informed of his actions. He considered Alexander's role was to meet his logistical requirements, to act as a buffer with those who would otherwise distract his attention, and to command with the very loosest rein, all of which Alexander obligingly did.

The British successes against Rommel were a tonic to Churchill whose political position was shaky in mid-1942. Not only were his critics silenced but the Prime Minister looked like a genius for having placed Montgomery in command of the Eighth Army at exactly the right moment. Moreover, the favourable publicity became a useful tool to raise the morale of the British people who

---

[1] *The Path to Leadership*, London (Fontana edition), 1963, p. 112. In the same essay Montgomery noted that 'Brooke was the best soldier produced by any nation during Hitler's war'.

[2] The third was Lady Clementine Churchill. (Cf. Carlo D'Este, *Decision in Normandy*, New York/London, 1983, pp. 397–8, and Colville, *The Churchillians*, p. 156.)

[3] *The Path to Leadership*, op. cit., p. 109.

* The Monty–Brooke correspondence may be likened to that which occurred between Eisenhower and Marshall. Monty's letters always began with 'My Dear CIGS', or 'My Dear Brookie', while letters from Eisenhower to Marshall always began more formally with 'Dear General'. *No one* ever called Marshall 'George' except his wife and the irascible General 'Vinegar Joe' Stilwell. FDR once made the mistake of calling Marshall 'George' and was so intimidated by Marshall's stony reply that from then on he always addressed him as 'General'.

had been accustomed for so long to bad news from the war front.

The transformation of the Eighth Army from its nadir in the summer of 1942 to the triumphant force that marched into Tunisia in early 1943 was exemplified by the victory parade organized by Montgomery when his troops reached Tripoli in February 1943. After over two years of defeat piled upon defeat, it was a moment to be savoured. Both Churchill and Brooke attended and, as the Prime Minister's personal assistant described it, 'On the seafront the greater part of the 51st Highland Division was lined up. They looked magnificent. We had last seen them on their arrival in Egypt, pink as lobsters from their first painful days in the African sun. Now they were bronzed and fit ... Silhouetted against the clear blue sky, a lone kilted soldier stood motionless on top of Mussolini's triumphal arch as the troops marched past with pipes playing. It was a sight I shall never forget. Nor will the PM, who was in tears.'[1]

Standing beside Monty, Churchill addressed the troops and told them, 'When anybody asks you what you have done in the Great War, it will be enough to say you marched with the Eighth Army.'[2] He also reminded them that:

> Yet nightly [we] pitch our moving tent
> A day's march nearer home.[3]

As the North African campaign drew to a close the Eighth Army was at the peak of confidence and cockiness, which itself was a reflection of its dynamic commander. While it is true that some of his officers and men disliked the autocratic little man who had so dominated their lives since the previous August when he had drawn the line at Alamein and thundered that henceforth there would be NO WITHDRAWAL, NO RETREAT, and NO SUR-RENDER, most recognized that a dynamic new broom had swept away not only the failures of the past, but had instilled a new sense of confidence in, and an identification with, the best-known for-

---

[1] Notes of Commander C. R. Thompson, quoted in Gerald Pawle, *The War and Colonel Warden*, London, 1963, p. 229. Colonel Warden was the cover-name for Churchill. From 1940 to 1945 Thompson was one of his Personal Assistants.

[2] Quoted in Harry Llewellyn, *Passport to Life*, London, 1980, p. 138.

[3] Quoted by Churchill in *The Hinge of Fate*, Boston, 1950, p. 720. Brooke too was deeply moved and later recalled, 'As I stood by Winston watching the division march past, with the wild music of pipes in my ears, I felt a large lump in my throat and a tear run down my face. I looked round at Winston and saw several tears on his face.' (Quoted in Bryant, *The Turn of the Tide*, p. 578.)

mation in the British Army. Churchill later wrote to King George that the Eighth Army had 'perhaps the best troops in the world'. Many years later one of Monty's staff reminisced, 'He made you better than you thought you were. Monty absolutely deserved all the credit he could get for the way he changed us. I mean, we were different people. We suddenly had a spring in our step.'[1] Another noted, 'Everybody felt, more and more, disproportionately perhaps, this tremendous upsurge, that you were the "chosen", you were the élite, that you were with this guy and he was with you.'[2]*

Montgomery's recipe for successful command was to translate his enormous confidence in himself to his troops. He was able to instil in them the firm belief that they simply could not lose under his leadership, and that their commanders throughout the chain of command had done everything possible to ensure victory with the minimum loss of life. What he did was to 'bring a completely new spirit to the Eighth Army when he assumed command. He showed who was master. He inspired his will . . . Monty *did* dominate the

---

[1] Quoted in *Monty: The Making of a General, 1887–1942*, op. cit., p. 629. The 51st Highland Division was an excellent example of the resurgence of the British Army. Most of the original Highland Division was lost in France in 1940 and forced to surrender to Rommel and his 7th Panzer Division at St-Valéry-en-Caux. One of the more poignant photographs of the war depicts Rommel accepting surrender from the division commander at St-Valéry. The proud, battle-tested Highland Division at Tripoli was unmistakable evidence of just how far a British Army under Montgomery's leadership had progressed since the dismal days of Dunkirk.

[2] Quoted in *Monty: Master of the Battlefield, 1942–1944*, op. cit., p. 221.

* Montgomery was totally unlike the stuffed-shirt caricature of himself who was thought to be stiff and humourless. On the contrary, he exercised command of his Army with the loosest of reins. For example, as he proved by the many unauthorized uniforms he wore throughout the war, he was never a stickler for uniform regulations or for bombarding his troops with memos. In fact, he was notorious for never issuing written orders. In Sicily one of the few directives sent to his troops was with tongue in cheek. As he impishly noted in his *Memoirs*, the humidity of Sicily took its toll and his men were in the habit of discarding their clothing during the heat of the day. 'Some even took to wearing the wide-brim Sicilian straw hat. I well remember an incident that occurred one day as I was driving in my open car up to the front. I saw a lorry coming towards me with a soldier apparently completely naked in the driver's seat, wearing a silk top hat. As the lorry passed me, the driver leant out from his cab and took off his hat to me with a sweeping and gallant gesture. I just roared with laughter. However, while I was not particular about dress so long as the soldiers fought well and we won our battles, I at once decided that there were limits. When I got back to my headquarters I issued the only order I ever issued about dress in the Eighth Army; it read as follows: "Top hats will not be worn in the Eighth Army"' (*Memoirs*, p. 185). According to Monty's Canadian liaison officer, Colonel Dick Malone, the culprit was a Canadian sapper operating a bulldozer, stripped to the waist. It was common practice for the soldiers of Eighth Army to yell and wave their hats whenever they spotted Montgomery, who returned their attention by standing up in his open staff car and waving back. As Malone recounts, it was 'truly an unusual relationship between private and Commanding General'. (Cf. Colonel Dick Malone, *Missing From the Record*, Toronto, 1946, p. 46.)

collective consciousness of the British Army so that all felt when "that little man" – sometimes spoken with exasperation as well as affection, but always with strong feeling – when "that little man" was in control all would, in the end, be well . . . By uncompromising strength of mind he dominated men and events.'[1]

The exercise of leadership is in part an intangible combination of factors that sets a leader apart from those he is responsible for. These invisible qualities are far more than the authority that automatically devolves from rank or position. Clausewitz has called it resolution and strength of character. 'The forerunner of resolution,' said Clausewitz, 'is an act of the mind making evident the necessity of venturing and thus influencing the will. This quite peculiar direction of the mind, which conquers every other fear in man by the fear of wavering is what makes up resolution in strong minds. . . .' Strength of character he defined as tenacity of conviction and the will to stick to that conviction despite the great distractions and unpredictability of war.[2]

Montgomery's philosophy of command was outlined in a letter to Brooke shortly after Alamein:

> Determined leadership is vital; and nowhere is this more important than in the higher ranks. Other things being equal the battle will be a contest between opposing wills. Generals who become depressed when things are not going well, and who lack the drive to get things done, and the moral courage and resolution to see their plan through to the end, are useless in battle. They are, in fact, worse than useless – they are a menace – since any lack of moral courage, or any sign of wavering or hesitation, has very quick repercussions down below. To win battles you require good Commanders in the senior ranks and good senior staff officers; all of these must know their stuff. You also require an Army in which the morale of the troops is right on the top line. The troops must have the light of battle in their eyes; if this is not so you can achieve nothing.[3]

The problem, lamented Montgomery, was that there were too few generals able to measure up to this standard. 'I have serious misgivings when I think of the large Army in England, commanded by Generals who do not know the practical technique of

[1] General Sir David Fraser, 'Montgomeries', *London Review of Books*, 22 December 1983–18 January 1984.
[2] Carl von Clausewitz, *On War*, Pelican edition, 1968.
[3] Letter, Montgomery–Brooke, 11 November 1942, PRO (WO 214/19).

modern battle fighting, many of whom have not seen a shot fired in this war, who do not know the "feel of the battle", who have no practical experience of the stresses and strains of the battle, and who thus have mostly got a wrong sense of values.'[1]

The rolls of the British Army became littered with the names of officers whose leadership failed to measure up to Montgomery's exacting standards. Some might be described as 'quite useless' and unfit for further command of any sort, while others would be recommended for specific assignments which would, in his opinion, provide them with the requisite experience and groom them for a later return to service under his command.* After Alamein several senior officers of the Eighth Army were sacked. One was the gallant and colourful former cavalry officer who commanded 10 Corps, Lieutenant-General Herbert Lumsden. The outspoken Lumsden commanded Montgomery's *corps de chasse*, but the two had fundamentally divergent views over the employment of armour and when Lumsden consistently followed his own course of action he was summarily relieved. After being informed he was sacked, Lumsden caustically remarked that 'this desert is not big enough to have two such shits in it as Monty and myself at the same time'.[2]

Montgomery's major flaw was that too often he carried a simple philosophy to absurd extremes. After the war he would sometimes

[1] Letter, Montgomery–Brooke, 5 January 1943. Brooke himself had written in the dark days of 1941 that: 'It is lamentable how poor we are in Army and Corps commanders; we ought to remove several, but Heaven knows where we shall find anything very much better. . . . The flower of our manhood was wiped out some twenty years ago and it is just some of those that we lost then that we require now.' (Quoted in Bryant, *The Turn of the Tide*, op. cit., p. 239.)

[2] Llewellyn, *Passport to Life*, op. cit., p. 132. Lumsden, a noted horseman, was later sent to the Far East where he was killed in early 1945 when a Japanese *kamikaze* aircraft struck the battleship USS *New Mexico*. Montgomery was unrepentant about dismissing Lumsden and not long after wrote to Alexander, 'I understand that LUMSDEN has been given command of a Corps of two armoured Divisions which is to go overseas to fight in Europe. He must NOT be allowed to command a corps in battle on the continent; he will merely let the show down. We have made many mistakes in our senior commanders; do not let us go on doing it – especially when we have seen the red light once.' (Letter of 17 March 1943, Montgomery Papers.)

* An example of Monty's ruthlessness occurred during operations to bridge the River Sangro in Italy. The six bridges erected under the supervision of a senior engineer were washed away when the river rose fifteen feet overnight and flooded, creating severe problems. The engineer was invited to tea with Monty, who politely enquired why after ten days not one single bridge was left in operation. Suddenly raising his voice he said, 'You are useless . . . quite useless. Ten days and not a single bridge going . . . here I have a little geography book about Italy . . . it says it isn't unusual at this season for the rivers in Italy to rise even twenty feet in one night. . . . Get out . . . you are fired.' Half an hour later a new engineer was placed in charge. (Quoted in *Missing From the Record*, op. cit., p. 55.)

boast – to the dismay of his former subordinates and friends – that he had never lost a battle. He once pompously advised, 'Military history? They'd better just read my campaigns. It's all they'll need.'[1]

Quite naturally, Monty's traits of character intensely annoyed the old guard of the British Army. Modesty was never a part of his makeup; candour, however, was and he was never hesitant about stating his views, no matter how blunt or outrageous. An eminent military historian has written that: 'The trouble with Monty was that he was anything but a "nice chap", as Tedder said disparagingly of the desert generals who preceded him. He was cocky, boastful, exaggerated his successes and refused to admit to the slightest error, of which he made a number, as generals will, ran down his contemporaries and was in a very un-English way, unabashedly his own PR man.'[2]

Yet it was this outrageous behaviour and complete disregard for the consequences that catapulted Montgomery to fame. Fortunately, Churchill not only condoned but encouraged individualism which mirrored his own eccentric behaviour and in Montgomery and Mountbatten he had two masterful examples. A critic once complained to Churchill that Monty was in violation of Army regulations by wearing badges on his bush hat, to which the Prime Minister is said to have replied: 'If I thought that badges would make my other generals as good as Monty I would order them all to wear badges.'[3]

Montgomery was such a larger-than-life character that his flaws were glaringly evident. The line between extreme confidence and arrogance is thin and his habit of speaking his mind regardless of the consequences delighted his critics and caused even a staunch friend like Brooke to wring his hands in dismay over his lack of tact. Particularly irksome were Monty's relations with Americans, who never warmed to him. As one of his subordinates has observed, the bond of understanding that existed between Monty and his troops simply did not exist with the Yanks.[4]

Nowhere was this more evident than in the relationship between Monty and Eisenhower. Their first meeting occurred in late

[1] Fraser, 'Montgomeries', op. cit.
[2] Shelford Bidwell, 'Monty, Master of the Battlefield or Most Overrated General?', *RUSI Journal*, June 1984.
[3] Quoted in 'The Monty Legend', *LIFE*, 15 May 1944.
[4] Malone, *Missing From the Record*, op. cit., p. 87.

March 1943 at Monty's TAC HQ near Gabes.* Both men came away wary of each other. Montgomery had never made a secret of his disdain for Lieutenant-General K. N. Anderson and his First British Army and, according to his biographer, 'Monty's searching questions and his evident contempt for what he knew was at fault on the First Army side of Tunisia must have been painful to the Supreme Commander...'[1] Indeed, it was only a few days later that Eisenhower wrote confidentially to Marshall that:

> Montgomery is of different caliber from some of the outstanding British leaders you have met. He is unquestionably able, but very conceited. For your most secret and confidential information, I will give you my opinion, which is that he is so proud of his successes to date that he will never willingly make a single move until he is absolutely certain of success – in other words, until he has concentrated enough resources so that anybody could prac- tically guarantee the outcome. This may be somewhat unfair to him, but it is the definite impression I received. Unquestionably he is an able tactician and organizer and, *provided only that Alexander will never let him forget for one second who is the boss, he should deliver in good style.*[2] (Author's italics)

At the same time Montgomery was writing to Brooke:

> Eisenhower came and stayed a night with me on 31 March. He is a very nice chap. I should say he is probably quite good on the political side. But I can also say, quite definitely, that he knows nothing whatever about how to make war or to fight battles; he should be kept away from all that business if we want to win this war. The American Army will never be any good until we can teach the Generals their stuff. Everyone is trying to teach the soldiers, and to have Battle Schools, and so on. But the soldiers won't fight, *because they have no confidence in their Generals*;

---

[1] Hamilton, *Monty: Master of the Battlefield, 1942–1944*, op. cit., p. 211. Both Brooke and Alexander were repeatedly advised to sack Anderson whom Montgomery considered quite unfit to command an army. Not only were they told of Anderson's failings – the kindest remark Monty ever made about him was that he was a 'good plain cook' – but he suggested his replacement be Lieutenant-General Oliver Leese, his 30 Corps commander. Alexander evidently agreed that Anderson should be replaced but was unable to bring himself actually to do so. (See Chapter 20.)

[2] Letter, Eisenhower–Marshall, 5 April 1943, Eisenhower Papers.

* They had met briefly in May 1942 during Eisenhower's first visit to the United Kingdom. Montgomery was conducting a large field exercise in southern England and during his briefing Eisenhower made the mistake of lighting a cigarette. Montgomery, who detested cigarette smoke, promptly ordered the chagrined American major general to put it out at once. In his trip report Eisenhower noted only that Montgomery was 'a decisive type and appears to be extremely energetic and professionally able'. (See *The Eisenhower Papers*, op. cit., Vol. I, p. 319.)

they would fight all right if the Generals would put them in to battle properly; therefore teach the Generals.[1]

The unfortunate outcome of these crucial first impressions was that neither man really understood the other and, as subsequent events would clearly demonstrate, the misunderstanding would only harden.

Within days of their first meeting Montgomery's insensitivity led to a contretemps which greatly embarrassed Eisenhower. Monty was fond of betting small sums on practically anything. The unwary who spent time at his TAC HQ soon found themselves signing his betting book and opening their wallets. One such unwitting victim was Eisenhower's no-nonsense chief of staff, Bedell Smith, who had agreed to provide Montgomery with a B-17 Flying Fortress, complete with American crew, if Eighth Army captured Sfax by 15 April. When Sfax fell on 10 April a jubilant Montgomery despatched a MOST IMMEDIATE cable to a mystified Eisenhower demanding immediate delivery. Unable to contain himself, several hours later he sent another cable. Both Eisenhower and Bedell Smith were acutely disconcerted by this incident. Bedell Smith had not even been aware he had been hoodwinked until Montgomery – like a spoiled child – began peppering AFHQ with demands that the bet be honoured at once. Monty got his Flying Fortress along with a scorching rocket from Brooke who clearly saw its negative impact on the still-embryonic Anglo-American relations. It was, Brooke wrote in his diary, 'crass stupidity' for its harmful effect.[2] After complaining about the matter to Brooke, Eisenhower was never heard to mention the matter again, but it was never forgotten.

Other than the streak of child-like impishness that was very much a part of Montgomery's character, the incident was an omen of future misunderstandings of a far more serious nature that clouded his relations with senior American commanders for the remainder of the war. So far as Monty was concerned the whole affair was a delightful gambol in which he had successfully tricked the unsuspecting Americans out of an aeroplane that he very likely could have obtained merely by asking for it.

[1] Letter, Montgomery–Brooke, 4 April 1943, Montgomery Papers. According to the Eighth Army Chief of Staff (then Brigadier Francis de Guingand), 'They got on well.' Monty's verdict on Eisenhower was: 'good chap; no soldier!' (Quoted in Richardson, *Flashback*, op. cit., p. 155.)
[2] Alanbrooke Diary, 3 June 1943.

Brooke was quick to sense that Monty's abrasive manner would cause untold problems with senior American officers. The B-17 incident was one of those occasions when Brooke employed stern measures to curb Monty's impetuousness. He was a master at the art of rebuking errant subordinates while still retaining their admiration and respect.* Montgomery was ordered to cut short a leave in England and return to North Africa where an unhappy Brooke delivered a stern rebuke:

> He requires a lot of education to make him see . . . the war as a whole outside the Eighth Army orbit. A difficult mixture to handle; brilliant commander in action and trainer of men, but liable to commit untold errors, due to lack of tact, lack of appreciation of other people's outlook . . . It is most distressing that the Americans do not like him, and it will always be a difficult matter to have him fighting in close proximity to them. He wants guiding and watching continually and I do not think Alex is sufficiently strong with him.[1]

To make matters worse, certain of Montgomery's remarks became public knowledge and contributed to the impression that he was insufferable and virtually uncontrollable as a field commander. For instance, in Sicily he related to Patton the now frequently quoted remark: 'George, let me give you some advice. If you get an order from Army Group that you don't like, why, ignore it. That's what I do.'†

There was no evidence of the frivolous side of Montgomery during the planning for HUSKY. As the end of April approached and the Allies still had not agreed upon a plan for the invasion Montgomery issued a fresh challenge that not only precipitated the gravest crisis yet but sparked animosities that plagued the Allied leadership for the remainder of the war.

---

[1] *The Turn of the Tide*, op. cit., pp. 640–1.

* Lieutenant-General Sir Frederick 'Boy' Browning, the Allied airborne commander at Arnhem, once emerged from Brooke's office, his face scarlet, to say, 'I've had the biggest dressing down of my life – but My God he's a great man!' (Quoted in *Alanbrooke*, op. cit., p. 215.)

† This quote has appeared in numerous accounts, including Bradley's *A Soldier's Story*.

CHAPTER 5

Montgomery Takes Charge

I am prepared to state on whatever reputation I may
possess as a fighting man that the plan put forward
by me will succeed.   MONTGOMERY

Monty thinks of himself as Napoleon.   TEDDER

Three months had passed since the Casablanca decision to invade
Sicily and still the Allies had no approved plan for the invasion.
The Allied commanders remained at loggerheads; decentralized
planning, a leaderless planning staff at Force 141 and the distraction of Eisenhower, Alexander, Montgomery and Patton with the
campaign to defeat Rommel and von Arnim had all contributed to
a situation that was clearly out of control and which threatened
the timetable for HUSKY. Churchill and Roosevelt had insisted the
invasion take place in June but the unexpected length of the
campaign in Tunisia until mid-May and the requirements of the
logisticians had forced postponement of the invasion which was
now scheduled for the early July full-moon period.

By early April, Montgomery was the only senior Allied ground
commander who believed that the time had come for HUSKY to
take priority over North African operations, and he blamed Alexander's distraction squarely on General Anderson whose generalship he had criticized for months in letters and cables to Alexander
and Brooke. Even though unable to devote his full attention to
HUSKY it is clear from both the official and unofficial records of the
campaign that Montgomery repeatedly and sometimes slightly
hysterically criticized what he perceived to be the failure of the
Allies to place someone qualified and responsible in charge of
HUSKY *before* it was too late.

Throughout the month of April his concern had risen to a crescendo of denunciation of the Force 141 plan and the dire consequences of continued indifference. On 12 April he complained to Brooke that:

> 18th Army Group ... ought to be giving very clear and definite directions about HUSKY. But they don't do so; they have to exercise operational command of a part of the front [Anderson's First British Army] ... trying to unravel the awful mess there. In war a commander cannot do someone else's job as well as his own. It merely means he neglects his own job and the show suffers ... The HUSKY planning is in a hopeless mess. We have made such a mess of it so many times in this war that it makes me quite angry to see us drifting the same way now. I should have thought we had learnt our lesson after nearly 4 years of war. But apparently not.[1]

Nor was Montgomery the only senior officer in the Mediterranean to become alarmed by the lack of direction of HUSKY. 'Jumbo' Wilson also sent Brooke a warning on 1 April that 'it would appear planning in Algiers is suffering from lack of a full-time commander on the spot, and is relying on snap decisions from those who are fully engaged (in Northwest Africa) and you may wish to send someone out here to sort things out'.[2]

Brooke's hands were tied. He had no one capable and available to fill the void, nor could he interfere directly in an Allied operation without working through the Combined Chiefs of Staff. To have interfered would have been an open vote of 'no confidence' in Eisenhower's leadership and quite likely would have resulted in the new Allied commander's resignation and an even worse crisis. A resolution to the problems of HUSKY would have to come from within. As much as Brooke agreed with Montgomery, the problem was essentially beyond his immediate control. Like it or not, the CIGS could only remain on the sidelines and use his influence wherever possible.

Even Deputy Prime Minister, Clement Attlee, who was rarely heard from during the war, asked Churchill '... have we anyone of directing mind and commanding will-power directly in control of the joint planners? Should not their deliberations be directed to essentials by some ruthless and forceful personality?'[3]

[1] Letter of 12 April 1943, Montgomery Papers.
[2] Quoted in *The Mediterranean and Middle East*, Vol. V, op. cit., p. 20.
[3] Ibid.

Try as he might, Montgomery had failed to convince Alexander to act. Now, he flew to Algiers where on 19 April he took his case directly to Eisenhower and Alexander at a private meeting at which he cautioned the two commanders that time was running out and it was imperative that some responsible commander take over HUSKY to guide the planning in a firm and sensible manner. With characteristic bluntness Montgomery said, 'It is my definite opinion that if we go on in this way any longer we may have a grave disaster ... Therefore some sort of compromise is essential in order to get ourselves out of the mess we are now in. "To compromise" is a well-known British habit, and we shall have to adopt it.'[1]

The compromise Montgomery had in mind was to withdraw Leese's 30 Corps Headquarters and the 50th and 51st Divisions from the front in Tunisia and send them to the rear to begin preparing for HUSKY. With de Guingand in Cairo as an acting major-general to guide the planning, and several other experienced staff officers to see that it was carried out, there would at long last be a common sense approach taken to the Eighth Army effort. Occasionally, Montgomery himself would take time from his duties at the front to visit Cairo to satisfy himself that the planning did not falter.[2]

'I had a very satisfactory conference at Algiers yesterday,' he wrote to Brooke the following day. 'The whole thing is very far from satisfactory *really*; but my suggestions as to the only possible compromise were agreed to. If HUSKY is to come off there is no solution other than the one put forward by me ... In theory Alex should be doing it. In practice Alex is hopelessly involved in keeping First Army on the rails. In fact the whole underlying cause of the mess we are now in is that we chose a man to command First Army who was not fit for the job; then having discovered he was not fit for the job, we still keep him on.'[3]

Montgomery came away from this meeting incorrectly believing he had been given a mandate to take over HUSKY, an assumption which was quickly proven a fantasy.[4]

---

[1] 'Notes on "HUSKY"', 19 April 1943, Alanbrooke Papers.
[2] Ibid.
[3] Letter of 20 April 1943, Montgomery Papers.
[4] *Monty: Master of the Battlefield, 1942–1944*, op. cit., p. 252.

Three days later Montgomery made a secret trip to Cairo to see de Guingand and reported to Brooke that:

> HUSKY is in a fearful state. I became so alarmed at what was going on that I went to Cairo on 23 April to be put fully into the picture by my Chief of Staff. And for the first time I learnt what the planning staffs suggested I should do. I immediately wired to Alex and said that the proposed plan would involve us in a first-class disaster. I suggested a plan that would be a success ... My remarks on the plan have caused the most frightful tornado at Force 141, and it is clear to me that I am regarded there as a most unpleasant person ... They want me to operate in little B[riga]de G[rou]ps all over the place. I refuse. They say there will be only slight resistance. I say that here in Tunisia the Italian is fighting desperately; he has never done so before; but he is doing so now. To operate dispersed means disaster. We cannot go on in this way. Unless we get a good and firm plan *at once*, on which we can all work, *there will be no* HUSKY *in July*. [1]

Small wonder then that Montgomery deplored his battles with Force 141 as 'far more exhausting than my battles against the Germans'. The 'proper answer' he told Brooke:

> is to bring two USA Divisions in to land at CENT and DIME (Scoglitti and Gela), on the south coast, and get the aerodromes. And chuck the Palermo landing for the present. If this were agreed to, then we could all go ahead. The operation would have every prospect of being a first-class show. The effort at present is too dispersed. We have got ourselves into a real high class mess, and I feel the judgement of history will be that we have only ourselves to blame. No one is sitting right back, and thinking out quietly the various moves in the game – and doing the high level stuff – for the Tunisian war or for HUSKY ... As far as I can make out the trouble with HUSKY has been that no experienced fighting commander ever even read the proposed plan made out by the Planning Staff in London. And yet Algiers accepted it almost in toto. [2]

The day after Montgomery's visit to Cairo he signalled Alexander that he refused to carry out the proposed HUSKY plan so long as it remained in its present form. Without concern for the consequences, Montgomery now placed his reputation on the line by an act of calculated insubordination. Although his critics were outraged by his impertinence and audacity, the truth was that *no one* was satisfied with the plan. For well over two months the Allies

[1] Letter of 30 April 1943, Montgomery Papers.
[2] Ibid.

had vacillated over what to do, providing more than adequate substance to the notion that war by committee is an exercise in futility. In short, the Navy wanted ports, the Air Force wanted airfields, both wanted dispersion of their forces and Montgomery wanted a concentration of land forces mutually supporting one another. Thus, Cunningham disliked any plan which did not include an eastern and western invasion; Tedder was willing to compromise so long as the final plan guaranteed capture of the Gela airfields; Alexander wavered, and attempted to accommodate each proposed change. Eisenhower had been notably unsuccessful in steering his subordinates into a resolution of a problem that was virtually out of control. If Eisenhower could not do it, then someone else had to step in and compel the top brass to pull their act together. By necessity rather than by choice that person was Montgomery whose signal to Alexander on 24 April defined in clear terms both the problem and his proposed solution:

> Planning so far has been based on the assumption that opposition will be slight and that Sicily will be captured relatively easily. Never was there a greater error. Germans and also Italians are fighting desperately now in Tunisia and will do so in Sicily. To go ahead on this assumption with all the consequent tactical repercussions such as dispersion of effort which is a feature of all planning to date will land the Allied Nations in a first class military disaster. We must plan the operation on the assumption that resistance will be fierce and that a prolonged dogfight battle will follow the initial assault. I am prepared to carry the war into Sicily with the Eighth Army but must do so in my own way. The fight will be hard and bitter.[1]

One of Alexander's planners, Sir David Hunt, later challenged Montgomery's interpretation, stating that the Force 141 planners actually overestimated Italian resistance by two divisions and that Montgomery was guilty of the same thing by asserting that the Italians would fight desperately in Sicily. Montgomery's 'principal argument for a change of plan was based in fact on a purely temporary phenomenon, the nature of the fighting on the Enfidaville line ... the Italians were at that time putting up quite a good show. From this Montgomery deduced they would do even better on their home ground.'[2]

---

[1] Cable, Montgomery–Alexander, 24 April 1943, HUSKY Planning Papers, Middle East Forces, PRO (WO 201/2833).
[2] David Hunt, A Don at War, op. cit., pp. 190–1.

The heart of Montgomery's plan was for Eighth Army to operate with its corps and divisions within supporting distance of one another. 'The first thing to do is to secure a lodgment in a suitable area and then operate from that firm base. Time is pressing and if we delay while above is argued in LONDON and WASHINGTON the operation will never be launched in July. Whole planning work in Cairo is suffering because everyone is trying to make something of a plan which he knows can never succeed.'[1]

Without waiting for his approval Montgomery brazenly informed Alexander that he had already issued orders that planning within Force 545 was proceeding along these lines and that Admiral Ramsay was in complete agreement: '... together we are prepared to launch the operation and see it through and win ... I want to make it clear that I shall require for this battle the whole of Eighth Army ... the above solution is the only possible way to handle the E[astern] T[ask] F[orce] problem with the resources available.'[2]

Montgomery's ultimatum generated shockwaves which ranged from outrage to elation that at last someone was doing *something* to shake the Allied command from its malaise. Tedder and Cunningham were furious, and the latter complained that 'Monty is a bit of a nuisance: he seems to think that all he has to do is to say what is to be done and everyone will dance to the tune of his piping. Alex appears quite unable to keep him in order. Tedder is also absolutely opposed to this new plan.'[3]

Both Tedder and Cunningham favoured the concept of dispersed landings, and Cunningham in particular was bothered by the fact that Montgomery's plan left thirteen airfields in southeastern Sicily uncaptured, which placed his ships lying offshore in even greater jeopardy. Tedder's quarrel with Montgomery was precisely the same one which later caused a similar storm of controversy in Normandy: *airfields*. The Monty plan, argued Tedder, took no account of air force requirements, and unless the Army

---

[1] Cable, Montgomery–Alexander, 24 April 1943, loc. cit.
[2] Ibid.
[3] Letter, Cunningham to the First Sea Lord, 28 April 1943, PRO (AIR 8/1346). General Gairdner recorded that 'A.B.C. ... was very angry when he heard that planning was going on on the new plan without any reference to him'. Ramsay was ordered by Cunningham to proceed no further without his permission.

was prepared to capture these airfields he was solidly against the plan.[1]

Although the earlier problem of obtaining an extra division for Eighth Army had been resolved, neither Tedder nor Coningham (whose task it was to provide tactical air cover for the invasion) were satisfied with Montgomery's latest proposal. Coningham pointed out that by leaving thirteen airfields in Axis hands, enemy aircraft could operate over the assault area for up to forty-five minutes in every hour while his own Malta-based aircraft were limited to a mere fifteen minutes. These airfields must not only be denied to the enemy but captured for use by Allied tactical air.[2]

Montgomery's rebuttal was that once ashore Eighth Army must be in a position to fight and to do so required *both* airfields and ports. Under the existing plan he could not accomplish both missions. However, without airfields the Air Force could not provide the level of support required by both the Army and the Navy. It was a Catch-22 impasse.

In Algiers on 29 April Montgomery was to present his case to Alexander, Tedder, Cunningham and Patton, who was now back from command of II Corps in Tunisia as the Western Task Force Commander. At the last minute Monty became ill and sent de Guingand to represent him, but his plane crash-landed en route. Fortunately, no one was killed but de Guingand received a concussion and had to be scratched as Monty's spokesman. The 30 Corps commander, Oliver Leese, was sent at the last minute and when no one met him at the Algiers airfield, Leese was forced to hitchhike and arrived at the flag-bedecked conference tired and dirty in his battledress.[3] However, without Monty's personal presence neither Tedder nor Cunningham was prepared to accept Leese's presentation which was greeted with open hostility.

Montgomery had correctly anticipated passionate opposition to his plan and had again written to Alexander in an attempt to prevent what he was certain would be further vacillation. However, the time had come when Alexander was finally forced to make a decision and he did so in favour of the Montgomery plan,

[1] 'The Sicilian Campaign', unpublished RAF operational narrative by T. Milne, Air Historical Branch, December 1955, PRO (AIR 41/52).
[2] Ibid.
[3] *Monty: Master of the Battlefield, 1942–1944*, op. cit., p. 257.

even though Tedder was of the opinion that no compromise was possible.[1]

'Really gentlemen,' Tedder told the assembled brass, 'I don't want to be difficult but I am profoundly moved. Without the capture of these airports, the operation is impossible ... We are all in it, it is not an army show, but three arms are in it. Besides we can't support Patton unless we get these [air]fields.'[2] Cunningham replied for the navy, 'From the naval point of view, the massing of so many ships in the Siracusa area is to invite disaster, and besides the chief merit of amphibious attack is to do so on a broad front and disperse enemy effort. I am definitely opposed to the plan.'[3]

Patton spoke up to say that under Montgomery's plan his force would be split by 45 miles and that without the airfields, 'While I may get ashore, I won't live long.'[4]

All the pent-up frustrations of months of deadlock were let loose during one of the most acrimonious high-level debates of the war. Opinions were sharply divided during the meeting which lasted nearly three hours. Patton recorded with considerable understatement that the argument got 'quite hot'. An exasperated Cunningham finally blurted, 'Well, if the Army can't agree, let them do the show alone. I wish to God they would.'[5]

Alexander was quite unable to restore any semblance of control or generate a compromise. At a complete loss for a solution to this disagreeable quarrel, he suggested that perhaps they ought to send a wire to Churchill. A more absurd course of action cannot be imagined than an open admission that HUSKY was incapable of being run by its own commanders. One can easily picture the chilling reaction from the Prime Minister who was already dismayed by the indecision emanating from Algiers. Finally, Cunningham restored some common sense to the proceedings by suggesting that the proper course of action was to query Eisenhower; 'After all, he is Commander-in-Chief.'

Even sillier was the suggestion that Alexander, Tedder and Cunningham form a delegation to visit Monty to discuss the matter. A stickler for protocol, Cunningham would have nothing

---

[1] Tedder, *With Prejudice*, op. cit., p. 433.
[2] Diary of General George S. Patton, Jr., 29 April 1943, Patton Papers, Manuscript Division, Library of Congress.
[3] Ibid.
[4] Ibid.
[5] Ibid.

to do with such a scheme, noting acidly that, 'I also have something to do.'[1]

The meeting broke up in complete deadlock when Alexander was summoned away and never returned. Patton's dismay undoubtedly mirrored the feelings of all present that the impasse was 'all due ... to lack of force on the part of Alexander, who cut a sorry figure at all times. He is a fence walker.'[2]

Tedder ordered Coningham to accompany Leese to Eighth Army to explain the air force point of view to Montgomery and perhaps arrive at some last minute compromise. Coningham reported that he found Montgomery 'obstinate' and the problem continued to fester for three more days while yet another meeting of the HUSKY commanders was hastily arranged for 2 May. A weary and discouraged Montgomery took his frustrations out on the hapless Leese who was told he had failed in his mission and was 'no good' as a negotiator. To Brooke he wrote, 'this is really quite frightful'.[3]

Montgomery arrived in Algiers with a prepared set of notes, but this time Alexander was unavailable and the proposed meeting threatened to dissolve into another interminable postponement when Tedder and Cunningham refused to attend without Alexander present.

Whether or not the debate had transcended honest differences of opinion and was now strictly a blood feud is difficult to tell, but the evidence suggests it was impossible to separate the two any longer. Not long afterwards Cunningham ordered that Montgomery's name was never again to be mentioned in his presence. Tedder was stung by Montgomery's strong opposition to the air force plan to provide initial tactical air support from the RAF's Malta Command instead of from Air Vice-Marshal Harry Broadhurst's Western Desert Air Force, whose involvement was to begin only when the Axis airfields in southeastern Sicily were captured and operational. Montgomery, who thoroughly understood the need for close air–ground co-operation, had exceptional confidence in Broadhurst and considered any break-up of the successful team that fought in the desert as 'suicidal and criminal'. 'A change-over of command now is not only highly undesirable; it

---

[1] Ibid.
[2] Ibid.
[3] Letter, Montgomery–Brooke, 30 April 1943, Montgomery Papers.

is dangerous. We have so little time available that we must go for SIMPLICITY ... We cannot consider seniority and sentiment.'[1] Tedder refused to relent and Broadhurst, who in Normandy was to find himself caught between Tedder and Montgomery, now had a foretaste of that contention between two powerful personalities whose growing hostility to one another eventually escalated throughout the remainder of the war and during the postwar years when both men were the Chiefs of their services.[2]

Monty was not to be dissuaded by Alexander's absence on 2 May, and in what was surely one of the most unorthodox and comical encounters of the war, the crisis which had stirred rancorous debate and delayed the completion of an outline plan for three months was suddenly resolved in the AFHQ lavatory where Monty had 'run to ground' Bedell Smith.[3] The AFHQ Chief of Staff's influence upon Eisenhower far exceeded his relatively junior rank, and while he was aware of the planning rift, Montgomery's diary claims that when he heard the Eighth Army commander's side of the story he was 'much upset about the whole thing we discussed in the lavatory!! He said that for *political reasons* it was absolutely essential to reach a firm decision, and to get on with it.'[4]

The politics of HUSKY was of no concern to Montgomery, and he presented to Bedell Smith the *military* reasons why there must be a new plan. The solution he outlined was to cancel entirely the Palermo operation and shift the US effort to the southeast in the Licata–Gela–Scoglitti region to capture the airfields required by the air force and to ensure unity of effort.

Bedell Smith was only too aware of the growing pressures from Washington and London and any further delay beyond the July moon period was unthinkable. Churchill had already amply demonstrated he would tolerate no further delay or excuses; only the previous day Marshall had cabled Eisenhower to question the timing of HUSKY and insist the operation be carried out as soon as

---

[1] 'Notes on "HUSKY"', 19 April 1943, Alanbrooke Papers.
[2] Cf. *Decision in Normandy*, op. cit., Chapter 13. In 1946 when Montgomery became CIGS and Tedder Chief of the Air Staff, the two men would rarely appear together at a meeting. One or the other would find an excuse not to attend.
[3] Montgomery, *Memoirs*, p. 177.
[4] Diary entry of 6 May 1943. In the film *Patton*, a pompous caricature of Monty in a paisley scarf outlines his plan on the mirror of the lavatory, adding credibility to the false image of Monty as a buffoon intent upon usurping Patton's role in HUSKY.

possible, emphasizing the beneficial effects of boldness and surprise.[1] Smith was a hard-headed realist who understood clearly the
immense pressures on his boss to get HUSKY back on course. What
Montgomery told him that fateful morning in an Algerian privy
was immediately conveyed to Eisenhower, who concurred.

Eisenhower apparently had never understood the full extent of
the planning rift until he read a copy of Monty's 24 April cable to
Alexander and, when he did so, his naval aide records he sided
with Tedder and Cunningham. 'Ike sides with Air and Navy
viewpoints and may have to referee the inter-service British scrap.
Then "Monty" could appeal to his home government, worse still,
says he won't attack if it isn't done his way! ... The quarrel
amongst the three British services is accentuated by the wilful
cocksureness of Monty who at the moment is riding on a high
wave of public popularity ...'[2] Although Captain Butcher accurately reflected the growing anti-Monty sentiment within AFHQ,
he and many others failed to comprehend that while the dispute
itself was essentially *British*, the commanders involved were all
Allied, and the time had come for Eisenhower as the Commander-
in-Chief to intervene and resolve it.

Bedell Smith later claimed that the reason for Eisenhower's
sudden change of heart was that the Palermo operation 'did not
please us' and was strategically useless except for its port. 'So the
changes desired by Monty were readily conceded despite the
inherent supply problems if Palermo was left for later capture.'[3]
More plausible, however, is the fact that Eisenhower undoubtedly
realized there would have to be a compromise, and Montgomery's
plan, while not perfect, was an acceptable alternative. Although
Eisenhower refused to approve the change formally until he had
consulted Alexander, the deadlock was at last broken. The plan to
invade western Sicily was to be scrapped in favour of an invasion
by Patton's force in the Gela–Licata area.

Even though he had won acceptance of his plan, Montgomery
insisted on addressing the conference which both Tedder and
Cunningham prudently elected to attend. In his prepared notes*
Monty admitted he could be a 'tiresome person', but defended his

[1] Butcher Diary, 1 May 1943.
[2] Butcher Diary, 27/28 April 1943.
[3] George F. Howe, interview with Lieutenant General Walter Bedell Smith, 12 May 1947,
USAMHI.
    * Reproduced verbatim in his *Memoirs*.

actions towards the HUSKY commanders in that 'I have seen so many mistakes made in this war, and so many disasters happen, that I am desperately anxious to try and see that we have no more; and this often means being very tiresome. If we have a disaster in Sicily it would be dreadful.'[1]

While Monty's prescription for HUSKY's ills may not have been palatable to all present, it was a model of clarity which very cleverly and deliberately avoided creating a British versus American problem by addressing the overall military problem and how he believed it ought to be overcome.

Eisenhower ordered Force 141 to begin an immediate examination of the operational implications of Montgomery's plan. Tedder did a *volte face* by later insisting that Monty's emphasis on the importance of the early capture of the airfields was nothing new. 'It was a plan which had been examined weeks before. Personally, I had always favoured it, owing to my doubts about the whole Western Task.' His report to Portal noted that 'the mental gymnastics of some of our Generals would be amusing if it were not for the effect on their reputation and authority. Appears, however, there is sporting chance of reasonable escape from the deadlock.'[2]

Eisenhower's decision took Alexander off the hook and he was only too pleased to concur with Monty's proposal. On 3 May Alexander issued formal orders to proceed and a cable was sent to Montgomery that, 'Your plan has been approved by the C-in-C.'[3] Several days later Eisenhower wrote confidently to Marshall that 'HUSKY planning is at last going ahead on clear cut and definite lines at full speed.'[4]

Neither Patton nor Gairdner had the slightest impact on the decisions reached in Algiers. Bedell Smith had alerted Patton after seeing Montgomery but he was unable to arrive in Algiers until the following afternoon – too late to participate in the debate. Eisenhower had not seen fit to consult Patton, who was informed,

---

[1] 'Remarks Made at Conference in Algiers on 2 May 1943 by General Montgomery', Butcher Diary.
[2] Quoted in *With Prejudice*, op. cit., pp. 434–5.
[3] Cable, Alexander–Montgomery, 3 May 1943, PRO (CAB 106/368). Curiously, Eisenhower's office records show him absent all day on 2 May, but the British official history and supporting archival documents confirm his presence, along with Butcher's diary which contains a copy of Montgomery's notes. (Cf. PRO [AIR 41/52].)
[4] Butcher Diary, 8 May 1943.

'George, I knew you would do what you were ordered without question and I told them so.'[1]

Patton's demeanour throughout the HUSKY crisis was almost tranquil and in vivid contrast to Montgomery's outspokenness. While decrying what he called 'war by committee', Patton wrote to his wife Beatrice that 'I intend to do a hell of a lot of listening, but will not sacrifice American lives to save my job.' Patton's placid façade masked his inner fury at what he considered a betrayal of American forces by Eisenhower. Upon receiving his new orders from an anxious Alexander, Patton replied by saying, 'General, I don't plan – I only obey orders.'[2] Before returning to Morocco, Patton met with Cunningham who was still smarting over Monty's success and the changes made to HUSKY. After castigating Montgomery 'in the most outspoken terms' the crusty admiral urged Patton to protest his new mission. Patton adamantly refused, saying, 'No, Goddammit, I've been in this Army thirty years and when my superior gives me an order I say "Yes, Sir!" and then I do my Goddamndest to carry it out.'[3]

Later, when he returned to his headquarters at Mostaganem where the Western Task Force HQ had moved on 26 April, Patton finally vented his anger, telling his staff, 'This is what you get when your Commander-in-Chief ceases to be an American and becomes an Ally.'[4] Alexander later attempted to soften the intense disappointment by writing in his campaign despatch that Patton's attitude was 'an impressive example of the spirit of complete loyalty and inter-allied co-operation which inspired all operations with which I was associated in the Mediterranean.'[5]

Under Montgomery's plan, American forces were to land at Gela and Scoglitti, and capture the three important airfields of Ponte Olivo, Biscari and Comiso, while a smaller task force commanded by Major General Lucian K. Truscott assaulted the small port of Licata to the west. Patton fully understood that his new mission relegated him to the secondary role of protecting Montgomery's left flank while the British made the main effort towards

[1] Patton Diary, 3 May 1943.
[2] Quoted in Ladislas Farago, *Patton: Ordeal and Triumph*, New York, 1963, p. 273.
[3] Ibid., p. 273, and Morison, *Sicily–Salerno–Anzio*, op. cit., p. 20.
[4] Ibid., p. 273.
[5] Alexander despatch: 'The Conquest of Sicily', 9 October 1945, Alexander Papers, PRO (WO 214/68). Also published in the 2nd Supplement to the *London Gazette*, 10 February 1948.

Messina. Outwardly, Patton accepted this subordination with good grace; only those close to him knew his real feelings.

Moreover, inasmuch as no specific mention had been made of a post-invasion strategy, Patton felt justified in insisting that Alexander produce a signed document, 'with the binding effects of a treaty', which would establish a clear-cut boundary between his forces and Eighth Army, provide for supplies through the port of Syracuse and allocate sufficient airborne troops to accomplish what Leese's 30 Corps staff had previously called an 'impossible task'.[1] Patton's demand was fully backed by Bedell Smith who recalled Field-Marshal Lord Gort's remark about Montgomery: 'In dealing with him one must remember that he is not quite a gentleman.'[2]

Patton's biographer, Martin Blumenson, believes that his real contribution to the planning of the Western Task Force invasion was to make clear the concept of the operation and then to leave his planners to get on with their job. Bradley, however, was harshly critical of Patton for what he considered his timid acceptance of Monty's plan, his failure to interest himself in the details of HUSKY and his apparent willingness to accept without demur any plan so long as it contained a role in it for himself – an allegation refuted by the evidence of Patton's diary and letters. Bradley's complaint was that, 'George is spectacular. Does not like drudgery. And planning is drudging work.'[3]

Patton did come away from Algiers with one heartening result when Eisenhower recommended to Marshall that he should have equal status with Montgomery. Marshall readily approved the proposal that Patton's I Armored Corps become Seventh United States Army on D-Day.

Gairdner found himself unable to continue serving effectively as Chief of Staff of Force 141. Monty's refusal to implement his plan had been received with gloom. 'If it is backed by General Alex (and I think it will be) it will lead to a first class crisis in my opinion. It is impossible to treat admirals of the fleet and air chief marshals as if they were ignoramuses in the art of war. Furthermore, the Ameri-

[1] Patton told Gairdner that although he had the highest respect for the valour of American fighting troops, he did not rate them so superior to the British that he could succeed with only one-third as many troops in attack, 'which the XXX Corps considered impossible'. (Cf. *The Patton Papers*, Vol. II, p. 241.)

[2] *The Patton Papers*, Vol. II, op. cit., p. 239, and Patton Diary, 5 May 1943.

[3] Bradley Commentaries.

cans are beginning to feel that the British Empire is being run by Monty ... I can't understand how democracies wage war.'[1]

When Alexander did finally back the plan, Gairdner told him that he saw no useful purpose in remaining as his Chief of Staff. 'General Monty will not accept anything I say unless it happens to coincide with his wishes. Patton and his staff and [Admiral] Hewitt came and put forward their demands for parachutists, supplies, etc. I couldn't give a decision and am really in an insufferable position.' It took Alexander five days before agreeing to his request and when the axe finally fell, he passed into obscurity, his tenure a bitter failure. Although ineffectual in an exceptionally demanding post, the fault lay mainly with Alexander. Gairdner rightly lamented that some of the blame must be shared by his superior. 'This is the first time in my Army career that I feel I have definitely failed – and really a great part of the fault should lie with General Alex – who on no single occasion either backed me up or made an independent decision of his own. History will show, although nothing succeeds like success, and the Generalship of the North Africa campaign, which I should have thought was far from good, is already being hailed as a masterpiece!'[2]

Strangely, despite the disappointing change of mission and the domination of recent events by Monty, Patton's opinion remained favourable. 'Monty is a forceful, selfish man ... ,' he remarked, 'I think he is a far better leader than Alexander and that he will do what he pleases, as Alex is afraid of him.' Of the new Seventh Army mission, Patton's diary recorded that 'the new operation, from every standpoint except supply, is easier than the old [plan]'.[3]

The perception of Montgomery as an arrogant, insufferably pompous, glory-seeking egomaniac intent on capitalizing upon his new found fame as the vanquisher of Rommel and the vaunted Afrika Korps is untrue. In seeking to alter the HUSKY plan and the role of the Eighth Army, his motivation was not to enhance his own position at the expense of Patton and the United States Army. The wealth of documentation about HUSKY effectively demolishes any allegation that his motivation was self-advancement. In fact, the evidence suggests quite the opposite: what Montgomery did in

[1] Gairdner Diary, 24 April 1943.
[2] Gairdner Diary, 24 May 1943.
[3] *The Patton Papers*, Vol. II, op. cit., p. 244.

the face of powerful opposition and potential ruin was an act of courage, which rather than enhance his role might well have destroyed it. While many like Cunningham were never satisfied by the cancellation of the western assault and believed the earlier plan was better, there is no evidence that Monty's motivation was based on any but military grounds.

Many years later, on the eve of his death, Montgomery's 13 Corps commander, the officer who commanded Second British Army in Normandy, General Sir Miles Dempsey, would call this 'his finest hour'.[1] His biographer has praised his determination that 'after three months of Allied muddle, indecision, revision and confusion, he would dictate a simple plan in which the soldiers would have confidence'.[2]

What has distorted our understanding of Montgomery's motivation and left justifiable doubts about his intentions was his unfortunate tendency to insensitivity, a trait that so disturbed Brooke. Fresh from the capitulation of the Allied high command to his demands, Montgomery now made a blatant attempt to seize control of the overall ground command at the expense of Alexander and Patton, first by attempting to persuade Alexander to place Patton's corps* under his command, and second, to remove Alexander as the Allied ground commander. Alexander, as usual, failed to nip this intemperate suggestion in the bud and in so doing unleashed a torrent of demands and recommendations from Monty which culminated in this proposal to Brooke: 'The proper answer is to let Alexander finish off the TUNISIAN war, and to cut him right out of HUSKY. I should run HUSKY. With the new plan it is a nice tidy command for one Army HQ and Eighth Army should run the whole thing.'[3]

While the evidence does not suggest that Montgomery aspired to higher command at the expense of Alexander or that there were sinister motives. This incident – the first of many before the war's end – displayed his remarkable inability to grasp that this was no longer a British war but now an Allied coalition endeavour. It never occurred to him that such a command arrangement was out of the question or that American commanders were still smarting

[1] Ronald Lewin, *Montgomery as Military Commander*, London, 1971, p. 150.
[2] *Monty: Master of the Battlefield, 1942–1944*, op. cit., p. 254.
[3] Letter, Montgomery–Brooke, 2 May 1943, Montgomery Papers.
* At this time Montgomery was unaware that I Armored Corps was to become Seventh US Army on D-Day.

over the patronizing attitude of the British, and their criticism of US leadership and fighting proficiency on the battlefield. Montgomery quite correctly exposed the chaos in planning and the absence of firm leadership at the top, but this further proposal struck at the very heart of American morale.

On purely military grounds the proposal was not without merit: unity of planning and command and one overall commander on the spot to guide the ground campaign. In short, the concept advocated by Montgomery was a corrective to the many ills that had plagued HUSKY to date. In view of what was to follow in Sicily the idea cannot be dismissed as the ravings of a megalomaniac bent on acquiring power. Both Montgomery and Patton had no faith whatsoever in Force 141 or Alexander. Patton called Force 141 'a mess' and Alexander 'weak' – and Monty had even less faith in Alexander's ability to plan and command HUSKY ground operations. 'Every plan put up by the [Force 141] Planning Staff has been agreed to by Alexander, and I do not think he had ever had the full operational requirements put before him by anyone qualified to do so. But he agreed with all the plans. And then when I went in and disagreed, and said the plan would result in a military disaster, and substituted an alternative plan – he agreed with me also.'[1] When Alexander failed to act, Bedell Smith did, and emphatically rejected any scheme that HUSKY should be an all-British operation under Montgomery.[2]

The well-known controversies which later ensued in Italy and Northwest Europe which have dominated the postwar histories of these campaigns had their roots in the planning for Sicily and in the campaign itself. Among the less fortunate results of Anglo-American warfare were the problems of command that began in North Africa, were carried into Sicily and then bedevilled the final, decisive campaigns of the war. Montgomery's biographer has written that however politically correct Bedell Smith's decision, it finally opened the door 'to coalition battle not seen since the fateful days of spring 1940, when British, Belgian and French Armies each went their separate ways to destruction. For the creation of *two* Allied Armies for Sicily, instead of Monty's preferred single Army, now ushered into Allied operations a political

[1] Montgomery Diary.
[2] The full story of Montgomery's bid for control of HUSKY is in *Monty: Master of the Battlefield, 1942–1944*, Part III, Chapter Two.

principle that committed the Allies to failure upon failure, since no overall commander could be found with both the tact to combine the separate national wills of their forces *and* the military genius to command them in the field.'[1]

Patton observed that combined Allied commands could not work, 'Allies must fight in separate theaters or they hate each other more than they do the enemy.'[2]

By the time the Allies finally settled their differences the HUSKY plan had been through seven different permutations and even then it was far from satisfactory in the eyes of Cunningham and others. One of the Naval C-in-C's main criticisms was the lack of centralized planning, '... three months' delay in the production of the final overhead plan for the operation should never, and need never, have occurred'.[3]

By its very nature the concept of coalition warfare is synonymous with compromise and the plan finally agreed by the Allies in early May proved a classic example. The problems that had troubled the planning of HUSKY did not end with Montgomery's intervention. Alexander's approach to high command did not change even when he was finally freed of the burden of the now concluded Tunisian campaign. Under his direct command were two of the most stubborn and independent-minded men ever to command armies in battle. Montgomery he knew well; the other was an officer whom, despite his Anglophobia, Alexander came to like and admire: George S. Patton, Jr.

---

[1] *Monty: Master of the Battlefield, 1942–1944*, op. cit., p. 270.
[2] Quoted in *The Patton Papers*, Vol. II, op. cit., p. 234.
[3] Quoted in Oliver Warner, *Cunningham of Hyndhope: Admiral of the Fleet*, London, 1967, p. 198.

CHAPTER 6

'An Old Man of About 60'

It is my destiny to lead . . .

GEORGE S. PATTON, JR.

Lieutenant General George Smith Patton, Jr. had long passionately believed that he would one day lead an American army into battle and win a famous victory. Despite the bickering over HUSKY which resulted in his Army being assigned a secondary role for the conquest of Sicily, Patton was convinced that destiny would eventually deal him a favourable hand.

The character and career of Patton are as controversial and misunderstood as those of Montgomery. In Britain, he is generally seen as a dashing, vulgar American general with a vastly overrated reputation. Patton provided ideal copy for the press and never denied its portrait of him, because he believed it helped get across to his troops the image he wished to present. The result was two Pattons: one which fulfilled American thirst for a swashbuckling hero, the other an intensely private man whose commitment to the profession of soldiering was as profound as that of Montgomery. The public perception of Patton has evolved upon a false foundation, with the result that he has become a stereotype bearing scant resemblance to the real Patton.

Patton's public image was a carefully crafted façade he created for himself to compensate for a lifelong sense of inadequacy which, in part, was the result of dyslexia.* As his biographer has written:

> Shy and withdrawn by temperament, tending easily to tears of emotion, unsure of himself, sensitive to natural and artistic beauty, he scorned these characteristics ... Seeing himself to be

* A reading impairment which causes the printed characters on a page to appear jumbled or upside down. Among the symptoms of this disorder are feelings of inadequacy and a need to compensate by high achievement in other endeavours. (Cf. Martin Blumenson, *Patton: The Man Behind the Legend, 1895–1945*, New York, 1985, pp. 16–17.)

unfit because he lacked what he considered to be the military virtues, he struggled with single-minded devotion to remake himself, to alter his inner nature into his image of the fighting man ... Toward the end of his life, even he could barely distinguish his real self from the portrait he had deliberately faked.[1]

Descended from a lineage that produced a number of distinguished soldiers who fought for the Confederacy during the Civil War, Patton believed it was his familial obligation to continue that tradition by becoming a great soldier. Heritage and a sense of inferiority generated a burning ambition to emblazon his name alongside the great captains of military history. 'But what set him apart from those who were similarly schooled and obsessed was his ability to transmit to his soldiers a driving will to win. It was the essence of his leadership.'[2]

Patton saw himself as the modern embodiment of his heroic Confederate cavalry forefathers. Originally commissioned in the cavalry, Patton was one of the first Army officers to become an advocate of its natural successor, the tank. He became deeply involved in the first US tank operations in France in 1917–18. After serving in Pershing's HQ, he later moved to the newly formed Tank Corps and established the first training centre for armour near Langres. His exploits during the battle of the Meuse-Argonne in September 1918 are now legendary. In command of the 1st Brigade, Tank Corps, Colonel Patton was on foot directing his tanks during the first day of the battle when he was wounded. A long-time friend who was present and also wounded during the same engagement remembers that, 'Our infantry was not moving forward. He ordered those near him to charge a machine gun nest that was holding up the advance. Patton led the charge. He found after a short time that he and his runner, Angelo, were all that were left. It was a suicidal mission and he was hit in the leg by the machine gun and fell in a shell hole. He said that on this charge he seemed to be looking at himself as if he were a small detached figure on the battlefield, watched from a cloud on high by Confederate kinsmen and his grandfather whose daguerreotypes he had studied as a boy.'[3] It was part of the enigmatic nature of Patton

[1] Ibid., pp. 12–13.
[2] Ibid., p. 12.
[3] Harry H. Semmes, *Portrait of Patton*, New York, 1955 (paperback edition), 1970, p. 63. Brigadier General Semmes was Patton's friend and associate for more than thirty years and a distinguished armour officer in his own right.

that despite his bravery on the battlefield, he would always nurture doubts about his courage.

When the war ended Patton was a full colonel, the holder of the Distinguished Service Cross, and one of the few authorities on tanks and tank warfare in the United States Army. During the tedious inter-war years Patton became one of the few advocates of armoured warfare in an Army dominated by cavalrymen. It was during these years between the two world wars that he refined his concepts of leadership.

The manner in which Patton exercised his leadership has been the subject of endless debate. He believed a commander must influence the action on the battlefield both by his personal presence and by gaining the attention and confidence of his troops. Nothing could get him emotional more quickly than a discussion of the American fighting soldier and his bravery. 'These things make me emotional, maybe too emotional sometimes,' he said. Part of Patton's genius was his instinctive understanding of his men: 'You've got to get the feel of troops to lead them. You've got to know how much is left in them and how much more they can take. I know just how much more by looking at their faces.'[1] Armchair generals like Fredendall had no place in a Patton command.

It is one of the ironies of the story of the Sicily campaign that the two ground commanders for HUSKY were more alike than either would have cared to admit. On the surface, Patton and Montgomery were wildly dissimilar generals: Patton the thruster, the architect of the free-wheeling offence and the hastily improvised defence; Monty the cautious organizer who thoroughly planned his battles and went to his grave claiming that all of them had gone exactly according to plan. A closer examination reveals that their leadership techniques were surprisingly comparable. Monty adopted the bush hat and the black beret as his symbols and Patton did the same with his impeccably neat uniforms and the pair of ivory-handled Colt Frontier model .45 calibre revolvers worn strapped to his waist.*

[1] Quoted by John P. Marquand in Colonel Charles R. Codman, *Drive*, Boston, 1957, p. xvii.
* Patton's revolvers were no mere window dressing; he knew how to use them, as he proved during his service with Pershing along the Mexican border during the punitive raid against Pancho Villa in 1916. Most who write of Patton refer to his revolvers as 'pearl-handled pistols', a mistake he would have quickly taken issue with. He once said that only a pimp in a New Orleans cat-house would wear pearl-handled pistols! His marksmanship

Each instinctively understood that the successful leader must do what he does best to the point of *exaggeration*. Patton, for example, 'was always the figure in shining armour on the coal black charger. That was his style. No one could touch him in the role which came naturally to him, and in the role which he schooled himself.'[1]

Lieutenant General James M. Gavin first met Patton in Sicily and remembers that his mannerisms were intended to impress his troops. 'He had the wit, as Field-Marshal Rommel once expressed it, to make himself distinctive, so that he stood out at all times and was recognized by soldiers wherever he appeared. He liked to talk to junior officers about the rather ordinary problems that sometimes perplexed them.'[2]

Like Monty, Patton made a deep impression upon his soldiers. He frequently spoke to his troops in assembly hall fashion and the men remembered what he said as much for the colourful, profane manner in which he said it as for what he actually said. Patton believed in expressing his ideas in terms his troops were not likely to forget. He tended to describe his tactics in sexual terms, and while his methods were often embarrassingly crude, Patton could be confident his message had been received. 'They laughed at the elaborate pornography of his pep talks, but also blushed.'[3] Generally, the essence of Patton's message was this: 'Now, I want you to remember that no son-of-a-bitch ever won a war by dying for his country; he won it by making the *other* dumb son-of-a-bitch die for *his* country.'*

Some, like Bradley, were privately revolted by Patton's excesses, particularly his vulgar language, and there were occasions when he

---

[1] Brigadier General Harry H. Semmes, 'General George S. Patton, Jr.'s Psychology of Leadership', *Armor*, May–June 1955.

[2] General James M. Gavin, 'Two Fighting Generals, Patton and MacArthur', *Atlantic Monthly*, February 1965.

[3] Ibid.

* Many will recall actor George C. Scott uttering these same words in the opening scene of the film *Patton*. The portrayal was accurate as General Gavin and others have attested.

---

saved his life in May 1916 when, in command of a ten-man detachment during a foraging expedition near Rubio, Mexico, he and his patrol engaged in a wild gun fight with three Villistas. When the dust had settled, Patton and his men found they had killed all three. For several weeks he became a national hero and the story received wide publicity in newspapers across the United States. For the remainder of his life the Colt .45 revolver became a part of Patton's uniform and a symbol of good fortune. (For a full account of the Rubio incident, see Martin Blumenson, *The Patton Papers*, Vol. I, Boston, 1972, Chapter 16.)

did carry his methods to intemperate extremes, but, on balance, his technique generally achieved its aim.* His men *did* listen and, even if this saved only one life in the future, Patton would have argued that it was worthwhile.

Patton was an uncommonly complex man who consistently proved a study in contrast, as an incident in the early days of the war illustrates:

> One time at [Fort] Benning when he was in command of the 2d A[rmored] D[ivision] there was what we used to call a 'smoker' for the officers of the division. There was booze, music and dancing girls. As the evening wore on the girls got rid of most or all of their clothes, and put on some obscene dances. At this point General Patton got up and walked out. The next day he told us there would be no more such activities and gave us a lecture about obscenity, etc. A few hours later he was explaining a tactical maneuver in the most obscene language! How do you characterize such a person?[1]

How, indeed! And yet, there was a very different side to Patton that remains relatively unknown. One who knew him exceptionally well was his former commander at Fort Myer, Virginia, Major General Kenyon A. Joyce, who describes him:

> George Patton was a rare soul ... colorful, incorrigible, unexplainable ... He had a fire burning within him and that fire surged to white heat on occasions. He was highly emotional but

[1] General I. D. White, letter to the author, 2 September 1985.

* One occasion when it did not work occurred in North Africa. Lieutenant Colonel (later Lieutenant General) John A. Heintges had just reported to the 3d Infantry Division when Patton drove up in his command car, stopped at the entrance to the division HQ Company and summoned the Headquarters Commandant, Major James K. Watts: 'You, man, come over here.' As Major Watts began walking over to Patton he said, 'You son-of-a-bitch! When I tell you to come, I want you to run.' Watts reported to Patton who demanded, 'Where the —— hell is your headquarters?' After telling Patton where to find General Truscott, Major Watts boldly said, 'Sir, I resent being called a son-of-a-bitch. I think you owe me an apology.' Patton agreed and said he was sorry.

Heintges' first formal encounter with Patton took place on the north coast of Sicily as the 3d Division was driving toward Messina. His infantry battalion was halted outside a village which was under heavy German artillery fire from a nearby ridge. Suddenly, Patton appeared on the road above him in his command car. 'He stood up in his command car and looked down at me, and he said, "You man, who are you?" And, I said, "I'm the 3d Battalion commander, sir, Lieutenant Colonel John A. Heintges." And, he said, "Well, you son-of-a-bitch, why the —— damn hell aren't you moving?" I said, "Sir, we are temporarily halted here because the Germans have us under observation from that ridge about 600 yards in front of you." And I said, "You have no business being here. You must have gone through my guard on the other side of that village behind us." And, just then the German artillery opened up and I have never seen anybody turn around on a narrow road as quickly as he did. His driver turned around on a dime and left nine cents change. And, that was Patton....' (Oral history interview of Lieutenant General John A. Heintges, 1974, USAMHI.)

instead of the instability that usually accompanies emotion, he had a tactical sense that approached genius, and the ability to make sound deductions that might be expected from one who was cold and calculating ... In reality, he was a deeply religious man, although he was blasphemous to a degree ... he was human with a tender side that enabled him to project himself into the woes of others. With all his interior complex, he had a rough outside and was truly a hard soldier, who could not forgive lack of standards, dereliction of duty or failure of courage. He was impatient with anything except a matchless performance of any task.[1]

Unlike Montgomery, who infuriated nearly every American commander with whom he had contact, Patton the profane swashbuckler possessed gentlemanly qualities that enabled him to charm even a potential enemy. In Tunisia he became incensed at what he considered was grossly inadequate air support of II Corps, and soon made his displeasure known at the highest level. When the Allied tactical air commander, 'Mary' Coningham, sent a rude signal to every Allied HQ in Tunisia which, in effect, called Patton a liar and the allegations 'a false cry of wolf', Eisenhower decided to intervene and personally ordered Coningham to II Corps to pacify Patton. When Coningham arrived at Patton's Command Post he was greeted with barely concealed hostility by a smouldering Patton who quickly unleashed his wrath upon the airman, and the two exchanged shouts. Patton argued that he and all American troops had been slurred by Coningham's remarks. Both men finally realized this was no way to resolve the problem and Coningham said, 'I am awfully sorry. What can I do to make amends?' Patton suggested that a public message of retraction would do nicely. Patton wrote in his diary that upon leaving Coningham said, 'I can't thank you enough. You have been very generous.' Patton replied: 'It is always easy to be generous to a gentleman who admits his mistakes.'[2]

Patton's version was confirmed the next day when Coningham

[1] Major General Kenyon A. Joyce, unpublished manuscript, Joyce Papers, USAMHI. Joyce commanded the 3d Cavalry Regiment and was one of the first to sense future greatness in Patton. In his 1934 efficiency report on Patton, Joyce wrote: 'I believe this officer could be counted upon for great feats of leadership in war.' He repeated this judgment in 1935 and in 1938, when Patton was a colonel and Joyce a brigadier general: 'Because of his innate dash and great physical courage and endurance he is a cavalry soldier from whom extraordinary feats might be expected in war.' (Extracted from Patton's official 201 file, 1918–1957, Accession # 17,250, Reel 1, Patton Papers.)

[2] Patton Diary, 4 April 1943. See also Chapter 8.

wrote to his higher HQ that 'I like him very much, he is a gentleman and a gallant warrior. But on the slightest provocation he breathes fire and battle, and as I also like fighting I could not resist the challenge when he turned the barrage on to me ... After settling the business at Gafsa we had a friendly lunch and talked of work, and we both now consider the matter closed.'[1]

This was not an isolated incident. Major Harry Llewellyn, the senior liaison officer of the Eighth Army Chief of Staff, de Guingand, recalls his trepidation in Sicily at orders to interview Patton about a matter of tactical co-ordination. Unable to gain access to him, a disgusted Llewellyn finally marched up to Patton's tent and announced: ' "Major Llewellyn, Liaison Officer, sent by General Montgomery." Without any formality a soft voice said, "Come inside", where I found Patton stripped to the waist. He said: "Excuse me Major, but it's kinda hot." ' Both men were expert horsemen and this was quickly sufficient to cement their relations, with Patton assuring the young British officer that he did not need written permission to visit Seventh Army units. 'Just say, I am a friend of the General's.' As Llewellyn observed, 'I believe there were two Pattons, the really tough, thrusting cavalry officer and the soft-spoken gentle man – perhaps I was lucky only to see the latter side.'[2]

There was, unfortunately, an *enfant terrible* within Patton's complex makeup which not only tended to confirm the public perception of him, but which on more than one occasion threatened to destroy his career. Marshall had long since committed Patton's name to his little black book but there were times

---

[1] Letter, Coningham–Air Vice Marshal H. E. P. Wigglesworth, 5 April 1943, PRO (AIR 23/7439). The following day Patton wrote to Coningham: 'Please accept on the part of myself and the officers and men of II Corps our most sincere appreciation of your more than generous signal ... to me you exemplify in their most perfect form all the characteristics of the fighting gentleman.' (Letter of 5 April 1943, Patton Papers.)

[2] Quoted in Llewellyn, op. cit., pp. 149–50. Llewellyn had placed second in the Grand National of 1936. In 1952 he won Britain's only Gold Medal in the Helsinki Olympic games in showjumping. He also knew Montgomery well and was always addressed as 'Harry' until Sicily, when Llewellyn told him he did not intend to stay on as a Regular soldier after the war. Thereafter, he was addressed as 'Llewellyn'. Like the elephant who never forgets, Monty would after the war *always* call him 'Llewellyn' whenever they would meet.

Among those who never warmed to Patton was Brooke who, after their first meeting at Casablanca on 16 January 1943, wrote: 'I had heard of him, but must confess that his swashbuckling personality exceeded my expectation. I did not form any high opinion of him, nor had I any reason to alter this view at any later date. A dashing, courageous, wild and unbalanced leader, good for operations requiring thrust and push but at a loss in any operation requiring skill and judgment.' ('Notes On My Life', Alanbrooke Papers.)

when Patton failed to use good judgment around the Chief of Staff who, like his British counterpart, Brooke, was not overly blessed with a sense of humour.

An example was an unpublicized incident shortly after the TORCH landings which nearly proved ruinous. A member of his staff – inexplicably with his personal approval – sent a letter home which provided details of US operations near Casablanca. The letter was duly intercepted by a censor in Washington and was brought to the attention of a furious Marshall. What angered the Chief of Staff was not so much the divulgence of important information, but rather that Patton had condoned a violation of clear War Department orders. Eisenhower recalls that when Marshall arrived in North Africa for the Casablanca Conference in January 1943, 'he described to me the circumstances and suggested that, as an example to others, I remove Patton from his command and send him home'.[1] Luckily, Marshall firmly believed in delegation of authority and left the matter in Eisenhower's hands. With American fortunes in North Africa approaching a low ebb, Eisenhower declined to sack Patton, knowing his dash and *élan* would be sorely required in the days ahead.

Shortly before the invasion of Sicily, Patton's tendency to excess did him no good when, in the presence of both Marshall and Eisenhower, he raged at a squad of 1st Division infantrymen who had just made a practice assault landing. In a paroxysm of anger he demanded: 'And just where in hell are your goddamned bayonets?' As Bradley later described the incident, 'George blistered them with oaths. Eisenhower (and Marshall) stood within earshot in embarrassed silence ... An officer on Eisenhower's staff whispered to me, "Well, there goes Georgie's chance for a crack at higher command. That temper of his is going to finish him yet." '[2]

Although this particular incident was another of Patton's acting performances (moments later he remarked to Bradley, 'Chew them out and they'll remember it.'), there were, as will be seen, other occasions when his emotions did indeed get the better of him and the consequences proved extremely serious. It was impossible for most people to distinguish between Patton's charades and his true emotions. Both Patton and Montgomery were consummate actors, and most of what they did in public was for the purpose of impressing their troops. Monty claimed to have practised his public speeches in front of a mirror. 'I rehearse it. I take immense trouble over what I say. I write it down beforehand, I practise it in front of the mirror when I'm shaving.'[1]

Patton's tendency to impulsive, self-destructive acts, his carefully crafted façade, and the use of the press to enhance that image, increased his reputation as a colourful, brilliant but utterly unpredictable commander. His relations with superiors and subordinates were frequently stormy. Had Patton not had – as Monty had in Brooke – a powerful ally in Secretary of War Henry L. Stimson, and been given the benefit of the doubt from the pragmatic Marshall on several occasions during the war, it is unlikely he could have avoided being relieved and sent home. He was doubly fortunate that, in Eisenhower, he had both an old friend and a tolerant commander, able to see beyond the irrationality of Patton's outbursts.

Their friendship had been deeply forged during the inter-war years when the two officers served together at Camp Meade, Maryland, where both had done pioneering work in the development of the tank and its future tactics. There would, unfortunately, be many occasions when Patton exasperated Eisenhower's patience – sometimes to the breaking point – yet Eisenhower retained a genuine fondness for the brash general. As Brooke did with Monty, Eisenhower never hesitated to haul Patton over the coals for his transgressions. Patton, in turn, always reacted humbly to these scoldings. Early in the Tunisian campaign Eisenhower was irritated by something Patton said. Patton wrote to him:

> Let me start by assuring you I do want your advice. I want it for two reasons, because you are my Commanding General and because you are my friend ... For years I have been accused of indulging in snap judgments. Honestly, this is not the case because like yourself, I am a profound military student and the thoughts I express, perhaps too flippantly, are the result of years of thought and study ... I realized for sometime that I do not present myself in the best light to my seniors. I feel that thanks to your thoughtfulness in writing me frankly, I shall in the future do much better. At least it shall be my constant study to follow your advise [sic].'[2]

Like Monty, Patton's lack of tact was the one flaw in his character

---

[1] Quoted in *Monty: The Making of a General, 1887–1942*, op. cit., p. 490.
[2] Letter, Patton–Eisenhower, date unknown, Eisenhower Papers.

which consistently landed him in hot water. Fortunately, some of his more outrageous remarks were confined to the privacy of his letters and diary. In June he met King George VI whom he pronounced 'just a grade above a moron. Poor little fellow'. When the Secretary of State for War, Sir James Grigg, told him that Alexander had confidently predicted that American troops would soon be the best in the world, Patton replied they were *already* the best. Patton's Anglophobia also led him to write that despite his impoliteness, 'it is the only way to talk to an Englishman'.[1]

With regularity Eisenhower reminded Patton of his shortcomings, and while the two men retained their long-standing friendship, the HUSKY period was certainly not one of its high points. In turn, Patton was becoming more and more disillusioned by what he perceived was the Allied commander's loose hand on the reins of command and what seemed to him blatant indifference to American prestige and the US role in HUSKY.

Since his death at the end of World War II the mythology of Patton the man and Patton the warrior – which he himself largely created – has not been altogether enhanced by the Academy Award-winning film *Patton*, seen by millions and still often shown on television in many countries. Although accurate in many respects, its most glaring flaw is the portrayal of Patton as a bloodthirsty warrior, bent on fulfilling his destiny at the expense of his troops. The film was largely General Omar Bradley's version of Patton and was based on Bradley's best-selling war memoirs, *A A Soldier's Story*.* Bradley was never sympathetic towards Patton; moreover, his memoirs are openly anti-Patton, and his personal papers reflect a deep personal dislike of Patton the man, and a professional disdain for Patton the soldier.†

---

[1] *The Patton Papers*, Vol. II, op. cit., p. 265.

* *A Soldier's Story* was published in 1951 to great acclaim and considerable publicity, including serialization in *LIFE* Magazine. Bradley acted as a paid adviser to the film.

† So different were these two men in everything from temperament to the exercise of leadership that Bradley occasionally failed to give Patton credit where it was due. A case in point occurred when Patton assumed command of II Corps. From the onset he was not happy with the performance of the 1st Armored Division commander, Major General Orlando Ward. Bradley later wrote that: 'Patton pushed Ward constantly to break through at Maknassy and seemed unreasonable toward Ward for his failure to break through. This was climaxed when Patton called Ward one evening and said, "Goddamn it! I want that hill in front of you. Get off your ass; get a pistol in your hand, and lead that attack yourself." Ward did lead a night attack at the head of his infantry. Ward was wounded slightly in the eye. He probably would have preferred to have been killed that night.' (Bradley Commentaries.)

Bradley's version does not do justice to the problems facing Patton when he took over II

Perhaps the best example of the stereotyped image of Patton was his nickname, 'Old Blood and Guts'. The mythology holds that this nickname was the result of his love of war and his willingness to spill the blood of his men to enhance his own reputation. The truth is that the sobriquet was acquired in 1941 while Patton was commanding the 2d Armored Division. His task had been to turn an inexperienced, newly formed division into a battle-ready force. It was his habit to lecture his officers on military subjects. During one of his talks he attempted to describe what they might expect when the Division went into combat. Out came the comment that 'war will be won by blood and guts alone'. Word soon got round the Division. As Harry Semmes later recalled:

> Some able, but forgotten, artist, caught the spirit of it in a gay crayon sketch. Resplendent in his then famous green dragon costume, Patton, excelsiorlike, dragged forward into battle a rearing, frantic horse, which merged centaurlike into a tank. In his other hand was a shot-torn guidon with his battle cry of 'Blood and Guts' sewn on it. The spirit of his men was sketched in a lone figure of a wounded tanker being carried off on a stretcher as he madly fired his revolver at the enemy. It embodied the idea of George Patton in the eyes of the officers of the Division.[1]

Another little known side of Patton was a trait he shared with Montgomery: both were serious students of military history. Although the Army languished during the inter-war years, Patton did not. His thoughtful mind, trained in the lessons of past wars,

---

[1] *Portrait of Patton*, op. cit., p. 13.

Corps. The 1st Armored Division had been the prime victims of Rommel at Kasserine Pass and Patton considered its leadership too timid and in need of a solid jolt to restore morale and confidence. His decision to force Ward to lead the attack, while heartless at first impression, was less so in light of the circumstances. Nor was Patton as callous as Bradley has portrayed him. The decision was not made without considerable trepidation. In his diary that night Patton wrote: 'Now my conscience hurts me for fear I have ordered him to his death, but I feel that it was my duty. Vigorous leadership would have taken the hill the day before yesterday. I hope it comes out all right.' Even though it failed, Patton decorated Ward with the Silver Star. 'I believe his action would have merited the DSC [Distinguished Service Cross] except for the fact that it was necessary for me to order him to do it.' (Patton Diary, 24 and 25 March 1943, Patton Papers.)

Bradley's opinion may have derived from the fact that Patton relieved Ward not long after this incident. However, Patton's loss of confidence in Ward was based on his belief that Ward was not the man to lead the division. Nor is there evidence that Patton was influenced by the unfavourable comments of Alexander who was unimpressed with Ward and had written privately to Brooke that he found Ward 'quite useless'. (Letter, Alexander–Brooke, 3 April 1943, loc. cit.)

and his prolific pen produced numerous articles on leadership, the use of mechanized forces and a brilliant essay on 'Success in War' in which he argued that the dominant factor is not technology, but the commander 'as a living presence, an all-pervading, visible personality'. With some justification he complained that 'volumes are devoted to armament; pages to inspiration'.[1]

Patton's private papers contain an impressive array of notes and observations on the subject of war and how its lessons could be applied on future battlefields. They ranged from a study of Frederick the Great to Napoleon, the Civil War, the Boer War and World War I. Here, one can discover the roots of his philosophy of leadership and war which he put into practice during World War II. An example was his fundamental belief in the will of a commander to influence the outcome of a battle:

> Shrewd critics have assigned military success to all manner of things – tactics, shape of frontiers, speed, happily placed rivers, mountains or woods, intellectual ability, or the use of artillery. All in a measure true, but none vital. The secret lies in the inspiring spirit which lifted weary footsore men out of themselves and made them march forgetful of agony, as did Masséna's division after Rivoli and Jackson's at Winchester ... The ability to produce endurance is but an instance of that same martial soul which arouses in its followers that resistless emotion, defined as *élan, the will to victory*.'[2] (Author's italics)

Patton would have scorned the American architects of the Vietnam war who placed such store by the technological superiority of the United States. In 1931 he had already learned the lesson mostly forgotten in the years following World War II: 'We must avoid that adoration of the material as exemplified by scientists who deny the existence of ought they cannot cut or weigh. In war tomorrow we shall be dealing with men subject to the same emotions as were the soldiers of Alexander; with men but little changed for better or for worse from the starving shoeless Frenchmen of the Italian campaign; with men similar, save in their arms, to those whom the inspiring powers of a Greek or a Corsican changed at a breath to bands of heroes, all-enduring and all-capable.'[3]

[1] Major George S. Patton, Jr., 'Success in War', *Cavalry Journal*, January 1931. Patton had been reverted to the grade of major during the drastic cutbacks in the Regular Army which took place after World War I.
[2] Ibid.
[3] Ibid.

A study of the essays of Patton the military thinker is an education in what Semmes later termed 'The Psychology of Leadership'. Using a blend of historical example and his own precepts developed in the years since his graduation from West Point in 1909, Patton's writings are a model of clarity that are as meaningful to soldiers of the 1980s as they were fifty years ago.

Anyone studying Patton's inter-war essays can discern some powerful clues to the principles he would follow in the next war:

> Courage, moral and physical ... fosters the resolution to combat and cherishes the ability to assume responsibility for successes or failures ... [as] Lee did at Gettysburg ... These traits are of no value if concealed. A man of diffident manner will never inspire confidence. A cold reserve cannot beget enthusiasm ... the leader must be an actor ... he is useless unless he lives the part. Can man then acquire and demonstrate these characteristics? The answer is they have – they can. For 'As a man thinketh so is he.' The fixed determination to acquire the warrior soul, and having acquired it, to conquer or perish with honor, is the secret of success in war.[1]

Patton was also a firm believer in history as a tool of learning. He read vociferously and his personal library was varied and large. He could quote verbatim from various accounts of ancient campaigns as well as from poetry in which he also took a serious interest. Here, Patton was ever the pragmatist, insisting history be read for its lessons of leadership:

> To be a successful soldier you must know history. Read it objectively – dates and even the minute details of tactics are useless. What you must know is how man reacts. Weapons change but man who uses them changes not at all. To win battles you do not beat weapons – you beat the soul of man, of the enemy man. To do that you have to destroy his weapons, but that is only incidental. You must read biography and especially autobiography. If you do you will find that war is simple. Decide what will hurt the enemy most within limits of your capabilities to harm him and then do it. TAKE CALCULATED RISKS. That is quite different from being rash. My personal belief is that if you have a 50% chance, take it because the superior fighting qualities of the American soldiers led by me will surely give you the extra 1% necessary.[2]

[1] Ibid.
[2] Patton quoted in Semmes, 'General George S. Patton, Jr.'s Psychology of Leadership', op. cit.

Patton said, 'The most vital quality a soldier can possess is SELF-CONFIDENCE, utter, complete and bumptious. You can have doubts about your good looks, about your intelligence, about your self-control, but to win in war you must have NO doubts about your ability as a soldier.'[1]

His principles of war were summed up in four simple tenets:

First – surprise; find out what the enemy intends to do and do it first.

Second – rock the enemy back on his heels – keep him rocking – never give him a chance to get his balance or build up.

Third – relentless pursuit – *à l'outrance* the French say – beyond the limit.

Fourth – mop him up.[2]

Ironically, despite winning the Army's second highest decoration for bravery on the battlefields of France, the private Patton beneath the tough exterior was a warrior constantly plagued by an inferiority complex, a fear of disgracing himself by failing to live up to the lofty goals he set for himself. His diary and letters are filled with questions about his courage, his physical stamina and his ability. None of this was ever to be publicly visible, for Patton confined his trepidations to a small circle of trusted friends and confidants. He unerringly practised his precept that a commander must always radiate the highest level of confidence. Before the invasion of Normandy in June 1944, he sent his corps and division commanders several 'Letters of Instructions' which might well serve as models for good leadership. At the end of one letter, under a section headed 'Courage', he wrote simply: 'DO NOT TAKE COUNSEL OF YOUR FEARS'[3]

Nineteen forty-three was undoubtedly the most turbulent year of Patton's military career. During the period of the Sicily cam-

---

[1] Ibid.
[2] Ibid.
[3] George S. Patton, Jr. *War As I Knew It*, New York/London, 1946, p. 402. Published posthumously, the book was based upon Patton's diary and personal papers and was edited by his wife, Beatrice, with the assistance of Patton's erstwhile Deputy Chief of Staff, Colonel (later General) Paul D. Harkins.

paign he rose to the command of an Army during the largest amphibious operation ever mounted, tasted the fruits of victory and nearly ruined his career by the two most self-destructive acts of his life – all in the space of little over one month.

Before departing for North Africa in 1942 Patton had told his nephew: 'It is my destiny to lead the biggest army ever assembled under one flag and to smash the Germans with it.'[1] Prior to Sicily the Germans knew virtually nothing of Patton; after Sicily they were unwavering in their conviction that he was the most competent and formidable of all the Allied generals against whom they fought in the West. For the general Monty had characterized an 'old man of about 60', Sicily was to propel him to the forefront of American commanders during the most bitter-sweet campaign of his career.

[1] Fred Ayer, *Before the Colors Fade*, London, 1964, p. 116.

CHAPTER 7

The Invasion Plan

> Seldom in war has a major operation been under-
> taken in such a fog of indecision, confusion and
> conflicting plans.
>
> BRADLEY[1]

The damage done by the weeks of bickering and indecision that
had so divided the Allied high command was not easily forgotten
even during the period of intense preparations before the invasion, now scheduled for the early morning of 10 July.

The problems at the military level in the Mediterranean were
duplicated at the TRIDENT Conference in Washington in mid-May,
when the Allied leadership failed to reach agreement on the
strategic considerations left unresolved at Casablanca. The bone
of contention was the same: the American demand for a limit on
Mediterranean operations in favour of the cross-Channel invasion, and the British avowal that the route to France lay through
Sicily and Italy, which would force Germany to expend her
dwindling military strength defending southern Europe. Marshall
once again led American opposition by telling Brooke bluntly that
he had not lost his distaste for Mediterranean operations, which he
believed generated a 'suction pump' effect at the expense of OVER-
LORD. 'I find it hard even now not to look upon your North
African strategy with a jaundiced eye.'[2]

Churchill hoped for a quick end to the Sicily campaign and
pressed for a commitment to continue with operations to knock
Italy out of the war. The British official historian maintains that
the British penchant for the Mediterranean was 'the spirit of the
chase and not any dedication to "peripheral strategy" – much less

---

[1] *A General's Life*, op. cit., p. 167. Bradley died before he could approve the World War
II portion of the story written by his collaborator, Clay Blair. Nevertheless, this comment is a
fair reflection of Bradley's attitude towards HUSKY.
[2] *The Turn of the Tide*, op. cit., p. 620.

any calculation of post-war political advantage – which led the British now to urge impatiently that their recent victories in North Africa should be exploited to the full'.[1]

When Marshall resisted and King agitated for a larger Pacific commitment, Brooke despaired of finding some common ground to break the impasse. But with Dill's deft diplomacy a series of 'off the record' meetings produced a subtly worded, face-saving compromise which placated the two sides but – once again – failed to settle the persistent question of an invasion of Italy after Sicily; but which *implied* such action.

To demonstrate their determination to invade Italy, Churchill, Eden, Ismay and Brooke visited Algiers immediately after TRIDENT to press the British case. They were accompanied by Marshall, who was there to protect American interests and dispel any hint of undue British pressure upon Eisenhower. Marshall considered the trip a waste of time, contending that Casablanca had authorized and anticipated an exploitation of a victory in Sicily by the Allied Commander-in-Chief. 'Marshall was', said Eisenhower, 'plainly annoyed by the need for making the long journey; he hinted to me that he would veto anything that smacked of the adventurous in designating future missions for my Headquarters . . . he obviously meant that he would never consent to any effort to build up the Mediterranean campaign into the main effort against the European Axis.'[2]

When Eisenhower reported the conversation to Marshall, the Chief of Staff replied that he had suspected that Brooke had not

[1] Ibid. The Eisenhower manuscript disputes this by claiming that during their 'walk in the garden' in Algiers, Brooke had said, 'the European Fortress, defended by the Axis was, in a practical sense, invulnerable to any attack from the West. This suddenly presented evidence that Brooke was flatly opposed to the entire Overlord concept was news. At the moment I didn't attempt to argue, but to say that I was startled is a weak description of my reaction. He went on to explain that the proper role of the Western Allies in the European war was not to commit great land forces to bloody battlefields ... We should "thrust and peck" around the Axis perimeter, always threatening and feinting, but never attempting a major invasion. He had no objection to an attack on lower Italy but he argued that the destruction of Hitler's land forces was the business of the Soviets – while Allied contributions of our air and naval operations would progressively make the Soviet task easier.' When asked if he was expressing Churchill's views, Brooke replied 'no', that 'his convictions were based on military factors only, while the Prime Minister had to consider political factors, including ... the continuing need for cooperation with the American President'. (Eisenhower manuscript.) After this version appeared in *Crusade in Europe*, in 1948, Brooke claimed that he had either been misunderstood or that Eisenhower's memory was at fault. Both Churchill's account and Brooke's diary support the British official historian's version that the Mediterranean was considered an essential part of Allied strategy for OVERLORD.

[2] Eisenhower manuscript.

(yet) accepted OVERLORD as a wise strategic plan and would do anything to postpone or cancel the operation. American suspicion was heightened by Churchill's visit, whose sole purpose was to thwart any American attempt to shut down Allied operations in the Mediterranean after Sicily. As Eisenhower made clear, 'The Prime Minister frankly said that he wanted to do his utmost to see that no such "disaster" – as he called it – would occur.'[1]

Churchill's motives only hardened Marshall's resolve to oppose any threat to OVERLORD: 'We were both deeply convinced that the direct and shortest route to Hitler's destruction ran across the northern avenues of Europe – not across the Alps, and neither of us could accept General Brooke's concept of our proper course of action.'[2]

The British came away from Algiers without any formal agreement on post-HUSKY operations but with Eisenhower's assurance that he proposed to exploit its success by continuing across the Strait of Messina into southern Italy and that he would notify the Combined Chiefs in ample time for them to concur without a break in military operations.[3]

Among those deeply disturbed by these quarrels was the prescient Brooke who foresaw that Anglo-American personality problems would not disappear with the agreement over the invasion plan. The CIGS rarely disagreed with Montgomery's military logic but he was painfully aware that his lack of tact and single-minded pursuit of victory was frequently misunderstood as self-aggrandizement and was offensive to others.

The Allies were now hastening preparations to carry out the plan which was essentially the Montgomery version. This, Eisenhower told the Combined Chiefs of Staff, merited the increased risk of concentrating all of the Allied forces along Sicily's southeastern coast. The plan approved by the CCOS on 13 May called for the capture of Sicily in five phases:

---

[1] Ibid.
[2] Ibid. Butcher's diary contains references to Eisenhower's growing belief that continued operations in the Mediterranean were not the answer, and that 'we're only nibbling at the edges when we peck off Sicily ... [Ike] insists we must put not just divisions but armies ... ashore on the continent.'
[3] Minutes of Meeting at AFHQ, 31 May 1943, Eisenhower Papers.

I – Preparatory measures by the air and naval forces to gain air supremacy and to neutralize the Axis naval effort.

II – Airborne and glider landings on the night of 9/10 July, to disrupt enemy movement and communications and to help secure the important airfields in the Gela sector. Beginning in the pre-dawn hours (approximately 0245 hours), assault forces of Seventh and Eighth Armies would land along nearly 150 miles of the southeastern coast of Sicily to seize the airfields and the ports of Syracuse and Licata.

III – The establishment of a secure lodgment as a base for further operations.

IV – The capture of the ports of Augusta and Catania and the Gerbini airfields.

V – The reduction of Sicily.[1]

The means by which Phase V was to be carried out was deliberately vague, even though both Montgomery and Patton always assessed the aim as the capture of Messina and the sealing off of the Axis lifeline to mainland Italy. Alexander's preference was to allow the land battle to develop before any decisions were made about specific measures by each of the two armies. This was later to cause untold problems. For the present, however, there was no doubt within Eighth Army that Montgomery's intention was to capture and isolate Messina, and on 9 June General Leese was told personally by Montgomery at a planning conference that the Eighth Army objective was 'to dominate the Messina Straits as soon as possible'.[2] The subject of Messina would shortly become the dominant problem of the Sicily campaign.

Eastern Task Force (Force 545) (Eighth Army)

Eighth Army's mission was to assault the area located between Syracuse on the east coast and Pozzallo on the southeast coast with four divisions and one independent brigade, supported by glider troops of the 1st Airborne Division. The 1st Airlanding Brigade

---

[1] PRO (AIR 41/52). See also *The Mediterranean and Middle East*, Vol. V, op. cit., pp. 28–9, and *Sicily*, op. cit., Chapter V.
[2] Quoted in G. W. L. Nicholson, *The Canadians in Italy, 1943–1945*, op. cit., Chapter IV.

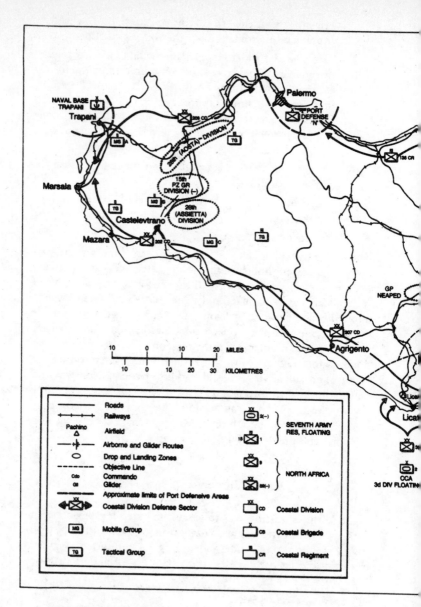

FINAL INVASION PLAN

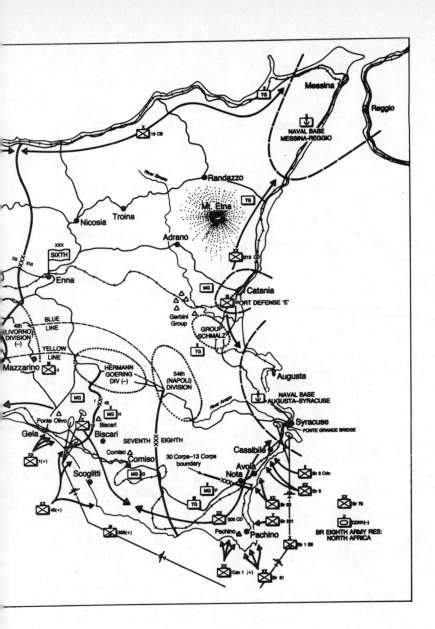

would land its glider-borne troops in the early hours of 10 July with the task of seizing the important Ponte Grande bridge over the Anapo River south of Syracuse to prevent its destruction, block enemy attempts to interfere with the invasion to the south and to ease the capture of the city by 13 Corps.

The main Eighth Army objectives were to capture the port of Syracuse and the landing grounds around Pachino. Once ashore, Eighth Army was to establish a front along the general line Syracuse–Pozzallo–Ragusa and to make contact with Seventh Army. These forces were then to push rapidly forward to carry out their Phase IV mission of capturing Catania and the Gerbini airfields.

Montgomery organized his forces into 13 and 30 Corps.* Dempsey's 13 Corps, consisting of the 5th and 50th Divisions, would assault on a three-brigade front between Avola and Cassibile in the Gulf of Noto. Once a beachhead was secured this force was to advance as rapidly as possible to the north to seize Syracuse, Augusta, Catania and the Gerbini airfields near the River Simeto along the western edge of the strategically important plain of Catania.

Leese's 30 Corps, consisting of the 1st Canadian and 51st (Highland) Divisions and the (independent) 231st Infantry Brigade, was to assault both sides of the southeastern tip of Sicily: the Pachino peninsula. 30 Corps would then relieve 13 Corps, first at Avola, then at Syracuse, by advancing along a northwesterly axis to make contact with Patton's Seventh Army at Ragusa.

An important element of the plan was a series of diversionary manoeuvres against Catania on the night of D-Day by naval, air and airborne forces to contain and disrupt enemy reserve forces in and around the plain. Remaining in Tunisia in Eighth Army reserve were the 78th Division and the 1st Canadian Tank Brigade.

Montgomery recognized that the key to any successful advance to Messina by Eighth Army was the plain of Catania. Mountains and rugged hills cover most of Sicily but the plain of Catania, located directly south of Mount Etna, is a broad, marshy lowland through which flow numerous streams and rivers from the mountains to empty into the Gulf of Catania. The flat plain measures twelve miles wide by eighteen miles long, has excellent visibility and is bisected by the longest river on the island, the Simeto, which

---

* See Appendix B for the Order of Battle of the Allied land forces.

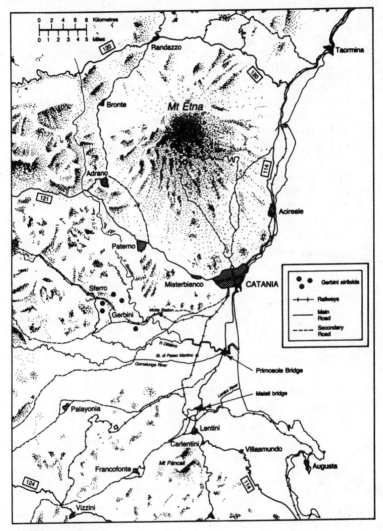

PLAIN OF CATANIA

drains a huge watershed on the southern slopes of the Caronie Mountains and meets the sea immediately below the port city of Catania. Summer temperatures and humidity are exceptionally high and mosquitoes abound, increasing the threat of malaria.

Immediately to the north of the plain rises Mount Etna, one of the world's largest (10,925 feet)* and most active volcanoes, whose last major eruption had occurred in 1928. Etna forms a circular cone nearly 25 miles in diameter:† its slopes increase in steepness with elevation and its flanks are covered with boulders and blocks of broken rock, long tongues of rough-surfaced lava and numerous steep-walled, impassable ravines. At its summit is a yawning crater which in 1669 spewed more than 100 million cubic feet of lava down its slopes. The area around Etna is totally unsuitable for cross-country movement of motor vehicles but on its lower slopes there are many dirt roads which make possible the restricted deployment of armoured vehicles and artillery.

Etna stands as an impenetrable barrier to the movement of an army towards Messina which is possible only along a narrow coastal shelf running through Catania. Movement around Etna to the west is difficult and the mountainous terrain restricts vehicular mobility to the few roads. An enemy force controlling the plain of Catania could dictate the ability of an attacker to move northeast towards Messina. In particular, control of the Simeto riverline and the terrain leading into Catania would be crucial.

Western Task Force (Force 343)
(Seventh Army)

Seventh Army was to make its assault over a seventy-mile section of the Gulf of Gela, stretching from Licata in the west to Pozzallo in the east. The main landings were to be at Gela, Scoglitti and Cape Scarmina. A secondary simultaneous assault was to be directed against Licata by a separate sub-task force. Patton's principal objectives were the port of Licata, its airfield and the

---

* Etna's height has varied with its many eruptions. The ancient Greeks believed the mountain was the home of the fire god Hephaistos (Vulcan) and of Cyclops, the mythological one-eyed monster.

† The circumference around the base of Etna is approximately 125 miles. The richness of its soil produces extensive crops of lemons, oranges, and tangerines, as well as grapes, olives, almonds and figs. Along its slopes are forests of eucalyptus, oak, umbrella pine and pistachio trees.

three important airfields at Ponte Olivo, Biscari and Comiso. After making contact with Eighth Army, Seventh Army was to protect the airfields and Monty's left flank from enemy interference.

The two assault forces were Bradley's II Corps and Truscott's 3d Division (Reinforced),* supported by an off-shore floating reserve consisting of the 2d Armored Division (less Combat Command 'A') and a Regimental Combat Team (RCT)† of the 1st Division.

The Licata assault – code-named JOSS – had the mission of seizing both the port and its airfield northwest of the city by the night of D-Day. After making contact with II Corps, JOSS Force was to protect the left flank of Seventh Army against any interference from the northwest. Included was token Free French representation provided by a 900-man battalion of Moroccan Goums.‡

Omar Bradley's II Corps consisted of the 1st Division ('Big Red One'), called DIME Force, and the 45th Division of the Oklahoma National Guard, called CENT Force. The 1st Division was to assault Gela and the 45th Scoglitti with the object of capturing Ponte Olivo airfield by daylight on D+1, Comiso airfield by daylight on D+2, and Biscari airfield by dark on D+2. Also assigned to II Corps were three Ranger battalions, one of which was commanded by Lieutenant Colonel William O. Darby, whose exploits in North Africa had already earned the Rangers considerable prestige.§ Over the objections of the senior Allied air commanders who were at this stage of the war not yet convinced of the potential of airborne operations, an airborne task force of the 82d Airborne Division was to parachute into the Gela sector. The reinforced 505th Regimental Combat Team commanded by Colonel James M. Gavin was given the mission of parachuting into Sicily about midnight on 9 July to the north and east of Gela to secure the high ground northeast of the town in order to block a likely enemy approach from that direction. Gavin's men were also

---

* See Appendix B.

  † A Regimental Combat Team was an infantry regiment augmented by the attachment of additional forces deemed essential for a specific mission. In this instance, the two RCTs of the 1st Division were supported by field artillery, anti-aircraft artillery, engineers, and a platoon of Sherman tanks. (See Appendix B.)

  ‡ The Goumiers were native Moroccan irregulars, mostly recruited from the fierce Berber tribes of the Atlas Mountains, and were under the command of French officers and NCOs. The Goums were to land on D+5 to act as part of JOSS Force.

  § See Chapter 15.

to disrupt enemy communications and assist the 1st Division to capture Ponte Olivo airfield.

For the air movement to Sicily, the 82d Airborne was to receive two-thirds of all available troop carrier aircraft and the 1st Airborne the remaining one-third. The remainder of the 82d Airborne was to be moved to the Gela–Licata sector beginning on the evening of D-Day.

As Patton studied the terrain in his sector he became convinced that the key to establishing a successful Seventh Army beachhead was to capture and hold the high ground directly inland which formed a dome-shaped plateau that faced the assault beaches. Extending from Enna, 37 miles north of Gela, to the town of Piazza Armerina, this terrain feature became the focus of Patton's planning:

> The obvious strongpoint on which to base the beachhead on the west was a secondary ridge east of the Salso River, which would provide a further obstacle to enemy intrusion. . . . The high ground Piazza Armerina would delineate the beachhead. Possession of this terrain would deprive the enemy of ground overlooking the assault beaches and give the Seventh Army protection for building up its strength preliminary to a push inland . . . the key to the entire problem remained the high ground at Piazza Armerina, which was not only commanding terrain but also carried the main road [Highway 117] leading from Enna to Gela and Syracuse. The enemy would most certainly utilize this road in shifting his forces from the western and central portions of the island to oppose the Allied landings. To get to this high ground quickly became the basic motive of Seventh Army planning.[1]

The result was the designation of two phase lines, Yellow and Blue. By D+3 Patton expected to control this critical terrain. The Yellow Line marked the attainment of a secure beachhead and possession of the Blue Line ensured that Seventh Army could fend off any determined interference by counterattacking Axis forces, especially German armoured formations (see pages 146–7).

Finally, in Seventh Army reserve in North Africa would be Major General Manton S. Eddy's 9th Infantry Division which had participated in TORCH and received its baptism of fire in Tunisia. The 39th Infantry Regiment and the division artillery were to be ready for movement to Sicily whenever required after D-Day.

[1] *Sicily*, op. cit. p. 97.

The Naval Plan

Even by the later standards of the Normandy invasion, the forces assembled for the invasion of Sicily were enormous. Never before had the numbers of ships and men been equalled in an amphibious operation.[1] The armada of 3,200 ships assembled for HUSKY was in fact the most gigantic fleet in the world's history.[2]

Cunningham's naval forces were likewise organized into two naval task forces to support each assaulting army. Ramsay's Eastern Task Force consisted of three assault forces designated 'A' (5th and 50th Divisions); 'B' (231st Infantry Brigade and 51st Division); and 'V' (1st Canadian Division). A support Force 'K' was to provide convoy escort and naval gunfire support of the landings; later it was to protect the northern sea flank of the task force. Force 'V' would stage the 1st Canadian Division directly from United Kingdom ports on Scotland's River Clyde and sail non-stop to its rendezvous with the fleet off the Sicilian coast on 9 July.

Vice Admiral Hewitt's Western Naval Task Force was organized into a Control Force and three Attack Forces: CENT, DIME and JOSS. CENT Force would stage the 45th Infantry Division from the United States, with a brief pause in North Africa for practice landings. The other two forces were to stage from Tunisian ports.

A submarine force would be on patrol to intercept the Italian fleet should it choose to put to sea from its main ports in Sardinia and challenge the invasion fleet. Seven other submarines were to act as beacons to guide the task forces to their release points off the beaches.[3]

All of the landings except for those of the 3d and 51st Divisions were to be ship–shore, that is, men and equipment would be carried to points offshore where they were to be transferred to landing craft for the assault. The other two divisions were equipped with a new amphibious shore–shore craft called the DUKW which was capable of delivering both men and their equipment directly on to the beaches.[*]

[1] *The Mediterranean and Middle East*, Vol. V, op. cit., p. 31.
[2] Vice Admiral H. K. Hewitt, 'Action Report: The Sicily Campaign, Operation HUSKY, July–August 1943', PRO (AIR 23/5642). Also Naval Historical Center, Washington, D.C.
[3] *The Mediterranean and Middle East*, Vol. V, op. cit., pp. 30–1.
[*] In addition, a number of new craft were to play the first of many important amphibious roles in landing men and equipment: the Landing Ship Tank (LST); Landing Craft Tank (LCT); Landing Craft Infantry (LCI); and the Landing Craft Vehicle/Personnel (LCVP). These ingeniously designed craft were solutions to the most pressing problem of amphibious

On 21 June the Allied commanders met in Algiers to present their plans to Eisenhower and to each other. Patton recorded his impressions in his diary, beginning with Eisenhower's ten-minute opening speech which he thought failed to assert his authority as the Commander-in-Chief. More impressive was the Royal Navy presentation, but Patton was disappointed in the air commanders whose avoidance of specific support commitments to the Army and Navy did not inspire his confidence. Tedder apparently slept through most of the presentations, perhaps because another of the senior airmen blundered through a dreary speech. An American general called the entire presentation 'boring' except for that of Force 343 which bore Patton's imprint and was 'short, beautifully illustrated and carefully rehearsed'.[1] Montgomery was hosting a visit to Eighth Army by King George and his plan was presented by de Guingand.*

The Algiers conference was one of many in the weeks leading up to the invasion as Allied preparations grew in intensity with each passing day. Montgomery held a similar conference at Force 545 where the invasion plan was not only thoroughly briefed but tested and war-gamed, a practice that he carried over into OVERLORD with great success.† Back from his brief rest in England, Montgomery began a tireless round of visits to speak to every Eighth Army unit participating in HUSKY, a custom begun in the desert. These generally took place near his jeep where the troops were summoned to gather around informally while their Army Commander standing on the bonnet delivered a pep-talk on the importance of *their* particular mission. His officers would normally be given a more formal lecture-hall presentation. Typically, Montgomery would begin by stating his principles for the successful conduct of war, followed by the purpose of the invasion of Sicily and his utter confidence in its success. As de Guingand relates, his method invoked 'no bombastic rhetoric, no pompous boasts, but plain common sense given out by one who was obvi-

---

[1] Diary of Major General John P. Lucas, Lucas Papers, USAMHI.

* During his four-day visit to Eighth Army, King George VI bestowed a knighthood upon Montgomery for his victory at Alamein.

† Exercise THUNDERCLAP held in London over a two-day period in April 1944.

---

warfare: the ability to shift troops and material rapidly from ship to shore or from shore to shore. (Cf. *Sicily*, op. cit., pp. 103–5.)

ously a master of his craft. No notes were used throughout. At the end there were spontaneous cheers . . .'[1]

During June, 13 Corps carried out practice assaults in the Gulfs of Suez and Aqaba; 30 Corps conducted similar rehearsals. All of these realistically drove home just how much there was left to accomplish in the short time left before the invasion. American practice landings by the 1st and 45th Divisions were poorly executed: units were landed in the wrong places, frequently many miles from their destination. Most of the naval landing craft were manned by inexperienced seamen participating in their first amphibious operation – and it showed. Bradley gloomily despaired over the dire consequences of such a performance on D-Day.[2] With time running out, the pragmatic Bradley was entitled to deep concern over an operation whose planning was 'literally mind-boggling'.[3]

Like Montgomery, Patton's philosophy of command was rooted in the belief that a commander's personal presence made a difference. In the days prior to debarkation he visited each of his Seventh Army units to inform and inspire his men. His approach was part pep-talk and part lecture in which he spoke to them about their fears, assuring them these were normal, and that as good soldiers they would overcome them – provided they received the leadership they were entitled to from their officers. 'All men are afraid in battle,' he noted. 'The coward is the one who lets his fear overcome his sense of duty.' With sirens screaming and motor-cycle escorts clearing the way, Patton sped from unit to unit imploring his men to follow his principles of fighting a war, and reminding them to 'make the other dumb son-of-a-bitch die for *his* country!' Patton attempted to instil his own pragmatic battle tactics, the essence of which was discipline, leadership, relentless attack and teamwork.

The development of teamwork between Army and Navy was sometimes painful and not without difficult moments, as Truscott relates in his postwar memoirs. The JOSS Force planners had determined that excellent use could be made of burros to carry

[1] Major-General Sir Francis de Guingand, *Operation Victory*, London, 1947, p. 287.
[2] *A Soldier's Story*, op. cit., p. 118, and *A General's Life*, op. cit., p. 174. The practice landing by the 45th Division was made directly from the ships that had brought the division from the US. Two of its three assault regiments were landed as much as 10–12 miles off-target.
[3] *A General's Life*, op. cit., p. 173.

ammunition during the drive inland into the mountains, and during a night exercise near Bizerte they were tested for the first time. The JOSS naval commander, Rear Admiral R. L. Conolly, was not told of this and the Army was ignorant of the naval tradition against the transport of livestock. A very angry admiral told the puzzled Truscott,

> 'General ... I am astounded to find that you have taken advantage of me. I thought that we were working together. Now what do I find? You have loaded a bunch of damn mules on my ships. And you have done it without saying a word to me! ... You have taken advantage of my spirit of co-operation. You are making a cavalry stable out of my ships. I will be the laughing stock of the Navy. The unsanitary mess will endanger your soldiers as well as the sailors. I am surprised at you. I won't stand for it.'

After apologizing for the obvious oversight Truscott offered to unload the burros. Conolly formally replied, 'Very well, General. I am glad that you agree.' An equally formal Truscott replied,

> 'But, Admiral, I don't agree. I have assumed that you were to land us complete with all of our weapons prepared to fight. Those "mules" as you call them are actually weapons which we think we need to accomplish this assault. You don't want them on your ships. I am going to have them off. But what I am wondering now is what I shall do tomorrow if you should object to carrying infantry mortars, or tanks, or any other item of equipment which the Navy does not usually transport.'

A chastened Conolly replied, 'Dammit, General, you are right. We will carry the goddam mules and anything else you want carried.'[1]

The Army was responsible for allocating priorities for space aboard the naval vessels, some of which was required by the air forces for use in establishing airfields. Bradley was presented with a requirement for 660 bulldozers and heavy trucks for use in repairing airfields which the airmen insisted be brought ashore during the first sealift. Bradley quite naturally denied the request with the reminder that this represented the same total allowed for a full assault division! He volunteered the assistance of his combat engineers but the stubborn airmen refused all compromise, whereupon Bradley – with Patton's full backing – replied, 'Very well then, you make the assault with your 660 trucks. Clear the

---

[1] Quoted in *Command Missions*, op. cit., p. 203. Truscott was right and the 'mules' proved a valuable asset in the tortuous terrain of Sicily's mountains. The effects of Truscott's decision are discussed in Chapter 29.

beach for us and we'll come in on a later lift. It's either you or the infantry. There's not lift enough for both....' When the airmen failed for the second time to get his message, a thoroughly annoyed Bradley replied if it was to be 'all or nothing' they would do without air support. Bradley won his point and the air requirement was pared back to a more reasonable 234 vehicles.[1]

Both army plans made sound use of resources and maximum use of the terrain to favour their operations. Less easily resolved were the complex problems of satisfying the enormous appetite of the armies for supplies, equipment, fuel and ammunition which had to be in the right place, at the right time, and in the right quantities. Until the ports were able to function and supplies stockpiled, which was expected to be about D+7 or D+8, the assault units had to provide for their own requirements. Logistics has been described as 'the practical art of moving armies and keeping them supplied'.[2] While successful military strategy is the art of the possible, logistics is more often than not the art of the impossible. Not only must the logistician anticipate the course of a battle and determine the needs of the armies but he must ensure these arrive when needed. Aviation gasoline was as useless to a tank unit as diesel fuel was to an air force fighter.

The logistics of HUSKY were made more difficult by the great distances involved, the multiple layers of command (Eisenhower was 'appalled by the number of headquarters seemingly required to run this sprawling theater')[3] and their insatiable requirements. British logistical plans called for the two corps to be self-sufficient for seven days. 13 Corps consisted of nearly 4,300 vehicles and 191 tanks and required 11,700 tons of supplies to subsist for that time. Though smaller, 30 Corps still required 8,300 tons.[4] US requirements were similar.

There were literally thousands of problems to be solved but the most vexing was to develop a plan* that would satisfy everyone who required a slice of the limited space aboard the supply ships

---

[1] A Soldier's Story, op. cit., pp. 116–17.

[2] Martin van Creveld, Supplying War, Cambridge, 1980, p. 1.

[3] Joseph P. Hobbs, Dear General, Eisenhower's Wartime Letters to Marshall, Baltimore, 1971, p. 114. Letter of 25 May 1943.

[4] The Mediterranean and Middle East, Vol. V, op. cit., p. 135.

* Merely preparing, printing and disseminating the operational orders was itself a major undertaking. The typing of the naval orders alone took twenty typists seven days and required the printing of 800 copies. (Cf. Rear-Admiral L. E. H. Maund, Assault From the Sea, London, 1949, p. 256.)

and landing craft. Bradley was not alone in having to plead, cajole and threaten before his planners were able to devise a plan that placated everyone.[1]

While training, logistics and many other problems were being thrashed out, for the most part successfully, another problem was defying solution. The development of the Allied air plan was responsible for continued distrust and bad feeling among the officers of the three services.

[1] *Sicily*, op. cit., p. 103.

CHAPTER 8

Internecine Quarrels

Army and Navy acted as 'one big family', to which they would gladly have admitted the Air Force if that junior service had not preferred to fight its own war.

ADMIRAL SAMUEL ELIOT MORISON[1]
Official US Naval historian

By early 1943 the expansion of Allied air power in the Mediterranean had reached explosive and unmanageable proportions. The Casablanca decisions made it necessary to reorganize the multiple British and American air commands that included not only the Mediterranean, Middle East and Africa, but also parts of the Atlantic and Indian Oceans, into a streamlined and integrated *Allied* air force. The responsibility for all these belonged to Sir Arthur Tedder, the unassuming Air Commander-in-Chief. Behind an unpretentious façade the soft-spoken Tedder possessed one of the most brilliant minds to emerge during the war. Although he carried four-star rank Tedder was always uninterested in military pomp and during his service in the Mediterranean could frequently be seen bringing up the rear of a flashy convoy of brass-hat limousines in a nondescript jeep, without a cap, contentedly smoking his famous pipe. He was a man who preferred listening to others rather than talking himself and could sometimes be seen sketching scenes about him with a pencil, playing the piano or reading poetry.

Those who came to know him were soon disabused of any foolish notion that his casual approach to sacred military protocol was evidence of an easy mark. A thoughtful and introspective man, Tedder was largely unknown to his airmen, which was not surprising considering his many assignments to high positions and his tendency to shun publicity.

---

[1] *Sicily–Salerno–Anzio*, op. cit., p. 143.

Few could ever claim to know Arthur William Tedder intimately even though he had been an airman since 1916 when he had exchanged his captaincy in the Dorset Regiment for the uncertain future of a Flying Officer in the fledgling Royal Flying Corps. In the years since then, he moved steadily upwards through the ranks of the Royal Air Force by excelling in virtually every sphere of his Service. He served as Director-General of Research and Development in the Air Ministry from 1938 until May 1940 when he became Controller of Research and Development under the volatile Lord Beaverbrook, who had been appointed by Churchill to head the emergency effort to produce aircraft to meet the threat of the Luftwaffe. A man of complete candour,* Tedder was never hesitant to clash with Beaverbrook whose policies he strongly opposed. Nor did he shy from bluntly informing the Prime Minister of what were in the early years of the war mostly unpleasant truths. Churchill not only never warmed to Tedder but in early 1945 attempted to have him replaced as Eisenhower's deputy by Alexander. Earlier, Tedder's veracity had nearly resulted in his removal as the RAF Middle East commander when his assessment of German strength before Operation CRUSADER offended Churchill, and it took the threat of Portal's resignation to avert his dismissal.[1]

As AOC-in-C, Middle East, Tedder organized and directed the victory of the Royal Air Force over the Luftwaffe, which ultimately made it possible for Montgomery to lead Eighth Army to victory over Rommel at El Alamein. Now, as the new Allied Air

---

[1] John Terraine, *The Right of the Line: The Royal Air Force in the European War 1939–1945*, London, 1985, pp. 354–5. This long-awaited account of the Royal Air Force fills an enormous void in the literature of the Second World War. With the exception of the superb four-volume series by Sir Charles Webster and Dr Noble Frankland (*The Strategic Air Offensive Against Germany, 1939–45*) the British official histories adopted an interservice viewpoint. This approach sacrificed what otherwise would have been a more detailed examination of the air role in the many campaigns of the war.

* One of Tedder's endearing qualities was his frankness, especially with the press. One time during a press conference in North Africa he indicated he would like someday to see US and British soldiers wearing the same uniform. When asked if this was 'off the record' Tedder said, 'Certainly not. That is my sincere hope, and I am not ashamed of it.'

Tedder's relations with the press were excellent. Introduced to correspondent Demaree Bess, he exclaimed, 'Ah-ha! A correspondent! That means fresh blood. What do you know that I don't know? You know, I learn a lot from correspondents. They are not tied to one war theater as I am. Now, where have you been that I haven't been?' Bess soon found the tables turned and himself the object of the conversation: 'And as we sat down to dinner, he fired one question after another at me, while I tried to turn the conversation to some topic which would induce him to do the talking.' (Demaree Bess, 'Eisenhower's Flying Scot', *The Saturday Evening Post*, 26 February 1944.)

C-in-C, his task was to preside over the merger of the RAF and the USAAF which were commanded by ambitious airmen whose forceful opinions on the proper conduct of aerial warfare were frequently at variance with his own views. The creation of a new air command called the Mediterranean Allied Air Forces embodied Tedder's conception of how a unified air command should be organized. However, to accomplish this he had to find a common ground between two competing air doctrines.

Within the ranks of the RAF and the USAAF there existed two schools of thought concerning the proper application of air power. One of these has been described as the 'Victory-through-Air-Power-School'. As Tedder's biographer observes, this doctrine propounded the notion 'that a strategic Air Force could win a whole war provided that the Army secured its aerodromes and the Navy its supplies. Having, as a prerequisite, attained air superiority, the Air Forces were to batter the whole German industrial machinery until it came to a standstill.'[1]

The principal British architect of this strategy was Air Chief Marshal Sir Arthur Harris, the single-minded czar of Bomber Command who from February 1942 controlled the operations of Britain's strategic bombers with an iron-fisted determination and the absolute conviction that Germany could be brought to her knees by saturation bombing of her industrial, war-producing targets, while her will to fight was shattered by the wholesale destruction of her cities. While less hard-line in its advocacy, the Air Ministry generally supported this approach, as did the USAAF. A directive issued in June 1943 by the Combined Chiefs of Staff – called POINTBLANK – became the basis for the great combined bomber offensive against Germany and was misused by both Harris and his American counterpart, Lieutenant General Carl A. 'Tooey' Spaatz, as their *carte blanche* to pursue the capitulation of the Third Reich by air action alone.

In 1944 Harris and Spaatz violently opposed OVERLORD as 'a vast, gratuitous, strategic misjudgment', totally unnecessary, 'when Germany was already tottering on the edge of collapse from bombing'.[2] These strongly held convictions about the role of air

[1] Roderic Owen, *Tedder*, London, 1952, pp. 196–7.
[2] Max Hastings, *Bomber Command*, London, 1979, p. 327.

power established a doctrine which was eventually to be proved false. However, at this stage of the war it was not only some airmen who were misled, but also the Joint Intelligence Sub-Committee of the War Cabinet which, in April 1943, concluded that if the capture of Sicily in July failed to knock Italy out of the war, a concentrated programme of bombing key targets could force the Italians to sue for peace.[1]

Tedder never succumbed to the lure of this fantasy and with the backing of the equally pragmatic Portal, who could always be counted upon to support him, Tedder became the proponent of the doctrine of Theatre air power, which saw successful warfare as a joint, inter-service effort. 'I never felt that the [strategic] air effort against Germany wasn't vital, but I did see the continual necessity for having to call on air effort to support the land campaign.'[2]

The basis of this doctrine was for the air forces to concentrate on the destruction of Axis air power and to cripple its airfields. The slogan of Tedder and his principal disciple – Coningham – became, 'to seal off the beachhead'.[3] The problem was that Tedder's philosophy was in sharp contrast to the expectations of the ground and naval commanders.

The roots of this conflict stemmed in large part from the bitter wrangles in London in 1942 between the War Office and the Air Staff when the Army demanded that air support be organized into what the airmen caustically called 'penny packets' under the control of the ground commander. While in agreement that full support of the ground forces was essential, the airmen were adamant they retain their independence which, in turn, meant the flexibility to concentrate air power when and where it was most required.*

As the role of air power increased it was inevitable there would be fundamental differences of opinion between the airmen and their Army and Navy brethren. Tedder's problem was twofold: how to reach an accommodation with the American air chiefs like Spaatz and, at the same time, satisfy the Army and Navy. The extent of the problem can best be understood by the fact that there

[1] J.I.C. Paper, 'Defeat of Italy by Air Attack Alone', 16 April 1943, PRO (WO 201/2833).
[2] Tedder, op. cit., p. 197.
[3] Sicily–Salerno–Anzio, op. cit., p. 21.
* Brooke had attempted to impose Army control of close air support when he became CIGS but was vigorously opposed by Portal and the Air Staff. For the RAF version, see Marshal of the Royal Air Force Sir John Slessor's Central Blue, London, 1956, Chapter XV.

was little agreement amongst the airmen themselves, much less with the other services, over the definition of the terms 'strategic' and 'tactical'.

Tedder's first priority was to get his own house in order. The need for this became evident during the early months of the Tunisian campaign when some very disturbing trends threatened to cripple the new Anglo-American military coalition. Co-operation and liaison between air and ground forces was deplorable.* TORCH had been planned separately and in isolation by British and American airmen while Tedder's Middle East Command played no meaningful role.[1] The grumbling over lack of air support only added to the wretched baptism of fire of American forces. With Patton's arrival the problem exploded with his widely disseminated signal of complaint that II Corps was receiving inadequate air support. Whenever Eisenhower toured the front his men reminded him in colourful language that the Germans still maintained air supremacy over the battlefield: 'Where is this bloody Air Force of ours? Why do we see nothing but Heinies?'[2] What Tedder observed was not only troublesome and disheartening, but reinforced his determination to revamp the air structure.

The criterion employed by Tedder throughout HUSKY was the principle that the war in the Mediterranean had to be fought as a *whole*. The fact that in the spring of 1943 there were two separate campaigns being fought in Tunisia mattered little to him, and he organized the Allied air forces around the concept that it was all *one* campaign. In broad terms, his solution was to group his commands by a mixture of functional and geographic missions. The all-RAF Malta and Middle East Air Forces were placed directly under the new Mediterranean Air Command, along with newly created Northwest African Air Forces under Spaatz, which were designed with support of the forthcoming Sicily campaign in mind. In turn, Spaatz controlled the Tactical, Coastal and Strategic air forces and the Troop Carrier and Air Service Commands.† Tedder's success in creating a genuine, integrated *Allied* air command was in no small part due to his policy of appointing

---

[1] Terraine, *The Right of the Line*, op. cit., p. 390.

[2] Eisenhower, *Crusade in Europe*, New York/London, 1948, p. 134.

* The shining exception was the Desert Air Force and Eighth Army, which remained outside the TORCH sphere until the latter part of the Tunisian campaign.

† The air Order of Battle is depicted in Appendix C. For an even more detailed depiction, see *The Mediterranean and Middle East*, Vol. V, Appendices 1 and 4.

British and Americans to alternating layers of command within his HQ and Spaatz's command.

The air reorganization was a major turning point in the airmen's quest for independence and recognition. Henceforth, Tedder employed the principle – shared by virtually every senior officer in the RAF and USAAF – that the air force mission could best be accomplished by complete autonomy from the ground forces. Despite apportioning command, the RAF unquestionably emerged as the dominant force in Mediterranean air operations. The RAF commanders never forgot their distaste of the inter-service rivalries of the inter-war years and now that their voice could be heard, they became even more deeply committed to independence as the key to their survival.

With an American (Spaatz) in command of the African air forces, Tedder ensured that command of the Tactical air forces was given to an RAF officer, Air Marshal Sir Arthur Coningham. Born in Australia but raised and educated in New Zealand, Coningham considered himself a New Zealander and was proud of the nickname 'Maori' which eventually simply became 'Mary'. In World War I he won the DSO, MC and DFC as a pilot in the Royal Flying Corps, and in 1925 set a long-distance record by leading a flight from Cairo to Nigeria which inspired the opening of the African air routes.

In North Africa, Coningham began his association with Tedder who put him in command of the Desert Air Force supporting Eighth Army. He and Tedder became apostles of the concentration of air power and full partnership in the desert war. What had been merely theory was put to practical use with spectacular results. Their solution was close co-operation with the Army and the training of RAF squadrons to be so versatile that they could respond with alacrity to any type of situation or target. This concept of concentration of force and the flexibility to react through a high state of mobility became the standard for tactical air operations in the Royal Air Force. Working side by side and integrating its operations with Eighth Army, the Desert Air Force became the model for air–ground co-operation.

The tall, hard-driving and handsome Coningham became known as a decisive commander and a brilliant strategist who was quick to grasp a situation and react with sound judgment. Unfortunately, the honeymoon between him and Montgomery was short-lived. The enormous publicity accorded Montgomery and Eighth Army after Alamein stung Coningham who believed that his airmen had not received due credit for their contribution. While the public acclaimed Monty who became the darling of the press, there was, as former BBC correspondent Chester Wilmot noted, 'little but a passing round of applause for Coningham and the Desert Air Force. The headlines stung. Speaking to war correspondents one day, Coningham burst out, "It's always 'Monty's Army', 'Monty's Victory', 'Monty Strikes Again'. You never say 'Coningham's Air Force'." [1]

What had once been harmonious relations eventually worsened to a level of bitterness towards Montgomery unequalled by any of the better-known quarrels of the war. The official SHAEF historian later remarked that Coningham was 'the bitterest critic of Monty that I have heard speak', and his postwar despatch as the commander of the 2nd [British] Tactical Air Force was so critical of Montgomery that the Air Ministry declined to publish it.[2] Nor was Coningham an easy subordinate, as Spaatz soon learned.[*]

As D-Day drew nearer a growing number of complaints began to be heard from the naval and ground commanders who were

[1] Chester Wilmot, *The Struggle For Europe*, London, 1952, p. 374. Senior Eighth Army officers considered Coningham a prima donna who had to be handled with kid gloves. During Auchinleck's tenure as Eighth Army commander they considered Coningham to have been 'bloody-minded'. Although it has been given scant recognition, Monty's goal was to encourage a team atmosphere and he was always generous in his praise of the Desert Air Force. (See *Monty: Master of the Battlefield, 1942–1944*, Part Two, Chapter Six, and Richardson, *Flashback*, op. cit., p. 131.)

[2] Dr Forrest C. Pogue, interview with Air Marshal Coningham, 14 February 1947, USAMHI and 'Report of Operations, 2nd TAF' (1945), PRO (AIR 37/876). It was, as John Terraine points out, a sad commentary that Montgomery and Coningham, who had only months earlier 'established their close and fruitful accord at Alam Halfa', should now be so far apart. (*The Right of the Line*, op. cit., p. 779.)

[*] Within the Northwest African Air Forces, relations between Coningham and Spaatz were, at best, uneasy. According to Lord Zuckerman, who knew both men well, Coningham had little respect for Spaatz. One day in the garden of Spaatz's villa at La Marsa, Coningham demonstrated the extent of his feelings by suddenly leaving a discussion and picking the blossoms from a nearby hibiscus.

He then returned and bent down on one knee in front of Tooey saying, as he proffered the flowers, 'Master, I bring you these.' Tooey was not amused. He knew well enough that the gesture was Mary's way of indicating that he had nothing to learn from an American general who had been in the war for less than a year. It was the first occasion on which I saw personal Anglo-American relations go wrong at that level. (*From Apes to Warlords*, London, 1978, p. 204)

As will be seen, Coningham's subordination to Spaatz tended to be mostly titular. For his part, Coningham was equally blunt in his demands upon his airmen. Soon after taking deeply concerned that the air forces had presented them with only the vaguest description of their plans for the air support of the invasion. The plan outlined by Tedder was less a plan than a concept. Operations were divided into three phases: preliminary strategic bombing, support of the assault forces and air operations to assist in the capture of Sicily.

Phase I began at the conclusion of the Tunisian campaign when the Allied air forces began applying steady pressure upon selected targets in Sicily, Sardinia and Italy and air strikes against Axis shipping. Key targets were Naples, Messina and Palermo, along with the important Axis airfields on Sicily and the mainland. The object was to interfere as much as possible with any attempted enemy build-up in Sicily *without* providing any indication that Sicily itself was the next Allied target.

Starting on D minus 7 (3 July) the air effort was to be directed against the German and Italian Forces to minimize their ability to interfere with the Allied landings a week later. Primary targets were Luftwaffe bases, although the Superaereo was not to be ignored. Attacks were to be directed against those airfields capable of launching attacks against the Allied fleet. At the same time, according to an unpublished RAF account, 'increasing attention was to be paid to land, sea and air communications leading into Sicily'. The ports of Catania and Palermo were included but the primary focus was on Messina where, 'at a favourable time near the approach of D-Day a maximum scale of day and night bombing attacks would be directed ... with a view to neutralising it as a supply base and as a channel for reinforcements'.[1]

Concurrently, Bomber Command was to initiate heavy bomber strikes from its United Kingdom bases against Italian communication and industrial targets, including the northern industrial cities of Turin, Milan and Genoa and the important rail centre of Bologna.[2]

[1] T. Milne, 'The Sicilian Campaign', PRO (AIR 41/52), loc. cit.
[2] Ibid.

---

command of the Northwest African Tactical Air Force, Coningham issued an operational directive the thrust of which was that only superior pilots could win the air battle. The efficiency of the 'human machine' was the basic requirement for success. 'The inculcation of the offensive spirit is of paramount importance. Spirit and confidence will spring from good leadership ... The weak men of low morale are not to be tolerated in units as they taint the atmosphere. You are to remove such personnel immediately on discovery...' (General Operational Directive, n.d., Box 11, Spaatz Papers, Manuscript Division, Library of Congress.)

Phase II was to coincide with the assaults to gain control of the air by denying the Luftwaffe and Superaereo the skies while at the same time pounding their airfields. The other vital mission of the second phase was to protect Allied shipping day and night.

Phase III was the establishment of air support on Sicily itself, utilizing the airfields captured by Seventh Army. As the first squadrons left Malta for Sicily, their place was to be taken there by five RAF squadrons and two USAAF support groups from Tripoli. The air effort would then continue both in tactical support of the ground forces and, strategically, to prevent enemy reinforcement through Messina. The heavy bomber offensive against Italy would also intensify.

What became increasingly worrisome to the ground and naval commanders was the absence of specific details about how the air force intended to support the invasion forces. During May and June these and other questions were repeatedly raised but satisfactory answers were not forthcoming from the air chiefs. Aerial photographs required by the army planners were time and again requested but never produced for reasons that included incomprehensible decision-making at AFHQ. Truscott's JOSS Force planners were forced to prepare for the invasion of Licata with maps whose sole value was their qualification as relics dating to 1883! Daily requests for photo coverage were routinely turned down by Brigadier Kenneth Strong, the AFHQ Intelligence Officer (G-2) on the dubious grounds that such a mission might compromise the security of HUSKY, even though dozens of missions were being flown each day against Sicilian targets as part of the pre-invasion air offensive. 'I was desperate,' wrote Truscott. 'This photographic intelligence was essential to our planning.' In despair, Truscott finally was forced to shun normal command channels and appeal directly to Major General James H. 'Jimmy' Doolittle for assistance.* Without fuss the problem was solved at once by the RAF who honoured an official request from the USAAF.[1]

The widening gulf between the senior air commanders and their ground and naval counterparts was a manifestation of the growing air independence. Tedder's long-time Personal Assistant, Wing-Commander Leslie Scarman,† recalls that the events in

[1] Truscott, *Command Missions*, op. cit., p. 200.
* Commander, Northwest African Strategic Air Force.
† Later, Lord Scarman, a Lord of Appeal on Britain's highest judicial tribunal.

North Africa in late 1942 and early 1943 generated an atmosphere of achievement and impending victory despite the success of Rommel's retreat and the problems in Tunisia:

> If anything, they were extremely arrogant in their view of the competence of the Ground Force commanders ... They thought that the Ground Force commanders did not understand how to operate Air Forces or the limits necessarily put upon their capacity to co-operate due to such matters as engineering, repairs and the need for protected air bases. I remember Tedder saying that the trouble with the Ground Commanders was that they did not understand the 'nitty gritty' problems of maintaining an Air Force in the air.

The real difficulty was that

> Tedder was not prepared to have either the Ground Force commanders or the Naval commanders dictate to him either the strategy or the deployment of the Air Forces under his command. His attitude then, as always, was 'Tell me what you want done and I will deliver in my own style.' I fear this did not contribute to harmony on a personal basis between Air Force and other commanders but ... they were striving to maintain the independence of the Air Force. The British commanders were very alive to what they regarded as the structural subordination of the American Air Forces to the Navy and the Army.[1]

Not all the problems were inter-service; there were disagreements within the air forces over tactics. One of Coningham's principal subordinates was Air Vice-Marshal Harry Broadhurst who had succeeded him as commander of the Desert Air Force and who is widely regarded as one of the most innovative tactical air commanders produced by the RAF during the war. As he rose in rank, Broadhurst, himself a fighter pilot and veteran of the Battle of Britain, refused to become a desk-bound commander. In North Africa, and later in Sicily, Italy and Normandy when he was not flying his own Spitfire, Broadhurst could be observed darting about the front in an unarmed German Storch observation aircraft which he had painted bright yellow.*

---

[1] Letter to the author, 2 April 1985.
* The Storch had originally been captured behind British lines in the desert by several soldiers who found it on the ground with its engine running while the pilot was away cutting telephone lines. It was given to Coningham and as Broadhurst relates: 'It was a marvellous aircraft for hopping around and required no runway. It could land right next to an HQ. And so, the time came when Coningham left and his ADC got drunk and creamed it taking it to Cairo to have it boxed up and sent home to England. He broke it but the depot managed to

While Senior Air Staff Officer (SASO) of the Desert Air Force, he clashed with Coningham during the pursuit of Rommel after Alamein. Broadhurst was deeply committed to the doctrine of close air support of the ground forces and he brought to the desert an open mind and fresh ideas which he was anxious to see implemented. Broadhurst recalls: 'I wanted to use the whole of the Desert Air Force in low-level attacks against the German and Italian armies who were retreating along a single road and were particularly vulnerable at a point called Sollum (on the Eyptian–Libyan border).'[1] Coningham refused and Broadhurst believed this cost the British a great opportunity. At Mareth, Montgomery's successful left hook was made possible by Broadhurst who – in a return to the barrage tactics of 1918 – concentrated the aircraft of the Desert Air Force to paralyse the Germans, first by striking hard at their rear, and then by a massive aerial blitz which permitted a breakthrough by the ground forces. John Terraine writes that his performance at Mareth stamped Broadhurst as 'bold, original, creative and entirely unawed by Service orthodoxy'.[2]

Despite their considerable success, Broadhurst's aerial 'blitzkrieg' tactics did not endear him to his superiors, among then Coningham. As Terraine notes, 'The reason is not far to seek ... Coningham's first task [as the new Allied tactical air commander] had been to wean the armies from the old desire to see the sky full of supporting aircraft. His struggle was for the air superiority which would bring all else in its train; this was being achieved, and he obviously viewed with trepidation Broadhurst's total commitment to direct support.'[3]

Then and throughout the remainder of the war, Broadhurst found himself torn between loyalty to his RAF superiors who tolerated but never fully approved of his commitment to direct

---

[1] Letter to the author, 25 May 1985 and interview of 22 November 1979.
[2] *The Right of the Line*, op. cit., p. 398.
[3] Ibid, pp. 755–6.

---

repair it. I got a message it was mended and would I like to have it? So I had it. When we joined forces, 'Mary' Coningham *demanded* his Storch back. By then I'd got used to having it, but my ADC flew it over to him. Then the great day came when Coningham went to fly this Storch. He taxied it out and was just opening up the throttle when it broke in half! And he never really would believe I hadn't sabotaged it. But they had welded the thing together and it had gone at the weld. Had he been airborne he would have been killed ... Then in Italy, some Yugoslavs escaped in a brand new Storch. At the end of the war I had a letter from the Yugoslav government demanding their Storch back!' (Interview of 2 November 1983.)

support of the ground forces. Future wars in Korea, Vietnam and the Middle East would prove the validity of his philosophy even in the age of the supersonic, high performance jet aircraft. 'It was at this time,' says Broadhurst, 'that relations between Montgomery, Tedder and Coningham broke down. Tedder and Coningham were openly and publicly criticising Montgomery for failing to cut off the retreating armies, whilst themselves failing to use their complete air superiority to destroy the enemy transport in low-level attacks and thus block their retreat!'[1]

The USAAF, which was still nominally under the control of the Army, was somewhat more flexible and while claiming independence also accepted the role of close air support as a proper mission. Nevertheless, despite the example pioneered by the Desert Air Force, the air chiefs were insisting that their *primary* function was now to neutralize enemy air power.

This did not prevent Patton's air counterpart, Colonel Lawrence Hickey, an advocate of close air–ground co-operation, from paying dearly for his stance. Under the new air structure, all tactical aircraft of the XII Support Command were placed for HUSKY under the operational control of either the Malta Air Command or Coningham's tactical air force. Hickey elected to co-locate with Patton's HQ which apparently irritated Coningham, who intervened to cause Hickey's replacement on grounds that his relationship with Patton was 'invidious' and a 'weakness'.[2] Hickey and several other air force officers who espoused the theme of co-operation with the ground forces suddenly found themselves *personae non gratae*,[3] and this repudiation was not lost on Patton and his staff who saw it as proof of the indifference of the airmen to their requirements. Hickey was replaced by Major General Edwin House but by retaining operational control it was Coningham who exercised the real authority.

What so concerned Patton and Montgomery was that the air plan 'gave ground and naval commanders no concrete informa-

[1] Letter of 25 May 1985, loc. cit.

[2] Cable, Coningham–Spaatz, 3 June 1943, Box 12, Spaatz Papers. Coningham had a long memory for those who tangled with him and although Patton believed they had parted on friendly terms after the incident in Tunisia, it is possible there was a connection between this and Colonel Hickey's treatment. (See Chapter 6.) Coningham's signal in response to Patton's complaint that II Corps was receiving inadequate air support had led to a written reprimand from Tedder. (Spaatz Diary, 4 April 1943, Box 11, Spaatz papers.)

[3] *Sicily*, op. cit., p. 107.

tion on the amount and type of air support they could expect on D-Day'.[1] So vague was the final air plan that one American general derided it as a 'most masterful piece of uninformed prevarication, totally unrelated to the Naval and Military Joint Plan'.[2] In short, the problem was this: 'Ground and naval commanders had no idea of the degree of protection they could expect, and when the assault troops set sail for Sicily, their commanders [still] had not the faintest idea of when, where, under what circumstances, and in what numbers they would see their own aircraft.'[3]

The ground commanders never could relate this proposition to their own conception of air support and the unhappy result was that they became increasingly sceptical of the air chiefs. Their suspicions were confirmed when the airmen refused to co-ordinate their planning with either the Army or the Navy. The new Mediterranean Air Command thus became a mirror image of the independence being demonstrated by the RAF and the result was little or no full consultation at the planning level. Patton, for example, was vexed by the knowledge that despite having over four hundred planes at his disposal, Coningham refused to provide any assurance in advance to either the Army or Navy about what support they could expect on D-Day. This refusal stemmed, at least in part, from a reluctance to sacrifice flexibility: ' "Tactical" might be wanted to support "strategic" in action against enemy air forces.'[4]

A postwar history of the RAF points with pride to the amalgamation of the RAF and USAAF, a unity forged in the subjugation of Sicily and Italy in which 'every triumph was shared in equal measure by both Allies'.[5] However, neither this account nor the unpublished RAF narrative deals adequately with the vagueness of the air plan and the criticism of it by the naval and ground commanders. Tedder's war memoirs emphasize the success of Allied air power which by D-Day had left the enemy without a single operational airfield. 'It would be hard to imagine,' he wrote, 'a better demonstration of the flexibility of air power than that

---

[1] Ibid., p. 106.
[2] Ibid., p. 106. This comment is ascribed to Major General H. R. Bull, a senior American officer on the AFHQ staff.
[3] Ibid.
[4] Sicily–Salerno–Anzio, op. cit., p. 22.
[5] Denis Richards and Hilary St. George Saunders, The Fight Avails, London, 1954, p. 301.

provided by the attacks on airfields in the first nine days of July 1943.'[1] On D-Day he reported to Portal that our Air Forces are 'on top of the world'.

This optimism was not wholly warranted, for the air plan never achieved the successes claimed by the airmen. The first phase was very effective except against the crucially important targets along the Messina Strait. Here, the achievements of Allied air power were vastly overrated. Raids against the Messina and Reggio di Calabria marine dock facilities and supporting railway communications failed even to slow the movement of military supplies and equipment across the Strait, despite the enormous physical damage. The ports were crippled but the enemy compensated for this loss by the extensive use of barge ferries which were able to land directly on to the beaches north of Messina. The assertion by Tedder that 'fighters from Malta and North Africa, their sweeps carefully co-ordinated, hunted and assaulted the enemy's shipping....' is belied by the fact that Allied air power failed to choke off or even slow down the Axis lifeline across the Strait.*

This optimism was never shared by the naval and ground commanders, among them Patton whose dissatisfaction with the air plan led him to implore Admiral Hewitt to circumvent the airmen by obtaining naval carrier aircraft to take over the task. 'You can get your Navy planes to do anything you want; but we can't get the Air Force to do a goddam thing!'[2] Before the presentation of the final invasion plans in Algiers, Patton wrote to Alexander to complain about the lack of commitments for close air support. To bolster his case, he even quoted from a recently issued pamphlet by Montgomery entitled 'Some Notes on High Command in War' which mirrored Tedder's own doctrine: 'The greatest asset of air power is its flexibility and this enables it to be switched quickly from one objective to another.'[3]

Right up to the invasion Patton continued to express his unease

[1] *With Prejudice*, op. cit., p. 447.
[2] Quoted in *Sicily–Salerno–Anzio*, op. cit., p. 22.
[3] Memorandum of 19 June 1943, Wedemeyer File, Eisenhower Library. Wedemeyer was temporarily attached to Patton's staff for the invasion as a War Department observer, sent personally by Marshall. Wedemeyer too was distressed by the vague air plan and Patton persuaded him to write the 19 June memo to Alexander. According to Wedemeyer, Alexander agreed and 'directed the HUSKY air commanders to provide direct air support'. There is no evidence that Alexander had any influence on the airmen. (Quote from *Wedemeyer Reports!*, op. cit., p. 221.)

* A complete account is in Chapter 30.

about the air support for his Western Task Force despite reassurances from the air commanders. Patton went to see Tedder's Deputy Air C-in-C, Air Vice-Marshal H. E. P. Wigglesworth, but emerged feeling he would somehow be 'double-crossed'.[1]

On 22 June the Allied commanders were given an intelligence briefing, which was followed by a general discussion that centred on concern over the air plan. Patton's diary recorded that promises were made that were only forthcoming because of pressure from the invasion commanders. 'Here it was that Ike missed being great. He could have faced the issue but sat mute...'[2]

This dissension was in no small part the result of a Catch-22 situation: the airmen refused to commit themselves in advance to a specific level of fighter support which would depend upon the scale of enemy opposition. This, in turn, was wholly dependent upon the success of the Allied bombing offensive during Phase I.[3] The principal reason, however, was that Tedder was adamant in his conviction that without the early capture of the Gela airfields 'the entire [HUSKY] plan would prove abortive. Provisions for their speedy capture therefore became the guiding principle of our operational plans.'[4] Thus, direct air support became subservient to the attainment of air supremacy over Sicily. Yet, Tedder seems to have overlooked the fact that the greater the direct air support of the invasion forces, the better the chances were of early capture of the enemy airfields which the air force required in order to execute Phase III of the air plan.

By far the most serious schism was caused by the refusal of the airmen to provide the navy with the flight paths to be used by the troop carrier aircraft to transport the airborne and glider troops to Sicily. For their part, the air force was sceptical of the proposed airborne operations and predicted heavy aircraft losses.* When the problem went unresolved Cunningham became equally intransigent by refusing to provide assurance that the navy would not fire

---

[1] *The Patton Papers*, Vol. II, op. cit., p. 266.
[2] Ibid., p. 267.
[3] 'The Sicilian Campaign', loc. cit.
[4] Tedder quoted in Terraine, *The Right of the Line*, op. cit., p. 613.
* An example was a Memorandum sent to Spaatz by his planners on 6 April entitled 'Troop Carrier Operations for HUSKY' which considered the proposed operation too risky. (Box 11, Spaatz Papers.) For the remainder of the war the Allied airmen never lost their distaste for airborne operations. From Normandy, where Air Chief Marshal Leigh-Mallory attempted to persuade Eisenhower to cancel the airborne operations as too dangerous, to Arnhem where they insisted on using drop zones that all but guaranteed the failure of Operation MARKET-GARDEN, there was simply no great enthusiasm for these operations.

on the unarmed air convoys. Even though the problem had existed for weeks no solution was forthcoming until nearly D-Day, despite the fact that the US airborne commander, Major General Matthew B. Ridgway, warned that unless the navy was able to provide satisfactory guarantees he would recommend against the airborne operation.[1]

Ridgway's warnings went unheeded and it was not until *after* the convoys departed for Sicily that the air routes were finally revealed on 7 July, a mere three days before D-Day and far too late to ensure that all naval and ground forces were alerted. No satisfactory reason has emerged for this delay but the episode was one of the worst examples of inter-service co-operation of the war. The dire warnings were not exaggerated and had they been heeded the tragedy which occurred on D+1 might have been averted.

The evidence clearly establishes that the problem was known throughout the Allied high command. Eisenhower sent Major General John P. Lucas to Patton's HQ as his 'eyes and ears' and on 9 June he warned the Allied commander that all was not well. Ten days later came the strongly worded Patton-Wedemeyer memo to Alexander. Eisenhower claimed to have spoken frankly to Tedder of the importance of calming the fears of the ground commanders but without noticeable effect.

An observer's report published by Combined Operations Headquarters in October 1943 was very critical of the air planning and generated a furious reaction by both the British and American air chiefs who were stung by this censure. Speaking for the airmen, Air Marshal Sir John Slessor, while admitting that 'arrangements might have been better', ridiculed the suggestion that there had been a 'deliberate refusal on the part of the Air Forces to co-operate', a charge he termed 'fantastic'.[2]

---

[1] Papers of General Matthew B. Ridgway, USAMHI.
[2] Letter, Air Marshal Sir John Slessor–Vice-Chief of Air Staff, 12 March 1944, PRO (AIR 23/7539). COHQ sent an unidentified military observer (an army officer, probably a colonel or lieutenant-colonel) to Seventh Army to observe the planning and execution of HUSKY. His detailed 'Notes on the Planning and Assault Phases of the Sicilian Campaign' appeared as 'COHQ Bulletin No. Y/1' in October 1943. Among his observations on the role of the Allied air forces were these: (1) There was no single air representative on the JOSS Force 'Joint Planning Board'. (2) Aerial photographs of the assault area were not only wholly inadequate but the interpretations supplied by Force 141 were dangerously incorrect. (3) '... the almost complete lack of participation by the Air Force. An Air Plan ultimately arrived [which] ... gave Military Commanders no concrete information of what air support might be expected on the [D] day ... As regards targets for pre D-day bombing, I was informed that Army Headquarters had originally been asked to submit a list of require-

Whether or not they intended it, the failure of Tedder and Coningham to communicate even a measure of reassurance about close air support to their ground and naval counterparts conveyed an impression of arrogance and unco-operativeness that soured relations and unnecessarily perpetuated mistrust.

In their defence the airmen complained of being handicapped by their full commitment to the Tunisian campaign, the dispersal of their forces throughout North Africa and the Middle East, and by the constantly changing HUSKY invasion plan. Nevertheless, the same problems existed for the ground forces and the changes to the invasion plan had no impact on the strategy for the preliminary air operations. Moreover, while Malta provided an ideal base of operations for British support of Eighth Army, the capture of Pantelleria now provided the same for American support of the Seventh Army landings.*

Unquestionably, the air planners had to overcome considerable logistical problems which involved shifting aircraft and support facilities to Tunisia. Broadhurst's Desert Air Force, for example, had to be withdrawn *from* Tunisia to the Middle East where all its spare parts and equipment were located. Its long trek across North Africa in support of Eighth Army had simply left it too far away from its support bases to enable it to prepare for HUSKY.

The unpublished RAF narrative complains that planning was complicated by the armies 'who made no attempt to centralise their planning and expected the air forces to break what was

* See Chapter 11.

---

ments. This was done but in due course returned with the bald comment that the targets were unsuitable ... and that a further list was to be sent as a matter of urgency. A new list was thereupon contrived, but this again met with a similar response. Finally, on about D−25 a reasonably senior air officer was sent to Army Headquarters to make suggestions and to assist in the production of still another list of targets ... he was unable to understand why the previous lists were considered unsuitable.' (4) Targets for D-Day bombing were not even provisionally published by the time Seventh Army embarked for Sicily. The only concession to the ground commanders in the field was that after D-Day they could submit their requirements for the consideration of a 'Target Committee' sitting in North Africa, but that no such request would be considered with less than 12 hours' notice. (5) 'As regards fighter cover, no indication of the degree of protection to be expected was given, and the forces again sailed without any idea of when, where, under what circumstances and in what numbers they would see their own fighters.'

After strong remonstrations from the Air Ministry and senior airmen such as Slessor, COHQ hastily withdrew the offending document, Bulletin Y/1. After a considerable search the only copy located by the author is in the Truscott Papers, George C. Marshall Research Library, Lexington, Virginia.

essentially an over-all air problem requiring careful co-ordination into a number of detailed and uncoordinated tasks, each of which were expected to be discussed with minor Army formations spread over North Africa and the Middle East'.[1] Nevertheless, some of this wound was self-inflicted. An American air planning staff that was originally intended to be located at an early stage with Force 343 in Morocco remained in Algiers until relatively late in the planning. Had there been less separation of the inter-service planners much of the ill-will and misunderstanding about the air plan would never have occurred.

There were other obstacles as well, among them the disparity between British and American planning methods, which was worsened by the dearth of Americans with experience matching that of the RAF. So far, HUSKY was providing a harsh lesson in inter-service co-operation in combined operations, and the reason was not hard to find: the decentralization of the planning. Too many cooks were spoiling the broth; there was simply no way to satisfy everyone without the advantage of daily contact and eyeball-to-eyeball resolution of mutual problems. To make matters worse there were too many bloated bureaucracies in too many locations. Eisenhower became increasingly frustrated by the unseemly glut of headquarters. 'I have gotten so my chief ambition in this war is finally to get to a place where the next operation does not have to be amphibious, with all the inflexibility and delay that are characteristic of such operations.'[2]

Montgomery expressed the same scepticism in the air plan as Patton, and complained it was a grievous mistake to break up the successful air–ground team from the desert. However, the team was not really broken up: the most logical headquarters was Malta Air Command which was responsible for air support operations until the beachhead was secure, at which time operational control would pass to the tactical air forces. 'Moreover,' as Broadhurst notes, 'the decision had no impact on my own mission for the pre D-day period or the assault phase because my HQ was located alongside AOC Malta's HQ, and the two staffs and [Air Vice-Marshal Sir] Keith Park* and myself worked closely

---

[1] 'The Sicilian Campaign', loc. cit.

[2] Butcher Diary, 13 May 1943.

* Air Chief Marshal Sir Keith Park (1892–1975) was another of the outstanding tactical air commanders produced by New Zealand. Park was an artilleryman at Gallipoli and the

together. Also, I had a number of my squadrons from the Desert who were very experienced in supporting the 8th Army.'[1]

Montgomery's fears were considerably exaggerated for, as Broadhurst affirms, 'we and our staffs were together [with Eighth Army's] in Malta and continued to co-operate as in the past'. It is a tribute to the flexibility and experience of Broadhurst and Park that they continued to function exceptionally well despite a zany command structure. 'As far as the Desert Air Force was concerned,' writes Broadhurst, 'we had no part in the planning of the Sicily campaign except in the dispositions of the DAF squadrons in Malta and North Africa. We were still being administered by HQ, Middle East Air Forces in Cairo, were under the operational control of the North African Tactical Air Force in Tunis – and operating within the zone of Malta which was still under the administrative control of HQ, Middle East in Cairo!!'[2]

On the eve of D-Day Montgomery noted in his diary, 'I do not like the air plan.'[3] He was not convinced that the air force had accomplished their mission. 'It is an axiom in modern war, if you want to succeed, then you must win the air battle before you embark on the land or sea battle. In this operation we embarked for the invasion of SICILY without being quite certain that we *had* won the air battle; even the RAF could not say for certain we had won the air battle.'[4]

To his credit, he would soon change his tune, admitting that 'I was wrong':

> The Allied Air Forces had definitely won the air battle, and this was quite apparent from the first moment we stepped ashore in SICILY. The enemy air force was swept from the sky and was never allowed to inconvenience us, except for night bombing of

[1] Letter of 25 May 1985, loc. cit.
[2] Ibid.
[3] Montgomery Diary, 9 July 1943, Montgomery Papers.
[4] 'Some Reflections on the Campaign in Sicily, July/August 1943', Montgomery Papers.

Somme before joining the Royal Flying Corps. As the commander of No. 11 [Fighter] Group, Park provided air cover for the evacuation of Dunkirk and was in the vanguard during the Battle of Britain. An airman of great initiative, he was given command of the vitally important British base of Malta in July 1942. He was no stranger to close air support and, in addition to Sicily, Malta had provided similar support to the TORCH landings and in September would do the same for the Salerno landings. Despite his outstanding record, Park today remains little known, which John Terraine rightly calls 'something of a national disgrace' (*The Right of the Line*, p. 185). Fortunately, a long-awaited biography was published in 1984 which has helped to redress this neglect. (Cf. Vincent Orange, *Sir Keith Park*, London 1984.)

the ports. This was a remarkable achievement, and I wrote to Air Chief Marshal Sir Arthur Tedder and expressed the great appreciation of the Eighth Army in the matter.[1]

There was no such satisfaction in the Seventh Army sector where, as Bradley's troops would soon attest, close air support during the first critical hours of the invasion was an unfulfilled promise. Moreover, as the campaign unfolded, the air plan was shown to have serious flaws. The destruction of the Axis air forces and the neutralization and capture of its airfields would succeed brilliantly. Interdiction of the Axis ability to ferry reinforcements at will across the Messina Strait was another matter entirely.

[1] Ibid.

PART III

Point / Counter-Point

The question was, where would the Allies land ...
The Italians and OKW believed it would be in Sicily;
Hitler thought otherwise....

MATTHEW COOPER
The German Army 1933–1945

CHAPTER 9

Operation MINCEMEAT

... as astonishing and macabre as it was successful.

LORD ISMAY[1]

In the early morning hours of 18 April 1943 an unmarked Ford transit van arrived inconspicuously at the naval docks at Greenock, Scotland. The three men inside the van, one of whom was dressed in the uniform of a lieutenant-commander of the Royal Navy, dismounted and unloaded a specially constructed steel container which weighed about 400 pounds and was inscribed on the side with the words: 'Handle with Care – OPTICAL INSTRUMENTS – for Special FOS Shipment'. Also unloaded was an uninflated rubber liferaft of the type commonly used aboard British aircraft.

Men and cargo were ferried by launch to a submarine tender anchored in the waters of Holy Loch. Berthed alongside was the submarine HMS *Seraph* which was making final preparations for departure. There the men were met by the submarine's Commanding Officer, twenty-nine-year-old Lieutenant N. L. A. Jewell, RN. After a brief discussion the cargo was turned over to Lieutenant Jewell and the men departed. Orders were given for the proper storage of the mysterious cargo and as six ratings wrestled the heavy canister into position in a forward compartment of the submarine, they began to joke about its contents. The canister was no larger than a man and was soon mirthfully referred to as 'John Brown's body' and 'our new shipmate, Charlie'.

At 1800 hours the following night the *Seraph* cast away from the tender, slipped out of Holy Loch and disappeared into the darkness of the Firth of Clyde. Her official destination was listed as Malta; yet this was no ordinary patrol. Known only to her captain was the fact that the mission of the *Seraph* was anything but routine and that a number of very important people in London had an unusual interest in her patrol.

[1] *The Memoirs of Lord Ismay*, London, 1960, p. 292.

Lieutenant Jewell was no stranger to unconventional missions. Six months earlier he had safely delivered Lieutenant General Mark Clark to (and retrieved him from) a secret rendezvous at an isolated beach house outside Algiers, where covert negotiations took place between Clark and a group of senior French officers which cleared the way for Operation TORCH. Jewell and his crew acquired a reputation for getting the job done and now, by sheer coincidence, the *Seraph* was available for her current mission.

Eleven days later, in the early morning hours of 30 April, the *Seraph* lay close inshore in the shallow waters of the Gulf of Cadiz off the southern coast of the province of Andalucia, Spain. Nearby were the vessels of a Spanish fishing fleet. At 0430 hours the submarine surfaced little more than a mile off the point where the rivers Odiel and Tinto empty into the gulf at the town of Huelva. Lieutenant Jewell and four of his officers clambered up the ladder into the conning tower and on to the deck, followed immediately by crew members carrying the mysterious canister.

Only moments before, Jewell had told his crew the real purpose of their mission and then sworn them to secrecy, reminding them that the operation they were participating in was exceptionally important.

The moon had set and it was dark as the five officers struggled to open the bolts on the vacuum-sealed canister and removed its bizarre contents. Wrapped in a blanket, soaked from melted dry ice, was the soggy corpse of a man who appeared to be in his early thirties and was dressed in the uniform of an officer in the Royal Marines. Chained to his waist was an official black despatch case with the Royal seal affixed. The 'Mae West' life jacket worn by the corpse was inflated, and in a departure from his instructions the young captain offered what prayers he could recall from the Burial Service. The body was then pushed overboard where it began to drift inshore with the tide.*

When the submarine headed out to sea the wash of its screws forced the corpse even closer to its intended destination, the beach at Huelva. A half-mile to the south the officers pushed the now inflated rubber liferaft and a single paddle overboard upside

---

* There was considerable concern over what action to take if the tide refused to co-operate and swept the body back out to sea. Typically, it was Churchill who provided the final word: 'You will have to get him back and give him another swim.' (Quoted in Ronald Lewin, *Ultra Goes to War*, London, 1978, p. 370.)

down, along with the metal canister which was riddled by gunfire and sunk in over 300 fathoms of water.

Later that morning a brief MOST SECRET signal from *Seraph* was received in the office of the Director of Naval Intelligence in London and hand-carried to the same lieutenant-commander who had delivered the canister to Holy Loch two weeks earlier. The message confirmed that Operation MINCEMEAT had been carried out as planned.[1]

As the events of that day were later reconstructed, some time that morning a Spanish fisherman recovered the floating body which was removed to a nearby beach and turned over to Spanish authorities who identified it from its papers as that of a Major William Martin, Royal Marines. It seemed obvious from its condition that Major Martin's corpse had been in the water for several days, and was there as a result of some type of mishap off the coast of Spain, a common wartime occurrence.

While Operation HUSKY was being planned in the Mediterranean there were those in London whose task it was to develop methods of deceiving the Axis that the invasion would occur elsewhere. The practice of deception within the British wartime establishment was a counter-intelligence function assigned to MI5. Within MI5 was a group of top intelligence officers who operated under the umbrella of what was designated the XX Committee – later immortalized as the 'Double Cross System' by Sir John Masterman.[2] Members of the XX Committee were drawn from the War Office, GHQ, Home Forces, Home Defence Executive, Air Ministry Intelligence, MI6, Combined Operations Headquarters, and Naval Intelligence.[3] One of its seven functions was 'to deceive the enemy about our plans and intentions'.[4]

Within the Admiralty's Department of Naval Intelligence (NID) was Section 17M, whose mission was liaison with other intelligence activities. One of the officers who represented NID on the XX Committee was the officer who had delivered the mysterious cargo

---

[1] Ewen Montagu, *The Man Who Never Was*, New York, 1953. This account of Operation MINCEMEAT is based largely on Commander Montagu's bestselling book which became an equally successful film of the same title, starring Clifton Webb. Before his death in 1985 Montagu confirmed a number of details about the operation in a letter to the author.

[2] J. C. Masterman, *The Double Cross System*, New Haven, 1972.

[3] Ibid., p. 62. The composition of the XX Committee varied and later included representation from SHAEF in connection with the Normandy landings and the campaign in Northwest Europe.

[4] Ibid., p. xii.

to HMS *Seraph*, Lieutenant-Commander Ewen Montagu, RNVR, in peacetime a lawyer and King's Counsel. The son of Lord Swaythling, an internationally known banker, Montagu was educated at London's prestigious Westminster School, Trinity College, Cambridge, and Harvard University from which he obtained MA and LLD degrees.

The idea of planting a corpse carrying disinformation was the brainchild of Montagu and a colleague, Flight-Lieutenant Charles Cholmondeley, an Air Ministry intelligence officer. After informal discussions the two men dismissed the idea as an impossible scheme.* However, when no other feasible deception operation could be created the two intelligence officers turned once again to the use of a corpse to plant false information on the Germans. Under their tutelage the scheme grew into a full-blown plan approved by the XX Committee. Eventually it passed through the military bureaucracy and was sanctioned by the British Chiefs of Staff, subject to the final approval of Churchill himself. When the plan landed on his desk the Prime Minister expressed no misgivings that the plan might compromise HUSKY if it went wrong and he authorized Operation MINCEMEAT, thus clearing the way to its launch.†

The extent of the problem of deceiving the Germans was made plain by Churchill who upon approving the plan noted that 'Anybody but a bloody fool would *know* it is Sicily.'[1] How then could the Germans be persuaded that the Allies would not do the obvious? What started out as a 'wild idea' to plant a suitably genuine corpse with equally genuine papers containing false information that the Germans would accept as real had evolved into one of the most brilliant deception operations ever undertaken. Thus was born Operation MINCEMEAT.

As Commander Montagu later wrote, 'It was decided that we could not hope to persuade the Germans that we were not going to attack Sicily, but we *might* persuade them that we would try to surprise them by capturing Sardinia first and then come down to Sicily afterwards, from the north. And, if we were very successful,

---

[1] Montagu, *The Man Who Never Was*, op. cit., p. 24, and *Beyond Top Secret Ultra*, New York, 1978, p. 143.

* This Trojan horse idea was undoubtedly based upon an actual incident which occurred in 1942 when ULTRA revealed that a corpse had washed ashore on the Spanish coast and the contents of its pockets passed to the Abwehr.

† Eisenhower was informed of the plan and had he objected it would have been scrapped.

we *might* get even the professional German High Command to believe that we were going to be rash enough both to try that and begin a Balkan invasion almost simultaneously.'*

Montagu had after a lengthy search located the body of a recently deceased young man and obtained the permission of his next of kin to use the corpse in return for a guarantee that his identity would never be revealed. It was decided that the 'man who never was' should be a Royal Marine officer assigned to Mountbatten's Combined Operations Headquarters staff en route to Gibraltar when his plane crashed in the ocean off southern Spain.

Every trapping of authenticity was provided to make the corpse into a genuine 'Major William Martin' – the name of a real officer on the rolls of the Royal Marines. Ticket stubs, photographs of a fictitious fiancée and all the other accoutrements of a man's private life were obtained – and where necessary forged – and planted on the body. The real problem was: what would it take to convince the Germans that the secret documents carried by Major Martin were genuine? Who would write them and what would they say? Despite bureaucratic obstruction in many forms – Montagu later said that 'to deceive the German High Command was nothing like as difficult as it was to persuade their British opposite numbers that we could do that' – one senior officer in the War Office was enthused by the scheme. He was Lieutenant-General Sir Archibald Nye, the able Vice-Chief of the Imperial General Staff. It had been decided that a fake letter must be planted on Martin from a high-ranking officer in London to General Alexander which would convincingly discuss an invasion of Greece by the Allies. Nye agreed to compose such a letter.

Nye had risen from the ranks and was well respected within the Army. He had been considered by Churchill as a replacement for Field-Marshal Sir John Dill as CIGS until Nye himself had told the Prime Minister that General Sir Alan Brooke, then commanding the Home Forces, was 'the only one conceivable choice'.[1]

Nye rose admirably to the occasion and produced a brilliant and wholly believable fabrication in the form of a 'Dear Alex' letter in

---

[1] Quoted in *Alanbrooke*, op. cit., p. 202.

* There has, of course, been considerable speculation over the identity of the 'man who never was'. Montagu will only say that it was the body of a young man who had died of pneumonia, and that 'he was a bit of a ne'er-do-well, and that the only worthwhile thing he ever did he did after his death'. Some believe the individual had died in a prison. It is doubtful whether his true identity will ever be known.

which he purported to smooth over and explain that General Sir Henry 'Jumbo' Wilson, C-in-C, Middle East, was getting troops originally earmarked for Alexander. Thus, under the guise of explaining a painful decision to Alexander, Nye reviewed the fictitious plan to invade Greece with two British divisions and the cover plan to confuse the Germans into believing the target was really Sicily. To make the letter even more believable, Nye went on to discuss the sort of routine matters that two such high-ranking officers would exchange, such as how the War Office was regrettably unable to furnish a brigadier specifically requested by Alexander owing to the man's illness. The letter was a dazzling *tour de force*, which subtly implanted the deception that the British *wanted* the Germans to believe the target in the western Mediterranean was Sicily – 'so *that* obviously *can't* be the real target'.[1]

To further authenticate Major Martin and why he was carrying such a sensitive letter, two additional letters signed by Mountbatten were included in his official despatch case, one of which passed him off as a top expert in amphibious operations whom Mountbatten was anxious to have back once Alexander was finished with his services.

Huelva was chosen because there was known to be an Abwehr agent active in the area. Within hours of its discovery the body of Major Martin was presented by Spanish authorities to the British vice-consul. Happily there was *no* despatch case accompanying the body. The following day he was buried with full military honours in the local cemetery, having dutifully fulfilled his role in the operation.

To keep up the façade, urgent signals flowed from London expressing grave concern over the missing despatch case and its secret contents. The British Naval Attaché was instructed to make strong representations to the Spanish authorities to return the case without delay. Finally, on 13 May the Spanish returned the case and papers. Tests in London revealed with certainty that the envelopes had indeed been tampered with and intelligence from Spain revealed considerable activity by the Abwehr agent, leaving no doubt that Major Martin's secrets had been passed on to the Germans.*

---

[1] *The Man Who Never Was*, op. cit., p. 55.
* The first German acknowledgement of Major Martin's false documents occurred on 7 May 1943 when the war diary of the Operations Division of the German Naval staff

On 4 June, *The Times* recorded Major Martin among the casualties in its latest listing. By coincidence an aeroplane had been lost in the vicinity at about the same time and the death of those on board appeared in the same list. As predicted, the local Spanish medical examiner failed to detect that Major Martin had not died of drowning.

The operation was essentially over and the bait successfully dangled for the Germans to take. And take it they did. Within days copies of the counterfeit letters were on their way to Berlin where they were given very special attention. Not until after the war would captured documents reveal the full extent of the success of Operation MINCEMEAT. It had been hoped that perhaps the Germans might be induced to take their eye off Sicily, even for a brief moment, if that might eventually save Allied lives. However, no one was prepared for what was revealed in these captured documents.

They reveal how Hitler and OKW were unaware that their decisions in the period before HUSKY were powerfully influenced by Operation MINCEMEAT which quickly began to produce the intended results. By 7 May the German Naval staff was summarizing its contents. Through its captured war diaries one can follow the evolution of how the German high command fell for this poisoned bait. The initial reaction was predictably cautious: 'No judgment can be passed at present on the authenticity of the document' (General Nye's letter to Alexander).[1] Four days later a meeting between Grand Admiral Karl Doenitz* and Hitler is reported in which the Fuehrer decides to hold Sardinia with all available forces. An invasion of Sicily is considered less likely.[2]

By 13 May the Germans had clearly taken the bait: 'It can be gathered from [Nye's letter] that a landing operation on a large scale is to take place in the western Mediterranean in the course of

[1] War diary, Operations Division, German Naval staff, 11 May 1943, microfilm reel G, Naval Historical Center. A substantial portion of the original 'Kriegstagebuch der Seekriegsleitung' covering the entire war has been translated and is now on sixteen reels of 35-mm microfilm. These documents provide a fascinating view of the war from the German side.

[2] Ibid., 11 May 1943.

* Doenitz had commanded the German U-boats and had only recently succeeded Grand Admiral Erich Raeder as C-in-C of the German Navy.

recorded: 'A British courier who crashed over Spain carried on himself a personal communication from the Chief of the Imperial General Staff to General Alexander . . . (contents summarized).' (War diary, German Naval staff, Reel G, Naval Historical Center, Washington, D.C.)

which Sicily is to be attacked as a mock objective ... the main landing will take place ... apparently on Sardinia ... *In the judgment of the Army General Staff the documents are without a doubt authentic. . . .*'[1] (Author's italics.)

The Germans also congratulated themselves that they had deceived the British that Major Martin's briefcase had not been tampered with and their 'secrets' were safe. This was, of course, exactly what British intelligence had intended:

> The Armed Forces High Command, Intelligence Division, had furnished an exact report on the way in which the British documents fell into Spanish hands, and that following their perusal the documents were treated with special care in a manner which made it impossible to recognize that the papers had been opened. The papers were returned to the British via the Spanish Ministry of Foreign Affairs in the original state.[2]

The great success of MINCEMEAT was in no small part attributable to the success of the large-scale strategic deception effort of the Allies in the Mediterranean whose purpose was to convince the Germans that the next target of Allied forces after North Africa was a major new campaign in the Balkans. Code-named BARCLAY, this theatre deception plan aimed at hoaxing the Germans into believing the Allies intended to invade western Crete and the Peloponnese in late May, and Pantelleria and Lampedusa in early June.* The British force that would carry out these operations was a bogus Twelfth Army Group composed of eleven divisions. Several days later a large American force was to invade Sardinia, Corsica and southern France. The Germans were fed information to confirm the threats to these targets, followed by two postponements that justified Allied inaction.[3]

With Washington's approval BARCLAY was conceived and carried out by a British organization based in Cairo called 'A' Force, originally the brainchild of Wavell, who in the dark days of 1940

---

[1] Ibid., 13 May 1943.

[2] Ibid., 19 May 1943.

[3] Charles Cruickshank, *Deception in World War II*, London, 1979, p. 52. Patton was to command the American Army which would invade Sardinia and Corsica while Alexander led a second Allied force invading southern France. The architects of this deception were thus able to provide the Germans with a plausible justification for the activities of the Allied units scattered across the breadth of North Africa.

* The Pantelleria and Lampedusa deception was eventually abandoned. However, the Allied capture of the island in late June undoubtedly served the same purpose as the original deception scheme.

created it in an attempt to help offset the enormous Axis advantage in the Mediterranean.* BARCLAY was designed not only to lure German forces away from the western Mediterranean to the Balkans but also to weaken their garrisons in the Dodecanese and the Aegean so as to lay the groundwork for a real operation in this region which Churchill intended later in 1943.†

To be successful a deception programme must possess elements of reality and the phony operation in the eastern Mediterranean were made more plausible by a number of other deceptions designed to reinforce the German belief that this was the next Allied target. CASCADE was an operation first begun in 1942 and designed to produce a fictitious 50% increase in the strength of Allied forces in the Mediterranean. ANIMALS was a series of raiding and photo reconnaissance operations in the Balkans which was effective in strengthening the German conviction that the Allies intended to invade sometime in the late spring of 1943.‡

Through the use of double agents throughout the Mediterranean who were under 'A' Force control and in Britain by agents turned and controlled by the Double Cross (XX) System, the Abwehr was fed carefully prepared rumours and items of information. This spider web of interlocking deception operations produced a network of deceit, bluff and double-bluff that fed the German appetite for information.§

* 'A' Force was commanded by Brigadier Dudley Clarke, a gunner whose fertile mind spawned what later became a virtual deception industry in the Mediterranean and Middle East. Among Clarke's many accomplishments was his role in the establishment of the Commandos. (See Anthony Cave-Brown, *Bodyguard of Lies*, London, 1976, p. 49.)

† Churchill saw an attack in the Aegean as another means of gaining access to Germany via the 'soft underbelly' and later in 1943 attempted to persuade Eisenhower to divert forces for an attack on the island of Rhodes. Backed by his senior commanders plus Marshall and Roosevelt, Eisenhower rejected the British attempt to launch yet another campaign in the Mediterranean.

‡ A recent investigation by a student at the US Army War College provides valuable new insight into Allied deception operations in the Mediterranean in 1943. See Joseph E. Browne, 'Deception for Operations: Sicily 1943', 1986 (unclassified), US Army War College, Carlisle, PA.

§ The full extent of Allied deception measures can only be hinted at here. Among the actions taken were radio deception and demonstrations and feints designed to hold Axis forces away from Sicily once the invasion began. Dummy landing craft and aircraft were set up in Cyrenaica and Egypt, where Abwehr agents could verify the presence of invasion fleets. Aerial attacks against Greek targets occurred in the period prior to the real D-Day for HUSKY. Greek troops were given special training by the British; false radio links were established and fake message traffic established between the equally phoney invasion forces. Rumours and false information were spread from Capetown to Switzerland and Sweden, where even the 'cocktail circuit' was employed to feed the deception. The troops bound for Sicily were prepared for combat in a country which spoke Greek and maps, currency and phrase books prepared and issued. To support the other fake operation AFHQ arranged the

The Germans were already inclined to believe the Allies would eventually strike in the eastern Mediterranean, and Operation MINCEMEAT thus became the *pièce de résistance* which not only convinced Hitler and OKW but served to muddy the waters further. Instead of one major operation they were now led to believe there would be two: Sardinia and the Peloponnese. In mid-May, OKW cabled Kesselring and other commands that it possessed 'absolutely reliable' information of large-scale landings in both the eastern and western Mediterranean.[1]

The Italian commander in Sicily and the Comando Supremo never fell for this massive Allied deception and never doubted that the pattern of Allied air attacks pointed to an invasion of Sicily or Sardinia. The fake MINCEMEAT documents may have swayed Hitler and sprung the trap so carefully baited by the British but they appear to have had no impact on Italian thinking. In fact, it was not so much the Allied deception measures that fooled the Germans but that they reinforced what the Germans themselves *already believed*. They had for some time been aware that the Allies were practising large-scale deception in the Mediterranean. Yet the strategic deception begun by BARCLAY and the subsidiary operations enhanced the believability of MINCEMEAT. The extent of Allied success became known in early June when a German signal was intercepted showing that the full-strength 1st Panzer Division was being shifted from its base in southern France to the Peloponnese.[2] A unit whose presence in Sicily might have been decisive was thus shunted on a wild-goose chase a thousand miles away. Any lasting doubts of the effects of Allied deception were later dispelled by documents captured by Canadian forces which revealed that OKW sent the following order on 21 May to Kesselring: 'THE MEASURES TO BE TAKEN IN SARDINIA AND THE PELOPONNESUS HAVE PRIORITY OVER ANY OTHERS.'[3]

---

[1] *British Intelligence in the Second World War*, Vol. III, Pt I, op. cit., p. 78.
[2] Ibid., p. 120.
[3] 'Information from German Sources', PRO (CAB 44/285). This document is a compendium of information about Axis forces in Sicily prepared for the official Canadian historians.

---

issue of French currency and maps. Clarke cleverly led 'A' Force to play a double-bluff whereby it was intended to make the Germans believe the shift of the Allied high command to Malta was in reality a deliberate Allied bluff to focus their attention on the central Mediterranean and away from the Peloponnese. (Browne, loc. cit.)

The gullibility of German intelligence and OKW in swallowing hook, line and sinker evidence that *could* have been an Allied ruse contradicted the accuracy of an OKW appreciation made long before the fall of Tunisia:

> The enemy will direct his operations against places where he believes that inferior defences will permit a quick realization of important aims. Short sea routes will also appear desirable. . . .
> *The idea of knocking Italy out of the war after the conclusion of the African campaign, by means of air attacks and a landing operation, looms large in Anglo-Saxon deliberations . . . Sicily offers itself as the first target.*[1]

The official histories later paid tribute to the enormous success of this strategic deception which had begun as a fantasy and ended as a *ruse de guerre* that may well never again be equalled in audacity or success. For the time being, however, British intelligence had to be content with the knowledge that the fabricated documents carried by the non-existent Major Martin were safely in German hands.

Churchill's knowledge of and interest in every aspect of the war is now legendary, and none more so than the audacious operation he had sanctioned some months earlier. By mid-May when it had become certain that the Germans had taken the bait, the Prime Minister was in Washington for the TRIDENT Conference. Nevertheless, not long after his arrival there a cryptic and prophetic message was delivered to him. It was from London and it read simply: 'MINCEMEAT SWALLOWED WHOLE'.[2]

---

[1] Ibid. Quoted from an appreciation titled 'Future Anglo-Saxon Operative Possibilities', submitted by the Foreign Armies West section of OKW on 8 February 1943.

[2] Quoted in *The Man Who Never Was*, op. cit., p. 117.

CHAPTER 10

A Difference of Opinion

Kesselring judged the situation optimistically ...
[Guzzoni's] pessimism was quite justified.

GENERAL FRIDOLIN VON SENGER UND ETTERLIN

Generale d'Armata Alfredo Guzzoni, the commander of the
Italian Sixth Army and the officer responsible for the Axis defence
of Sicily, was then sixty-six years old and had been in retirement
since 1941 until recalled by the Comando Supremo to assume
responsibility for Sicily on 20 May. It did not take Guzzoni long to
learn that he had inherited insurmountable problems. Not only
were Sicily's defences woefully inadequate to protect its more than
600 miles of coastline from invasion, but there existed a fundamental disagreement between himself and the German Supreme
Commander in the Mediterranean, Field Marshal Albert Kesselring,* over how the island was to be defended.

A good many Italian commanders were unfit to hold their
positions; some were not only incompetent but also cowards.
Guzzoni was not one of them. He had commanded both a division
and a corps before the war and in 1939 was the Commander-in-
Chief of the Italian Expeditionary Force during the invasion of
Albania. After the calamitous beginning of the campaign in Greece
in 1940, Guzzoni was relieved and returned to Rome as the vice-
chief of the Army General Staff and the Undersecretary of State for
War. In May 1941 he resigned both positions and vanished into
retirement. He was a rather small, heavy-set man, known as an
ambitious politician who enjoyed a reputation for knowing what
he was doing and for pursuing it with determination. Unlike many
other senior Italian officers, Guzzoni maintained sound relations
with the Germans.

Guzzoni was also an able strategist, and when he took over the
defence of Sicily he found the island's naval defences virtually

* *Oberbefehlshaber Süd* – abbreviated to OB South.

non-existent, its air defences inadequate and the ground forces poorly trained – in some units officers did not know how to operate their own guns – and badly positioned to repel an enemy invasion. Although on paper there were adequate numbers of troops, the state of morale of the Italians ranged from poor to dismal. And, as Allied intelligence noted, the coastal divisions displayed 'an almost unbelievably low standard of morale, training and discipline'.[1]

From Hitler downwards, the Germans tended to view their Axis partner with an attitude of haughty disdain and frequently unconcealed scorn. The Italians were considered the weak link in the Berlin–Rome axis forged between Hitler and Mussolini by the Pact of Steel in May 1939. Rommel had typified the German attitude in North Africa by disregarding the orders of the Italian C-in-C under whom the Afrika Korps was assigned whenever it suited him.

The problem with the Italian Army, observed Rommel, was that it had acquired a very considerable inferiority complex. Their training was poor and unrealistic, their weapons inadequate, obsolete and unreliable and many of their officers were disillusioned to find that war was not the pleasant romantic adventure portrayed by Mussolini in his Fascist vision of empire.[2]

Rommel's problems with his Italian ally in North Africa were typical. The Italian approach to war was far too frequently one of leisure, lack of initiative and the use of antiquated doctrines of war. Italian organization was cumbersome, over-staffed and generally unable to react at more than a snail's pace to urgent military matters which required decisiveness and efficiency. The bureaucracy in Rome meddled in affairs that were properly the business of commanders.

The most serious defect of the Italians was the weakness of their officer corps which, while it contained some excellent commanders and officers, was far too politicized. Corruption and intrigue in Rome resulted in the appointment of too many unqualified officers who demonstrated little interest in the morale and welfare of their men. The unsoundness and corruption of the officer corps was fortunately not found in the Italian soldier who showed that if properly trained and led he could often perform splendidly.

[1] G-2 Intelligence Notes, No. 18, 1 August 1943, AFHQ Papers, PRO (WO 204/983).
[2] *The Rommel Papers*, op. cit., p. 134.

Rommel sympathized with the plight of the ordinary soldier: 'Rations were so bad that the Italian soldier frequently had to ask his German comrade for food. Particularly harmful was the all-pervading differentiation between officer and man. While the men had to make shift without field-kitchens, the officers, or many of them, refused adamantly to forgo their several course meals. Many officers, again, considered it unnecessary to put in an appearance during battle and thus set the men an example ... It was small wonder that the Italian soldier, who incidentally was extraordinarily modest in his needs, developed a feeling of inferiority which accounted for his occasional failure in moments of crisis.'[1]

What Guzzoni found in Sicily was scarcely better than what Rommel had observed in North Africa, and in mid-June he personally attempted to convince Mussolini of the seriousness of Sicily's position, but like Hitler, Il Duce was uninterested in reality or the truth and 'sounded off with one of his eloquent orations in which he predicted that the Italian Army would defeat the enemy "at the water's edge"'.[2]

Later portraits of Mussolini would show Il Duce as one of the most savage and astonishingly incompetent war leaders of modern history. Had he bothered to visit Sicily he might have recognized that such bravado was wishful thinking. A brief look at the state of the Italian 206th Coastal Division provides a good example of the calamitous state of readiness. The 206th Division was responsible for defending the precise area of southeastern Sicily chosen by the Allies for the invasion.

Discipline and training were almost non-existent; some company commanders were accustomed to taking leave without bothering to place an officer in charge during their absence. Sundays and Feast days were taken off by officers to be with their families, most of whom were not authorized to be there in the first place. The XVI Corps commander, General Carlo Rossi, noted sarcastically that the enemy certainly did not take the day off. Nor did the division commander (Generale di Divisione d'Havet) have any illusions about his own command. During surprise visits guards were found asleep at their posts, telephones inoperable and at one battalion headquarters the duty telephonist was found

---

[1] Ibid., p. 262.
[2] Quoted in Samuel Eliot Morison, *Sicily–Salerno–Anzio*, op. cit., p. 48.

sleeping soundly. A mortar unit had never had any practical training. Officers acted more like strutting Roman gigolos in sun glasses. 'Wherever I go,' he lamented, 'I see company commanders behaving like cinema actors and leaving their men to engage in some childish occupation.'[1]

The Italian Sixth Army had been based in Sicily since the autumn of 1941 and was responsible for all of the island and a small portion of Calabria across the Messina Strait. Until the spring of 1943, however, Sicily had been neither on a wartime footing nor had its defences been strengthened in any way. Rome considered the neighbouring island of Sardinia to the north as the most likely Allied target and concentrated on its defence. Only when it became evident that the days of Axis forces in North Africa were numbered did the Comando Supremo finally begin to pay some attention to Sicily.

In February 1943 a former chief of staff of the Italian Army, General Mario Roatta, assumed command of the Sixth Army. Roatta found an impossibly tangled command structure that divided command authority among seven military and nine civilian agencies. The Italian system was based on co-operation and co-ordination and forced a commander to rely on persuasion and liaison to obtain support and co-ordinate dispositions. Roatta found he was a commander with no authority over the Italian Navy (Supermarina), the air force (Superaereo), the Militia or any of the forces used to conduct para-military functions by the prefects of the civilian administration; and only partial control of the territorial anti-aircraft defences of the Fascist Militia.[2]

Roatta's first successful action was to obtain unification of command from the Comando Supremo who approved the redesignation of Sixth Army as Armed Forces Command Sicily,* leaving him in complete control of all military and civilian elements, including all German ground troops on the island.[3] Roatta's tenure was brief and in May he was replaced by Guzzoni.†

[1] G-2 Intelligence Notes No. 18, 1 August 1943, AFHQ Papers, PRO (WO 204/983).
[2] Magna E. Bauer, Manuscript # R-127, 'The Assault Upon Sicily', USAMHI. Bauer was a researcher employed by the US Army official historians to develop a comprehensive picture of the Axis side of the Sicily and other campaigns. Her unpublished manuscripts provide a valuable portrayal of events on 'the other side of the hill'.
[3] Manuscript # R-127.
* Hereafter the term 'Sixth Army' is used to designate both the army and the Armed Forces Command Sicily.
† One of the reasons for Roatta's removal was the ancient Sicilian concept of honour,

Although the Germans were hoaxed by the fake Major Martin's secrets, the astute Guzzoni was certain that the next Allied target was to be Sicily. Moreover, Guzzoni correctly surmised that the invasion would take place in the southeastern corner of the island. Recognizing that he could not protect the entire coastline of Sicily from invasion, his next best option was to form a powerful counterattack force, utilizing as its core the armour of the two German panzer grenadier divisions then in Sicily. These mobile forces would be positioned in the eastern half of Sicily safely out of range of the naval gunfire of the invasion armada, poised to deliver a crushing blow while the invaders were still vulnerable. While Guzzoni was certainly under no illusion that he could actually defeat a mighty Allied invasion force with the troops at his disposal, later events would give the Allies cause to be thankful that Kesselring prevented the Italian general from implementing his strategy.

Field Marshal Albert Kesselring was, apart from Hermann Goering, the most powerful officer in the Luftwaffe and one of the outstanding German generals of the war. An artillery officer in the First World War, Kesselring rose quickly and without fanfare to the rank of major general in the Reichswehr during the inter-war years. Quick to sense the prospects in the new air arm, he transferred to the Luftwaffe in 1933 and was one of the architects of its rise to prominence. Kesselring was considerably responsible for the effectiveness of the Luftwaffe in Poland in 1939 and France and Norway in 1940, for which he was rewarded by Hitler with a promotion to field marshal in 1942 and the assignment to command German operations in the Mediterranean and North Africa as Commander-in-Chief, South.

Kesselring's genius lay in his ability to understand and effectively employ both air and land forces. One of his few flaws was an almost incurable sense of optimism, which became the source of his nickname 'Smiling Albert', and this led him to overestimate the ability of Axis forces to thwart an invasion of Sicily. It is probable that he overrated the ease with which the Anglo-Canadian raiding force had been defeated at Dieppe in August 1942 and the fact that

---

when one of his proclamations was interpreted by the population as a slight to their patriotism. Even in wartime Italy under a Fascist dictatorship Rome was sensitive to the ire of the Sicilians. (Cf. *Sicily*, op. cit., p. 77.)

this was as much a failure of Allied planning as it was a triumph of German skill.

Although Kesselring had no control over the Comando Supremo, in practice he made his influence as Hitler's senior representative in the central Mediterranean firmly felt. He settled questions of Axis strategy by unilateral decisions which clearly reflected his own strategic and tactical thinking without regard for Italian plans or intentions.[1]

Within the Comando Supremo[2] there was a sharp division of opinion over the use of German troops to defend the Italian homeland in 1943. In February Mussolini had appointed General Vittorio Ambrosio* as the new Chief of the Comando Supremo. Unlike his predecessor, General Cavallero, who advocated close co-operation with the Germans, Ambrosio not only despised the Germans but actively pursued a policy of ending Italy's dependence upon Germany. To attain this goal he also attempted to return as many Italian Army units to Italy as possible.

The first half of 1943 saw tensions between Germany and Italy grow perceptively worse. Mussolini was beginning to press Hitler to sue for peace with Russia and on the military side the once warm relations between Kesselring and the Italians turned formal and frosty under Ambrosio. Italian intransigence and growing signs of independence led Hitler to an attitude of grave distrust and mounting suspicion that his ally would sell out to the Allies at the first opportunity.

General Roatta who was once again the Army Chief of Staff was a pragmatist who recognized that neither Sicily nor the Italian mainland could be defended without the participation of German ground forces on a major scale.[3] His views coincided with those of

---

[1] Kenneth Macksey, *Kesselring: The Making of the Luftwaffe*, New York, 1978, Chapter 8.
[2] See Appendix F for the organization of Comando Supremo.
[3] Howard McGaw Smyth, 'Command of the Italian Armed Forces in World War II', *Military Affairs*, Spring, 1951. Roatta was a fifty-seven-year-old infantryman who had been a staff officer almost exclusively since the First World War where he won three medals for valour. An ardent Fascist of high standing with the party leaders, Roatta was almost universally despised as an intriguer completely without scruples – both by the Germans and within the Italian Army. A former British military attaché who knew Roatta in Rome called him 'A very plausible rogue'. An Allied intelligence summary issued a week before D-Day noted that his military ability was probably not great and that as the commander of the 'Frescia' Division of the Italian Expeditionary Force in Spain in 1938 his misjudgments during the Aragon offensive led to his recall to Italy. He also was less than successful in dealing with insurgents in Yugoslavia. Roatta was, however, a first-class organizer and his

Field Marshal Kesselring. 'Thus it frequently happened in May and June 1943 that Roatta would urge more German divisions in Italy while Ambrosio resisted German offers of troops. There was no unified front by the Italian High Command against the Germans.'[1]

Like Guzzoni, Kesselring also believed the Allies would land in the southeast, and he used his authority as the representative of the dominant Axis partner to overrule Guzzoni and arrange Axis dispositions in Sicily to reflect his thinking. While it is probably true that this demonstrated an unrealistic appraisal of the fighting ability of the Italian Army, Kesselring appears to have had two sound reasons for placing most of his second mobile German division – the 15th Panzer Grenadier – in the western part of the island. He could not rule out a primary invasion in the west or even a secondary landing, but of equal importance was German distrust towards their Italian ally. Hitler was by now nearly paranoid over the possibility of Italian treachery, and the obvious deterioration of Italian morale undoubtedly caused Kesselring to consider the possibility of a betrayal and wholesale surrender of the Sixth Army. He therefore prudently dispersed his forces so as to be able to disarm the Italians in the event they defected.

At Kesselring's insistence the strategy eventually adopted was this: the decisive battle was to be fought along the coast by the coastal divisions aided by local reserves under division or corps control. 'Mobile reserves ... relatively close to the coast in small groups, were to be ready to pounce as soon as the Allies set foot on shore; finally the German divisions were to clean up.'[2] The expectation that the Allies would land in several separate places at the same time was correct. Axis defensive strategy was to prevent the

[1] Ibid.
[2] *Sicily*, op. cit., p. 87.

---

long staff experience gave him a wider background than most Italian officers. (Cf. AFHQ Intelligence Summary No. 45, 3 July 1943, PRO [WO 204/967].)

After the campaign, Churchill's political envoy to the Allied High Command, Harold Macmillan, wrote in a confidential report that Roatta's brains 'were more developed and effective than his guts. Nor would I trust his loyalty to any cause that should show remote signs of becoming a lost one. A natural coward; he can be bullied if necessary.' (Cf. Memorandum by Harold Macmillan, 17 September 1943, Eisenhower Papers.)

* Generale d'Armata Ambrosio began his career as a cavalry officer and fought in the Libyan war in 1912–13, became the chief of staff of a cavalry division and later an infantry division in World War I. He was appointed an army commander at the outbreak of World War II and Chief of the Army General Staff in early 1942.

establishment of a solid, continuous front by committing the mobile reserves at what Guzzoni called 'that fleeting moment' when the beachheads were not yet linked up and could be dealt with piecemeal and destroyed.[1] The drawbacks to this strategy would soon become evident on D-Day.

On the surface the Axis defence of Sicily looked impressive: four Italian and two German divisions, somewhere between 300,000 and 350,000 total troops. There were, however, some less than obvious flaws. There was, for example, a desperate shortage of transport to move troops and supplies. Lines of communication on the island were under almost constant Allied air attacks and the terrain of Sicily made movement over mountainous roads hazardous.

The sudden attention given to the defence of Sicily was for more than military reasons. Hitler saw the possible defection of Italy as a destabilizing influence that would force him to give priority to the Mediterranean at a time when the Wehrmacht was particularly hard-pressed on the Eastern Front. By committing reinforcements to Italy Hitler was taking a positive step towards bolstering his Italian ally and protecting an area of obvious threat from the Allies. While Roatta and Guzzoni were struggling to improve the defences of Sicily, the Fuehrer continued to demonstrate his concern by summoning in mid-June the commander of the 17th Panzer Division from the Eastern Front to the Obersalzberg. The general, a diminutive former Rhodes scholar who had studied at Oxford during 1912–14 and spoke excellent English, was one of the many Prussian officers who had elected to fight for Germany despite their abhorrence of Hitler and the Nazis. This officer did not relish his forthcoming encounter with the man he loathed.

Anyone meeting General Fridolin von Senger und Etterlin for the first time was unlikely to forget him. 'His high forehead, under black hair receding at 53, bisected by a prominent vein, and his great beak of a nose between deep-sunk dark eyes, gave him in profile the look of a hawk. In repose his face was austere, but when he smiled, as he often did, the effect was attractive; and his hands with their long fingers with which he gestured eloquently, were those of a pianist.'[2]

[1] Ibid. Not for the last time would a difference of opinion divide their enemy and aid the Allies. Eleven months later essentially the same scenario was enacted on the battleground of Normandy where only the cast of German commanders had changed.

[2] David Hapgood and David Richardson, *Monte Cassino*, New York, 1984, p. 39.

As he awaited the Fuehrer's beckon, the first thing von Senger noted was the sterility of Hitler's famous retreat high atop the Bavarian alps overlooking the Königsee and the picturesque town of Berchtesgaden. 'The interior of the house had that mixture peculiar to all Nazi official dwellings ... conventional ... furnished with good things ... conveying the impression of a rather bourgeois setting. It all looked new and clean and ... nowhere was there any feminine touch.'[1]

Recalling that day, von Senger remembered that 'the personal sway that Hitler was alleged to hold over so many people made absolutely no impression on me. It could hardly be otherwise, since I detested him for all the misfortune he had brought upon my country.'[2] In attendance at Hitler's daily situation conference were Field Marshal Wilhelm Keitel,* the fawning Chief of the OKW, and General Walter Warlimont. Hitler's purpose in summoning von Senger soon became evident: he was to become the German liaison officer to the Italian Sixth Army in Sicily. As was so often the case with Hitler, the assignment given von Senger was imprecise:

> Discoursing on the possibilities of defending Sicily, his great knowledge of detail was, as always, impressive. He deliberated whether or not the island could be defended by two German divisions without calling on Italian forces. One of these divisions was already established there, the other on its way ... Hitler was already reckoning with the early defection of Italy ... Turning a mistrustful eye on me, he added: 'You, of course, know the Italians.' Then he held forth on the strategy of the Allies, who 'through failing to leap across to Sicily immediately after their landings in North Africa, had already lost the struggle in the Mediterranean'.[3]

Despite its vagueness, Hitler's intent was for von Senger to become the defender and saviour of Sicily. He was one of the many outstanding generals produced by the German Army and one of

---

[1] Von Senger, 'The Sicilian Campaign – 1943', *An Cosantoir* [The Irish Defence Journal], June 1950.

[2] Von Senger, *Neither Fear Nor Hope*, New York, 1964, p. 126.

[3] Ibid.

* Keitel was an irresolute, colourless Nazi whose selection by Hitler to head OKW (*Oberkommando der Wermacht* – the High Command of the German Armed Forces) was mainly due to his ability to carry out faithfully the orders of his Fuehrer. Sneeringly referred to behind his back as *Der Lakaitel* (lackey), he was frequently the butt of Hitler's sarcasm and contempt.

the most unlikely candidates for the role thrust upon him by Hitler. A man of great intellect, he was 'more at home talking history or music with a Frenchman or an Englishman or an Italian – in each case in the other person's language – than he was discussing current events with his fellow officers'.[1]

Born of minor Baden aristocracy in 1891, von Senger seemed destined for a far different career when World War I intruded. He survived the Western Front as a field artilleryman and the chaos of postwar Germany which included the loss of his family land. This led to his choice of the cavalry as a career and he was good enough to become one of only a handful of Reserve officers to be retained in the German Army under the severe terms of the Treaty of Versailles which permitted only 100,000 men. Until 1934 he served continuously with his cavalry regiment at Göttingen. Even though he had passed the competitive examinations for admission to the élite General Staff, he was considered too old for General Staff training until 1934 when the German Army began to flex its muscles under Hitler and expand in open defiance of Versailles. From 1934 to 1938 he served in the Operations Division in Berlin and then returned to Göttingen as the commander of his former regiment which along with others was being converted from horse cavalry to mechanization.

By this time it was clear Hitler was steering Germany on a course towards war, and von Senger was forced to grapple with the burden which haunted so many members of the German officer corps. As his daughter has said, the devoutly Catholic von Senger 'had to go or stay, and he believed that in spite of Hitler he should remain with his people'.[2]

Suddenly the good years of hunting and horseback-riding with his wife and the undemanding duties of a cavalryman were over. May 1940 found von Senger's unit, now a full brigade, participating in the Blitzkrieg across France. After racing through Holland and Belgium and pursuing the retreating British across France his unit captured Cherbourg on 19 June ahead of Rommel's 7th Panzer Division. There followed a respite of two years that most soldiers only dream of: occupation duty in Normandy during which he ate and drank well from the sanctuary of a requisitioned

---

[1] *Monte Cassino*, op. cit., p. 39.
[2] Ibid., p. 40.

chateau and mingled easily with the local French gentry who looked favourably upon a man of his intellect, taste, and above all, his ability to converse easily in their language.

This was followed by an equally agreeable assignment in Turin where he served as the senior German liaison officer to the Franco-Italian Armistice Commission. The autumn of 1942 brought orders to the Eastern Front which ended once and for all the good life. With a promotion to major general came command of the 17th Panzer Division, then part of the Fourth Panzer Army, and a series of winter engagements during the life and death struggle to rescue von Paulus' trapped Sixth Army at Stalingrad. Von Senger was appalled by the magnitude of the butchery taking place in Russia. In this frozen hell there were no amenities, only misery and death. The terrible brutalities that had been inflicted on the Russians were now being repaid in kind by the Red Army who needed no education in the art of barbarism.

By June 1943, von Senger understood that Germany would not win the war, nor was he under any false illusions about his ability to defend Sicily against an Allied invasion. Both Keitel and War-limont were sceptical of the ability of Axis forces to hold Sicily. Warlimont believed the best option was to evacuate Sicily if the Allies launched a major attack, even though he recognized that it was unlikely they would be able to take their equipment with them. Von Senger recalled that 'this appreciation and definition of my task were not in line with those of Hitler'.[1]

Three days later when he met Kesselring in Rome, von Senger found the Field Marshal unjustifiably optimistic:

> Kesselring was evidently still impressed by our successful repulse of the small landing operation at Dieppe in 1942. Commanders of German land forces were usually prone to underestimate the chances of a landing by an opponent possessing naval and air superiority. Such an opponent will always enjoy the dual advantages of surprise and superior mobility. Kesselring, moreover, was like certain other optimistic German higher commanders in failing to recognise the Allied invasion of North Africa as the first example of a major landing that must open an entirely new phase of the war. Not wanting to believe in the danger, they consoled themselves with the fact that the landing was made against an opponent reluctant to defend himself.[2]

[1] *Neither Fear Nor Hope*, op. cit., p. 126.
[2] Ibid., p. 127.

To add to his problems, von Senger's next conference with Field Marshal von Richthofen, the C-in-C of Luftflotte 2 (the German Air Forces in Italy), revealed that the main defences of the GAF had been moved to Sardinia where von Richthofen believed the Allies would attack. Von Senger came away convinced the Luftwaffe was, as was its habit, once again going its own way.[1]

'At Berchtesgaden I had been told that I was to lead the campaign exclusively with German forces, although I was nominally attached to the Italian Army Commander, who was C-in-C in Sicily. Hitler's directive was founded on the likelihood of Italian treason. How I was to lead a campaign on the isolated island when the bulk of the Italian forces could not be relied upon was a question which did not seem to harass Hitler much ... [his] arguments ... were at any rate a fine example of the strategy of wishful thinking.'[2]

Kesselring's view was that for both political and tactical reasons von Senger should co-operate closely with Guzzoni and encourage the same between German and Italian troops. Not only would this carry out a mutual agreement between Germany and Italy, but would involve the Italians in the defence of their own country.[3]

On 26 June, Kesselring and von Senger flew to Sicily to confer with Guzzoni. What he found, convinced von Senger of the immense difficulty he faced in carrying out Hitler's orders. The Italian Sixth Army had been unable to make the transition from peacetime footing to the serious business of preparing for war. Still worse, von Senger found that Kesselring and Guzzoni were in complete disagreement over the tactics to be employed to repel an Allied invasion. Although Allied intelligence was unaware of the chaotic state of affairs in Sicily in late June 1943, the state of Axis defences were so disorganized and incomplete there was no possibility of a co-ordinated defence of its lengthy coastline. The Germans had a word for it – *Riesenauri* – which loosely translated means 'one hell of a mess'.

The mess in Sicily was symptomatic of what in reality was the dissolution of the Berlin–Rome axis. The shattering losses in Tunisia left both Berlin and Rome without a coherent strategy for defending the Mediterranean in the period immediately following

---

[1] Ibid., p. 128.
[2] Von Senger, *An Cosantoir*, op. cit.
[3] Ibid.

the surrender of nearly 250,000 troops. Much to Hitler's disgust the Italians began to make onerous demands for aircraft, guns and equipment that the Germans were unable and unwilling to fulfil.

The alliance had been largely based upon Hitler's personal faith in Mussolini, but the spring of 1943 found Mussolini beginning to act independently and as Hitler's influence over his ally began to wane so too did his confidence in Il Duce and Italy. This led to a series of harsh exchanges during which Mussolini expressed an unwillingness to accommodate additional German units in Italy. Mussolini wanted the Italian Armed Forces to defend Italy and desired German assistance only in the form of badly needed war material. As Warlimont later explained, the 'large and completely impossible demands for delivery of German war material continued to arrive; they began to look more like a pretext to get out of the war than evidence of a determination to make a new start'.[1]

As Hitler's suspicion grew into an obsession with the alleged traitorous elements within Italy, all hope of developing a joint strategy evaporated. When Kesselring told Mussolini he was forming three new German divisions, Il Duce waved him away with the comment they would make no difference; what he needed was aircraft and tanks. However, he relented in mid-May and agreed to accept the divisions but forbade the movement of two others to Italy, and it was not until nearly the end of June that his generals succeeded in reversing this policy.[2] Roatta's warning that there could be no defence of Sicily without German participation went essentially unheeded. In late June a group of Italian officers inspected the Sixth Army and, finding no improvement, confirmed that the defence of the island would have to be undertaken by German armoured formations.[3]

With the Italians bereft of modern equipment, with only a few reliable fighting troops in Sicily, with no one able to agree where the Allies would strike next, and with the movement of German reinforcements to Italy stalled by indecision and disagreement,

---

[1] Walter Warlimont, *Inside Hitler's Headquarters 1939–1945*, New York, 1964, p. 335. Italian demands were for the immediate delivery of 300 tanks, 50 AA batteries, aircraft for 50 fighter squadrons (later raised to 2,000 aircraft as a result of Roatta's pessimistic assessment of the defence of Sicily). In June, demands from Comando Supremo rose to 17 tank battalions, 33 self-propelled artillery battalions, 18 anti-tank battalions and 37 mixed AA battalions.

[2] Ibid., p. 332.

[3] 'Information from German Sources', PRO (CAB 44/285), loc. cit.

precious weeks were lost when the situation might have been improved. The Germans wanted the greatest number of fresh units in Italy but, as long as the Italians resisted, there was no common strategy for defence against the next Allied move.

An OKW appreciation concluded that in addition to the Balkans, the Italian islands and southern and possibly central Italy were the most likely Allied targets. German strategy was to keep the Allies away from the frontiers of the Reich and their large military presence in the Mediterranean signalled that Western Europe was free of an invasion threat for the time being. With the aid of the natural barriers of the Alps, German strategy could now only be defensive.[1] Hitler seems to have agreed but, undoubtedly influenced by Allied deception measures, decided Sardinia and the Peloponnese were the most likely targets. However, as Warlimont and others have recorded, after his initial depression over the setback in Tunisia, Hitler swung back to the view that Festung Europa should be defended everywhere a threat existed; and despite the worsening problem on the Eastern Front he decreed that preparations be undertaken to meet Mediterranean requirements by moving six panzer/panzer grenadier divisions to Italy.* Now in better health after his ordeal in North Africa, Rommel was ordered to prepare to take over as C-in-C Italy in the event of an Italian collapse.

Hitler's decision to appoint von Senger may well have been a direct result of several pessimistic first-hand reports in May. On 5 May the OKW representative in Rome presented Hitler with a candid appraisal of the woeful state of the Italian armed forces: 'The core of the Italian Army has been destroyed in Africa, Greece and Russia.' Italian troops were now 'not up to the burdensome problems of a major struggle; they are only of value as a weak stop-gap of a strong ally ... the Italian Army alone is not in a position successfully to ward off a major assault on its metropolitan territory. This can only be expected with strong German support and central mobile reserves.'[2]

Two weeks later Hitler received a similar gloomy assessment

---

[1] Warlimont, op. cit., p. 318.
[2] F. W. Deakin, *The Brutal Friendship*, New York, 1962, pp. 283–4.
* This decision by Hitler came at the time of a renewed spring offensive against the Red Army called Operation Citadel. Although postponed until early July, what became the largest tank battle in history took place around Kursk and resulted in a decisive German defeat which gave the Red Army back the initiative which they never again lost.

from Baron Konstantin von Neurath, the former Foreign Minister and now Reich Protector of Bohemia who had just returned from Sicily and Italy to report on his discussions with the Italians. General Roatta had bluntly told von Neurath he had little confidence in the possibility of defending Sicily. Even at this early date the effects of Allied air strikes were taking their toll, particularly on the Sicilian railways, which Hitler was told 'the English busily shoot up daily', making it virtually impossible to ferry replacement locomotives across the Strait.

Hitler considered Roatta a prime example of the intriguers who had been sabotaging the alliance from its inception.[1] While he understood the need for German troops to defend Sicily, Hitler saw no great urgency in reinforcing the island because of his conviction it was not the next target of the Allies.

Kesselring and Grand Admiral Doenitz urged that Hitler counter the Allied moves in North Africa by moving German forces into neutral Spain against Gibraltar as a means of regaining the initiative and posing a threat to the Allied flank. However, Hitler was uncertain of obtaining Franco's assent and chary of the consequences of a guerrilla war with the Spaniards. Moreover, the boundaries of the Third Reich were already spread too thinly and much of Germany's precious manpower had already been fed into the Russian meatgrinder. As much as he admired the Spaniards whom he termed 'the only tough Latin people', Hitler would only agree to a modest build-up of German forces in Sicily.[2] After needlessly sacrificing the Afrika Korps and Fifth Panzer Army, Hitler now hedged his bets even though aware it was scarcely possible that Italian forces in Sicily would put up more than token resistance.

Nevertheless, it was decided to reinforce the German garrison in Sicily by one additional division. One combat-ready division already existed there, the newly formed 15th Panzer Grenadier

[1] Minutes of Fuehrer Conference, 20 May 1943, S.L.A. Marshall Military History Collection, University of Texas at El Paso Library. Known generally as the Hitler transcripts. In May 1945 counter-intelligence agents of the 101st Airborne Division recovered fragments of Hitler's daily conferences near Berchtesgaden. In May 1942 Hitler created a Stenographic Service to record everything he said, mainly for the purpose of the history he planned to write after the war. Although all but less than 1% of the Hitler transcripts were burned, there were some fifty-three fragments recovered and translated, most of them the Fuehrer's daily situation conferences. Unlike the fake Hitler Diaries hoax of 1983, the authenticity of these documents has never been in question. Copies can be found in various archives and portions appear verbatim in Warlimont's account.

[2] *Grand Strategy*, Vol. IV, op. cit., p. 463.

Division commanded by the able Generalmajor Eberhard Rodt.*
Although not entirely mobile the 15th Panzer Grenadier was
battle-ready, capable of fairly rapid deployment and was outfitted
with enough supplies for twenty days of combat.[1]

The other major German unit sent to reinforce Sicily was the
Hermann Goering Division,† a Luftwaffe division which had been
originally formed as the personal bodyguard of the Luftwaffe
boss. Its commander, Generalmajor Paul Conrath, was a favourite
of Goering and an aggressive, experienced commander.‡ When
briefed before the invasion by Kesselring about the importance of
a speedy reaction, Conrath had growled in reply, 'If you mean go
for them, Field-Marshal, then I'm your man.'[2]

For unknown reasons Goering permitted only two of its four
panzer grenadier regiments to be shifted from France to southern
Italy and thence to Sicily in June. A company of Mark VI Tiger
tanks originally assigned to the 15th PzG was stripped away and

[1] *Sicily*, op. cit., p.81, based on MS # C-077, German Report Series, USAMHI (Rodt's
personal account of his division's operations, May–Aug 1943). Von Senger disputed the
claim of mobility and later wrote the division was 'more or less immobile', an incorrect
observation.

[2] Field Marshal Albert Kesselring, *A Soldier's Record*, Greenwood, Ct. (reprint of 1954
edition), 1970, p. 194. Kesselring recalls returning home 'pretty confident' after hearing
Conrath who, as a Luftwaffe commander, was answerable only to Goering except in tactical
matters.

* The original 15th Panzer Grenadier Division fought in North Africa and was lost in the
Axis capitulation in May at Tunis. Known as the Division Sizilien, the reconstituted 15th
PzG consisted of scattered German units on Sicily which had originally been destined for
Tunisia. The officer responsible for organizing and training this unit was Colonel Ernst-
Guenther Baade (see Chapter 30). Baade's tenure lasted until 5 June 1943 when General-
major Rodt assumed command.

† The official designation of this unit was Parachute Panzer Division Hermann Goering
[German designation: Hermann Goering Panzer Fallschirmjäger Division]. It was, however,
neither a parachute *nor* a panzer division. The term 'parachute' was honorary and its single
panzer regiment made it another mechanized division similar to the other panzer grenadier
units of the German Army. A substantial portion of the original Hermann Goering Division
was sent to von Arnim in Tunisia and ultimately lost. Most of the personnel were Luftwaffe
recruits or Air Force ground personnel. Many of its officers were former Luftwaffe personnel. The division was deficient in all aspects of training and had no combat experience.
Training effectively began only when the division began arriving in Sicily in mid-June. As
well as missing an entire armoured infantry regiment, several artillery batteries and the
engineer and reconnaissance battalions contained only two companies each.

‡ Conrath had considerable combat experience and had begun his military career as a
2nd lieutenant of artillery on the Western Front in 1914. From 1920 to 1935 he served as an
officer of the State Police in Berlin before transferring to the new Luftwaffe as a major in a
flak regiment. In 1937 he became a battalion commander in the General Goering Regiment
and the following year the senior adjutant to the Luftwaffe boss. From 1940 to 1942 he
fought first in the French and Balkan campaigns and later on the Eastern Front during the
battles for Kiev and Briansk as the commander of the General Goering Regiment, earning
the Knight's Cross. The regiment was re-designated as a brigade in mid-1942 and expanded
to a division in October, with Conrath as its commander.

sent to the Hermann Goering, to the dismay of von Senger. Without regard for the consequences it was decided to send the Tigers
to the Hermann Goering because of its then undeserved reputation
as an élite fighting division.[1] 'Everybody – the Italians included –
expected miracles from the Tiger tanks and therefore the "Hermann Goering" was to have them.'[2]

By July the transfer of the Hermann Goering to Sicily was
completed. Division headquarters was established at Caltagirone,
20 miles northeast of Gela, along with about two-thirds of its
units, with the other one-third based around Catania. The 15th
Panzer Division was fragmented into three regimental elements,[*]
one in the west with the Division HQ, one in the centre of Sicily
near Caltanissetta as part of a Sixth Army reserve, and a third
group in the east which was attached to the Hermann Goering as
part of a strong mobile reserve force (Group Schmalz).[†] Once
positioned astride the invasion routes of both Allied armies, the
Hermann Goering Division contained about 100 tanks. To its left
was the 54th (Napoli) Infantry Division along the southern edge of
the plain of Catania, and to its right the 4th (Livorno) Light
Division which occupied the objectives of JOSS Force north of
Licata.

Von Senger was not pleased with this arrangement and would
have reversed the positioning of the two German divisions. Rodt's
troops were better equipped and trained than the Hermann Goering which he wanted employed *in toto* in western Sicily. Not only
was the Hermann Goering deficient in infantry but its leadership

[1] As will be seen, the reconstituted Hermann Goering Division was – initially – hardly in
the same category as their comrades lost in North Africa. The Hermann Goering was one of
the last units to surrender in Tunisia in May 1943. The men of its Reconnaissance Battalion
defiantly held out until 10 May. Fearing a trick and ever defiant, the commander demanded a
certificate stipulating they were the last Germans to lay down their arms. An equally
hard-nosed American battalion commander of Harmon's 1st Armored Division replied that
if the Germans did not come down from the caves where they had entrenched themselves
'we'll carve that certificate on your headstone'. Only after this threat did the Germans
surrender. (Howe, *Northwest Africa: Seizing the Initiative in the West*, Chapters XXXIII
and XXXIV and Richard Collier, *The War in the Desert*, Alexandria, Virginia, 1977, p. 195.)

[2] Von Senger, 'The Sicilian Campaign – 1943', *An Cosantoir*, op. cit.

[*] *Kampfgruppe* Ens, *Kampfgruppe* Fullreide, and *Kampfgruppe* Koerner. The last was
sent to *Kampfgruppe* Schmalz, the element assigned to eastern Sicily. These formations were
the equivalent of an Anglo-American task force, that is, a temporary grouping of units to
accomplish a specific mission. Throughout the text each of these *Kampfgruppen* is referred
to as 'Group'.

[†] Named for its commander, Colonel (later Lieutenant General) Wilhelm Schmalz, it
consisted of an infantry battalion and two artillery batteries of the HG and the 115th PzG
Regiment of the 15th PzG Division.

was later found to be so poor that soon after the invasion Conrath relieved a regimental commander and von Senger sacked the commander of the armoured regiment. 'Similar shortcomings appeared among other officers.'[1]

Guzzoni and Kesselring clashed over the employment of the German forces. The Italian did not waver in his conviction that the next Allied target was the southeastern corner of Sicily. His preferred strategy was to keep *both* German divisions together in the east as fully mobile reserves. While the two Italian divisions fought to delay the Allied advance the Germans would mount a counterattack. However, after Kesselring's decree that German units be sent to western Sicily there was little Guzzoni could do. Kesselring would later admit that he and Guzzoni agreed on only one point, the need to counterattack at once before the invaders could establish themselves ashore – the same strategy Rommel fruitlessly advocated in Normandy. 'It makes no difference whether or not you get orders from the Italian Army at Enna,' Kesselring told the German commanders, 'you must go into immediate action against the enemy the moment you ascertain the objective of the invasion fleet.'[2]

With Guzzoni's reluctant agreement, the Axis strategy at the end of June called for the defence of Sicily to be fought in three phases. Coastal units and local reserves would provide the initial resistance; the mobile Italian divisions would then attack, followed by the Germans who would complete the task of destroying or driving the invader back into the sea.

Only Guzzoni seemed to have grasped that the one and only possibility of a successful counterattack would come at the 'fleeting moment' when Allied intentions were clear but the beachheads yet unjoined.[3]

With the 26th and 29th Panzer Grenadier Divisions moving into southern Italy and the XIV Panzer Corps established to take over German operations in Sicily, time had run out for the Axis. The 30,000 German troops and 200,000+ Italians in Sicily mistakenly believed they had at least another week before any Allied attack.

The air forces were a shambles. The Italian RAF all but ceased to exist as a fighting force and the Luftwaffe had taken a terrible

[1] *Neither Fear Nor Hope*, op. cit., p. 132.
[2] Quoted in *A Soldier's Record*, op. cit., p. 194.
[3] *Sicily*, op. cit., p. 87.

hammering from Tedder's air forces. Goering's leadership of the Luftwaffe was by now all but non-existent as he grew increasingly isolated from the top German leadership. A hopeless drug addict, his body bloated by his excesses, Goering's influence was on the wane[1] and consisted mainly of ceremonial morale-boosting of his airmen who adored him. An example of the fantasy world in which Goering lived was provided as he worsened the situation by misunderstanding that Luftwaffe losses and Allied air superiority were due to inferior German aircraft and not the ineptitude of his own airmen. The men of Luftflotte 2 received this scathing censure from their leader:

> I can only regard you with contempt. I want an immediate improvement and expect that all pilots will show an improvement in fighting spirit. If … not forthcoming, flying personnel from the commander down must expect to be remanded to the ranks and transferred to the Eastern Front to serve on the ground.[2]

Once the Italians recognized they must have German help in defending Sicily the Comando Supremo agreed to compromise. In return for Italian control of all troops in Sicily, Kesselring would gain control of all Axis forces in mainland Italy. Left in the cold was von Senger who was a commander without full authority or adequate communications and with a pitifully inadequate staff. Von Senger's new role as the defender of Sicily was another figment of Hitler's imagination.

Italian morale was fading noticeably and was lowered even further by the fall of Pantelleria and Lampedusa which had allegedly surrendered on Mussolini's personal orders.* To make matters worse there was little likelihood of the outgunned Italian Navy leaving its sanctuary at La Spezia to challenge the Allied fleet. The German fleet was hampered by an oil shortage and recent losses to escort vessels left it unable to respond to any Allied naval movement with its capital ships.

*   *   *

[1] Albert Speer, *Inside the Third Reich*, New York, 1970, pp. 265–6, inter alia.
[2] Quoted in *Sicily*, op. cit., p. 83.
* According to Kesselring's Chief of Staff, General Siegfried Westphal, the Pantelleria commandant alleged a shortage of water which made resistance impossible. Westphal called the excuse contrived and Mussolini's facile agreement, in almost indecent haste, inexplicable. The OKW representative to the Comando Supremo, General Enno von Rintelen, found the decision 'astonishing'.

Although we can never know what each man felt in the days before the Allied invasion, the letter of an Italian officer to his father may be representative:

> The only thing left for us is unconditional surrender ... The Germans don't trust us any longer and are afraid, so they keep us down by this so-called occupation. If you move, you are a dead man, that is the situation ... It is all clear as daylight, simply to place us in the position of a hostage ... Our fatherland is in a tragic situation. Don't misunderstand me, I pray that the Allies will win, because only then will we be able to breathe a little. Otherwise, if before we were a lot of beggars, afterwards we would be a bunch of wretches; because, and remember it well, *that* victory would never belong to Italy but Germany. ... *Only to Germany* ... What have our strategic retreats gained us? We lost 180,000 men in the last battle alone (Tunisia). These errors are unpardonable! You'll see that our government will remain stained throughout history, and the greatness that was Rome will be blotted out. We, who boasted to the four winds, trying to build on an historic inheritance which, although we are Italians and Romans, we have no claim to ... we threw it away in three years. Of what use is Heroism from a cripple?[1]

The morale of German troops was also mixed. The constant Allied air raids, the heat and bad rations were beginning to be felt and nerves becoming strained. The diary of a panzer grenadier engineer lance corporal reflects the anticipation of invasion:

21 *April* – Punishment drill because two men were found drunk. The heat is telling on their lordships.

3 *May* – Tommy and the Americans come almost every day and drop their blessings all around.

24 *May* – ¾ hour punishment drill because a man talked in ranks. The lieutenant stands with a whistle in his mouth. Every time he blows it once we have to lie down, every time he blows it twice we have to stand up. That for ¾ hour. We could all see him in hell. 'We'll string you by the feet and let the lice eat you.' That is one of the little flatteries he lavishes on the squad.

15 *June* – One wave after another of four-engine American bombers. They drop their bombs everywhere around us ... Tommy comes day and night.

---

[1] Appendix A to Eighth Army Intelligence Summary No. 527, 3 August 1943, PRO (WO 169/8519).

4 *July* –   Tommy bombs this accursed island day and
night. Bombs fell near us but we work
boneheadedly on. It is to be hoped that Tommy
lands soon on Sicily. The wish of all the boys.[1]

---

[1] Intelligence Notes No. 20, 15 August 1943, AFHQ Papers, PRO (WO 204/983).

CHAPTER 11

The Die is Cast

We were committed to the assault. There was
nothing more we could do for the time being.
ADMIRAL ANDREW B. CUNNINGHAM

In June the Allies decided to capture the Italian-held islands of
Pantelleria and Lampedusa, a decision which received the strong
backing of Eisenhower who, for perhaps the first time, was beginning to show signs of asserting his authority as Allied
Commander-in-Chief.

For some months AFHQ had been studying the feasibility of
capturing these two islands, the largest of a small chain of wind-
swept, barren volcanic atolls lying approximately fifty miles off
the Tunisian coast, some 120 miles west of Malta and directly in
the path of the Allied convoys heading toward Sicily. They had
since 1937 been a forbidden zone established by Mussolini as a
counter to the British fortress of Malta. The islands' importance
had grown in Italian eyes and by 1943 were garrisoned by 12,000
men of Guzzoni's Brigata Mista Pantelleria, and the 8½ by 5½ mile
Pantelleria was now defended by fifteen battalions of coastal guns,
pillboxes and other defensive works. While the island's ack-ack
was formidable, its defenders were largely over-age, ill-trained
soldiers whose morale grew steadily worse when the Allies began
their campaign of saturation bombing in mid-May. Pantelleria
was proved a paper tiger once the combined might of Allied
bombing and naval gunfire began pounding the island starting on
7 June 1943. The prize offered by its seizure was a large, well-
equipped airfield which Tedder required for air operations against
Sicily. The aerial campaign against Pantelleria actually began in
mid-May and increased in intensity, eventually severing its communications with the outside world.

Eisenhower had always favoured an operation to neutralize
Pantelleria and, in his despatch, argued that because it was imposs-

ible to gain strategic surprise in Sicily it was increasingly important to gain tactical surprise. With the Malta airfields at saturation point with Allied aircraft it became vital to establish a forward base from which close air support could be provided during the critical early stages of HUSKY. As Eisenhower wrote, 'The North African airfields were out of effective range for the purpose; the airfields on MALTA and [nearby] Gozo could not accommodate the total number of short-ranged fighter aircraft required. Five squadrons based on Pantelleria would greatly ease the situation.'[1]

Pantelleria had long been an Axis listening post equipped with RDF* stations that had proved troublesome to Allied shipping and aircraft. In Eisenhower's judgment, 'left in the enemy's hands, they would be a serious menace; secure in our hands they would be a most valuable asset'.[2] The decision to invade Pantelleria and Lampedusa was Eisenhower's and was as much a reaction to recent stinging criticism from Marshall of his 'lack of adaptability' as it was for military reasons.[3] Although the British had since 1940 desired to eliminate this threat to their shipping, Eisenhower's proposal met with outright resistance from Alexander, who feared failure and its possible effect upon Allied morale. Both Tedder and Cunningham were doubtful at first but were quickly swayed into supporting Eisenhower, who remained adamant that the operation be launched.

The plan to seize the two islands was developed by a task force specially formed for the operation (code-named Operation CORKSCREW). The planners were assisted by Professor Solly Zuckerman, a renowned zoologist who had become an expert in devising bombing policy, and who was later to play an important role in developing the bombing strategy for Normandy. Originally a member of Mountbatten's Combined Operations staff, Zuckerman was summoned at short notice to the Mediterranean by Tedder and directed to assist the joint planners for the Pantelleria/Lampedusa operation.†

[1] Eisenhower despatch, 'Pantelleria Operations, June 1943', Zuckerman Papers.
[2] Ibid.
[3] Sicily, op. cit. p. 70.
* [R]adio [D]irection [F]inders were devices which located targets by means of radar. The powerful RDF stations on Pantelleria could detect any aircraft or ship movement for North Africa or in the Sicilian straits.
† For the remainder of the war Zuckerman served as Tedder's scientific adviser. His report on Pantelleria and later on the bombing of Sicily became the basis for Allied bombing

The Allied plan called for massive air and naval bombardments, to be followed by an amphibious invasion of Pantelleria by a brigade-sized force of the British 1st Division, commanded by Major-General W. E. Clutterbuck, whose gloomy assessment of the possible outcome so vexed Eisenhower that he exclaimed in disgust to Cunningham, 'Andrew, why don't you and I get into a boat together and row ashore on our own. I think we can capture the island without any of these soldiers.'[1]

Eisenhower and Cunningham did the next best thing on 7 June when they boarded the British cruiser Aurora and viewed first-hand the shelling of Pantelleria which was pulverized by air and naval bombardments that all but obliterated the tiny island in a pall of smoke and fire. In one of the greatest examples of overkill of the war the air forces in three weeks dropped 6,400 tons of bombs during 5,218 bomber and fighter-bomber sorties against targets on Pantelleria.* On 11 June the invasion began at noon but, before the first British troops landed, the Italian governor, Admiral Pavesi, having initially rejected a formal call for surrender in order to save face, ordered the garrison to capitulate. The following day, after also refusing to surrender, white flags appeared on Lamped-usa and this brief footnote to history was over almost before it began. Allied intelligence which had predicted that an opposed landing would produce heavy casualties[2] severely overestimated

[1] Quoted in Major-General Sir Kenneth Strong, *Intelligence at the Top*, London, 1968, p. 97. Strong replaced Brigadier Mockler-Ferryman as the AFHQ (and later SHAEF) intelligence chief (G-2). Clutterbuck's reaction stemmed at least in part from grave doubts about the extent of his air support. In a letter to Eisenhower on 6 June, he pointed out that during a dress rehearsal for CORKSCREW on 4 June communications with the Air Force failed entirely and on 5 June the problem had still not been resolved, with the result that there was no way to request close air support. 'As all chances of success depend entirely on the efficient working of this close support aircraft (an airborne command post) after landing, I view the situation with considerable alarm and the Commanders in this Division have had their confidence very much shaken by this lack of co-operation through faulty communications.' Clutterbuck argued it was not an improvement in communications but rather 'a transformation that is required'. (Letter, Major-General W. E. Clutterbuck–Eisenhower, 6 June 1943, Box 12, Spaatz Papers.)

[2] *British Intelligence in the Second World War*, Vol. III, Part I, op cit., p. 85.

* Between 6 and 11 June, 5,324 of the 6,400 tons were dropped on Pantelleria by 3,712 of the 5,218 sorties flown by the Allied air forces.

policy in 1944. Still an active adviser to the British government, he is now Lord Zuckerman, OM. His autobiography, *From Apes to Warlords*, provides an insider's account of the Allied air war.

the Italian will to resist.[1] Clutterbuck's troops took 11,399 POWs; the single British casualty was a soldier bitten by a mule![2]

The Pantelleria operation seemed to return Eisenhower's self-esteem and according to his biographer he would thereafter point with pride to this operation on the same basis as he did to the great invasion of Normandy.[3]

Unhappily, the ease with which Pantelleria and Lampedusa fell added to the growing delusion of some senior airmen that air power alone could single-handedly change the course of the war. The elation and considerable over-reaction to the rapid fall of this so-called Italian 'Gibraltar' greatly disturbed Tedder, who saw the operation as merely 'a field for experimental study' of the possibilities of concentrated bombing. Writing to Portal, Tedder lamented that the operation had fulfilled his worst fears. 'Despite all I have said . . . even Eisenhower has now begun to say, can't we possibly do something like this for "Husky"? In short, I can see Pantelleria becoming a perfect curse to us in this manner.'[4]

The chief American advocate of the strategic bombing gospel was the air commander for the operation, Spaatz, who inadvisedly overrated the results by claiming that 'the application of air [power] available to us can reduce to the point of surrender any first-class nation now in existence, within six months from the time that pressure is applied'.[5] Spaatz's belief mirrored that of Harris, who kept his Bomber Command staff busy filling reams of paper in defence of this dogma despite mounting evidence to the contrary.

Spaatz, whom Churchill completely distrusted, totally misread the significance of the capitulation without serious enemy air opposition of the beleaguered and depressed Italian garrison and thereby helped to perpetuate the mythology that two decades later was still deluding a new generation of airmen directing the air war in Vietnam.

* * *

[1] Sicily, op. cit., pp. 72–3.
[2] Ambrose, The Supreme Commander, op. cit., p. 215.
[3] Ibid., p. 216, and Eisenhower: Soldier, General of the Army, President-Elect, 1890–1952, op. cit., p. 248.
[4] Letter, Tedder–Portal, 14 June 1943, quoted in With Prejudice, p. 443.
[5] Letter, Spaatz–General H. H. Arnold, 18 June 1943, Box 11, Spaatz Papers. According to Spaatz, 'Any conception of modern Warfare which does not fully recognize the foregoing is marking time in place. We will win the War no matter what methods we use, but any other method is equivalent to building a bridge with the safety factor of forty when five will suffice.'

No one was more pleased to play a key role in the invasion than the commander of II Corps, Major General Omar Nelson Bradley, whose meteoric rise to high command in World War II closely paralleled that of his friend and West Point classmate, Dwight Eisenhower. Both men were products of the farm belt of middle America and both spent their boyhoods in exceptionally modest circumstances that engendered no thought of a military career.

Bradley was born in 1893 and grew up in rural Missouri, far too poor to attend college. When someone suggested that he might qualify for an appointment to the United States Military Academy at West Point where he could receive a paid education, Bradley seized the opportunity, entering the Academy in 1911 and graduating in the class of 1915, which later became known as 'the class the stars fell on'.*

After World War I, Bradley, like all career Army officers, found himself in the backwater of the US Army of the inter-war period. During the war, while most of his contemporaries were serving with the AEF in France, Bradley had commanded a guard company in the copper mines of Butte, Montana. He worried, needlessly as it turned out, that this would harm his career. In 1929 he graduated from the Command and General Staff College at Fort Leavenworth, Kansas, and began a tour of duty at the Infantry School as a major instructing in tactics. It was here that he first met George Marshall, who impressed the junior officer by his practice of permitting his officers to get on with their jobs without meddling, a trait for which he was to become renowned as Chief of Staff. Bradley would later write that 'From General Marshall I learned the rudiments of effective command. Throughout the war I deliberately avoided intervening in a subordinate's duties. When an officer performed as I expected him to, I gave him a free hand.

---

* From this illustrious class of 163 graduates came six future division commanders in the European Theater of Operations, two chiefs of staff of the Army and two five-star generals, one of whom also became the thirty-fourth president of the United States. Those who achieved divisional command were: Major Generals Charles W. Ryder, 34th Infantry Division (Northwest Africa/Sicily); LeRoy Irwin, 5th Infantry Division (NW Europe); Leland S. Hobbs, 30th Infantry Division (NW Europe); John W. Leonard, 9th Armored Division (NW Europe); James A. Van Fleet, 4th and 90th Infantry Divisions, II Corps (NW Europe); and LeRoy Watson, 3d Armored Division (NW Europe). Other well-known members of the Class of 1915 were Generals Joseph T. McNarney, Joseph A. Swing, George Stratemeyer, and Henry S. Aurand. Van Fleet also became a four-star general and later commanded Eighth US Army during the Korean War. (Source: *Register of Graduates*, USMA.)

When he hesitated, I tried to help him. And when he failed, I relieved him.'[1]

Nothing impressed Marshall more than a man who could think for himself and produce some innovation. Bradley demonstrated imagination, attention to detail, and a willingness to make decisions. In his endorsement to Bradley's 1929–30 efficiency report, Marshall said simply: 'Quiet, unassuming, capable, sound common sense. Absolute dependability. Give him a job and forget it.'[2]

By 1940 Bradley was a lieutenant colonel in the War Department and Marshall soon had him transferred to his office as an assistant Secretary of the General Staff, where he went to work for Walter Bedell Smith, with whom he had served at Fort Benning. His job consisted mainly of presenting to Marshall oral précis on papers that had come to his office for decision. In late 1940 Bradley was promoted by Marshall from lieutenant colonel directly to brigadier general and sent to the Infantry School as the new Commandant. The man he replaced was another of those whose name appeared in Marshall's renowned little black book,* Brigadier General Courtney Hodges, who was later to command First Army under Bradley in Northwest Europe.

By now it was clear that the United States would soon become directly involved in the war, and six months later Marshall ensured that the Army's junior brigadier general was given command of the 82d Infantry Division which was soon to be reorganized as the first of the new airborne divisions. During his brief period of command the division was visited by Medal of Honor winner Sergeant Alvin York, who described Bradley as too nice to be a fighting general. 'You will never hear from him.'[3]

At the time of the TORCH landings Bradley had helped to organize and train not only the 82nd Division but also the 28th Infantry Division, a National Guard unit that had been called to active service in 1941 and was still ineffective after being constantly stripped of its cadre to form other units. Bradley's task was

---

[1] *A Soldier's Story*, op. cit., p. 20.
[2] Bradley Commentaries, loc. cit.
[3] Ibid.
* During his tenure as Assistant Commandant of the Infantry School from 1927 to 1932, Marshall began recording the names of promising officers in a small, black notebook, along with the names of those who displeased him. When he became Chief of Staff the black book became an indispensable reference in the selection of officers to fill the most important roles in the wartime Army. Among those whose names appeared were Eisenhower, Bradley and Patton.

THE DIE IS CAST 219

to turn an understrength, clique-ridden and demoralized unit into a first-class fighting division, which he did with the efficiency and ruthlessness that was to characterize his later performance.

Bradley's accomplishments with the 28th Division brought him to the attention of the commander of Army Ground Forces, Lieutenant General Lesley J. McNair, himself another of Marshall's astute choices for high command. One of Marshall's most difficult tasks when he became Chief of Staff was to create a large modern army and McNair's special quality was an outstanding ability to organize and train troops. In him Marshall found exactly the right man for the daunting task of preparing the Army for combat. McNair became the driving force behind a total reorganization of the Army's fighting units and the initiation of a realistic training programme for both units and men.

One of McNair's valuable services to Marshall was to help him identify promising officers for higher command. He reported to Marshall that Bradley had proved himself as a division commander and was now ready for the command of a corps. However, Marshall again intervened, deciding there was a more important assignment for him. Marshall could see from what was happening in Tunisia that Eisenhower needed all the competent help he could get. Bradley had passed every test of leadership given to him and Marshall firmly believed that Eisenhower needed someone he could trust implicitly to act as his 'eyes and ears'. When Marshall and Eisenhower had first discussed the names of officers who might fill such a position, Bradley's name had been casually mentioned by the Chief of Staff. Eisenhower's immediate reply was, 'Go no farther.'[1]

Marshall's orchestration of Bradley's assignment to Eisenhower was one of the shrewdest decisions he made during the war, for as Marshall's biographer has written: 'Of all the officers sent to Eisenhower by Marshall none brought stronger recommendations . . . Unlike the Pattons and Allens who won the general's eye by dash and color, or the Eisenhowers who gained attention by their personal charm and geniality, the undramatic, somewhat diffident Bradley was likely to be overlooked by anyone giving a quick appraisal of a group of potential leaders. Those who accused Marshall of snap judgments in selecting officers forgot the men

[1] Dwight D. Eisenhower, *At Ease*, London, 1968, p. 261.

who gained his approval by steady performances of high quality.'[1]
When Bradley reported to Eisenhower at the new Allied headquarters in Algiers on 24 February 1943 it was the first time the two had served together since their graduation from West Point twenty-seven years earlier.

Bradley had more than justified Marshall's confidence and Eisenhower's trust in what was the first major step en route to one of the most distinguished military careers of any officer of the US Army of World War II. In Sicily he was to be challenged by a difficult mission and by his increasingly strained relations with Patton.

In early July the Allied convoys began forming in ports along the Tunisian and Moroccan coasts and in the Middle East. Montgomery moved his tactical HQ to Malta on 3 July. On 4 July Bradley was piped aboard the flagship of Admiral Alan R. Kirk's DIME Force, the *Ancon*. The same day Truscott boarded the *Biscayne* which slipped out of Bizerte harbour to join the other 276 vessels of Admiral Conolly's JOSS Force. Patton, accompanied by Ridgway and Lucas, boarded Admiral Hewitt's flagship the *Monrovia* on the morning of 6 July.

The western Mediterranean became one gigantic floating traffic jam as vessels joined to form the elements of the Western Task Force. They were joined temporarily by the Royal Navy's Force 'V' carrying the Canadians on the final leg of their long journey from Scotland. As ships darted about, forming themselves into the intricate patterns that comprised a naval task force, LSTs, LCIs, minesweepers, attack transports, cargo ships, destroyers and cruisers dotted the horizon as this mighty force sailed east along the Tunisian coast. To any enemy eyes the fleet appeared to be en route to some unknown eastern Mediterranean target.

Once past Lampedusa the task forces slowly swung their helms to port and began moving toward Malta where they were joined on 9 July by the Royal Navy task forces bearing Eighth Army. After converging off the tiny island of Gozo (off the northern tip of Malta), where US engineers had just completed a new airfield for

---

[1] Forrest C. Pogue, *George C. Marshall, Ordeal and Hope, 1939–1942*, London, 1968, p. 409.

the RAF in the record time of thirteen days,* the American fleet moved off into the night towards the Gulf of Gela, while the British steamed to the east towards their invasion stations off the southeastern tip of Sicily. The enormous bottleneck off Gozo known as the 'marshalling yards' was negotiated without incident.

Aboard the *Monrovia* Patton had marvelled at the sight of the fleet and ruminated, 'I hope God and Navy do their stuff.'[1] In a brief but moving ceremony Hewitt presented Patton with his first Seventh Army flag. The motto of the Seventh Army became:

> Born at sea,
> Baptized in Blood.

Reporter Hal Boyle saw a 'fire of pride' in Patton's eyes, writing later that 'it was to him not a ship's deck he stood upon, but a peak of glory'.[2]

A message from Cunningham went out to all naval forces exhorting them to take whatever risks necessary to ensure that 'no flinching in determination or failure of effort . . . will hamper this great enterprise'.[3] The new Seventh Army commander's first message carried a similar appeal. 'When we land we will meet German and Italian soldiers whom it is our honor and privilege to attack and destroy . . . The glory of American arms, the honor of our country, the future of the whole world rests in your individual hands. See to it you are worthy of this great trust.'[4]

The afternoon of 9 July the Allied fleet was suddenly buffeted by

---

[1] Quoted in *The Patton Papers*, Vol. II, op. cit., p. 274. Ernie Pyle wrote, 'There is no way of conveying the enormous size of that fleet. On the horizon it resembled a distant city. It covered half the skyline, and the dull-colored camouflaged ships stood indistinctly against the curve of the dark water, like a solid formation of uncountable structures blending together.' (Cf. *Brave Men*, New York, 1943, p. 11.)

[2] Quoted in Morison, op. cit., p. 64.

[3] Quoted in *A Sailor's Odyssey*, op. cit., p. 551.

[4] *The Patton Papers*, Vol. II, op. cit., pp. 274–5.

* The amazing story of the Gozo airfield convinced at least some sceptical British of American ingenuity. The terrain on the island was so ill-suited that British engineers said there was no possibility of completing an airstrip in time for Sicily. An American engineer whose specialty was airfield construction told the Malta air commander, Air Vice-Marshal Park, the job could be done in about ten days with the proper equipment. Park considered this nonchalant response an American joke in bad taste. However, when the engineer convinced the sceptical Park he was deadly serious, things began to happen. After a hasty scramble to locate and move an engineer construction unit to Gozo, the astonished British saw the first aircraft take off exactly thirteen days after its arrival. 'This story was told to me over and over again,' said Eisenhower, 'by British officers on the island whose admiration for the American engineers was scarcely short of awe.' (Cf. *Crusade in Europe*, op. cit., p. 189.)

strong winds that grew to Force 7 (over 40 mph) and the seas grew ominously high and rough, making manoeuvre difficult and many soldiers and sailors seasick. With the assault craft barely able to make 2½ knots and others all but swamped by the high waves, it was a period of sheer misery. Correspondent Ernie Pyle was aboard a headquarters ship and recorded that 'never in my life had I been so depressed. I lay there and let the curse of a too-vivid imagination picture a violent and complete catastrophe for America's war effort – before another sun rose.'[1]

Eisenhower, Alexander and Cunningham met in Cunningham's office on Malta in an atmosphere of increasing anxiety. With the weather so uncertain and some convoys running late, what should Eisenhower do? In a scenario that anticipated the momentous hours of 5 June 1944 before D-Day in Normandy, the Supreme Commander had to decide at once whether or not to postpone HUSKY. The presence of Mountbatten to observe the landings did little for Eisenhower's bleak mood. Butcher's diary noted that the 'self-advertised expert on the Mediterranean weather' remarked, 'to be perfectly honest, it doesn't look too good'. A message from Marshall asked if HUSKY was 'on' or 'off'. Undeterred, Eisenhower met with the Royal Navy's meteorologists and decided HUSKY would go ahead as planned; there would be no postponement. A message to Marshall read, 'The operation will proceed as scheduled in spite of an unfortunate westerly wind that may interfere somewhat with the landings of US troops.'[2]

Near midnight Cunningham went to the cliffs overlooking the sea to catch a glimpse of the gliders of the 1st Airborne. 'They were flying at only three or four hundred feet in pairs of towing aircraft and gliders, sometimes in twos and threes, sometimes in larger groups, with their dim navigation lights just visible. In the pale half light of the moon they looked like flights of great bats. Occasionally we could hear the drone of engines above the howling of the wind.'[3]

Nearby Montgomery was confiding his mixed emotions to his diary: 'My Army is in tremendous form, the soldiers are very enthusiastic, and are soberly confident of the issue. So am I myself. But I am under no illusions as to the stern fight that lies ahead . . .

[1] Pyle, *Brave Men*, op. cit., p. 20.
[2] Butcher Diary, 9 July 1943.
[3] *A Sailor's Odyssey*, op. cit., p. 550.

I consider that we shall require all our resources to capture SICILY. . . .'[1]

Eisenhower rubbed his seven lucky coins and 'offered up a silent prayer for the safety and success of all the troops under his command'.[2]

Bradley who had been indulging his passion for ice cream during the voyage was seasick and like the other HUSKY commanders forced to trust in 'God and the Plan'.[3]

Patton wondered what the future held and conveyed his own uncertainties to his wife: 'I doubt that I will be killed or wounded, but one can never tell. It is all a question of destiny . . . I have no premonitions and hope to live forever.' After meeting with the chaplains for prayer Patton slept restlessly. Forty minutes before H-hour he appeared on deck and thought to himself that despite his own anxiety the Italians must be scared to death.[4]

Shortly after 2100 the fleet had passed the Gozo marshalling yards and by 2230 were just over the horizon in waters suddenly and mercifully grown calmer.

Midnight came and went and the anxious HUSKY commanders awaited word of the landing of the glider and airborne troops. At 0115, 10 July, the heavy guns of the Royal Navy began bombarding targets in Catania.

For Axis forces the first warning that Sicily was about to be invaded came at 1630 on the afternoon of 9 July. Three hours earlier reconnaissance aircraft of Luftflotte 2 on routine patrol in the Mediterranean Sea had spotted five enemy convoys in the waters south of Malta. When word of this discovery finally reached Guzzoni's headquarters at Enna, it was stated that the convoys were headed in the direction of Sicily and that each consisted of 150–180 landing craft and warships, escorted by at least two battleships.[5] Shortly after 1800, another report revealed the approach of additional convoys and confirmed the presence of the two battleships, one aircraft carrier, four cruisers and considerable air power.

Guzzoni was in no doubt that the long-anticipated Allied strike against a Mediterranean target was about to fall upon Sicily. At

---

[1] Quoted in *Monty: Master of the Battlefield, 1942–1944*, op. cit., pp. 295–6.
[2] *Sicily*, op. cit., p. 109.
[3] *A Soldier's Story*, op. cit., p. 127.
[4] *The Patton Papers*, Vol. II, op. cit., p. 275.
[5] Bauer, Manuscript # R-127, 'The Assault Upon Sicily', loc. cit. Appendix D contains a complete listing of the Allied naval forces engaged in Operation HUSKY.

1900 he ordered a preliminary alert and three hours later he placed all Axis garrisons on the island on full alert.

The US official history records the mood in Sicily the night of the invasion:

> At nightfall on 9 July the waters off Sicily seemed deserted. Yet despite the windy weather and rough sea, the coastal defenders were aware of the presence of a huge fleet of vessels somewhere in the darkness. Filled with American and British soldiers, the ships were moving towards the island. The Italian and German island defenders could do little except await the resumption of Allied air bombardments that would signal the start of the invasion.[1]

Even Hitler found himself powerless to make much more than a token gesture when the news of the Allied convoys was brought to him by an officer of the OKW staff at Rastenburg. He ordered the Luftwaffe to place the 1st Parachute Division on alert for immediate air movement to Sicily from its base near Avignon, in southern France. Beyond this one decision there was for the moment little Hitler or anyone else could do to stop the powerful Allied force from invading Sicily.

The same sense of frustration gripped the Allied high command. Some time after midnight Eisenhower and Cunningham fell exhausted into bed in their clothes for a brief rest before H-hour. As Cunningham later wrote: 'The die was cast. We were committed to the assault. There was nothing more we could do for the time being.'[2]

---

[1] *Sicily*, op. cit., p. 111.
[2] *A Sailor's Odyssey*, op, cit., p. 550.

PART IV

Invasion

You are entering the greatest sporting competition
of all times . . . for the greatest prize of all – victory.

PATTON

It will be a hard and very bloody fight.

MONTGOMERY

CHAPTER 12

The 'Flying Coffins'

> I thanked God that I went to battle by parachute and
> not by glider.
>
> BRITISH PARATROOP OFFICER

The invasion of Sicily began shortly after 2200 on the night of 9
July 1943 as the Red Devils of the British 1st Airborne Division's
1st Airlanding Brigade* arrived off Cape Passero in a vast aerial
armada. Three hundred feet behind each of the tow aircraft was a
glider carrying the men of Brigadier Philip H. W. 'Pip' Hicks'
brigade. As they approached the Sicilian coast they could see
below them elements of the Allied fleet lying silently offshore
awaiting H-hour.

The primary mission of the 2,075 glidermen was to land outside
Syracuse and to seize and hold the vital Ponte Grande bridge over
the River Anapo until relieved the following day by Major-
General H. P. M. Berney-Ficklin's 5th Division.

The men of the 1st Airborne Division had earned their name the
'Red Devils' the hard way: from their enemy. In their distinctive
red berets these men comprised an all-volunteer force of three
parachute brigades and Brigadier Hicks' glider brigade. The division had been commanded by Lieutenant-General 'Boy' Brown-
ing† who had been recently promoted and had turned over command to Major-General G. F. Hopkinson who had persuaded

---

* The 1st Airlanding Brigade consisted of the 1st Battalion, The Border Regiment; the
2nd Battalion, The South Staffordshire Regiment; and the 9th Field Company, Royal
Engineers. Other than their individual weapons, the Brigade went into Sicily with only six
jeep-towed six-pounder anti-tank guns and ten 3-inch mortars.

† Lieutenant-General Sir Frederick 'Boy' Browning was Britain's most senior airborne
expert, the first commander of the 1st Airborne Division, and a pioneer in the evolution of
British airborne operations. His assignment to the new airborne force was considered a
positive sign of the importance placed upon this new concept by the War Office. The
nickname Red Devils was earned by the men of the 1st Parachute Brigade during operations
in North Africa, primarily during the battle of Tamara in March 1943. It soon became
applied to the 1st Airborne Division as a whole. When Alexander formally acknowledged
the name 'Red Devils' at the end of the Tunisian campaign, Browning, now Eisenhower's

Montgomery that his men could seize and hold Ponte Grande bridge and thus solve a knotty problem that had been worrying the Eighth Army commander. Unlike the glidermen of the 82d Airborne who were disgruntled at being left out of HUSKY, the Red Devil glidermen were to spearhead the British invasion of Sicily. Their American counterparts were regarded as poor cousins to their more élite parachute brethren, but the British glidermen were full-fledged members of the airborne team as were the men of The Glider Pilot Regiment, a little-recognized group who flew the ungainly and fragile gliders which were generally referred to in the gallows humour of the combat soldier as 'flying coffins'.*

Hopkinson, the ambitious former commander of the 1st Airlanding Brigade, was an amateur pilot and a glider enthusiast who was determined to prove that the gliderman could be as effective as the parachutist. He was also resolved that the 1st Airborne Division play a meaningful role in Sicily. Without consulting anyone he

---

* The Glider Pilot Regiment was created in 1942 to carry troops of the newly formed airborne force into battle. The officer who commanded the Regiment and guided its development was a former RAF pilot and infantryman, Colonel (later Brigadier) George Chatterton. The men of this regiment were all volunteers and trained not only as glider pilots but also as infantry soldiers capable of operating any infantry weapon, wireless set, tank, jeep or lorry used by the British Army. By Chatterton's rigid standards and under the tutelage of two veteran sergeant-majors from the Brigade of Guards, this unique regiment became a vital part of the British airborne forces. The early experiences of The Glider Pilot Regiment were exceptionally difficult and frustrating and included a lack of aircraft, inadequate time for training and the usual lack of understanding that plagues any new organization without a previous history or doctrine. In the months preceding Operation HUSKY many of the glider pilots were engaged in the hazardous task of ferrying their gliders from England to North Africa. These flights of some twelve hours required the RAF tugs (usually Albemarle or Halifax medium bomber aircraft) and their gliders to run the gauntlet of German air interference in the Bay of Biscay and in the Mediterranean. The only lifeline the glider pilot had was a frequently unreliable intercom cable attached to the fragile tow rope. The American-made Waco gliders were made of steel and fabric, while the larger British Horsas were fabricated entirely from wood.

The regiment participated in all of the major operations of the war in which British airborne troops were involved. At the time of the Sicily campaign the regiment consisted of the 1st Battalion in North Africa and another battalion undergoing organization and training in England. In addition to Sicily the 3,302 officers and NCOs of this superb regiment saw action and distinguished themselves in Normandy, Arnhem and during Operation PLUNDER, Montgomery's massive operation to breach the Rhine river in March 1945 during which over 100 pilots were killed, wounded or missing. Overall, 551 men of The Glider Pilot Regiment gave their lives during World War II. Brigadier Chatterton later wrote an account of the formation and exploits of the regiment in *The Wings of Pegasus*, London, 1962. See also Gerard M. Devlin, *Silent Wings*, New York, 1985, Chapter 4.

---

airborne adviser, cabled the men of his former unit that 'such distinctions are seldom given in war and then only to the finest fighting troops'. (Cf. Major-General John Frost, *A Drop Too Many*, London, 1982, p. 168.)

presented a strong case for their participation to Montgomery who was concerned that a night airborne operation could easily go awry and leave the important Ponte Grande bridge in enemy hands. Montgomery's problem was to find a means of ensuring that Eighth Army was not impeded in its rapid drive to seize Syracuse. Its port was urgently required to resupply not only his Army but also (initially) Seventh Army.

The major obstacle to the capture of Syracuse was Ponte Grande bridge. Its retention in enemy hands would severely restrict the movement of all vehicular traffic and doom Montgomery's plan to failure. Hopkinson's proposal to use glider troops in advance of the Eighth Army assault forces thus came as a welcome solution. Montgomery was not yet familiar with the capabilities and limitations of the new airborne force and gave his assent much to the surprise of his staff and key advisers, several of whom attempted to dissuade him. 'Montgomery's decision to use a glider force shocked experienced airborne subordinates. Glider resources in Africa could best be described as a hodge-podge of available, marginally available or non-existent disparate airborne resources, unsuitable for launching any reasonably successful airborne operation. To expect it to be made by gliders at such short notice made the outcome of a glider assault in Sicily highly doubtful.'[1]

When the operation was explained to him by Hopkinson, Chatterton was shocked by what he later described as 'this frightening operation'.[2] It was already the first day of April and he was being required less than three months later to make a night landing in terrain wholly unsuitable for glider operations. When he examined photographs of Sicily, Chatterton found to his dismay that the Sicilian beaches were rock-strewn, fenced in by large cliffs and that the fields where the landings were to be made were dotted with stone walls.[3] To make matters worse, his pilots were woefully unprepared for night flying with the devilishly tricky gliders. At this time there were no airfields, no gliders, no tow aircraft and no pilots in North Africa.

Hopkinson was in no mood to entertain Chatterton's objections and made it clear that if he was not prepared to support the

[1] James E. Mrazek, *The Glider War*, New York/London, 1975, p. 81. Also, *Silent Wings*, op. cit.
[2] *The Wings of Pegasus*, op. cit., p. 42.
[3] Ibid., p. 41.

operation he would be immediately relieved and replaced with someone who would. Chatterton was the only experienced officer in the entire regiment and knew that his departure could only worsen matters. Thus, Hopkinson's well-intentioned but fatally flawed plan stood, despite quite separate objections from a senior RAF adviser to the British airborne command.[1]

The plan that Hopkinson unfolded was both dangerous and bold. The entire force was to arrive over its three landing zones at approximately 2200, land and fight in battalion groups. The main focus of the operation was Ponte Grande bridge which was to be captured by a *coup de main*. Eight Horsa gliders were to land on both sides of the bridge along the two canals formed from the Anapo River which emptied into Syracuse harbour about half a mile further east.[*] A company of the South Staffordshire Regiment would immediately seize the bridge before its defenders could react.

In the time remaining before D-Day, what little training that could be given to the tug and glider pilots was inadequate. Chatterton's pleas for his men still in England to be given night training failed. Nor was there an opportunity to develop the essential teamwork under combat conditions between tug and glider pilots, and certainly no opportunity to do so in gale-force winds. Everything that could be accomplished in so short a time was attempted, but Chatterton and others knew that despite their best efforts the force that took off from the dusty airstrips in Tunisia on the evening of 9 July was pitifully unprepared to land over 2,000 men in the darkness of a hostile landscape – a terrain utterly devoid of landmarks and navigational aids, that offered few suitable landing sites and was buffeted by winds up to 35 miles per hour. The stage was thus set for a calamity.

The operation, code-named LADBROKE, called for the South Staffs to seize the bridge shortly after 2300, 9 July, while the Border Regiment, which was to arrive about 0100, was to seize and hold the city of Syracuse until relieved by the 5th Division the following day.

The 1st Airlanding Brigade embarked from six airfields around

---

[1] *The Glider War*, op. cit., p. 81.

[*] The area where river and harbour meet was covered by saltpans and the canals were too deep and too wide to ford, and thus impassable to troops. (Cf. *Sicily–Salerno–Anzio*, op. cit., p. 160.)

Kairouan in the early evening of 9 July in 137 Waco and ten Horsa gliders piloted by the men of the 1st Battalion, The Glider Pilot Regiment, led by Chatterton. About 100 of the gliders were towed by C-47s of the 51st USAAF Troop Carrier Wing, the remainder by RAF Halifaxes and Albemarles. The official British historian has written that the two major problems which had not been overcome were that 'glider pilots had learned little of the very difficult art of judging distance across the water off a coastline, and the tow pilots had insufficient practice in night navigation. These shortcomings were to have grievous consequences.'[1]

By the time the glider force approached Sicily the winds were still running at 30–35 miles per hour. As the lead elements approached, heavy ground fire from Italian AA batteries forced the pilots to take evasive action away from the flight paths to their landing zones. At this point the operation became unravelled as planes and gliders broke their formations. To make matters worse, smoke from the heavy flak was pushed by the stiff winds over the LZs and the lights of the Italian flares ruined the night vision of the pilots. Some tug pilots released their gliders prematurely, forcing them to ditch into the sea.

The ships of the Allied fleet were under orders to hold their fire during the passage of the glider force, but near Cape Passero a gunner on a merchant ship began firing at a C-47 while another ship several miles away did the same.

The disintegration of the convoy was now complete as aircraft and gliders flew aimlessly in a dozen different directions. Most simply had no idea where they were. The essential ingredient for any successful airborne or glider operation at night is for the pilots of the tow aircraft to remain in their assigned formation – no matter what happens. Once off course at night it becomes virtually impossible to reorganize an aerial convoy so close to the release point of the gliders. The factors of inexperience, wind and enemy flak were a fatal combination and enough to ensure that Operation LADBROKE would be a first-class disaster.

Of the 147 gliders that departed from Tunisia, nearly half – sixty-nine – crash-landed into the sea, drowning 252 Red Devils. Fifty-nine gliders landed over a 25-mile area between Cape Passero (Sicily's southeastern tip) and Cape Murro di Porco, outside Syracuse. Two gliders were shot down by ground fire, ten were forced

[1] Molony, *The Mediterranean and Middle East*, Vol. V, op. cit., p. 79.

to turn back to Tunisia, and exactly twelve gliders landed on their assigned landing zones, one within 300 yards of Ponte Grande bridge.[1]

The grim aftermath revealed the full extent of the disaster.* Most of the gliders had been released over the sea and, unable to maintain sufficient airspeed, were forced to ditch into the choppy Mediterranean waters. Most of the glidermen and Red Devils who were lost that night never had a chance. Here, in the words of the survivors, are some representative examples of what occurred:

Glider No. 2: Waco	Glider was almost uncontrollable for 5 minutes over Malta . . . Tug altered course near target area twice and flashed lights for glider to release . . . too far out to sea. To avoid crashing into a 100-foot cliff, pilot ditched in sea off Cape Murro di Porco.
Glider No. 20: Waco	Glider landed in sea approximately 3–4 miles offshore. All missing with exception of two passengers.
Glider No. 39: Waco	Glider unable to make land and came down in sea 1–2 miles off coast. 1st pilot all right, all others believed drowned.
Glider No. 93: Waco	Glider just cleared cliff and hit a wall. Crew surrounded by Italians after a few minutes. 2 pilots killed, 6 wounded.
Glider No. 99: Waco	Glider landed in sea about 4 miles off-shore, hitting water hard and filled up immediately. 13 missing believed drowned.
Glider No. 124: Waco	Glider hit cliff and fell back into sea. Severe crash into sea. 3 wounded, 9 believed drowned.
Glider No. 134: Horsa	Left wing hit by tracer fire, crash-landed into wall southwest of Syracuse. Left wing burning, thick smoke in glider, men trapped by exploding ammunition, intense heat and enemy small arms fire made extraction of men difficult. 2 pilots, 12 ORs killed, 7 wounded.[2]

[1] Ibid., p. 80.

[2] 'Summary of Glider Reports on Operations at Syracuse', War Diary, 1st Airlanding Brigade, PRO (WO 169/8666).

* LADBROKE was one of the most thoroughly documented operations of the war. In addition to obtaining the accounts of most of the surviving pilots and glidermen, the disaster

The glidermen had left North Africa in a high state of morale; now many were dead, injured or missing in the rough waters of the Mediterranean. Those who had survived attempted to save those who were injured or trapped inside their flimsy 'flying coffins'. Some succeeded, others found there was little they could do.[1]

There were one or two examples of black humour amid the grimness. One glider landed intact and as its men organized themselves in the darkness to move towards their rendezvous point they got into an argument with two men who pulled up in a jeep and demanded to know what the hell they were doing. The young platoon commander replied that he was not far from his assigned LZ near Syracuse, and what business was it of this chap anyway? A voice from the jeep answered dryly, 'We are sorry to inform you that you are *not* in Sicily, but on the main airstrip at MALTA, and what's more, you are blocking one of the runways and the fighters cannot take off. So, please take the jeep and pull, not only the trailer, but also this bloody glider 200 yards in that direction!'[2]

Major J. C. Gibbon was in one of the gliders which was forced to ditch into the sea. One of the two pilots disappeared but their passengers survived and inflated their Mae West life jackets. Major Gibbon wondered what would happen, particularly since five of his men were poor swimmers. They decided there was no

---

[1] With typical bluntness, Montgomery privately blamed the pilots of the towing aircraft for losing their nerve. Montgomery Diary, 'The Invasion of Sicily: 1st Phase, 10 July 1943 to 21 July 1943', Montgomery Papers.

[2] Major J. C. Gibbon, MC, 'Operation Husky', *The Border Magazine*, September 1954. The discouraged glidermen thought theirs was the only one to have strayed off course. The men of another glider thought it strange that Sicily was all sand, especially inasmuch as they had been led to believe there was some vegetation and trees. They thought it even odder that the men of a British mobile bath unit who picked them up off the road could have beaten them to Sicily. They soon found they had landed back in North Africa near the Mareth Line.

An even more bizarre incident occurred to the survivors of another glider which crashed into the sea. They decided to swim for a cruiser which suddenly appeared and anchored some distance away. No one noticed the men who climbed up the anchor chain and wandered around the decks of what appeared to be a deserted ship. Suddenly, near a forward gun turret hatchway, a sailor appeared with a slop bucket in his hand. When he saw the twelve wet and bedraggled figures the sailor shouted for help, whereupon the hapless Red Devils were beaten nearly senseless and cursed by Royal Navy sailors before managing to convince an officer they were really British glider troops. After profuse apologies the Navy insisted the Army understand that if airborne troops were to *swim* to Sicily then HM ships ought to be advised!

---

was investigated at several levels of the Allied command. Most of this documentation appears in the war diaries of the 1st Airborne Division and its subordinate formations. (See PRO, series WO 169.)

other choice except to try to swim ashore. After two hours in the water they were picked up by an Italian motor launch whose crew although military seemed friendly. After persuading the Italians to take them to Syracuse the boat began a strange odyssey. As it entered Syracuse bay in the early dawn light, Major Gibbon could see gliders everywhere with men standing on their wings. 'Without more ado we went from glider to glider, collecting men. Eventually the ship was crowded to capacity with, I should think, over 100 men aboard.'[1]

One of the gliders that crashed into the sea contained the division commander, Major-General Hopkinson, who was fortuitously plucked from the sea exhausted and wobbly by the flagship of the 'Bark East' invasion armada. Its commander, Captain Lord Ashbourne, later recalled:

> We were stopped in HMS *Keren* off the beaches. I saw a body floating in the sea, almost alongside and evidently alive. I told the captain of the *Keren* to pick him up. A few minutes later a dripping soldier arrived on the bridge. He turned out to be Major-General G. F. Hopkinson commanding 1 British Airborne Division. The last time I had seen him was in 1922 when I had rowed in the same boat with him at Cambridge [Caius College]. We wrung out his clothes, gave him a plate of eggs and bacon, and then sent him off ashore to catch up the rest of his soldiers.[2]

Despite the disastrous turn of events the small groups of survivors who did manage to land intact began harassing the Italians by cutting telephone lines and ambushing patrols.

Glider No. 133 was a thirty-seater British Horsa containing Lieutenant Louis Withers and twenty-six men of his platoon of the 2nd Battalion, The South Staffordshire Regiment. After being cut loose from their tow plane the pilot* had become hopelessly lost in

---

[1] Ibid.

[2] Captain (later Vice-Admiral) Lord Ashbourne is quoted in S. W. C. Pack, *Operation 'Husky'*, London, 1977, p. 87. 'Bark East' was the landing sector of Brigadier Robert E. Urquhart's 231st Infantry Brigade. Chatterton, who was piloting the lead glider, and his principal passenger, Brigadier Hicks, were forced to ditch off the coast when they came under heavy tracer fire from Italian positions ashore. Both Hicks and Chatterton were among the survivors.

* The pilot, Staff-Sergeant D. P. Gilpin, was later awarded the Distinguished Flying Medal for his bravery. Another pilot has described Gilpin as 'an immensely powerful man of tremendous character [whose] aggressiveness, determination and courage couldn't fail to influence anyone with whom he came in contact'. For his courage in flying on despite his wing being on fire, the RAF tug pilot, Flight-Lieutenant Tommy Grant, was awarded the DSO.

the darkness and unable to find his LZ until an obliging Italian searchlight lit up the night sky. Not only did the light illuminate the LZ dead ahead but also the nearby outline of their target, Ponte Grande bridge. Lieutenant Withers soon realized the other gliders of his company were not going to arrive and that he would have to carry out the task of seizing the bridge with only his platoon: their original mission had been to neutralize one of the pillboxes protecting the bridge.

Fortunately Withers was familiar with the company plan which had been thoroughly rehearsed. He soon encountered a Royal Engineer lieutenant and while this officer organized the removal of the demolition charges attached to the stone pillars of the bridge, Withers with five men swam the canal and successfully attacked the pillbox guarding the north end of the bridge as the rest of the platoon attacked from the south. After a short but sharp firefight the bridge was captured intact and the charges dismantled. This tiny force was now in possession of the primary target of the 1st Airlanding Brigade. During the night other groups of Red Devils and glider pilots, including one American, made their way to the bridge and by the time dawn arrived there were about eighty-seven men defending Ponte Grande bridge from what was certain to be a determined effort by the enemy to retake it.[1]

Nearby another *ad hoc* force succeeded in seizing the radio station at Cape Murro di Porco but only after its frightened occupants had been able to broadcast the arrival of the glider force. Another small group from Brigade Headquarters captured a coastal battery of five guns at Caderini Point in Syracuse harbour. Led by the Deputy Commander of the Red Devil brigade, Colonel O. L. Jones, they had bided their time and late on the morning of 10 July attacked and overwhelmed the Italian defenders with small-arms fire and grenades, and then blew up the guns and an ammunition dump.*

[1] William B. Breuer's *Drop Zone Sicily*, Novato, 1983, *The Wings of Pegasus*, and *The Glider War* all contain useful accounts of the action at Ponte Grande bridge.

* Colonel Jones later received the DSO for this action. After successfully swimming to shore from his ditched glider, Colonel Chatterton attached himself to a group of assaulting SAS men. After the fall of Syracuse he encountered Colonel Jones who related how, after destroying the coastal guns, he decided to 'capture' a nearby villa out of which walked a lovely American girl whose Italian husband was hiding in the cellar. The woman asked Jones to lunch and suggested he bring a friend. 'But what about transport?' queried Chatterton. Whereupon Jones led Chatterton to a nearby shed where there reposed a gleaming, brass-fitted 1900 vintage fire engine behind which was attached a six-pounder anti-tank gun. 'Collecting several men we all climbed on the fire engine, armed to the teeth,

About 0800 the following morning the Italians struck back at Ponte Grande bridge in force. The corps commander, General Rossi, had previously ordered an immediate counterattack when he heard the warning from the Cape Murro radio station, but his orders were never received. Nevertheless, a force was dispatched from Syracuse by the local commander to deal with the British threat. The first encounter was tragi-comic. Shortly before the main force arrived '. . . a large Italian staff-car stopped at the barricade of the bridge and the officer in charge, resplendent in gold braid and fancy uniform, proceeded haughtily to command the barrier to be lifted. He obviously had no idea that the British had captured the bridge. But a second afterwards pandemonium was let loose as every single weapon was fired into the wretched car. The prisoners were put into the blockhouse on the bridge . . .'[1] where they were killed soon afterwards by fire from the attacking force.

A furious exchange developed as the Italian troops supported by mortars and four armoured cars attempted to dislodge the stubborn, heavily outgunned British. The battle raged for over seven hours as the British were repeatedly attacked with mortar fire and raked by six machine guns. As casualties mounted, those not dead or wounded finally ran out of ammunition and at about 1530, with the survivors now down to about fifteen, they threw their weapons into the river and surrendered. Marched off in the direction of Syracuse, they were soon freed by a patrol from the 2nd Battalion, The Northamptonshire Regiment, and speedily turned the tables on their captors. About thirty minutes after the British had lost control of Ponte Grande bridge it was recaptured by one of the advance elements of the 5th Division, the 2nd Battalion, Royal Scots Fusiliers, who stormed the bridge with Bren carriers. 'The Italians, to judge by the numbers of their dead who now littered the bridge itself and its surrounds, had paid a very high price for their half hour or so of triumph.'[2]

[1] Account of Captain A. F. Boucher-Giles, DFC, quoted in *The Wings of Pegasus*, p. 87.
[2] Ibid., pp. 88–89.

and sped down the lanes to lunch with an American lady. It was an amazing sight, and when we roared into the courtyard the owner and his entourage set up a cheer. With sentries at strategic points we then proceeded to a wonderful lunch, while all around us were the sounds of the diminishing battle, the rattle of machine guns and explosions. I don't know how many bottles of Chianti we drank that afternoon, or how much spaghetti we ate, but it was a very large and very, very good lunch.' (*The Wings of Pegasus*, op. cit., pp. 95–6.)

Despite its tragic aspects, a handful of men led by a resourceful young lieutenant had saved the day for the British. Montgomery later paid tribute to the bravery of the Red Devils by claiming that the capture of Ponte Grande bridge had saved him seven days.[1] There were, however, the inevitable recriminations. Among the angriest was Hopkinson who, from the moment of his rescue by Lord Ashbourne, 'cursed the [51st Troop Carrier] Wing with every breath he could muster. His men did not hesitate to accuse the troop carriers of flinching from enemy anti-aircraft fire, and the charge was later to bring about brawls between troop-carrier and airborne men in many an English tavern.'[2]

The truth was that inexperience was only one of the problems that plagued the operation. As glider expert James Mrazek points out, 'Even if all the pilots had had nerves of steel and eyes like owls, many would have failed through an error in planning. The altitudes prescribed for the gliders were not sufficient to enable them to reach their landing zones against the strong wind . . . As it was, the glider pilots had to make the best of a bad situation.'[3]

The British assault near Syracuse was only half of a two-pronged Allied airborne/glider assault on the eve of D-Day. To the west the reinforced airborne regiment of the 82d Airborne Division was being parachuted into the Gela sector. What they endured during the first hours of the invasion, like Operation LADBROKE, bore no resemblance whatever to the Allied plan.

[1] *The Glider War*, op. cit., p. 97.
[2] Ibid., p. 96.
[3] Ibid., p. 97.

CHAPTER 13

Invaders from the Sky

Gory, Gory:
What a helluva way to die!
Popular ditty*

The commander of the airborne force that spearheaded the Seventh Army landings was Colonel James M. Gavin. An orphan who was raised by foster-parents in the austere coalfields of northeastern Pennsylvania, he joined the Army at age seventeen with only an eighth-grade education and fifteen months later had earned himself a competitive appointment to West Point. By early 1941 Gavin had visualized the potential of airborne operations and had applied for assignment to an airborne unit. As one of the architects in developing the tactics and operations of airborne forces, he moved rapidly from captain to colonel and command of the 505th Parachute Infantry Regiment† in the span of two short years. Ridgway, his commander in Sicily, would later say of Gavin that he 'developed into one of the finest battle leaders, and one of the most brilliant thinkers, the Army has produced'.[1]

The first of Gavin's paratroopers spilled into the skies over Sicily shortly before midnight, 9 July, and for an hour they floated to earth throughout the southeastern portion of the island. It had taken some 266 C-47 aircraft (affectionately called 'Goony Birds') of the 52d Troop Carrier Wing [USAAF] to ferry Gavin's paratroopers to Sicily from their base in Tunisia. The manner in which the men of the 82d Airborne Division arrived at their destination was unlike anything ever envisioned in the pre-D-Day planning.

---

[1] *Soldier: The Memoirs of Matthew B. Ridgway*, New York, 1966, p. 62.
* Sung to the tune of 'The Battle Hymn of the Republic'.
† For this operation the 505th was reinforced with additional supporting units. Designated the 505th Regimental Combat Team (RCT), it consisted of the 505th Parachute Infantry Regiment (1st, 2d and 3d Battalions); 3d Battalion, 504th Parachute Infantry Regiment; 456th Parachute Field Artillery Battalion; Co. B, 307th Airborne Engineer Battalion; and miscellaneous Signal, Medical, Naval and Air support detachments.

The 3,045 paratroopers were to have landed in four drop zones northeast of Gela. Several hours earlier they had been preparing for take-off in the intense heat and dust of North Africa when a messenger brought Gavin unpleasant news. A 35-mile-per-hour west–east wind was expected in Sicily. Parachute jumps were normally never made into winds of over 15 miles per hour, but this was no training jump and Gavin did not enjoy the luxury of being able to wait for better jumping conditions. He could only shrug his shoulders and carry on; wind or no wind, Operation HUSKY was still on.[1] Orders had long since been given to all pilots and troops that every jumper and every single piece of equipment was to be dropped into Sicily – without exception. 'No one would be returned. If a pilot or jumpmaster could not locate the exact drop zone, the troops would jump and fight the best way they could.'[2]

Most of Gavin's men were not even aware their destination that night was Sicily until moments before take-off from Tunisia. To preserve the secrecy of HUSKY from the prying eyes of Axis agents, the troopers were not told of their objective until each was handed a mimeographed sheet which read:

Soldiers of the 505th Combat Team

Tonight you embark upon a combat mission for which our people and the free people of the world have been waiting for two years.

You will spearhead the landing of an American force upon the island of SICILY. You have been given the means to do the job and you are backed by the largest assemblage of air power in the world's history.

The eyes of the world are upon you. The hopes and prayers of every American go with you . . .

The term American Parachutist has been synonymous with courage of a high order. Let us carry the fight to the enemy and make American Parachutists feared and respected through all his ranks. Attack violently. Destroy him wherever found.

I know you will do your job.

Good landing, good fight, and good luck.

Colonel Gavin[3]

---

[1] James M. Gavin, *On to Berlin*, New York, 1978, pp. 19–20.

[2] Major General James M. Gavin, 'Paratroopers over Sicily', *Infantry Journal*, November 1945.

[3] Quoted in Gerard M. Devlin, *Paratrooper!*, New York, 1979, p. 219.

The men of the 505th were so anxious to escape their North African hell-hole that they could not have cared less where they parachuted so long as it had less heat and dust.

The decision to jump into Sicily at night had been taken primarily to avoid interception by enemy fighters and visibility to enemy ack-ack, a deadly peril in daylight that the airborne planners believed fully justified the risk of undertaking the first major Allied airborne operation at night.

Exactly one month earlier Gavin and two of his battalion commanders had flown a personal reconnaissance in night fighters over the planned air route during a similar full moon period. Although displeased by the refusal of the pilots to fly close to the Sicily coastline, Gavin was reassured when the checkpoints were all visible and believed there would be no problem on the night of 9 July.[1]

The 505th's mission was to establish an airhead between Caltagirone, where Allied intelligence had noted there were considerable enemy reserves, and the assault beaches of the 1st Infantry Division. The area chosen was south of Niscemi where the paratroopers would have the advantage of occupying defensible key terrain to enable them to block any enemy movement in the direction of Gela and the vulnerable invasion force. There was special concern that the airborne gain control of a strong point called Piano Lupo which consisted of sixteen pillboxes and blockhouses controlling all access to Gela via the Gela–Caltagirone and Gela–Vittoria highways.[2]

What was to have been an orderly aerial convoy from North Africa to Sicily became a chaotic mess no one had been able to foresee and which could only have been averted by more training of the aircrews. The flight plan called for the aircraft to fly in a straight line from their ten airfields near Kairouan, Tunisia, to the tiny island of Linosa and then to Malta where they were to turn ninety degrees to the left. Normally blacked out against enemy attack, Malta was deliberately lit this night as a navigational aid for the airborne and glider forces en route to Sicily. Gavin remembers sitting in the cramped cockpit of his C-47 to help guide the

[1] Ibid., pp. 217–8. A paratroop lieutenant made an unauthorized daylight reconnaissance of Sicily aboard his brother's B-25 bomber and returned convinced that Sicily's rough terrain was ill-suited for major airborne operations.
[2] Gavin, 'Paratroopers over Sicily', op. cit.

pilot as they searched in vain for the friendly beacon provided by the lights of Malta. As in many other aircraft, they had somehow missed the island.[1]

Having missed Malta entirely, most of the aircraft flew too far to the east before making their left turn towards Sicily. Everyone had been instructed that Sicily was first to appear on the *right* side of their aircraft as they approached the island, but because of the earlier navigational error, most made landfall with Sicily on their *left*. Clearly, something had gone dreadfully wrong.

A combination of the strong winds and the inexperienced aircrews, most of whom were participating in their first combat operation in support of the new airborne arm of the Army, resulted in the dissolution of the neat V-formations into a confused jumble over a huge area of southern Sicily.

Sicily was the first major Allied airborne operation of the war and like any radical new form of military endeavour was exceedingly crude. The use of pathfinders to land first and mark the drop zone with homing devices had not yet evolved, nor had the employment of more sophisticated navigational aids used in later operations. Navigation was visual and thus subject to the vagaries of human error and the unpredictability of the weather.

After flying at a hazardous 200 feet (some pilots flew so low that salt spray spattered their windshields), the C-47s were to climb to 600 feet for the jump. But when the pilots made landfall they were not only miles off course but totally confused by a pall of smoke and haze from Allied bombings over much of southeastern Sicily. Unable to fix their locations, many flew back out to sea to regroup before once again heading inland to find their drop zones. When they did so they came from all directions. Eight were shot down by enemy anti-aircraft fire but all managed to disgorge their paratroopers before crashing. Only moments before their jump, Gavin's aircraft was rocked by automatic-weapons fire from the ground.

With confusion now omnipresent, checkpoints were missed, directions confused and the sometimes intense ack-ack fire forced the pilots to take evasive action, further compounding the problem of resuming the proper flight path. Aware that there were serious problems the paratroop commanders were anxious to jump before their airborne taxis were shot from the sky or exploded in mid-air.

[1] Interview with Lieutenant General James M. Gavin, 2 August 1984.

Nothing could be done to reconstitute the formations and the object now became to jump successfully almost anywhere into Sicily. In the hour between midnight and 0100, 10 July, the men of the 505th ended up dispersed over more than a thousand square miles of the island. Some jumped from altitudes as low as 300–400 feet, causing a number of broken bones. Many landed in the Eighth Army sector but most arrived in the area from Santa Croce Camerina (south of Comiso near the sea) to Gela. The majority dropped into the 45th Division invasion sector and only one unit, Major Mark Alexander's 2d Battalion, landed more or less intact but still some twenty-five miles off target.[1]

Major Alexander's plane was still well out to sea when the red warning light came on and as he stood in the doorway it was soon inexplicably followed by the green light. Alexander had to fight off his own men behind who attempted to push him out of the door. After a blast from the angry major, the pilot quickly turned off the warning lights.[*]

When Gavin jumped he had no idea if he was going to land in Sicily, Italy or somewhere else in the Balkans, but the sound of gunfire and the glow of shells bursting in the distance quickly provided reassurance he was indeed in Sicily. Rounding up a small band of troopers, Gavin heeded one of the first lessons taught him at West Point: he began marching towards the sound of the guns in the distance.[2]

Another small formation of aircraft flashed their green lights at 1,500 feet at a speed of 200 miles per hour instead of at 600 feet and 100 miles per hour. Sergeant Frank Herkness remembered being the last to jump from his aircraft. 'The plane seemed to be going unusually fast. My chute snapped open with a terrific jerk and my carbine disappeared . . . so the only weapon I had was a long trench knife.' Alone on the ground, Herkness encountered two

---

[1] *Sicily*, op. cit., p. 117; *On to Berlin*, op. cit., pp. 22–3.

[2] *On to Berlin*, op. cit., p. 24. One of those who jumped into Sicily with Colonel Gavin was *Chicago Tribune* war correspondent John H. 'Beaver' Thompson, a veteran of more combat jumps than the men he accompanied. Thompson had jumped into North Africa in November 1942 as part of TORCH when the 509th Parachute Infantry Battalion jumped onto Youks-les-Bains airfield. Resplendent with an enormous beard, Thompson was the first civilian reporter ever to parachute during a combat operation. Although he had left it behind in North Africa, when he landed Thompson found to his amazement that his battered portable typewriter was part of the airborne baggage that followed the troopers from the aircraft. (Cf. Breuer, *Drop Zone Sicily*, op. cit., Chapter Five.)

[*] It was airborne practice for an officer to act as the jumpmaster and to jump first when the green light flashed.

surprised civilians, one of whom had a long stiletto visible in the moonlight. His first combat was a vicious knife fight with the Sicilian which he lost when he slipped and fell and was stabbed in the right leg clear to the bone. His life was undoubtedly saved when he fell into a deep ditch and was knocked unconscious. His lieutenant was not so fortunate. Captured immediately on landing along with another trooper, the two Americans were tied hand and foot and subsequently executed by an Italian officer moments before British soldiers stormed the farmhouse where they were imprisoned.[1]

Private Lawrence O'Mara landed in a tree in the British zone and dangled helplessly, his chute tangled in its limbs. As he was attempting to work himself free from his chute, he was approached by three German soldiers with fixed bayonets. His Tommy gun was still firmly strapped to his chest so O'Mara decided to remain deathly still in the hope he could somehow escape detection. His luck ran out when a startled German saw him and automatically reacted by stabbing the American in the leg. The injured trooper was freed, given first aid and taken to a nearby farmhouse where an English-speaking German doctor tended his wound. O'Mara was told by the doctor he would have to be put to sleep while his wound was treated, and O'Mara lost consciousness not knowing if he would ever awaken again. The following day he was rescued by a British patrol which found him alive and well and alone in the farmhouse which only moments before had been hastily abandoned by the Germans.[2]

The fact that this was no training exercise was starkly driven home to some of the paratroopers when they heard the story of trooper Mike Scambelluri, who was captured by some Italians who stripped him of his weapons and valuables and tied his hands behind his back. When they discovered he could speak Italian he was called a traitor and a bastard by a captain who began firing at the helpless trooper with his revolver at point-blank range. Shot seven times, Scambelluri's own grenades were thrown at him when he defiantly refused to die, and his body was punctured by shrapnel. Somehow he survived and several hours later was able to identify one of his captors from a group of newly seized Italian POWs. Three angry paratroopers took the protesting Italian over

[1] Sergeant Frank Herkness, 'Sicily was no Picnic', *American Magazine*, October 1943.
[2] *Paratrooper!*, Chapter 9, *passim*.

a nearby hill where shots were heard. One later noted the man had been shot attempting to escape. Several days later Scambelluri died of his wounds in a hospital in North Africa.

While nearly all of Gavin's men landed safely, they were so dispersed that they posed no threat as a major fighting force; but they quickly discovered that by assuming a guerilla role they were able to raise havoc all over southeastern Sicily. The tough training given to this élite force now began to pay enormous dividends as they demonstrated their ability to disrupt an enemy force. Enemy patrols were ambushed, telephone lines cut, weapons captured and turned on the enemy, leaving most convinced they were being attacked by a massive force that was all around them.

When Major Alexander's troops began to receive machine gun and sniper fire from nearby high ground on the night of 10 July, Alexander decided to see if he could establish contact with a British cruiser that had been anchored for most of the day in the Gulf of Gela. He summoned his signal officer, Lieutenant Arthur Miller, and instructed him to try to establish contact with the cruiser by flashlight. The lieutenant obliged his CO while everyone waited nervously to see if the British would notice and respond. Suddenly there was a flash from the cruiser and two accurately placed salvoes smashed the enemy positions.[1]

Wherever they landed, the paratroopers used various enterprising means of solving their immediate problems. Some 'rented' horses and carts to transport their wounded, using specially issued 'invasion money'. Others stole or captured transport, but most walked, looking for their comrades and for likely targets to harass.

A cocky German officer from the Hermann Goering Division later loudly complained that the paratroopers did not fight fairly. 'Our people will cut the throats of these parachutists if they capture them', he boasted. 'It has been unsafe to use the roads for the past forty-eight hours.' One lieutenant landed near some German troops and lay helpless on the ground expecting to be shot. Three Germans led by an officer came up to the startled lieutenant and the officer said in perfect English: 'We surrender', later explaining: 'For three years and eight months we've been fighting all over Europe, Russia and North Africa. That's long enough in any army. We're sick of it all.'[2]

---

[1] Breuer, op. cit., pp. 129–30, and Gavin, op. cit., p. 23.
[2] Quoted in *Drop Zone Sicily*, op. cit., p. 83.

Company 'I', 3d Battalion, 505th Parachute Infantry Regiment, landed on its assigned DZ and was able to accomplish its mission in addition to reducing pillboxes and a blockhouse and taking prisoners. On 10 July sixty men of Company 'G' (3d Battalion/505th) with the aid of three guns of Battery 'C', 456th Field Artillery, became the first troops into the town of Vittoria where they reduced the Italian garrison, took prisoners, and captured numerous vehicles and arms. One officer, Lieutenant William J. Harris, was captured and held by the Italians for several hours. The loquacious young officer managed to convince the defenders their situation was precarious and that they would be unable to resist the advancing 45th Division. The Italian commander raised a white flag and surrendered with nearly eighty men.[1]

A group of about seventy-five troopers landed near Avola on the east coast, one of the D-Day assault objectives of the British 50th Division. Commanded by a group of lieutenants, the force decided to attack the nearby city of some 22,000 where they quickly became embroiled in heavy street fighting during the morning and early afternoon of 10 July with Italian snipers and troops manning machine-gun nests. It never occurred to these men that it is not a routine operation of war for seventy-five lightly armed men behind enemy lines to attack and capture a city the size of Avola.[*] During the bitter fighting which took place the Americans realized they had bitten off more than they could chew. Fortunately, Major-General Sidney Kirkman's 50th Division came to the rescue when a Bren carrier arrived in mid-afternoon and blasted the Italian machine gunners who had pinned the GIs down in a square. When the cheering subsided the Americans realized their ordeal would not be over until they could safely identify themselves to a group of advancing soldiers who opened fire, forcing them to dive for cover. Finally, after waving several helmets on the ends of their rifles and shouting they were Americans each side recognized the other without being killed. One Tommy exclaimed, 'What the bloody 'ell are you Yanks doing 'ere?'[2]

No one had thought to exchange passwords with the British and for those paratroops roaming the British sector in the early hours

[1] 'Report of the 505th Parachute Combat Team in the Landing on Sicily, July 10, 1943', Ridgway Papers, USAMHI.

[2] Herkness, 'Sicily was no Picnic', op. cit.

[*] The paratroopers' armament consisted of eight machine guns, two light anti-tank guns and some Tommy guns.

of 10 July extreme caution was necessary. Most were shot at by the British and one trooper was forced to jump a British soldier in order to identify himself and obtain the British password.*

Near Biscari there was another outstanding example of improvization when Lieutenant Peter J. Eaton of the 3d Battalion, 504th Parachute Infantry, organized some fifty men and set out to accomplish his battalion's mission of blocking any enemy reinforcement towards the beaches where Patton's infantrymen were to land. After capturing several 57 mm anti-tank guns this small force dug itself in, mined the Biscari–Nisemi road and settled back to await developments. During the afternoon of D-Day, a battalion-sized column of the Hermann Goering Division arrived accompanied by a small tank. Eaton's force disposed of the tank and began to rake the column with fire, causing the enemy troops to disperse in total confusion.

General Conrath had ordered this task force to thrust towards Gela to disrupt the invaders. However, between Allied air strikes and harassment from the paratroops of the 82d Airborne this element of the Hermann Goering failed miserably in its first test of combat against an outgunned, inferior force of paratroopers. Postwar investigation revealed that Conrath was forced repeatedly to intervene personally to keep his green troops and equally inexperienced commanders from panicking. This was to be only the first round. In the next thirty-six hours the Hermann Goering and the 82d Airborne were to get to know one another well.[1]

When the 505th Regimental Combat Team parachuted into Sicily neither Gavin nor his superiors were aware they would soon be engaging the Hermann Goering Division. As Gavin was later to discover to his dismay, this omission was deliberate. ULTRA had duly noted the arrival of the Hermann Goering in Sicily and this information appeared in the AFHQ Weekly Intelligence Summaries which were distributed to Army level and in some instances to the corps. It is impossible to pinpoint, but at some level – most likely Seventh Army – a decision was made to withhold this information from the 82d Airborne Division. Consequently, when

[1] Bauer, MS # R-133, 'Axis Tactical Operations in Sicily'.
* In future operations the password was always the same for all airborne and ground elements in order to avoid any possible repetition of the Sicily experience.

Gavin was briefed prior to D-Day he was told to expect only Italian formations. Other than some 'technicians', there were no German combat units anywhere near the beaches and his drop-zones. Gavin recalls his reaction on D-Day when he spotted a destroyed German scout car: 'I had a peculiar feeling in the hollow of my stomach, because no German scout cars were supposed to be in the area, and the one that I saw might well have been, and I assumed it was, a forerunner of a Panzer division.'[1]

From December 1942 to March 1943 there were several cases of near compromise of ULTRA which caused 'an almighty flap' lest the Germans somehow become aware that the Allies had cracked what they believed to be their most secure cypher system, the Enigma machine. This led to correspondence at the highest level, warning of the crucial need to safeguard ULTRA information. In May, Eisenhower received a personal TOP SECRET letter from Marshall reiterating the need for stringent security precautions. ULTRA experts had originally feared that German message traffic via wireless would dry up at the end of the North Africa campaign where, once relocated in Italy and Sicily, most would be sent via landline. There was considerable elation when their fears proved groundless and ULTRA continued to yield valuable intelligence (including the German Order of Battle in Sicily) on an increasing scale. These two factors made the authorities, who were by nature highly cautious, doubly determined that no unneeded risks be run which might result in ULTRA's compromise.

This seems to be the reason why it was considered necessary to deliberately withhold the presence of the Hermann Goering Division from Gavin, even though it was undoubtedly an agonizing decision. In *Ultra Goes to War*, historian Ronald Lewin pointed out that 'Patton's staff had strict instructions not to inform Gavin's command because of the likelihood of their being captured. D-Day for Husky vividly illustrates, in fact, Ultra's inescapable limitation. It was impossible to risk disclosing its intelligence to those in actual contact with the enemy, or liable to capture for other reasons, even though the knowledge might improve their chance of success or survival.'[2]

---

[1] Letter to the author, 8 October 1985.
[2] *Ultra Goes to War*, op. cit., pp. 280–1. Unlike the 82d Airborne, the 1st Division was informed of the presence of the Hermann Goering Division and their pre-D-Day preparations took this probability into account. (Interview with General Robert W. Porter, USA Ret., 15 September 1985.)

The mission of Lieutenant Colonel Arthur ('Hardnose')*
Gorham's 1st Battalion, 505th Infantry, was to seize and hold the
high ground overlooking the road junction (called the 'Y' by the
airborne), where the Gela–Vittoria highway (Route 115) met the
secondary road leading to Niscemi and the nearby Ponte Olivo
airfield. The twin hills which dominated this road junction were
known as Piano Lupo and had long been a major concern to the
American planners for their extreme tactical importance. In enemy
hands they constituted the easiest and most direct route to the 1st
Division landing beaches and were certain to be used in the
expected enemy counterattack. The problem was that few of
Gorham's troops had landed anywhere near their drop zone several hundred metres northwest of Piano Lupo. Only Captain
Edwin B. Sayre's Company 'A' had even come close and by 0230
hours he had managed to assemble only fifteen men. His position
was several thousand yards north of the Piano Lupo road junction,
on the Niscemi road. Machine guns from a nearby Italian strongpoint had fired on Sayre and his men as they jumped.

Undaunted, Sayre with his tiny force decided to assault the
machine guns at 0300 with grenades, but was repelled without
loss. By 0530 Sayre's force had grown to approximately fifty and a
second attack with grenades and two 60 mm mortars routed the
defenders who surrendered. They turned out to be about forty
Italians and a ten-man German team from the Hermann Goering.
In addition to controlling a useful blocking position along the
Niscemi road Sayre's force seized twenty machine guns and nearly
half a million rounds of ammunition.[1]

Barely thirty-six hours earlier the men of the 82d Airborne had
been dreaming of getting away from the oppressive heat of North
Africa. Before embarking in the *Monrovia* with Patton, General

---

[1] Major Edwin B. Sayre, 'The Operations of Company "A" 505th Parachute Infantry (82
Airborne Division) Airborne Landings in Sicily, 9–24 July 1943', 10 November 1947. This
first-hand account was originally written for the Advanced Infantry Officer Course, Fort
Benning, Georgia. Copy furnished the author by Colonel Sayre, USA, Ret. Captain Sayre
personally led the attack by carrying his carbine in his right hand, a grenade in his left, and
another between his teeth. After the door to the Italian bunker was blown open by a rifle
grenade, Sayre threw one of his grenades inside which quickly induced the survivors to
surrender. (82d Airborne Division G-2 Historical Record, Microfilm Reel 2000, USAMHI.)

* For the operation each battalion commander was assigned a code-name; Gorham's
was 'Hardnose'.

Ridgway decided that his men had earned a reward for the weeks of gruelling training they had undergone in the furnace-like heat of North Africa. First, there had been a dustbowl in Morocco, and now an equally unpleasant staging area in Tunisia near Kairouan. The barren site near Oudjida, Morocco, had been chosen by Ridgway because it resembled the area of Sicily his men were to attack. Over and over again the men of the 82d were drilled. There were practice jumps in which a great many troopers were injured, glider landings, mock attacks and physical training which tested the stamina of these hardy young soldiers and their officers to the limit. The paratroop elements of the division were all volunteers and received the princely sum of fifty dollars extra per month in compensation; their officers received 100 dollars.*

Dysentery was rife, tempers dangerously frayed and, as Ridgway later wryly noted, 'By take-off time for Sicily, the men were so lean and tough, so mean and mad, that they would have jumped into the fires of torment just to get out of Africa.'[1] Ridgway had arranged to reward the men of the 505th with a rare feast by spending 1,000 dollars from regimental funds for beer and beef, enough for each trooper to have one pound of beef and a bottle of beer. An unusual gesture perhaps, but then neither Ridgway nor the 82d Airborne was ordinary. Along with the 1st Infantry Division, the 82d 'All American' Division had established a reputation as one of the great fighting units of World War I. It was the division of the Meuse-Argonne and St Mihiel, and of the legendary Medal of Honor winner, Sergeant Alvin York, the Tennessee sharpshooter whose unparalleled feat had thwarted the attack of an entire German battalion. Reactivated in 1942 under the command of Bradley, it was selected to become the first of the new airborne divisions and placed under Ridgway's command when Bradley moved on to command another division.

The career of Matthew B. Ridgway and that of his invasion

---

[1] *Soldier*, op. cit., p. 66.

* The glidermen of the 325th Glider Infantry Regiment were not volunteers but were assigned to the unit on the basis of being good soldiers. They received no hazardous duty pay and were mostly regarded with disdain by the cocky paratrooper comrades. One disgruntled gliderman was heard to rage, 'I would give a year's pay if the desk-bound son of a bitch in Washington who decided crash-landing in one of these canvas coffins isn't hazardous duty would go up with us just once.' To make matters worse, the glidermen were not authorized to wear any of the distinctive insignia of the paratroopers. The men of the 325th were bitterly disappointed at being excluded from the D-Day operations of the 82d Airborne. (Cf. *Drop Zone Sicily*, op. cit., pp. 5–6.)

commander James Gavin are classical American success stories. Considered one of the ablest soldiers produced by the US Army, Ridgway was a tough commander who believed physical and moral courage were essential qualities in any leader and who never hesitated to relieve even his former West Point classmates if they failed in combat. Outspoken in opposing any military operation which needlessly wasted his men, Ridgway never shrank from speaking his mind to a superior officer.* A one-time choirboy who could curse like a stable boy, Ridgway was an officer who took care of his men and they knew it. He had learned very quickly in his military career as a brand-new second lieutenant fresh from the plains of West Point that 'one of the attributes of military leadership is knowing when to get rid of a sorehead, or a subordinate who is dragging his feet'.[1]

Ridgway despised ambitious officers who would sacrifice their men for some worthless purpose or piece of terrain, and always pointed with considerable emotion to Passchendaele as a classic example. Throughout a sensational career that later included command of an airborne corps in Northwest Europe, Eighth Army in Korea, Commander-in-Chief of the United Nations Command, Supreme Commander of NATO and Chief of Staff of the US Army, Ridgway never lost his respect for the ordinary soldier. In his memoirs he wrote, 'I shall go to my grave humbly proud of the fact that on at least four occasions I have stood up at the risk of my career and denounced what I considered to be ill-conceived tactical schemes.'[2]

Nor was he among those senior American officers who disliked Montgomery. On the contrary, while noting that Monty was a free spirit who was sometimes a bit hard to restrain, Ridgway called him 'a first-class professional officer of great ability . . . and Monty could produce . . . I don't know anybody who could give

---

[1] Ibid., p. 29.

[2] Ibid. and Robert C. Alberts, 'Profile of a Soldier: Matthew B. Ridgway', *American Heritage*, February 1976. Ridgway would bristle at the mere mention of Haig's Passchendaele offensive in 1917 which he called 'a pointless sacrifice of British soldiers'. In Ridgway's eyes a commander could commit no graver sin.

* Shortly before D-Day Ridgway thoroughly annoyed Eisenhower and Bedell Smith when he locked horns with Ike's airborne adviser, 'Boy' Browning, on several occasions. Ridgway was told Browning was to visit him to check his plans for Sicily. Ridgway cabled back there were no plans until such time as Patton approved them and they would not be available to inspection by Browning or anyone else until that time. Although he later softened this incident in his memoirs, the truth was he deeply resented the patronizing attitude of some senior British officers, among them Browning.

me more complete support than Monty did when I was under British command twice . . . I had no trouble with Monty at all.'[1]

Ridgway and Gavin were firm exponents of leadership by example and throughout the war were always to be found prowling the front lines. In Normandy, Ridgway became known as 'The Causeway Kid' for his fearlessness in exposing himself to hostile fire. He is reputed to have said once to his aides, who were attempting to keep him away from the front lines, that it wouldn't hurt for the troops to see a dead general occasionally. A correspondent for *Time* magazine who had jumped into Normandy on D-Day with the 82d later wrote: 'I remember seeing the two of them walking down a road in Normandy with all sorts of stuff flying around. I was creeping along down in the ditch by the side of the road, and when they saw me, they yelled simultaneously, "Get up here and walk like a man!" And I did.'[2] Their men knew neither officer would require them to perform any task they would not do themselves. In the twilight of their distinguished careers both men would refuse to compromise their ideals or their integrity and would oppose policies they believed wrong or misguided. Both were outspoken in their opposition to the folly of massive American involvement in Vietnam.

Now, in the dawn hours of 10 July 1943, Gavin and Ridgway were each suffering from intense frustration. Gavin had no idea where he was and without a radio had no way of determining what had happened to his men. His regimental Operations Officer (S-3), Major Benjamin Vandervoort, remembers Gavin's intensity during those first hours when they landed near Vittoria, more than twenty miles from the intended drop zone:

> In the moonlight he rounded up eight combat-green troopers. I was one of them. He would have rather found a radio. He had no idea where his regiment was and only a vague idea as to exactly where he was. We walked all night.
>
> Mid-morning [10 July], we ran into an Italian thirty-five-man anti-parachute patrol seventy yards in front of us. An intense fire fight ensued. Two of our troopers were hit and lay very still. In the length of time it takes to fire two dozen aimed shots with a carbine, the Italians were driven to cover behind a stone wall. In the lull, we disengaged straight back, one at a time, the others

---

[1] *Soldier*, p. 251, and Oral History, USAMHI. As the postwar NATO Supreme Commander, Ridgway became Monty's boss, 1952–3.

[2] Quoted by Tim Clark in 'Trained to be a Soldier', *Yankee*, June 1984.

covering. The colonel was the last man to withdraw from the position. . . . We were sweaty, tired and distressed at having to leave wounded behind. The colonel looked over his paltry six-man command and said, 'This is a hell of a place for a regimental commander to be.'[1]

While Gavin and his tiny band of men began to converge northeast of Gela where they would shortly lock horns with the men of the Hermann Goering Division, Ridgway paced anxiously aboard the *Monrovia*, awaiting some news of his men. The high seas and high winds were a source of great worry and the radio silence in effect throughout the Allied fleet meant that there could be no news of Gavin's regiment until it was lifted. Ridgway was all too aware that the potential for disaster was high, but what he could not know at this moment was that the unfortunate course of events during the night of 9/10 July was turning the first major Allied airborne operation of the war into what some would later call 'the best executed snafu in the history of military operations'.[2]

The ordeal of the Red Devils had been brief but brutal. Most who survived were soon evacuated back to North Africa. The airborne troopers of Gavin's 505th RCT were not so fortunate. For the men of the 82d Airborne this was to be their first test of combat and in the next several days the weeks of strenuous training in North Africa would begin to pay important dividends.

Although isolated from his men and uncertain of the situation he faced, Gavin would have been somewhat less apprehensive had he known of the panic his men were creating. Reports began filtering in to Guzzoni's Sixth Army Headquarters in Enna of parachute and glider troops all over southern Sicily. According to the reports the enemy was everywhere, from as far away as 140 miles to the west in Castelvetrano, to Gela, where 'thousands' of parachutists were reported to be roaming the hills and valleys.[3]

---

[1] Letter, Colonel Benjamin H. Vandervoort to the author, 23 September 1985. Vandervoort later went on to command the 2d Battalion, 505th Parachute Infantry Regiment in Normandy, Holland and the Ardennes before being severely wounded in early 1945. He became one of the legendary battalion commanders of the 82d Airborne and his loss to the Division was deeply felt not only by Gavin and Ridgway but by all who had served with him. (Cf. Clay Blair, *Ridgway's Paratroopers*, New York, 1985, p. 499.)

[2] 'Snafu', which entered the GI lexicon during World War II, means 'situation normal, all fouled up'. Gavin first heard the term applied to Sicily about D+5. (Major General James M. Gavin, *Airborne Warfare*, Washington, 1947, p. 16.)

[3] *The Mediterranean and Middle East*, Vol. V, op. cit., p. 81. Italian estimates ran to as many as 20,000–30,000 paratroopers.

It would be days before all the survivors of Gavin's force were reunited. Some continued to roam the hills in small bands;* others were able to join units of the invasion force which began coming ashore in strength as dawn broke to reveal that D-Day – 10 July 1943 – would be a clear, sunny day across the ancient land of Sicily.†

* What none of the men of the 82d Airborne ever knew was what the Germans had to say about them. In a report issued by OB South on 20 July, the German High Command said:
Paratroops have greatly delayed the advance of our own troops and have inflicted considerable casualties on our troops. Small groups of parachutists who had jumped into overgrown country made themselves noticed in a particularly unpleasant manner. In the future this fact must be taken into account through the setting aside of security detachments in every formation for the purpose of guarding the zone of the advance and to give battle to appearing paratroops without creating a substantial delay of the marching troops. (Report of LXXVI Panzer Corps in 'Information from German Sources', loc. cit.)

† A very few paratroopers took the easy way out and went to ground. Colonel White of 2d Armored writes: 'My aide and jeep driver and I rounded up many of them out of cellars. In one cellar we found about a dozen of them. This cellar had a number of wine casks but rather than using the bungs the paratroopers had fired a shot into the end of a cask and filled their canteens and were whooping it up as the good red wine poured out of the bullet hole!' (General I. D. White, letter to the author, 7 August 1985.)

CHAPTER 14

The Eighth Army Assault

We are sailing to take part in the greatest combined
operation in history.

REAR-ADMIRAL SIR PHILIP VIAN
(Commanding Force 'V')

During the months leading up to the invasion a series of daring and
hazardous operations took place along the coast of Sicily. There
were many nights when a British submarine would surface offshore and launch usually two-man teams from a select group
called Combined Operations Reconnaissance and Pilotage Parties
– Royal Navy officers and ratings and men of the Royal Engineers
– in collapsible canvas canoes called 'folbots'. Their task was to
reconnoitre along the 105 miles of coastline that comprised the
Allied assault area. Each of the twenty-six main assault beaches
had to be investigated and every detail of importance recorded.
Some of the reconnaissance was carried out by submarines cruising at periscope depth close inshore while the pilotage officer
sketched details of what he saw into a notebook, but most of it was
accomplished by these two-man teams. One would remain in the
'folbot' several hundred yards offshore while the other would
swim ashore to observe shore batteries, beach defences, buildings,
earthworks, searchlight locations and RDF facilities. Other
important details were recorded, such as the gradients and composition of the beaches.

Operating in the utmost secrecy, the Pilotage Parties were one of
the lesser-known contributions of Mountbatten's Combined
Operations Headquarters. Few details have emerged about these
operations but it is known that by March 1943 eleven of the
thirty-one men who carried out these missions had been lost.[1] The
large quantities of information with which they furnished the
assault planners enabled the Allies successfully to land sixty-nine

[1] *The Mediterranean and Middle East*, Vol. V, op. cit., p. 56.

battalions of infantry along with supporting artillery, engineer, signal and medical units.[1]

Unlike the later invasions of Salerno, Anzio, the great invasion of Normany and the many amphibious operations in the Pacific which were preceded by naval bombardments, the assault upon Sicily must rank as one of the least tumultuous in history. There were no lengthy, thunderous barrages prior to the launching of the assault units from their troopships. Other than diversionary shellings by the cruisers *Aurora* and *Penelope*, the awesome firepower of the Allied warships remained silent in anticipation that the invasion might at least achieve tactical surprise.[*]

The Royal Navy convoys of Ramsay's Eastern Task Force had rendezvoused about fifty miles south of Malta on the afternoon of 9 July. Losses en route were small and occurred only to Force 'V' which lost three ships to U-boat torpedoes in the western Mediterranean.[†] The Canadian 1st Division (Major-General Guy G. Simonds) lost some 500 vehicles and important signals equipment belonging to Division headquarters.

By the early hours of 10 July many of the men had been in their small landing craft for a number of hours and were wet, cold and very seasick in the rough sea. One man in the 51st Division actually died of seasickness. Approximately 2½ hours had been allotted for disembarkation from the transports to landing craft which were to form into flotillas at designated Release Positions before heading for their respective assault beaches.

---

[1] One of the participants who recorded his experiences was Lieutenant Ralph Neville, RN, in *Survey By Starlight* (London, 1949). Among the many accomplishments of these remarkable men was the marking of the British and Canadian assault beaches on D-Day by a canoe showing a light. In his autobiography Admiral Cunningham noted the debt owed to these gallant young men. (*A Sailor's Odyssey*, op. cit., p. 557.)

[*] Strategic surprise was lost when the Allied fleet was discovered during the afternoon of 9 July. (See Chapter 11.)

[†] The number of U-boats operating in the Mediterranean had steadily declined in 1943, mainly due to Allied success in choking off the only access through the Strait of Gibraltar. No U-boat reinforcements had penetrated since the months of April and May when four were successful. The total number of U-boats in the Mediterranean was now down to 17. Nevertheless, the U-boat fleet there posed a very substantial threat to the vulnerable Allied convoys en route to Sicily which were forced to maintain fixed routes. There were also about 45 Italian submarines available for operations, although they did not sink a single Allied vessel in 1943. Apart from the U-boat menace, Allied shipping was also vulnerable to Axis air attack and during their passage to Sicily, the Eastern Task Force passed within striking distance of Italian naval bases in southern Italy. Germany's naval chief, Grand Admiral Doenitz, had fruitlessly attempted to persuade the Italians that to fight, even if they lost, was better than their policy of relative inaction. (Cf. Captain Stephen W. Roskill, *The War at Sea, 1939–1945*, Vol. III, Part I, London, 1960, Chapters II and VI.)

Offshore were seven British submarines which acted as inshore beacons, one for each of the seven task forces. One of these was positioned directly off Scoglitti to guide the landing craft of the 45th Division (CENT Force) to their destinations. Its name was HMS *Seraph*, whose crew were unaware of the major contribution they had already made to the operation now about to take place.[1]

In addition to the conventional assault forces of 13 and 30 Corps, Eighth Army was augmented for the invasion by the 1st Special Raiding Squadron of the 2nd Special Air Service (SAS) Regiment,* No. 3 Commando, and Nos 40 and 41 Royal Marine Commandos. The mission of these specially trained units was to seize targets in advance of the main invasion. The SAS and No. 3 Commando were to destroy the coastal artillery batteries at Cape Murro di Porco and Cassibile. The Royal Marines were to land west of Ponte Castellazo in the Pachino peninsula to anchor the extreme left flank of Eighth Army.

As the official historian has described them, the British landings were for the most part anti-climactic. Although the Allies expected a hard fight on the beaches, the ill-equipped and ill-trained Italian coastal defenders were never equal to the task and generally put up only a cursory defence before either surrendering or melting away into the night. As we now know, the Italian plan never envisioned a stout defence of the beaches and certainly none was forthcoming. Prudently, the British had prepared for the worst. 'The British

---

[1] The *Seraph*'s Commanding Officer, Lieutenant Jewell, later wrote of the sight of the great Allied fleet that 'the English language needs a new descriptive noun to replace the hackneyed word *armada*'. (Quoted in *Secret Mission Submarine*, New York, 1944, p. 114.)

* The distinguished forerunners to the modern-day SAS of anti-terrorist repute, the SAS of World War II were trained for guerilla-type operations by air, land or sea. The 1st Special Raiding Squadron was a battalion-sized unit consisting of 16 officers and 238 men. The Commandos and the Royal Marine Commandos were also élite forces trained primarily for special assault operations. The SAS in Sicily was commanded by a remarkable Irishman, Major R. B. 'Paddy' Mayne. Colonel Chatterton, who was with the SAS for a time after swimming ashore on the night of 9/10 July, witnessed two examples of why the SAS was feared and respected. Not long after landing, Major Mayne was going forward to accept the surrender of a group of senior Italian officers when a shot rang out from somewhere inside the group. Mayne drew his pistol and, shoving an Italian officer aside, fired at an officer in the rear rank who fell. 'There was no more trouble, but it left no one in doubt as to the character of Paddy Mayne.' In another, the SAS were escorting some Italian POWs when a shot rang out and an SAS trooper fell dead. Another SAS man who saw the incident as he turned at the sound immediately pushed his way into the column and stopping in front of one man suddenly lifted his rifle by its barrel and violently crushed the skull of the Italian. When asked why he had killed the man, the trooper replied, 'Didn't you see the bastard ... He was up that tree. He shot my chum in the back and then dropped into the column. I happened to turn round just as he dropped.' (Cf. *The Wings of Pegasus*, Chapter 4.)

medical services were prepared to receive about 10,000 battle casualties in the first week (in fact, 1,517 were received); and the orders of most of the Army formations outlined action to mitigate catastrophes such as the sinking of key vessels and the loss of units embarked in them ... no walkover was imagined.'[1]

Despite a general lack of resistance the landings were not altogether smooth. The transfer of troops to the assault craft proved difficult and mix-ups resulted in many units landing behind schedule and sometimes in the wrong locations. When H-Hour (0245 hours) arrived, Allied air forces had already been hard at work bombing Axis airfields. As the Canadians assembled off the Pachino peninsula the assault troops could clearly see the flak and fire against the medium bombers attacking Pachino airfield. The 2nd Brigade landed without incident, although two assault battalions landed on the wrong beaches, but the 1st Brigade experienced considerable delay and when, by 0315, the operation had not begun an exasperated Admiral Vian signalled his Senior Naval Landing Officer, 'Will your assault ever start?'[2]

The SAS and No. 3 Commando carried out the silencing of their respective coastal batteries and were followed by the 5th Division which assaulted the beaches at Cassible. The 15th Brigade was late and unable to find its correct beaches. Harassment by Italian artillery was a problem until knocked out by the destroyer *Eskimo*.

Near Avola, Kirkman's 50th Division assault force, the 151st Infantry Brigade, encountered considerable difficulty. The wind and heavy seas made the launching and assembly of the assault flotilla difficult, and there was so much confusion that the troops landed in scattered groups on the wrong beaches. Kirkman later prepared a scathing report in which he charged that 'had enemy resistance on the beaches been at all determined the landings might well have resulted in complete failure with heavy casualties'. Part of the 6 Durham Light Infantry landed on a 5th Division beach to the north. Inexperienced naval personnel landed their troops an average of 1,000 to as much as 6,000 yards off target. Kirkman assailed the lack of training of the flotilla crews and suggested that unless there were better training in combined operations it would

---

[1] *The Mediterranean and Middle East*, Vol. V, op. cit., p. 52.
[2] Nicholson, *The Canadians in Italy*, op. cit., pp. 69–70.

one day lead to a 'very considerable military disaster'.[1] These events and those which were to occur on 11 July would serve as a warning of just how much improvement in inter-service relations and training was required.

Major-General Douglas Wimberley's Highland Division assaulted the southern tip of the Pachino peninsula. The rough sea led the senior naval landing officer to urge the abandonment of the assault on one of the division's two assigned beaches and the transfer of its forces to the other. Wimberley refused, as did Leese, and the operation was carried out as scheduled.[2]

Throughout the day as Eighth Army units continued to stream ashore, steady progress was made in both corps' sectors. The Royal Scots Fusiliers had disposed of the short-lived Italian occupation of Ponte Grande bridge and the 17th Brigade of the 5th Division had pushed on towards Syracuse where resistance was rapidly crumbling. Beginning at dawn, Allied aircraft appeared off the British beaches to provide air cover and to pound all roads leading into the assault area. The few feeble attempts by Italian artillery or coastal batteries were rapidly snuffed out either by air or naval gunfire. The Canadians found Pachino airfield abandoned and the runway ploughed up, but by early afternoon it was usable for emergency landings.* With a minimum of resistance, four divisions, the 231st Brigade, the SAS and the Commandos were safely ashore in Sicily where the beaches were now jammed with artillery, vehicles and increasingly large masses of other equipment.

By mid-morning the success of the Eighth Army landings was conveyed to an anxious Montgomery who was so jubilant at this reassuring news that he momentarily forgot the savage battles with Tedder and Cunningham. In his diary, Monty admitted that he had been wrong about the air forces; they had mastered the skies over Sicily and he wrote to Tedder to convey his appreciation

---

[1] '50th [N] Div Landing in Sicily', 30 July 1943, copy furnished by Brigadier James A. Oliver. Kirkman's report was sent to the 30 Corps Commander, Oliver Leese, who ordered it shown unofficially to Mountbatten. Kirkman's chief complaint was that LCT skippers had not been properly briefed, were without clear orders and had no knowledge of what to do when the unexpected occurred as it did that morning, when enemy shellfire caused some to head for the nearest safe beach, regardless of whether or not it was the correct one.

[2] 'Scottish Soldier', the unpublished autobiography of Major-General Douglas Wimberley, furnished by Brigadier James A. Oliver. A copy is also in the archives of Churchill College, Cambridge.

* Like so many unsung units, the airfield construction engineers were able to work near-miracles in creating or repairing airfields.

for their achievement. The performance of the Royal Navy Montgomery deemed 'quite first class' and at 1030 he personally went to Cunningham's Malta headquarters 'to express my great appreciation of the work of the Navy'.[1] For the moment the success of Operation HUSKY had exceeded his wildest expectations.

[1] *Monty: Master of the Battlefield, 1942–1944*, op. cit., pp. 297–8.

CHAPTER 15

The Seventh Army Landings

> I want those sons of bitches! I won't go on without them!
>
> PATTON

The landings of Seventh Army in the Gulf of Gela were successful but not without problems. The easiest of the three landings occurred at Licata where Truscott's JOSS Force encountered feeble resistance from the Italian 207th Coastal Division. The launching of the LCVPs proved difficult in the heavy sea and nine men were drowned when a davit on an LST broke and dumped a boatload of troops into the sea. The first wave did not land until 0330, approximately 45 minutes late. For the men of the 2d Battalion, 7th Infantry Regiment, the assault on Red Beach was no picnic when the LCIs ferrying the battalion came under heavy artillery and small-arms fire. Once ashore the battalion quickly by-passed the enemy gunners and by 1000 had successfully established itself on its objectives and broken up a lacklustre Italian counterattack against their roadblock established at Station San Oliva, some 3½ miles northwest of Licata. Shortly after dawn the 10th Field Artillery Battalion landed and was quickly able to provide valuable close support fire to the assault troops.[1]

Truscott intended to attack and capture Licata from two directions. The left pincer was the 3d Ranger Battalion which landed a mere 12 minutes behind schedule at 0257 and established defensive positions on the western flank of Green Beach. Troops from Yellow and Blue Beaches to the east of Licata were in better position to squeeze the town as the right pincer, and once the threat posed by an Italian railway battery on the Licata break-

---

[1] *Sicily*, op. cit., Chapter VI. The commander of one of the artillery battalions in the follow-up 9th Infantry Division was a young lieutenant colonel named William C. Westmoreland who so impressed the 82d Airborne artillery commander, Brigadier General Maxwell D. Taylor, that his name went into Taylor's notebook as an officer to watch.

water was silenced by naval gunfire the city quickly fell. By dawn Truscott was encouraged by the fact that his infantrymen were either on or about to take their assigned objectives. With fewer than 100 casualties that morning, Truscott's force was well on its way to accomplishing the mission of anchoring Patton's left flank.[1]

Perhaps the closest call to JOSS Force came at sea about 0200 when four searchlights suddenly came on and began sweeping the sea around Licata, coming finally to rest on Admiral Conolly's flagship *Biscayne* which was firmly impaled on their beams at a range of less than 7,000 yards. Truscott was anxious to avoid any action that might imperil the achievement of tactical surprise and he managed to convince the Admiral not to open fire unless Italian coastal guns did so first. Incredibly, nothing happened and after about twenty minutes in the glare of searchlights so bright that Truscott recalled one could read a book in them, the lights just as suddenly flickered out and the threat passed.[2]

Yellow Beach, east of Licata, was assaulted by a tank-infantry task force which encountered scant opposition. Most of the Italian defenders had scattered, including those manning the local command post. One of the first war correspondents ashore was Michael Chinigo of International News Service. Upon entering the command bunker the field telephone rang and Chinigo, who spoke fluent Italian, picked up the receiver. To his surprise there was an Italian general on the other end. The general had been awakened with the news that American forces were invading the Licata sector. 'Please, I beg of you, say it isn't so.' Chinigo told his caller in an authoritative voice that all was well. The Italian general hung up obviously believing he had been given false information about an invasion.[3]

Major General Troy Middleton's 45th Division had practised amphibious operations off Cape Cod, Massachusetts, the previous summer and autumn and now his three infantry regiments

---

[1] Ibid., pp. 133–5.
[2] Truscott, *Command Missions*, op. cit., p. 212.
[3] Donald G. Taggart (Ed.), *The History of the Third Infantry Division in World War II*, Washington, 1947, p. 51. Truscott's version is that Chinigo had only spoken to some agents in an inland town who had heard that the Allies were landing. Chinigo was later accorded the rare honour for a civilian of being decorated with the Silver Star for gallantry during the landings. He accompanied the 3d Division throughout the Sicily campaign and became the first war correspondent to enter Palermo and Messina. (*Command Missions*, op. cit., p. 217.)

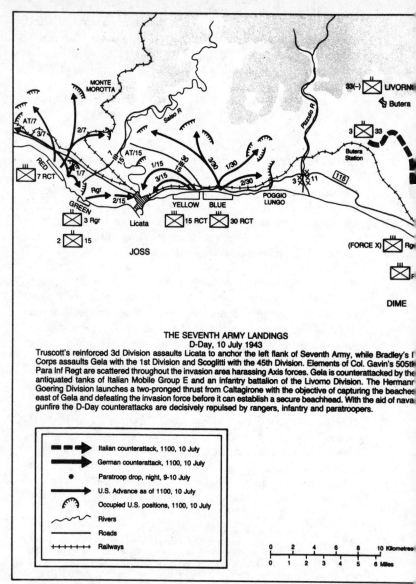

THE SEVENTH ARMY LANDINGS
D-Day, 10 July 1943

Truscott's reinforced 3d Division assaults Licata to anchor the left flank of Seventh Army, while Bradley's II Corps assaults Gela with the 1st Division and Scoglitti with the 45th Division. Elements of Col. Gavin's 505th Para Inf Regt are scattered throughout the invasion area harassing Axis forces. Gela is counterattacked by the antiquated tanks of Italian Mobile Group E and an infantry battalion of the Livorno Division. The Hermann Goering Division launches a two-pronged thrust from Caltagirone with the objective of capturing the beaches east of Gela and defeating the invasion force before it can establish a secure beachhead. With the aid of naval gunfire the D-Day counterattacks are decisively repulsed by rangers, infantry and paratroopers.

▄▄▶	Italian counterattack, 1100, 10 July
▬▶	German counterattack, 1100, 10 July
●	Paratroop drop, night, 9-10 July
➤	U.S. Advance as of 1100, 10 July
⌒	Occupied U.S. positions, 1100, 10 July
∿	Rivers
──	Roads
┼┼┼┼	Railways

SEVENTH ARMY LANDINGS

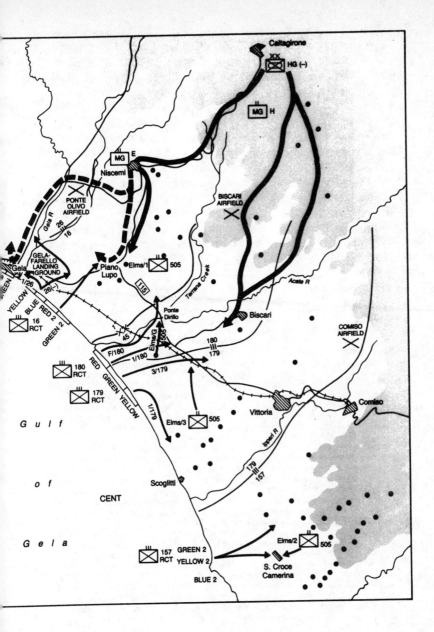

landed on the sandy beaches east and west of the dreary little fishing village of Scoglitti.* Two of the regiments landed at the correct beaches but the third landed far to the west in complete disarray.[1]† One wave of the 157th RCT came to grief on the rocks at Point Braccetto where two landing craft capsized, drowning 27 men in the heavy surf. The 157th RCT operated as virtually an independent task force, with its landing beaches some nine miles east of the other two regiments and more than fifteen miles from the Canadians in the Pachino peninsula. The mission of Colonel Charles M. Ankorn's force was to drive quickly ten miles inland to Comiso where the regiment was to join forces with elements of Colonel Robert B. Hutchins' 179th RCT to attack and seize Comiso airfield.

As the landings were taking place the paratroopers scattered over the 45th Divison's sector were beginning to become effective against a variety of enemy targets. On D-Day the 45th Division

---

[1] Frank James Price, *Troy H. Middleton: A Biography*, Baton Rouge, 1974, pp. 148–9. Troy Middleton, the fifty-three-year-old commander of the 45th Division, enlisted in the Army in 1910 as a private and was commissioned a 2d lieutenant of Infantry in 1913. By 1918 Middleton was the youngest colonel in the AEF and had commanded an infantry regiment in the Meuse–Argonne. In 1937 he retired after a distinguished 37-year career. In 1940 he wrote to his old friend from World War I, George Marshall, and volunteered to return to active service if Marshall and his nation needed him. Marshall declined but wrote across the top of Middleton's letter: 'This man was the outstanding infantry regimental commander on the battlefield in France.' His brief retirement years as the comptroller of Louisiana State University ended after Pearl Harbor when Middleton was recalled to active duty as a lieutenant colonel. By the autumn of 1942 he was a major general commanding the 45th Division. Middleton's experience and leadership were to validate Marshall's judgment and before the war ended he would rise to the command of a corps in Northwest Europe and in 1945 would once again retire, this time as a lieutenant general with the distinction of having served more days in combat than any other general officer in the US Army.

* Nicknamed the 'Thunderbirds', the National Guardsmen of two of its three regiments consisted of large numbers of Cherokee, Seminole, Choctaw, Apache and Sioux Indians. During their training in Massachusetts there was considerable publicity generated by an Indian war dance on Boston Common in support of a war bond campaign. (*Sicily–Salerno–Anzio*, op. cit., p. 128.) The 45th Division sector was plagued by submerged rocks; in addition, throughout the American invasion sector were sandbanks which made it impossible for all landing craft to make it to the beaches. A number of landing craft were grounded when they ran foul of these underwater obstacles.

† The inexperience of the 45th Division manifested itself in many forms. The division had arrived from the US, combat-loaded with two barracks bags per man. There was no way they could be stored and it was impossible, of course, for the troops to carry them into combat. The result was that southern Sicily became littered with these precious objects which included, among other things, extra socks for the troops. Fortunately, an Italian depot was captured that was found to be well stocked with socks which II Corps ordered issued to the 45th Division. The more experienced 1st Divison carried such supplies in mobile (truck) depots. By the time of Normandy the lesson still had not been learned and the causeways and roads near the D-Day beaches again became littered with barracks bags. (Bradley Commentaries.)

managed to push nearly seven miles inland.* About 1600 Lieutenant Colonel Earl A. Taylor's 3d Battalion, 179th Infantry, and
some stray paratroopers were encamped outside the town of
Vittoria. Colonel Taylor failed in an attempt to induce a Sicilian to
enter the city and return with the mayor or military commander to
discuss surrender in lieu of needless destruction and loss of life.
What he did not know was that there were three captured paratroopers already inside the city. Two were hopelessly drunk but
the third was the previously mentioned Lieutenant William J.
Harris of Alexander's 2d Battalion, 505th Parachute Infantry, and
for hours he had been arguing with his Italian captors that they
would do better to surrender rather than die. Moments before
Taylor's men were to bombard and storm the city, Harris won his
point and white flags marked the peaceful fall of Vittoria.[1]

Nearby two forces had earlier that afternoon coincidently
attacked the town of Santa Croce Camerina at the same moment.
The 1st Battalion, 157th Infantry stormed the town from the west
just as Major Alexander's paratroopers did so from the east. The
Italian garrison promptly surrendered. An infantry company then
drove east and entered Ragusa by early evening where there was
yet no sign of the Canadians. Around Comiso other elements of
the 157th Brigade seized Hill 643 overlooking Comiso airfield.[2]

One of the attributes of a successful leader is the ability to select the
right commander and formation for a particular task. Such was
the example of Patton's choice of Terry Allen's 1st Infantry Division for what he envisioned would be the most difficult of the three
assault landings: Gela. Patton was no stranger to either Allen or
the 1st Division when both had come under his command in
Tunisia. The stormy friendship between Patton and Allen dated to
early in the inter-war years when both were still cavalrymen and
led directly to the division being given the toughest job in Sicily.

---

[1] *Sicily*, op. cit., pp. 155–6.
[2] Ibid., p. 156.
* More than troops came ashore on D-Day in the 45th Division sector. For reasons never
explained, the Division paymaster, Lt Col. R. C. Routh, was ordered ashore along with his
six field safes containing some $2,000,000 in cash. The colonel and his safes became
separated and a frantic search failed to turn up the cash until the following day when the
errant safes were found submerged offshore where they had been dumped by a Navy
coxswain whose LCVP had been unable to land. The soaking wet greenbacks were laid out
to dry on the roof of the local fascist headquarters. (*Sicily–Salerno–Anzio*, op. cit., p. 143
and *YANK*, The Army Weekly, 13 August 1943.)

The saga of the legendary 1st Division in World War II was of a division that was consistently given the most difficult assignments which were just as consistently carried out with brilliance and *élan*.

The 'Big Red One'* (so named for its large red '1' on the division shoulder patch) was the oldest active division of the US Army. Formed in 1917 as part of America's commitment to General John J. Pershing's Allied Expeditionary Force, the great tradition of the 1st Division was moulded in France at St Mihiel, Picardy and the Meuse–Argonne where its battle honours were won.†

The 1st Division is undoubtedly best remembered for the more publicized drama which occurred on 6 June 1944 when the division stormed ashore on Omaha Beach: yet, Omaha was only one of the many battles fought by the division during the war, one of which was Gela. Both were occasions where the 'perversity'‡ of the 'Big Red One' won the day against a powerful and determined enemy force. The unit which never understood the meaning of the word failure reflected the character of its colourful commander, 'Terrible Terry' Allen.

The US Army of the Second World War era produced its fair share of mavericks, men of independent mind and conduct whose superior ability and accomplishments stamped them as a breed apart from their contemporaries. Generally, such men are impervious to attempts to induce conformity of thought or deed in them, and their brilliance is frequently negated by their abrasiveness. On a very senior level Patton and Montgomery come immediately to mind, as do Wingate and 'Hobo' Hobart. A number of others played influential roles in the Sicily campaign.§

---

* Also known throughout the US Army as 'The First Team'.

† The 1st Division had accompanied Pershing to France and during that war was known as 'Pershing's Own'. Its World War I strength was about 28,000, compared with 15,000 in World War II. Two of its three infantry regiments – the 16th and 18th – were first organized during the Civil War and participated in most of its major battles, as well as in the Spanish–American War and the Philippine Insurrection. Two of its artillery units, the 5th and 6th Field Artillery Regiments, date to the Revolutionary War.

‡ It was altogether appropriate that the code-name assigned to the 1st Division was DANGER. The forward Command Post thus became DANGER FORWARD.

§ Major General Matthew B. Ridgway, the brilliant commander of the 82d Airborne Division, was something of a maverick himself. When he became the US Army Chief of Staff after the Korean War, he once said at a dinner for four or five very senior officers of the various services: ' "What do you suppose the most important job of the Chief of Staff is?" No one knew. "To protect the maverick," said Ridgway, "because only the maverick makes progress." ' (Quoted by Lieutenant General James M. Gavin in Clark, 'Trained to be a Soldier', op. cit.)

The 1st Division was unique in that it was led by *two* mavericks, Allen, and his assistant division commander, Brigadier General Theodore Roosevelt, Jr.*

Terry de la Mesa Allen was a horse cavalryman who had earned his spurs the hard way. Born on April Fool's Day 1888 at Fort Douglas, Utah Territory, the son of an artillery colonel and a mother of Spanish descent, he grew up an 'Army brat' on dusty military posts throughout the western United States, most of them in Texas which he later adopted as his home. During his youth Allen's companions were often soldiers who taught him the ways of the world.[1]

It was inevitable that young Allen would follow his father to West Point, which he did in 1907. Although the United States Military Academy has produced its share of mavericks it has never looked kindly upon those who do not conform to its rigid rules of discipline and behaviour. As indifferent to discipline as he was to scholarship, Terry Allen's name appeared with great regularity on

[1] One officer's son was spanked for playing with Allen who later reminisced that 'My opinion of myself went up like a rocket'. (Cf. A. J. Liebling, 'Profiles', *The New Yorker*, 24 April 1943.)

* Eldest son of President Theodore Roosevelt (1859–1919), Teddy Roosevelt was one of the most distinguished citizen-soldiers to serve in the US Army. He also struggled throughout his life to live up to the image expected of a son of one of America's most fearless men and popular presidents.

Most of Roosevelt's military career is identified with the 'Big Red One'. In France in 1918 he commanded one of its infantry battalions at the age of 30, was wounded twice and gassed leading his men. During one of his hospitalizations he went AWOL to return to his unit. By war's end he had not only become the first non-Regular Army officer to lead a regiment into battle but also was the recipient of a DSC, the Silver Star, the French Croix de Guerre and the Legion of Honor, along with seven battle stars on his Victory Medal.

During the inter-war years Roosevelt successfully carried on his family's long tradition of public service that included the posts of governor of Puerto Rico and governor-general of the Philippines. In the spring of 1941 he again returned to military service as a colonel in command of his former regiment, the 26th Infantry. Promotion to brigadier general elevated him to the position of Allen's second-in-command.

No officer was more devoted to his unit than Teddy Roosevelt was to the 1st Division. In North Africa a general was heard to complain that Roosevelt and Allen 'seem to think the United States Army consists of the 1st Division and 11 million replacements', which caused T.R. to retort, 'Well, *doesn't* it?'

Roosevelt was also a study in contradiction. One of the most fearless officers ever to wear the uniform of a US Army officer, he was a beloved figure in the 1st Division. Yet, as his aide remembers, 'He was the most disreputable-looking general I ever met. Half the time he'd forgotten his helmet, which he didn't like to wear anyhow, and in his combat fatigues ... he looked like the most beat-up GI you ever saw ...' Now, at the age of fifty-six, Roosevelt, who inspired his men almost as frequently as he infuriated his superiors, was once again providing his unconventional leadership to the battle for Sicily. (Quotations and background material from Lt Cdr Maxwell Hamilton's profile of Roosevelt in 'Junior in Name Only', *The Retired Officer*, June 1981.)

the Commandant's punishment list. A rumour circulated within the Corps of Cadets that 'Terry' really stood for 'Terror', and he became known by the nickname 'Terrible Terry'. During his senior year Allen's casual attitude in the classroom finally cost him dearly when he failed a mandatory class and was dismissed.

Allen had to earn his Army commission the hard way. After a stern lecture from his father he resumed his studies at Catholic University in Washington, DC, where 'he studied with fiendish earnestness for a year ... the first real mental effort of his life'.[1] After passing a competitive examination he was commissioned a 2d lieutenant of cavalry.

His early years in the Army set the tone for what became an extraordinary career best remembered for inspired leadership and uncommon individualism. Allen fought rustlers and bandits along the Mexican border and participated in Pershing's punitive expedition against Pancho Villa. When the United States entered World War I he had obtained his captaincy and was desperate to join the AEF. His failure to be assigned to France was an oversight he remedied by contriving to join an ammunition unit en route there.

Pershing required all arriving officers to undergo refresher training before assignment to a front-line unit. With typical audacity Allen quickly found a combat training centre about to graduate a class, and – so the story goes – slipped into the line of officers receiving their diplomas. The commanding officer regarded him with puzzlement and said, 'I don't remember you in this class.' Allen boldly replied, 'I'm Allen, why don't you?' He obtained the requisite certificate and an assignment to the 90th Infantry Division where he was given command of an infantry battalion.[2]

Terry Allen's philosophy was *never* to sacrifice needlessly the lives of his men. In the Argonne his battalion was ordered to make an early morning frontal assault after the usual artillery bombardment. In Allen's opinion such an attack would be suicidal and, on his own initiative, he ordered his unit to attack the night before. 'We took the position with a loss of twenty killed, and if we'd done it by day we would have lost three hundred.'[3]

[1] Ibid.
[2] Colonel Bryce F. Denno, 'Allen and Huebner: Contrast in Command', Army, June 1984.
[3] Liebling, op. cit. According to Allen, he pulled his pistol and shot one protesting company commander in the buttocks. His replacement, a 2nd lieutenant, took over and 'he did fine'.

He was wounded three times; one occurred at St Mihiel in September 1918 from shell fire. After regaining consciousness on a litter near an aid station, Allen 'rolled off the stretcher, gathered together a group of soldiers who had become separated from their units, and led his "pickup" command forward until he encountered German machine gunners. In the ensuing firefight, Major Allen caught a bullet in the mouth which smashed his jaw and teeth.'[1] Despite the seriousness of his wounds Allen managed to return to the front and ended the war as an acting regimental commander and the recipient of a Silver Star from Pershing for exceptional gallantry.

During the inter-war years Allen continued to go his own way. As a student at the Command and General Staff College at Fort Leavenworth, Kansas, in 1925–26, he managed to start off on the wrong foot the very first day by ignoring his first tactical problem in order to keep a tennis date with a senior officer's attractive blonde daughter. Not surprisingly the commandant referred to Allen as the 'most indifferent student ever enrolled there'.[2]

Some years later as a student at the Infantry School at Fort Benning, Georgia, he came under the scrutiny of Marshall and among the names that found their way into Marshall's black book was Terry Allen's. Marshall's biographer later wrote that Allen was a 'swashbuckler' who gladdened his heart. 'Orthodox leaders of the Army never understood why Marshall gave his backing to the doughty cavalryman, and they liked to repeat the story that only the timely announcement of Allen's promotion to general saved him from court-martial.'[3] By 1942 Marshall saw to it that Allen was given command of the 'Big Red One' for TORCH. Thus, the unconventional, feisty Allen not only had outperformed his former West Point contemporaries by becoming the first man from his former class to be promoted to general officer, but had been given one of the most coveted assignments in the Army.*

During the first months of the Tunisian campaign the 1st Divi-

---

[1] 'Allen and Huebner', op. cit.

[2] Liebling, op. cit. Allen graduated 221 of 241. First was an ambitious young major named Dwight D. Eisenhower.

[3] Forrest C. Pogue, *George C. Marshall: Ordeal and Hope, 1939–1942*, op. cit., 1965, p. 407. The day of his promotion on 1 October 1940 Allen was undergoing disciplinary action for some infraction of Army regulations.

* Despite a reputation as the Army's champion rebel, Terry Allen nevertheless won promotion from lieutenant colonel directly to brigadier general, the same recognition given to Bradley – who was not similarly promoted until February 1941.

sion was fragmented, with its infantry battalions attached to other American units and even to British and French units, a move which left Allen seething with frustration and anger. Always a pragmatist, he noted that 'A soldier doesn't fight to save suffering humanity or any other goddamn nonsense. He fights to prove that his unit is the best in the Army and that he has as much guts as anybody else in the unit. Break up the unit and incentive is gone.'

When Patton assumed command of II Corps it was inevitable that these two charismatic and iron-willed men would clash, even though they were old friends. During the battle of El Guettar they squabbled endlessly over tactics. On one occasion Patton was visiting the 1st Division when he spied slit trenches which had been dug around the perimeter of the CP. 'What the hell are these for?' demanded Patton. Allen replied they were for protection against air attack from the Luftwaffe who were active at that time. 'Which one is yours?' When Allen pointed it out to him, Patton walked over, unzipped his fly and proceeded to urinate into it. 'There,' said Patton, 'now try to use it.'[1] It was an ugly incident, a humiliating experience for Allen and one that did no credit whatever to Patton who always seemed to over-react when they were together.

Prior to Sicily when the weather became increasingly humid and hot, Allen went to Patton's headquarters to demand his men be issued khaki uniforms to replace their woollen ones. A blistering argument ensued. ' "The yellow bellies of the 1st Division don't need khakis," Patton was yelling in his high-pitched voice. "Tell you what I'll do," he continued sarcastically. "If you get a third of your sons of bitches across the sands, I'll see that those that are left get some khaki uniforms." Allen wheeled and stalked out of the room in silent, resentful, smouldering anger.'[2]

As Allen's chief of staff later noted, Patton delighted in taunting him, 'I don't know why, but Patton just loved to tease Terry....'[3] Yet, beneath the bravado and acts of outrageous behaviour there is solid evidence of genuine friendship and mutual respect. The friendship between the two men had deep roots in their cavalry backgrounds. Allen's G-2 in Sicily was Lieutenant Colonel Robert W. Porter, Jr., also a former cavalry officer who served under both men at the Cavalry School at Fort Riley, Kansas, in 1938. Allen and

[1] Quoted in A General's Life, op. cit., p. 140.
[2] 'Terry Allen and the 1st Infantry Division', unpublished account of Allen, written by former members of the 1st Infantry Division. Terry Allen Papers, USAMHI.
[3] Ibid.

Patton were both instructors and maintained a robust but friendly rivalry, particularly over a manual Allen was writing about cavalry tactics. The two would argue furiously and often came to Porter and said, 'You're a young lieutenant, what do you think?' Porter would attempt to hedge, but this tactic rarely succeeded and he would frequently get telephone calls in the middle of the night from Allen demanding an opinion on some point. 'Terry was more unconventional than Patton', but despite its intenseness their rivalry was never acrimonious and Patton never lost his admiration and respect for Allen's leadership ability.[1]

Far more alarming were Allen's relations with Omar Bradley. While the Patton–Allen relationship was one of rivalry and the natural emotion of two mavericks, Allen's relations with Bradley were born from what one witness has described as a 'classic, visceral personality conflict':

> Bradley and Allen could not have been more unalike in personality. Allen was given to profanity; Bradley was not. Allen was gregarious and liked to talk and drink; Bradley was restrained and abstemious. Allen was direct, impatient with theory; Bradley was a thinker. Bradley had been a good student at West Point; Allen ... had flunked out in 1911 ... Bradley was infantry, Allen a polo-loving cavalryman ... Neither, in short, was the other's kind of man. Allen, never a subtle man in personal relationships, made no effort to hide his lack of liking and respect for Bradley. There was an argument on the phone between them during the North African campaign, for example, in the course of which Bradley said to Allen, 'Allen, let me remind you I am your Corps Commander', at the end of which Allen angrily hung up, calling Bradley 'a phony Abraham Lincoln'.[2]

Even though Allen's penchant for drink reputedly did not extend to combat operations, there is no doubt that Bradley's intense disapproval of those who were intemperate was *the* key factor in their unhappy relationship.*

---

[1] Interview with General Robert W. Porter, Jr., USA Ret., loc. cit.

[2] 'Terry Allen and the 1st Division', loc. cit.

* As Bradley's biographer, Clay Blair, points out, 'You have to remember Bradley came from a strict, teetotaling Christian Church, small town, Midwest background. He did not even *taste* alcohol until he was thirty-three-years-old. [His wife] Mary Bradley did not drink at all ... and *detested* anyone who was even a moderately heavy drinker.' Bradley did not believe that anyone was capable of thinking clearly either under the influence of alcohol or with a hangover. Allen's excesses were common knowledge and in Bradley's judgment affected his ability to command the 1st Division. For the remainder of his life Bradley remained critical of Allen's intemperance. In his research Blair discovered that no heavy drinkers ever got anywhere with Bradley, with the lone exception of Colonel B. A. 'Monk'

As he does with Patton, Bradley damns Allen with faint praise in *A Soldier's Story* and *A General's Life*, leaving no doubt he considered the rebellious Allen one of his least favourite subordinates. Bradley believed there was a very serious discipline problem in the 1st Division. Noting that both Allen and Roosevelt suffered from the same weakness – 'utter disregard for discipline, everywhere evident in their cocky division' – Bradley claims to have entertained doubts from the start that either man 'had the inner toughness to impose the discipline and training or the willingness to take orders from and play on the same team with higher command.'[1]

Discipline and team play were the bedrock of Bradley's experience and later became obligatory for those under his command. Those who failed this test were soon replaced. 'It was hard to get the 1st Division to follow an order, to play on the team...'[2] Bradley remembers Allen as 'stubborn'. 'He was possibly the most difficult commander I had to handle throughout the war.'[3]

Two incidents especially irked Bradley. After the Tunisian campaign the 1st Division celebrated by leaving a trail of looted wineshops and outraged local officials in Oran, which the division considered its personal fiefdom. There was bad blood between the rear-echelon troops and the 'Big Red One' veterans. Clubs were closed to the 1st Division, which was deeply resented and led to a second 'liberation', rioting and a great many bashed and bleeding heads. The division was thereafter banned from Oran.

The other incident had taken place near Bizerte near the end of the Tunisian campaign. Bradley's version is that 'Terry Allen foolishly ordered his division into a completely unauthorized attack and was thrown back with heavy losses. From that point forward, Terry was a marked man in my book... Had we not been on the threshold of our first important US Army victory in Africa I would have relieved him – and Teddy Roosevelt – on the spot.'[4]

The Oran incident further soured Bradley and appears to have convinced him that 'Terry Allen was not fit to command, and I was

---

[1] *A General's Life*, op. cit., p. 136.   [2] Bradley Commentaries, loc. cit.
[3] Ibid.   [4] *A General's Life*, op. cit., p. 158.

Dickson, the II Corps G-2 whom he greatly admired. Nevertheless, in Northwest Europe, Dickson was the only officer on Bradley's First Army staff who failed to be promoted to brigadier general. (Quotation and comments in letter, Clay Blair to the author, 11 March 1986.)

determined to remove him and Teddy Roosevelt from the division as soon as circumstances on Sicily permitted.'[1]

As unconventional and outrageous as Allen's behaviour may at times have been, he was nevertheless a deeply serious professional soldier whose judgment was sound. There was ample reason why his officers and men held him in such high esteem. One of his junior infantry officers recalls the effect Allen had upon his men. During a lull in the fighting:

> General Allen assembled small groups of 1st Division officers and men and described the battle they had just won ... Speaking quietly and without heroics or even gesticulation, he told us how proud he was of the way we had performed and how privileged he considered himself to command men of our courage and competence. At no time did he so much as mention his own role in the battle. As he concluded his remarks, I glanced around me and I realized that he had captured every man in his audience.[2]

Bradley was not entirely correct when he criticized the lack of discipline in the 1st Division. The real problem lay in their reaction to non-divisional authority which most of them accepted only reluctantly. The extraordinary loyalty and esprit of the soldiers of the 'Big Red One' was visibly illustrated one day in Sicily when Bradley was en route to the 1st Division and stopped to pick up several soldiers outside Palermo. He learned they were 1st Division troops who had been in a field hospital nearby and rather than risk being put into the replacement pool and most likely end up in another division, they had gone AWOL from the hospital and were hitchhiking back to their unit.[3]

The notion that Allen encouraged or condoned acts of indiscipline is utterly false. He was, in fact, noted as a stern disciplinarian who after the Oran incident summoned Roosevelt and in the strongest language ordered him to root out and court-martial the culprits. Even though both Allen and the 1st Division were known to go their own way in matters Bradley considered indicative of the quality of a good unit, the lax leader pictured in A Soldier's Story simply did not exist.*

[1] Ibid., p. 173.
[2] Letter, Colonel Bryce F. Denno to the author, 1 July 1984.
[3] Bradley Commentaries.
* Among the less publicized incidents that contradict Bradley is one in which some men of the 1st Division were accused by a French wine grower of despoiling his precious vineyards. Word reached AFHQ in Algiers where Eisenhower was known to have been furious over an earlier incident in which a division MP punched an Arab. He sent his deputy,

The other side of Allen that Bradley sometimes did not observe was of firmness and tact. An incident in early 1943 illustrates this point. By February Allen had become so deeply frustrated by the continued fragmentation of his infantry units that, accompanied by Porter, he finally went to Algiers and uttered his now famous remark to Bedell Smith, 'Is this a private war or can anyone get in?' Allen obtained permission to visit his 18th Infantry Regiment, then attached to the British 1st Guards Brigade (78th Division), to find out for himself the truth about a report sent to AFHQ by the [British] V Corps commander, which said that the regiment had performed badly during a battle the previous December.

Allen's investigation produced a far different picture and he immediately went to see the corps commander, Lieutenant-General C. W. Allfrey, and presented his written report. Allfrey said he had accepted in good faith what he had been told. It was a tense moment and after a long silence Allfrey shrugged his shoulders and replied, 'I can't comment.' At this point, Terry Allen could easily have turned this incident into a major Anglo-American row. Instead, he ripped up the report and said to Allfrey, 'Please tell General Alexander we're doing the best we can under difficult circumstances and we need to get along and not knock heads.'*

In retrospect it was evident that the voluble Allen and the taciturn Bradley were on a collision course. Their disharmony was to grow worse in Sicily and contribute to one of the most controversial and misunderstood incidents of the campaign. However, even Bradley was unable to avoid acknowledging the contribution of Terry Allen and the 1st Division during the invasion of Sicily.

Early in the HUSKY planning it had been intended to use the 36th Infantry Division (a Texas National Guard unit) as one of the US

---

* Porter wrote the report and was present throughout Allen's trip to the front. One of Allen's traits that Porter most appreciated was his candour. When he became the 1st Division intelligence officer, Allen bluntly told him, 'You're my G-2 as long as we win; if we lose I will fire you.' (Porter interview, loc. cit.)

Major General Everett S. Hughes, to conduct an investigation. Not only did Hughes exonerate the 1st Division, but he reported that the discipline and military courtesy he observed were the best he had seen in North Africa. (Patton Papers.)

invasion forces. Patton already had a similar unit in the 45th Division and did not want two-thirds of his invasion force consisting of untested divisions. This led to his plea to Eisenhower that 'I want those [1st Division] sons of bitches.'[1]

The 1st Division assault against Gela began at 0200 when Rangers of Lieutenant Colonel William O. Darby's Force X converged on the Gela beaches.* While Darby's men created a powerful diversion by striking directly at Gela itself, the main effort of the 1st Division took place across the three miles of beach due east of the city. The Rangers came under intense fire from enemy rifles and machine guns and lost an entire platoon before clearing the beach defences around dawn. An Italian coastal battery was captured intact and used in support of the invaders. The 16th RCT was spotted by enemy searchlights and was hit by scattered but heavy fire from pillboxes, but otherwise the landings were uneventful. By mid-morning the Rangers had cleared Gela and taken 200 Italian prisoners while the remainder of the 1st Divison began to move towards their primary objectives inland.

If proof were needed that the invasion was not to be free of the painful price of war, it came early the morning of 10 July when the destroyer USS *Maddox* on anti-submarine patrol outside the Gulf of Gela was sunk by a direct hit from a Stuka dive bomber with a

---

[1] Quoted in 'Terry Allen and the 1st Division', loc. cit.

* The Rangers were the American counterpart to the British Commandos: élite, volunteer soldiers trained in every aspect of ground fighting. The Rangers were trained for the most dangerous missions that required daring, speed and the ability to fight under the most adverse conditions. Among the most highly motivated and disciplined troops of the US Army, the first Ranger battalion was formed in Northern Ireland in 1942 under then Major William O. Darby (USMA, Class of 1933) who would lead them to rapid recognition in Tunisia where he organized two additional battalions and commanded what was known as 'The Ranger Force'. At El Guettar, Darby's 1st Ranger Battalion won a Presidential Unit Citation. Although perhaps better known for their exploits in Italy at Salerno, Anzio and Cisterna, the Rangers played a major role in the invasion of Sicily. Darby's Force X was attached to the 1st Division and consisted of the 1st and 4th Ranger Battalions, a battalion of combat engineers, three chemical mortar companies and an Engineer Shore Regiment. Darby and his men provided a superb example of what a highly trained force can accomplish. Three times during his illustrious career Darby spurned promotion in order to remain with his beloved Rangers. At Gela, Darby personally held off an attack by Italian light tanks with a machine gun. Then, along with a Ranger captain, he manned a captured anti-tank gun that destroyed one tank as it bore down on his Ranger CP. Several days later Patton presented Darby with America's second-highest decoration for bravery, the Distinguished Service Cross, and offered him a promotion to full colonel and the command of a regiment of the 45th Division. Darby declined and an amazed Patton wrote in his diary, 'This is the first time I ever saw a man turn down a promotion. Darby is really a great soldier.' Truscott, who later succeeded Mark Clark as Fifth Army commander in Italy, said of Darby, 'Never have I known a more gallant, heroic officer.'

loss of 8 officers and 203 hands. On a distant ship an officer described the scene as 'a great blob of light [which] ... reddened the sky, tearing the night into shreds'.[1] Within two minutes the *Maddox* was gone beneath the waves, leaving only debris where she had once been.[2] Only minutes later the minesweeper *Sentinel* was severely damaged by a series of air attacks and sank soon after dawn with a loss of 10 dead and 51 wounded.[3] Total Allied naval losses in Sicily eventually totalled 48,685 tons, most of which were British coastal vessels, landing craft and merchantmen. In addition to the *Maddox* and *Sentinel*, the US Navy lost two LSTs and one merchant ship. The majority of these losses were from enemy air attack rather than U-boats.[4]

The Navy staged two diversions to confuse the enemy, one by the Royal Navy in the Ionian Sea, reinforcing the impression that the Peloponnese was the target predicted by Major Martin's fake documents. The other took place off western Sicily and, while it undoubtedly raised serious worries for the Sixth Army, it did not dissuade Guzzoni from deciding some time during the morning of 10 July that he must order 15th Panzer Grenadier Division, who had just completed their move to western Sicily, to return at once to take up blocking positions in the area Canicatti–Caltanissetta.[5]

As the day wore on, favourable reports began to flow from the assault units back to anxious commanders aboard ships anchored nearby. One by one the word 'success' was flashed from every beach in Eighth Army by 0530.[6] Despite the foul-ups on various beaches the spirit of co-operation between Army and Navy was excellent. The operations of CENT Force have been cited as a model of inter-service co-operation. Even though the 45th Division landings were difficult, Middleton admired the spirit and perseverance

---

[1] Quoted in John Mason Brown, *To All Hands*, New York, 1943, p. 131.

[2] Nine officers and 65 men were later plucked from the sea. (Cf. *Sicily–Salerno–Anzio*, op. cit., pp. 100–1.)

[3] Hanson Baldwin, 'The Sicilian Campaign', in *Battles Lost and Won*, New York, 1966, p. 211.

[4] Roskill, *The War at Sea*, Vol. III, Pt I, op. cit., p. 139.

[5] Bauer, MS # R-127, 'Immediate Axis Reaction to the Allied Landings'. Along with 15th PzG, Guzzoni also ordered the move east of the Italian 162nd Artillery Battalion, a self-propelled unit in Army reserve guarding the approaches to Cape St Vito at the northern end of the Gulf of Castellammare. The transfer began the night of 10 July by road and rail and the first German units arrived in the Canicatti area on 11 July.

[6] *Sicily–Salerno–Anzio*, op. cit., p. 152.

of the navymen and Admiral Kirk returned the compliment by noting the division was admirably led and full of dash.[1]

The men of the British and US merchant fleets who manned the lightly armed and vulnerable cargo ships displayed a fine spirit, discipline and a calm determination which drew praise from Cunningham for their work in ferrying large numbers of men and huge tonnages of supplies and equipment to Sicily.

Throughout D-Day there were numerous acts of bravery that did not go unnoticed: during the Licata landings an artillery observer flew his Piper Cub aircraft from an improvised fifty-foot runway on a landing ship and for the remainder of the day circled over the beachhead, calling in continuous support fire despite several hits to his plane. An LCT skipper found the water too shallow to land his cargo of troops. Undaunted, he rammed his vessel onto the beach and silenced enemy machine-gun fire with his 20 mm cannons. Brigadier General Wedemeyer was frustrated in his role as an observer and asked Patton to reduce him to colonel so that he might be given command of a regiment. Patton refused to demote Wedemeyer but did give him command of a regiment of the 45th Division for several days.[2]

By the end of D-Day the British had yet to make serious contact with German forces; the Americans were beginning to collide with a German counterthrust aimed at dislodging Allen's 1st Division from the Gela sector. While there was indeed cause for elation at the success of the Allied landings, the sporadic initial resistance came from second-line troops. The multitude of successful landings across a broad front had already left the Italian strategy for the defence of Sicily a useless vestige of wishful thinking.

During the first two days of Operation HUSKY the beaches served as the entry points into Sicily for 80,000 men, 7,000 vehicles, 300 trucks and 900 guns.[3] Men and equipment came ashore in seemingly endless waves.

Across southeastern Sicily there were scenes which left an indelible image of the latest war to engulf the embattled island. Dead Italians littered the roads in many places. Bradley's aide wrote in his diary that, 'Refugees simply pass the dead by, walking around

[1] Ibid., p. 143.

[2] *The Patton Papers*, Vol. II, p. 285. Patton called this an outstanding act (unpublished essay in the papers of Guy V. Henry, USAMHI); Wedemeyer modestly neglects to mention his brief regimental command in his war memoirs, *Wedemeyer Reports!*

[3] Eric Linklater, *The Campaign in Italy*, London, 1951, pp. 26–7.

them, make no attempt to bury them. They believe in the evil eye and refuse to touch their own dead. First batch of prisoners coming in already and the civilians appear stunned. An old Italian colonel in fancy uniform sitting on the steps of Scoglitti city hall weeping.'[1]

Correspondent Ernie Pyle went ashore at Licata and found Sicily far different than he had conjured from the guidebooks. Instead of a lush, green, picturesque island, he found 'a drab, light brown country, and there weren't many trees. The fields of grain had been harvested and they were dry and naked and dusty. The villages were pale grey and indistinguishable at a distance from the rest of the country. Water was extremely scarce.'[2]

American troops who landed at Licata had expected a grim struggle but had encountered only token resistance. Of the heat and dust, many GIs were heard to grumble, 'Hell, this is just as bad as Africa.' Their talk was not of wine or women but of fields of ripe tomatoes which were treated like finds of gold![3]

When Patton went ashore the following day it was with thoughts of the ancient empires that had ruled Sicily in its heyday. He was not impressed with the natives who inhabited this part of the island and whom he called 'the dirtiest of all Sicilians'. As he drove to the front he could smell the enemy dead. 'The people of this country,' he wrote, 'are the most destitute and God-forgotten people I have ever seen.'[4]

Those Sicilians living along the coast awoke that morning to the extraordinary sight of hundreds of ships anchored off their once tranquil coastline. War had once again come to the shores of Sicily.

[1] Diary of Lieutenant Colonel Chester B. Hansen, USAMHI.
[2] *Brave Men*, op. cit., p. 31.
[3] Ibid., pp. 29–31.
[4] Patton, *War As I Knew It*, op. cit., p. 59.

CHAPTER 16

The D-Day Counterattacks

Hermann Goering Division is ordered to destroy the
enemy.
Order from OB South
[10 July 1943]

The announcement of the Allied glider landings from the Syracuse radio station came as no surprise to Guzzoni when the Commandant of the Messina naval base notified Sixth Army of the message they had monitored. It had already been a very long and difficult night for the old general, and the arrival of the British confirmed what he had expected all along. At 0415 he notified both his corps to expect amphibious landings that night in the Gela sector and along the southeast coast. His first orders were to Rossi, the XVI Corps commander, to reinforce immediately the threatened naval bases at Augusta and Syracuse.

Guzzoni considered it a hopeless waste of time to attempt to react to the multitude of Allied landings; the best he could do was commit his reserves to the most critical sectors. While Syracuse represented the most serious weakness, Guzzoni believed that between them, Group Schmalz and the Napoli Division could prevent a successful Allied thrust into the plain of Catania. He therefore ordered the main counterattack to be launched by Conrath's Hermann Goering Division against the Gela landings.[1]

By the morning of 12 July Guzzoni was dismayed to find that the defences protecting the Syracuse fortress area had ignominiously collapsed and the breakdown was rapidly spreading in the direction of Augusta. Rossi had been unable to muster anything resembling a useful counter to the swift British advance. Spearheaded by the 5th Division,* the British were everywhere

---

[1] *Sicily*, op. cit., pp. 120–1.
* The 5th Division (Major-General H. P. M. Berney-Ficklin) was the only Regular British division to participate in the Sicily campaign. It had been part of the BEF and in the ensuing three years had fought in Madagascar, followed by postings to India, Persia and Syria. The 50th and 51st Divisions were both Territorial units.

consolidating their grip and thrusting to the north. 30 Corps had cleared the Pachino peninsula of what little resistance remained. The 23rd Armoured Brigade under the control of the 51st Division was outside Vizzini by dusk on 12 July. The same day the Canadians had driven to Ragusa and made contact with units of the 45th Division. The US rifle company that had seized the town had captured not only the mayor and chief of police but also the main city switchboard. While awaiting the arrival of the Canadians some of them had 'amused themselves by answering phone calls from anxious Italian garrisons that wanted to know what was going on near the beaches'.[1] One astute war diarist noted that 'the myth that the Italians would fight with great fortitude in defence of their country was exploded'.[2]

Once Montgomery was assured of the success of the Eighth Army landings he began to exhort both corps commanders to push on as fast as possible. Leese was instructed to 'operate with great energy' towards Noto and Avola while Dempsey was told in the same words to head for Syracuse, and then Augusta.[3] Together with an excited Mountbatten, Montgomery came ashore near Pachino early on 11 July and to his delight learned that not only had Syracuse fallen to 13 Corps but that its port had been seized intact and undamaged. The most important of the Sicilian ports was now safely in Allied hands.

Montgomery's first moments ashore in Sicily were very nearly his last. Mountbatten describes what happened:

> We came to a long, narrow village which had a main road running through the centre, where it forked. Monty was sitting beside the driver; his ADC, I and my staff officer, Brigadier Antony Head, were sitting in the back. Suddenly there was a rat tat tat of machine guns and we saw a Messerschmitt flying down the main street gunning all the vehicles. All of us at the back immediately flung ourselves down, but not so Monty who sat bolt upright and didn't even turn his head to look at the Messerschmitt. As luck would have it we reached the fork just before the aircraft reached us; we went down the right hand fork and the aircraft went down the left hand fork and so we were missed. But Monty never turned a hair and didn't seem to be afraid.[4]

[1] Ibid., p. 189.
[2] War Diary of the 2nd Battalion, The Wiltshire Regiment (13th Brigade/5th Division). Quoted in *The Mediterranean and Middle East*, Vol. V, op. cit., p. 82.
[3] War Diary, HQ, Eighth Army, PRO (WO 169/8494).
[4] Quoted in Philip Ziegler, *Mountbatten*, London and New York, 1985, p. 204.

As Montgomery's biographer has revealed, 'far from being the reluctant general beloved of American military caricaturists, Monty was now almost indecently concerned with making haste rather than consolidating the bridgehead'.[1] Indeed, the image of the careful, cautious Monty was thoroughly dispelled in the early days of Sicily only to return several days later after the savage battles on the plain of Catania led to an unexpected and controversial change of plan for Eighth Army.

The 5th Division collided with part of Group Schmalz near Priolo on the Syracuse–Augusta highway, but the Germans were unable to do little more than delay the British advance. In three days Eighth Army captured all of southeastern Sicily, raising the expectation that the campaign might be a walkover after all. Despite their early successes, both British and American soldiers quickly learnt that Sicily was going to be an infantryman's war. In the first three days of the campaign the men of the 17th Brigade of the 5th Division marched nearly 100 miles in salt-water laden boots and in the next thirty-five days would march a great deal further.

The performance of the US 3d Division is an example of the extraordinary foresight of its commander. Truscott had anticipated just such a situation and upon assuming command of the division in March found his units deficient in marching ability. 'I had long felt that our standards for marching and fighting in the infantry were too low, not up to those of the Roman legions nor countless examples from our own frontier history, nor even to those of Stonewall Jackson's "Foot Cavalry" of Civil War fame.'[2] His intense programme to train his men to march at four miles per hour rather than the standard rate of two and a half miles per hour became known as the 'Truscott Trot' and his division was later rated as the best trained and disciplined of Patton's Seventh Army units. Truscott's insistence on tough physical training for his men eventually enabled most battalions to march fully combat-loaded at up to five miles per hour, and in Sicily this was to pay enormous dividends: the 3d Division marched the length and breadth of the island, from Licata to Agrigento, to Palermo and eventually to Messina under the most gruelling conditions.

[1] Nigel Hamilton, *Monty: Master of the Battlefield, 1942–1944*, op. cit., p. 298.
[2] Truscott, *Command Missions*, op. cit., pp. 175–6.

At the headquarters of the Hermann Goering Division at Caltagirone, German–Italian communications proved inefficient and Conrath heard officially of the Allied landings only through the German network from Kesselring's headquarters in Rome. Although unable to establish contact with Sixth Army, Conrath had already placed his division on full alert at 2200 hours the previous night. In a telephone conversation with von Senger, Conrath outlined his plans for a counterattack against Gela on the morning of 10 July. Both officers were unaware that Guzzoni had ordered the Hermann Goering to be attached to XVI Corps for what was to have been a co-ordinated counterattack by the Germans and the Livorno Division. It was the first of many mistakes the Axis defenders of Sicily committed in the days ahead.

In preparation for their first engagement Conrath organized the Hermann Goering into two *Kampfgruppen*, each a reinforced regiment: one infantry-heavy, the other tank-heavy.* The intent was to unleash both forces simultaneously against the 1st and 45th Divisions. Beginning at first light (0400), the division began to move from its bases around Caltagirone.

The western element was the tank-heavy task force under the command of the regimental tank commander, Oberst (Colonel) Urban. It was to move south via Niscemi on the secondary road which joined the Gela–Vittoria highway [Route 115] at Piano Lupo.

The infantry-heavy eastern task force was on the move via two secondary roads to a point just north of Biscari where they were once again to merge for an attack that was intended to carry them to the beaches where the main elements of the 45th Division had landed.

Conrath knew that his attack had to commence before 0900 if the Germans were to avoid the problem of attacking directly into the sun and thus favouring the Americans. However, 0900 passed as the two task forces were harassed by Allied aircraft and on the ground by panicking Italian troops fleeing into the mountains, who spread alarming and frequently confusing reports of advances in the Scoglitti sector. Their advance was further delayed

---

* The infantry task force consisted of two truck-mounted infantry regiments, an armoured artillery battalion and a company of seventeen Tiger tanks mounting an 88mm gun as main armament. The other force consisted of two battalions of Mark III and IV medium tanks both mounting 75mm guns, two armoured artillery battalions, an armoured reconnaissance and an engineer battalion which were fighting as infantry.

by the narrow twisting roads which slowed movement to crawling speed. When by 1000 the attack still had not begun, the western task force commander was relieved on the spot by Conrath, who assumed personal command.[1]

In war, plans seldom work in the manner intended and the experience of the Hermann Goering Division on 10 July was no exception. At the time the Hermann Goering was thought to be a well-trained, first-rate unit and some Allied correspondents covering Sicily were fond of using the term 'the crack Hermann Goering Division'. At this early stage of the Sicily campaign the division was mediocre, possessed an undeserved, inflated reputation and generally inept leadership which led von Senger to deplore its commitment to eastern Sicily instead of the better-trained and -led 15th Panzer Grenadier Division.[2] Only the artillery were seasoned troops; the rest were poorly trained and (with the exception of Group Schmalz which was operating as a virtually independent force to the east, led by the very able Colonel Wilhelm Schmalz) commanded by inexperienced officers. Had it not been for Conrath's timely presence the western task force might well have panicked and fled even before commencing its attack.[3]

Tanks and infantry were not accustomed to working together and the leaders of the Hermann Goering demonstrated no understanding of such a need in terrain which, for the most part, was wholly unsuitable for armoured warfare. Despite its shortcomings the division constituted a potentially lethal force when pitted against the vulnerable American units whose only support during the first forty-eight hours came from the United States Navy.

The Germans soon discovered that Sicily was ill-suited for the lumbering sixty-ton Tiger tanks, whose deployment was difficult. The steep hills, rugged mountains and many stone walls often forced these behemoths on to the poor Sicilian roads where they became easy targets for the Allied air forces. The Tigers also had considerable difficulty manoeuvring through the narrow streets of the Sicilian villages. The Tiger commander whose unit was attached to the eastern task force complained that his tanks were frequently separated from their protecting infantry, with the result that some Tigers which might otherwise have been salvaged and

[1] Bauer, MS# R-137, 'The Counterthrusts on the First Day, 10 July 1943'.
[2] Von Senger, *Neither Fear Nor Hope*, op. cit., p. 133.
[3] Bauer MS # R-137.

repaired had to be abandoned. In the first three days of fighting ten Tigers had to be blown up by their crews.*

Unknown to the German commanders, an Italian force from XVI Corps called Mobile Group E was already ahead of the Hermann Goering and about to launch a counterattack from the direction of Niscemi. The Italian commander had likewise split his force into two elements. One was to move from Niscemi towards Ponte Olivo airfield and then drive south along Route 117 which led directly into the northeastern edge of Gela. The other was ordered to move south down the same secondary road leading to the Piano Lupo road junction that Conrath had selected for his tank force. While the Germans were still struggling southwards the Italians began their advance towards Gela shortly before 0900.

The events occurring on the Niscemi road on the morning of 10 July have been the subject of considerable confusion and contradiction and offer an excellent example of what is meant by the term 'fog of war'. Not only were Mobile Group E and the Hermann Goering unaware of each other's presence but some of the men of the 82d Airborne were certain they were being attacked by Germans. The first enemy force to launch its attack down the Niscemi road about 0900 hours was the left pincer of Mobile Group E's two-pronged counterattack against Gela. Depending upon their location and the time, some of the 82d paratroopers might have engaged German troops. Some Germans were present at the Italian strongpoint captured several hours earlier by Captain Sayre; others were apparently reconnaissance elements of the western counterattack force of the Hermann Goering. Nevertheless, the German accounts are clear that their main force was at that time still getting itself disentangled in and around Niscemi.

Navy Lieutenant C. G. Lewis who was flying a light observation aircraft from the cruiser *Boise* first spotted Mobile Group E about 0900 some three miles from the Piano Lupo road junction. At 0910, Lieutenant Lewis called in naval gunfire from the *Boise*. This is supported by the postwar report prepared by the Historical Office of the Italian Army which states that the commander of Mobile Group E split his force of light tanks (an estimated thirty-two ten-ton Renaults, sixteen three-ton tanks and several even smaller

---

* The Tiger tank company was part of the 215th Tank Battalion which had been originally assigned to the 15th Panzer Grenadier Division, but had remained in southeast Sicily when the division was ordered to western Sicily by Kesselring.

World War I tanks) in half. Other naval gunfire answered a call for assistance from the 16th Infantry which was advancing inland from the beaches to join the paratroopers along the Niscemi road and at the 'Y'.* Other warships in the Gulf of Gela shelled the Italians advancing towards Piano Lupo. The 16th Infantry eventually broke up the Italian tank attack which had succeeded in advancing as far as the 'Y' and was heading towards Gela on Route 115 when two of its twenty tanks were knocked out and the advance stalled. Shortly thereafter the remainder withdrew into the foothills northeast of Gela.[1]

Soon after Captain Sayre and his tiny band of paratroopers of Company 'A' had seized the Italian strongpoint on the Niscemi road earlier that morning he was joined by Lieutenant Colonel Gorham and thirty more paratroopers, bringing the American force to approximately 100 men. After thwarting the initial enemy counterattack, Gorham recognized that his force could not hold off a more determined attack and that the time had come to withdraw to the south and seize his original objective of the Piano Lupo road junction. Captain Sayre was given the task of capturing the large pillbox complex guarding the road junction but, instead of attacking, he sent one of his Italian POWs as an emissary to demand surrender. The Italian defenders were told the paratroopers controlled the naval gunfire and if they failed to surrender at once that fire would be directed their way. As Sayre relates, 'The prisoner was evidently an eloquent speaker for in a very few minutes after he entered the first pillbox, all occupants of the three pillboxes in the area came out with their hands up.'[2]

The paratroopers were soon joined by the lead elements of the 1st Division's 16th Regimental Combat Team who had the same objective. This unit was Lieutenant Colonel Joseph Crawford's 2d Battalion and together with Gorham's paratroopers this combined force established defensive positions along the high ground astride the Piano Lupo road junction.

Nearly five hours later than planned the Hermann Goering Division finally launched its counterattack towards the beaches

---

[1] *Sicily*, op. cit., pp. 150–2; *Sicily–Salerno–Anzio*, op. cit., pp. 103–4; 1st Infantry Division G-3 Journal, 10 July 1943; 82d Airborne G-2 Historical Record; Sayre account and Bauer MS # R-137.

[2] Sayre, 'The Operations of Company "A", 505th Parachute Infantry (82d Airborne Division) Airborne Landings in Sicily, 9–24 July 1943', loc. cit.

* See Chapter 13.

and Gela. The tank-heavy task force driving south along the Niscemi road struck the 1st Division/82d Airborne force at Piano Lupo while the infantry-heavy eastern task force was moving from its assembly point west of Biscari under orders to cross the Acate River and attack Piano Lupo from the east.* The stage was thus set for the first showdown between German and American forces in Sicily.

This engagement was strictly one-sided as a deluge of naval gunfire broke up the tank attack, and small-arms fire from dug-in paratroopers and infantrymen dispersed the German infantry, creating so much chaos that even Conrath's personal presence failed to provide the incentive for the force to regroup and continue their attack. Despite their superior numbers the Hermann Goering had no counter to the steel curtain provided by the US cruisers and destroyers offshore in the Gulf of Gela. The western task force slowly withdrew to the north towards Niscemi, while a gleeful 1st Division officer reported, 'Tanks are withdrawing; it seems we are too much for them.'[1]

To the east the Hermann Goering task force collided head-on with Lieutenant Colonel William H. Schaefer's 1st Battalion, 180th Infantry, assisted by some stray paratroopers who had joined up with his battalion. The German task force had long since lost contact with Conrath and had no idea of the situation to the west. In the ensuing battle a greatly inferior American force blunted the German advance, in no small part because the supporting Tigers were unable to manoeuvre in the terraced terrain of dense groves of olive trees.[2]

After the stinging rebuke delivered by Schaefer's men, Conrath sent his chief of staff to investigate and this officer found that not only had one of the two infantry battalions been inexplicably held in reserve but that the tanks and infantry were not co-operating with one another. Under his prodding, the force regrouped and began a fresh attack which overwhelmed the Americans. Schaefer and most of his men were captured and those who escaped were forced to retreat towards the coastal highway. The gallant Colonel

[1] G-3 Journal, 1st Infantry Division, 10 July 1943, Modern Military Field Branch, National Archives, Suitland, Maryland.

[2] Sicily, op. cit., p. 154, and von Senger, 'The Sicilian Campaign – 1943', Part II, An Cosantoir, July 1950.

* Biscari was formerly called Acate and on postwar maps appears under its original name.

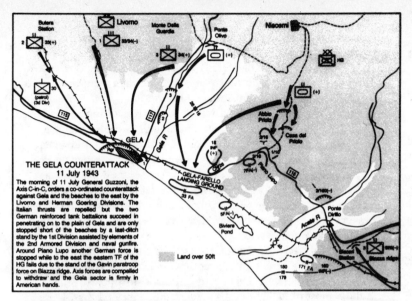

THE GELA COUNTERATTACK
11 July 1943

The morning of 11 July General Guzzoni, the Axis C-in-C, orders a co-ordinated counterattack against Gela and the beaches to the east by the Livorno and Herman Goering Divisions. The Italian thrusts are repelled but the two German reinforced tank battalions succeed in penetrating on to the plain of Gela and are only stopped short of the beaches by a last-ditch stand by the 1st Division assisted by elements of the 2nd Armored Division and naval gunfire. Around Piano Lupo another German force is stopped while to the east the eastern TF of the HG fails due to the stand of the Gavin paratroop force on Biazza ridge. Axis forces are compelled to withdraw and the Gela sector is firmly in American hands.

THE GELA COUNTERATTACK 11 JULY 1943

Schaefer was well known in the 45th Division for his frequent exhortations to his troops not to take foolish chances and become a prisoner of war. 'A captive can't fight,' he would tell his men. Schaefer remained a POW until liberated in 1945 from a German prison camp. General Middleton recalls receiving a brief but poignant note written on brown paper which read: 'Dear General, I'm sorry I got captured. Schaefer.'[1]

The Germans had now found an open gap in the American defences and circumstances were occurring which could have placed the beaches of the 1st Division in grave jeopardy. It was precisely the sort of opportunity Conrath and von Senger were seeking. However, instead of a German triumph, Schaefer's sister (3d) battalion was able to break up the attack. Once again, the leadership of the Hermann Goering Division was found seriously wanting as the Germans panicked and fled to the rear in complete disarray. During the night, while his men were engaged in an attack, the commander of the task force abandoned his troops and

[1] *Troy H. Middleton*, op. cit., p. 148; *Sicily*, pp. 154–5, and Bauer MS # R-137.

returned to Division HQ to justify his actions to Conrath. He was immediately relieved, later court-martialled, and his place taken by the chief of staff.[1]

Although the Italians had fared equally badly, they could at least claim to have posed a far more serious threat than their German ally. When Mobile Group E launched its attack to the west, a battalion from the Livorno Division began advancing towards Gela. Had the combined German and Italian forces been able to co-ordinate their attacks and strike the 1st Division about 0900, there might have been a far different outcome. But, as we now know, neither force was aware of the presence of the other, and the delay in the German attack provided the 1st and 45th Divisions with valuable time to push further inland and away from the beaches where they would have been exposed and far more vulnerable to counterattack.

The Italian attacks against Gela itself were savagely repelled by Darby's Force X. The right pincer of Mobile Group E penetrated into Gela from Ponte Olivo and although disrupted by naval gunfire, most of its light tanks made it intact into the city. Once again, the inability of the enemy infantry and tanks to work together as a team produced dire results as the Italians tangled with Darby's men in the streets of Gela in a lethal game of hide and seek. Using the buildings as cover, the Rangers, now in the role of defenders, used hand grenades and rocket launchers against the tanks. Some Rangers worked from the rooftops, throwing stick grenades at the tanks. When two of them ran out of grenades they lugged 15 lb blocks of TNT to the top of a building from where they were dropped on the tanks.[2] The rigorous training given the Rangers in Ulster was demonstrated again and again as the Italians got more than they bargained for from Force X which gave no quarter and always did the unexpected. It was during this engagement that Darby won the DSC for unhesitatingly taking on and destroying an Italian tank.

The battalion from the Livorno Division was cut to pieces when

---

[1] MS # R-137 and *Sicily*, p. 155. According to von Senger's account, he had personally asked for the replacement of the two task force commanders. However, von Senger's authority as an Army liaison officer over a Luftwaffe unit was at best tenuous, but Conrath was obviously embarrassed and dismayed by the performance of his troops and he needed no prodding from von Senger to replace both commanders.

[2] *Sicily*, p. 152, and William O. Darby and William H. Baumer, *We Led the Way: Darby's Rangers*, New York, 1985, p. 99.

it advanced in a formal parade-ground formation reminiscent of nineteenth-century warfare. The Livorno was considered the best Italian unit in Sicily but its tactics were a sad illustration of the ineptitude of the Italian Army. Patrols later surveyed the carnage and found the bodies and equipment littered over a large area of the battlefield. As one Ranger officer later wrote, 'The poorly led Italians had paid an extravagantly high price for their failure.'[1]

So ended the first unsuccessful attempts by Axis forces to crush the US landings, and while it was evident the counterattacks had been badly bungled there was little doubt they had been merely a preliminary skirmish and that the real test was yet to come. The American commanders were certain the following day would see a renewal of the German and Italian counterattacks.

[1] Lieutenant James J. Altieri, *Darby's Rangers*, Durham, N.C., 1945, p. 50.

CHAPTER 17

D+1: The Crucial Day

The Panzers came with all their tanks
And thought that we were sunk.
Bazookas, guts and one-oh-fives
Turned them into junk.

Verse from 1st Division song[1]

The night of 10/11 July was spent preparing once again to resist an all-out effort by the Hermann Goering and Livorno Divisions to push the 1st and 45th Divisions back into the sea. The threat posed by the Hermann Goering on D-Day afternoon led Patton to order his floating reserve ashore in support of the 1st Division. This was Major General Hugh Gaffey's 2d Armored Division (less Combat Command A, which was acting as Truscott's floating reserve) augmented by the 1st Division's own 18th Regimental Combat Team. Patton also considered ordering a second airborne drop that night but postponed it because of the unstable situation ashore.

By the morning of 11 July only four battalions of reserve infantry were ashore. The landing of the armour and artillery was impeded by offshore sandbars and mines found on several beaches. Operations had to be improvised and moved to other beaches when a combination of high tides, congestion, enemy interference and a lack of exit ramps caused extremely serious problems and inordinate delays on the assigned beaches.[2]

---

[1] 1st Division song: words and music by Lieutenant Colonel D. McB. Curtis.

[2] *Sicily*, op. cit., Chapter VII. Moving vehicles across the soft sand and onto firmer ground proved a nightmare as did the lack of suitable exits. The official history has called the situation in the 45th Division sector 'most deplorable' and it was scarcely better at Gela. The poor situation in the CENT sector was worsened by the Army Engineers who comprised the shore parties. They were mostly misfits and rejects from combat units and, on the whole, were so ineffective that Middleton characterized them as 'rabble'. These men were 'untrained and insubordinate; some even devoted their energies to rifling soldiers' barrack bags and the personal baggage of officers'. So bad was this unit that its commander was court-martialled. (Cf. *Sicily–Salerno–Anzio*, op. cit., pp. 139–40.)

At dusk on 10 July, von Senger visited the battlefield and saw for himself the extent of the failure of the Hermann Goering. Conrath was told, presumably by von Senger, that his division was now attached to XVI Corps and was to mount a co-ordinated counterattack at 0600 the next morning in conjunction with the Livorno Division and the remnants of Mobile Group E. Their object was to push the Allied invaders back into the sea at Gela. Each division would attack with three separate task forces.[1]

The same night Guzzoni's order for a co-ordinated counterattack was affirmed by Kesselring who sent similar orders via Luftwaffe channels for the Hermann Goering to resume its attack and destroy the invaders the following day. For operations on 11 July, Conrath elected to attack with three elements. The tank force was split in two and ordered to converge on the Gela plain and attack US forces on the beaches. One tank battalion was to attack via Ponte Olivo while the main effort was again to be down the Niscemi–Piano Lupo road where the other tank battalion was to seize the two dominant hills overlooking the road junction. The infantry force was to resume its attack from the vicinity of Biscari, drive across the Acate River and join the two tank forces near Piano Lupo where all three would then roll up the 1st Division beachhead from east to west, while the Livorno Division struck from the west to complete the task.[2]

Terry Allen was renowned for his successful employment of night attacks and he had no intention of waiting for the Hermann Goering to strike first. He ordered two regiments to attack at midnight towards the main divisional objective, the Ponte Olivo airfield. By dawn the 2d and 3d Battalions of the 26th Regiment were dug in along Route 117 leading to the airfield. On the Niscemi road two blocking forces had been set up at Casa del Priolo and amid the orchards on the ridge 1000 yards further north at Abbio Priolo.

This time the attack jumped off only fifteen minutes late at 0615, backed by German and Italian aircraft which pounded the beach areas and attacked the US ships anchored offshore. The graphic evidence provided by the events of 11 July attests to the validity of

---

[1] MS # R-137, loc. cit. There is some confusion where Conrath got his orders. He claims to have visited Sixth Army on 10 July but it more likely was XVI Corps where General Rossi briefed Conrath and General Chirieleison, the Livorno commander, on the forthcoming attack.

[2] MS # R-138, 'The Counterattack on the Second Day, 11 July 1943', USAMHI.

the RAF historian's conclusion that the air support provided Seventh Army on this most critical of days was wholly inadequate. On D-Day there had been six requests for direct air support of the assault forces, *none* of which was ever flown. On 11 July the 1st Division would request five more of which only one was flown in the late afternoon.[1]

In their absence, the most desperate battles of the Sicilian campaign were fought on 11 July as men of the 1st Division and Gavin's paratroopers bore the brunt of a series of fierce enemy counterattacks all across the Gela front. The Allied air forces were scarcely to be seen and their promises of adequate and timely support never materialized; it was the US Navy which came to the rescue and helped save the day.

Italian and German tank forces launched parallel attacks on both sides of the Ponte Olivo road. Heavy artillery and mortar fire halted the Italians short of Gela but most of the panzers escaped serious losses and despite naval gunfire support successfully debouched onto the Gela plain and headed east towards the crucial Piano Lupo road junction.

A savage encounter took place at Abbio Priolo as outgunned paratroopers and infantrymen duelled with German tanks at point-blank range and repelled the first enemy thrust with the accurate assistance of close artillery support from the 7th Field Artillery Battalion and nearby anti-tank guns.[2]

Conrath was again in personal command of this action and, still smarting over the setback a day earlier, was determined to crush the American force. He ordered the attack to be renewed and this time it was too powerful to be resisted. The embattled defenders of Abbio Priolo were forced to withdraw to their previous day's positions at Piano Lupo.[3]

To the east, where Route 115 crosses the Acate River at Ponte Drillo, the 180th Regiment was in an equally precarious state. A small force of infantry and paratroops was forced to withdraw to the beaches despite the excellent fire support of the destroyer *Beatty* which hurled nearly 800 rounds of five-inch shells into the advancing German column.

While this was taking place, Colonel Gavin's quest for the

---

[1] *Sicily*, op. cit., p. 167.
[2] Ibid., pp. 166–7.
[3] Ibid., p. 168.

battlefield was finally ended when he made his way to Route 115 about 0830 hours, 11 July. As he headed west on foot along the Vittoria–Gela road Gavin began rounding up scattered groups of paratroopers and infantry from the 45th Division and succeeded in attacking a ridge overlooking the Biscari road and the Biscari–Gela road junction. Called Biazza Ridge by the Americans, it held the same critical importance as the Piano Lupo site further west, and it became the place where Gavin and his men made a valiant stand against an overwhelmingly superior enemy force. Supported by only a few 81 mm mortars and two 75 mm howitzers, Gavin ordered his men to establish defensive positions pending the arrival of help. When Gavin and his men attempted to dig protective foxholes for protection against the attacking German infantry and Tiger tanks they found the hard shale of the ridge virtually impossible to penetrate. Gavin's entrenching tool bent and even using his heavy steel helmet it was all he could do to scrape out a small trench deep enough to avoid the treads of the Tigers. Even worse was the lack of effect his bazookas were having on the heavily armoured Tigers: the projectiles would bounce harmlessly off the steel plates while they continued their relentless advance. Over forty years later the sense of frustration and determination was still evident in Gavin's voice.[1]

By chance, Gavin and his pathetically small band of men found themselves the only Allied force between the Germans and their unhindered exploitation of the exposed left flank of the 45th Division and the thinly held right flank of the 1st Division. Against Gavin was the entire eastern task force of the Hermann Goering Division: over 700 infantry of the 1st Panzer Grenadier Regiment, the armoured artillery battalion and the company of Tiger tanks.

Fortunately for the paratroopers the Germans were still paying for the disastrous lapse of leadership which had stalled their attack the previous day. As Major Vandervoort points out, 'They had more than enough capabilities to wipe us off the ridge had they wanted to do so. Either their mission was to defend or their commander was lousy.'[2] Vandervoort was correct on both counts.

---

[1] Interview of 2 August 1984. Gavin himself had come within ten feet of a Tiger and had fired a bazooka only to see the projectile bounce away like a ping-pong ball. Gavin considered the American bazooka so useless that he and his paratroopers employed the more lethal and reliable German *panzerfaust* whenever one was captured.

[2] Letter, Colonel Benjamin H. Vandervoort to the author, 23 September 1985.

According to the postwar account of a Hermann Goering staff officer, the men were still nervous and 'the units were brought into it [the attack] in confusion. The situation on the left Division flank had to be considered dangerous.' Consequently, the left task force assumed a largely defensive posture throughout 11 July and 'it was possible to use these troops in defence only because the enemy did not press forward'.[1]

The two sides exchanged fire throughout that terrible day when Gavin's tiny force held out despite fierce German pressure and steadily mounting casualties. The defenders of Biazza Ridge had been told by their commander that 'we're staying on this god-damned ridge – no matter what happens'.[2] Gavin's men had acquired two pack 75 mm howitzers both of which were now being employed as direct-fire anti-tank weapons. 'One anchored our right flank. The other was on the military crest of the ridge – maybe seventy-five yards in from the road. That one hit a Tiger tank, stopping it from moving forward on the road.' Despite the vast mismatch between the two sides, Gavin continued to display his unique brand of leadership:

> There was a large concrete culvert under the road 100 yards in back of the geographic crest of the ridge. A man could stand upright in it. With people getting killed in their foxholes because of tree bursts, I suggested we move the command group back into the cover of the culvert. Colonel Gavin said, 'Ben, you don't appreciate what is at stake here.' He was a very brave commander and dedicated to the belief that the commander's presence was an inspiration to the troops. The culvert became a quick-stop Aid Station.[3]

By early evening the situation had become very grim when relief arrived in the form of six Sherman tanks which suddenly appeared to the accompaniment of loud cheers from the weary paratroops. 'It was a very dramatic moment,' recalled Gavin.[4] Throughout the day individual paratroopers had materialized to join the fray. About mid-afternoon a platoon of Company 'B', 307th Airborne

[1] Colonel Hellmut Bergengruen, 'Division "Hermann Goering" in Sicily (10–14 July 1943)', translation of MS # C-087a, Papers of Rear Admiral Samuel Eliot Morison, US Navy Historical Center.
[2] Quoted in *Drop Zone Sicily*, op cit., p. 142.
[3] Vandervoort, loc. cit.
[4] *On to Berlin*, op. cit., p. 33. The tanks had arrived courtesy of Bradley who was present at Middleton's CP when Gavin's representative, Captain Albert Ireland, reported the urgent need to send immediate help to the men on Biazza Ridge.

Engineers, arrived in time to drive off an attempt by German infantry to outflank the airborne positions. 'It was remarkable,' remembers Vandervoort, 'the way the scattered troopers came in on the sound of the guns.'[1]

Using every man he could round up – infantry, engineers, clerks, cooks, truck drivers, even two Navy fire control officers – Gavin decided at dusk the time had come when he could strike back at the Germans whose attempts at advance – however inept – had been held up by a vastly inferior, outgunned force of American paratroopers. Gavin launched his attack with the Shermans in close support. Things began to happen quickly. Lieutenant Harold Swingler caught and killed the crew of a Tiger outside their tank and captured the sixty-ton monster intact. Others overran and captured twelve 120 mm mortars. Although the Germans had not been inclined to be aggressive at Biazza Ridge on 11 July, they had nevertheless posed a severe threat and there is little doubt that the furious defence of the ridge deterred the German commanders from pressing their considerable advantage.

After the battle, brief services were held on Biazza Ridge for the American dead. A sombre Gavin stood with head bowed in prayer and tears in his eyes as the chaplain prayed for their immortal souls.[2] Gavin's valour and superlative leadership on Biazza Ridge earned him the Distinguished Service Cross.

Although the defenders of Biazza Ridge did not know of it, a decision to break off the counterattack had already been made. At 1600 the German situation report read:

> The counterattack against enemy landings has failed. Support by Italian forces can no longer be counted on, nor can Italian orders be expected. The enemy is continually being reinforced and is beginning to surround the HG Panzer Division from the west

[1] Vandervoort, loc. cit.

[2] *Drop Zone Sicily*, op. cit., p. 149. The chaplain who performed the service was the Reverend George B. Wood who later earned the distinction of being the only chaplain in the US Army to make four combat jumps. Wood aided in the burial of thirty-four dead Americans and he remembers Biazza Ridge as a gruesome experience. 'The hot Sicilian sun made it all the more so. But all of us by our training were literally combat veterans. We could not stop and mourn over the dead. We had to go on to our other objectives. And I had been in the ministry five years and I was professionally experienced. I had met death before, but this was a little different. These were my friends!' A monument dedicated to the valour of the defenders of Biazza Ridge was later erected by the local Sicilian community. (Letter, Reverend Wood to the author, 10 July 1985.)

and east. Continued defence in present positions would result in the annihilation of the Division. Effective resistance is possible only in a shorter continuous defence position of all German units in Sicily in terrain favourable to defence.[1]

Elsewhere on 11 July battles raged all across the Gela front. Darby's Rangers, aided by the cruiser *Savannah*, rained fire on the advancing columns of the Livorno Division attacking Gela, devastating the Italians in a dreadful scene reminiscent of the previous day. Later it was learned this action had completely finished the Livorno as a fighting force.[2]

Earlier that morning Patton could no longer stand being cooped up in the *Monrovia* and made his first appearance in Gela where he waded ashore, to the whir of Signal Corps cameras, in an immaculate uniform complete with necktie, knee-length polished black leather boots and twin ivory-handled revolvers. En route to Allen's 1st Division Command Post, Patton spied Darby's CP and was able to witness the attack by Italian tanks. When he saw the advancing tanks he demanded of a young naval officer standing nearby with a radio, 'If you can connect with your Goddamn Navy, tell them for God's sake to drop some shell fire on the road'. Tanks of both the Hermann Goering and the Livorno Division were thrusting down both sides of the Ponte Olivo road. Soon shells from the cruiser *Boise* began to hammer the advancing tanks.[3] Before departing from the Ranger CP, Patton instructed Ranger Captain James B. Lyle to 'kill every one of the goddam bastards'.[4]

The main German effort remained east of Gela where the 1st and 2nd Tank Battalions had now joined forces in a thrust intended to take them across the Gela plain towards Highway 115 and the beaches beyond. In the process the two panzer units had overwhelmed several 1st Division units and their guns were causing considerable damage. Colonel George A. Taylor, commander of the 16th Infantry who later won fame and a DSC on Omaha Beach, ordered that 'Everyone stays put just where he is . . . Under no circumstances will anyone be pulled back. Take cover from

[1] Bergengruen in MS # C-087a, loc. cit.
[2] *Sicily*, op. cit., p. 170, and MS # R-138.
[3] *Patton*, op. cit., p. 291.
[4] Quoted in *Sicily*, p. 170.

tanks. Don't let anything else get through . . .' However, as the situation grew more and more grave, Taylor was forced to signal the Division CP that 'We are being overrun by tanks. In our 2d Battalion area, the enemy has ten tanks in front of the battalion and has ringed them with an additional thirty; we have no idea what is going on to the east of us.'[1]

By early afternoon the panzers had penetrated the centre of the 1st Division's defences and were loose on the Gela plain, threatening even the Division CP.* During the afternoon Patton turned up at the CP but found that the 1st Division commander was away. When the dog-tired Allen returned he found a euphoric Patton sitting with a big cigar in his mouth, his feet propped up on a field desk. How was the division doing? asked Patton. Allen replied that it was no tea party and the division was doing OK but needed additional artillery support. With a wave of his hand Patton said, 'I'm now an Army commander; take this up with Keyes.'[2]

During his visit to Allen it was evident that Patton either failed to appreciate the dilemma of the 1st Division or was engaging in his long-standing habit of baiting his old friend. Allen was one of the most attack-minded men ever to command a US division but at that moment his one and only concern was to ensure his battered division somehow survived the fury of the German counterattack. Patton, however, felt it necessary to use the occasion to express his displeasure that the 1st Division had failed to take Ponte Olivo airfield.

For reasons which are still unexplained, Conrath mistakenly assumed he was about to win a great victory, for he signalled that the 1st Division had been forced to re-embark temporarily to

---

[1] Unpublished account of Major General Terry Allen, Terry Allen Papers, USAMHI, and *Danger Forward: The Story of the 1st Division in World War II*, Washington, D.C., 1947, Chapter III.

[2] Porter interview, loc. cit.

* The counterattack on 11 July by the Hermann Goering Division was not unexpected. On D-Day Allen had ordered every available unit forward to meet the expected Axis attack. The commanders and staff of the 1st Division knew of the presence of the Hermann Goering and that they could expect a co-ordinated tank–infantry counterattack some time soon after the assault landings. Porter was fortunate to have working in his G-2 section a young officer (Captain Klotz) whom he had recruited in Tunisia. Klotz prepared an excellent terrain map of the invasion area complete with lights and obstacles. According to Porter this enabled the 1st Division staff to work out in detail the best terrain for enemy tanks, what routes they were likely to employ and how long it would take for them to reach the beaches. The regimental commanders were then brought in and briefed, using the map. (Porter interview, loc. cit.)

escape his counterattack.* At Sixth Army this raised false hopes in Guzzoni and von Senger who long after the war still believed the tale.[1] There was never any such action by the 1st Division nor any message to that effect intercepted by the Germans. Moreover, as Conrath would soon learn, his panzers were unable to breach the tree-lined Gela highway where American artillerymen joined the fray by depressing the tubes of their howitzers over the dunes and firing point-blank at the panzers. Engineers, infantry and several Shermans of Colonel I. D. White's† Combat Command B, 2d Armored Division, were finally able to get free of the beaches and add their support. The ferocious fire poured into the Gela plain stopped the panzers of the Hermann Goering Division dead in their tracks.

The US official histories ascribe most of the credit for defeating

---

[1] MS # R-138 and *An Cosantoir*, July 1950, op. cit. Von Senger claims to have seen American troops re-embarking when he visited the battlefield on the afternoon of 11 July. He very likely was witnessing the *debarkation* of reinforcements. The US official history is emphatic that no American troops were re-embarked as a result of the German counter-attack on 11 July. The sights which greeted von Senger as he prowled the front during the first three days of HUSKY mirrored Eisenhower's first impressions. On 12 July both observed the scene in the Bay of Gela from vantage points only a few kilometres apart. In his report to Marshall, Eisenhower observed that 'I must say that the sight of hundreds of vessels, with landing craft everywhere . . . was unforgettable'. (Manuscript # C-095, 'Liaison Activities with Italian 6th Army', based on von Senger's personal war diary, German Report Series, USAMHI copy.)

* The story of the alleged 1st Division withdrawal first appeared in the postwar account of Guzzoni's Chief of Staff, Colonel (later General) Emilio Faldella: *Lo Sbarco e la Difesa della Sicilia* (Rome, 1956), which was written with the full approval of the Italian Army Historical Office. According to Faldella, at 1130 hours, 11 July, Patton sent a message in the clear ordering the 1st Division to prepare for re-embarkation. This message was allegedly intercepted by Sixth Army and immediately passed to Guzzoni who, along with Faldella, recalls the message reading: 'Bury the equipment on the beaches and be ready to re-embark – Patton.' The original document did not survive the war but appeared in the Army war diary. There are sufficient witnesses to establish that Sixth Army did indeed intercept a message but its source is a mystery. A British account by Hugh Pond (*Sicily*, London, 1962) suggests that 'some senior officer in the Gela bridgehead took it upon himself to issue such a message' (p. 99). Patton came ashore from the *Monrovia* at approximately 0930 hours, 11 July, and remained in and around Gela until approximately 1900 hours. That Patton or any member of his staff issued such a message is preposterous. The senior commanders ashore – Darby, Allen and I. D. White (2d Armored) – were strong-minded leaders who had no intention of surrendering their foothold in Sicily. In separate letters to the author both the G-2 (Porter) and General White deny that any such message was ever sent. As Porter relates, 'There was no, repeat *no*, thought on the part of General Allen of leaving our beachhead at Gela'. (Letter of 18 November 1985.)

Not only were naval personnel ashore ordered by Patton himself to 'get all hands up here to fight', but the operational records of the units who fought in the Gela battle are singularly devoid of any evidence that a re-embarkation order/message ever existed.

† I. D. White was a 1922 graduate of Norwich University, Vermont, who commanded the 2d Armored Division during the last six months of the war and later became one of the few non-graduates of West Point ever to rise to four-star rank.

the German counterattack to the Navy. However, as a recent account reveals, the role of the tiny force of the 2d Armored Division was significant. Four tanks of First Lieutenant James A. White's third platoon, 'C' Company, 82d Reconnaissance Battalion, had at last struggled free of the nightmare of the soft sand which threw their tracks, and the chicken wire matting which thoroughly fouled both the tracks and drive sprockets of the Shermans. Colonel White ordered them to occupy positions along the Gela–Vittoria highway where they were soon joined by an itinerant 105 mm howitzer of the 32d Artillery Battalion. Some 4,000 yards to the north were the thirty to forty panzers comprising Conrath's main striking force. The CCB executive officer, Lieutenant Colonel Briard P. Johnson, stood on the rear deck of a Sherman pointing out targets for the Shermans to engage. 'The tanks scored hits against the approaching German panzers at the same time that indirect fire from artillery batteries, 4.2-inch mortars and perhaps naval gunfire was landing in the area. The huge amount of indirect fire concealed the presence of direct fire weapons . . . During the battle, two tanks had stoppages or malfunctions with their main gun. The sergeant tank commanders calmly got out of their tanks and cleaned the bores of their weapons while under fire. One commander led his tank to a better firing position.'[1]

As other tanks came ashore they were rushed into service. When the Executive Officer of the 3d Battalion, 67th Armored Regiment, Major Clifton Batchelder, reported to Colonel White he was told to move his tanks inland and engage the panzers. When asked what the plans and orders were, White brusquely replied, 'Plans hell! This may be Custer's last stand!'[2]

Ultimately, no German tank ever penetrated beyond the Gela highway. The fighting was so close and so intense that the naval guns were temporarily silenced for fear of hitting friendly forces. Nevertheless, under the intense shelling from artillery, mortars, Shermans and anti-tank guns the Germans found their attack had run its course. Unable to counter the hail of fire being relentlessly showered upon them, they began slowly to pull back towards the foothills to the north. As they did so the US Navy supplied

---

[1] Donald E. Houston, *Hell on Wheels*, The 2d Armored Division, San Rafael, 1977, pp. 165/7.
[2] Ibid., p. 166.

the *coup de grâce* by chasing them with naval gunfire. On the battlefield the Germans left behind the burning wreckage of six-teen panzers whose oily black smoke served as mute evidence of what a near-run thing the battle had been.[1]

An equally desperate battle was fought around Piano Lupo where Taylor's 1st and 2d Battalions and Gorham's paratroopers had managed to knock out four of the six tanks that had broken into their positions. Using a trick later effectively employed by the Germans in Normandy, the Americans let the tanks roll over their positions and then struck them from the rear. 'Hardnose' Gorham, the courageous paratroop commander, was killed in a similar engagement on 12 July when he deliberately exposed himself as bait as he stalked a panzer with a bazooka.[*]

Eight hours into the second major counterattack in two days Conrath once again acknowledged failure. More than a third of his tanks had been lost, the eastern task force was being thoroughly stymied by Gavin's paratroopers and was never a factor in the main battle; it was evident the momentum of the attack could not be successfully maintained. While the western elements withdrew to the north, bitter fighting continued east of the Acate River until well into the night as the Gavin force struck back at its tormentors.

Guzzoni also recognized the counterattack had failed and he now ordered XVI Corps to turn its attention to the British sector where there was grave concern at the ease with which Syracuse had fallen to Eighth Army. The Hermann Goering was ordered to shift its main elements to the east to assist Group Schmalz and the Napoli Division.

Conrath blamed the German setback on poor leadership and issued this stinging rebuke to his officers and men:

---

[1] *Sicily*, op. cit., pp. 170–1. Another unit that played a key role in thwarting the panzers was the 32d Field Artillery Battalion whose guns poured direct fire across the tops of the sand dunes. Today, a few hundred metres north of the battleground runs a portion of the multi-lane *autostrada* which now encircles the entire coastline of Sicily.

[*] Lieutenant Colonel Gorham was one of several Americans who traded their lives for a Mark IV tank. While the bazooka was virtually useless against a Tiger, it was lethal when employed against the more lightly armoured Mark IV. Gorham stalked a Mark IV and drew its attention while several other bazooka teams moved in to ambush the unwary tank crew. In the exchange of fire Gorham was killed. Moments later the tank was destroyed by bazooka fire. Some accounts have suggested Gorham's men tangled with Tigers around Piano Lupo, but the only Tigers engaged on 11 July were attached to the eastern task force near Biscari. Gorham was posthumously awarded two Distinguished Service Crosses for his gallantry on 10, 11 and 12 July.

Panzer Division Hermann Goering
Commanding General   DIV HQ 12 Jul 43

I had the bitter experience to watch scenes, during these last few days, which are not worthy of a German soldier, particularly not of a soldier of the Panzerdivision Hermann Goering.

Persons came running to the rear, hysterically crying, because they had heard the detonation of a single shot fired somewhere in the landscape. Others, believing in false rumours, moved whole columns to the rear. In one instance, supplies were senselessly distributed to soldiers and civilians by a supply unit that had fallen victim to a rumour. I want to state in these instances, that these acts were committed not only by the youngest soldiers, but also by NCOs and warrant officers.

Panic, 'Panzer fear', and the spreading of rumours are to be eliminated by the severest measures. Withdrawal without orders, and cowardice, are to be punished on the spot, and, if necessary, by the use of weapons.

I shall apply the severest measures of court-martial against such saboteurs of the fight for freedom of our nation, and I shall not hesitate to give death sentences in serious cases.

I expect that all officers will use their influence in order to suppress such an undignified attitude in the Panzerdivision Hermann Goering.

/s/   CONRATH
                       Commanding General
                       Hermann Goering Division[1]

Back aboard the *Monrovia* that night Patton's chief of staff confided in his diary the opinion that Patton's personal presence at the front lines that day had much to do with the failure of the German counterattack.[2] Patton's presence and that of Bradley on 11 July had little to do with the successful American stand. Throughout the remainder of the Sicily campaign, Patton's longstanding policy of visiting his troops at the front had mixed effects on troop morale. When Gavin met Patton on a bluff overlooking Gela harbour on 12 July the Seventh Army commander took one look at the tired and dirty paratroop colonel and immediately took out his silver flask and passing it over said, 'Gavin, you look like

---

[1] AFHQ Intelligence Notes No. 18, 1 August 1943, AFHQ Papers, PRO (WO 204/983).
[2] *The Patton Papers*, Vol. II, op. cit., p. 278.

you need a drink – have one.'[1] Gavin considered Patton's personal presence positive, but, as we shall see, others felt it sometimes had a negative impact.

The Rangers, infantry, paratroopers, artillerymen and tankers – in fact, virtually anyone with a weapon – contributed, along with the magnificent support of the Navy, to withstanding the Axis counterattacks. Everywhere that day were American heroes. Bradley believed the Navy deserved special credit for helping to save the day by their relentless fire on the enemy armour.[2] Conspicuous by their absence were the Allied air forces.

When word of the Allied invasion was flashed to Rome the first reaction was to order Axis aircraft to attack the invasion force from bases in Italy. Although there were scattered air attacks against the Western Task Force on D-Day these were largely ineffective and never posed a serious threat. The official US naval historian claims this was indeed fortunate, arguing that there was virtually no air cover in evidence until 12 July and those aircraft which did appear were ineffectual. Unlike the Eastern Task Force, which received excellent air support from Malta- and Pantelleria-based aircraft, air cover for the Gela force was the object of considerable criticism. Admiral Morison vehemently charged that the system of requesting air support from the fleet to Cunningham's HQ in Malta to Tedder's HQ in Tunis and finally to the air command[s] concerned was cumbersome and generally obsolete by the time help arrived.

> Combat air patrol over DIME [Gela] never amounted to more than two to eight planes at any time during the first two crucial days, and for the most part none were present. These few and far-between friendlies were of slight assistance, because, in the first place, no Air Force officer embarked with Admiral Hewitt had any authority over them, and, second, because the Army [Air Force] fighter-director team in [the] *Samuel Chase* [flagship of Rear Admiral J. L. Hall, Commander Task Force 81, DIME Attack Force] did not know its business. The fighter-director unit in *Monrovia* did a little better, but was apt to announce 'Red' alerts without stating the direction from which the attackers were approaching. A formation of 32 German planes once

---

[1] Gavin, *On to Berlin*, op. cit., p. 43.
[2] Papers of Lieutenant Colonel Chester B. Hansen, USAMHI, and *A General's Life*, op. cit., p. 183.

flew over the transports without any interference from Allied fighters that were supposed to be protecting them.[1]

According to Morison, Admiral Ramsay, like Admiral Hewitt, was hampered by lack of Air Force representation and had sailed for Sicily still uncertain as to exactly what support his fleet would receive from Spaatz's Northwest African Air Forces. In his despatch Hewitt was especially critical of the poor air support for Admiral Kirk's CENT Force, noting that the naval and ground commanders had sailed for Sicily with no knowledge whatever of what the Air Force would do in the assault thereafter. 'They were not informed of the general air situation nor was this information broadcast to them at sea . . . up to the time of sailing neither the Naval nor Army Commander was informed of what bombing support, if any, could be expected.'[2]

Opinions tended to split along national lines, with the British generally satisfied with their support and the Americans highly critical. The official British naval historian has taken the pragmatic view that although the air plan was flawed and suffered from a lack of co-ordination, the overall air performance nevertheless was impressive.[3] Admiral Cunningham later wrote in his official despatch that it seemed 'almost magical that great fleets of ships could remain anchored at the enemy's coast within forty miles of the main aerodromes with only such slight losses'.[4]

After the war the official [US] air historians struck back, calling the naval criticism a result of the 'usual differences of opinion'.[5] The Northwest African Air Forces insisted they had done the job required of them and pointed to the statistics which reflected they had flown 1,092 Spitfire and P-40 sorties on D-Day. The real problem, they contended, lay in the differing concepts of what constituted close air support. The Admiralty supported the airmen by affirming that losses were far less than anticipated.[6]

[1] *Sicily–Salerno–Anzio*, op. cit., pp. 101–2.
[2] Vice Admiral H. Kent Hewitt, 'Action Report: The Sicily Campaign, Operation HUSKY, July–August 1943', loc. cit.
[3] Roskill, *The War at Sea*, op. cit., p. 140. '. . . the success of the expedition,' said Roskill, 'was achieved at far less cost than we had anticipated, and even the troublesome enemy counterattacks from the air never came near to wrecking the undertaking.'
[4] Cunningham despatch, published as a supplement to the *London Gazette*, 25 April 1950. Also quoted in Roskill, op. cit., p. 140.
[5] Wesley Frank Caven and James Lea Cate (Eds.), *The Army Air Forces in World War II*, Vol. II: *Europe: Torch to Pointblank, August 1942 to December 1943*, Chicago, 1949, p. 451.
[6] Ibid., p. 452.

Closer examination of what occurred during the first two days of HUSKY reveals that there is substance to the criticism of the air force. Enemy air attacks began as early as 0424 hours, 10 July, when Me109s, Ju88s and Italian fighter bombers began to drop flares and attack troops of the 45th Division. Dive bombers attacked the cruisers *Philadelphia* and *Jefferson*, followed by attacks in the JOSS area. Throughout 10 July enemy aircraft attacked the American beaches. About 1930 the 1st Division reported having been subjected to dive bombing attacks for more than two hours. These attacks continued throughout the night of 10/11 July and during the daylight hours of 11 July, with almost continuous attacks against shipping and troops. At 1546 there was a large raid by sixteen *Focke-Wulf* 200 and *Heinkel* 111 bombers escorted by eight fighters which attacked in and around the 1st Division area. The raiding continued with formations of sixteen or more aircraft continually attacking shipping and was not limited to daylight hours.[1] Spaatz's aircraft may have flown a large number of missions but the fact remains that they were ineffective against Axis interference that was far more intense than they portrayed. Although the Navy may have been overly sensitive to what it considered inadequate air cover, the claims of the Air Force seem wildly exaggerated. Moreover, even the unofficial RAF history readily concedes that 'It is surprising to note the large number of sorties the enemy were able to make in view of the heavy-scale bombing to which their airfields had been subjected in the preliminary phase of operation Husky, and finally *one is forced to conclude that the American fighters failed in their task of protecting the shipping and the troops on the beaches*'.[2] (Author's italics.)

The airmen argued that although there were adequate aircraft available, the long distances from their bases left only about thirty minutes of flying time over the combat area. Therefore, there would be continuous protection only for the first two and last one and one-half hours of daylight. During the first three days of HUSKY the two US fighter groups supporting the Licata and Gela

---

[1] 'The Sicilian Campaign', unpublished RAF operational narrative, PRO (AIR 41/52).
[2] Ibid. The night of 11 July the 1st Division again came under heavy bombing and not for the first time made a request for additional protection.

sectors flew more than 1,000 sorties; some planes flew as many as three per day.[1]

There is no question that very large numbers of aircraft were in the air during the first three critical days, but most appear to have been engaged in interdiction missions to impede enemy reinforcements from reaching the assault areas. The official air historian has claimed that the attacks delivered along the eastern coastal road and the the roads radiating from the main Axis area of concentration around Enna were 'especially effective'. It is stated that on 12 July interdiction was so effective that it 'left the roads of Sicily blocked with burned trucks [and] seriously hampered the enemy's road movements'.[2]

Without consulting Patton or any of the other commanders, the air chiefs elected to place their priority of effort upon interdiction instead of close air support of the assault forces. The large numbers of sorties are a misleading statistic for what amounted to nothing less than a serious breakdown of close air support. The events of 11 July speak for themselves. Air support did little to impede the advance of the Hermann Goering and Livorno Divisions on 10 July and even less on the crucial day of 11 July. Conversely, on 11 July, 198 Italian and 283 German aircraft flew missions against the Allied beachhead – most of them in the Seventh Army sector.[3]

The panzers on the Gela plain were sitting ducks had air support appeared to assist the hard-pressed ground forces. Their absence at the critical moment revealed the ineffectiveness of close air support and justified Admiral Hewitt's comment that 'Close support of aircraft in amphibious operations, as understood by the Navy, did not exist in this theater'.[4]

The system for requesting prompt air support was virtually useless and left the airmen with the final decision whether or not a requested mission was flown. The requests from the 'Big Red One' were anything but frivolous and went unanswered. If the air had been a positive factor on 11 July the panzer capability of the Hermann Goering Division might well have been terminally crip-

---

[1] Craven and Cate (Eds.), *Europe: Torch to Pointblank*, op. cit., pp. 451–3. The official air historian who wrote the account of the Sicily campaign was Dr Albert F. Simpson.

[2] Ibid., p. 453.

[3] *Sicily*, op. cit., p. 177.

[4] Vice Admiral H. Kent Hewitt, 'Action Report: The Sicily Campaign, Operation HUSKY, July–August 1943', loc. cit.

pled. Had it not been for the Navy the Axis counterattacks on 11 July might have turned into a tragedy for Seventh Army.

Patton's actions this day marked the beginning of a perceptible decline in his relationship with Omar Bradley who later accused him of meddling when the Seventh Army commander countermanded an order previously given to Allen. Bradley was aware of the dangerous gap between his two divisions and wanted it secured as a matter of priority. Patton reversed this by issuing instructions to by-pass this German pocket without consulting the II Corps commander. When a furious Bradley learned what Patton had done he immediately sent a portion of the 2d Armored Division to protect the 1st Division's flank, and later confronted Patton who apologized for interfering. Patton was, however, nettled by Bradley's criticism and when he met with Eisenhower the following day he remarked that Bradley was 'not aggressive enough'.[1] Bradley, in turn, considered Patton's remark a slur that he could never quite forgive.[2] From that day on relations worsened between the two commanders.

Patton's major achievement that dramatic day was not his personal presence on the battlefield* but his initiative months earlier to persuade Eisenhower to switch the 1st Division with the 36th Division, a decision whose soundness was proven by the fiasco at Salerno in September 1943. 'In doing so,' said Bradley, '[Patton] may have saved II Corps from a major disaster.'[3] Despite his antipathy to Allen, Bradley praised the 1st Division for its stand at Gela. 'Only the perverse Big Red One with its no less perverse commander was both hard and experienced enough to take that assault in stride.'[4]

[1] Bradley Commentaries; *A General's Life*, op. cit., p. 183.

[2] Ibid.

[3] *A Soldier's Story*, op. cit., p. 130.

[4] Ibid. When he met Allen the afternoon of 11 July, Bradley asked the exhausted 1st Division commander, 'Do you have it in hand, Terry?' Allen replied, 'Yes, I think so. But they've given us a helluva rough time.'

* As the Army Commander, Patton's presence ashore on 11 July was justified. One whose presence was not was the head of the OSS, Major General 'Wild Bill' Donovan, a man who carried in his head the deepest and most sensitive secrets of Allied intelligence and sabotage operations. His capture would have been a calamity, yet in violation of direct orders from both Roosevelt and Marshall that he was to stay away from battlefields, Donovan, a hard-headed, fearless Irishman who had won the Medal of Honor in World War I, inveigled himself ashore where later that day he momentarily shared a foxhole with Bradley. Another OSS agent who accompanied Donovan into Sicily disappeared against orders behind enemy lines to establish an agent network. The agent vanished under mysterious circumstances and was never seen again. (Cf. Anthony Cave Brown, *Wild Bill Donovan: The Last Hero*, New York, 1982, pp. 351–2.)

The aggressive Allen was not content to rest upon his laurels. He ordered another co-ordinated attack for midnight backed by concentrated artillery and naval gunfire support. Throughout the 'Big Red One' went the word to 'Sock the hell out of these damned Heinies, before they can get set to hit us again.'[1] With the 18th Infantry Regiment back in the fold again, the 1st Division seized Ponte Olivo airfield the following morning.

Comiso airfield fell to Middleton's 45th Division the afternoon of 12 July but the bitter fight to secure Biscari went on between the division and the Hermann Goering until 14 July. Unaware of its capture, the pilot of a *Ju*88 was fired upon by US anti-aircraft artillery as it landed at Comiso. The enraged pilot taxied to a halt and emerged from the cockpit shaking his fist at what he thought were his own inept gunners. Several Spitfires were also fired upon, causing Bradley to send his aide, Chester Hansen, to inform the AA commander that if he fired so much as a single round at a friendly aircraft, 'he might just as well take off over the hills and give himself up at Messina'.[2]

The triumphant American stand at Gela on 11 July was marred by tragedy that night when the aerial convoy ferrying Colonel Reuben H. Tucker's 504th Regimental Combat Team was shot to pieces by Allied naval forces. What ought to have been a milk run in which the 2,300 paratroopers of Tucker's force were to be dropped as reinforcements into the Gela bridgehead turned into a nightmare. The story of Ridgway's grave misgivings has already been told.[*] For this operation, assurances were given that if the 144 aircraft of Brigadier General Paul L. Williams' 52d Troop Carrier Wing flew the prescribed route which would take them into Sicily at Sampieri, near the Seventh Army/Eighth Army boundary, they would not be fired upon. The convoy would then fly over friendly territory to the drop zone on the Gela plain.

The Navy had been under aerial attack for most of the day and less than an hour before the arrival of the transports, Axis aircraft launched their largest strike of the day at the fleet. Only minutes

---

[1] Unpublished account of the 1st Division in Sicily, Terry Allen Papers, Eisenhower Library.
[2] A *Soldier's Story*, op. cit., p. 135.
[*] See Chapter 8.

after the attack had abated the unsuspecting troop carrier pilots appeared. The first serial made it to Gela without incident but a nervous machine gunner, no doubt spooked by the constant air attacks and the sight of the nearby Liberty ship *Robert Rowan* whose cargo of ammunition had taken a direct hit and exploded in mid-afternoon, opened fire on the second serial and before anyone could stop it, indiscriminate fire began from virtually every AA gun ashore and afloat. The hapless columns of slow-flying aircraft were trapped in a hail of 'friendly' fire that quickly took a frightful toll. The pilots attempted to take evasive action as the convoy disintegrated in a sad and desperate scene. Twenty-three aircraft were lost and never seen again; thirty-seven others were severely damaged and sixty pilots and crewmen died, as did eighty-one paratroopers. One hundred and thirty-two more were wounded and sixteen went missing. Among those lost was the Assistant Division Commander, Brigadier General Charles L. Keerans, Jr. Some troopers managed to bale out before their aircraft were shot down, and several others managed to crash-land in nearby fields. Colonel Tucker's aircraft was one of those that survived but was later found to have more than 1,000 shell holes in its fuselage.

Patton, Ridgway and the naval commanders had all attempted to ensure that all units were notified of the time and route of the airborne convoy but some clearly failed to get the word. Ridgway personally visited six AA crews and found that one of them had not been informed. Several hours earlier Patton had noticed that the AA gunners were jumpy and attempted unsuccessfully to postpone the drop. 'Am terribly worried,' he wrote.[1] Before the invasion Patton had directed all ground and naval commanders to be aware that there might be flights of friendly troops during any of the first six nights of HUSKY. Patton's worst fears came true; Ridgway awaiting his men at the drop zone, was forced to watch in agonizing frustration while they were blown out of the sky.

This tragic incident not only cost precious lives but nearly became the death knell to the future employment of airborne forces. Those who either misunderstood the potential of airborne warfare, or who disapproved of its use, now believed they had found an axe to grind. Eisenhower sent Patton a cable 'cussing me out' for the tragedy and ordered a halt to further operations until a formal inquiry was conducted. Not surprisingly, criticism

[1] Patton Diary, 11 July 1943, Patton Papers.

abounded as each side blamed the other. The US air chief, General 'Hap' Arnold, blamed the Army for laying on a needless operation and complained they ought to have been sent to Sicily by sea. Coningham criticized the operation as a rather amateurish 'soldier's air operation' rather than an airman's.[1]

The Navy responded to criticism of its actions by noting that the operation was too dangerous and laid on too hastily. The official historian observed that 'It seemed incredible that the Air Force would lay on so hazardous a flight at low level – over an assault area heavily committed in combat, where enemy raids had been frequent for two days – and for no sound purpose . . . And what if an enemy air raid were taking place when the transport planes arrived? Nobody seemed to have thought of that.'[2]

In the following weeks there was a furore over the future employment of airborne troops. One of the most vigorous supporters of the airborne concept was the unflappable Bradley. Gavin recalls 'Bradley's excitement upon coming upon the Biazza battlefield. He was particularly impressed by the knocked-out Tigers . . . After that experience, he insisted upon the paratroopers going in first.'[3]

The thorough investigation which followed was at best inconclusive, but it did establish stringent guidelines for future operations that established 'safety corridors' ten miles in width. Nevertheless, it was a bitter and depressing end to the most crucial day of the Sicily campaign.

---

[1] Craven and Cate (Eds.), *Europe: Torch to Pointblank*, op. cit., p. 455.

[2] Morison, *Sicily–Salerno–Anzio*, op. cit., p. 120.

[3] Letter, Lieutenant General James M. Gavin to the author, 8 October 1985. Other things about Bradley impressed the young airborne commander: 'Not long after reporting to [Lieutenant-General Sir Frederick E.] Morgan's Cossac headquarters [in 1944], Bradley sent for me to sit down with him and go over the Normandy air photo coverage. He asked me questions as though he were a battalion commander. The sort of questions he asked had to do with specific commitments of small units . . . Bradley had a fine appreciation of the tools of his trade. He knew how good a unit was and how long it could withstand heavy tank and artillery attacks, and next, when to counterattack, and what should be its objective. I have never known a senior officer so steeped in tactical hands-on knowledge.'

Bradley carried his commitment to airborne operations into the Normandy campaign. When the Allied air C-in-C, Air Chief Marshal Sir Trafford Leigh-Mallory, attempted to scrap the US airborne landings in the Cotentin peninsula on grounds that they would lead to yet another disaster, Omar Bradley resolutely refused, stating that he would not make the invasion without them.

CHAPTER 18

The Axis on the Defensive

The situation has become more acute.
Despatch by OB South

When news of the setback near the Gela beaches reached Rome it brought gloom to Mussolini and the Italian high command. The swift fall of Syracuse was followed on 11 July by the bitter news that Augusta too had fallen virtually without a fight, leaving a second major port in Allied hands. Even worse was the scandalous conduct of the Italians responsible for defending Augusta. The Italian commander, Admiral Leonardi, falsely claimed that Augusta was being invaded from the sea as an excuse which the Italians used for destroying their guns and firing their fuel and ammunition dumps before fleeing north towards Catania in complete disarray. Colonel Schmalz submitted a scathing report that every single officer had abandoned his troops and that Italian soldiers were drifting aimlessly around the countryside, some in civilian clothes.[1] Many units of the 206th Coastal Division had surrendered *en masse*, including the division commander and his staff on 11 July. The following day the commander of the 54th Napoli Division was captured by an Eighth Army unit.[2]

Equally bleak was an OB South dispatch on 12 July which proclaimed: 'The situation has become more acute ... HG Div. is

---

[1] David Irving, *Hitler's War, 1942–1945*, London, 1983, p. 535; *Sicily*, op. cit., p. 240.
[2] Montgomery Diary, 'The Invasion of Sicily: 1st Phase, 10 July–21 July 1943'. One pint-sized Italian general who surrendered to the British was escorted along with several other senior Italian officers to the minesweeper *Antwerp* which had ferried both Montgomery and Mountbatten to Sicily. When he learned of Mountbatten's presence the general demanded to be taken before the admiral. The general told Mountbatten that his father had been awarded the MC in the First World War by the British and he felt he was entitled to the same recognition for having surrendered so quickly to the Allies. The incredulous Mountbatten was not amused but soon saw the humour in this bizarre demand. The Italian general was advised he should consider himself fortunate merely to be alive and was removed to an Allied POW camp. (Sir Harry Llewellyn, interview of 18 September 1984 and letter of 29 July 1985.)

310

withdrawing under strong enemy pressure from the southeast into the area southeast of Caltagirone–Vizzini ... The Italian forces in the area under attack are almost a total loss. The German forces at the moment are not sufficiently large to carry out a decisive attack against any one of the enemy bridgeheads...'[1]

The German commanders roundly condemned the performance of the Italian Army in Sicily with the lone exception of the artillery troops whose actions were considered praiseworthy. The wretched performance of the Italians only deepened the gloom. Mussolini continued to exist in his own fantasy world and, although he was shocked by Kesselring's 13 July report of the situation in Sicily, appeared outwardly unworried.[2] Before the invasion the Italian press had on his orders trumpeted his grand plans to annihilate any Allied force that dared land in Sicily and when inaccurate reports reached Rome that the counterattacks on D-Day had been successful, there was great rejoicing.[3]

These false hopes were soon dashed when the true picture emerged. A week after D-Day as the Allies continued to make fresh gains, Mussolini decided the blame lay with Axis troops and continued to insist that his plans for a counterthrust to throw the Allies back into the Mediterranean were in hand.[4] Soon gone, however, were any further war bulletins proclaiming the elimination of the Allied beachhead. Instead, the new operative word became 'containment'.[5] The failure of the Axis counterattacks against Seventh Army and their complete inability to launch such an attack against Eighth Army signalled a perceptible shift from a strategy of counterattack to the defensive.

Mussolini's reveries were no substitute for leadership and the result was that the Italian ship of state was in serious trouble. German disgust at the indifferent fight put up by Italian forces in Sicily soon led Hitler unsuccessfully to seek a new leader to replace Mussolini. Without German support Sicily was indefensible, and when the two leaders met at Feltre on the Italian–Swiss border on 19 July, Hitler dominated the meeting with a two-hour diatribe of Italian shortcomings while Mussolini sat mute as his ministers

[1] 'Information from German Sources', loc. cit.
[2] Bauer, Manuscript # R-139; *Mussolini* p. 340.
[3] Ibid.
[4] *Mussolini*, op. cit.
[5] Bauer, loc. cit.

looked on in embarrassment and disgust. The next day Ambrosio tendered his resignation only to have it refused.[1]

Hitler accepted as a *fait accompli* the inability of the Axis to dismiss Allied forces from Sicily, which was a departure from the usual 'hold to the death' demand that pervaded so many of the German campaigns. Western Sicily he ceded to the Allies and it was to be along the Etna defence line that German forces were to stop the Allied advance. Hitler's growing disdain for Mussolini and the Italians was exacerbated by the ease with which Augusta had fallen. In one sense the invasion of Sicily was a relief to the Germans for it signalled the certainty that there was no present threat of an invasion of northwest Europe; it also meant there were formations now available for reinforcement of either Italy or Sicily.[2]

Once again, the effects of Operation MINCEMEAT entered into the German reaction. The spectre of an Allied invasion of Greece and Schmalz's report of the Augusta incident dampened the enthusiasm of both Hitler and OKW who were loath to take any big decisions regarding the reinforcement of Sicily other than to order the immediate movement of the 1st Parachute Division. On 16 July, Hitler approved a large reinforcement of AA batteries, but permission to move the 29th Panzer Grenadier Division which had earlier been moved into Calabria was not given until 18 July. Also activated were German contingency plans to move the headquarters of the XIV Panzer Corps to Sicily. Its commander was General der Panzertruppen Hans Valentin Hube, a veteran of the Russian campaign who had commanded the 1st Panzer Army under von Manstein, and was considered one of the ablest of the German armoured commanders.* Hube's corps HQ had also been held in

[1] Mussolini could barely understand what Hitler was saying until furnished a written summary later. He continued to insist privately that one day he would free Italy from the German hold, but not now if it meant the end of the Fascist state. (Cf. *Mussolini*, op. cit., p. 341.)

[2] *Grand Strategy*, Vol. IV, op. cit., p. 468. By as early as 14 July, Allied decrypts of German message traffic established that western Sicily was being abandoned by the enemy. (Cf. *British Intelligence in the Second World War*, Vol. III, Pt I, op. cit., p. 90.)

* A World War I veteran, Hube lost an arm in the battle of the Marne. The impression he made on Guzzoni was of a Teutonic warrior who had left his armour, helmet and spear outside. He seemed to be less amenable and communicative than Kesselring but purposeful and rather stubborn. With great determination he presented and held on to his point of view and rarely entered into an argument, usually merely stating his conclusions. (See Bauer, MS # R-117, USAMHI.)

readiness in Calabria to move to Sicily in the event of an Allied invasion.

Hube received his orders personally from Kesselring on 16 July. German forces were to establish a solid defensive line in front of the Etna *massif*, even if it meant giving ground initially to the Allies. Here the Germans would make their stand in Sicily. To assist Hube, Kesselring ordered the Luftwaffe heavy flak units to be placed under his command. Even though it defied the normal axioms of command, Kesselring's rationale was clear: 'Hube could hardly count on any air support in the daytime, so to compensate I was anxious to leave no stone unturned to accelerate the arrival of the 29 Panzer Grenadiers.'[1]

Hitler's biographer, David Irving, relates that Hitler's intention was to tempt the enemy to pour huge numbers of reinforcements into Sicily, so that the Luftwaffe could destroy the supply ships and starve the Allies into submission in a reverse Tunis. However, for this strategy to be successful, the Italians would have to participate actively and effectively in Sicily's defence.[2]

This was, of course, a wildly improbable scheme that reflected just how far out of touch with reality Hitler was, despite accurate reports from the front and OB South. Kesselring remained far too optimistic, even though claiming to have told Hube that he was 'reckoning with the evacuation of Sicily, which it was his job to postpone as long as possible'.[3]

The situation which had developed by mid-July convinced both the senior German commanders in the field and the senior staff officers at OKW that there was very little possibility of holding Sicily for an extended period and even less to be gained from a needless sacrifice of German formations. Even though Kesselring was telling Mussolini that everything possible would be done to hold Sicily, the real German intentions were to establish a bridge-head in northeastern Sicily under Hube which would later permit a deliberate evacuation of the island when the time came.[4]

---

[1] *A Soldier's Record*, op. cit., p. 197.

[2] *Hitler's War, 1942–1945*, op. cit., p. 541.

[3] *A Soldier's Record*, op. cit., p. 197. Von Senger later charged that, as late as 17 July, Kesselring envisioned the arrival of the 29th PzG Division – enabling Axis forces to take the offensive 'much like the good old days of the African war where the offensive had been taken now by the Allies, now by the Axis'. ('The Sicilian Campaign – 1943', *An Cosantoir*, July 1950.)

[4] *The Mediterranean and Middle East*, Vol. V, p. 91, and *Sicily*, op. cit. Chapter XI.

Hube's appointment as the tactical commander of all German forces in Sicily now effectively reduced von Senger's role to that of a figurehead despite *his* new appointment by OKW as commander of all German army formations. Guzzoni had no voice in the new arrangement which had been made between Kesselring and Roatta, who was now the Chief of the Italian Army High Command. On 16 July Hube assumed tactical control over all sectors where German troops fought, replacing Sixth Army whose role, like that of von Senger, was reduced to insignificance. By 2 August Hube was in full control of the entire Sicily front.*

Kesselring left Sicily convinced that in Hube he had the right man in the right place.[1] He had earlier made another astute appointment, that of an Army officer, Colonel Ernst-Guenther Baade, to control all German operations across the Messina Strait, including the AA defences on both sides. The accomplishments of the brilliant and unconventional Baade who became known as the 'Commandant of the Messina Strait' will be more fully explored later.

The German response to the invasion was rather half-hearted and reflected the contradiction of committing German forces to what most recognized as an indefensible situation. Hitler's mixed emotions were understandable; his desire to keep a firm hold in Italy was offset by a leadership crisis of such serious proportions that it now threatened to topple Mussolini by *coup d'état*. The result was a compromise: the Italian plea for more air support was fulfilled by the transfer of four bomber groups and one fighter group from other theatres.

Kesselring and others had expected the Allies would also invade Calabria to bottle up Axis forces in Sicily and he was frustrated by Hitler's refusal to commit the 29th PzG Division sooner, Nevertheless, Kesselring was on the whole satisfied.† He met with Guzzoni, in part to reassure the old general that the defence of Sicily was not

---

[1] A Soldier's Record, op. cit., p. 198.

* Unknown to the Italians were the secret orders given to Hube at Hitler's instigation. In conjunction with von Senger, Hube was unobtrusively to exclude the Italians from further planning and, in addition to taking over full control of all operations in the bridgehead, was to gain control of all Italian units still in Sicily. To this Jodl added his own secret instructions that Hube was to conduct his operations with an eye to saving as much German manpower as possible for future operations. Jodl's action was prompted by his long-standing doubt that Sicily could be defended by the Axis; his guidance to Hube was to prove significant as the campaign unfolded. (*Sicily*, op. cit., p. 214.)

† Von Senger privately disagreed and felt the wisest course of action was the immediate evacuation of Sicily. Comando Supremo was equally pessimistic and Ambrosio told Musso-

entirely hopeless. Inexorably the Germans took control and on 31 July Comando Supremo directed Guzzoni to hand over to Hube command of all German and Italian troops in the battle zone. As Montgomery in particular was soon to recognize, the easy time enjoyed by Eighth Army was about to end.

On the battlefield, the first days of the campaign saw the Allies carve out a sizeable bridgehead while Axis forces scrambled to block their advance by all possible means. On 12 July, the 15th Panzer Grenadier Division made its first appearance opposite the 3d Division which had enlarged its bridgehead as far north as Canicatti where, supported by Brigadier General Maurice Rose's CCA (2d Armored Division), it made Truscott's overall front some fifty miles long.

To the east, the Hermann Goering, still smarting over its set-backs, was withdrawing grudgingly and on 12 July still had not fully disengaged from contact with American units in the Gela–Scoglitti sector; this despite two urgent messages from von Senger ordering Conrath to speed up his move to the east to reinforce the Napoli Division and Group Schmalz. While Conrath seemed lacking in any sense of urgency, the situation on the fringes of the plain of Catania was becoming increasingly precarious.

Group Schmalz was the only reliable fighting force left in the Eighth Army sector but it was too weak to take the offensive and was forced to fight a delaying action as it withdrew towards Lentini, leaving the approaches to Augusta undefended. Colonel Schmalz, who was cut from sterner cloth than the other senior commanders of the Hermann Goering, used his task force at Lentini to delay the British advance until reinforcements arrived. With a large gap between himself and Conrath, and with no reserves behind him, Schmalz skilfully employed his task force to prevent a British breakthrough into the plain of Catania and certain disaster. While the Italians were crumbling at Augusta and elsewhere, Schmalz was blocking the advance of the 5th Division north of Syracuse.

Lentini sat astride the final British obstacle to an unhindered

---

lini on 14 July that Sicily's fate was sealed and he should consider ending the war to spare Italy further agony. (*Sicily*, op. cit., Chapter XI.)

march towards Messina and a quick Allied victory. It is no exaggeration to state that the fate of the Axis in Sicily rested in the
capable hands of Schmalz whose capacity to continue holding off
the British without reinforcements, and to establish a defensive
line before the British arrived in force, was now diminishing
hourly. Catania and its plain now became the most critical objective in Sicily. Whichever side controlled this terrain could dictate
the actions of the other. If the British broke through there would be
no way to reinforce Axis units from Messina, and the forces in
central Sicily would be vulnerable to a double envelopment from
east and west. By attacking from both flanks and continuing to
exert heavy pressure northwards from Gela–Scoglitti, the Allies
could soon render the Axis position in Sicily untenable.

Dempsey's 13 Corps was preparing for a major thrust into the
plain of Catania beginning the night of 13 July, and consequently
the absence of a serious attack enabled Schmalz to hold south of
Lentini. That night, reinforcements in the form of an airborne
infantry regiment* plus two infantry battalions which had arrived
in Sicily on 11 July now turned Group Schmalz into a far more
formidable force. Schmalz had finally been able to establish contact with Conrath and the two agreed they would be able to join
forces on the morning of 15 July when the division would resist
along a forty-mile line running from Leonforte to Catania.

The morning of 12 July, elements of the Hermann Goering were
still in contact with the 1st Division around Piano Lupo which
once again became a bloody battleground as a German infantry
attack supported by Tigers tore into units of the 16th and 18th
Regiments. Particularly hard hit was the 2/18th Infantry where the
battalion commander was badly wounded. All morning the two
sides slugged it out and although the German threat was erased,
the 2d Battalion was reduced to about 200 men and its rifle
companies were at less than one-half strength.[1]

The 45th Division's drive to capture Biscari airfield also met
bitter opposition from the retreating Hermann Goering who
alternated effective delaying actions with occasional small
counterattacks which severely impeded the American advance to
the Yellow Line.

[1] *Sicily*, op. cit., pp. 188–9.
* Part of the 1st Parachute Division. See Chapter 21.

The protracted fight for Biscari airfield generated the first odious incident of the campaign. In two separate episodes seventy-three Italian POWs were massacred by a captain and a sergeant of the 180th Regiment/45th Division. The engagements beginning on D-Day between the two opponents had been fierce around Highway 115 which the GIs soon renamed 'Adolph's Alley'. Before the invasion Patton had personally spoken to the entire division and warned its troops what to expect in Sicily. Wedemeyer who was present recorded that:

> He admonished them to be very careful when the Germans or Italians raised their arms as if they wanted to surrender. He stated that sometimes the enemy would do this, throwing our men off guard. The enemy soldiers had on several occasions shot our unsuspecting men or had thrown grenades at them. Patton warned the members of the 45th Division to watch out for this treachery and to 'kill the s.o.b.'s' unless they were certain of their real intention to surrender.[1]

Once ashore the inexperienced troops of the 45th Division found there was considerable truth in Patton's admonition as evidenced by a series of incidents reminiscent of what later took place in Normandy near Bayeux between the 3rd Canadian Division and Kurt Meyer's 12th SS Panzer Division.* One lieutenant recalled that 'German atrocities were rampant and so were ours in retaliation. My driver was captured, was tied to a tree and shot by the Goerings. Then we encountered another German trick. They would rise without weapons, waving their hands in the air and shouting "Kamerad!" Then, when we went to round them up, they would fall flat and other Germans, concealed behind them, would open up on us. We lost many men due to this. Casualties were severe, and the procedure of taking prisoners was abandoned by both sides.'†

---

[1] *Wedemeyer Reports!*, op. cit., p. 226.

* Patton's concern is substantiated by Canadian reports of Germans faking surrender. After the war General Rodt complained that the Canadians during the battle for Leonforte shot a number of German POWs. According to Rodt this incident increased German determination to resist. (Pond, *Sicily*, p. 172.) The 3rd Division had numerous unpleasant experiences, particularly with the Italians. As one battalion commander later recalled, 'I had a hell of a lot of casualties because of these ruses they pulled on us'. (Oral history interview of Lieutenant General John A. Heintges, loc. cit.)

† Quoted in Farago, *Patton*, op. cit., p. 399. Farago also points out that because of their inexperience Patton felt that they needed one of his most dynamic pep talks – of the sort seen in the film *Patton* – and on 27 June, after intense preparation, he delivered the speech in two shifts to the men of the 45th Division.

Near Biscari airfield on 14 July an infantry force began drawing heavy machine-gun and sniper fire. During the ensuing firefight twelve men were wounded by sniper fire before the small enemy force surrendered. They turned out to be a group of approximately thirty-six Italians, several of whom were dressed in civilian clothes. The infantry company commander ordered the prisoners shot, whereupon they were lined up along the edge of a nearby ravine and executed by a group of infantrymen. The same day another infantry company captured an estimated forty-five Italians and three Germans. An NCO was ordered to escort thirty-seven of the Italians to the rear for interrogation by the regimental S-2. About a mile down the road the sergeant ordered the group halted and moved off the road where they were lined up. Saying he was going to kill the 'sons of bitches', the sergeant borrowed a Thompson sub-machine gun from his 1st Sergeant and calmly gunned down the hapless Italians.

When Bradley heard of the incidents he was horrified and promptly reported them to Patton who, he said, cavalierly dismissed the matter as 'probably an exaggeration'. Patton instructed Bradley 'to tell the officer responsible for the shootings to certify that the dead men were snipers or had attempted to escape or something, as it would make a stink in the press and also would make the civilians mad. Anyhow, they are dead, so nothing can be done about it.'[1]

Bradley quietly refused and ordered the two men to face a general court-martial for the premeditated murder of seventy-three prisoners of war.* Their defence attorneys argued they had only been following Patton's orders and cited his 27 June speech to the 45th Division as evidence. Although this defence was rejected, Patton did become the object of an official Inspector General investigation and an investigating officer was sent from Washington to England prior to the Normandy landings. Patton was grilled by the IG whose report concluded there was no culpability on his part and that the defence lawyers had used 'quite unethical

---

[1] Patton Diary, 15 July 1943.

* The two men who were tried were Sergeant Horace T. West (Company 'A', 180th Infantry Regiment) and Captain John T. Compton, who commanded Company 'C' in the same regiment. An account of their trial and subsequent events are documented in Appendix K.

methods' by attempting to create a smokescreen with Patton as its source.*

Patton was also the target of criticism by Eisenhower, at a private dinner in England, who said: 'George, you talk too much.' Patton defiantly replied: 'If you order me not to, I will stop. Otherwise I will continue to influence the troops the only way I know, a way which so far has produced results.' To his wife he wrote scornfully that 'the friends of freedom' were attempting 'to cook up another incident about some unnecessary killings – if killings in war are ever unnecessary'.[1]

Sicily was the low point in the long-standing Eisenhower– Patton friendship. When Eisenhower learned of the airborne tragedy he immediately sent a very angry cable to Patton demanding action against those responsible and implying that the fault lay within Patton's command. Eisenhower was still irritated when he visited Patton aboard the *Monrovia* the following day, 12 July. According to his naval aide, 'Ike spoke vigorously to Patton about the inadequacy of his reports of progress reaching headquarters at Malta.' Patton was also castigated for absenting himself ashore the previous day. Eisenhower contrasted Seventh Army's reporting with that of Eighth Army which obviously satisfied the Allied commander. However, Eisenhower's observer, General Lucas, could not understand Eisenhower's displeasure, noting that he personally checked the reports and 'they seemed to me to be as complete as they could well be under the circumstances'.[2]

This unpleasant encounter illustrates the extent of the deterioration in relations between the two commanders. 'Ike had stepped on him hard. There was an air of tenseness. I had a feeling that Ike was disappointed. He said previously that he would be happy if after about five days from D-Day, General Bradley were to take over because of his calm and matter-of-fact direction.'[3] Not once during his visit did Eisenhower ever compliment Patton on any aspect of Seventh Army operations. Moreover, his criticism of

---

[1] Patton Papers.
[2] Diary of Major General John P. Lucas, loc. cit.
[3] Diary of Captain Harry C. Butcher, loc. cit., entry of 13 July 1943.
* The notes of Bradley's aide record that when informed by Bradley of the incident, Patton replied, 'Try the bastards.' (Hansen Papers, USAMHI.) According to Hansen, during the campaign Patton raised the question whether or not an enemy soldier who shoots until his ammunition is exhausted and then gives up, loses his right to surrender. There is no evidence that this was anything more than a rhetorical question or that it was ever said in the presence of any of his troops.

Patton's alleged reporting failures may have been misplaced, for the chain of command was through Alexander's 15th Army Group.* What Alexander's headquarters did with Patton's reports was outside the control of the Seventh Army commander. As Lucas observed, 'The C-in-C should have mentioned the fact that a most difficult military operation was being performed in a manner that reflected great credit on American arms.'[1]

Butcher also wrote in his diary that 'When we left General Patton I thought he was angry.' Patton was indeed livid but resigned himself that the incident merely represented a further example of Eisenhower's pro-British bias.

Patton's confrontation with Eisenhower and the C-in-C's angry reaction to the 82d Airborne incident on 11 July could not have come at a worse moment. They left Patton uncharacteristically reluctant to act at the very moment when he should have challenged the most misguided decision made by the Allies in Sicily.

[1] Lucas Diary.
* 15th Army Group (the former Force 141) was officially activated on D-Day.

CHAPTER 19

The Great Boundary Line Dispute

> General Bradley executed this preposterous order
> silently and skilfully, but inwardly he was hot as
> Mount Etna.
>
> COLONEL B. A. 'MONK' DICKSON
> G-2, II Corps

As events began to unfold in Sicily both Army commanders found themselves without either a firm plan of action or guidance from Alexander. There existed no overall master plan of campaign, no agreed strategy (however loosely defined) for the conquest of Sicily. During the planning phase Patton and Montgomery never met to discuss strategy and there was no co-ordination between their Army headquarters or from Alexander's 15th Army Group staff. Thus, among the three senior ground commanders there was not even a common agreement on campaign strategy. Alexander preferred to await actual developments before asserting himself and, from his own extensive interview given to the official US historians in 1949, he has indicated that he had no intention of doing so until Seventh Army had seized its assigned airfields and Eighth Army had control of the ports of Syracuse, Augusta and the plain of Catania.

What passed for strategy can be summed up in Alexander's *idée fixe* that Patton would be the shield in his left hand while Eighth Army served as the sword in his right.[1] As one of Montgomery's senior staff officers later wrote, 'The two armies were left largely to develop their operations in the manner which seemed most propitious in the prevailing circumstances. When there is a master plan, the subordinates exercise their initiatives within its framework, and there is thus greater cohesion in seeking to achieve the superior commander's object.'[2] Alexander never made a secret of the fact that prior to the invasion he had not prepared detailed

---

[1] *Sicily*, op. cit., p. 91.
[2] Major General David Belchem, *All in the Day's March*, London, 1978, p. 167.

plans or possessed any firm convictions about the exploitation phase and how it ought to be conducted. It would depend, he said, on what the Germans did and how they used their reserves.[1] The British official history observes that Alexander had no master plan; 'rather, chance and the reactions of competent commanders to the circumstances of an encounter battle decided his moves'.[2]

Bradley's later recollection of the strategy of the campaign was that the first objective was to push inland, take the high ground, protect the beaches and get the airfields. Once securely established the Allies were to cut Sicily in half, face east and roll up Axis forces trapped between them and Mount Etna and the eastern coast.[3] How this was to occur was left unanswered.

Beyond this generalized purpose lay an expectation that the overall Allied objective was Messina. During the pre-invasion planning, AFHQ called Messina the key to the island[4] but this headquarters was not responsible for planning strategy and what remains indisputable is that Alexander never saw fit prior to D-Day to orient his two Army commanders or to provide even the vaguest guidance. There is no evidence that Alexander ever seriously considered assuming the reins of control over his two Army commanders, nor did he evince having anticipated the speed with which the two armies would secure such sizeable bridgeheads.

The inevitable result was that his two strong-willed subordinates began to act independently of Alexander and each other. Montgomery had, in fact, impudently cabled Alexander on 11 July that 'Everything going well here ... No need for you to come here unless you wish. Am very busy myself and am developing operations intensively so as to retain the initiative. Have no news of American progress. If they can press inland and secure Caltagirone and Canicatti and hold firm against any action from the west I could then swing hard with my right with an easier mind. If they draw enemy attacks on them my swing north will cut off enemy completely.'[5]

Montgomery's overconfidence was unfounded, for his Army had yet to fight its first serious battle with a front-line German unit

---

[1] Alexander interviews with Sidney T. Mathews, 10–15 January 1949, USAMHI.
[2] *The Mediterranean and Middle East*, Vol. V, op. cit., p. 93.
[3] Bradley Commentaries.
[4] Ibid.
[5] Alexander Papers, PRO (WO 214/22).

and had so far encountered only token resistance. And, as his biographer notes, 'This was to be the first of Monty's imperious "suggestions" for the way Alexander should run the Sicilian campaign. Meekly, Alexander complied – and the stage was set for the historic rivalry between Patton and Montgomery that would become an almost manic obsession with Patton, as well as spawning books and films for decades after his death.'[1]

Alexander's dormant leadership was compounded by the mistaken conviction that American fighting ability was inferior to that of the British Army. Alexander refused to acknowledge that the US Army now fighting in Sicily bore no resemblance to the Army that had been humiliated at Kasserine a scant five months earlier. The 15th Army Group commander entered the Sicily campaign firmly believing that the troops of Eighth Army were more experienced and reliable than Patton's Seventh Army, and he was therefore receptive to Monty's veiled suggestions as to what he should be permitted to do.

Even Sicily failed to change Alexander's mind about the ability of the American combat soldier. His anti-American bias consistently manifested itself well into the Italian campaign when, as the US official history notes, the situation was radically altered and 'American troops in Italy had to bear the brunt of the fighting because of the exhaustion of British divisions.'[*]

In their eagerness to influence the action both Army commanders broke tradition by issuing orders directly to their division commanders and in at least one instance Monty issued instructions to a brigade commander of the Highland Division. Kirkman, the 50th Division commander, was a gunner who as a brigadier had been personally appointed by Montgomery to take over the Eighth Army artillery before Alam Halfa. Kirkman's outstanding performance earned him a promotion and command of the

[1] *Monty, Master of the Battlefield, 1942–1944*, op. cit., p. 301.

[*] In early 1945 this sore subject sparked a clash between Alexander and Marshall. He considered Alexander's attitude insufferably patronizing when he remarked, 'Of course, your American troops are *basically trained*.' Marshall who never shared Eisenhower's enthusiasm for Alexander replied glacially: 'Yes, American troops start out and make every possible mistake. But after the first time, they do not repeat their mistakes. The British troops start in the same way and continue making the same mistakes over and over for a year.' Churchill, who was present, quickly changed the subject. Nevertheless, Marshall found Alexander's attitude widespread. Even King George once said how nice it was to have Eisenhower in nominal command with Monty at his side. (*Sicily*, op. cit., p. 210; Alexander interview, and interview by Smyth and Mathews with Marshall, 25 July 1949, USAMHI.)

Northumbrian Division. Most of his men had been forced to walk when the bulk of the divisional transport was lost to successful enemy bombing offshore. The division had so far met little opposition and the tenacious Kirkman was determined not to let up, even though his troops badly needed rest. He told his lead brigade commander, 'You're not going to sit down and rest. There's no one in front of you at all, the place is empty. You go on till you drop if necessary – occupying this ground which you'll have to fight for tomorrow. Get 'em all on the move, go on, go on ... Use your [Bren] carriers as tanks, get on, get on. I don't care how tired the men are – walk!'[1]

Summoned by Montgomery, Kirkman was given an identical order: move north into the plain of Catania with all speed. As will be seen, Montgomery had in mind an aggressive and daring scheme to achieve a quick and decisive victory in Sicily.

The problem plaguing Eighth Army during the first days of the campaign was a chronic lack of transport. Competition for space and priorities had relegated the bulk of the general transport vehicles to later lifts. When enemy resistance unexpectedly crumbled across the entire Eighth Army front, the troops were forced to march in the broiling Sicilian heat with not only their basic load but water and food as well. Enterprising Tommies commandeered any form of transport they could lay their hands on, from the motley to the practical, including carts, mules, bicycles and, in the Highland Division, even perambulators. Although the men were generally very fit, the many miles the troops had marched heavily laden since D-Day took a toll.[2]

Alexander's broad strategy seems to have been that once a solid bridgehead was created, the island should be split in half – with the first stage being the seizure of the road net around Enna* and Caltanissetta which would effectively block enemy movement from the main routes connecting east and west Sicily. This was to be followed by a second thrust north to cut the next main east–west axis, the Nicosia–Adrano highway. The final phase would

[1] Quoted in ibid., p. 302.
[2] Cf. Wimberley Memoirs, loc. cit. Nearly all the Eighth Army infantry had marched an average of forty miles since D-Day.
* Enna was of strategic significance as the main road hub of central Sicily, from which roads fanned out in all directions into the rugged mountains that dominated central and eastern Sicily.

see Sicily sliced in two and the Palermo–Messina coast road in Allied hands.[1]

In the absence of formal guidance from Alexander, Montgomery had in early June formulated his own definition of Eighth Army's role after the capture of Catania:

> The Allied Plan after landing ... is for the Americans to form a firm base on the West covering the aerodromes, and for 13 Corps to drive on relentlessly in order to seize Syracuse, Augusta and Catania with the least possible delay. From these bases the Eighth Army will strike with its right in order to secure crossings over the Straits. The general conception is thus to hold on the left and strike on the right. By this means we should cut off and isolate the enemy still holding out round Palermo and in the West of the island.[2]

Although Messina was the obvious final Allied objective, only Montgomery seems to have articulated the point. On 12 July he suggested what Alexander had envisioned all along: that Eighth Army make the main Allied effort to cut Sicily in two. Montgomery's severest critics, Patton and Bradley, believed his motivation was to enhance his reputation and that of his Army by asserting *de facto* control of the campaign when Alexander failed to act.

In his diary Montgomery remarked on 12 July that 'It was becoming clear that the battle in SICILY required to be gripped from above. I was fighting my own battle, and 7th American Army was fighting *its* battle; there was no co-ordination by 15th Army Group (ALEXANDER). Without such co-ordination the enemy might well escape; given a real grip on the battle I felt convinced we could inflict a disaster on the enemy and capture practically all his troops in SICILY. I therefore sent the following cipher telegram to ALEXANDER, giving him my views as to how the battle should be fought:

> My battle situation now very good. Have captured Augusta and my line now runs through Sortino–Vizzini–Ragusa–Scicli. Intend now to operate on two axes: 13 Corps on Catania and northwards; 30 Corps on Caltagirone–Enna–Leonforte. Suggest American division at Comiso might now move westwards

---

[1] *The Mediterranean and Middle East*, Vol. V, op. cit., p. 87; Alexander despatch, copies of which can be found in numerous British and American archives, including the PRO (Alexander Papers, WO 214/68).

[2] Quoted in *The Canadians in Italy*, op. cit., p. 87, based on a letter from Leese to GOC, 1st Canadian Division (General Simonds), 10 June 1943.

to Niscemi and Gela. The maintenance and transport and road situation will not allow two armies both carrying out extensive offensive operations. Suggest my Army operates offensively northwards to cut the Island in two and that American Army hold extensively on line Caltanissetta–Canicatti–Licata, facing west. The available maintenance to be allocated accordingly. Once my left Corps reaches area Leonforte–Enna the enemy opposing the Americans will never get away.'[1]

Montgomery was acutely aware that the ineffectual enemy resistance could not be expected to last indefinitely and that he must take advantage of his present superiority of force or lose the initiative. What took place as a result of his prodding of Alexander may have smacked of insufferable arrogance towards Patton and the American role in Sicily, but his motives were to gain the upper hand before the enemy could do anything about it. He sensed an opportunity existed to win quickly by employing a *coup de main* on the plain of Catania while at the same time Leese's 30 Corps sliced the enemy and the island in two, isolating and dooming all enemy forces trapped in the eastern half of Sicily. That in doing so Monty would radically recast the role Patton and the American commanders envisaged for themselves does not seem to have entered his mind. Rather, the evidence strongly suggests he viewed the entire problem within a larger context of how the Allies could best win the battle for Sicily. Naïvely, Montgomery tended to view the problem across a spectrum that did not include an equal division of the spoils and of battle honours.

What Montgomery had in effect proposed to Alexander was for Seventh Army to hold fast as a protective shield while 30 Corps encircled and trapped all Axis forces in southeastern Sicily. The practical effect of this scheme was to relegate Patton to the role of interested bystander.

In proposing this change of mission for Eighth Army he required the Vizzini–Caltagirone highway* which belonged to Seventh Army. The inter-Army boundary ran through Vizzini to the Yellow Line leaving the highway exclusively within the 45th Division's zone. Nevertheless, Montgomery directed the Canadians to attack from Vizzini towards Caltagirone at the same time as

[1] Montgomery Diary, 12 July 1943. A copy of this message is also quoted in *The Mediterranean and Middle East*, Vol. V, op. cit., p. 88.
* Route 124.

Middleton's 45th Division was about to advance along the same road for the same purpose.

The evening of 13 July Montgomery signalled Alexander that 'unless something is done there will be a scene of intense military confusion on road Vizzini–Caltagirone. Suggest 45th Division moves Gela area and whole American effort is directed on Caltanissetta to Canicatti to Agrigento.'[1] What Montgomery neglected to point out was that he had yet to capture Vizzini which was proving a very tough nut to crack and that he would not be in a position to thrust towards Caltagirone until the morning of 15 July.

However, within hours (at 0230, 14 July) Alexander confirmed that he had *already* (as of 2000, 13 July) issued these exact same instructions to Patton: the Vizzini road now belonged to the British.[2] Alexander later defended his action as being consistent with the original invasion mission given to both Armies.[3]

On the basis of Montgomery's cabled suggestions, Alexander at a stroke lit the spark for one of the most unfortunate episodes of the European war. Not only were Patton and the entire American army in Sicily reduced to a nebulous secondary role – a humiliation never forgotten, or forgiven, by him and Bradley – but it was a decision the tactical soundness of which was decidedly questionable.

That same day – 13 July – Alexander visited Seventh Army and learned first-hand of its progress. As we know, previously Alexander could claim to have lacked adequate information about Seventh Army, but as a result of his visit he was fully aware that American forces were well positioned for a deep thrust to the north.

The previous evening, elements of Brigadier G. W. Richards' 23rd Armoured Brigade had reached the outskirts of the mountain city of Vizzini* which sits 2,000 feet above sea level at the intersection of three major roads on a knife-like ridge. The town can only be approached along a steep, winding road. Held by reconnaissance elements of the Hermann Goering, which had been reinforced

---

[1] Quoted in *The Mediterranean and Middle East*, Vol. V, op. cit., p. 88.
[2] Ibid., pp. 88–9.
[3] Alexander interview.
* Vizzini was typical of the towns in the mountains of Sicily. Over the centuries its inhabitants had built their homes so as to create a fortress for defence against invaders and bandits. The Germans soon became expert at using these natural fortress towns to their advantage.

by a newly arrived panzer grenadier battalion from the mainland, Vizzini presented a serious problem for the 51st Division whose task it was to take the town. The division was spread over a large area and its men exhausted. General Wimberley had expected to find Vizzini undefended; instead the Germans held out against a series of attacks for two days and it was not captured until the early hours of 15 July.[1] Montgomery then gave the Highlanders a new mission and ordered the Canadians to pass through them and continue to thrust northwest toward Caltagirone.

When Alexander was briefed by Patton he obviously declined to accept the premise that the 45th Divison – whose leading elements were then some 1,000 yards south of the disputed highway – might be in a better position to carry out the mission of seizing Caltagirone. The Americans were poised to strike at Vizzini early on the 13th when they encountered units of the 51st Division even though at this time (approximately 1700, 13 July) Alexander had yet to approve Montgomery's request to cede the highway to Eighth Army. Once the orders were issued transferring the disputed road to Eighth Army, the 45th Division was given strict instructions not to fire their artillery within one mile of the road to ensure that no British forces were accidentally shelled. On 15 July a Canadian brigade moving towards Grammichele (midway between Vizzini and Caltagirone) was held up by rearguard German elements. Not only were two of Middleton's brigades better positioned to take both Grammichele and Caltagirone, but the divisional artillery was in perfect position to fire in support of the Canadians. However, because of its strict orders the artillery could do nothing.[2]

Patton was surprised to get the order and wrote with disgust in his diary that Alexander and members of his staff 'gave us the future plan of operations, which cuts us off from any possibility of taking Messina. It is noteworthy that Alexander, the Allied commander of a British and American Army, had no American with him. What fools we are.'[3]

It is clear that Alexander had already made up his mind to relegate Seventh Army to a secondary role *before* visiting Patton on 13 July and *before* he appears to have been fully knowledgeable

---

[1] Wimberley Memoirs, loc. cit.
[2] *Troy H. Middleton*, op. cit., pp. 150–2.
[3] Patton Diary, 13 July 1943.

about its situation and capabilities. Moreover, the evidence strongly suggests that Alexander had already decided to switch the inter-Army boundary before his visit, a decision he would formalize that same night. Yet he declined the opportunity to inform Patton personally at a time when he might have at least smoothed what were certain to be ruffled American feathers. Instead, Alexander remained silent, and the incident unnecessarily permitted a severe setback for mutual trust and goodwill within the Anglo-American leadership.

Alexander's lack of grip was felt as early as 12 July when Truscott was poised to launch an attack either to the west towards Agrigento or north to Caltanissetta. However, Truscott was powerless to move without guidance from Patton, and Patton himself had received no instructions from Alexander. It took all of Patton's powers of persuasion to convince a reluctant Alexander to permit him to send Truscott west towards Agrigento, and then only if he went in the nature of a reconnaissance in force. Alexander made it clear Patton was not to become heavily engaged in doing so.[1]

Alexander, whose concept of future operations remained at best vague, continued to focus his attention on the Enna road axes through which he felt certain the German reserves would pass for what still might be a powerful German counterattack. Should this occur he clearly preferred Eighth Army's chances to those of Patton's army.[2]

His apprehensions notwithstanding, the truth is that Alexander was simply not prepared to entrust Seventh Army to any meaningful role at this time, regardless of how well they had performed. Neither does he appear to have paid sufficient attention to the enemy situation. The 15th PzG Division had yet to be committed, and the Hermann Goering Division was on the defensive and withdrawing to the east in both Army sectors. Although the 1st Parachute Division began arriving the same day and further German reinforcements from mainland Italy were sure to follow, for the moment the threat of anything more than a local Axis coun-

---

[1] Alexander interview, loc. cit.

[2] Ibid. Montgomery agreed with Alexander over the importance of the limited road network in Sicily. 'The battle in SICILY is a battle of key points. The country is mountainous and the roads poor. The few big main roads are two-way and very good; these run North–South and East–West, and once you hold the main centres of inter-communication you can put a stranglehold on enemy movement and so dominate the operations.'

terattack was non-existent. Furthermore, as we now know, from 13 July on, the Allies were the recipients of plentiful enemy signal intelligence about Axis ground operations. As the official history records, there was 'no lack of Sigint, about either the enemy's intentions or the state of affairs on the battlefront, for transmission to the Allied commands'.[1] Moreover, the steady flow of intelligence continued to show 'the Axis forces to be under heavy pressure on the whole front between 13 and 17 July'.[2] Alexander's actions can only have been governed by an innate mistrust of American forces and his fear that Patton must not be permitted to initiate any premature exploitative thrusts that could conceivably result in a threat to Montgomery's left flank.[3]

Bradley was thunderstruck when told by Patton of Alexander's decision. He was outraged at what he considered Montgomery's monumental insolence and perplexed by Patton's apparent apathy in meekly submitting to Alexander without a fight. Lucas was equally incensed:

> I think the fact that General Alexander had no American staff officers with him when he came to see us was an act of deep discourtesy. As he does not lack intelligence I am forced to the conclusion that it was deliberate and an attempt to belittle the American effort. It is disturbing to note that his instructions to Patton, which definitely limit our advance, is a step towards the assumption of a purely defensive role by the American Seventh Army. It is too bad because the momentum which we have gained by so much effort on the part of everyone will be lost and, once lost, momentum is difficult to regain.[4]

Bradley pleaded with Patton to demand at least that the 45th Division be permitted to use the Vizzini–Caltagirone road to move to the left of the 1st Division and avoid having to go clear back to the Gela beaches. 'My God, you can't let him do that,' argued Bradley. 'Sorry, Brad,' Patton replied, 'but the change-over takes place immediately. Monty wants the road right away.' Patton's lame reason was that it was already too late to reverse Alexander's order, which was not the case.[5] Bradley countered by pointing out

---

[1] *British Intelligence in the Second World War*, Vol. III, Pt I, op. cit., p. 90. Sigint (Signal Intelligence) is defined as 'the general term for the processes of interception and decryption and the intelligence they produced'.

[2] Ibid., p. 91.

[3] Alexander interview.

[4] Lucas Diary, 14 July 1943.

[5] *A Soldier's Story*, op. cit., p. 136, and *A General's Life*, op. cit., p. 189.

that not only was II Corps in an excellent position to break out of the rapidly expanding American bridgehead but that Middleton's brigades were better positioned to accomplish the task of seizing Vizzini and Caltagirone. Bradley's entreaties fell upon deaf ears and the 45th Divison was forced to make the long and disruptive return to the beaches. Bradley later thought that he might well have disobeyed the orders which erased the threat to the German defences posed by the presence of the 45th Division and which concurrently placed the Canadians in a position where it was impossible for them to outflank the Germans. 'I was very peeved, obeyed my orders, but often wondered if I received such orders now, would I really obey them? They were so obviously wrong and impractical. We should have been able to use that road, even if we would have shifted to the left – used it to move to the left.'[1]

Bradley believed, with some justification, that Patton's reticence to challenge Alexander stemmed from his lack of understanding of the British way of doing things where such an order could be challenged without being insubordinate,[*] and his fear that Eisenhower was on the verge of sacking him. Coming on the heels of their acrimonious meeting of 12 July was the cable from Eisenhower implying that Patton was responsible for the airborne tragedy. There is no evidence whatever to suggest that Eisenhower even considered Patton's relief, nor is it likely the Allied commander was even aware of the paranoid effect he was having upon Patton. However, an evaluation written in June 1943 does suggest that Eisenhower considered it necessary to keep a tight rein on his impetuous subordinate.[†] The unfortunate decline in their relations came at a critical moment when Patton ought to have challenged Alexander's precipitate decision.

Had Alexander seen fit to voice his plans during their meeting Patton could have at least made a case for a major thrust north in conjunction with the Eighth Army drive into the plain of Catania. However, once the order was issued, Patton accepted it without

[1] Bradley Commentaries.
[*] Which later led to Montgomery's now famous remark that Patton ought to do what *he* did when he got orders he didn't like: ignore them.
[†] Eisenhower praised Patton's performance of duty but noted that 'He talks too much and too quickly and sometimes creates a very bad impression. Moreover, I fear that he is not always a good example to subordinates, who may be guided by only his surface actions without understanding the deep sense of duty, courage and service that make up his real personality.' ('Memorandum for Personal File', 11 June 1943, Eisenhower Papers.)

question. Patton's reserve was characteristic of those occasions when he found himself in Eisenhower's doghouse and expected to be relieved and sent home.

The problem lay neither with Monty's impetuousness nor with Patton's apathy but with Alexander's unwillingness to take control of the ground campaign at its most critical moment. While there is no question that the role of Eighth Army was always to drive up the east coast to Messina, there were a number of possible roles for Seventh Army, which Alexander ignored in his fixation that his American army could not be trusted with a mission other than protecting Monty. Napoleon would have argued that here was a classic example of his principle that 'War is waged only with vigour, decision and unshaken will; one must not grope or hesitate.'[1] Bold leadership was not forthcoming and the unhappy result was that Montgomery was permitted to dictate a course of action only because it came closest to Alexander's own imprecise definition. But mainly it came down to Alexander's blindness to the fact that American leadership had made enormous strides since the previous February at Kasserine Pass. The decision shattered all pretence of cohesiveness and led to a situation whereby the two Army commanders virtually dictated conflicting and divisive courses of action for their respective armies and created an absurd and unnecessary personal rivalry.

As for the disputed highway, even Leese later admitted that it would have made more sense to have left the road in American hands. Said Leese, 'I often think now that it was an unfortunate decision not to hand it over to the Americans. Unknown at any rate to 30 Corps, they were making much quicker progress than ourselves, largely owing, I believe, to the fact that their vehicles all had four-wheel drive. They were therefore far better equipped to compete quickly with the endless deviations with which we were confronted, as a result of the destruction of every bridge by the Germans. We were still inclined to remember the slow American progress in the early stages in Tunisia, and I for one certainly did not realize the immense development in experience and technique which they had made in the last weeks of the North African campaign. I have a feeling now that if they could have driven

[1] Quoted by Dr Jay Luvaas in 'Napoleon on the Art of Command', *Parameters*, Vol. XV, No. 2, Summer 1985.

straight up this road, we might have had a chance to end this frustrating campaign sooner.'[1]

Even though what ensued is now a matter of record, precious little is really known of Alexander whose reputation has been shrouded in myth for over four decades. To delve behind the myth is to encounter a commander whose reputation has been vastly overrated.

[1] Unpublished memoirs of General Sir Oliver Leese, copy supplied the author by Nigel Hamilton.

CHAPTER 20

Alexander: The Great Enigma

> Alexander has acquired a false reputation as a great
> commander in the field, and as a great strategist.
>
> MONTGOMERY

In the more than forty years since the battles and campaigns in
the Mediterranean there is now enough new evidence upon which
to base serious reassessments of the principal military leaders.
Among them is General (later Field-Marshal) Sir Harold Alexander, a man whose true character and accomplishments have
eluded historians and even his own biographer, who confessed he
was unable to probe successfully beneath the outer shell of Alexander the general in an attempt to discover Alexander the man.[1]
Known affectionately and simply as 'Alex', he was one of the most
respected and popular of the Allied generals, a modest, unassuming commander who was far more content to remain in the
shadows rather than bask in the limelight of publicity, as did
Montgomery.

Alexander held the distinction of being Churchill's favourite
general, and of all the British generals it was Alexander who
commanded the greatest American admiration and respect, starting with Eisenhower who praised his generalship and esteemed
him as a friend. Where Montgomery had rough edges, Alexander
was smooth and polished; where Montgomery was controversial,
Alexander barely caused a ripple. As Montgomery observed, 'He
has all those fine qualities that I lack myself.'[2]

Alexander was every inch a soldier. Born of Northern Irish
Protestant nobility, he followed a traditional path to his calling:

[1] Nigel Nicolson, *Alex*, London, 1976 (Pan edition).
[2] 'The "HUSKY" Problem', Montgomery Papers. This was a personal chronicle of the
events leading up to the approval of the operational plan for HUSKY and was written in May
1943.

(l-r) Marshall, Arnold, two unidentified officers, Wedemeyer, Ismay, Mountbatten, Pound, Brooke, Portal (partially obscured), Dill

The HUSKY C-in-Cs at Casablanca: (l-r) Eisenhower, Tedder, Alexander and Cunningham (*in background l-r*) Macmillan, Bedell Smith, unidentified officer and AVM H. E. P. Wigglesworth (Tedder's Deputy Air C-in-C)

American assault troops receiving final briefing aboard an LST enroute to Sicily

USS *Robert Rowan* exploding off Gela on 11 July

Troops of the Big Red One storming ashore at Gela on D-Day, 10 July 1943

US self-propelled artillery rolling inland about D+1 as curious Sicilians watch

Bradley and Patton

The II Corps commander,
Lieutenant General Omar N. Bradley

Lieutenant General George S. Patton, Jr.
aboard the *Monrovia*, 11 July 1943
(r. Brig. Gen. Gay, C/S, Seventh Army)

Colonel Wilhelm Schmalz

General der
Panzertruppen
Hans Valentin Hube

Field Marshal Albert Kesselring,
Commander-in-Chief, South

Generale d'Armata Alfredo Guzzoni

The changing of the guard at Troina:
Major General Clarence R.
Huebner (l.) replaces Major General
Terry de la Mesa Allen (r.), 8 August
1943

Generalleutnant Fridolin
von Senger und Etterlin

Generalleutnant
Paul Conrath

The Plain of Gela after the battle. Note destroyed panzers, bottom right

German engineer paratroops of the 1st Parachute Division defending the Fosso Bottaceto, 19 July

Highway 114 at the southern end of Primosole bridge, scene of the most crucial battle of the Sicily campaign in mid-July

Montgomery and Lieutenant-General Sir Oliver Leese, commander 30 Corps

Major General Lucian K. Truscott, Commander, US 3d Infantry Division

82d Airborne paratroopers under fire near Abbio Priolo, 11 July (D+1)

A British officer observing enemy positions on the Plain of Catania. Mt. Etna in background

Royal Artillery gunners firing salvos on the Catania front

(l-r) Major General Troy H. Middleton confers with Bradley and Patton

Air Marshal Sir Arthur Coningham, Allied Tactical Air commander

13 Corps commander, Lieut-General Miles Dempsey (l.) with Major-General Guy G. Simonds, commander 1st Canadian Division (r.)

The Eighth Army commander, General Sir Bernard Montgomery

Major-General Vivian Everleigh, GOC, 78th Division (l.) shares a light moment with Colonel H. A. 'Paddy' Flint, CO, 39th Infantry Regiment (r.) when the two allies met outside Randazzo

US artillery forward observation post directing fire on Troina

Troops of the 1st Infantry Division entering the ruins of Troina, 6 August 1943

Monty explaining his strategy for the capture of Messina to Patton, Alexander and Bedell Smith on 25 July, 1943

The British move forward in the centre of the island, probably Sferro, to try to break through the Etna Line, 25 July

General Sir Harold Alexander and General Dwight D. Eisenhower

Patton delivering his apology to the 1st Infantry Division, 27 August 1943

Major General Geoffrey Keyes accepting the surrender of Palermo from Generale di Brigata Guiseppe Molinaro the evening of 22 July

Among the 137,000 Italians captured by the Allies were the commander of the Napoli Division, General Porcinari, shown here with several members of his staff

The citizens of Palermo greet troops of the 2nd Armored Division, 22 July

A rare scene of joy as Sicilians join US troops to celebrate the liberation of Messina, 17 August 1943

Harrow, Sandhurst, and in 1911, at the age of nineteen, a commission in the Irish Guards.

During the First World War he gained a reputation for fearlessness in battle and in less than a year rose from platoon leader to battalion commander, and in the process became one of the youngest lieutenant-colonels in the Army. For a brief period in 1918 when he was twenty-six years old, he even commanded a brigade. 'He was in action throughout the war, except when recovering from wounds or on courses. He was twice wounded (the first time seriously), and three times decorated. He was mentioned five times in despatches. He served alternately in each battalion of the Irish Guards, and reached his peak during his year in command of the 2nd Battalion, which made him indisputably the most highly regarded officer in his regiment.'[1]

Unlike Montgomery he never showed any sign that the grim horror of the Western Front ever disturbed him. In fact, as his biographer notes: 'Alexander enjoyed the First World War, and was not ashamed to admit it. He was happy doing what was expected of him and knowing that he could do it well. To his mother he wrote in 1916, "There's something terribly fascinating about it all, the starlights at night which one shoots out of a pistol to light up the ground, the rattle of musketry, and then the sound of big guns. I wouldn't miss it or be out of it for anything." '[2]

War was a business like any other and as a soldier he would do his best and not involve himself in moral questions. Alexander once remarked that 'War is horrible, but it is often necessary. It will probably always be necessary. If I see a fly, I do not crush it but let it out the window. But if I see an enemy army, my whole purpose is to destroy it. There are certain things which are evil, in a way that a fly is not evil, and we must fight those things, first by argument, then if argument fails, by war.'[3]

Alexander commanded the 1st Division of the BEF in 1940, and when the evacuation of Dunkirk commenced he was chosen by Lord Gort to command 1 Corps which was responsible for covering the evacuation. With characteristic calm Alexander successfully accomplished his mission and was the last Englishman to leave Dunkirk. In recent years, questions have been raised about

[1] Nigel Nicolson, *Alex*, op. cit., p. 48.
[2] Ibid., p. 52.
[3] Ibid., p. 279.

why Alexander failed to carry out his written mandate to ensure that French troops were evacuated in equal numbers to the British. When he made his final tour of the beach area on the night of 2 June not one single Frenchman had been evacuated, even though 10,000 French troops were nearby and might have been evacuated with available British ships. Instead, they were left behind while British ships sailed for England empty. Alexander's role in this affair is ambiguous, but he bears some responsibility for the muddle which followed the final evacuation of the BEF which has left a legacy of bitterness on the part of the French who believed the British were concerned only with saving their own hides.

Command of a corps in southeastern England in 1940–41 followed Dunkirk. However, the increasingly desperate Allied position in Burma led Churchill to send Alexander to assume command of the Burma Army in early 1942. Within days of his arrival he barely escaped capture by the Japanese and was forced to evacuate his forces from the capital of Rangoon. When Churchill made his long-expected change of command in North Africa in August 1942, Alexander was summoned to replace Auchinleck as C-in-C, Middle East.

One of Alexander's greatest admirers was a future prime minister, Harold Macmillan, then Churchill's British Minister Resident in North Africa. His diary reveals his growing impressions of Alexander:

> 28 April 1943 – The more I see of him the more I like and admire him.
>
> 14 June 1943 – He is really a first-class man.
>
> 17 July 1943 – He is really a remarkable character – his simplicity, modesty and firmness make up a most charming and impressive whole. Like so many men of his responsibilities, he is dependent on a simple but complete faith in the certainty of victory and the guidance of Providence.[1]

That these two men would have much in common is no surprise: they were fellow Guardsmen and British gentlemen. For most of the Sicily campaign, Alexander's HQ was outside Tunis in a large seafront house which operated more like a well-run English country estate than a military headquarters. Macmillan observed that,

[1] Harold Macmillan, *War Diaries*, London, 1984, *passim*.

in this stately atmosphere, conversation was preferred to listening to the 'wireless':

> The conversation in the usual form of educated (and there are some *very* well-educated) Englishmen – a little history, a little politics, a little banter, a little philosophy – all very lightly touched and very agreeable ... very occasionally an officer comes in with a message to the 'Chief'. After pausing sufficiently for politeness the conversation in hand – the campaign of Belisarius or the advantages of classical over Gothic architecture, or the right way to drive pheasants in flat country to show them well, or whatever it may be – General Alex will ask permission to open his message – read it – put (it) into his pocket – continue the original discussion for a few more minutes and then, perhaps, if the message should call for any action, unobtrusively retire, as a man might leave his smoking-room or library after the ladies have gone to bed, to say a word to his butler, fetch a pipe or the like.[1]

Eisenhower's first encounter with Alexander took place in London in August 1942, and for the newly designated Allied commander it was a case of impressing a living legend. Eisenhower's diary shows he was deeply concerned about making a suitable impression on the man who was to become his ground commander in North Africa. He needn't have worried, for the two men hit it off from the start. Returning from lunch Eisenhower remarked, 'That guy's good! He ought to be Commander-in-Chief instead of me!' In turn, Alexander had told Eisenhower: 'You're off to a good start.'[2]

Another contemporary of Alexander, General Sir William E. Morgan, has suggested that he possessed two essential assets to successful generalship: unbounded optimism and very good health, including 'a damn good digestion'. 'Alexander had all the best qualities of an aristocrat: generosity without extravagance, tolerance and a tremendous sense of duty.'[3]

Alexander's success as a general emanated primarily from his personal leadership on the battlefield rather than as a result of brilliant planning; by personal example rather than the execution of a well-thought-out strategy. In short, for his entire career Alex-

---

1 *War Diaries*, op. cit., p. 154.
2 Harry C. Butcher, *Three Years with Eisenhower*, London, 1946, p. 37.
3 Papers of General Sir William Morgan, Imperial War Museum. After service in the UK from 1940 to 1944, he became Chief of Staff to the Supreme Allied Commander, Mediterranean, in 1945. He is no relation to General Sir Frederick Morgan, the architect of the COSSAC plan for Operation OVERLORD.

ander had simply done what came naturally, with scant thought to the evolving role an officer assumes as he rises in rank. He was quite content to be seen rather than heard. He was also one of the most intellectually lazy men ever to hold high command; he loathed detail and paperwork and was never comfortable articulating strategy or in outlining guidance to his staff. As a result, planning at 15th Army Group was chaotic and his staff found it almost impossible to obtain guidance or decisions; Alexander never seemed to know what he wanted.

Montgomery later said of him – more in sorrow than animosity – that 'when he has a conference of commanders, which is very seldom, it is a lamentable spectacle; he relies on ideas being produced which will give him a plan; he does not come to the conference with *his own* plan, and then give out clear orders. No one gets any orders, and we all do what we like.'[1]

As he progressed to higher positions of responsibility, Alexander never varied his approach and does not seem to have expressed the slightest interest in doing so. While his technique of command worked well at lower levels, the power of personal example by itself was no substitute at Army Group level for a firm hand in planning overall strategy and ensuring it was carried out.

Alexander's detached style of command can best be illustrated during the Allied invasion of Anzio in January 1944. The task force commander, General Lucas, was *never* given specific guidance by Alexander as to what the landing was to accomplish. Nor was Lucas told whether to move aggressively to the heights of the Alban Hills some twenty miles inland or to play it safe and firmly establish his force ashore before attempting offensive action. Alexander and General Mark Clark held opposing points of view. Nevertheless, 'it was the responsibility of Alexander, the superior commander, to make his desire clear and prevailing. *Instead, because of his own lack of decision or because of his inhibitions in the coalition command, he allowed the venture, like the entire operational strategy in Italy, simply to develop.*'[2] (Author's italics.) Such was the case in Sicily.

The most serious flaw of Alexander's generalship was his consistent failure to grasp the reins of higher command, to make the distinction between interference in the actions of his subordinate

---

[1] 'Reflections on the Campaign in Italy, 1943', Montgomery Papers.
[2] Martin Blumenson, *Mark Clark*, op. cit., p. 171.

Army commanders and the necessity to impose his will at the right *time* and *place*; to use the power of his personality and position to influence the action while still permitting them the necessary initiative and latitude to carry out their respective missions.

Alexander's inability to control his subordinates was not, as generally thought, confined to Montgomery and Patton. Montgomery's successor and personal choice as Eighth Army commander in December 1943 was Lieutenant-General Oliver Leese. Like Alexander, the tall, hearty Leese was a Guardsman* who was a popular commander of the 30 Corps in Sicily. His background included considerable experience in command of troops, which equipped him admirably for corps command. His senior operations officer, Lieutenant-Colonel (later General) Victor Fitzgeorge-Balfour, believes 'he was far and away the best *Corps* Commander that the British Army produced during the war'.[1] In the desert Leese had already proved he could get the most out of such diverse and idiosyncratic commanders as Freyberg and Wimberley. Besides being a familar figure to his troops, they had confidence in him and considered him a 'lucky' general.[2]

As an Army commander Leese was less successful, partly because of his tendency to emulate Montgomery. Leese, however, lacked Montgomery's stable temperament and was, on occasion, given to intemperate outbursts. Broadhurst recalls that Leese 'was terrified of Monty. On his own he was a bully; used filthy language. He used to lose his temper and shout at his officers. And I've seen him in full flow while waiting for a corps commanders' conference, beating hell out of his staff, calling them all the rude names under the sun. And Monty walks in and he suddenly stands smartly at attention and only pearls would fall from his mouth.'[3]

Alexander's impotence as a commander is illustrated by this incident in early 1944 in Italy:

> Leese and myself were called over for a meeting under Slessor who was then Air Commander (RAF, Mediterranean and Middle East) and Alex. Leese was bleating about his airmen not

[1] Letter, General Sir Victor Fitzgeorge-Balfour to the author, 17 May 1984.
[2] Ibid.
[3] Interview with Air Chief Marshal Sir Harry Broadhurst, 2 November 1983. A Canadian officer later described Leese as 'a smooth-faced baronet with about as much personal appeal to Canadian troops as a suet pudding in a Sam Browne belt'. (Cf. Strome Galloway, *The General Who Never Was*, Belleville, Ontario, 1981, p. 180.)

* Leese was commissioned in the Coldstream Guards in time to serve in the 1914–18 war where he won the DSO, was wounded three times and mentioned in despatches twice.

being with him for this [forthcoming] operation in which an American airman was going to be in charge of air support. And Leese said, 'I have been brought up only to work with my airmen in close support. Any other way and we'll get in a muddle.' Slessor said, '. . . Broadhurst is going home for Normandy.' Whereupon Leese lost his temper and accused the airmen in this foul language he always used when Montgomery wasn't there – in front of Alex – and raved away about the bloody airmen, lot of crooks, couldn't trust them. And he got up and stalked out. Had he done that with Monty, he'd not only have gone out but been on the first aeroplane home. There was an awful silence for about a quarter of an hour, then Alex got up, walked out and persuaded him to come back. Then Slessor said: 'If only you'd waited before losing your temper; I didn't know Broadhurst was going until just now.' He didn't either, because I hadn't told him [the signal had only arrived that morning] . . . An example of Alex's complete inability to control his commanders.[1]

Later in the war the British Chiefs of Staff would develop grave doubts about Alexander's ability to fulfil the role of a supreme commander. Cunningham, the First Sea Lord, described him as 'totally unfitted for the job' and Brooke's growing doubts are reflected in numerous unflattering entries in his diary.[2] Alexander was universally liked but this has not muted the opinions of his associates. Lieutenant-General Sir Ian Jacob who served at Churchill's behest as the Chief Staff Officer to Alexander when he was the postwar Minister of Defence (1952–54) recalls without malice that Alexander never produced a single original idea in the time he knew him.[3]

The truth is that beneath the delightful outer façade lay a shallow intellect which was rarely ever stimulated by the study of war or interest in military matters. The myth of Alexander's greatness as a military leader has taken root from a mistaken public perception that equates soldierly bearing with military eminence and exceptional personal courage to great generalship.

---

[1] Ibid.

[2] Cf. the diary of Admiral Sir Andrew Browne Cunningham, The British Library, and the Alanbrooke Diary and Papers, University of London, King's College.

[3] Interviews with Lieutenant-General Sir Ian Jacob, 1979–84. General Jacob served under General Sir Hastings Ismay as a military assistant in the War Cabinet and was privy to events at the highest level throughout the war. When Churchill was returned to power as Prime Minister in October 1951 he summoned Jacob for the specific purpose of keeping a firm grip on Alexander during the early months of his ministership. Jacob later became Director-General of the BBC from 1952 to 1960.

In short, Alexander's deeds have never matched his reputation.
Even his own biographer said of his subject recently:

> I don't think he was a very clever man, Alex. I don't think he had
> great imagination. He had great courage but not much daring.
> You can never see in any of Alex's battles or campaigns some-
> thing that makes you gasp with admiration. You see how much
> he . . . depended on advice from very, very brilliant subordinate
> generals who often disobeyed his orders, but brought it off!. . .
> He was an English country gentleman, almost uneducated, who
> never read a book or had any interest in the arts at all, except for
> his painting – not other people's painting . . . He had no
> philosophy, you see. He had no politics. He wasn't interested in
> the causes of war, or the cause of that particular war in which he
> was fighting.[1]

Montgomery genuinely liked Alexander and thought of him as a
friend. But when it came to his military ability Montgomery was
characteristically blunt in his assessment. 'Alexander is a very
great friend of mine, and I am very fond of him. But I am under no
delusion whatsoever as to his ability to conduct large-scale operations in the field; he knows nothing about it; he is not a strong
commander and he is incapable of giving firm and clear decisions
as to what he wants. In fact, no one ever knows what he *does* want,
least of all his staff; in fact, he does not know himself . . . The
whole truth of the matter is that ALEXANDER has got a definitely
limited brain and does not understand the business; the use of air
power in the land battle is a closed book to him. Defensively he is
good, and will pull a bad situation out of the fire . . . He does not
understand the offensive and mobile battle; he cannot make up his
mind and give quick decisions; he cannot snap out clear and
concise orders. He does not think and plan ahead . . . He has never
commanded an Army or a Corps in the field. He loves battle
schools and minor tactics. The higher art of war is beyond him . . .
And so ALEXANDER has acquired a false reputation as a great
commander in the field, and as a great strategist.'[*]

Montgomery's opinion of Alexander's generalship was devoid
of envy or even the slightest animosity:

[1] Nigel Nicolson, quoted in *Monty, Master of the Battlefield, 1942–44*, op. cit., p. 472.
Note Macmillan's completely contrasting assessment on p. 337.

[*] Montgomery was in the habit of writing candid opinions either in his diary or in
memorandums which he retained in his personal papers. His comments about Alexander
appear in a document entitled 'Reflections on the Campaign in Italy 1943', Montgomery
Papers. Numerous other similar remarks appear in his papers for the Sicily period.

I often wish he would take more of a grip of things . . . when the table has to be 'thumped' he relies on me to do it. I do so, and take all the mud that is then slung about!! He is very ignorant of the air aspect of operations and is seen off by the RAF . . . On the level of high command in war ALEXANDER is not good, and definitely requires someone handy to tell him what to do . . . His character is pure gold . . . If he were more forceful, and was clever, he would be a superman.[1]

What Alexander needed, lamented Montgomery, was a stronger staff around him:

I am afraid it must be admitted that throughout the preliminary planning stage, and during the actual operations in SICILY, 15 Army Group has been completely and utterly ineffective. The CGS [Major-General A. A.] Richardson is definitely out of his depth. The MGA [Major-General C. H.] Miller is also out of *his* depth . . . There is no one at 15 Army Group, from ALEXAN-DER downwards, who really knows the battle end of the business . . . The staff . . . is far too big; it is a clumsy and unpractical set-up. They total some 480 officers and a great many other ranks – which is definitely a great waste, and in fact a scandal. A further trouble is that ALEXANDER cannot make a decision when faced with a difficult and complex problem. Therefore his staff have a very difficult time.

He is so used to reaching agreements by compromise, and to finding a formula that will suit all parties, that he has lost the gift of quick decision – if he ever had it.

He will take action at once when the line of country is given him by me, or by someone else whose opinion he trusts . . . ALEX-ANDER requires a Chief of Staff who is the 'cat's whiskers', and who will tell him what is wanted. Given this he would be excellent. But he has not got one.[2]

For the Americans who never warmed to Monty's bluntness, Alexander was a welcome change and represented the quintessence of the British officer and, with the exception of Mark Clark, who never trusted him, they embraced him as one of their own. Even Patton, who was strongly anti-British, liked and respected

[1] Memorandum, 'The "HUSKY" Problem (23 April–6 May 1943)', 9 July 1943, Montgomery Papers.
[2] 'Some Reflections on the Campaign in Sicily – July/August 1943', Montgomery Papers. During the Italian campaign Alexander got exactly the Chief of Staff suggested by Montgomery: Lieutenant-General A. F. (later Field-Marshal Lord) Harding, former commander of the 7th Armoured Division and a desert veteran. Harding was sent by Brooke specifically to bolster Alexander, a task which he fulfilled admirably.

Alexander from the time of their first meeting in March 1943 in Tunisia. (The anger of Patton and Bradley over the boundary line change was vented more upon Montgomery than Alexander.) Bradley would later record that 'Alexander proved to be all that I had heard: a patient, wise, fair-minded, shrewd, utterly charming professional soldier with a firm strategic grasp of the whole Mediterranean–North African Theater. His combat experience was intimidating to all American officers . . . He had been thrust into a difficult position in Tunisia, a job requiring the utmost tact, diplomacy, tolerance and discretion. He was clearly the man for the job and he bore the responsibility with disarming modesty.'[1]

Alexander's relations with the Allied air and naval commanders in the Mediterranean were occasionally frosty. He never seems to have had much faith in the Royal Navy, who he felt were far more concerned with avoiding losses than in assisting the Army. In Sicily he and the volatile Admiral Andrew Cunningham clashed.* Nor did he care much for Tedder. At Salerno, Tedder, in a sharp and unpleasant manner, refused air support requested by Alexander on the premise the ground forces were in no danger. Always the gentleman, an exasperated Alexander said to Tedder: 'Well, Arthur, I'd just like you to go up to Salerno, stay with the men in an infantry battalion for one month, share their life and then see what you would say!'[2]

A lengthy unpublished postwar interview given to several American official historians is the only known occasion on which

---

[1] A General's Life, op. cit., p. 134.

[2] General L. L. Lemnitzer, interview with Sidney T. Mathews, 16 Jan 1948, USAMHI. Lemnitzer also noted this incident as an example of how Eisenhower played the role of conciliator. After their exchange 'Ike spoke to Alexander and told him not to mind what Tedder had said – that was the way Tedder was, and that we were all anxious to reach the same end. Also that he would get the air support he needed.'

* Shortly after D-Day Alexander and Cunningham locked horns over Alexander's signal section which was mistakenly landed by the navy at Gela instead of Cassibile. Alexander was angry and sent a 'hot' message to Cunningham stating that his signal section had been lost by the navy and landed at the wrong place and what was he going to do about it? Cunningham was a very old-fashioned officer who believed that protocol should be strictly followed. Thus, an angry 'ABC' went to see Alexander and said, 'General, I received your telegram. Do you know what I do with telegrams like that? I throw them in the wastebasket. There was some little mistake about your signals but I don't have to take that sort of message from you.' Alexander replied, 'Well, Admiral, we're going to have a big scrap if you don't get my signals back to me here,' which Cunningham eventually did. (Alexander interview with official US historian George Howe, n.d., USAMHI. This lengthy three-part interview was given by Alexander in Ottawa some time during his tenure as Governor-General of Canada (1946–52). None was ever given to the official British historians who did not believe in the use of interviews and apparently never approached Alexander.)

Alexander permitted a glimpse behind the polished public persona. His private views of senior Allied commanders are blunt and often scathing. Descriptions such as 'thoroughly useless' and 'an old woman' were more reminiscent of Monty. He admitted having scant respect for his later superior in the Mediterranean, Field-Marshal Sir Henry Maitland 'Jumbo' Wilson, and that he politely ignored all his suggestions unless they happened to coincide with his own views.[1]

His correspondence with Brooke shows the same candour and, on occasion, a compassionate side. When Montgomery sacked the commander of the 10th Armoured Division, Major-General A. H. Gatehouse, in December 1942, Alexander wrote a letter to Brooke about both Gatehouse and Lumsden, the 10th Corps commander, who was also relieved:

> I think he [Gatehouse] is a borderline case. There is no doubt that he is slow and stupid. Against this he has more experience of actually fighting armour than anyone else. He has the confidence of his subordinates . . . I have seen both [men] alone . . . and I have tried very hard to convince them that we are not sending them away because they are failures – but because they are due for a rest from the battlefield . . . But if you could spare a few moments to send for them when they arrive, the sooner after they arrive the better, and say how pleased you are to get them back . . . I sincerely hope they can be found suitable roles, otherwise they will feel they are not wanted and all of this valuable experience is very much wanted.[2]

Montgomery would have scoffed that both men had failed as commanders and that Lumsden in particular was a menace who should under no circumstances be given any further combat command. In the gentlemanly tradition of the British Army, Alexander went out of his way to inject a good word on their behalf with Brooke who rarely had kind words for failed commanders. While this was certainly an example of Alexander's compassion, it was also symptomatic of another flaw in his generalship, one that Eisenhower had detected early in their relationship. In a June 1943 confidential evaluation of his senior officers, Eisenhower wrote presciently of Alexander:

> He has a winning personality, wide experience of war, an ability

[1] Alexander interview.
[2] Letter, Alexander–Brooke, 10 December 1942, Alanbrooke Papers.

to get along with people, and sound tactical conceptions. He is self-effacing and energetic. The only possible doubt that could be raised with respect to his qualifications is a suspected unsureness in dealing with certain of his subordinates. At times it seems he alters his own plans and ideas merely to meet an objection or a suggestion of a subordinate, so as to avoid direct command methods. This I must say is only a feeling. I have no proof that in the cases where he has apparently changed his mind rather radically, that he was swayed by anything except further reflection on the problem.[1]

A case in point was the British First Army Commander, Anderson. By his own admission Alexander found him sorely lacking, yet for weeks he vacillated over whether to recommend his relief. For some time Montgomery had been advising his replacement and Alexander himself had agreed; nor had he liked what he had seen during his first visit to the Tunisian front as the new Allied ground forces commander in February 1943, and although he later admitted he had not considered relief at that time, the more he saw of him, the more he was convinced Anderson ought to be removed.[2] On 12 March he cabled Brooke:

> Undoubtedly Anderson has had immense difficulties to contend with in the past but a bigger man could have overcome them. He is a good plain cook and not of the calibre we must now look for in our army commanders. He will carry his present job through with help and assistance from above and there is no use in making a change unless I am certain that his successor will be what I want.[3]

Brooke refused to interfere and Alexander was forced to bite the bullet. Privately, he maintained he would have replaced Anderson if Montgomery had given him Oliver Leese.[4] Montgomery had, in fact, attempted on 17 March to persuade Alexander to do exactly that, in response to a cable from Alexander, who later claimed that Montgomery could not spare Leese during the battle for the Mareth Line.[5] *After* the Mareth battle Montgomery again offered Leese to take over First Army, but Alexander wavered and kept, for the remainder of the Tunisian campaign, a commander in whom he admittedly had little confidence.

---

[1] Eisenhower, 'Memorandum for Personal File', 11 June 1943, Eisenhower Papers.
[2] Alexander interview.
[3] Cable, Alexander–Brooke, 12 March 1943, Alanbrooke Papers.
[4] Alexander interview.
[5] Ibid.

Alexander's role in the Sicily campaign was crucial. As the Army Group commander it was his responsibility to develop the invasion plan and to mastermind the strategy for the ground campaign to follow the assault landings. It was a time for firm and aggressive leadership from a commander who knew what he wanted and was prepared to fight for it. Instead, there emerged a commander whose attitude towards American commanders and troops was powerfully coloured by their early failures in Tunisia. By electing to distance himself from his subordinates, the campaign soon developed virtually into two private wars fought by Patton and Montgomery to their own ends, while Alexander stood mutely on the sidelines.

The ultimate irony of the American love affair with Alexander was that this most popular of British generals proved in the end to be one of their biggest detractors over the course of three campaigns: Tunisia, Sicily and Italy.

PART V

The Battle for Sicily

In war nothing is achieved except by calculation.
Everything that is not soundly planned in its details
yields no result.

NAPOLEON

CHAPTER 21

The Bridge over the Simeto

> I intended to make a great effort to reach CATANIA
> by nightfall on 14 July; given some luck I felt it could
> be done; but I must have the luck.
>
> MONTGOMERY

For three days the Eighth Army had advanced with only minimal opposition. Now, as a result of a bold decision by Montgomery, the entire focus of the Sicilian campaign came to rest upon an ugly, nondescript 400-foot-long steel girder bridge known as Ponte Primosole. Approximately seven miles south of the port city of Catania, Highway 114 passes over the River Simeto en route to the city of Lentini which lies some ten miles further south on the edge of the plain of Catania. Spanning the muddy Simeto in 1943 was Primosole bridge which resembled a Bailey bridge of the type frequently erected by Allied combat engineers during the war.

At this point in its journey from the mountains of central Sicily the river winds sluggishly from the west in a series of loops which eventually carry it to the Gulf of Catania, approximately 1½ miles east of the bridge, in a marshland devoid of cover. On both sides of the bridge the river is about 30 yards wide, with muddy banks overgrown with patches of tall reeds.

At each end of the bridge were protective concrete blockhouses that baked their occupants in the sizzling sun of the Sicilian summer. Near the northern edge of the bridge was a series of farm buildings, and for more than a thousand yards to the east and west of Highway 114 were rows of vineyards, olive and fruit trees which extended to a depth of some five hundred yards. 'It was a hole-and-corner area, very "blind", full of lurking places.' On the northern edge of the vineyards a sunken track ran westward, while to the north the plain again became bare and filled with gullies. Approximately 2½ miles north of the bridge, Highway 114 crossed a large, dry irrigation canal called the Fosso Bottaceto which marked the southern edge of the formidable defences of the Catania airfield.[1]

Primosole bridge, this heretofore obscure speck on the harsh Sicilian landscape, became the pawn in a deadly game between British and German forces which was to alter the course of the campaign.

During the pre D-Day planning, Montgomery had pinpointed Primosole bridge as the key to securing the vital Catania plain and city. The bridge was the vital point in any assault against Catania itself but would be a dangerous bottleneck in a successful British advance. The collapse of the Italian defences had, as we have seen, left only Schmalz's task force between the British and the virtually undefended city of Catania. While there were known to be Italian defenders between the bridge and the city, Montgomery was confident that a *coup de main* was possible before either the Italians or Germans could react.

In early May, General Hopkinson was alerted to prepare the 1st Airborne Division to accomplish three separate missions, one of which was a brigade-sized parachute/glider operation to seize Primosole the night of D+2/3 several hours ahead of a ground force which would drive rapidly north to relieve the paratroopers about dawn, 14 July.[2]

During the first 48 hours of the campaign the progress of Eighth Army had been so favourable that Montgomery succumbed to the false conviction that he could successfully advance on two fronts: a main thrust up the coast to slice through the plain of Catania and seize the city, and a secondary attack inland by Harpoon Force* to capture Vizzini, Caltagirone, Enna and Leonforte. While Patton's troops choked off the counterattack at Gela this force would drive behind the Hermann Goering Division and trap Conrath's forces

[1] Description contained in *The Mediterranean and Middle East*, Vol. V, op. cit., pp. 100–2.

[2] War Diary, 1st Airborne Division, 'Draft Outline Plan of 1 (Br) Airborne Division', 12 May 1943, PRO (WO 169/8666). The instructions read: 'An airborne force will be dropped the night of D+2/3 or any subsequent night with the object of seizing and holding the river crossing PONTE DI PRIMOSOLE ...' The other two tasks given the 1st Airborne were the seizure of Ponte Grande bridge on D-Day by the 1st Airlanding Brigade and the seizure of a key river crossing north of Augusta the night of D/D+1, which was aborted when it fell with unexpected swiftness to ground troops – a fortunate occurrence, notes Major-General John Frost, as the DZs were non-existent and would have produced very heavy casualties and the scattering of the unit far and wide. (Cf. *A Drop Too Many*, p. 176.)

* A task force consisting of the 23rd Armoured Brigade, the infantry of 51st Division and, on the left, the 1st Canadian Division.

between Bradley's II Corps and Leese's 30 Corps. A telegram to Alexander on 12 July displayed Montgomery's enthusiasm and expectations: 'Hope to capture CATANIA and its airfields by about 14 July.'[1]

The secondary thrust failed when the lead units of Harpoon Force ran into unexpectedly stiff resistance at Vizzini from the Hermann Goering which held the city until the morning of 15 July. Therefore, Montgomery turned his attention to the primary coastal thrust. The 1st Airborne, still on standby at its base outside Kairouan, was alerted that the airborne assault to seize Primosole bridge was 'on' for the night of 13/14 July.

Montgomery's audacious plan was uncomplicated: the night of 13/14 July the 1st Parachute Brigade would parachute on to drop zones around Primosole bridge, followed three hours later by a small glider-borne force carrying two troops of light artillery (10 guns). At the same time No. 3 Commando would land by sea and capture the bridge at Malati, which spans the Lentini River about three miles north of the city of Lentini. While these forces held the two bridges, the 50th Division (then at Sortino), reinforced by Brigadier J. C. Currie's recently landed 4th Armoured Brigade, was to thrust rapidly north towards Carlentini, then continue the drive, capture Lentini, and quickly race the remaining eight miles to Primosole bridge. En route they would relieve the commandos and, at the Simeto, also the paratroopers who would help them establish a bridgehead north of the river by nightfall, 14 July. The following day, this powerful airborne–infantry–armoured force would complete the operation by seizing Catania.

Kirkman was summoned at midday on 13 July by Montgomery and Dempsey. It was Montgomery who did the talking. Kirkman was to spearhead the drive with 50th Division and was to get forward with 'all possible speed' to ensure the airborne were relieved early on 14 July.[2] To accomplish its mission the division would have to punch through all enemy opposition and advance some thirty miles in less than twenty-four hours to Primosole bridge. Concurrently, the 5th Division was to advance north along the coastal belt from Augusta and join forces with the 50th Divi-

[1] Eighth Army narrative, 9–31 July 1943, PRO (WO 201/473).

[2] *Monty: Master of the Battlefield, 1942–1944*, op. cit., pp. 302–3, and Major-General Sidney Kirkman, 'Account of 50th Division Operations – Sicily', PRO (CAB 106/473). Although Dempsey, the 13 Corps commander, was present, Kirkman's orders came directly from Montgomery who had taken full charge of Eighth Army operations.

sion at Carlentini. One brigade would then occupy the high ground to the west and protect the left flank of both divisions from enemy interference.[1]

The task of seizing Primosole bridge fell to Brigadier Gerald Lathbury's 1st Parachute Brigade.* Lathbury's plan called for Lieutenant-Colonel Alastair 'Jock' Pearson's 1st Battalion to carry out the *coup de main* north and south of the bridge while Lieutenant-Colonel E. C. Yeldham's 3rd Battalion landed some 1,000 yards north where the river looped towards the sea and established a bridgehead which would permit the paratroopers to counter any attack from the direction of Catania. To the South, Lieutenant-Colonel John Frost's 2nd Battalion was given the task of securing the high ground south of the river. Code-named JOHNNY I, II and III, these three small but vitally important hills controlled all access to the bridge from the south.[2]

While the 1st Airborne were busy preparing for the operation the Germans were at last beginning to respond with reinforcements for the beleaguered Schmalz. Once word of the invasion was flashed to Berlin, Fliegerkorps XI – OKW's most powerful mobile reserve, consisting of 30,000 highly trained parachute troops – was placed on full alert. The commander of German airborne forces, General Kurt Student, had 3,000 paratroopers standing by and he now suggested their immediate deployment directly into the assault area to smash the Allies while they were

---

[1] 13 Corps narrative, Middle East Forces Papers, PRO (WO 201/619).

[2] Outline Plan, War Diary, 1st Airborne Division, loc cit., and Frost, *A Drop Too Many*, op. cit., p. 176. Frost recalls that Lathbury's orders were crystal clear and the DZs easily distinguishable from the air. He also recounts how Montgomery had inspected his battalion on 8 July and found the men of the 2nd Parachute Battalion extraordinarily fit. Before leaving, Monty reminded the men that there were some people who believed the Italians nice people. Personally, he thought they were very nasty people. 'The Eighth Army had killed quite a lot of them – they were easy to kill.' (War Diary, 2nd Parachute Battalion, PRO [WO 169/10344].)

* Lathbury, who became a full general after the war, was a Regular officer (Sandhurst 1924–25) who had previously commanded the 3rd Parachute Battalion and was a leading exponent of airborne operations. In 1944 he had the distinction of being one of the very few foreign officers ever to be awarded America's second highest decoration for bravery, the Distinguished Service Cross.

His sergeant-major was the legendary John C. Lord, a 6' 2" former Grenadier Guardsman of awesome presence, who was known as a stern disciplinarian of great fairness and impartiality. His usual greeting to new drafts reporting in was: 'My name is Lord – Regimental Sergeant-Major – my initials are J.C., but don't let that deceive you, for I'll have no mercy upon you.' Lord later was awarded an MBE for his leadership in a German stalag after being taken prisoner at Arnhem in September 1944. (Quote from Robert Smith, 'The Red Devils in Sicily', *Stand-To*, March 1952.)

at their most vulnerable. Student's proposal was rejected as too dangerous.[1]

Instead the commander of the 1st Parachute Division, Lieutenant General Richard Heidrich, was immediately summoned to Rome from his headquarters near Avignon.[*] Heidrich reported to Kesselring who informed him that his division was being sent to Sicily. The following day came a personal message from Goering himself, ordering Heidrich to send one parachute regiment at once to reinforce his hard-pressed Hermann Goering Division.[†]

The plan was to send Lieutenant Colonel Ludwig Heilmann's[‡] 3rd Parachute Regiment (FJR 3) to Sicily as an advance guard, followed by the Machine Gun Battalion and a Signal company. These units would soon be joined by the engineers, the anti-tank units and lastly by the 4th and 1st Parachute Regiments. About midnight on 11 July, Heilmann was summoned to the telephone. On the other end was Heidrich and he came straight to the point: Heilmann's regiment was to spearhead the reinforcement of Sicily by the 1st Parachute Division. 'You will personally reconnoitre the

---

[1] Volkmar Kuhn, *German Paratroops in World War II*, London, 1978, p. 181. 'Volkmar Kuhn' is the pseudonym of a successful German military writer.

[*] The 1st Parachute Division was formed in the early spring of 1943 mainly from the veteran 7th Air Division, and consisted of the 1st, 3rd and 4th Parachute Regiments (with three battalions each), an artillery regiment, an anti-aircraft artillery battalion (the 1st Parachute Machine Gun Battalion) and Engineer, Signal and anti-tank units. The disaster in North Africa led to the formation of two parachute divisions in southern France under the command of a parachute corps (Fliegerkorps XI) as part of an élite new German reserve. The morale of the men of the 1st Parachute Division was considerably lifted by new weapons, uniforms and intensive training which found them well prepared for their forthcoming role in Sicily.
Heidrich was a veteran parachutist and combat commander who had been a paratrooper since 1936. He had parachuted into Crete as a regimental commander and most recently had fought in the battle of Leningrad. A short, large-faced, blunt-jawed, soft-spoken officer, Heidrich's features were said to resemble those of a bull dog. He smoked cigars and was proud of his resemblance to Churchill. Under Heidrich's able leadership the 1st Parachute Division was soon recognized by the Allies as one of the very best divisions of the Wehrmacht.

[†] Since 1939 the German parachute troops had been under the control of the Luftwaffe. General Kurt Student, the founding father and commander of the parachute forces, had been in disfavour with Hitler since the German airborne operation in May 1941 which enabled the Germans to seize Crete. However, the excessively high casualties led Hitler to proclaim that 'the day of parachute troops is over' and, until Sicily, the airborne had been in limbo. Ironically, it had been the German success in Crete which had led the United States and Britain to form their own airborne and glider forces.

[‡] Heilmann, who was affectionately known as 'King Ludwig' to his men, was another of the wily, veteran officers who attained command in the German parachute forces. A soldier since his eighteenth birthday in 1921, Heilmann was attracted to the new parachute arm of the Luftwaffe and commanded a company during the Polish campaign and in France. As the commander of the 3rd Battalion of the 3rd Parachute Regiment, Heilmann led his men through the bitterly fought battles in Crete and later in Russia.

landing zone. The Field Marshal [Kesselring] will provide you with a swift combat aircraft. Start at 0500 hours in the morning [12 July]. Conduct yourself according to the situation. We ourselves don't know what is going on over there. Good luck....'[1]

With a small advance party consisting of Captain Franz Stangenberg and Captain Specht, a logistical officer, Heilmann departed from Avignon for a non-stop flight to Sicily. As his aircraft approached Catania, Heilmann could see the city was under Allied air attack. Thick black clouds of smoke rose into the morning air from the city. Heilmann's pilot was forced to seek cover by flying at low altitude in the foothills surrounding Mount Etna. As Heilmann later recalled, the pilot acted like an infantry-man as he wove into Catania whose airport still had fresh, smoking craters from the recent air attack. High above the airfield RAF Spitfires circled as the pilot landed. His landing was 'a work of art, as was the take-off'. When the three officers stepped from their aircraft, 'We saw for the first time the face of the hot ground of Sicily and felt more than before that we are actually only bits of dust on this earth.'[2]

While Specht went off to organize the necessary transport to move Heilmann's regiment to Lentini where it was to join the severely beset Group Schmalz, Heilmann and Spangenberg began to reconnoitre south of Catania for a suitable drop zone. At one point they were forced to take cover in a ravine during another of the incessant Allied air raids against targets in and around Catania. The drop zone eventually selected turned out to be the open ground directly to the east of Route 114, between the Gornalunga and Simeto rivers and only a few hundred metres north of Frost's DZ.*

Stangenberg barely had time to telephone the co-ordinates of the DZ before FJR 3 took off for Sicily. En route the He111 troop carriers were attacked by twenty P-38 Lightnings over the Strait of Messina and a disaster was averted only when low fuel forced the US planes back to their North African bases.[3]

---

[1] Generalmajor Ludwig Heilmann, 'Fallschirmjäger auf Sizilien', *Der Deutsche Soldatenkalender Nr. 7*, 1959. Heilmann's vivid recollections of the Sicilian campaign provide an excellent perspective of the German side of the battle.

[2] Ibid.

[3] Kuhn, op. cit., p. 182.

* On postwar maps the DZ appears as Statione di Passo Martino. (See Touring Club Italiano, 'Sicilia', Sheet No. D19, 1:200,000.)

Heilmann's first hours in Sicily had been anything but encouraging. The sight that greeted him on landing had been a steady stream of Italian soldiers fleeing north towards Catania. No Luftwaffe escorts accompanied the flight of FJR 3 to Sicily and, while admitting that the German airmen were brave, Heilmann wondered why they seemed to be everywhere *but* Sicily. His first reaction had been hope, followed by anger. In the end he knew his men would need some sort of miracle to land successfully in Sicily.[1]

At 1800, fires were lit to mark the drop zone and then came the answer to Heilmann's prayers: the Allied air force had gone home for dinner! Instead of having to land under aerial attack, the men of FJR 3 were allowed to parachute unmolested. Allied predictability, not for the first time, was to cost them an opportunity; in this case to destroy the unarmed German troop carriers. At 1815, the first German paratroopers to land in Sicily were the 1,400 men of the 3rd Parachute Regiment who made a near-textbook jump. High winds blowing in off the Gulf of Catania caused some injuries, but otherwise the drop of his regiment was a great success. Within forty-five minutes of landing Heilmann and his men had rendezvoused with the transport arranged by Captain Specht and were en route to Lentini – where they were to come under the operational control of Group Schmalz. At 2000, Heilmann met Schmalz outside Lentini and was told his 2nd Battalion was to be sent to Francofonte where they were to help plug the gap between Group Schmalz and the Hermann Goering force defending Vizzini. The remainder of the regiment was ordered to take up defensive positions between Carlentini and the sea.*

The following day – 13 July – saw the arrival of further reinforcements in the form of the 1st Parachute Machine Gun Battalion which was airlanded at Catania airfield in the midst of yet another Allied air raid.† The CO, Major Schmidt, ordered his

---

[1] Heilmann, op. cit.

* The story of German operations at Primosole bridge is based on a composite of published and unpublished accounts, including: Kuhn, op. cit.; Helmut Wilhelmsmeyer, 'The Battle for Primosole Bridge', *British Army Review*, Parts I and II, April and August 1985; and 'German Paratroopers and the Primosole Bridge, Sicily, 1943' by Georg Schmitz, edited by John Hillyer. Schmitz is a veteran paratrooper who served in Sicily as an NCO in the engineer battalion, and in Italy as a lieutenant in the same unit. This document was prepared for the author by Schmitz during the summer of 1985 and is based on a combination of his own experiences and several published German sources.

† Despite their enormous aerial supremacy, the Allied air forces never managed to cripple Catania airfield completely. Soon after the campaign the *R.A.F. Mediterranean Review*, No. 4, July–September 1943, recorded that 'As a result of bombing the GERBINI and

second-in-command, Captain Laun, to move the battalion south towards Primosole bridge while he drove to the FJR 3 CP near Carlentini where he was told by the astute Heilmann that: 'Something is bound to happen tonight. The enemy will try to sneak through to the Catania plain, and to do so he'll send in more troops – either by sea or by air. If he manages to land them in our rear and to dig in, then we're cut off for sure. So your battalion will remain south of Catania. Hold the bridge over the Simeto and put one company between there and the sea.'[1]

While Schmidt was away, Captain Laun was deploying the battalion to a point some 2,000 metres south of Primosole bridge where they dug in on the edge of an orange grove along the west side of Highway 114. Laun selected positions well concealed from aerial observation, and thereby set the stage for a showdown between the Green Devils* of the 1st Parachute Division and the Red Devils of the 1st Airborne Division for the control of Primosole bridge.

Heilmann's men were a welcome sight to Schmalz who was beginning at last to acquire some muscle and now made the most of his new paratroop reinforcements to gain additional time around Lentini, at the very moment when 13 Corps launched its drive north towards that town and the plain of Catania. There was very heavy fighting on 13 July as the Germans took advantage of the terrain around Mt Pancali where Kirkman's lead element, the 6th Green Howards, collided head-on with Group Schmalz. The spearhead of 50th Division was the 69th Brigade (Brigadier E. C. Cooke-Collis) – the same unit Kirkman had so vigorously prodded the previous day. By now the men of 69th Brigade were spread

[1] Quoted in Kuhn, op. cit., p. 184.

* The 1st Parachute Division, which later fought at Cassino, acquired the nickname Green Devils. According to German historian Helmut Wilhelmsmeyer (himself a veteran paratrooper), this sobriquet was bestowed by Churchill. 'After that, General Heidrich gave the order to paint a symbolic little devil on the cars as a sign of recognition.' (Letter to the author, 14 October 1986.)

CATANIA landing grounds [the latter also having been subjected to bombardment from the sea] were now untenable. ...' The arrival of the German parachute reinforcements on 13 July resulted in the loss of a number of anti-tank weapons and personnel when a number of German aircraft were either damaged or destroyed while on the ground at Catania airfield, including two Me321 GIGANT transport aircraft. Other losses to the anti-tank element of the division had occurred during the transfer to Italy from southern France. Several crashed on take-off or were lost en route. Thus, the main elements of the divisional anti-tank force were now gone, a serious loss. Schmidt's battalion arrived at Primosole with considerably less firepower than anticipated.

thinly over a large area and bone-tired. Monty's timetable had decreed that Lentini be captured during the night of 13/14 July, but when he came forward to assess the situation personally it was clear to Kirkman that the timetable could not be met.[1]

Exhausted though his men were, Kirkman had no option except to demand still more of them by reinforcing the Green Howards who continued to attack throughout the night against exceptionally stubborn resistance. Delays in moving the artillery forward caused postponement of a fresh attack by the 7th Green Howards until about 0830, 14 July. A vicious battle ensued until Mt Pancali fell at 1000 hours. On the battlefield the British found many dead Germans and twenty-nine machine guns.[2]

On 13 July the 5th Division advancing toward Lentini from the southeast ran into a unit of the 115 PzG Regiment and the two remaining battalions of Heilmann's paratroopers who held up the 15th Brigade all day. Monty's bold masterstroke was off to a rocky start.

While the infantry were battling their way towards Lentini, the commander of No. 3 Commando (Regiment), Lieutenant-Colonel J. F. Durnford-Slater, was summoned on very short notice to report to Syracuse on the afternoon of 13 July. On the quay he reported to Dempsey. To the side stood Montgomery and Rear-Admiral Roderick McGrigor, commander Naval Force 'B'. In the midday heat Durnford-Slater found the three commanders in high spirits. For a change it was Dempsey who did most of the talking: 'We've got a new operation for you tonight. It's an ambitious one but I think you'll like it.' What Dempsey had in mind was one of the most perilous missions ever given to this élite unit.*

[1] Kirkman account, loc. cit.
[2] Ibid. None of the accounts of this furious encounter specify the number of Germans killed on Mt Pancali. Among the Germans captured was a desert veteran who told his captors: 'I have been against many British attacks, but that was the finest I have ever seen. I congratulate you.' (Cf. Ewart W. Clay, *The Path of the 50th*, Aldershot, 1950, p. 177.)
* In mid-1940 Durnford-Slater was a Regular officer of the Royal Artillery who craved something more exciting than the duties of an adjutant of a training regiment. He got his wish when the War Office began recruiting men for a new Commando force and became one of its first soldiers as the CO of No. 3 Commando which he raised and trained. There were few guidelines and no precedent for this force but it was tempered by months of intensive training and trial and error in the form of raids against Guernsey, Norway and Dieppe. Recruitment was at first survival of the fittest. On one occasion Durnford-Slater and another colonel were to select new recruits at the Commando Replacement Depot in Scotland. However, Durnford-Slater arrived early and persuaded one of his former NCOs to identify the best men who were then put on a fatigue detail dressed in their oldest clothes while all others were smartly turned-out in their best battledress. The unsuspecting other colonel

That same night the commandos were to be put ashore by the infantry assault ship HMS *Prince Albert*, in bright moonlight, behind enemy lines in the Bay of Agnone. Once ashore they were to march five miles rapidly across country to seize intact the Ponte dei Malati, the highway bridge spanning the Lentini River four kilometres north of the town. The bridge was of crucial importance to the success of Montgomery's plan.

The terrain north of Lentini consists of small hills, gullies and ravines and is totally unsuitable for rapid off-road movement by tanks and vehicular traffic. The bridge and its causeway comprised about 300 yards of Highway 114 – the main route linking Lentini and Catania, and the only direct road to Primosole bridge. Its capture was obligatory if Montgomery's timetable was to be met. After being briefed by Dempsey, Durnford-Slater and the commandos had less than three hours to plan their attack and brief the participants.[1]

The British were not aware of the arrival of Heilmann and his paratroopers and Durnford-Slater was told to expect only Italian opposition on the beaches. The Commando leader was less certain ('I have an instinct for danger and ... that bridge was the only road linking the German and Italian armies with their bases in the Messina area. It seemed likely to me that Jerry would want to make sure it was well guarded.') but was reassured by Montgomery who had the last word: 'Everybody's on the move, now. The enemy is nicely on the move. We want to keep him that way. You can help us do it. Good luck, Slater.'[2]

As things turned out, it was Dempsey who was closer to the mark. Before leaving he said to Durnford-Slater, 'If, by any

---

[1] Hilary St George Saunders, *The Green Beret: The Story of the Commandos, 1940–1945*, London, 1949, p. 160.
[2] *Commando*, op. cit., p. 139.

---

naturally selected the smart-looking troops while Durnford-Slater gleefully chose the men he wanted.

When No. 3 Commando was sent to North Africa in mid-April, Durnford-Slater was appalled by the indifference and pompous atmosphere he found in AFHQ. 'Never before or since have I struck anything so bad,' he later wrote. At Force 141 he was shown the early plans for HUSKY. 'This is one of the worst plans I have ever seen,' he told his second-in-command, Major Peter Young. No. 3 Commando found a far different atmosphere in Eighth Army where they were warmly welcomed by both Montgomery and Dempsey. On D-Day his men knocked out an Italian AA battery in eighty-five minutes. Durnford-Slater had promised Dempsey the Commandos would accomplish the mission in ninety minutes. (Cf. Brigadier John Durnford-Slater, *Commando*, London, 1953.)

chance, 50 Division, who will be our leading troops, don't get through to you by first light tomorrow morning, clear off and hide up for the day.'[1]

When the first commandos landed about 2200, instead of encountering scattered Italian defenders, they of course ran headlong into Heilmann's tough paratroopers. And, as they would soon learn, the high ground between the landing site and Lentini was held by the 3rd Battalion of the Hermann Goering Regiment. From the time they landed until reaching the bridge about 0300, 14 July, the commandos were engaged in constant firefights. The first troops to reach the bridge were under the command of Major Peter Young.* The few Italian defenders were quickly routed as the bridge came under British control. Demolition charges were removed and, as Durnford-Slater later recalled, in the hour or so before dawn 'we had a marvellous time shooting up everything which came and causing complete confusion'.[2]

Now that No. 3 Commando had control of the bridge, the problem was to retain control until the 50th Division arrived. Not only was Highway 114 crucial to the British, but it was also the main resupply route for all German units fighting south of the Lentini River and their principal evacuation route to the north. The German reaction was predictable and very unpleasant.

The 50th Division was to have relieved the heavily outgunned Commando force at about dawn but the stiff German resistance left them still some miles to the south battling Group Schmalz and Heilmann's paratroopers. As the day wore on, commando casualties rose to alarming numbers from a Tiger tank stationed near the bridge and from intense fire of heavy mortars. And still there was no sign of the 50th Division. The Tiger was positioned out of range of the British Piats† and could not be approached over the open ground. After holding out for the better part of 14 July the survivors were finally forced to break into small groups and fight their way out of what would have been certain death or needless capture. For the Germans were throwing an ever-tightening noose

---

[1] Ibid.

[2] *The Green Beret*, op. cit., p. 164.

* Later Brigadier Peter Young, DSO, MC. Young was one of the original commandos and participated in nearly every major commando operation of the war, including Dieppe and Normandy. After the war he taught at Sandhurst and has become one of Britain's best-known military historians.

† Projector, Infantry, Anti-Tank weapons operated by a two-man team; the British equivalent of the American bazooka.

around the Malati bridge in order to remove this grave threat to their withdrawal to the north.[1]

Fierce fighting continued in the hills and rocky gullies as the commandos used all of their considerable skills to break through to the safety of friendly lines. One wounded major was taken prisoner but persuaded his captors he was too near death to be moved. The regimental adjutant removed his badges of rank and pretended to be just another private not worth the bother; both were among those later rescued.

About 1700 on 14 July the 5th Battalion, East Yorks (69th Brigade), became the first 50th Division unit to reach the Ponte dei Malati which the hastily retreating Germans had not had time to destroy.* That evening Dempsey said of No. 3 Commando, 'The men of No. 3 are the finest body of soldiers I have ever seen anywhere.'† However, the valour of No. 3 Commando was not without a high cost: 28 killed, 66 wounded and 59 missing.[2]

By dusk a troop of tanks of 4th Armoured Brigade were a mile south of Primosole bridge and, along with the 9th DLI, would soon join forces with what was left of the 1st Parachute Brigade.

The parachute drop of the 1st Parachute Brigade on to the plain of Catania turned out to be the third costly airborne fiasco of the four-day-old campaign. Like its predecessors, very little went according to plan. Operation FUSTIAN‡ began on the night of 13 July with 145 aircraft – 126 carrying paratroopers and 19 towing

[1] Ibid., pp. 164–5.
[2] Ibid., p. 168.
* At this point, 151 Brigade replaced the exhausted 69th Brigade as the spearhead force. 151 Brigade consisted of the 6th, 8th and 9th Battalions of the Durham Light Infantry (DLI).
† Among the commandos lost was Captain Bill Lloyd, one of their early recruits. Gravely wounded in both feet by an exploding mortar round, Lloyd insisted on continuing the fight. Despite a bone protruding from one of his fractured ankles, Captain Lloyd rode off on a bicycle, aided by troopers. Still propped up on his bicycle he led an attack on a German machine-gun nest and was cut down. Durnford-Slater called it 'my most serious personal loss of the war', and paid this tribute to his fallen comrade: 'Bill died fighting mad. He was a quiet man normally; courageous but unspectacular. He died in a spectacular way.' Montgomery was moved by the valour of the commandos and called the operation 'classic'. 'I want you to get the best stonemason in the town,' he ordered. 'I want you to have him engrave "No. 3 Commando Bridge" on a good piece of stone. Have this stone built into the masonry of the bridge.' (*Commando*, Chapter X.) The Malati bridge for which so many men died became known as 'No. 3 Commando Bridge' and the plaque ordered by Monty was duly placed and remained on the bridge after the war.
‡ The code-word that the operation was 'on' was 'Marston To-Night' and it is by this name that the operation is more commonly known.

the large Horsa gliders containing the anti-tank guns of the parachute artillery. Lessons had been learned from the earlier experiences of the glider landings and the two 82d Airborne parachute operations, and the flight path of the troop carriers was to keep the planes five miles off the east coast of Sicily, well away from the naval gunners of the Allied fleet. They were not to turn towards land until parallel with the mouth of the Simeto. The drop was to take place at a height of 500 feet commencing at 2200 hours and the gliders were to land starting at 0100, 14 July.*

Once again, the airborne were fired upon by friendly naval vessels and the various war diaries record a depressingly familiar tale. Some of the 'friendly' flak came from vessels lying off Malta, others from ships off the Sicily coast. Heavy flak from Axis batteries added to the chaotic scene which resulted in the dispersal of the aerial convoy. Fifty-five of the aircraft and seventeen gliders recorded being fired at by Allied ships and twenty-six returned to their North African base without dropping their troops. Fourteen planes were lost, eleven from flak; others managed to drop their troops before crashing, some into the sea, others on land. Thirty planes managed to drop their troops on to the correct DZ; nine dropped their loads nearby and forty-eight were off the mark by anything from half a mile to twenty miles. Four of the gliders landed on the DZ and seven of the remaining thirteen managed to land in various spots around the plain of Catania. The commandos encountered some of the Red Devils near the Malati bridge. Of the 1,856 officers and men who departed from Kairouan, only 12 officers and 283 men landed at or near Primosole bridge.[1]

The experience of Lieutenant-Colonel Yeldham's 3rd Battalion was typical. Only a handful of his men actually made it to the bridge, and these excerpts from the war diary typify the experience of many:

[13 July]

2210   Plane fired on by our own flak ships somewhere between between Malta and Sicily.

2250   Ran into heavy flak, this time the enemy's.

[1] *The Mediterranean and Middle East*, Vol. V, op. cit., pp. 95–6, and 1st Airborne Division War Diary (WO 169/8666).

* In addition to its three parachute battalions, the 1st Parachute Brigade consisted of the 1st Airlanding Anti-Tank Battery (RA); 1st Parachute Squadron, Royal Engineers; detachments of the 21st Independent Parachute Company and two Naval Bombardment Detachments.

| 2300 | Red light–green light – we float down into a world of searchlights, tracer bullets and burning corn stalks. |
| 2320 | 3rd Battalion consists of CO and Batman, RSM and Batman, intell sgt and one pte. Realise we are dropped on wrong DZ ... No sign of remainder of Bn.[1] |

Medic Robert Smith later wrote that, 'Dante's inferno would be an apt simile to describe the scene which greeted my eyes as my parachute opened ... Fires were burning to the four points of the compass, and I could see the bridge shining in the light of the moon . . . The machine-gun and small arms fire intensified as I approached Mother Earth; then I was on the ground, hugging it grimly in a depression that was not nearly deep enough ... As I lay on the ground a plane was hit in the under-belly and I saw a pinpoint of flame almost simultaneously as she exploded.'[2]

Major G. H. Seal, then a signal sergeant, recalls that 'as the green light came on, I went out like a bomb. My parachute opened and I hit the ground immediately* on a hillside. We never saw anything of the others in our stick ... I set off walking into the darkness. It was clear that the dropping zone was not in this neighbourhood ... At first light I identified a north-facing strip of the east coast and realised that the bridge was several miles north of my position. An Italian commando captain, with his sixty or so armed men, came up and pleaded with me to take them all prisoner. I asked him to get lost, which he did.'[3]

Another Red Devil who landed north of the Simeto encountered what he thought was another trooper in the dark. The password/countersign was 'Desert Rats' and the response 'Kill Italians'. Instead of the expected reply, the soldier asked in German if his Schmeisser had been found!

Frost's 2nd Battalion met with mixed success. The HQ and a portion of 'A' Company were dropped with great precision exactly on to their assigned DZ southwest of the bridge. Frost landed in a shallow ditch and wrenched his knee. From the ground he could see the drama being played out overhead:

---

[1] War Diary, 3rd Parachute Battalion, PRO (WO 169/10345).

[2] 'The Red Devils in Sicily', op. cit.

[3] Quoted in Pack, *Operation 'Husky'*, op. cit., pp. 139–41. Italian morale continued to crumble and on 13 July the Italian garrison guarding Catania harbour deserted, forcing German paratroopers to spend valuable manpower protecting the waterfront from possible amphibious landing.

* Most paratroopers were dropped from a dangerously low height of 300 feet.

There could be no doubt that few of the other squadrons had flown in as staunchly as ours had done. In fact we saw no other aircraft flying in formation anywhere. Some Dakotas flew over the general area at varying heights. Most of these were going flat out and some were weaving through the air in desperate evasive action. On one occasion two of them approached each other from opposite ends of the dropping-zone. We watched with bated breath, for a really sickening crash seemed inevitable. However, they tore past each other, perhaps not even knowing how near they had been to disaster ... The odd glider came in almost silently. One caught in a searchlight was riddled with machine-gun fire and crashed ...[1]

Flak and artillery fire filled the northern plain with a Fourth of July atmosphere: 'The DZ area was burning in many places where incendiary bullets had set it alight.'[2] By 0100 Frost had managed to assemble 112 men and began moving towards the three battalion objectives. A short time later, hobbling painfully with the aid of a stick, he encountered Brigadier Lathbury who was celebrating his thirty-seventh birthday in a very disagreeable fashion. Lathbury was one of many dropped in the wrong place and like Frost he had scant idea of the situation at Primosole bridge. About 0530, with a force now numbering 140 men, the 2nd Battalion was in position around JOHNNY I. His force, as Frost later matter-of-factly remarked, was poised for all-round defence but was totally without either supporting weapons or communications.[3] With the first light of a new day came the German response: a deadly machine-gun and mortar attack. Once again, Frost was to find himself leading his paratroopers in a desperate battle.*

[1] A Drop Too Many, op. cit., pp. 178–9.
[2] War Diary, 2nd Parachute Battalion, loc. cit.
[3] A Drop Too Many, op. cit., p. 180.
* By the end of the war the name of Lieutenant-Colonel John Dutton Frost became synonymous with the grit and determination of the British airborne soldier. Best known for his leadership of an airborne raid against a German radar station at Bruneval (near Le Havre) on 28 February 1942, and for his epic stand with 2nd Parachute Battalion at Arnhem bridge in September 1944, Frost was commissioned from Sandhurst into The Cameronians (Scottish Rifles) in 1932, thus joining a distinguished Lowland regiment whose battle honours are traced back to the Battle of Blenheim.

His erstwhile adjutant, Major Victor Dover, MC, has described the unassuming Frost as made of steel, a shy officer whose calm, inspired leadership and refusal ever to accept a situation as hopeless could be seen in his 'apparently sleepy eyes [which] could flash with a suddenness that made a man move faster than he would have believed possible'. Frost believed a commander's task in combat was to direct the actions of his men and he never carried a personal weapon into battle, carrying instead a shooting-stick and a hunting-horn which he used to rally his troops. In Tunisia, his unit fought a savage battle at Oudna and was forced to withdraw under heavy artillery fire. Like Gavin and Ridgway, Frost was

Pearson's 1st Battalion had as its primary task the seizure of the bridge by *coup de main*. Pearson was a Territorial officer who had joined the Parachute Regiment in 1941 and had been decorated with several DSOs and the Military Cross in eighteen months and was now at the age of twenty-seven a battalion commander. Only a small portion of his battalion landed on or near the correct DZ, and like the 2nd Battalion, nearly all of their Vickers machine guns, mortars, Piat anti-tank weapons and wireless sets had been lost. One of Pearson's troopers who did land on the designated DZ was Lance-Corporal Coster whose fall was broken by a conveniently placed haystack under which were hiding six Italians who, upon seeing the menacing figure towering above them with a Sten gun in his hand, 'ran like hares'.[1]

The presence of Italian troops caused some unexpected difficulties. About 0330, 14 July, an intelligence officer and three men of the 1st Battalion carried out a short patrol north of the bridge and returned with thirty Italian engineer POWs, the first of what proved to be an unwelcome flood. At 0700 the 3rd Battalion war diary was recording that: 'Italians waving white rags are coming out of hiding places they bolted to when they saw us drop the previous night.'[2] Others began arriving, baggage in hand, asking to be taken prisoner. They came from everywhere and were of all ranks and services (including the Air Force and Navy). The presence of these defectors proved an increasingly serious nuisance to the paratroopers who had more important problems. To the south of the bridge the steady stream of Italians became a great irritant to Colonel Frost's 2nd Para. More than 130 had surrendered around JOHNNY I. They were finally herded into a nearby farmyard which was turned into a makeshift (but unguarded) POW cage.

[1] Hilary St George Saunders, *The Red Beret*, London, 1950 (paperback edition, 1978), p. 119.

[2] War Diary, 3rd Parachute Battalion, loc. cit.

utterly fearless and seemed to lead a charmed life in battle. Dover recalls that during this withdrawal his men were 'wading through water up to their chests (in a river bed indelicately dubbed "Shit Creek") with their firearms held high above their heads ... Johnny Frost on the other hand walked along the bank calling encouragement and urging us on like the cox of a university boat crew. Just how he survived the shellfire only the angels knew and they must remain mystified.'

Great leaders exude an indefinable air of authority and charisma. Anyone meeting General Frost is instantly aware of being in the presence of a man of rare dignity who despite his fame remains almost painfully shy. Major Victor Dover's quotes are from *The Silken Canopy*, London, 1979. Dover's portrait of Frost at Arnhem bridge, painted in 1978, and reproduced in his book, captures better than words the aura of this outstanding British commander.

Eventually more than 500 Italians surrendered to the 2nd Battalion.[1]

About 0500, Lathbury and a small group of about forty men moved towards the bridge. The airborne commander had no idea what he would find and was preparing to use his tiny force to carry out the task of seizing Primosole with nothing more powerful than their Sten guns. 'There were no sounds of fighting from the bridge and there appeared no reason to suppose that it had been captured.' Near the southern end Lathbury could see a glider which had crash-landed less than 100 yards from the river.[2] Thirty yards from the bridge he encountered a paratrooper who reported that it had been captured by a small band of Pearson's men who had landed on the north bank. As Lathbury was crossing the bridge several grenades were lobbed from a German truck towing an 88 mm gun parked at the northern end which no one realized had not been neutralized. Lathbury was slightly wounded in the fray.[*]

About three hours earlier a band of fifty Red Devils under Captain Rann had attacked and seized Primosole bridge intact from the Italian security force which fled in panic when one of the gliders had collided with the bridge.[3] A Royal Engineer officer and nine sappers then dismantled the explosives strapped to the girders and threw them into the Simeto. Pearson arrived before dawn and took charge of establishing the airborne defence of the prize with a pathetically small force numbering about 120 men from his battalion, two platoons of the 3rd Battalion and three anti-tank guns. Matters soon improved considerably when Major David Hunter delivered an assortment of Italian and German weapons he had collected using a captured vehicle.[4]

[1] Frost, A Drop Too Many, op. cit., Chapter 12; War Diary, 2nd Parachute Battalion.

[2] Brigadier G. W. Lathbury, 'Marston To-Night', The Oxfordshire and Buckinghamshire Light Infantry Chronicle, Vol. XLVIII, 1946. Three of the nineteen gliders crash-landed near the bridge. One crashed into the river bank and broke in half, gravely injuring the crew of an anti-tank gun. The two pilots were thrown through the perspex windows of the cockpit and were found mangled and bleeding on the grass.

[3] Helmut Wilhelmsmeyer, 'The Battle for Primosole Bridge', Part I, op. cit.

[4] Ibid., Part II, op. cit., and War Diary, 1st Airborne Division, loc. cit.

[*] Despite the parachute drop, the heavy flak and automatic weapons fire along many points of the plain of Catania, there was still convoy traffic on Highway 114 between Catania and the Lentini area. Lathbury observed headlights passing in both directions during the night. On the assumption that the troops guarding the bridge had to remove road blocks to permit the convoys to get through, Lathbury planned to await a convoy, then attack with grenades and Stens. Immediately after the ambush of such a convoy Lathbury was wounded by one of the German drivers who reacted by fighting back and throwing grenades at the paratroops. (See Peter Stainforth, Wings of the Wind: The Story of the 1st Parachute Division, London, 1954 edition, pp. 158–9.)

The enemy defences on the north bank of the Simeto consisted mainly of several ineffective Italian battalions while to the south the German machine-gun battalion awaited developments. Schmidt and his men were veteran troops and during the first hours of the battle they had been responsible for many of the British losses and had forced the pilots into taking evasive action which contributed to the erratic drop of the 1st Parachute Brigade. Captain Laun had unwittingly chosen his positions well and the gunners found themselves placed on the exact line of approach of most of the Allied aircraft. Throughout the landing operations this force caused considerable havoc. One platoon accounted for three gliders, while another shot down three British Dakotas. On the ground the Germans were rapidly collecting prisoners and by midnight eighty-two of the Red Devils had been captured.[1]

Although confusion continued throughout the night, it diminished as a fine dawn arrived on the morning of 14 July. It was the calm before the storm and very soon the struggle for control of Primosole bridge would begin in earnest. It would be only the second encounter of the Second World War between opposing airborne forces.* The outcome would determine the success or failure of Montgomery's gamble to seize Catania and end the campaign quickly.

---

[1] Kuhn, *German Paratroopers in World War II*, op. cit., pp. 186–7, and Schmitz, 'German Paratroopers and the Primosole Bridge, Sicily, 1943'. The German gunners had been emplaced exactly on the flight path of two of the four DZs and the single glider LZ.

* During the battle of Tamara (March/April 1943) in Tunisia, the 1st Parachute Brigade fought under the command of the 46th Division. One of their toughest foes was the German 21st Engineer Parachute Battalion, under the command of Major Rudolf Witzig, a veteran of the daring 1940 attack on Fort Eben Emael.

CHAPTER 22

The First Battle for Primosole Bridge

It was bitterly disappointing.
LIEUTENANT-COLONEL JOHN FROST

Frost's 2nd Parachute Battalion bore the brunt of the German counterattacks during the first hours of daylight on 14 July. His 140 men were dispersed on JOHNNY I but, with no communications, he had no idea of the situation at the bridge. About 0630 Schmidt's gunners began a deadly mortar and machine-gun barrage which claimed a number of casualties. The Green Devils and the Red Devils fought around JOHNNY III, which soon fell to the attackers. To their astonishment the British found their main opposition to be *German paratroops* who were attacking from the west. Not only was such stiff opposition wholly unexpected but the presence of crack *German* troops south of the Simeto was the real surprise.*

From JOHNNY III the Germans began delivering withering machine-gun fire. A patrol was sent to deal with the problem but

---

[1] Quoted in *A Drop Too Many*, op. cit., p. 179.
* Since this engagement both the official and unofficial accounts of the battle for Primosole bridge have incorrectly identified the German participants. The 2nd Parachute Battalion War Diary, for example, records their opposition the morning of 14 July as the 4th Parachute Regiment (FJR 4). However, that regiment did not arrive in Sicily until the night of 16/17 July. Under the command of Lieutenant-Colonel Erich Walther, it parachuted from He111s around Acireale, north of Catania. The 2nd Battalion's opponents were the 1st Parachute Machine Gun Battalion who, as we now know, had taken up positions early the previous night between JOHNNY I and JOHNNY III as a blocking force to any British attempt to seize Primosole bridge via Route 114. The British official history states that the attacks against the 2nd Battalion on 14 July came from machine-gun, signal and engineer troops. At this time the division Signal Company was still in Catania and the engineer battalion did not arrive in Sicily until that night. In *Sicily*, Hugh Pond erroneously claims Heilmann and his men fought at Primosole bridge and that the airborne commander was later captured by the Durham Light Infantry on 17 July. Not only was Heilmann never captured but he won lasting fame at Monte Cassino and later commanded the 5th Parachute Division as a major general during the Ardennes counter-offensive in December 1944.

was spotted and forced to withdraw with further casualties from three armoured cars which had joined the fray. The war diary of the 2nd Parachute Battalion records a scene of growing concern:

> 0800 – Forward troops are withdrawing inside the perimeter. At this time it was apparent that we were under MG fire from three sides and the enemy were closing in on us, not in very great strength but with heavy fire power and considerable skill. A great deal of sniping had taken place on both sides.[1]

A half-hour later and with typical understatement, the war diary recorded the situation was becoming 'rather serious'. Casualties rose as German accuracy began to improve. The dry grass to the south caught fire and the heat from the flames forced the surrounded paratroopers into a dangerously constricted perimeter.[2] With ammunition running low it was clear that the 2nd Parachute Battalion could not withstand a co-ordinated enemy counterattack.[3]

Accompanying the battalion was a Royal Artillery gunnery officer, Captain Vere Hodge, who was acting as a Naval Forward Observation officer for the six-inch guns of the cruiser HMS *Newfoundland** which was lying offshore. For some time Hodge's attempts to gain wireless contact proved fruitless. Finally, about 0900, he succeeded and 'almost immediately the high-velocity medicine began to arrive with a suddenness and efficiency that completely turned the scales . . . What seemed like imminent defeat was staved off and from then on the danger receded.'[4] Still, there was no sign of Eighth Army and artillery fire could be heard far to the south, providing ample confirmation that the ordeal of the Red Devils was far from over.[5]

Colonel Pearson's defenders were left relatively unmolested during the morning. About mid-morning a squadron of *Focke-*

---

[1] War Diary, 2nd Parachute Battalion, loc. cit.

[2] A *Drop Too Many*, op. cit., pp. 180–1. Frost notes that the smoke was effectively used by the Germans to improve their positions.

[3] War Diary, 2nd Parachute Battalion, loc. cit. Casualties for the morning were forty-two killed and an equal number wounded.

[4] A *Drop Too Many*, op. cit., p. 181.

[5] War Diary, 2nd Parachute Battalion. About 1100 hours, Frost's men took possession of an abandoned German howitzer and ammunition which was later turned on their tormentors.

* Flagship of Rear-Admiral C. H. J. Harcourt, commander of a Royal Navy support force. On 23 July the *Newfoundland* was damaged by a torpedo from an Italian submarine.

Wulf 190s appeared and strafed the area around the bridge but did little damage.[1] Beginning at noon there was heavy shelling from German 88s which lasted nearly an hour. At 0930 Lathbury held a brief wireless conversation with an Eighth Army unit and learned the grim news that the 50th Division was encountering stiff opposition around Lentini and its time of arrival was very uncertain. Pearson had dispersed most of his small force north of the river, facing Catania, and it was here that the Germans launched the first in a series of counterattacks to recapture Primosole bridge.

These counterattacks came about as a result of the outstanding initiative of one officer, Captain Franz Stangenberg who, it will be remembered, had been part of the advance party two days earlier. Around 1030 a German despatch rider carrying a message to Colonel Heilmann was halted north of the bridge by a hail of fire and returned to Catania where he reported to Stangenberg the presence of British troops blocking Highway 114 and in control of Primosole bridge. Unwilling to accept this news without confirmation, Stangenberg immediately drove south towards the bridge, whereupon he was rudely greeted by automatic-weapons fire. Undaunted, he collected about twenty men and again began moving towards the bridge. This time the British reaction was far more violent and he was obliged to beat a hasty retreat to safety. His worst fears had been confirmed and with the reinforcements not due until that night, Stangenberg knew he would have to deal personally with the unhealthy situation at Primosole bridge if disaster was to be averted.[2]

Stangenberg returned to Catania determined to raise an *ad hoc* force to deal with the British. The only unit available was Captain Erich Fassl's Signal Company* which had been airlifted into Catania airfield the previous afternoon. The early arrival of this unit had been for the purpose of establishing communications for the division but, when they landed, Strangenberg was reluctantly forced to send them to guard Catania harbour, which had been hastily abandoned by its Italian defenders and was now vulnerable

---

[1] War Diaries, 1st Parachute Brigade, and Wilhelmsmeyer, Part I.

[2] Ibid. The 1st Parachute Battalion War Diary vividly describes Stangenberg's initial foray: 'Enemy seen approaching from the North in two trucks which stopped about 1½ miles from the bridge to allow the troops to debus. The troops then advanced along both sides of the road until about 1 mile away, when our mortars opened up and placed five or six bombs very close to them, causing some casualties. The remainder withdrew with speed.'

* Official designation was the 1st Company, 1st Parachute Communications Battalion.

to attack from the sea. He reported the crisis by telephone to Heidrich at Kesselring's headquarters in Rome and was given permission to withdraw Fassl's signalmen for commitment to a counterattack against Primosole bridge.[1]

In the meantime several NCOs had been rounding up every German soldier who could be spared. Most were headquarters personnel – clerks, cooks, mechanics and drivers. The result was a force of about two hundred men, 'a rather motley crew, rapidly thrown together'.[2] By chance, Stangenberg had met two flak officers during his first trip south and had learned that there was a heavy flak battery located south of Catania, and wireless lines were laid to this unit which was to provide supporting fire for the counterattack. In all, Stangenberg had succeeded in a remarkably short time in forming a force of nearly 350 men (200 in his task force and about 150 in Fassl's Signal Company).[3]

With the flak* prepared to support them, Stangenberg led his force down both sides of Route 114 while Fassl's men were deployed to the east with instructions to cross the river and attack the British right flank.

Shortly after 1300 the attack came and was repulsed without too much difficulty. It was followed by another from the right flank, forcing Pearson to order his defensive perimeter shortened. In addition to the two 88 mm guns firing from near Catania airfield, the Germans had also managed to bring up a self-propelled 88 and several anti-tank guns and for two hours they rained down a hail of fire against the British paratroopers. While they were in no imminent danger of being overrun, ammunition was beginning to run short and casualties were mounting from the heavy artillery fire. A surgical team of the 16th Parachute Field Ambulance Company set up near the southern end of the bridge and were miraculously able to perform seventy-two operations relatively unmolested. One medic, Staff Sergeant E. G. Stevens, RAMC, earned the Military Medal for his actions in evacuating wounded from the forward aid station to the main dressing station located in a farmhouse half a mile southeast of the bridge. Stevens had 'liberated' a recalcitrant Sicilian mule from a nearby farmyard and

---

[1] Kuhn, p. 187; Wilhelmsmeyer, Part II, pp. 70–1; and Schmitz.

[2] Wilhelmsmeyer, Part II, op. cit.

[3] Schmitz.

* The flak support consisted of one 88 mm gun and an ancient 5 cm Italian field gun operated by a German crew.

had harnessed it to an ancient farm cart. The wounded were placed inside and, with Stevens running by its side, a gauntlet of fire was run until the contraption was safely in the rear.[1]

The real threat came from Fassl's Signal Company which attacked from the east against the right flank and took its first prisoners. As Major Rudolf Böhmler later wrote, there was considerable mutual respect between the two opponents. They were, he said later, 'splendid fellows, each single one an athletic type. Now it was clear the British had airlanded and we were involved with "colleagues"! Really a pity that one had to fight against such spirited types so similar to our German paratroopers, and who did not seem to be annoyed that they had been captured by their German "brothers-in-arms".'[2]

The only British radio contact with the outside world was made at 0930 by Major David Hunter, the Brigade Major, who spoke with an unidentified unit of the 4th Armoured Brigade and informed them the bridge had been captured intact. The unit replied that they were having difficulty getting through to relieve the 1st Parachute Brigade and then the conversation continued in code, much of which could not be deciphered correctly. At 1000, the radio came to life again as the unit reported they had passed the information about the capture of the bridge to higher headquarters. Then Major Hunter's set went dead and all contact with the outside world was severed and never regained.[3]

The notoriously inefficient British wireless sets were all too frequently the bane of the Army during the war, and Primosole bridge and Arnhem are but two vivid examples. During the battle the only contacts with Frost to the south occurred when Major Hunter personally visited JOHNNY 1, and later when Brigadier Lathbury managed despite his painful wounds to make his way to the 2nd Parachute Battalion position.

As the two airborne forces continued to blood each other along the Simeto and to the south around JOHNNY 1, there was no thought of the strategies preached in their respective war colleges; the battle was fought at the most elemental level as a fight for survival. Had the British had the leisure of reflection they would

---

[1] *The Red Beret*, op. cit., p. 121; and Robert Smith, 'The Red Devils in Sicily', op. cit.
[2] Rudolf Böhmler, *Monte Cassino*, Darmstadt, 1955, p. 56. Major (later Lieutenant-Colonel) Böhmler was the CO, 1st Battalion, FJR 3, in Sicily and Italy.
[3] War Diary, 1st Airborne Division, loc. cit.

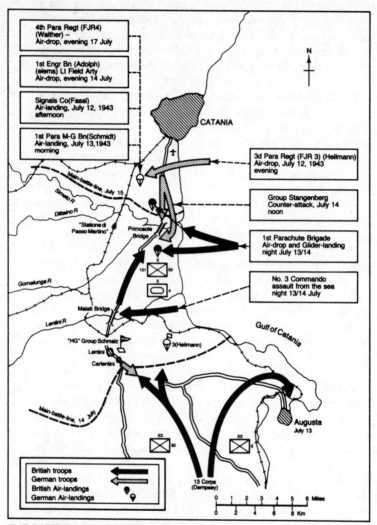

**4th Para Regt (FJR4)
(Walther) –
Air-drop, evening 17 July**

**1st Engr Bn (Adolph)
(elems) Lt Field Arty
Air-drop, evening 14 July**

**Signals Co(Fassl)
Air-landing, July 12, 1943
afternoon**

**1st Para M-G Bn(Schmidt)
Air-landing, July 13,1943
morning**

CATANIA

**3d Para Regt (FJR 3) (Heilmann)
Air-drop, July 12, 1943
evening**

Main-battle-line, July 15

Simeto R

Dittaino R

"Stazione di
Passo Martino"

Primosole
Bridge

**Group Stangenberg
Counter-attack, July 14
noon**

**1st Parachute Brigade
Air-drop and Glider-landing
night July 13/14**

151   50

4

**No. 3 Commando
assault from the sea
night 13/14 July**

Gornalunga R

Malati Bridge

Lentini R

Gulf of Catania

"HG" Group Schmalz

3(Heilmann)

Lentini

Carlentini

Main-battle-line, 14 July

Augusta
July 13

50

5

British troops
German troops
British Air-landings
German Air-landings

13 Corps
(Dempsey)

0 1 2 3 4 5 6 Miles

0   2   4   6   8 Km

THE BATTLE FOR PRIMOSOLE BRIDGE
Situation 12 – 18 July

have realized that they were fortunate the Germans had had no time to develop and implement a master plan for the defence of the plain of Catania. Instead, as the British official history records: 'Chance, and the reactions of competent commanders to the circumstances of an encounter battle decided [German] moves.'[1] The German high command was aiming for the establishment of the Etna Line but this was still several days off and for the moment it was purely a case of improvisation, of which one campaign after another bore out the German mastery. While Schmalz and the portly Heilmann were giving the 5th and 50th Divisions a bloody nose around Carlentini and Lentini, the actions of junior officers like Schmidt and Stangenberg were earning the German paratroopers the complete respect of their British opponents.

In both besieged positions the Red Devils waited in vain throughout the day for some sign of the relieving force. Without wireless contact the *Newfoundland* was unable to assist. Colonel Pearson realized he lacked both the manpower and the firepower to withstand the increasing German pressure. Even more disturbing was the nearly exhausted supply of ammunition. At 1730 the situation had deteriorated so badly that he had no other option except to order the positions on the north bank of the river abandoned. This was accomplished under heavy fire and the positions on the south bank were consolidated. Fortunately, stragglers had been turning up throughout the day, bringing the strength of the 1st Battalion up to about 160 men.[2]

Lathbury was acutely aware that, if relief did not arrive soon, the British hold on Primosole bridge was not only hopeless, but his men would be surrounded. The Brigadier's decision was clear when the Germans succeeded in moving an 88 mm gun up to the north bank where at point-blank range it proceeded methodically to destroy the two pillboxes on the south side which formed the bulwark of the airborne defence.

With his hold on the bridge increasingly hopeless, Lathbury ordered a withdrawal to the small hills comprising the JOHNNY positions some 1,200 yards to the south where, it was hoped, a link-up could be made with the 2nd Battalion, from whom there

---

[1] *The Mediterranean and Middle East*, Vol. V, op. cit., p. 93.
[2] War Diary, 1st Parachute Battalion, loc. cit. About 1500 hours a direct hit from the *Newfoundland* struck an enemy artillery battery west of Catania and the explosion of its ammunition could be seen from the bridge and JOHNNY I. Another battery in the same area was not silenced but the harassment forced it to change positions regularly.

was only an ominous silence.[1] If contact could not be made, the Red Devils were to use escape and evasion tactics to avoid capture as they headed south towards friendly lines. At 1830 the order was given, and after sixteen hours in British hands Primosole bridge was ceded to the enemy.

The situation at JOHNNY I remained quiet and, although the survivors of Pearson's battalion failed to make contact with Frost, about fifteen men from Yeldham's 3rd Parachute Battalion managed to filter in and join the 2nd Battalion.[2] About 1930 the first Sherman of the 4th Armoured Brigade appeared in an olive grove south of JOHNNY I, followed two hours later by a company of the 6th DLI who were on foot. As Frost notes, 'The DLI had covered some twenty miles during the heat of the day and were in no shape for offensive operations for the time being.'[3] Not for the first time the chronic lack of transport within Eighth Army had a crucial effect on the outcome of a major offensive.

A former lieutenant of the 2nd Inniskillings (13th Brigade/5th Division) has written a graphic memoir of life in Sicily as an infantryman. He describes what faced the DLI:

> Plodding along mile after dusty mile in a temperature of 95° in the shade ... I can still vividly recall the view that greeted us when I went forward with the CO to the crest of the ridge to look down for the first time on the Catania Plain. The panorama before us was magnificent. Thirty miles to the north, dominating the horizon was the huge, misty, snow-capped conical mass, 10,000 feet high, of Mount Etna. On the plain itself we could see through our binoculars the Simeto River curling irregularly from the west down to the sea ... Along the coast, past the Simeto, the city of Catania was dimly visible, shimmering in the heat. All this would have constituted a picture of great beauty and tranquillity, had it not been for the thud of shells, with their tell-tale puffs of black smoke, exploding near the river. The reality was that down in front of us, concealed in slit-trenches and ditches and sheltered behind buildings and whatever cover they could find, two armies were facing each other in mortal conflict.[4]

Ideally, this would have been the moment for a swift strike against the Germans before they could consolidate their hold on the

---

[1] Lathbury, 'Marston To-Night', op. cit.
[2] War Diaries, 1st Parachute Brigade, passim.
[3] A Drop Too Many, op. cit., p. 184.
[4] Sir David Cole, Rough Road to Rome, A Foot-Soldier in Sicily and Italy, 1943–44, London, 1983, pp. 43–4.

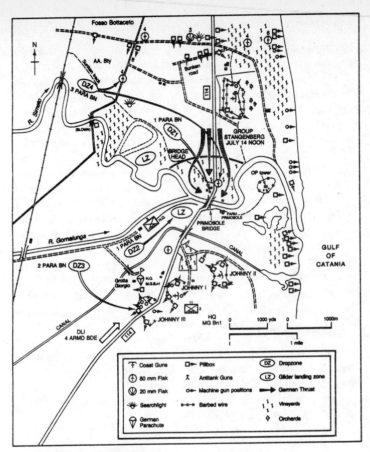

THE PRIMOSOLE BRIDGEHEAD

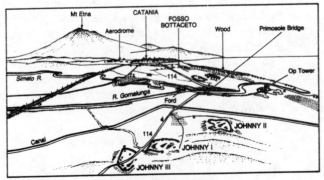

AERIAL VIEW OF THE PRIMOSOLE BATTLEFIELD

bridge. With close tank support the possibility existed for a surprise attack to retake Primosole bridge. Moreover, now that a
ground force had arrived it would presumably have been possible
to re-establish wireless contact with the *Newfoundland* for direct
fire support. The arrival of the Shermans of the 44th Royal Tank
Regiment caused the Germans to withdraw to the north bank
where they made preparations for what was now certain to be an
all-out British attempt to push through to Catania. Despite this
opportunity, Brigadier R. H. Senior, the commander of the
Durham Light Infantry Brigade,* was unable to take advantage of
it and mount an attack that night. The leading battalion – 9th DLI
– did not close in until 2130, the remaining infantry elements of the
brigade were strung out far back towards Lentini, and the last unit
did not arrive until midnight. With only one small break, the DLI
had been marching continuously since the D-Day landings. With
his artillery support also still en route and unable to make a
reconnaissance of crossing sites over the Simeto, Brigadier Senior
elected to wait until the following morning before launching his
attack.[1]

It had only been at the insistence of Frost's intelligence officer
that the DLI sent forward a company of infantry to augment the
paratroop force on JOHNNY I; the original intention had been to
bivouac two miles further south to prepare for the attack the
following morning.[2] Both sides passed a quiet night in anticipation
of the forthcoming battle.

To the south the men of Lieutenant Colonel Heilmann's FJR 3
were undergoing their own ordeal. They had first helped frustrate
the 5th Division advance towards Carlentini, after which the
regiment had pulled back to its present positions northeast of
Lentini. When Lentini fell, Schmalz ordered Heilmann to withdraw his paratroopers behind the Simeto west of Primosole
bridge. Heilmann refused to withdraw until assured of the safety
of his 2nd Battalion which had not been heard from since being
sent to Francofonte by Schmalz. Finally, when it became imposs-

[1] Brigadier R. H. Senior, 'The Durham Light Infantry at the Primosole Bridge', *The*
[British] *Army Quarterly*, October, 1944.
[2] War Diary, 2nd Parachute Battalion.
* 151st Infantry Brigade.

ible to delay his withdrawal any longer, the last of Heilmann's vehicles began heading north as the tanks of the 4th Armoured Brigade were rolling up the highway behind them. Heilmann had hoped to escape towards Catania via a minor road up the coast but soon found this escape route sealed off by constant shellfire from the Royal Navy.

Forced to abandon their transport and heavy weapons, the paratroopers marched northwest through the night of 14/15 July and by dawn on 15 July found themselves southeast of the Malati bridge, their intended escape route firmly blocked by British troops and tanks. Heilmann ordered his men to lie up in a nearby orange grove until nightfall. An unsuspecting British patrol managed to pass through the grove without detecting the German presence and a unit which selected the same sweltering orange grove for its HQ was none the wiser. Leaving some seventy British POWs behind in the care of some wounded paratroopers, Heilmann led his men stealthily across the Lentini River and most had successfully slipped undetected under the very noses of the British guarding the bridge when the 1st Battalion, bringing up the rear, was seen. By then it was much too late to impede them seriously, and after a brief firefight FJR 3 were at last free of their current trap but still far from friendly lines. Again they went to ground, at a deserted airstrip northwest of the bridge, throughout 16 July, while columns of British tanks rumbled north towards Primosole bridge.

Late on 17 July, Heilmann led his 900 men to safety across the Simeto where they were warmly greeted by a greatly relieved Heidrich and by Kesselring who was visiting the front.* Von Senger was also present, and Schmalz complained to him that Heilmann had needlessly jeopardized the men of his regiment, who had been in great danger of being lost, because its commander 'was too proud to obey a withdrawal order'. Von Senger agreed and wrote that 'such independent decisions and disregard of orders was a result of the nature and training of the parachute troops. During all the fighting between 14 and 17 July this urgently

---

* The account of the escape of FJR 3 is based on Kuhn, pp. 188–9, and Heilmann, 'Fallschirmjäger auf Sizilien', op. cit. The morale of these remarkable men remained high even amongst those captured. Sir David Cole writes, 'Once we passed a party of German prisoners – paratroops – going back to Syracuse. Unlike the Italians, they looked fit, marched smartly and sang lustily, no sign of defeat written upon their faces.' (*Rough Road to Rome*, op. cit., p. 43.)

needed regiment was absent; furthermore, it could not be committed immediately after its return because it had lost all its heavy weapons.'[1]

From the moment of their arrival in Sicily, relations between Heilmann and Schmalz had been frosty. Heilmann's displeasure at being placed under the command of a 'straight leg' infantry commander was typical of the disdain that élite troops of all armies felt for anyone (no matter how competent) who had not shared the danger and exhilaration of being an airborne soldier. When Schmalz had ordered him to withdraw, Heilmann had tersely replied, 'Wherever German paratroopers are, there will be no retreat.' Schmalz was distressed by this attitude but could only shrug his shoulders and observe that Heilmann was 'at least practising what he preaches'.[2]

Heilmann's stubbornness put Schmalz's neck into an uncomfortable noose. When he arrived on the morning of 17 July, Kesselring directed his displeasure at Schmalz for the necessity of reporting the missing FJR 3 to the OKW. Somehow, Schmalz managed to conceal from Kesselring the *real* reason why the regiment had gone missing. When a messenger sent through the lines by Heilmann reported their imminent arrival, Schmalz recalled, 'it was as if a stone had fallen off my heart'.[3]

No German commander contributed more to the defence of Sicily than Schmalz, whose skill and initiative were responsible for blunting the British advance north of Syracuse during the early days of the campaign when the situation on the Axis eastern flank was nothing short of desperate. A hard-driving officer, he earned the complete respect of his men and was idolized by his personal staff who had served him loyally for some years. Schmalz was a veteran of the campaigns in Poland, France, the Balkans and Russia, and was, as his driver has said, 'as solid as a rock'.[4] Throughout the Sicily campaign he continued to employ his considerable skills to frustrate repeatedly his British opponents.

Relations between the senior paratroop commanders and the Hermann Goering Division remained strained; privately, Heidrich was enraged and bitter at what he considered the abandonment of

---

[1] Von Senger in MS # C-095, 'Liaison Activities with Italian 6th Army'.
[2] Quoted in Pond, *Sicily*, op. cit., pp. 141–2.
[3] Ibid.
[4] Ibid., p. 149.

his men by Schmalz. Moreover, Heidrich believed the break-up of his division under the Hermann Goering a wasteful employment of crack airborne troops. The arrival of Hube as the new German ground commander brought a renewed attempt by Heidrich to regain control of his division and more frustration, for Hube provided no satisfaction and maintained that since Heidrich's forces were so few they must remain under the operational control of the Hermann Goering Division.*

For the gallant men of the 1st Parachute Brigade, Primosole bridge was a bitter pill. A mere sixteen per cent of the 1,856 men who had set out from North Africa on the night of 13 July ever saw action. More than one-third were never dropped at all. One stick dropped along the slopes of Mount Etna and was almost entirely captured; the exceptions were Captain Victor Dover and a signaller, who survived for twenty-four days on a diet of apples and enlivened their ordeal by raiding enemy installations and ambushing three despatch riders.[1]

An unknown number went missing and a good many of those were captured. Brigade casualties among those who participated in the battle of Primosole bridge numbered approximately 115, including twenty-seven killed. With understatement, Brigadier Lathbury called the operation 'disappointing'. After holding the bridge for far longer than called for, he was understandably angry and disgusted when the tanks of the 44th RTR sat atop the high ground south of the bridge without making the slightest attempt to come forward.[2] His men had bled and died for that miserable hunk of steel and concrete and he found the reluctance of the tanks to come forward insufferable.

FUSTIAN marked the third airborne operation of the brief campaign to go badly awry and once again the results boded ill for the once-promising future of airborne operations. On 15 July all further operations by 1st Airborne were suspended pending

[1] The Red Beret, op. cit., p. 126, and Dover, The Silken Canopy, op. cit., Chapter 3.
[2] 'Marston To-Night', op. cit.
* On 22 July the remaining division anti-tank units arrived from Italy, but the 1st Parachute Regiment (FJR 1) was sent to Salerno and the supply troops never left Rome. The result was that Heidrich and his staff sat uselessly in Italy with nothing whatever to do. Heidrich's account is contained in a Special Interrogation Report, a copy of which is deposited in the archives of the USAMHI.

further inter-service co-ordination and additional training. A week later Eisenhower convened a board of officers to review all three operations and present him with the lessons learnt and recommendations for the future employment of the Allied airborne forces. For the moment, the future of the airborne concept remained seriously in limbo.*

The first phase of the battle for Primosole bridge bears an uncanny likeness to its more famous successor, Operation MARKET-GARDEN, the ill-fated Allied airborne operation in mid-September 1944 to seize a bridgehead across the Rhine at Arnhem, Holland.

Had the men of the 1st Parachute Brigade been dropped at full strength at Primosole bridge and been relieved promptly by the tank–infantry force, the situation on the night of 14 July would most certainly have been far different. Frost's observation that had Montgomery elected to employ the entire 1st Airborne Division† at Primosole bridge the campaign might have been won in ten days has considerable merit, but only if they could have been successfully dropped on the correct DZs. Otherwise it would have undoubtedly resulted in an even more serious fiasco from the heavy 'friendly' and enemy flak. Although the operation wrote an undeniably illustrious chapter in the story of the 1st Airborne Division, the fact remains that, in the end, Primosole was also 'a bridge too far'.‡

Their job done, the Red Devils turned the battle over to the DLI. Later, as Colonel Pearson led his exhausted and bedraggled paratroopers from the battlefield he was stopped by a large staff car containing a staff captain who emerged immaculately dressed with a Sam Browne belt and gleaming boots. The captain imperiously enquired of Pearson, who was not wearing any badges of rank, whose uniform consisted of an old army pullover and muddy boots, and whose face was caked with two days' growth of

---

* Fortunately, common sense prevailed and the joint Anglo-American board of officers submitted their report to Eisenhower on 29 July with numerous practical recommendations. Eisenhower sent the report to Marshall with the observation, 'I think you will agree that, considering the magnitude of the operation, the inexperience of personnel, and the unfavorable weather conditions encountered, the results were most promising for the future effectiveness of this powerful arm of opportunity.' (Letter of 29 July 1943, *The Eisenhower Papers*, Vol. II, p. 1303.)

† The 2nd Parachute Brigade was uncommitted and available in Tunisia.

‡ The title of the late Cornelius Ryan's superb book about the operation at Arnhem which later became a film of the same name, directed by Sir Richard Attenborough.

beard and dirt: 'Who are you, my man?' Pearson, a Glaswegian, replied in a deliberately pronounced accent: 'A'm the commander o' the Furrst Parachute Battalion.' The flustered captain saluted and said, 'Jolly fine show, sir. What tactics did you use?' To the great amusement of his men, Pearson leisurely looked the officer up and down and then replied, 'I don't know what bloody tactics I used, but they were bloody well successful.'[1]

By chance, Montgomery was driving up Route 114 to Kirkman's Command Post at the time when most of the airborne were being convoyed on the first leg of their long journey back to Kairouan. He stopped the convoy and 'recognising the parachutists, he went to each truck, congratulating the men on the wonderful, heroic fight, whilst his aide followed, handing out "Victory" cigarettes to all and sundry. It was marvellous to see the effect of his praise on the paratroopers' morale.'[2]

Frost was bitter about the outcome and believed that once again senior officers were squandering the valuable talents of the airborne:

> During the planning it had been thought that having taken, held and handed over the Primosole bridge, we of the 1st Parachute Brigade would advance on Catania as part of the 8th Army. Now we, like the 1st Airlanding Brigade, were to be shipped back to Africa useless and unused for the remainder of the campaign. It was yet another humiliating disaster for the airborne forces and almost enough to destroy even the most ardent believer's faith.[3]

For the German airborne of the 1st Parachute Division there was to be no such relief; their ordeal had only begun. The arrival of the Durham Light Infantry and the 4th Armoured Brigade had brought momentary joy into the breast of Captain Stangenberg whose task force now held a small bridgehead around the southern end of Primosole bridge. To his dismay he found it was not Heilmann's FJR 3 coming to relieve him, but instead the Durhams coming to relieve his enemy![4]

Thus ended the first phase of the struggle for Primosole bridge. It had been a frustrating thirty-six hours since Montgomery had confidently boasted to his liaison officer, Major Robert Henriques,

---

[1] Quoted by Robert Smith in 'The Red Devils in Sicily', op. cit.
[2] Quoted in Pond, *Sicily*, op. cit., pp. 130–1.
[3] *A Drop Too Many*, op. cit., p. 185.
[4] Schmitz, loc. cit.

that 'I shall be in Catania tonight [13 July].'[1] Despite the exhortations of both Montgomery and Dempsey to keep moving at all costs, the relieving ground force was not equal to the challenge. A combination of the lack of transport, the dreadful heat and the long foot-marches of the infantry had conspired to rob the Eighth Army commander of a rapid relief of the airborne force at Primosole bridge.

Moreover, the first signs were beginning to appear of a frame of mind that was to plague the British Army in Italy and the long campaign in Northwest Europe which would begin on 6 June 1944 with the long-awaited cross-Channel invasion of Normandy. Hugh Pond describes the attitude which prevailed in Sicily among the veteran units of the western desert:

> Very few troop carriers were included in the initial assault . . . [and] they were limited to the speed of the marching infantry, which was tired, bloody tired, of marching and of war. They had seen enough in North Africa to last them for a long time; trudging in the summer heat along dusty rutted roads was not their idea of how the victorious Desert Army should be treated. Possibly fresher troops, as some of the Americans proved, would have moved faster and with a little more enthusiasm; but Montgomery had insisted on using his battle-proven veterans, and they were fatigued and browned off. So several vital days were lost, during which it would have been possible to drive almost unopposed up the coast to Messina and to carry out the plan of trapping the enemy between the two armies.[2]

Despite the urgent exhortations to press on, it was unlikely the 50th Division could have advanced much faster, especially without adequate transport. Nevertheless, if the success of Monty's plan had been judged on the results of the first two days of the operation, the future was indeed bleak. If he was to continue to retain the initiative, the ground forces would have to win a spectacular battle *quickly*. That responsibility now rested squarely upon the Durham Light Infantry.

Just before last light on the evening of 14 July more He111s appeared over Catania airfield where three companies of the 1st Fallschirm-Pionier Bataillon (the division engineer battalion) leapt into the reddish-orange sky. The German pilots were inexperi-

---

[1] Quoted in Pond, *Sicily*, op. cit., p. 115. Henriques was the Eighth Army liaison officer to Patton's Seventh Army.
[2] Ibid.

enced in airborne operations and flew much too fast over the drop zone, resulting in some of the paratroopers and their equipment landing as much as three kilometres away. It took nearly two hours for Captain Paul Adolff to assemble the 450 men of his battalion and begin moving with urgency to the south. Destination: Primosole bridge.

During the night, while the engineers were relieving Stangenberg (who returned to Catania with the Signal Company and his pro tem force), Schmidt moved his machine-gunners back across the Simeto where they took up new positions to the west of Primosole bridge. Adolff positioned two of his companies astride Route 114 at the southern end of the bridge, while the third 150-man company defended the northern end.[1] Stangenberg had succeeded in retaking Primosole bridge and now it was the sole responsibility of the newly arrived engineers to hold it for as long as possible.

[1] Schmitz, 'German Paratroopers and the Primosole Bridge, Sicily, 1943'. Captain Adolff was the acting commander in the absence of the regular CO who was attending a staff course in Paris. The other two companies of the battalion did not arrive in Sicily until later in the campaign.

CHAPTER 23

Stalemate

It was a very bloody killing match.
MONTGOMERY

A deadly quiet hung over the entire Primosole bridge sector during the first hours of daylight on the fine morning of 15 July as both sides finalized preparations for the coming battle. At 0730, the 24th and 98th Field Regiments of the Royal Artillery began raining down fire from their 25-pounders on suspected German positions. Thirty minutes later the British attack began as the lead troops of Lieutenant-Colonel A. B. S. Clarke's 9th DLI emerged from behind the protection of JOHNNY II, 1,200 yards to the south, and began moving up Highway 114 towards the bridge, supported by Shermans of the 44th RTR. For the tired Durhams it was another in the long, seemingly endless list of battles they had fought in this war.*

Lieutenant-Colonels Frost and Pearson had been relegated to the status of spectators and they were both able to observe first-hand a desperate drama being played out as the conventional infantry assault of the 9th DLI was cut to pieces by the German paratroopers. Frost describes what happened:

* The Durham Light Infantry traced their distinguished lineage nearly 200 years to 1756. During World War I the Regiment spawned thirty-seven Regular, Territorial and Service battalions, and during World War II there were fourteen battalions in active service. In 1908, when the Territorial Forces were created, four battalions of the DLI – 6th, 7th, 8th and 9th – were merged to form the 151st Brigade of the 50th (Northumbrian) Division. In 1936 the 7th Battalion was converted into an AA searchlight battalion but otherwise the Brigade had remained intact. The Durham Light Infantry Brigade fought in the battle of France as a part of the BEF and were evacuated from Dunkirk in May 1940. In 1941 it became one of the first Territorial units sent to the Middle East with 50th Division, first to Syria and Iraq. Later, it joined Eighth Army in time to participate in the great desert battles under Auchinleck and Montgomery, followed by the assault against the Mareth Line. At Tobruk, Private Adam Wakenshaw, a gunner assigned to the 9th DLI, won the VC in a battle which saw most of his battalion overrun and killed or captured. 151st Brigade led the D-Day assault in Sicily and none of the units now involved in the battle for control of Primosole bridge was a stranger to close combat against the Germans. (See David Rissik, *The D.L.I. at War: The History of the Durham Light Infantry 1939–1945*, Durham, 1952.)

384

We had never taken part in such an operation and having seen this [one] were determined never to do so. It all went according to plan. There was a massive expenditure of ammunition on suspected enemy positions. Medium machine-guns kept up continuous pressure and tanks were interspersed with the infantry. There was a smoke-screen to cover the last and most dangerous stretch. The infantry plodded remorselessly on with bayonets fixed for the final assault across the river. The Germans held their fire until the Durhams were within some fifty yards, more or less point-blank range, then mowed the leading platoons down. Then they engaged the follow-up platoons. They fired burst after burst of machine-gun fire at the tanks, which had the effect of forcing them to remain closed down and therefore unable to identify enemy targets. The enemy anti-tank fire appeared nevertheless to be ineffective, but, without protection, the infantry attack just faded away and both Durhams and tanks came back.[1]

The DLI were simply no match for the well-prepared paratroopers. So few made it across the river that they never had any chance of penetrating the German positions. According to the regimental history, 'many were drowned in the river as they crossed'.[2] There were 100 casualties that morning, including 34 killed (9 of whom were officers), while the 44th RTR lost three tanks. The dead and wounded had to be left behind on the north bank. After the disaster the two sides remained facing one another while the DLI regrouped and it was decided how and when the attack would be renewed.

Despite their initial success the Germans appear to have forfeited an excellent defensive position when Lieutenant Cords inexplicably withdrew his 1st Engineer Company back across the Simeto without orders. This unit had occupied a sound salient to the south and east of Highway 114 where it approaches the bridge. This controversial decision has been the subject of mixed feelings among German veterans but the explanation seems to be that the inexperienced lieutenant's orders were unclear and, after a runner failed to find the Battalion CP, Cords mistakenly assumed he had been abandoned and decided to save his men by withdrawing. Sergeant Schmitz who served in this unit is harsher in his judg-

[1] A Drop Too Many, op. cit., p. 184.
[2] The D.L.I. at War, op. cit., p. 125.

ment: 'The fact is that 1. *Kompanie* held an ideal defensive position and gave it up without just cause.'[1]

Nevertheless, the 3rd Engineer Company continued to hold a small bridgehead along the southern approaches to Primosole bridge. Even though the withdrawal of the 1st Engineer Company permitted the DLI to move up to the south bank of the Simeto, it did them little good during the first attack. Had they succeeded in crossing the river in force, the DLI would have encountered a nearly impossible situation. Not only had the Germans selected their defensive positions with great skill but the dense vineyards on the north bank made movement confusing and nearly suicidal in daylight. The vineyards were dotted with olive trees which extended to a depth of 300–400 yards. Behind these vineyards ran a sunken track later dubbed 'Stink Alley' by the British, though at this time they were unaware of its existence. Visibility beyond the vineyards when lying down was virtually nil except between the rows of vines where one could see about ten yards.[2]

About 1000, General Kirkman arrived at Senior's CP and promptly ordered a fresh attack that afternoon, this time with heavier artillery support. Later, Pearson and Frost sat silently observing a similar meeting between Lathbury, Brigadier Currie, the CO, 4th Armoured Brigade, and Lieutenant-Colonel R. P. Lidwell, the CO, 8th DLI, who was to lead the next attack. When the decision to mount another daylight attack was announced, the outspoken Pearson could no longer contain himself and muttered loud enough for all to hear: 'I suppose you want to see another battalion written off too!'[3] Lathbury successfully pleaded for them to listen to what Pearson had to say, whereupon it was decided to postpone the attack until that night. This was a welcome decision to Colonel Lidwell who, though he had grave misgivings about the order, was fully prepared to carry it out. Equally welcome was Pearson's offer to show the DLI commander an alternative route across the Simeto.[4] Later that afternoon Kirkman returned to the

---

[1] Schmitz, loc. cit. The men of the company swam the Simeto while a flat barge was used to move the equipment. New positions were established 600 metres east of the bridge. Soon afterwards the company was heavily shelled by the Royal Navy and Lieutenant Cords seriously wounded.

[2] Kirkman account, loc. cit.

[3] Quoted in *A Drop Too Many*, op. cit., p. 185.

[4] Pond, *Sicily*, op. cit., p. 135.

151st Brigade CP and approved the recommendation to delay the attack until that night.[1]

The decision was a victory for common sense, for not only did the inadequate cover around the southern end of the bridge make another daylight attack absolutely suicidal, but in the interim the Germans had managed to bring up two 88 mm guns which were now firing down the road from the north bank. With Pearson's knowledge of the battle area, a night attack across a fordable reach of the Simeto about 400 yards upstream at least offered a reasonable prospect of success.

More often than not, battles are a hodge-podge of rumour and misinformation, and the reports reaching Montgomery that morning were typical of the confusion over what was actually happening at Primosole bridge. At 0800, he was told the Germans had succeeded in blowing the bridge. 'This was bad news,' he wrote.[2] He might well have used even stronger language had he known of the rebuff to the DLI that grim morning. Throughout the afternoon and early evening he continued to receive misleading reports. In mid-afternoon came the news that the bridge had not been blown after all but had been successfully recaptured by the DLI. Four hours later the second part of this too was exposed as false.[3] In reality, Montgomery had as yet no clear picture of the situation at Primosole bridge. At this point about all he knew for certain was that the airborne performance was 'magnificent' and '[They] undoubtedly saved the bridge for us'.[4]

During the lull on 15 July the Germans received further reinforcements when Captain Fassl returned with his company of signalmen. After returning to Catania the previous night, Fassl had found the city all but deserted. Ships of the Royal Navy were visible close offshore and the streets of Catania eerily quiet. 'The harbour area was pitted with craters. Electrical power lines were

---

[1] Kirkman account. See also Ewart W. Clay, *The Path of the 50th*, op. cit., p. 183.

[2] Montgomery Diary, 15 July 1943.

[3] Ibid.

[4] Ibid. Nevertheless, he decreed there would be no further operations by the 1st Airborne Division during the Sicily campaign, complaining that 'the big lesson is we must not be dependent on American Transport aircraft, with pilots that are inexperienced in operational flying; our airborne troops are too good and too scarce to be wasted. We must have our own aircraft, and our own RAF pilots; in fact it must be an all-British show, the air part being handled properly by the RAF and not by a different Army who do not know our ways.' Clearly, the failure of two British airlanding and airborne operations had led Montgomery to the same worrisome conclusions as Eisenhower: that, while airborne operations still held great potential, something had to be done to improve pilot training.

hanging down all over the place and British naval guns were firing into the town from the sea.'[1]

Catania at this time was virtually undefended and the few Italian units that had been there had either fled or were in the process of doing so. Another golden opportunity existed to seize the city. With the support of naval gunfire, a seaborne invasion force could have easily taken Catania and then squeezed the German defenders of Primosole bridge between them and the tank–infantry force of the 50th Division/4th Armoured Brigade. Such a move would at a stroke have negated the precious time lost in attempting to get past the Primosole bottleneck so successfully established by the German airborne. Dempsey finally did propose such an operation for the night of 16/17 July which, as will be seen, was postponed and then eventually aborted.

Fassl was quick to grasp that it was utterly hopeless for his tiny force to waste their time attempting to defend Catania from a determined seaborne landing. He could, however, make a meaningful contribution to the defence of Primosole bridge and during the afternoon, on his own initiative, he returned there with his unit and established positions to the northwest, thus adding considerable depth to the defences of Adolff's engineers.[2]

At 0100, 16 July, the DLI launched their second attack to retake Primosole bridge. British gunners laid down a withering fire and an hour later, with the assistance of Colonel Pearson, two companies of Lidwell's 8th DLI succeeded in fording the river and gaining a foothold on the north bank, catching the Germans by surprise. The DLI soon had control of the north end of the bridge, but then the operation began to become unravelled. The plan was that once the bridge was back under British control the remainder of the battalion and a squadron of the 44th RTR were to cross over immediately, and together this tank–infantry force would carve out a bridgehead for 1,000 yards to the north. However, not for the last time in the war, British wireless sets failed at a crucial moment and, despite *four* alternative plans for making contact, *none* worked and it was dawn by the time this force crossed the disputed bridge.*

---

[1] Wilhelmsmeyer, Part II, op. cit.
[2] Ibid.
* In spite of the well-laid plans by the DLI it was not until – incredibly – a War Office observer by the name of Major Wagram wandered up riding a bicycle that the problem was resolved. He returned to bring the remainder of the battalion and the tanks forward. Earlier,

By then it was too late: the momentum had been lost, the Germans were given too much time to react, and they stubbornly denied any further movement northwards. The area around the northern end of the bridge became a graveyard for British tanks. The first two Shermans to cross on 16 July quickly became the victims of a nearby 88 which fired at point-blank range. Before the day ended this gun had claimed three more Shermans.[1] The British infantry were using a ditch running up both sides of Highway 114 as cover and, after moving several hundred yards, all hell let loose 'and the Battalion found itself engaged in the most savage hand-to-hand fighting it had ever experienced. Concealed Spandaus (MG 42s) opened up at point-blank range on the leading troops of "B" and "C" Companies, and but for the ditch hardly a man in either company would have survived. As it was the whole of "B" Company's leading platoon was written off.'[2] In the vineyards the DLI and Green Devils engaged in a deadly game of hide-and-seek. Bayonets were used, as were tactics of stealth. Some Germans were taken by Durhams who crept up behind them and shot or bayoneted them where they lay. At first light the Germans retaliated and another fierce hand-to-hand encounter forced the DLI back into a perimeter a mere hundred yards deep.[3] Heavy fog marred visibility until late morning and Kirkman, mindful of the previous day's setback, was reluctant to sacrifice another battalion in a lost cause. The British later learned that the main stumbling-block to their advance proved to be the unknown sunken track running west from Highway 114 several hundred yards north of the bridge from which the Germans delivered withering small-arms fire.[4]

This attack was part of a fresh scheme devised the day before by

---

[1] Wilhelmsmeyer, Part II, op. cit.
[2] The D.L.I. at War, op. cit., p. 127.
[3] Ibid., pp. 127–8.
[4] Lieutenant-Colonel L. P. Lidwell, 'Durham Light Infantry at the Primosole Bridge', Part II, op. cit.; The Mediterranean and Middle East, Vol. V, op. cit., p. 103; and Kirkman account.

Colonel Lidwell had himself gone back across the bridge in an attempt to carry out the final alternative plan, which was to relay the information via a tank wireless. Lidwell found a Sherman with its engine running but was unable to gain the attention of the tank commander whom he tapped on the head with his swagger stick. The tank commander, thinking he was hit by enemy fire, hurriedly slammed shut his hatch, leaving the frustrated Lidwell alone. Fortunately for the DLI the uproar on the north bank had not deterred Major Wagram from calmly riding his bicycle across Primosole bridge in order to 'observe' the battle first-hand.

Dempsey. Two battalions of Royal Marine commandos and the 5th Division's 17th Brigade were to make an amphibious landing at Catania the night of 16/17 July and establish a foothold in the German rear. In the meantime, the 50th Division would gain a bridgehead north of the Simeto and then thrust north towards Catania, taking advantage of the confusion in the enemy rear. Later, the remainder of the 5th Division would pass through the 50th Division and continue the attack to secure Catania and gain control for Eighth Army of the direct, undefended route to Messina.

The afternoon of 16 July both Montgomery and Dempsey came forward to observe for themselves the situation at Primosole bridge and as a result the amphibious operation against Catania was postponed until the night of 17/18 July. Kirkman was ordered to launch yet another attack to enlarge his small bridgehead that night.

This time, Kirkman and Senior decided on a stronger, two-pronged attack. While 8th DLI held firm, the 6th and 9th Battalions would cross the river by the same ford used the previous night. Once in position at the north end of the bridge, 6th DLI was to attack up the left side and 9th DLI up the right side of Highway 114 to their objective, a line extending east–west from the loop in the river, a distance of about 1,500 yards. The 3rd County of London Yeomanry would follow and exploit with their Sherman tanks. In support was the tremendous firepower of six regiments of artillery: ninety-five 25-pounders (88 mm), forty-eight 105 mm howitzers and sixteen medium guns – in all, 159 weapons.[1]

The third attack began at 0100, 17 July, after an easy river crossing by the two battalions. But as the DLI attempted to advance north the Germans contested every yard of ground. More savage fighting ensued and an entire platoon of 6th DLI was lost; 'A' Company of 9th DLI also lost a platoon and was soon down to less than fifteen men. Shortly after dawn the Germans launched a tank-supported counterattack which was only broken up by artillery fire. Supported by nine Shermans, a battle raged throughout the day. In places the fighting was again hand-to-hand. One sergeant was reduced to fighting with his fists against the Germans and an infantry company commander was captured and kicked by

---

[1] *The Mediterranean and Middle East*, Vol. V, op. cit., fn 1, p. 104; Senior, 'The Durham Light Infantry at the Primosole Bridge', Part III; Kirkman account.

a German private for carrying a German pistol. One after-action report summed it all up with this terse comment: 'I've never seen such carnage.'[1] One wounded paratrooper rose up from the ground and threw a grenade at some British troops. He was shot at once but, only wounded, rose up, shouted 'Heil Hitler!' and killed himself with a dagger. Senior recounts that 'another young German who took refuge up an olive tree spat on some of our troops who were trying to induce him to come down. He was given no further chance to spit on anyone.'[2]

The most frenzied battles occurred in the vineyards. Fassl's Signal Company claimed three more Shermans. But, as he has recently recorded, the full extent of the dreadful carnage could not be appreciated until daylight on 17 July. The battlefield was strewn with the broken bodies of dead and dying men. It was so awful that Fassl succeeded in arranging a temporary cease-fire with the British, and was fortunate that a DLI medic had inadvertently found refuge among his men. This is the story in Fassl's own words:

> ... When 'our' medical orderly had understood what I wanted, we both left cover with me close on his heels. Had we been fired upon, he would have shared my fate. He held a handkerchief aloft and waved it. The British may well have believed, at first, that we wanted to surrender, for immediately half a dozen flat steel helmets and caps appeared over there and I had the impression that they had clearly been waiting for this moment. However, they quickly understood what our real intention was and very soon search parties reached our positions. Then followed some very tense moments while the first of the seriously wounded men were recovered. Everyone realized, on both sides, that an unexpected move would cause catastrophe in a matter of seconds. Fortunately no one lost his nerve and the business of recovery went ahead. Germans and British called out to each

[1] Quoted in Andrew Graham, *Sharpshooters at War* (Regimental history of the 3rd, 4th and the [combined] 3/4 County of London Yeomanry), 1964.

[2] Senior, 'The Durham Light Infantry at Primosole Bridge', Part IV, op. cit. More so than any other German formation in Sicily, the tenacity of the men of the 1st Parachute Division stands out. Hugh Pond, who served in Sicily as a major, writes that those captured and taken to the rear for questioning 'remained arrogant and hostile in the face of all threats and interrogation'. Some spat in the faces of their captors, while others simply refused to respond with even their name or rank. Brothel tickets served as proof to Allied interrogators that the unit had been in southern France recently. (*Sicily*, op. cit. p. 142.)

One paratrooper who was having his wounds dressed at a British aid station plunged his teeth into the hands of an orderly. A lieutenant captured behind British lines was told he was liable to be shot for wearing civilian clothes. The lieutenant said, 'That is quite understood. I took the risk and failed – I deserve it – Heil Hitler.' (Cf. de Guingand, *Operation Victory*, op. cit., pp. 298–9.)

other to show where their seriously wounded lay. Everything went well and, finally, two long columns of wounded, some supporting others and all bound up with emergency field dressings, left the battlefield and disappeared into the dusty, glowing landscape. We allowed the prisoners to go with them. I asked 'our' British medical orderly to call a few words of thanks to the British and then let him leave with the last group of wounded. The flat steel helmets disappeared and we watched the wounded file over the bridge in the midday haze.[1]

Fassl was only too aware that his gesture had given the British a good look at his positions, but never hesitated in placing the welfare of the wounded of both sides first.[2]

For the German defenders 17 July was the turning point. Where other units might have broken, the brave DLI gave as good as they got and with his anti-tank weapons destroyed, the German engineer commander recognized the futility of any further attempt to hold his ground. The time had come to render Primosole bridge useless to the British and several determined attempts were made to drive explosive-laden trucks onto the bridge where it would detonate in the manner now in common vogue with modern-day terrorists. Fortunately for the British, these attempts all failed and during the final try Captain Adolff was gravely wounded. He died the following day.[3] Tanks overran many of the German positions and Captain Fassl vividly remembers a Sherman lumbering over his foxhole only moments before he became a prisoner. His unit had shrunk to seventeen men.

While those Germans who had escaped death or capture were withdrawing north to the safety of the Fosso Bottaceto (called by the Germans *Der Panzergraben* – The Tank Ditch) the DLI were surveying their losses. The British estimated that the Germans had left some 300 dead on the battlefield and that 155 more were taken prisoner, all of them members of the 1st Parachute Division.[4]

---

[1] Dr Ing Erich Fassl, Captain, German Army, retired, was interviewed by Helmut Wilhelmsmeyer for 'The Battle for the Primosole Bridge', Part II, op. cit.

[2] Ibid.

[3] Ibid., and Schmitz. Adolff was posthumously promoted to major and awarded the coveted *Ritterkreuz* for his valour in defending Primosole bridge.

[4] Kirkman account. In *Sharpshooters at War*, the CLY historian paid tribute to their foe: 'It is impossible not to admire the fanatical courage with which they had fought.' Among those killed at Primosole bridge was the CO, 3rd CLY, Lieutenant-Colonel Geoffrey Willis. Unfortunately the war diaries of the 1st Parachute Division did not survive the war, but Schmitz believes that the British estimate of 300 dead was far too high. The exact count will never be known.

Casualties to the DLI were equally severe: 120 to 6th DLI and 100 to 9th DLI. At last it was the Germans who cracked, but even as they pulled back the 4,000 yards to the Fosso Bottaceto, small comfort could be taken by the DLI in victory.

The DLI history records the scene:

> The area around the bridge was a regular hell's kitchen; it was littered with smashed rifles and automatics, torn pieces of equipment, bloodstained clothing, overturned ammunition boxes and bodies of British and German dead. It was a scene of terrible destruction and telling evidence of a bitter struggle in which neither side had asked or given any quarter. There can have been few better German troops in Sicily than those who held the bridge. They were Nazi zealots to a man, but they fought superbly well and as their Battalion Commander was led away into captivity [Lieutenant-]Colonel [Arthur] Clarke of the 9th Battalion quietly shook him by the hand.[1]

The picture that seems to emerge from various accounts is that the commanders and men of the 1st Parachute Division were fanatical Nazis. This impression is not altogether accurate. Within the ranks of the German parachute corps there existed a strong sense of patriotism and while it is true that leaders like Heidrich were impressed by Hitler, there is no evidence they were either Nazis or supported the excesses of the Third Reich, of which most appeared not to know. Their fanaticism stemmed not from Nazism but rather from a powerful sense of camaraderie and *esprit de corps*. Their use of 'Heil Hitler!' when captured was more often than not a matter of personal morale rather than political belief. A more accurate representation is of men who were constantly thrust into the most difficult situations and learned to rely on each other for support. Their behaviour towards their prisoners was, on the whole, excellent. When some of the men of No. 3 Commando were captured near Malati bridge, Heilmann recalls that they were treated by the German medics just as they would tend their own troops. The German paratroops had long since learned the lesson that the Wehrmacht survived primarily through improvisation, and what the men of Eighth Army saw as fanaticism was in reality an expression of their brotherhood.[2]

[1] *The D.L.I. at War*, op. cit., p. 130. The unlucky 9th Battalion lost its CO, Lieutenant-Colonel Clarke, and the second-in-command, Major Bill Robinson, two weeks later during a mortar attack near Mount Etna.

[2] Cf., Heilmann, 'Fallschirmjäger auf Sizilien', op. cit.; Wilhelmsmeyer, Part II, op. cit.; and Schmitz, loc. cit.

Tank–infantry co-operation during the battle for Primosole bridge proved clumsy and ineffective at first as each attempted to fight the battle in its own way, until each discerned the value of better co-operation.* It was also a confusing, very untidy battle fought mainly by small groups of men. And even though the German paratroopers had surrendered the bridge, the battle for Catania was far from over.

The night of 16/17 July brought more German reinforcements in the form of Lieutenant-Colonel Erich Walther's 4th Parachute Regiment (FJR 4), which moved into positions along the *Panzergraben* to bolster the decimated engineers. They were joined further to the west by elements of Group Schmalz in what was to become the eastern anchor of the Etna Line. The Germans were now in better defensive positions than they had been in and around Primosole bridge; and with a combination of fresh troops and the use of a great many weapons 'liberated' from British gliders and weapons canisters which landed north of the Simeto, they were able to turn Highway 114 into a death trap for any force attempting to thrust through to Catania.

Thus ended the latest chapter in the bloody battle for Primosole bridge. After three days of savage combat the 50th Division bridgehead extended a mere 1,000 yards north of the disputed bridge. It seemed like an eternity since Captain Rann's intrepid band of Red Devils had seized the bridge from its Italian defenders, and even though Primosole was firmly under British control it had been captured far too late. The 'luck' Montgomery had needed so badly never materialized and he was now about to abandon his strategy of forcing a breakthrough at Catania. The first evidence came that day [17 July] when Dempsey again visited Kirkman to

---

* Mutual co-operation and understanding between infantrymen and tank men was more often than not a slender reed, more so in the British Army than the US Army. Part of the problem lay in understanding each other's problems. For example, one of the common difficulties of tankers was simply answering the call of nature while cocooned inside a tank. The 44th RTR historian provides a vivid example of how such problems could influence co-operation. During the Italian campaign, 'a troop commander was crouching beside his tank discussing certain important tactical matters with the colonel of infantry with whom he was supposed to be co-operating. The mortar bombs had been falling for some time and for several hours it had been unhealthy to leave one's tank. As the two officers were conferring, the flap above the co-driver was opened and a hand emerged, holding an empty shell-case. The hand slowly turned and poured a steady stream of yellow liquid on to the colonel's tin helmet. He was not amused and co-operation between tanks and infantry suffered a temporary setback, until the colonel could be convinced that his discomfort had not been intentionally caused.' (Quoted in *A History of the 44th Royal Tank Regiment in the War of 1939–1945*, 1965, pp. 91–2.)

announce that the Catania landings were cancelled and 50th Division's task was to continue pressing forward another 2,500 yards to the Fosso Bottaceto, which marked the southern defences of Catania airfield.

The exhausted and decimated DLI had shot their bolt. When they counted the toll it revealed the brigade had lost 500 killed, wounded and missing.[1] They were replaced in the line by the 168th Brigade which launched another of the interminable attacks towards Catania on the night of 17/18 July, this time directly into the teeth of the enemy's main defences which had been prepared months earlier by the Italians and were now manned by the rejuvenated German paratroopers. This attack fared little better than its predecessors and brought the 50th Division to a point several hundred yards south of the Fosso Bottaceto. Due to a misunderstanding of their orders the 1st Battalion London Scottish on the right failed to close up during a planned artillery barrage and found themselves pinned down in an exposed position. The entrenched Germans were unscathed by the artillery fire and when the hapless British infantry attacked they were mown down. More than forty years later, Sergeant Georg Schmitz still vividly remembers the horrific scene: 'Heavy machine-gun and small-arms fire greeted the brave attackers who again suffered high losses. The dead and wounded lay in rows before the German position and the cries of the wounded were heard for the rest of the night.' The next morning some of the wounded British troops were rescued by the Germans.[2]

Kirkman was forced to order a withdrawal to a point well short of the Fosso Bottaceto. It had been a baptism of fire for the green 168th Brigade and their inexperience ensured that the first attempt to capture this key piece of terrain ended in failure.[3]

[1] *The D.L.I. at War*, op. cit., p. 130. Although their opponents were no longer paratroopers, the Green Devils of the 1st Parachute Division had a great respect for their foe, especially the men of the DLI. Sergeant Schmitz recalls a later incident when an elderly *Festungs-Btl* soldier (inexperienced men who were allocated to 'help' front-line troops) smashed a British POW in the head with a rifle butt. Fortunately, the POW wore a helmet and survived, but Schmitz was angered by this act and ordered the soldier to carry an ammunition box, saying this would not be so easy to 'fling about'. This incident illustrates the professional and moral attitude of the German paratroopers who fought in Sicily and Italy. (Cf. 'German Paratroopers and the Primosole Bridge, Sicily, 1943', loc. cit.)

[2] 'German Paratroopers and the Primosole Bridge, Sicily, 1943'. The survivors of Schmitz's engineer battalion were now under the command of the newly arrived 4th Parachute Regiment.

[3] *The Path of the 50th*, op. cit., pp. 198-9. Part of this failure was attributable to malfunctioning wireless sets.

With minor exceptions Eighth Army advanced no closer to the city of Catania – a scant three miles away – for the remainder of July. The city itself did not fall to the British until 5 August: twenty-two days after Primosole bridge was captured by the 1st Airborne Division.

The highest possible compliment to the German defenders of Primosole bridge came from the venerable *Times* of London: 'They were troops of the highest quality . . . fantastically courageous, to fight against them was an education for any soldier.'[1]

The battle for the plain of Catania was one of the bitterest fought by British troops during the war. A Royal Artillery captain long afterwards wrote of Primosole bridge that 'the fighting there was the bitterest I remember in the whole war and I can still remember the stench of decaying flesh on the banks of that river'.[2] Even Montgomery was forced to admit to Brooke that the battle 'has been quite some of the hardest we have ever had in my Army . . . it was a very bloody killing match'.[3]

Only days earlier Montgomery had been on the brink of a rapid and decisive victory in Sicily; now his dream of capturing Catania had turned to ashes. How did a small outgunned German paratroop force at Primosole bridge – devoid of naval support and air cover – prevent Eighth Army from rolling up the Axis left flank and thrusting unhindered clear to Messina?

The abortive airborne operation to seize the bridge, although an important element, was not the real reason for the British failure. What doomed the operation was the inexplicable decision by both Montgomery and Dempsey to cancel the amphibious invasion of Catania. Even though the 50th Division was unable to break the German defences along the Simeto, the attacks there served the purpose of drawing all of the available German forces away from Catania. Had Montgomery carried out his original intention he would, at a single stroke, have regained the initiative and been in control of the coastal route to Messina. The most vital link of the Etna Line would have been destroyed and the outcome of the campaign foreordained.

---

[1] *The Times*, 27 August 1943.
[2] Captain D. L. C. Price, RA, quoted in Pack, *Operation 'Husky'*, op. cit., p. 142.
[3] Letter of 27 July, Montgomery Papers.

Unfortunately, neither Montgomery nor Dempsey ever commented specifically about their reasons for cancelling the amphibious end-run. What is certain is that for five days Catania was undefended from an attack from the sea while German paratroops and (later) Group Schmalz fought savagely to block any British advance north of the Simeto.

There were other reasons: Eighth Army made poor use of the naval and air assets available.* At this early stage of their venture in battle coalition, Allied forces had yet to grasp fully the enormous potential of three-dimensional warfare. The Eighth Army attempt to force a lightning breakthrough to Catania was conducted in a one-dimensional environment. Although 200 requests for naval gunfire support were met by the Royal Navy in support of Eighth Army operations during the campaign,[1] Primosole bridge was an example where the Navy could have provided far more support if called upon.†

Throughout the advance on Lentini and the battle for Primosole bridge there is no evidence of the ground forces utilizing close air support. The air effort was primarily concentrated on eradicating enemy air resistance and interdicting communications. Nevertheless, there were ample aircraft available to support the most important army effort of the campaign. On 14 July, for example, the RAF recorded that thirty-four escorted Kittyhawk fighter-bombers operated against targets of opportunity near Caltagirone and Lentini.[2]

The use of the airborne against Primosole bridge was a scheme that went wrong at the top. Although true that the drive north by the ground forces was unimaginative (just as it would be at Arnhem) and that later on the Allies would make better use of their capabilities, the fact remains that the most crucial battle of the campaign was fought with only a fraction of the assets available to Eighth Army.

[1] Roskill, *The War at Sea*, Vol. III, Part I, op. cit., p. 138.
[2] 'RAF Mediterranean Review No. 4', July–September 1943. Copies are in the PRO, Air Historical Branch, MOD, and the Public Archives of Canada. Targets of opportunity were, as the name implies, any suitable enemy target that could be located on sweeps through an area by fighters and fighter-bombers. On 14 July the thirty-four sorties could just as easily have been in direct support of the Eighth Army offensive on the plain of Catania.
* The exception was the 1st Airborne whose dead radios stymied the use of naval gunfire.
† There is no better example of the powerful support possible from naval gunfire than the performance of the US Navy at Gela on 10–11 July 1943.

The official historians unfairly blamed the failure on the 5th and 50th Divisions:

> Nature gave the enemy a good position on the Simeto, and he used the gift well. When all is said, it is possible that seasoned troops might have hustled him more on the way to the Simeto, and broken him at it. For seasoned troops, at concert pitch, had a deliberate, rather awesome impetus – hard to define in words, but unmistakable and deadly in action. Neither 5th nor 50th Division had recently had the experience which gives this quality.*

As Hugh Pond has observed, the veteran troops of Eighth Army, which included both these divisions, were 'bloody tired' and 'browned off', but the performance of the DLI at Primosole bridge was certainly *not* such an example!

A major factor in the failure of the spearhead ground forces to make deeper and more rapid penetrations was the failure of the planners and logisticians to provide the necessary transport. The mountainous terrain of Sicily's interior limited movement largely to the few existing roads, which were well defended by an enemy who knew how to utilize the setting to maximum advantage. Without animal transport, schemes to outflank the enemy were virtually impossible. The result was that units were tactically slow and their advance sometimes resembled 'efforts to cram a number of corks into a bottle'.[1] The 30 Corps area of operations was nightmarish country for mechanized forces but ideal for pack animals. The original Eighth Army order of battle called for seven companies of pack mules, but a staff officer made the foolish decision to cancel the requirement, thus terminating any possible hope of organized pack support.[2]

The enormous distances covered by the units of Eighth Army

---

[1] *The Mediterranean and Middle East*, Vol. V, op. cit., p. 114.
[2] Ibid. Despite this blunder, attempts were made to organize pack trains with locally procured animals. Most proved too small except for limited use. Truscott, it will be recalled, brought mules to Sicily as an organic part of his 3d Division. During the drive on Palermo his troops captured a good many mules and some horses which were used for transporting water, ammunition and rations in areas inaccessible to vehicles. Old cavalryman Patton likewise favoured the use of pack animals, and the feared Berber Goumiers were all equipped with mules which were used to carry ammunition. Attached to every *tabor* [regiment] of Goums was a cavalry unit and each man in it owned his own horse. The enormous success enjoyed by these fierce soldiers in Sicily was due in no small part to their use of pack animals. The decision by Eighth Army not to use pack animals is one of the little-known but telling blunders of the campaign.

had, after ten days, left most troops sapped by the cruel heat and humidity. The decision not to allocate more transport to the first of the follow-up convoys would, in hindsight, appear to be as misguided as the decision not to employ pack transport.

Montgomery's decision to attempt a secondary drive with 30 Corps via Vizzini instead of launching a thrust towards the plain of Catania with the full resources of both his corps was a serious misjudgment. His official biographer calls his attempt at a breakthrough at Catania on a one-brigade front an eerie parallel to Mareth. By splitting his forces so far apart in a race against time before the Germans could form a defensive line, he could not at that stage have undone his mistakes even if he had chosen to do so. Instead, by design Monty persisted obstinately in the same futile strategy for which he had so roundly castigated Anderson in Tunisia – ' "the partridge drive" he had himself mocked so contemptuously'.[1]

What has been so misunderstood about the Sicily campaign was that the British failure at Catania was not a consequence of the usual criticism levelled at Montgomery – ponderous and determined concentration of force at a decisive point – but rather, as Nigel Hamilton observes, from mistakenly dispersing his thrusts over too large an area without a powerful reserve to exploit a favourable situation. 'For once Monty had let down his army by overambitiousness and his lack of ruthless adherence to his own rule of concentration in strength.'[2]

Eisenhower was only one of many who misinterpreted the battle of the Catania plain and blamed Monty's failure to break through on his reputation for overcaution.[3] To the contrary, the only opportunity missed during this battle was his failure to concen-

[1] *Monty: Master of the Battlefield, 1942–1944*, op. cit., p. 317.
[2] Ibid., p. 318.
[3] An example is the comment in *The Eisenhower Papers*, Vol. II, p. 1260: '. . . the assumption was that Montgomery would push up the coastal road past Mount Etna and into Messina. This did not happen, partly because of Montgomery's caution, partly because the Germans put up stiff resistance.' His G-2, Brigadier Kenneth Strong, complained that if Monty had been 'less conservative and his forces more mobile, he could probably have been to Messina during the first week'. (Butcher Diary, 4 August 1943.)

* The only inexperienced formation in the 50th Division was the 168th Brigade, whose participation in the battle commenced after the outcome of the battle had already been decided.

trate his abundant combat power against the weakly defended coastal sector where a breakthrough could have been exploited clear to Messina.

Eighth Army already had in action four divisions, one independent infantry brigade (a total of thirty-nine battalions of infantry), three independent armoured brigades (nine regiments of tanks) plus supporting machine-gun battalions, reconnaissance units, artillery, and engineers. Yet Montgomery's vital thrust to break the Catania defences relied on *one brigade* and at times a single battalion.

When the 50th Division ran out of steam at Primosole bridge, Montgomery began casting his eye westward. If 13 Corps could not succeed in the east, then Leese would surely do better by launching a left hook around Mount Etna to open the way to Messina. As the prospects of success dimmed along the Simeto, Monty began telling Alexander that he would continue to exert pressure there but would at the same time launch two other thrusts in the west: one by the Canadians against Enna, then northeast towards Leonforte and Adrano; the other by 51st Division towards Paterno. 'All indications point to the fact that the enemy is very stretched and we should press him strongly with thrusts on all sectors.'[1]

His diary reveals that by 17 July Montgomery had already written off a breakthrough at Catania and was determined to use 13 Corps as an anvil while 30 Corps became the hammer and captured Leonforte and Adrano, thus driving a deep wedge between the 15th Panzer Grenadier and the Hermann Goering Divisions which would have the effect of rendering the Etna Line untenable.

Although he knew by 16 July the Catania operation was a failure, it was not until he met Dempsey on the morning of 18 July that it became absolutely clear he had decided to abandon the entire operation by declining to continue pressing the costly attacks north of the Simeto.* The 5th Division was ordered to pass around the left flank of the exhausted 50th Division and attack Misterbianco, a small town near the western suburbs of Catania. If successful, this operation held the promise of enveloping the defenders of Catania. However, the tone of Montgomery's diary

---

[1] Montgomery Diary, 16 July 1943.
* Dempsey had already anticipated him and issued similar orders.

suggests he was merely going through the motions and in reality had no faith in its success:

> It was quite clear now that the enemy was going to fight with great determination to prevent me from getting possession of the CATANIA airfields. His troops opposing me were all Germans and he kept dropping small parties of very stout-hearted parachute troops in order to stiffen up his weak places.[1]

The truth was that the campaign in eastern Sicily was almost out of control and was being fought on four separate fronts:

(1) 50th Division astride Route 114, south of Catania.

(2) 5th Division on the left of 50th Division, attacking towards Misterbianco.

(3) 51st Division attacking towards Paterno.

(4) 1st Canadian Division attacking towards Leonforte and Adrano.

On 19 July Montgomery signalled Alexander that he hoped to reach Misterbianco and Paterno by the night of 20 July. 'Canadians will reach Leonforte area tonight. These four thrusts are very strong and the enemy will not be able to hold them all. If I can reach MISTERBIANCO and PATERNO tomorrow night and ADRANO by 21 July I will be well placed for extension of battle round either side of ETNA.'[2]

Two days later his optimistic prediction had turned sour. His diary entries reflect a combination of wishful thinking and growing frustration:

> The attacks put in last night by 50 Div, 5 Div and 51 Div did not make any great progress. Very determined resistance was met.
>
> We have definitely won the battle for the plain of CATANIA and we are in possession of the whole plain; our advanced troops have got a footing on the foothills of ETNA. . . .
>
> But the enemy is securely positioned in CATANIA itself, which is a strong bastion . . . My troops are getting tired as the heat in the plain of CATANIA is great. . . . He is also going to hold the CATANIA flank against me to the last.[3]*

---

[1] Montgomery Diary, 18 July 1943.

[2] Ibid., 19 July 1943.

[3] Ibid., 21 July 1943.

* Heat was not the only problem to plague the British on the plain of Catania. The Canadians, who had not been in the desert, suffered initially from sunburn in the hills, but on the plain the problem was malaria, and it claimed a great many victims. Monty's GSO 1,

'The proper answer to the problem,' he wrote, 'is now to reorganize; to hold on my right while keeping up a good pressure; to continue the left hook with 30 Corps using the Canadian Division. I will give 78 Div to 30 Corps and go hard for ADRANO and then Northwards round the West side of Mt ETNA.'[1]

By 21 July the battle for Primosole bridge had become the first of the bitter memories for the British of the Sicily campaign. Convinced he had no chance whatever of breaking the German defences at Catania, and having forfeited that opportunity by failing to capture the city while it lay undefended, Montgomery had reduced his options to the left hook by 30 Corps.

[1] Ibid.

Brigadier (later Major-General) David Belchem, has written that 'experts came from home to study the disease which, at one time, became so prevalent that one infantry division had to be taken out of the line, such was its debilitating effect on officers and men'. (*All in the Day's March*, op. cit., p. 168.) The official history notes that battle casualties in Eighth Army were about 9,000 and those from malaria 11,500 in Eighth Army and in Seventh Army about 9,800. Apparently the danger was foreseen but tough measures to enforce anti-malarial discipline do not appear to have existed. (*The Mediterranean and Middle East*, Vol. V, op. cit., pp. 145–6.) Bradley forced the men of II Corps to wear the woollen OG (Olive Green) uniform in Sicily and he mistakenly believed this somehow acted to minimize malaria casualties to American forces. (Bradley Commentaries.)

CHAPTER 24

The Left Hook

The left hook is now the thing.

MONTGOMERY DIARY
(21 July 1943)

The last ten days of July were a dismal period for Eighth Army as Montgomery's strategy came unglued.* Alexander played no role in Montgomery's decision to switch his main effort to the west and merely approved his action after the fact. Monty's optimism that he would capture several key places by 21 July proved illusory.

The Germans were at last beginning to pull together their defences along what became known as the Etna Line.† As we have seen, the 1st Parachute Division and the Hermann Goering Division stalemated Eighth Army at Catania, thus buying time for the remainder of the Etna Line to be established.

In a setting remarkably similar to the crucial battle for Caen in Normandy the following summer, Montgomery found his strategy thwarted by small but determined German forces who operated with great effectiveness independently of one another and without benefit of mutual support. By splitting his forces and pinning his hopes on the left hook by 30 Corps, Montgomery had stretched Eighth Army to a dangerously thin limit. 30 Corps was fighting in very rough country over an area far too large for effective offensive operations against a determined defender. The

---

* Montgomery's problems on the battlefield were aggravated by his troubles with the Canadian government when he forbade the Canadian C-in-C, General A. G. L. McNaughton, to visit the 1st Canadian Division or from even setting foot in Sicily. Monty's relations with the Canadians and the so-called McNaughton affair are discussed in Appendix L.

† Alternatively called the Hube Line, for the new German ground commander. The 'line' was in reality a series of defensive positions established at key points along the Etna *massif*. They began in the east along the Fosso Bottaceto, ran west along the general line of the Dittaino River, through Gerbini to Sferro and Statione di Dittaíno, about ten miles east of Enna. This sector was the responsibility of the Hermann Goering, except for the Fosso Bottaceto which was still defended mainly by the 1st Parachute Division. Group Schmalz occupied new positions along the Simeto to the west of Primosole bridge, while other sectors contained elements of the Livorno and Napoli Divisions, both of which had been decimated by mass defections of their troops. Further west, the 15th Panzer Grenadier Division was defending the line Leonforte–Nicosia where roads were virtually non-existent.

Army reserve, Major-General Vivian Evelegh's veteran 78th Division, was still in Tunisia, would not debark its first unit at Cassibile until 25 July and could not be committed to battle until 30 July.

The operations by 30 Corps turned out to be separate battles fought by the Canadians and the Highlanders, with neither supporting the other. Alexander had passed up a valuable opportunity to employ the 45th Division in the role now being enacted by the Canadians who were to carry out a strong left hook from Enna to Leonforte, and then to Adrano, a tall order for a division in its first combat and largely bereft of transport in mountainous country which favoured the defender. In theory, the concept of cutting off the Germans in the plain of Catania by seizing the key road centre of Adrano was sound; in practice, Leese's corps was stretched tenuously and lacked the ability to accomplish its mission without reinforcements. No thought seems to have been given to the possible employment of US forces towards Mount Etna. Instead, Montgomery – with Alexander's tacit blessing – persisted in carrying out his four divisional thrusts.

Instead of 'hustling' the Germans as Monty had claimed to Alexander, the four offensives all developed unfavourably as the Germans savagely resisted all attempts to crack their defences along the northern edge of the plain of Catania. With the exhausted 50th Division holding along the Primosole bridgehead, a series of assaults by the 5th Division to penetrate north of the Simeto and seize Misterbianco met with failure.

The 13th Brigade of the 5th Division was ordered to establish another bridgehead north of an unnamed bridge some six miles west of Primosole. Dubbed Lemon Bridge by the British, this sector now became the site of a series of fierce battles with Group Schmalz. The first to engage the Hermann Goering was the 2nd Inniskillings* who were severely mauled in a scene of 'terrifying confusion'.[1] Again, as at Primosole bridge, the best that could be attained was a tenuous foothold on the northern bank of the Simeto. The night of 19 July, the 15th Brigade was ordered to enlarge the foothold and in a 24-hour battle they too took very heavy casualties from intense German fire and were actually 'lost'

---

[1] Cole, *Rough Road to Rome*, op. cit., p. 52. The Inniskillings lost a quarter of its officers and many NCOs and men. 'C' Company, for example, started with 95 men and returned with 25.

* The Royal Inniskilling Fusiliers were an Ulster regiment.

for over five hours before being withdrawn under a barrage from nine Royal Artillery regiments. Misterbianco remained as distant and unattainable as Catania.

The effects of Montgomery's new strategy were rapidly evident elsewhere. The Canadian left hook which was to have taken them to Leonforte by the night of 19 July was blocked by the tough grenadiers of Rodt's 104th Panzer Grenadier Regiment who, along with the rest of the 15th Panzer Grenadier Division, fought a skilful delaying action between Assoro and Leonforte which kept the Canadians at bay until 22 July. It would take a bold and risky manoeuvre finally to crack the German defences around Leonforte.

The town anchored the western end of the Etna Line and the Germans were determined to protect it from the Canadians. The plan General Simonds put into effect on 19 July was for the 2nd Brigade to attack towards Leonforte while the 1st Brigade intensified the pressure by attacking Assoro, a mountain village several miles to the southeast which commanded the valley leading to Leonforte. Both brigades encountered very strong resistance.

When his commander was killed by an 88 mm shell, Major The Lord Tweedsmuir took command of the Hastings and Prince Edward Regiment.* Rather than attack Assoro by the most obvious means, the exposed road leading to the mountain-top town, Tweedsmuir elected to carry out a bold and exceptionally dangerous plan by scaling the steep and treacherous eastern face of the mountain hoping to catch the Germans by surprise. Under the cover of a diversionary feint and an artillery barrage, the specially formed all-volunteer assault force of one platoon from each of the rifle companies began to pick its way across some of the wildest terrain in Sicily, aided only by the bright moonlight. The regimental historian called it the most difficult forced march ever attempted in training or combat. The going was treacherous and at times terrifying. Tweedsmuir's brilliant gambit was so successful that not a single man was lost as the Canadians caught the Germans flatfooted, defending the ruins of an ancient Norman castle overlooking the village. When dawn came they found the site commanded a view for fifty miles.

Throughout 21 July, Tweedsmuir's men beat off a series of German counterattacks with the aid of artillery fire and by mid-

---

* Tweedsmuir was a Scot serving in the Canadian Army and the son of the former Governor-General of Canada, John Buchan.

day, 22 July, the town and the road leading up the mountain were cleared and Assoro indisputably belonged to the Canadians.[1] Despite the success of the unexpected assault, the capture of Assoro was a near-run thing. The assault force was totally isolated and in desperate straits from the repeated attacks of a larger German force. One trooper had managed to carry a radio set up the mountain and this became the lifeline which saved Tweedsmuir and his men. Accurate counter-battery fire opened up to silence the deadly barrage that had been raining over their positions around the castle.

The loss of Assoro knocked the props from the southern end of the German defences on the Assoro–Leonforte mountain ridge and eased the way for the capture of Leonforte which was very stubbornly defended until 22 July when the Germans were finally forced to withdraw. The cost to the Canadians in the operation was 275 casualties, most of them from the battle for Leonforte.

As the Canadians had been quick to learn, these two battles represented a turning point in German tactics. The Division intelligence officer noted that, until then, the German rearguard would voluntarily withdraw at a propitious moment to new positions some miles away. 'The fact that they are not voluntarily retiring from their latest strongpoint but are fighting for every yard of ground indicates we are nearing something like a serious defence zone. Beyond doubt they would have held Leonforte had they not been driven out of it.'[2] The Canadians had, of course, struck the western edge of Hube's new Etna Line and, as their official historian laments, they would make 'slow and difficult progress across the mountains during the next two weeks' and become 'bitterly familiar with "this resolute defence" by German panzer grenadiers and paratroopers'.[3]

As the struggle continued in both east and west, yet another series of bloody battles were being fought in the Highland Division sector. To attain Monty's stated objective of Paterno, the Highlanders had first to secure the crossings over the River Dittáino,

---

[1] *The Canadians in Italy*, op. cit., pp. 104–6. The brutal battles fought by the Canadians in the mountains of central Sicily are recorded in Farley Mowat's *The Regiment* (Toronto, 1973) and *And No Birds Sang* (Toronto, 1979).

[2] Quoted in ibid, p. 112.

[3] Ibid. Rodt, the commander of 15th PzG Division, no doubt recalling Assoro, wrote that British and Canadian infantry were very mobile at night, superior to his own troops in field craft and clever at surprise break-ins and night-time infiltration.

followed by the capture of the village of Gerbini, its railroad station, barracks and airfield. Gerbini is situated in the northwest corner of the plain of Catania directly astride the neck of a valley which carries the Simeto south from its headwaters deep in the mountains around Lake Pozzillo, to Paterno and thence to the plain. To gain access to the valley leading to Paterno, the 51st Division had first to dislodge either the Germans defending Gerbini or those holding Sferro, where an alternative route led to the Ponte la Barca spanning the Simeto approximately three miles below Paterno.

The plan of the Highland Division commander, Major-General Douglas Wimberley,* was to launch a two-brigade attack: 154th

---

* Major-General Douglas N. Wimberley (1886–1983), the somewhat eccentric Scot who commanded the 51st Division, was one of a long line of distinguished Scottish commanders. Lanky and rather ungainly, Wimberley gained the nickname of 'Tartan Tam' and was known and respected by the men of his division to whom he was always visible and accessible. On one occasion after Alamein, Wimberley was driving his jeep through a battalion position when a Jock asked: 'Could you tell us what is happening, Sir?' Wimberley stopped his jeep, dropped into the trench beside the startled soldier and proceeded to explain in great detail on his map the situation, most of which the battalion HQ was not even yet familiar with.

A Regular officer (Sandhurst 1915), Wimberley was commissioned in the Queen's Own Cameron Highlanders and as an infantry officer he fought at Loos, with the 51st Division on the Somme and at Ypres, St Quentin and Cambrai, followed in 1919 by service with the forgotten international force sent to Russia after the war. In 1942 he became commander of the newly constituted 51st Division sent to the desert to become part of Eighth Army. A staunch supporter of everything Scottish, Wimberley rebuffed all efforts to send non-Scots to the 'new' 51st Division, so much so that he became a source of intense annoyance within the War Office. He nevertheless succeeded in prying Scots loose from units all over England.

Tradition and pride were the backbone of Wimberley's methods and to emphasize this he enforced the wearing of the regimental tartan kilt on every possible occasion. He was equally fanatic about the Highland Division shoulder flashes and unit signposts, and the Division soon achieved the nickname in North Africa of 'The Highway Decorators'. At Alamein the division went into battle with its bagpipes blaring. Another of Wimberley's leadership traits was to insist, whenever time permitted, that every battalion commander construct a model of the battle area and rehearse each and every man.

Wimberley was known to defend fiercely his men and his division even if it meant butting heads with senior commanders, including Monty. Five of his brigadiers who had learned from him how battles should be fought went on to divisional command: Thomas G. Rennie – later killed in 1945 leading the Highland Division during the crossing of the Rhine; Douglas Graham, the 56th Division in Italy and the 50th Division in Northwest Europe, both of which he commanded with great distinction; Horatius (Nap) Murray, the 6th Armoured Division in Italy; Roy Urquhart, the 1st Airborne Division; and G. H. A. MacMillan, the 15th (Scottish) Division and the 51st Division after Rennie's death.

Brigadier James A. Oliver, who commanded the 7th Black Watch in Sicily and 154th Brigade in Northwest Europe, has said of Wimberley that 'he did more than anyone in the Regular Army to close the gap which existed pretty strongly between the Regular Army and the Territorial Army'. In the postwar years Wimberley never received the recognition routinely accorded others who had accomplished far less. Undoubtedly his tendency to place his men and his division before his own career, and his sometimes abrasive outspokenness, resulted in denial of a knighthood after the war.

Infantry Brigade to mount a left hook via the Sferro route and Arrow Force* to attack north via Gerbini. Wimberley retained a reserve consisting of his other two brigades (152nd and 153rd) for commitment whenever required. All went reasonably well the first day and night and Arrow Force succeeded in attaining a narrow bridgehead over the Dittaino, the first of three rivers which lay between the division and Paterno. On 18 July, Wimberley committed his reserves, the 154th Brigade toward a flyspeck on the Catania–Enna railway line called Motta Station (east of Gerbini) and 153rd Brigade on the left towards Sferro. 152nd Brigade now became the reserve to exploit success in either direction from the vicinity of Stimpato.

But success never came. Around the Gerbini airfield and in the village, the Hermann Goering had elected to establish its main defences to impede the British advance. By 19 July the left hook was thoroughly checked around Sferro, and some 2,000 yards south of Gerbini airfield 154th Brigade and Arrow Force were unable to cross the Simeto. Aware that this was clearly the strongest of the enemy's defences, Wimberley was nevertheless reluctant to concede his gains on both flanks despite the fact that the division was now dangerously overextended. As he later admitted, Wimberley now bit off more than he could chew by ordering a full-scale attack on Gerbini airfield the night of 20/21 July by Brigadier Rennie's 154th Brigade, augmented by tanks and the fire of three artillery regiments.

The 7th Argyll and Sutherland Highlanders spearheaded the attack. The fight was ferocious and the division history notes that the Argylls had everything imaginable thrown against them by the Hermann Goering, who had long since begun to regain the reputation lost during their inept performance at Gela. The Argylls encountered deep wire, machine guns and tanks. The 1st and 7th Black Watch on the left and right had a rough time but the Argylls were forced into a frontal attack into the teeth of the Gerbini defences around the railroad station and barracks. During three hours of fierce fighting the Argylls took their objective only to be dislodged the following morning by a savage counterattack.† The

---

* Arrow Force was a tank–infantry task force of Brigadier G. W. Richards' 23rd Armoured Brigade which was still attached to the 51st Division from the Vizzini operation.

† The enemy at Gerbini was thought to be two battalions of the 2nd PzG Regiment, a reconnaissance unit and most of the 2nd Battalion of the tank regiment – all units of the Hermann Goering Division.

Scots paid a fearsome price: the COs of the Argylls and the 46th Royal Tanks were both killed. Most of 'A' Company were either killed or captured and the battalion decimated with the loss of eighteen officers and 160 men, while the RTR lost eight tanks, five men and twelve more missing.[1]

Wimberley later admitted that:

> Emboldened by the speed at which we had gone forward we were now too hasty and took rather 'a bloody nose'. We found the Germans holding the airfields of Gerbini with wire and concrete belonging to the old aerodrome defences. We had come so fast that we had not been able to get the detailed aeroplane photographs which we obtained for more deliberate attacks, and I made the mistake of attacking the enemy within twenty-four hours of getting over the river.[2]

The increasing deterioration of the Eighth Army initiative was reflected in Montgomery's decision that same day when he learned of the setback at Gerbini. Wimberley's recollection is that:

> About the middle of the day Monty himself came to see me. He told me that he had decided to bring the 78th Division over to Sicily from Africa, and to stop attacking on the 13th Corps and Highland Division front, facing the Catanian low ground, while he now continued the offensive with the Canadians and the 78th as soon as they arrived, further to the west. It can be imagined that I was not sorry to get this, to me, quite unexpected news.[3]

Wimberley was acutely aware that the sudden termination of the 51st Division offensive after such heavy losses would inevitably be misunderstood and, in a gesture designed to save face on both sides, he asked Montgomery to confirm his decision in writing. 'I knew full well that my "Jocks" were more temperamental soldiers than the phlegmatic "Tommies", and it would never do, if they thought we had been brought to a full stop by enemy action, especially after the grand fight the Argylls had just put up.'[4]

Montgomery obliged by grabbing a pencil and writing on the spot a note of praise for the Scots:

[1] J. B. Salmond, *The History of the 51st Highland Division*, Edinburgh, 1953, p. 116, and *The Mediterranean and Middle East*, Vol. V, op. cit., p. 117. At full strength an infantry battalion consisted of 35 officers and 786 men. Officer casualties that grim day were 51% and were over 20% for all others. At Gerbini the Argylls suffered 86% of their total officer casualties for the *entire* Sicily campaign and 72% of casualties to the troops.

[2] Quoted in Salmond, op. cit., p. 115.

[3] Wimberley Memoirs.

[4] Ibid.

Eighth Army
21.7.43

My Dear Douglas,

I have decided to make the right flank of the Army Front a defensive front, and to pull in to the best positions – ready for offensive action at a suitable moment later on. Meanwhile I am pushing the offensive hard on the left, where the resistance is not so strong [sic]. In ten days we have captured practically the whole of Sicily, and the enemy is now hemmed in at the N.E. corner – rather like the Cape Bon peninsula. Please tell all your soldiers that I think they have done magnificently. They have marched and fought over a very long distance in great heat, and up to the best standards of the Highland Division. I am sending you 50,000 cigarettes as a present to the Division.

Yours Ever,

B. L. Montgomery[1]

An attempt by the 153rd Brigade to advance in the Sferro sector was met by another of the now familiar exchanges between two determined foes. Throughout 19 July, the 5th Black Watch spent 'a really damnable day' pinned down by intense fire in the excruciating summer heat and that night the 1st Gordons recorded the heaviest shelling they had received in either North Africa or Sicily. When Montgomery called off the offensive the two sides were eyeball-to-eyeball around Sferro.

With Montgomery's latest change of plan the 51st Division went over to the defensive. While Wimberley's tactics may have been questionable, the heroism of the Scots was not.* It will be recalled that Montgomery originally estimated the division would reach Paterno by 20 July and [he hoped] Adrano the day after. Wimberley's original objective of Paterno involved an advance of some twelve miles. He was later to write:

I must admit when I gave out these orders, I never expected to reach Paterno without some days of hard fighting, but little did I

---

[1] Ibid. Also quoted in Salmond, op. cit., pp. 120–1.

* The valour of Major K. W. Pooley of the Royal Artillery attached to the 5th Black Watch was one such example. Acting as the artillery forward observer, Major Pooley watched as the bridge at Sferro was seized the night of 19/20 July. Sensing an enemy counterattack, and knowing registration of his artillery was impossible in the darkness, Pooley walked across the bridge under a hail of enemy fire, contacted the infantry and walked back across the bridge through more fire and accurately registered his guns in time to break up the counterattack. Time and again the intrepid major repeated his trips across the disputed bridge which ensured it remained in British hands. (Cf. Salmond, op. cit., pp. 119–20.)

think, then, that it would be August before Highland Division troops entered that town.[1]

By the second week of the campaign it was evident that Alexander had no intention of taking control of the battle. The result was that his two Army commanders, each of whom had differing ideas, took matters into their own hands.

[1] Wimberley Memoirs.

CHAPTER 25

The Palermo Venture

If I succeed Attila will have to take a back seat.

PATTON

While Montgomery was struggling in the east, Patton was behaving like a caged lion desperately seeking its freedom. Ever since Alexander's visit on 13 July, Patton had been seething with anger and frustration as he continued to see the campaign slipping away before Seventh Army could assume a role more meaningful than merely guarding Monty's left flank. The decision to usurp Patton's boundary line and Alexander's apparent indifference not only left a sour aftertaste of indignation but, as his biographer notes, an air of 'practical cunning'. Patton had managed to wring only one concession from Alexander, in the form of permission to expand his operations to the west and to capture the ancient city of Agrigento which sits atop hills overlooking the Mediterranean about twenty-five miles west of Licata.* Alexander's only proscription was that Patton must on no account become embroiled in a major engagement which might risk exposing the Eighth Army left flank. Having got his foot in the door, Patton now sought a means of capturing Agrigento without incurring Alexander's displeasure.

On 14 July, Patton visited Truscott and told him that he needed to find some means of capturing the port city of Porto Empedocle but could not do so without first capturing nearby Agrigento. Despite Alexander's admonition, Patton made it clear he was 'extremely anxious to have that port'. Truscott immediately

---

* Agrigento was founded in 582 BC by the Greeks who built there the greatest Doric temples outside Greece. As a centre of Greek culture in the western Mediterranean, the walled city attracted poets such as Pindar. Agrigento was also the home of the philosopher Empedocles for whom the nearby port city is named. Before its decline under the Carthaginians and Romans, Agrigento was the jewel of Sicilian cities. Militarily, Agrigento was an important road centre and its capture was a necessary prerequisite to any Seventh Army operations in western Sicily.

understood and replied that he not only sympathized but could undoubtedly help. Surely the 15th Army Group could have no objection to a reconnaissance in force undertaken on his own initiative? 'General Patton, with something of the air of the cat that had swallowed the canary, agreed that he thought they would not.'[1]

Patton had been posing the same question to his staff: 'If I attack Agrigento, will I bring on a major engagement?' 'No, Sir,' he was told. As his G-2, Colonel Oscar Koch has recalled, Patton decided to go ahead. 'There were no whys, no interruptions of what a major engagement might be considered to be – no nothings. That was the estimate on which the decision was based. It represents the shortest estimate of the situation that could be given under any circumstances ever.'[2]

Truscott was as good as his word and by the afternoon of 16 July Agrigento belonged to the 3d Division and Porto Empedocle to Darby's Rangers.* Some 6,000 Italian prisoners were bagged during the brief battles, along with large numbers of vehicles, tanks, artillery and other weapons.

Now that he had Agrigento, Patton could begin to make a move towards attaining his real goal: the capture of Palermo. To do so he knew he would have to outscheme both Monty and Alexander once again. On 19 July he wrote to his wife that 'Monty is trying to steal the show and with the assistance of Devine Destiny [a snide reference to Eisenhower] may do so but to date we have captured three times as many men as our cousins.'[3] As Truscott remembers, 'Palermo drew Patton like a lode star.' After conferring with Lucas and Wedemeyer, Patton decided to fly unannounced to Tunis and attempt to persuade Alexander personally to grant him more latitude in the employment of Seventh Army. 'I am sure neither he nor any of his British staff has any conception of the power and

---

[1] *Command Missions*, op. cit., p. 218. Alexander, during his 13 July visit, had made a point of remarking that if Agrigento could be captured 'through the use of limited forces in the nature of a reconnaissance in force, he had no objections'. (Patton Diary, 13 July 1943.)

[2] Colonel Oscar Koch, 'A One Way Ticket', Koch Papers, USAMHI.

[3] Patton Papers. Patton's dyslexia was the reason for his tendency to misspell words.

* Three Americans won the Medal of Honor in Sicily: two young lieutenants of the 3d Division and a sergeant of the 1st Division. The day after Agrigento fell, 1st Lt. David C. Waybur's reconnaissance platoon was behind enemy lines attempting to locate an isolated Ranger unit when his three-vehicle patrol was attacked by four Italian tanks. Undaunted but thoroughly mismatched, Waybur, even though seriously wounded, stood in the middle of a moonlit road and with only a Thompson sub-machine gun killed the crew of the leading tank which crashed onto a bridge and into a stream bed.

mobility of the Seventh Army, nor are they aware of the political implications ... I shall explain to General Alexander on the basis that it would be inexpedient politically for the Seventh Army not to have equal glory in the final stage of the campaign.'[1]

While Patton was in Tunis, a disturbed Lucas flew to Algiers to report to Eisenhower. Although he wrongly ascribed the slowness of the British advance towards Catania to Monty's overcaution, Lucas was one of the first to sense the strategic advantages of a concentrated drive by Seventh Army towards Messina and the north coast. But when he arrived on 15 July, Lucas found that Eisenhower had not been in Algiers since 6 July and it would be five more days before he could report his misgivings to the Allied commander. When he did so on 20 July the conversation was illuminating:

> I told him frankly that I thought the situation was rapidly becoming very dangerous but that, from what Wedemeyer had told me, something was apparently being done about it. I said we were both Americans and so was Patton and that our personal welfare did not enter into the matter at all. I also said that Patton must stand up to General Alexander and fight for what he thought was right.

Eisenhower agreed but said

> that he had never found a case where the British had deliberately tried to put anything over on us. I didn't answer that ... I must try to put myself in Alexander's place. He first came in contact with American troops when the fighting at Kasserine and Gafsa was going on. They did so poorly that the British Command completely lost confidence in us as offensive troops ... In Sicily there were two new divisions, one, the 45th that has had no combat experience at all, and the other, the 3d, with very little. He should not be blamed too much for being cautious.[2]

The meeting ended with an incredulous Lucas being told by Eisenhower 'to see that Patton was made to realize that he must

---

[1] Patton Diary, 17 July 1943.

[2] Lucas Diary, 20 July 1943. Again, the following day, Lucas took both Eisenhower and Bedell Smith through the problems he saw in Sicily. Truscott and Bradley alone – not Patton – were singled out for praise from Eisenhower, which perplexed Lucas who believed jealousy on the part of many was at the root of things. 'I hope I can weave my way through this intricate web without getting my head cut off. What a hell of a job for a poor, ignorant soldier.'

stand up to Alexander and that he would not hesitate to relieve him from command if he did not do so'.[1]

Patton's unheralded arrival in Tunis on the afternoon of 17 July caught Alexander completely off guard, and in a tense atmosphere the Seventh Army commander delivered his appeal, aided by the presence of Wedemeyer and the abrasive Huebner. The confrontation took place in a civilized but deadly serious manner and there seems, from the impressions of eye witnesses, to have been no doubt in Alexander's mind that Patton had come for a showdown. To Patton's surprise Alexander quickly acceded to his plan to detach part of Seventh Army for a drive north to cut the island in two in conjunction with operations into western Sicily and north-west towards Palermo.

Once again, Alexander's poor leadership was painfully evident. Patton's diary for that day records that when he saw Alexander, the Allied ground commander explained that 'he planned to do just what I asked but that his chief of staff had failed to tell me (pretty weak) when issuing the order. He gave me permission to carry out my plan if I would assure him that the road net near Caltanissetta would be held ... If I do what I am going to do, there is no need of holding anything, but "it's a mean man who won't promise", so I did.'[2]

The order, issued the following day (18 July) by 15th Army Group, read that after capturing Petralia, Patton would:

> take advantage of the situation by pushing north a detachment to cut the coast road thereby splitting the island in two. As soon as you are firmly established on the general line CAM-POFELICE–PETRALIA–CATERINA–CALTANISSETTA–AGRIGENTO you will advance westwards to mop up the western half of Sicily, but this operation must not be started before you are ready to operate from a secure base as given you in the above.[3]

Patton had shrewdly recognized that geography and Montgomery's influence made it fruitless to attempt to alter the role of Eighth Army, but he could most certainly regain control of his own destiny as a commander merely by obtaining a green light from Alexander and letting the mobility of his Army carry American forces into Palermo. Patton's proposal to Alexander stressed

[1] Ibid.
[2] Patton Diary, 17 July 1943.
[3] Alexander Papers, PRO (WO 214/21).

two points: (1) that Palermo had been identified in the HUSKY planning as essential to the successful conclusion of the campaign, and (2) if Seventh Army were to continue carrying out Alexander's wishes [as outlined on 13 July, which effectively eliminated any possibility of capturing Messina], the campaign would end with US forces playing nothing more than a subsidiary role of acting as Montgomery's flank guard.[1]

Without a plan of his own, Alexander was clearly shaken by Patton's surprise arrival on his doorstep and, though imperturbable as always, he nevertheless had little choice except to accede, even though the most meaningful mission that could have then been given to Seventh Army was to strike hard northeast towards Mount Etna, trapping the main German forces between the Americans and Eighth Army. This could then have been followed by a drive to the northeastern coast and Messina where German evacuation from the island could be prevented.

Alexander, however, was still overly preoccupied with protecting Montgomery's left flank despite a steady flow of intelligence which clearly indicated that all that was left in western Sicily were Italian forces who had yet to mount even the slightest threat, and a few scattered German units. The British official intelligence history confirms that by 14 July the threat from Axis forces in western Sicily was non-existent. Moreover, not only was the enemy abandoning that part of the island *en masse* but he was known to be issuing a steady stream of orders to do so at once. On 15 July German elements in the Palermo area were ordered to evacuate immediately, and all landing craft available at Messina were sent to Palermo to remove supplies. The following day the Allied code-breakers intercepted an order naming the German general to be responsible for the orderly evacuation of all western Sicily.[2]

Though still mistrustful of giving American forces a more important role, Alexander caved in. He had, after all, set a precedent by giving in to Montgomery for *his* schemes in the east, and he now either had to do the same for Patton or else had to order Patton to implement a plan of his own, thus assigning a stronger

---

[1] Patton Diary, 17 July 1943.
[2] *British Intelligence in the Second World War*, Vol. III, Part I, op. cit., pp. 90–1, and War Diary, Captain Gustav von Liebenstein, Naval Officer-in-Charge, Messina Strait; the Papers of Rear Admiral Samuel Eliot Morison, Operational Archives Branch, US Navy Historical Center, Washington Navy Yard.

role to Seventh Army in the defeat of German forces and in the capture of Messina.

Alexander's decision, made not through established military procedure, but in the haste of unforeseen confrontation, doomed the Sicily campaign to a dreary and decidedly unhappy ending. It was a fateful decision, made on the spur of the moment and with scant consideration of the consequences. With stalemate daily approaching in the battle for control of the plain of Catania, it made even less sense to turn Seventh Army loose in western Sicily where the enemy threat was virtually non-existent. It should have been obvious that the campaign had to be won in the east and, once accomplished, it did not matter what enemy forces, most of whom were Italian, remained in western Sicily, for their fate would already have been settled.

There is clear evidence Patton well knew that Seventh Army could have altered the complexion of the entire campaign. His diary for 19 July reads:

> I think that the British have a bear by the tail in the Messina peninsula and we may have to go in and help. Had they let us ... take Caltagirone and Enna ourselves, instead of waiting for them, we would have saved two days and been on the north coast now.
>
> Alex has no idea of either the power or speed of American armies. We can go twice as fast as the British and hit harder, but to save British prestige, the XXX Corps had to make the envelopment, and now I think they are stuck. They attacked Catania with a whole division yesterday and only made 400 yards...
>
> Our method of attacking all the time is better than the British system of stop, build up, and start, but we must judge by the enemy reaction. I can do it here [judge the enemy reaction] – Alex can't in Tunis.[1]

Lucas agreed:

> The essence of this campaign is *speed*. I believe the Seventh Army could take Palermo in ten days. If it advanced in that direction the enemy would have to concentrate and fight or lose it. *It would be better to send it against Messina north of Mount Etna and let the British, after taking Catania which they have not done yet, move on Messina through the corridor east of the mountains.*[2] (Author's italics)

[1] Patton Papers.
[2] Lucas Diary, 15 July.

Patton's sudden willingness to challenge Alexander was a complete reversal of his earlier, almost stoical acceptance of the decision to give Montgomery the Vizzini highway. He had earlier failed to discern that a 'wish' expressed to him by Alexander need not represent an order which he was obliged to obey. Within the British Army this frequently meant nothing more than a basis for discussion or modification before it hardened into an order. Montgomery would most certainly have challenged such an order from Alexander and many believed Patton reacted too quickly and misunderstood the distinctions between British and American methods. Foremost among them was Omar Bradley who later wrote: 'Unlike the US Army where an order calls for instant compliance, the British viewed an order as a basis for discussion between commanders. If a difference of opinion developed, it would be ironed out and the order might be amended. In contrast, we in the American Army sought to work out our differences before issuing an order. Once... published it could not be changed except by the issuing authority.'[1]

His method of enhancing the American role in Sicily was coldly calculated and vintage Patton which he likened to the making of 'rock soup':

> A tramp once went to a house and asked for some boiling water to make rock soup. The lady was interested and gave him the water, in which he placed two polished stones. He then asked if he might have some potatoes and carrots to put in the soup to flavour it a little, and finally ended up with some meat. In other words, in order to attack we had first to pretend to reconnoitre, then reinforce the reconnaissance, and finally put on an attack...[2]

Having taken Agrigento by this method and then obtained Alexander's approval for a larger action in western Sicily, Patton now had the one ingredient he knew would unharness Seventh Army once and for all: mobility. Once his forces got rolling and began to gobble up chunks of Sicilian terrain, he knew it would henceforth become impossible for Alexander again to relegate American troops to a secondary role. Patton created a Provisional Corps consisting of the 3d Infantry Division, the 82d Airborne Division,

[1] A Soldier's Story, op. cit., p. 138.
[2] War As I Knew It, op. cit., p. 125.

the two Ranger battalions and the 2d Armored Division which was to follow the advance and exploit any breakthrough. Command of this force was given to his trusted deputy commander, Major General Geoffrey Keyes.* During the pre-D-Day planning Palermo had been considered a prize second only to Messina and now that he had a green light from Alexander, Patton lost no time in ordering an aggressive push across the 100 miles or more of rugged terrain to capture the capital of Sicily.

The 82d Airborne was ordered into western Sicily for mopping up operations which General Maxwell D. Taylor later said turned out to be 'a pleasure march'.[1] Truscott was ordered to move with all speed towards Palermo. His division was not to stop on any of the new phase lines established by Patton except the last, the area overlooking Palermo itself. The city was not to be entered without permission from Seventh Army. For the 3d Division this presented a daunting task, for not only were there sizeable Italian forces still operating, particularly around San Stefano di Quisquina in central Sicily directly north of Agrigento, but the route to Palermo was through some of the most tortuous terrain in Sicily, where mountains rose to heights of 4,000 feet or more and the wretched roads were laced with dizzying hairpin bends and bridges where ambushes and hidden demolitions could easily slow the advance and inflict considerable casualties. In places, the roads were little better than cart tracks. At his final briefing on 18 July, Truscott said he hoped to be in Palermo in five days. He and his commanders then toasted the 'American Doughboy' with a rare drink of Scotch whisky.[2]

The dash for Palermo officially began on the morning of 19 July. What followed was an amazing feat by the men of the 3d Division. Their first goal was to dispose of the bottleneck at San Stefano. One rifle battalion, Lieutenant Colonel Edgar C. Doleman's 3d Battalion, 15th Infantry, marched fifty-four miles over mountain

---

[1] Quoted in *Monty: Master of the Battlefield, 1942–1944*, op. cit., p. 319.

[2] *Command Missions*, op. cit., p. 224.

* Major General Geoffrey Keyes (1887–1967) was a 1913 graduate of West Point, a veteran cavalry officer and long-time friend and associate of Patton. Like him, Keyes was an intellectual soldier, widely read in history, who had spent considerable time in France during the inter-war years where he studied at the *Ecole de Guerre* and later taught French at West Point. He was hand-picked by Patton to be his Deputy CG of I Armored Corps for TORCH and later had been responsible for most of the planning for HUSKY. He later went on to command a corps in Italy and after the war became commander of Seventh Army, then on occupation duty in West Germany.

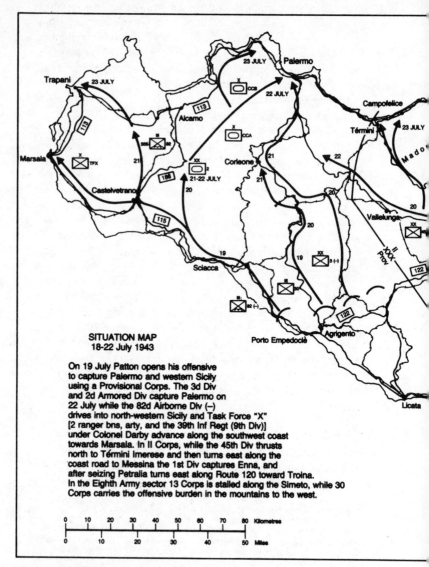

SITUATION MAP
18-22 July 1943

On 19 July Patton opens his offensive
to capture Palermo and western Sicily
using a Provisional Corps. The 3d Div
and 2d Armored Div capture Palermo on
22 July while the 82d Airborne Div (–)
drives into north-western Sicily and Task Force "X"
[2 ranger bns, arty, and the 39th Inf Regt (9th Div)]
under Colonel Darby advance along the southwest coast
towards Marsala. In II Corps, while the 45th Div thrusts
north to Términi Imerese and then turns east along the
coast road to Messina the 1st Div captures Enna, and
after seizing Petralia turns east along Route 120 toward Troina.
In the Eighth Army sector 13 Corps is stalled along the Simeto, while 30
Corps carries the offensive burden in the mountains to the west.

| 0 | 10 | 20 | 30 | 40 | 50 | 60 | 70 | 80 Kilometres |

| 0 | 10 | 20 | 30 | 40 | 50 Miles |

SITUATION MAP 18-22 JULY 1943

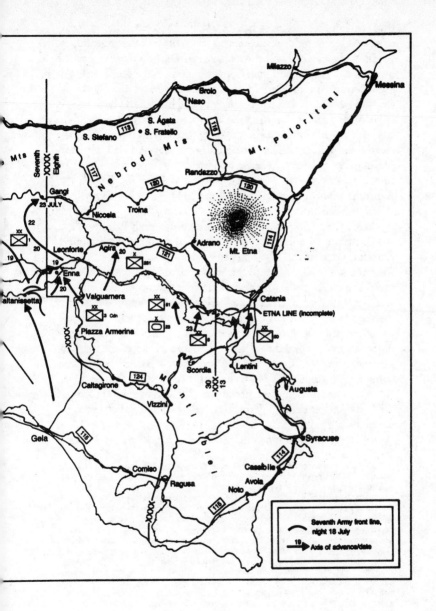

Milazzo

Messina

Brolo

Naso

S. Ágata
● S. Fratello

119

S. Stefano

118

Mt. Peloritani

Nebrodi Mts

117

120

Randazzo

120

Gangi

114

Seventh
XXXX
Eighth

23 JULY

Nicosia

Troina

Adrano

Mt. Etna

22

121

XX
1

20

Agira

20

X
231

19

19

Leonforte

Catania

XXXX

Enna

20

Valguarnera

ETNA LINE (incomplete)

XX
61

X
3 Cdn

O
23

XX
51

80

Piazza Armerina

23

aitanissetta)

XX
3

Scordia

Lentini

30
XX
13

Augusta

Caltagirone

124

Vizzini

M o n t i

Gela

115

Syracuse

Comiso

Ragusa

Cassibile

Avola

Noto

116

XXXX

Seventh Army front line,
night 18 July

19 ▶ Axis of advance/date

trails to San Stefano in 33 hours.* While the 15th Infantry Regiment was left to reduce San Stefano, Truscott sent the 7th Infantry Regiment in a right hook towards Prizzi. The 3d Division slashed its way to Corleone and then to the Blue Line – the hills overlooking Palermo and its splendid harbour. By noon on 22 July the 3d Division was poised to enter Palermo, and by evening both the 3d Division and the 2d Armored Division were prepared to attack the city, though that proved unnecessary: the Germans had already cleared out and the Italians defending the city had no interest in prolonging the war. A delegation of city fathers attempted to surrender Palermo to Brigadier General William W. Eagles, the Assistant Division Commander of the 3d Division but Eagles had other instructions and the offer was spurned.

There is still debate over which division entered Palermo first, with both the 3d Infantry and 2d Armored claiming the honour.† Certainly, one of the first units to enter was a patrol of the 82d Reconnaissance Battalion of the 2d Armored Division which captured the commander of the Italian defence forces. Soon afterwards a patrol of CCA (Combat Command A) entered Palermo without opposition and captured Generale di Brigata Giuseppe Molinaro, the scar-faced commander of the port defences.‡ Molinaro was not prepared to fight and offered to surrender the city. He was taken to Keyes and Gaffey, the 2d Armored Division commander. Keyes decided to accept. Escorted by a triumphant American procession, he entered the city and formally accepted the Italian surrender of Palermo at the Royal Palace about 1900 on the night of 22 July.

Although enemy opposition during the brief drive on Palermo

* Doleman was one of a number of 3d Division officers who later attained senior general officer rank in the postwar years. Others included William B. Rosson, Ben Harrell and John A. Heintges.

† The argument will likely never be settled, nor is it important except as a matter of unit pride. The 3d Division history claims patrols of the 7th Infantry were inside the city at 1400 hours, while 2d Armored claims the prize for CCA, insisting no other Americans were found inside Palermo during their foray. Palermo is the largest city in Sicily and in 1943 had a population of about 400,000; it is therefore not unreasonable to conclude that small patrols of both divisions might well have missed encountering one another. (See Taggert, p. 60; Will Weng's account in LIFE, 2 October 1944; and Hell on Wheels, p. 175.)

‡ The CCA patrol's mission was to capture an Italian battleship thought to be in Palermo harbour. The CO, 41st Infantry Regiment, Colonel Sidney R. Hinds, had been given this mission but soon found the mysterious ship had departed the day before. Hinds was understandably relieved since the capture of enemy battleships by ground troops had somehow never appeared in the curriculum of the US Army service schools! (See Hell on Wheels, p. 174, and Sicily, p. 254.)

had been scant, the 3d Division had advanced some 100 miles in a little over seventy-two hours, most of it on foot. When Patton arrived about 2100 the same night he found his dream a reality. The next morning Truscott reported to an ebullient Patton who greeted him by saying, 'Well, the Truscott Trot sure got us here in a damn hurry.'[1]

Life photographer Robert Capa was present during the entry of General Keyes and American troops and his camera recorded a series of dramatic photographs of the event. The Americans were greeted with a thunderous welcome by what seemed the entire population demonstrating their feelings about Fascist rule.[2] The two captured Italian generals, on the other hand, claimed they were pleased to have been captured because 'the Sicilians were not human beings but animals'.[3]

As Patton toured Palermo on 23 July his command car passed by a group of Italian POWs who first stood up, then saluted and cheered. Elsewhere he found himself the object of cheering and shouts of 'Down with Mussolini' and 'Long Live America'. The Royal Palace became his new HQ and he was soon visited by a representative of the Cardinal of Palermo and other supplicants who came to be presented to Patton as they would have to a king in times gone by.*

Others came to plead their case to anyone who would listen. A tank battalion bivouacked in a lemon orchard near Palermo with its tanks parked under the trees was visited by the owner who pleaded with the sergeant-major to protect his trees. When assured everything possible would be done but that in case of attack there could be no assurances, the well-dressed Sicilian fell to the ground, crying and tearing his silk shirt. The disgusted sergeant-major nearly 'took down his pants and spanked him'.[4]

On 24th July, Patton returned to Agrigento where he gave an off-the-record press conference during which he exulted that his

---

[1] *Command Missions*, op. cit., p. 227.

[2] 'The Surrender of Palermo', *Life*, 23 August 1943.

[3] 'Account of the Capture of Palermo', 23 July 1943, and letter to Beatrice Patton, 27 July 1943, Patton Papers.

[4] Quoted in Semmes, *Portrait of Patton*, op. cit., pp. 159–60.

* Patton's aide, Captain A. C. Stiller, suggested he be permitted to find his boss 'a nice modern house much better than this old dump!' However, the palace suited Patton's sense of history where he could 'eat K-rations on china marked with the cross of Saxony' in the huge State drawing room. Patton also 'got quite a kick about using a toilet previously made malodorous by constipated royalty'. (Letter to Beatrice Patton, 27 July 1943, Patton Papers.)

Army's achievement exceeded anything the Germans had ever done. 'Gentlemen,' he said, 'we had about 200 miles [sic] to go over crooked roads to get to Palermo.' He also produced the statistics: 6,000 (Italians) killed or wounded, 44,000 captured, 190 enemy aircraft shot down and 67 guns seized.[1] In his diary he wrote that 'future students of the Command and General Staff School will study the campaign as a classic example of the use of tanks'.[2]

Patton's exaggeration at a moment of personal triumph that ended days of frustration was understandable. While the rapid movement of the 2d Armored Division was indeed noteworthy, Patton might better have ascribed the American success to a combination of outstanding training and employment of *both* infantry and armour. Only a superbly trained unit like Truscott's 3d Division could have withstood the rigours of such a rapid advance in the heat, gagging dust and hostile terrain of Sicily.

One of the many myths surrounding Patton was that he attempted to hog the credit for capturing Palermo and even that he ordered that no Seventh Army troops enter the city until he arrived to lead a triumphal entry personally, as the conquering hero. While the capture of Palermo certainly generated considerable publicity for Patton, he generously gave full credit to the modest Keyes. To Eisenhower and to his wife he wrote, 'Geoff realy [sic] deserves most of the credit and I have handed it out to him via the press. I hope it gets through.' After Patton's death, Beatrice Patton revealed that 'General Keyes told me that he went to see Georgie the night before he was to enter Palermo, and that Georgie said, "You took it. You enter and I will enter it after you." '[3] In the *Life* article a month later there are six photographs of Keyes and none of Patton.[4] Keyes later counted 22 July 1943 as the proudest day of his life.[5]

[1] Quoted in Farago, *Patton*, op. cit., p. 300. Patton won a bet of a bottle of whiskey from Tedder's deputy, Air Vice-Marshal Philip Wigglesworth, that Palermo would fall by midnight, 23 July. The bet was promptly paid and the whiskey turned out to be Irish. About this time author John P. Marquand turned up at Patton's palace HQ and he offered it to his guest. 'Help yourself. I don't care for the stuff myself. It's a bet I won from the British.' (Quoted in Codman, *Drive*, p. xv. Codman became Patton's ADC after Captain Richard N. Jensen was killed in action at El Guettar.)
[2] Patton Diary and *War As I Knew It*, op. cit., p. 63.
[3] Quoted in *Portrait of Patton*, op. cit., pp. 160–1.
[4] 'The Surrender of Palermo', *Life*, 23 August 1943, op. cit. Patton's picture was on the covers of both *Time* and *Newsweek* on 26 July.
[5] *Portrait of Patton*, op. cit.

The Palermo venture might have had a different ending had Patton's loyal chief of staff, Brigadier General Hobart R. Gay* not practised a bit of trickery to protect Patton. On 19 July, Alexander received Montgomery's signal outlining his four divisional thrusts to break the German defences in the east, apparently realized that he had given Patton too loose a mandate and, belatedly, that he had probably erred in so doing. Consequently, he offered, and Monty refused, the attachment of an American division. This was followed by a new signal to Patton which appeared significantly to alter the terms under which Seventh Army could drive on Palermo. It stated that he was *first* to drive north from Petralia and cut Sicily in two before taking on Palermo. The line established by Alexander would protect the Eighth Army flank as Montgomery swung his left hook around Mount Etna. In short, 'Alexander was willing to let Patton exploit, but only on his terms, and not on the terms as laid down in the 17 July conference'.[1]

Although Patton was present at his headquarters when the cable arrived on the morning of 19 July, Gay decided that Patton must not see this message. He ordered dissemination of only the first portion (which called for the 1st Division to drive to the north coast) to II Corps. The remainder went into his desk while the signal section was directed to complain to 15th Army Group that the message had been 'garbled in transmission' and request a duplicate transmission. Gay's rationale was that Seventh Army could hardly be expected to carry out an order it hadn't received. By the time all of this took place it no longer mattered, for Seventh Army was about to enter Palermo. Patton did not learn of Gay's deception until some days later and, although he did not record his

---

[1] *Sicily*, op. cit., p. 246.

* Brigadier General (later Lieutenant General) Hobart R. 'Hap' Gay was a former cavalry officer and confidant of Patton whose loyalty sometimes ran to blind faith in his chief. Martin Blumenson calls Gay a plain man who was utterly devoted to Patton, 'a splendid companion who liked to ride and hunt, a superb staff officer who ran the military details of the headquarters with exceptional efficiency'. Gay acted as Patton's foil under any and all conditions. And he was effective. When Patton was in Washington in 1942 planning TORCH, it would sometimes become too noisy in the bullpen atmosphere of the Munitions Building where the War Department was headquartered while the new Pentagon building was being constructed. 'Tell 'em to stop that goddam racket. I can't hear myself think,' growled Patton. Gay would come out and say 'The General wants QUIET.' And that would be the end of the noise! The problem was that Gay 'lacked breadth and depth of intellectual capacity. His prejudices and politics paralleled Patton's, and as a consequence reinforced instead of correcting them.' (*The Patton Papers*, Vol. II, op. cit., p. 757 and Codman, *Drive*, op. cit., p. 12.)

reaction, he doubtless approved heartily of his Chief of Staff's decision.[1]

Gay's diary casts some doubt that Alexander was officially reneging on his agreement of 17 July. His entry for 19 July reads:

> General Huebner, while here, states that the message received last night at 2230 was merely confirming the verbal arrangements made by the Commander of the 15th Army Group and the Commander of the 7th Army. That it intended no restrictions on our movement other than to assume that the coast line was cut at or near CAMPOFELICE. [Approximately thirty miles east of Palermo.][2]

The ineptness of relations between 15th Army Group and the two armies was best illustrated by this remark made to Patton by Major Henriques: 'The Chief of Staff of the Eighth Army [de Guingand] said to pay no attention to any order from Alexander. Whether this is in good faith or as bait I did not and do not know. Nice people.'[3]

The only senior officer in Sicily who found no joy in Patton's dash to Palermo was Omar Bradley. On the contrary, he considered it nothing sort of insane. To begin with, Bradley totally misunderstood Patton's intentions when he flew to Tunis to see Alexander. He was certain Patton had gone to persuade Alexander to allot a great role for Seventh Army in the drive on *Messina*, and in particular, for a greater role for II Corps. When he learned the truth Bradley was dismayed, not because the scheme apparently left Messina to the British and Palermo to the Americans, but that militarily he rightly considered it a vain and useless exercise that would merely exacerbate the problem of winning a decisive victory in Sicily. In his memoirs he wrote: 'It was true that Palermo was to become essential to the logistical support of his Seventh Army but except for that single port there was little to be gained in the west. Certainly there was no glory in the capture of hills, docile peasants, and spiritless soldiers.'[4]

To Bradley, Patton's venture smacked of grandstanding, 'great theater' which generated the headlines he craved. Correctly surmising that Patton was never criticized for disobeying Alexander's

[1] Semmes, *Portrait of Patton*, op. cit., pp. 163–4. Gay has affirmed to Semmes that Patton had nothing to do with this act and that full responsibility rested with him.
[2] Diary of Hobart R. Gay, Gay Papers, USAMHI.
[3] Patton Diary, 24 July 1943. The conversation took place on 16 July.
[4] *A Soldier's Story*, op. cit., p. 140.

(alleged) order, he noted caustically that 'the victory and the headlines were too sweet. However meaningless in a strategic sense, it was our most dramatic and crowed-about "success" to date. It made our soldiers proud, lifted spirits at home, and impressed Alexander.'[1]

Truscott never agreed that Palermo had any importance as a port. Before the operation he had offered to send his 3d Division to capture the important road centre of Caltanissetta instead of Palermo:

> As to the need of Palermo as a port – we could have been supported from the beaches and ports we already had for two months after we took Agrigento and Porto Empedocle. It was the glamour of capturing Palermo – the biggest city in Sicily – that attracted Georgie Patton. Patton sold Alexander on the idea of cutting loose to capture Palermo and incidentally (with II Corps) to cut the island in two. It is my belief that the glamour of the big city was the chief thing that attracted General Patton.[2]

Another who supports this theory is British historian Shelford Bidwell who believes that 'Patton went to Palermo because no one was in charge of the battle. Patton not only had to *be* a good general but *seen* to be a good general through his deeds. Newspaper headlines were one way to achieve this end. Patton instinctively knew what to do.'[3]

Even though he had defied the odds and outfoxed Alexander, Patton was far from satisfied. He now cast his eye towards the real prize of Sicily: Messina, the only strategically significant objective of the Allies. There now began the most one-sided 'race' of the war as the final stage of the Sicily campaign began with Patton determined – by hook or crook – to beat Montgomery into Messina.

[1] *A General's Life*, op. cit., p. 193.
[2] Interview with Howard McGaw Smyth, 19 April 1951, USAMHI.
[3] Conversation with the author, 9 August 1984.

CHAPTER 26

Exit Mussolini

Italy has gone to pieces.
KING VICTOR EMMANUEL III

By mid-July the Italian government was on the verge of collapse from within. The woeful performance of the Italian Armed Forces and intense Allied pressure in the form of round-the-clock bombing of Italian and Sicilian targets led some to begin active conspiracies to remove Mussolini.

The blows had come with numbing regularity. First, there was the successful Allied invasion of Sicily, followed by the near total collapse of the Italian Army there as an effective fighting force. The usually respectable Italian Navy had added the precipitate abandonment of the key coast ports of Syracuse and Augusta to the list of Italian humiliations. Then on 19 July came a blow aimed directly at the heart of the Fascist state, the first Allied bombing attack against Rome. The decision to bomb the Eternal City was taken at the highest level by the Combined Chiefs of Staff, for sound military reasons. Rome's two huge marshalling yards (Littorio and San Lorenzo) were the hub of all rail movement between northern and southern Italy. Their destruction would be a serious setback to the movement of Axis supplies and at the same time was expected to have a powerful effect upon Italian morale. The two missions by 520 USAAF bombers which dropped 1,000 tons of bombs were undertaken in keeping with the most stringent guidelines in order to avoid damage to Rome's historical and religious sites. The night before the raids, four RAF Wellingtons dropped 864,000 leaflets warning the Roman populace of what was to occur. Only two aircraft were lost in the twin raids on the railway yards in the morning and the Ciampino airbases in the afternoon. Rail traffic in central Italy was disrupted for several days thereafter; Rome's precious landmarks were spared any damage.[1]

Mussolini had mistakenly supposed the Allies would never attack the city, and when they did so the result was not only considerable panic among the populace but a further deepening of the sense of gloom that had been hanging over the Italian dictator for months. During one of his recent weekly visits to Victor Emmanuel, 'The King at long last told him he ought to think of resignation – but . . . such words to the Duce was like talking to the wind.'[2] On 22 July the fall of Palermo became yet another nail in the Fascist coffin.

The deteriorating position of Italy as a middleman in the larger conflict between the Allies and Nazi Germany led to the hatching of two unrelated plots to remove Mussolini. One involved a group of senior Fascist leaders that included Mussolini's own son-in-law, the former Foreign Minister, Count Ciano.* These men were anxious for Italy to dissociate itself from Germany. Mussolini's steadfast refusal to alter the disastrous direction in which the country was heading ultimately led them to conclude that he must go. The more right-wing members of the Grand Council (the ruling corporate but hitherto ornamental body of the Fascist state) would have been content to see the Duce replaced by a more forceful Fascist leader.

The other plot principally involved three key Italian figures who were determined not only to rid Italy of Mussolini but also his Fascist government: General Vittorio Ambrosio, the anti-German head of the Comando Supremo; Field Marshal Pietro Badoglio, a former head of the Armed Forces and long-time opponent of Mussolini; and King Victor Emmanuel III, the man who had brought Mussolini to power in 1922.

Despite his largely ceremonial position as the Head of Government, it was to the King that the men of the Italian Armed Forces and the civilian Fascist government had nevertheless sworn allegiance, and he now used that power to remove the source of the cancer that had plagued Italy for so long. Beneath the cynicism and

---

[1] Craven and Cate, *Torch to Pointblank*, op. cit., pp. 463–5; and *The Mediterranean and Middle East*, Vol. V, op. cit., pp. 126–7.

[2] Dennis Mack Smith, *Mussolini*, op. cit., p. 342.

* Ciano had been forced to resign from his post six months earlier by Mussolini who had become alarmed by his independent and increasingly anti-German policy. Ciano was now the ambassador to the Vatican.

tyranny of Fascism there was a curious code of honour which bound these men to the King and his wishes, even though he was in practical terms virtually powerless otherwise. In Germany Hitler had used and then disposed of the figurehead presidency of von Hindenburg to consolidate the reins of power, but in Italy after more than twenty years of Fascist rule the King still remained a revered figure whose authority Mussolini never thought to question or usurp.

Mussolini's downfall began on 24 July when the Grand Council met for the first time in three and a half years. It had been summoned not by Mussolini but by several of its members ostensibly for the purpose of hearing the Duce's report of his disastrous meeting with Hitler at Feltre five days earlier. In the stifling heat of Rome in July the men of the Grand Council found their once-ebullient and dynamic leader 'detached and unexplainably apathetic, as if his soul had left him and he had become a worn-out automaton'.[1]

Mussolini had no intention of discussing Feltre and instead subjected the Council to a rambling two-hour diatribe which laid the blame for Italy's failures squarely upon his generals. The Council members were very much aware of the humiliation of Feltre and consequently were unprepared for 'this lame, ingenuous, pitiful attempt at self-justification, this passing of the buck, this condemnation of others for his mistakes . . .'[2] In the dialogue which followed, the once-proud dictator of Italy became the subject of a shower of criticism and scorn unlike anything he had ever experienced. Feltre had been the last straw that at last brought even his long-time supporters to outright rebellion. One of the most outspoken was the Council head, Dino Grandi, who delivered a scathing denunciation: 'You believe you have the devotion of the people. You lost it the day you tied Italy to Germany. You believed yourself a soldier – let me tell you, Italy was lost the very day you put the gold braid of a marshal on your cap . . . In this war we have already a hundred thousand mothers who cry: "Mussolini assassinated my son!".' After more than twelve hours of heated debate and continued flailing of the hapless Mussolini there came what amounted to a vote of no confidence in their leader

[1] Laura Fermi, *Mussolini*, Chicago, 1966 edition, p. 427.
[2] Ibid., p. 424.

which was passed by an overwhelming vote of nineteen to seven.[1]

Mussolini foolishly believed the King would back him in over-turning the vote of the Grand Council, but when he appeared before Victor Emmanuel the following afternoon his illusions were rudely shattered. Only the two men were present and accounts of exactly what was said vary considerably, but accord-ing to Fermi's account the meeting was short and the King, although in a state of extreme agitation, did not mince his words: 'Dear Duce, things don't work any more. Italy has gone to pieces. The army is morally prostrated. The soldiers no longer want to fight ... You certainly don't entertain any illusions about the Italians' state of mind. In this moment you are the most hated man in Italy.'[2] When told of his replacement by a caretaker government headed by Badoglio, Mussolini launched into a tirade of self-justification and insistence that Italy could not do without his leadership. In another version, Mussolini was dumbfounded when the King bluntly said, '*Il gioco e finito* – the game is over, Musso-lini ... you'll have to go. There's no other course open to me.' To which Mussolini was said to have replied, 'Sire, this is the end of Fascism.'[3] And indeed it was.

As he emerged from the royal villa outside Rome, Mussolini's real humiliation began. He was arrested by a *carabinieri* captain and taken away in a Red Cross ambulance to a secret location in Rome, ostensibly for his own protection. In his place the old King installed a military government headed by Marshal Badoglio* who immediately proclaimed, 'The war goes on' and that his country would 'keep faith with its pledged word', a rather vague pronouncement designed mainly to buy time without providing any real indication of the direction the new government would actually follow. Two days later Admiral Franco Maugeri was

[1] Ibid., pp. 425–7.
[2] Ibid., p. 431.
[3] Ibid.; and Admiral Franco Maugeri, *From the Ashes of Disgrace*, New York, 1948, p. 121.

* Field Marshal Pietro Badoglio was born in 1871 and fought in the Italian colonial wars of 1896 and 1911–12 against the Turks in Libya. He became Chief of Staff and led the Italian expeditionary force which conquered Ethiopia in 1936, and was once again Chief of Staff until December 1940 when he resigned after the abortive invasion of Greece. Harold Macmillan would write of the elderly marshal that he was 'honest, broadminded, humorous ... with the horse common sense and natural shrewdness of the peasant. A loyal servant of his King and country, without ambitions.' (Memorandum by Harold Macmillan, 17 Sep-tember 1943, Eisenhower Papers.)

informed he was being placed in charge of 'a little escort job' which turned out to be the secret movement of Mussolini into exile and house arrest on the tiny island of Ponza, about forty miles offshore from Naples to which previous enemies of the Fascist state had been banished.[1]

Late on 25 July the German ambassador was summoned to see Badoglio who informed him that he now headed the new Italian government and the Duce had resigned. The news of Mussolini's downfall came like a bombshell to the German leadership. A dismayed Hitler was heard complaining to Keitel, 'Badoglio has taken over. The blackest of our enemies!'[2] Hitler's reaction was predictable: righteous indignation at this Italian betrayal, and disbelief that Mussolini had gone voluntarily.

The immediate assumption at OKW was that Mussolini's downfall signalled an Italian capitulation to the Allies. According to Warlimont, Hitler now displayed 'a shocking and shattering exhibition of confusion and lack of balance . . . It was only with the greatest difficulty that Jodl was able to get any orderly military thinking done and turn Hitler's mind on to the urgent necessities of the situation.'[3] Surviving fragments of the Fuehrer conferences reveal that between outbursts of temper demanding retribution, Hitler issued a series of hasty orders. Fearful that the German garrison on Sicily would be trapped and lost, he ordered their immediate withdrawal. 'We must rescue the people . . . they must cross [the Messina Strait], particularly the paratroops and the Goering Division. The equipment doesn't matter a damn, they must blow it up or destroy it. But we must get the men back.'[4]

Hitler also ordered plans to be put in motion to carry out a *coup* against the new Badoglio government. Badoglio's pledge that the new Italian government would honour Italy's commitment to Germany as an ally brought a storm of derision from the sceptical Hitler who jeered, 'They say they'll fight but that's treachery! We must be quite clear: it's pure treachery!'[5] Cooler heads prevailed and Hitler was dissuaded from any attempt at a *coup* or from prematurely ordering Hube to evacuate Sicily. Instead, the Germans moved quickly to revive earlier contingency plans for a series

---

[1] Maugeri, ibid., Chapter 12.
[2] Quoted in David Irving, *Hitler's War – 1942–1945*, op. cit., p. 545.
[3] Warlimont, *Inside Hitler's Headquarters, 1939–1945*, op. cit., p. 343.
[4] Hitler Fragment No. 14, 'Briefing Conference 25 July 1943, 2130 hours'.
[5] Ibid.

of military actions to be taken in the event of an Italian collapse.[1] Rommel was hastily recalled from a special mission to Greece and given command of the newly formed Army Group B. For the moment there remained an uneasy truce between Germany and Italy, with neither side for one moment trusting the pledges of the other. In Sicily it was business as usual.

The fall of Mussolini brought wild celebrations from the people of Rome who demonstrated their detestation of Fascism by the systematic destruction of its public trappings, beginning with the posters and statues of Il Duce. Despite the conflict in Sicily, word spread rapidly throughout the island. Other than occasional resentment that their liberators had not brought enormous amounts of food with them, the Sicilians greeted the Allies as emancipators come to lift the evil burden of Fascism from their shoulders.[2]

Since the invasion there had been little for the population of Sicily to be joyful about, even though the struggle had by late July moved into the more lightly populated mountains of northeastern Sicily. For weeks the roads had become cluttered with Sicilians frantically seeking refuge further inland, away from the combatants. In scenes reminiscent of those repeated thousands of times during this dreadful war, there was chaos as men, women and uncomprehending, often screaming children fled with transport that ranged from hand-drawn carts to those pulled by animals. Allied aircraft on the hunt for enemy convoys were frequently unable to distinguish military traffic from the refugees and many of the roads were turned into charnel houses as the innocent died along with the combatants.[3]

Within two weeks of the invasion there were more than thirty-seven squadrons of Allied fighters and fighter-bombers based on captured Sicilian airfields, including Ponte Olivo, Biscari and Comiso, the key airbases taken by Seventh Army. These aircraft along with Malta-based heavy bombers and fighter-bombers

[1] *Grand Strategy*, Vol. IV, op. cit., p. 473.

[2] Pond, op. cit., p. 154. The news of Mussolini's fall brought this comment from Montgomery's eloquent G-2, Brigadier Williams: '... the ITALIAN ARMY, corrupt, ill-equipped and spineless though it is, has at last taken over from the Fascist satraps. The hooligans have had their privileges withdrawn; but they remain hooligans.' (See Eighth Army Intelligence Summary No. 519, 26 July 1943, PRO [WO 169/8519].)

[3] Pond, op. cit., p. 109, provides a description of these horrors. The victims were sometimes friendly forces. Major Llewellyn recalls soon after D-Day coming upon the flaming, smoking wreckage of what had moments before been a small column of British armoured vehicles that had been mistakenly bombed. (Interview of 18 September 1984.)

pounded targets in Sicily and Italy day and night. The communication centres of Palermo, Catania, Randazzo and Messina received special attention. Messina was the hardest hit, beginning on 14 July. An Italian official who was present in Palermo during the first days of the invasion recorded the chaos, particularly the non-stop bombardments by the Allied air forces. Initially, he reported the population of Palermo was inured to such bombings and the invasion was seen as inevitable, although it was believed it would quickly be repulsed. However, by 12 July when all communications with the outside world had been severed and there was no news of the Allies being thrown back into the sea, morale began to sink. 'Even Army officers betrayed a lack of confidence. Weary of waiting for communiqués, people began to tune in on the London and Algiers radio programmes and to absorb news broadcast by the enemy.'[1]

In Messina it was far worse. On the day of his arrival the official found

> the harbour still in flames, the city half destroyed and the population in a state of terror. No one seemed to have foreseen a disaster of such magnitude. At the prefecture, at the commissariat, and on the streets of the untouched higher sections of the city, there was open talk of betrayal at Augusta. Everyone, including the military, was in a confused and despairing frame of mind.[2]

The Allied bombings of Messina resembled those against German cities by Allied strategic aircraft during the great bomber offensive that was beginning about this time.

> We witnessed four frightful bombardments of Messina, Villa San Giovanni, and Reggio. Messina was destroyed beneath our very eyes. There was heavy anti-aircraft fire, but the aim was poor so that few enemy planes were brought down . . . We were surrounded by straggling, ragged bands of soldiers, sailors and airmen (particularly the latter two) making their way to the German ferries to the mainland . . . There were painful sights in the stations of Scilla and Bagnara. Crowds of soldiers and civilians were storming the trains. Soldiers, sailors and airmen from Catania, Riposto and Messina were elbowing their way

---

[1] Account by an official of the Ministry of Popular Culture in *The Fall of Mussolini*, New York, 1948, p. 40. Although this book is Mussolini's own highly subjective account of the events of the summer of 1943 (as previously published, unsigned articles in June and July 1943 in Italy's largest newspaper, Milan's *Corriere della Serra*), the descriptions of the war in Sicily are accurate. The raid on 14 July was carried out by ninety-six B-17 Flying Fortresses and eighty-three B-25 Mitchell bombers.
[2] Ibid.

through the mob, cursing as they went. *Defeat was in the air* . . .
officers failed to react to the behaviour of their men, displaying
the same low morale as they did.[1]

Allied soldiers found many of the liberated Sicilian towns and
villages all but abandoned. The relief of the populace at their
delivery from Fascism was contrasted by the empty slogans of the
regime which festooned the walls and sides of buildings in virtually
every village in Sicily.

From the time of the invasion the conduct of Italian forces on
Sicily was predictable.* Mass desertions left many units bereft of
fighting troops, many of whom roamed the countryside searching
for an Allied unit or soldier to whom they might surrender. Others
simply pillaged, frequently at gunpoint and in civilian clothes,
despite knowledge that capture could mean instant death. By the
end of the first week, Seventh Army had rounded up more than
22,000 POWs, at least a quarter of whom were Sicilians forcibly
conscripted into Italian units.[2]

Bradley was aware of the burden these burgeoning numbers of

[1] Ibid., pp. 40–1.
[2] Bradley, *A Soldier's Story*, op. cit., p. 141.

* Some was pure comic opera. One such example occurred on 11 July when a carrier
pigeon carrying a message from the 206th Coastal Division to General Mario Arisio's XII
Corps arrived unannounced on the deck of an American minesweeper. Part of the message
read:

> Heroic infantry and artillery still doing their duty after fifteen hours of fighting against
> tremendous odds in men and means. Cargo ships by the hundreds are discharging
> uninterrupted war materiel. No friendly air. Two of my soldiers ordered shot at
> PACHINO for desertion in the presence of the enemy and wearing civilian clothes. Send
> more pigeons. (Related in 'Report of Operations of II Corps in the Sicilian Campaign', 1
> September 1943. See [microfilm] Reel No. 102, 'Outline History of II Corps, 1918–1945',
> USAMHI.)

The division was responsible for the defence of the Pachino peninsula, and was one of the
sorriest of the Italian units in Sicily. The following day the commander, Major General
Achille d'Havet, surrendered to the Canadians, and this proved equally *opéra bouffe* when
the irascible Italian general refused to surrender except to an officer of equally exalted rank.
His escort to the Canadian 1st Division commander, Major-General Guy Simonds, to whom
d'Havet eventually surrendered, was Major Dick Malone, who later wrote:

> I was worried about leaving the [Italian] headquarters with all its valuable papers
> unguarded, so I told my jeep driver that he was to remain on guard. I can still see the
> wild-eyed look on the face of the driver as I drove off and left him, the only Allied soldier in
> the town, while lined up opposite him was the entire garrison of Italian soldiers . . .
> driving out of town the local inhabitants all booed the fat little general . . . A short
> distance further down the road . . . it suddenly occurred to me that I was sitting in a car
> loaded with Italian soldiers, and all of them were still armed. I politely suggested they
> should all give me their pistols but at this they all shouted, 'No! no!' . . . the general said
> that as his forces had put up such a gallant defence it was only fitting that he retain his
> pistol. As for his troops putting up a gallant show, I had never heard of such nonsense . . .
> Finally, we compromised. They agreed that I should take the clips of ammunition out of
> each of the pistols, then everyone was quite happy. (Colonel Dick Malone, *Missing from
> the Record*, op. cit., pp. 36–7.)

Italians and Sicilians posed to the hard-pressed and wholly inadequate American POW facilities. Moreover, he knew that without
men to harvest the ripening crops there would be considerable
problems for the US Army in feeding the hungry Sicilian population. About D+3, the capture of an Italian soldier in civilian
clothes near II Corps HQ sparked one of the most brilliant master-
strokes of the campaign, in which Bradley decided to gamble on
the idea of offering parole to Sicilian POWs instead of captivity.
He told his G-2, Colonel B. A. Dickson, ' "Monk", why don't we
see what happens if we pass the word around that any Sicilian
wishing to desert may go on back to their homes? We won't pick
them up as prisoners of war.' Seventh Army disapproved of the
scheme but by that time it did not matter as the rumours had
already spread and desertions were on the increase. When Caltanissetta fell on 18 July, Dickson enlisted the aid of the local
bishop whose efficient grapevine soon passed the news far and
wide. Ten days later, higher authority decided the idea had merit
after all and provided legal sanction for Bradley's scheme. Some
33,000 Sicilians of the 122,000 POWs captured by US forces were
eventually paroled to their villages. Thousands of others emerged
from the hills and valleys clutching leaflets that were their tickets
to freedom. The results were dramatic, as Bradley relates: 'In town
after town we entered Fascist slogans had been scrubbed from the
walls and the posters of Mussolini defaced. Angry mobs fell upon
local party headquarters to run their functionaries out of town and
make bonfires of their files.'[1]

Relations between German and Italian forces, never good,
deteriorated rapidly after the invasion as one Italian unit after
another either melted away or fought feebly. Scattered Italian
units did remain loyal and intact and even fought well but these

[1] Ibid., pp. 142–3. Many Americans had relatives in Sicily and there was understandable
concern when the invasion took place. Attempts were made by any available means to learn
of the safety of loved ones. One such case led to a bizarre but hilarious incident. At AFHQ all
cable traffic routinely ended with the words //SIGNED EISENHOWER//, although in actual
practice he saw only the most important messages. About D-Day 15th Army Group received
such a signal urgently requesting the whereabouts of a certain countess in Palermo. The
message was routinely passed to Seventh Army and forgotten. A follow-up signal quickly
found its way into the nearest wastebasket, but a steady flow of further messages began to
raise anxieties within Alexander's staff. His British officers were unaware that these messages had nothing to do with Eisenhower personally. Finally came yet another message
insistently demanding: 'UNABLE UNDERSTAND YOUR PERSISTENT REFUSAL TO
INDICATE WHEREABOUTS OF COUNTESS. ... REPORT AT ONCE STEPS BEING
TAKEN TO COMPLY. //SIGNED EISENHOWER//.'
The staff officer in charge of the countess affair was a former Oxford don, David Hunt,

were in the minority. At virtually all levels there was a whiff of suspected betrayal at everything the Italians did or failed to do. It was widely believed, for example, that Italian treachery was responsible for the order shifting the 15th Panzer Grenadier Division to western Sicily only days before the invasion. One German officer later wrote, 'The suspicion that premeditated treachery on the part of the Italians was not then suggested, but was later often expressed on grounds of subsequent events.'[1] None of these allegations has been proven true: it was always Kesselring's decision to overrule Guzzoni.*

Bradley's ploy caused great confusion and the rising tide of defectors included members of the Fascist militia. On 22 July an entire Blackshirt battalion deserted *en masse.* Although the rate of defections within the Aosta Division contributed to a premature withdrawal from Nicosia, the Livorno Division performed bravely, if ineptly, at Gela as did the Napoli Division when it was attached to the Hermann Goering Division. The Assietta Division and Group Schreiber also fought stubbornly. The overall performance of Italian artillery units was excellent and drew repeated praise from both Italian and German commanders.

The Germans too had their share of failures. At Catenanuova (northwest of Gerbini) the entire Fortress Battalion 923 (attached to the Hermann Goering) abandoned their positions on 31 July in a rare case of mass cowardice on the part of the Germans. A report to Kesselring read: 'The battalion fled in the direction of Centuripe in a shameful manner without enemy pressure. The immediate dissolution of the battalion has been ordered.' In September the

---

[1] Colonel Bogislaw von Bonin (Chief of Staff, XIV Panzer Corps), 'Considerations of the Italian Campaign 1943–1944', copy furnished the author by the Directorate of History, National Defence Headquarters, Ottawa.

* Among the German eyewitnesses was Lieutenant General Walter Fries, Commander, 29th Panzer Grenadier Division. See Fries' comments in MS # T-2, 'The Battle for Sicily', and in 'Report # 14', Historical Section (G.S.), Canadian Army HQ, 15 April 1947.

---

who did not always succumb to the overzealousness of things military. He composed a return cable to AFHQ in the form of a limerick which ended with the words, 'AM CONTINUING SEARCH. MEANWHILE WILL ANY OTHER WOMAN DO? //SIGNED ALEXANDER//.' This impudent cable *did* come to Eisenhower's personal attention and subsequent investigation revealed that a well-known New York café society count had used a friend in the Adjutant General's office in the War Department (reputed to be a very junior lieutenant) who was sending out similar cables addressed to AFHQ, '//SIGNED MARSHALL//' demanding news of the countess. The fall of Palermo ended the nonsense with this final cable reading: 'COUNTESS X DISCOVERED LIVING WITH BARON Y IN GOOD SPIRITS.' (Related by Sir David Hunt in *A Don at War,* op. cit., pp. 198–9. Sir David went on to a distinguished diplomatic career after the war.)

commander and his officers were court-martialled by order of
Field Marshal Keitel.[1]

On balance, however, the overall performance of Italian forces
in Sicily was woeful and it placed an at times intolerable strain
upon German forces who were given no respite from constant
attack on the ground and incessant bombing from the air. Those
defending the plain of Catania were also subjected to naval
gunfire. There were no reserves and precious few reinforcements.
Units decimated to the point of ineffectiveness were simply merged
into other formations and forced to carry on. Hot meals were an
unheard-of luxury and so exhausted were Schmalz's men that one
of his officers fell soundly asleep as he was taking dictation. As the
weary Schmalz toured the front each day he found his men miserable but determined to survive their ordeal.* The captured diary of
a German soldier provides an idea of what it was like:

> 19 July – Wakened by low-level air attack ... 1700 hrs we
> leave, going in the direction of CATANIA ... On the
> way the usual air raids. The food situation is lousy ...
> Have not had a warm meal for four days. The feeling
> among the boys is worse than bad.
>
> 21 July – Still near CATANIA. 2000 hrs heard German news on
> the wireless for the first time. The stuff they are putting
> over is beyond all description. The enemy has about
> half the island, and they talk about engaging enemy
> convoys off the coast. (Poor Germany!) We are almost
> surrounded again. We must withdraw. I hope we get
> out of it. The food is bad, especially the bread. They
> say we've got to move forward tonight again. It is a
> pretty hopeless business.
>
> 23 July – In the front line. Have settled down on a hill. It is to be
> held to the last round. Anyone who retreats will be
> shot ... We hold a height with a handful of men. The
> enemy has tried with all weapons to take it; but we've
> held out ... How long will all this silly monkey busi-
> ness go on? ... We've had no food for two days, and
> nothing to drink and nothing to smoke ... It is a lousy
> business.[2]

The chronic lack of reinforcements forced commanders like Conrath to comb their rear echelons for every man who could be

---

[1] Bauer Papers, USAMHI; and *The Canadians in Italy, 1943–1945*, op. cit., p. 141.
[2] AFHQ G-2 Intelligence Notes No. 20, 15 August 1943, AFHQ Papers. PRO (WO
204/(983)).
* Schmalz was interviewed by Pond for *Sicily*, and his recollections are in Chapter VI.

spared. MPs were ordered to round up all non-essential administrative personnel and anyone who resisted or attempted to abscond was ordered shot out of hand. The absence of the Luftwaffe hurt and as in other campaigns, most notably Normandy, the mere mention of the German Air Force would produce scornful criticism. In his despatch to Kesselring in mid-August Hube wrote that he 'would object most sharply to any possibly intended mention of the Air Force as giving immediate assistance to the troops on the ground. With all due respect to the few pilots, mostly reconnaissance pilots, the ground forces had practically to rely entirely upon themselves in their battles against the enemy on land and in the air. . . .'[1]

Throughout the war the Germans proved to be without equal when it came to fighting an improvised battle with units that ranged from small task forces to major units like Group Schmalz. Like the paratroop force at Primosole bridge, the Germans were adept at stopping an advance and just as they reached the point of being overwhelmed, skilfully disengaging. Although the terrain in Normandy was far different from that of Sicily, Max Hastings' observations are worth repeating: 'Another German skill, much in evidence in those days, was that of disengagement: fighting hard for a position until the last possible moment, then breaking away through the countryside to create yet another line a mile or two back, presenting the British yet again with the interminable problems of ground and momentum.'[2]

The outspoken Conrath later gave voice to German feelings towards their Italian ally:

> In Sicily the Italians virtually never gave battle and presumably they will not fight on the mainland either. Many units in Sicily either led by their officers or on their own, marched off without firing a single shot. Valuable equipment fell into the hands of the enemy in undamaged condition. The good intentions of some commanders and the good appearance of some officers and non-commissioned officers must not lead one to overlook the fact that 90% of the Italian Army are cowards and do not want to fight.[3]

Italian distrust of the Germans was mutual, particularly by men

---

[1] General Hans Valentin Hube, despatch of 14 August 1943 to Field Marshal Kesselring, 'Report # 14', loc. cit.

[2] Max Hastings, *Overlord*, London, 1984, p. 347.

[3] Generalleutnant Paul Conrath, 'Brief Experience Report on the Fighting in Sicily', 24 August 1943, 'Report # 14'.

who had fought in Russia or North Africa. They complained bitterly of being abandoned without warning. When the Germans withdrew from the Fosso Bottaceto for new positions north of Catania, a nearby Italian unit under Major Nina Bolla continued to fight on and still considered themselves under orders to fight to the death. Although a withdrawal order did eventually filter down, the Italians believed the worst. Bolla derisively told his officers, 'They buggered us like this in Russia . . . retreating without telling us.'[1]

Of all the unsavoury actions by the Italian armed forces in Sicily, none rankled more than the abandonment of Augusta and Syracuse by their respective garrisons. The strongest condemnation came from Schmalz who protested to OB South of the desertion of Augusta without a fight. Soon afterwards Major Bolla encountered some of these men fleeing north through his positions near Primosole bridge. Some of them were naked, others dressed only in pants. The scene disgusted him. Why, he asked, did they leave Augusta? Their pathetic excuses led Bolla to consider having them shot, and he was to regret not doing so, for instead of remaining to fight with his unit as ordered, the men deserted the following night. Schmalz correctly attributed the collapse of the Augusta garrison to a far deeper malaise, namely a lack of fighting spirit from leaders who had lost their will, and along with it, control of their situation.[2]

German forces in Sicily had now operated for so long without benefit of air support or Italian co-operation that few entertained any illusions about their ultimate fate. The high-level German decision for Hube to defend the island for as long as possible prior to the evacuation to mainland Italy had been deliberately withheld from the troops. Consequently, most assumed the fight would go on until they were either captured or killed.

The arrival of Hube and the successful establishment of the Etna Line now made the task of the final reduction of Sicily a formidable challenge for the Allies, as the recent experiences of Eighth Army had all too vividly shown. Although the people of Sicily could take comfort in the fall of Mussolini, it was to be some days yet before the guns of the warring sides fell silent.

[1] Pond, op. cit., p. 150.
[2] Ibid., p. 138. For his own good it was just as well Bolla spared these men, for in another incident the commander of the Italian garrison at Catania had a Fascist militia officer shot by a firing squad for abandoning his artillery battery. After the war the general was sued by the widow for 'unlawfully' killing her husband and won a judgment.

PART VI

The Race for Messina

We must take Messina before the British.

PATTON

CHAPTER 27

All Roads Lead to Messina

> If the 7th American Army puts in a full-blooded effort on my left then I believe the end should be in sight.
>
> MONTGOMERY[1]

The capture of Palermo by Seventh Army marked a clear turning point in the battle of Sicily. Not only were US forces now very much full participants but, thanks to both Patton and Montgomery, they were to dominate the final days of the campaign as the two Allied armies drove towards their final objective of Messina.

At Montgomery's invitation Patton flew to Syracuse on 25 July to discuss a common strategy for the final phase of operations in Sicily. It is noteworthy that it was Montgomery, not Alexander the Allied ground Commander-in-Chief, who took the initiative to make common cause with Patton. It was the first time the two generals had met since well before D-Day and the invitation had come from Montgomery who cabled, 'would be very honoured if you will come over and stay with me for a night and bring your Chief of Staff. We can then discuss the capture of Messina.'[2] The campaign was two weeks old and there was still no master plan for the Allied drive on Messina. Alexander continued to act without enthusiasm or firmness and seemed content to let his two Army commanders continue going their own separate ways. However, by 21 July, Montgomery had fully grasped not only the futility of his offensives to break the German defences in the Eighth Army sector, but had arrived at the cold realization that it was vital he and Patton co-operate.

Montgomery's initiative might well have been classified as leadership by default. Alexander's style of leadership in Sicily varied not one iota from his command of British Middle East Forces

---

[1] Letter to Brooke, 27 July 1943, Montgomery Papers.
[2] Cable, Montgomery–Patton, 23 July 1943.

where he had left the operations of Eighth Army to Montgomery. He would later assert that he was well satisfied with the way the campaign was developing, in particular by Patton's conduct of the exploitation into western Sicily. The timing of this operation, he told an official American historian, was about right. Alexander had wanted no setbacks to Eighth Army before he 'let Georgie go and exploit'. But his loose-rein approach to command brought a feeling that he could not have restrained Patton much longer than he did, in which case the Seventh Army commander would probably have said, 'To Hell with this' and gone ahead anyway. 'But it never came to that.'[1]

The same day that Patton had descended unexpectedly upon Alexander, Harold Macmillan was remarking in his diary of Alexander's dependence on a 'simple but complete faith in the certainty of victory and the guidance of Providence'.[2] This was not the first occasion when Alexander had invoked faith in a higher power. He had told Macmillan of the anxiety of the Allied commanders in Malta on the eve of D-Day, and how the weather had proved so helpful (one captured Italian general called the night of 9/10 July a real 'pyjama night' and thus quite safe from invasion). 'So you see,' Alexander told Macmillan, 'Providence was looking after us all the time and knew better than we did.'[3]

Patton arrived in Syracuse deeply suspicious of Montgomery's motives and their meeting began rather awkwardly as both made a show of hurrying to greet the other. This was soon forgotten as they quickly got down to business around Monty's staff car where a map of Sicily was spread across the bonnet. Patton fully expected there would be disagreement over priority on Sicily's sparse road network. The subject still deeply rankled with Patton and he was determined that Montgomery was not going to rob him of the initiative he had gained by the capture of Palermo.

Patton had already determined that if he was to capture Messina Seventh Army required the only two east–west highways which ran north of Mount Etna: Route 113, the coastal highway from Palermo to Messina, and Route 120, an interior mountain road running through central Sicily from Nicosia to Randazzo (see page 448).

---

[1] Alexander interview with George F. Howe, loc. cit.
[2] Macmillan, *War Diaries*, entry of 17 July 1943, p. 152.
[3] Ibid, pp. 152–3.

To Patton's utter incredulity Montgomery not only agreed with his concept but actually suggested that Seventh Army capture Messina rather than his Eighth Army![1] Montgomery even gave Patton *carte blanche* to cross his boundary line if the situation were to develop favourably in the north: 'If the Germans fought me hard in the area CATANIA–ADRANO, then the Americans should push on to RANDAZZO and down the coast to TAORMINA; we would then cut off the whole of two German Divisions,' he wrote in his diary.[2] A shocked and deeply suspicious Patton assumed Montgomery must have some ulterior motive and penned in his diary that night, 'He agreed so readily that I felt something was wrong but have not found it yet.' Although unable to subordinate his doubts, Patton never lost his innate mistrust of Montgomery's motives in what developed into one of the most misunderstood and historically distorted rivalries of the war.

Patton's suspicions were not unfounded. Ever since the D-Day landings Montgomery had behaved as if the Americans were not even present. His tactics at Vizzini, where he imperiously usurped Bradley's boundary, and his manipulation of strategy through a pliant Alexander who acceded to his every wish, smacked of an arrogance that only the British could win the important battles of the campaign.* What Patton in his frustration never understood was that by 25 July this was no longer the same cocksure Montgomery who had only days earlier sensed a quick victory, or that the farthest thing from his mind at this moment was to claim Messina for the British.

Montgomery's strategy of fighting separate battles by each of his corps had – after the calamitous failure to break through to Catania – verged on bankruptcy. What appeared to be a sweeping change of heart towards Patton was nothing more than a sobering awareness that this campaign was not going to be won by a spectacular unilateral British advance to Messina. Without strong American pressure against the northern end of the Etna Line, Montgomery's left hook around Mt Etna would have left 30 Corps vulnerable to a counterattack from the northwest.

[1] Montgomery Diary, 25 July 1943, and Hamilton, *Monty: Master of the Battlefield, 1942–1944*, p. 325.

[2] Montgomery Diary, 25 July 1943.

* Montgomery's plans on 13 July, which Alexander approved, gave Eighth Army the exclusive use of the four roads leading to Messina and effectively barred Seventh Army from any participation in its capture.

Montgomery's volte-face was not the result of an impetuous decision, but had evolved four days earlier when he had summoned Leese and Dempsey to announce the implementation of his latest change of strategy, the formal abandonment of a thrust to Messina via Catania. Having committed Eighth Army to the left hook by 30 Corps, Montgomery was anxious for his offensive to be complemented by an 'American thrust Eastwards along [the] North coast road towards MESSINA'.[1]

The new plan was to hold firm on the eastern flank on the plain of Catania and launch a hard left hook against the enemy's northern flank abutting Mt Etna where 30 Corps would 'go hard for ADRANO and then northwards round the west side of Mt ETNA', using the Canadians and the soon-to-arrive 78th Division from North Africa. This 'blitz attack' in conjunction with a thrust along the central and northern east–west axes by II Corps should, Montgomery cabled Alexander, be backed by 'the full weight of all power that can be made available from North Africa [and] must be turned on to the enemy army now hemmed in to the North-east corner of SICILY'. If this new battle plan were carried out, Montgomery was convinced German forces could never escape from Sicily; 'it was doomed if we acted properly.'[2]

Montgomery told Patton he would like to see two strong thrusts towards Messina by US forces:
- Two divisions along the axis NICOSIA–TROINA–RANDAZZO [via Route 120];
- Two divisions along the north coastal road [via Route 113]. 'This was all agreed,' wrote Montgomery, and soon afterwards Alexander arrived, and it was quickly evident he was in a testy mood. Patton recorded the scene in his diary:

> He looked a little mad, and, for him, was quite brusque. He told Monty to explain his plan. Monty said he and I had already decided what we were going to do, so Alex got madder and told Monty to show him the plan. He did and then Alex asked for mine...[3]

Alexander asked Patton if he knew that Huebner had been sacked, and Patton replied that he did. Somewhat defensively, Alexander said, 'I want to assure you that 15th Army Group is completely

[1] Montgomery Diary, 21 July 1943.
[2] Ibid. and cable, Montgomery–Alexander, 21 July 1943, copy in Diary.
[3] Patton Diary, 25 July 1943.

Allied-minded and favours neither Army.' 'I knew this was a lie,' wrote Patton, 'but said I felt that he was right – God pardon me!'*

The meeting broke up on a sour note with Patton complaining that, 'No one was offered any lunch and I thought that Monty was ill-bred both to Alexander and me. Monty gave me a 5¢ lighter. Some one must have sent him a box of them.'[1]

By validating the Monty–Patton agreement, Alexander tacitly acknowledged that Seventh Army was no longer the stepchild of 15th Army Group and had attained full equality with Eighth Army with whom it would now share the final battles for Messina. Three days later Montgomery, de Guingand and Broadhurst flew to Palermo in Monty's famous B-17 Flying Fortress to confer with Patton and very nearly lost their lives. The Palermo runway proved far too short to accommodate a B-17 and, had it not been for the extraordinary skill of the pilot, all aboard would undoubtedly have been killed. Montgomery's fun-loving ADC Johnny Henderson relates the harrowing experience:

> The most frightening thing that ever happened to me ... we went down this runway and it absolutely ate it up. The hangars were at the end and it wasn't long enough. I remember sitting in the glass dome in which I always sat, and I saw the hangar coming up – the pilot did the most amazing job. He swung the whole thing round and we landed on our side. I mean he put all the brakes on one side and revved one engine and swung the whole thing round – which wrote it off. That was the end of it. It collapsed on one side. We got out pretty shaken.[2]

Not Montgomery. Broadhurst recalls, 'It was hilarious to me: Monty was sitting there reading, quite unafraid of anything. We should never have gone there in that aeroplane ... He should never have had it but he adored it.'[3]

Patton was always a stickler for observing correct military protocol but pique over his treatment at Syracuse was manifest in his deliberate failure to greet Montgomery in person at Palermo

---

[1] Patton Diary, 25 July 1943.

[2] Captain John Henderson, quoted in *Monty: Master of the Battlefield, 1942–1944*, op. cit., p. 330.

[3] Broadhurst interview, 2 November 1983. Montgomery was given a USAAF C-47 to replace the written-off B-17.

* It is difficult to fault Alexander who considered Huebner ill-suited for his assignment. Huebner was never comfortable in a role that demanded diplomacy over emotion. He was a great soldier who never should have been placed in an assignment where tact was a prerequisite. (See Chapter 28.)

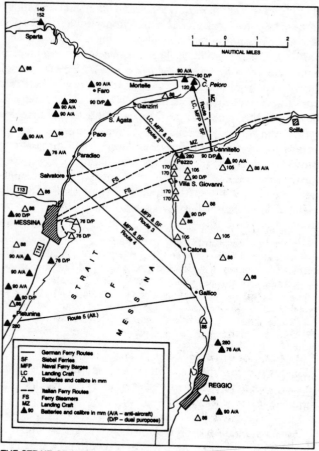

THE STRAIT OF MESSINA

airfield. However, when the party reached Patton's new headquarters at Palermo's splendid palace, the reception was vintage Patton: an escort of scout cars and motorcycles brought Montgomery into the courtyard where he was greeted by a band and inspected an infantry company honour guard. The ceremony was flawlessly executed in the best tradition of a Patton command. After an equally impressive lunch, both generals once again reviewed their plans to capture Messina and for the second time Montgomery emphasized the importance of the American thrust. 'Monty kept repeating that the move of the 45th Division along the coast was a most significant operation. I can't decide whether he is honest or wants me to lay off [Route] 120. On the other hand, he said that if we got to Taormina first, we were to turn south. Previously he had insisted that we not come as far as the [eastern] coast.'[1] Despite nearly losing his life Montgomery considered his visit a grand success. Patton had written, 'I hope Monty realized that I did this to show him up for doing nothing for me on the 25th,'; but if Montgomery took any notice it most certainly did not appear in his diary where he wrote, 'We had a great reception. The Americans are most delightful people and are very easy to work with ... their troops are quite first-class and I have a very great admiration for the way they fight.'[2]

Their second meeting in four days again left Patton wholly unconvinced of the sincerity of Montgomery's willing concession. He saw their relationship as a contest of adversaries and his immensely competitive nature could not accept that Montgomery would champion a course of action more beneficial to American forces than British. That night he penned a note to Middleton reflecting his scepticism: 'This is a horse race in which the prestige of the US Army is at stake. We must take Messina before the British. Please use your best efforts to facilitate the success of our race.'[3]

Why was Patton so mistrustful of what turned out to be a genuine proposal from Montgomery? The reasons are to be found in the months of British distrust and criticism of American troops which had left Patton with a burning desire to make the British eat their words. Nor was Patton alone: Bradley, Huebner, Harmon

---

1 Patton Diary, 28 July 1943.
2 Montgomery Diary, 28 July 1943.
3 Letter of 28 July 1943, Patton Papers.

and others all later made their feelings known. Patton's official biographer believes this condescending attitude on the part of Alexander, Montgomery and other senior British commanders left Patton smarting and obsessed with reaching Messina first 'not so much for his personal glory, although that was important, but rather to prove to the world that American soldiers were every bit as good as – indeed, better than – British troops'.[1] It can be argued with some justification that the equality achieved between Seventh and Eighth Armies only came about because of Patton's decision to strike for Palermo and by Montgomery's failure to break through at Catania.

Montgomery never viewed the capture of Messina in such terms. A year earlier when Eighth Army had been tired and frustrated after the disastrous setbacks at Gazala and Tobruk he might well have done so. Patton, however, reflected an extreme sensitivity to his Army being rated inferior to Monty's. In Patton's mind this demeaned the American fighting man and the only way this could be overcome once and for all was through a great American triumph, which in Sicily meant Messina.

American morale was scarcely uplifted by the bias of the BBC which repeatedly played up the exploits of Eighth Army at the expense of the American forces whose role was considered minor, with British troops fighting the bloodiest battles. One broadcast that sent Eisenhower's patience through the roof complained 'that the Seventh Army has been lucky to be in western Sicily eating grapes'.[2] The day after the 1st Division captured Enna the BBC baldly announced the British had taken the city! The snide reference to Seventh Army finally brought Eisenhower to boiling point and led to a strongly worded letter to Churchill criticizing the BBC for undermining his efforts to create a truly unified Anglo-American command in the Mediterranean.[*]

Had Montgomery wished to make Messina the object of Anglo-American competition it was evident that Eighth Army would have been in no position to respond, boxed in as it was on the southern slopes of the great Etna *massif*. More important in

---

[1] Blumenson, *The Patton Papers*, Vol. II, op. cit., p. 307.

[2] Cable, Eisenhower–Alexander, 5 August 1943, Alexander Papers, PRO (WO 214/22), and Butcher Diary, 6 August 1943.

[*] The BBC was the only source of news in English for Allied troops in the Mediterranean. BBC officials later claimed they had been misinterpreted. Nevertheless, there was a very rapid and noticeable improvement in their coverage.

Montgomery's mind at that time was to find an escape from the mess he found himself in after the abject failure at Catania. Although he continued to exude confidence that all was well, mounting casualty figures from both battle and the cruel Sicilian environment were quite enough to convince him that Eighth Army could no longer afford the luxury of carrying the brunt of the fighting without assistance.* The plain fact is that Montgomery no longer viewed the final conquest of Sicily through the rose-coloured glasses that ten days earlier had seen his army advancing as fast as his men could march. There were more difficult battles ahead before Messina fell and Montgomery was less interested who got there first, than in bringing the campaign to a speedy and successful conclusion. One searches in vain through Montgomery's notes, letters and diary for traces of rivalry with Patton. If prestige was at stake, it lay solely in the mind of Patton.

The most serious obstacle to the full-blooded offensive Montgomery desired from Seventh Army was its poor tactical position after the drive to Palermo. Keyes' Provisional Corps was hopelessly scattered throughout western Sicily, and of Bradley's two divisions the 45th was still driving northwest on 22 July to cut the north coast road near Términi Imerese. The 1st Division had been forced into a detour to capture Enna after another unpleasant incident between II Corps and Leese's 30 Corps.

The great walled city of Enna, until recently Axis tactical headquarters in Sicily, was to have been taken by the Canadians. However, they found the city heavily defended by a German force in the hills surrounding this ancient citadel which for centuries had been virtually impregnable. The inter-Army boundary ran due west of the town and when the Canadians ran into stiff opposition Leese ordered Simonds to bypass Enna to the east, which inadvertently left Bradley's extreme right flank unprotected. Bradley was still seething over the Vizzini incident a week earlier and was in no mood to let Leese's gaffe pass unnoticed, so despatched a terse

* On 27 July, Montgomery wrote to Brooke not only of the terrible battle fought along the plain of Catania but also of his mounting casualty figures: 400 officers and 5,400 other ranks. 'A marked feature is the high proportion of officers killed to other ranks killed; as high as 1 to 6 in some units; and averaging 1 to 9 in the whole army. It has never been more than 1 to 15 before.' The forthcoming battle 'will not be easy as [the enemy] is in ideal defensive country, and his troops are all Germans too – and very good and determined Germans too ... I am planning to develop a very heavy pressure about 2nd August directed towards ADRANO and if the 7 American Army puts in a full-blooded effort on my left then I believe the end should be in sight.' (Montgomery Papers.)

note informing him that II Corps would take Enna. Despite the sensitivity of the American, Leese grew very fond of Bradley and professed high respect for his ability as a corps commander. Though annoyed over the Enna incident, Leese replied at once with profuse apologies and several bottles of Scotch as a peace offering. A few days later Bradley reciprocated by serving the visiting Leese high tea from china embossed with the crest of the House of Savoy. When the 1st Division entered the city, Bradley's G-2 noted approvingly, 'Not bad, not bad at all. It took the Saracens 20 years in their siege of Enna. Our boys did it in five hours.'[1]

After the capture of Enna, the 1st Division had driven northwest and had made steady progress which brought them to Petralia on 23 July. As they retreated, the Germans mined the roads and left booby traps everywhere. Snipers were left behind in the wrecked planes at the airfields north of Gela and instances were reported of their own dead being wired with explosives. After the capture of Petralia, the 1st Division was ordered to turn east along Route 120 where they continued to meet only light opposition.

After completing their task of cutting the island in half, the 45th Division was also shifted east for a drive along Route 113. There the 45th Division ran into the 29th Panzer Grenadier Division and for a solid week encountered the toughest resistance since the battle for Biscari airfield. It proved difficult to advance in terrain that left little room for manoeuvre. East of Cefalu one regiment had to scale steep cliffs in order to dislodge the Germans whose positions blocked any further advance eastwards. It was a bloody business and the German defensive tactics repeatedly forced the Americans into costly and time-consuming battles. Over and over again, it was the same pattern the Germans would employ all across their front in Sicily: defences adopted to take maximum advantage of the terrain, skilful use of artillery, mortar and tank fire and occasional counterattacks designed to break up the American momentum. The 45th Division had acquitted itself well during its three weeks of combat but by the end of July Patton felt it was time for a change and ordered Truscott's 3d Division into the line. 'Middleton looked tired and his attacks have lacked drive.' He told Middleton, 'I think I will give the 45th a rest and use the 3d.' Truscott's men soon encountered the same problems that

[1] *A Soldier's Story*, op. cit., p. 143.

had plagued the 45th during a series of difficult battles during their two-week, 140-mile march to Messina.

Before they departed, Patton went to the front to praise Middleton's troops. 'I hope you know how good you are,' he told an infantry battalion, 'for everyone else does. You are magnificent.'[1] Considerable praise was also given to the combat engineers whose feats throughout the campaign were often astounding. The Germans had left Palermo harbour blocked by sinking forty-four vessels, yet within a week American engineers had reopened the harbour to nearly two-thirds capacity. At Cape Calavà, near Brolo, the Germans blew up a section of Route 113 which clung to a mountainside a hundred feet above the sea. Within eighteen hours the 10th Engineer Battalion had constructed a makeshift 'bridge in the sky' that permitted the 3d Division to resume its push towards Messina. Without the engineers the 3d Division's drive on Messina would have ground to a complete halt.[2]*

On 'the other side of the hill', as the third week of the campaign ended, General Hube had managed to tighten his defences to a point where the Etna Line now ran from Catania to Adrano, northwest to Troina and then to the north coast west of Sant' Agata, where it was known as the San Fratello Line. The two keys to collapsing the German defences were at Adrano in the Eighth Army sector and Troina in the American. Both were mountain towns from which ran the only roads towards Messina. The sudden loss of either anchor would have left the Germans open to encirclement. The Hermann Goering Division continued to hold the largest frontage from Catania to a point several miles southeast

---

[1] Patton Diary, 30 July 1943. The only problem Middleton ever had in Sicily with Patton was over Bill Mauldin, the famed cartoonist and war correspondent who got his start in Sicily. *The Forty-Fifth Division News* was the first division newspaper to appear during the war and Patton took great exception to the first of Mauldin's famous cartoons of Willie and Joe, the two archetypal GIs with whom millions of American soldiers came to identify. Patton developed a strong distaste for Mauldin in general and Willie and Joe in particular. He considered them 'damned unsoldierly' and told Middleton, 'I order you to get rid of Mauldin and his cartoons.' Middleton diplomatically replied, 'Put your order in writing, George.' No more was heard of the subject. (See *Troy H. Middleton*, op. cit., p. 160.)

[2] See *A Soldier's Story*, p. 148; *Sicily*, pp. 408–9; and *Command Missions*, pp. 241–2. A graphic account of the 'bridge in the sky' is in Ernie Pyle's *Brave Men*, pp. 65–73. The first convoys into Palermo harbour carried units of Major General Manton S. Eddy's 9th Infantry Division from North Africa.

* The slogan of the US Army Corps of Engineers was: 'The difficult we do immediately. The impossible takes a little longer.'

of Troina. The narrow front of the central highlands was held by Rodt's 15th Panzer Grenadier Division while the recently arrived 29 PzG had been slotted into defence of the San Fratello Line. There was no longer a need for Hube to be unduly concerned about depending upon the Italians. Elements of Aosta and Livorno Divisions held small sectors in the north but otherwise Hube now had full control of the defence of Sicily.

The fall of Mussolini had virtually no impact on German operations in Sicily. Guzzoni immediately appeared at Hube's CP to pledge his continued support and unconditional loyalty. The absurd charade that Guzzoni was still the Axis C-in-C continued, even though at no time did the Italians ever attempt to issue a single directive to Hube or attempt to influence his conduct of operations. Guzzoni was secretly pleased with Mussolini's removal and blamed him for the failure of Fascism. In the evenings he would dine in splendid isolation with the equally unimportant von Senger and discuss the collapse of Fascism. It was a pathetic scene: a small, fat, balding Italian general sitting in a specially fitted mobile dining van; behind him on the wall was a picture of the King and next to it an empty frame where Mussolini's portrait had once hung.[1]

To be certain, the German situation was serious, even critical, but there had not been a single day since the invasion when it had *not* been critical. Most noticeable was the absence of panic; even during the darkest hours of the battle for Sicily only the Hermann Goering Division had reacted badly. Three weeks of bloody fighting had hardened this division into a unit worthy of its fearsome reputation. A noteworthy parallel with German opinion in Normandy was the attitude of the German ground commanders towards the Luftwaffe. As von Senger has observed, Hube 'had bitter complaints about the Luftwaffe. No clear-sighted Army officer was inclined to blame the Luftwaffe for being no longer able to assist the ground forces. But what made them detestable to Hube and to me was the fact that they still availed of the better communications to Rome dating from the African campaign. Nobody was in a position to induce them to hand over these lines to the army who wanted them badly. On their part they kept them because they wanted them for the purpose of denouncing the ground leaders. It was one of those schemes invented by Goering,

[1] Von Senger, *An Cosantoir*, July 1950, op. cit.

who by denouncing others was trying to withdraw the attention from his own branch's deficiencies and total collapse ... Elements of the Luftwaffe ground forces began to set fire to dumps that might still be saved and thereby spread panic. They carried furniture with them – and left secret files behind! Hube implored me to report these facts to Kesselring and to Field Marshal von Richthofen in Rome after my return there.'[1]

Hube's most vulnerable point was the tenuous boundary between Rodt and Conrath southeast of Troina but the Germans with great skill managed again and again to keep the hole plugged by concentrating their defences around key terrain and obvious routes of approach.

Not only did the Germans have to contend with unending harassment from the air but they were rapidly feeling the effects of a growing shortage of supplies, ammunition and fuel, not from any interruption of the ferry service across the Strait of Messina but rather from Allied interdiction of the road and rail network in central and southern Italy. Hube's chief of staff recalls that:

> the flow of supplies began to dry up, and our supply situation on the island little by little became critical ... The supply dumps which had been dispersed in a foolish fashion all over Sicily in the course of preparations made in May and June, where they did not fall into the enemy's hands in the first days after the landing, and where we had not been obliged to destroy them, were just about exhausted. In short, from the end of July we lived from hand to mouth.[2]

Hube also knew that time was rapidly running out and that he would soon be obliged to order the evacuation of Sicily. Plans were already under way for a mass evacuation across the Strait and Hube's staff began to refine details of how they would conduct a series of delaying actions back to Messina.

While the Germans pondered their survival, the Allies after months of indecision had at last acted on Eisenhower's recommendation and authorized an invasion of Italy by an amphibious force near Naples at Salerno. There were to be two operations directed against Italy soon after Sicily fell. The corps-sized amphibious operation at Salerno (code-named AVALANCHE) was to be carried out by Mark Clark's recently formed Fifth US Army,

---

[1] Ibid.
[2] Von Bonin, loc. cit.

while the crossing of the Strait of Messina into Calabria (code-named BAYTOWN) was given to Eighth Army. There was considerable disagreement between the British and US Chiefs of Staff over the scope of AVALANCHE, but, for better or worse, the Combined Chiefs of Staff had at long last given Eisenhower the necessary directive to extend the campaign.

The generals on both sides had decided how the final battles would be fought. The centre of attention became the mountain town of Troina. During the last days of July, the 1st Division continued to advance eastwards across the axis of Route 120. The first of a series of mountain towns to fall was Gangi (which Patton aptly described as the queerest he had ever seen: 'It looks like plant lice on a rosebud'), followed by the crossroads town of Nicosia on 28 July. The next objective was Troina and it was here that American troops fought their bloodiest battle since Gela.

CHAPTER 28

The Battle for Troina

The most bitterly fought battle of the campaign.
BRADLEY[1]

For nearly a week Major General Eberhard Rodt's panzer grenadiers had been withdrawing slowly eastward along Route 120, avoiding all-out confrontation with the 1st Division while still successfully exacting a stiff price for each American gain. As the 1st Division shifted gears from a thrust to the north to an advance eastward along central Sicily the Germans resisted by defending each successive hill mass. Counterattacks were frequent and backed by strong artillery fire making the advance of Terry Allen's infantrymen a painful and expensive proposition.

The defence of Nicosia was particularly stubborn and the German tactics of attempting to force their attacker to drive them from each new position forced Allen to employ his infantry in tiring and time-consuming manoeuvres. Group Fullreide held two key hills west of Nicosia where a succession of bloody encounters took place over a four-day period. Allen was finally forced into employing a double envelopment, noting that, 'Had we kept up just a frontal attack, it would have meant just a bloody nose for us at every hill . . . This was about as stubborn as any resistance we've encountered so far.'[2] Before long Allen learned there was far worse to come.

The new eastward offensive by II Corps was severely handicapped by the harsh terrain. Between the two routes of advance lay [after Etna] the highest and most rugged mountains in Sicily, the Caronie chain, which ran from the vicinity of Troina almost to Messina. Immediately to the west were the equally rugged Madonie Mountains. These two mountain chains compartmentalized the II Corps advance into two completely independent milit-

[1] 'Report of Operations of II Corps in the Sicilian Campaign', 1 September 1943, in Reel 2, 'Outline History of II Corps, 1918–1945', USAMHI.
[2] Quoted in Richard Tregaskis, *Invasion Diary*, New York, 1943, p. 52.

ary actions, neither of which was capable of supporting the other. To the north the coastal route was bisected by a series of streams and ridgelines running from the mountains to the sea, each of which became an excellent defensive position. Along the 1st Division axis, mountains dominated both sides of Route 120 as it snaked up and down steep grades so sharp and narrow that large vehicles were forced into a series of backing and turning manoeuvres. No better terrain existed for a defender.[1]

Along the north coast, the 29th Panzer Grenadier Division was conceding ground in conjunction with Rodt's withdrawal even though there were instances when they could have held their positions longer. The delaying actions fought by 15th Panzer Grenadier coincided with Hube's concept of how German forces would fight the final battles of the campaign. Rather then attempt an all-out defence of the Etna Line, Hube elected to delay the Allied advance by establishing a series of mountain strongpoints, each of which would be defended until enemy pressure forced withdrawal to the next position. At Troina, Hube planned to defend a chain of hill masses of the Caronie chain that ran north–south across Route 120 as far as Randazzo. For as long as it could be held, the northern anchor of the Etna Line was to be the mountain town of Troina.

For some days American intelligence officers had been predicting that the Germans would merely pass through Troina en route to new positions some five miles further east near the town of Cesarò. No one had detected that 15th Panzer Grenadier had abruptly halted their retreat at Troina. Although the Etna Line was accurately described, II Corps intelligence assessments incorrectly assumed the Germans would defend and possibly even counter-attack from a final defence line further east, from which a withdrawal from Sicily via Messina might be protected. This comment by Colonel Dickson on 28 July indicates the extent of American misconception: 'The successful defence of Catania and the Catania Plain have raised German morale and hopes to the point where they are willing to gamble two or three more divisions to hold a Sicilian bridgehead.'[2]

Both II Corps and 1st Division intelligence estimates predicted

---

[1] *Sicily*, op. cit., Chapter XVI. At 3,674 feet (1,120 metres) Troina is Sicily's highest city.
[2] II Corps G-2 Intelligence Estimate No. 9, 28 July 1943, quoted in *Sicily*, op. cit., p. 325. Summaries emanating from AFHQ were closer to the mark. As early as 24 July came the

Troina would present no serious problem and that the state of the 15th Panzer Grenadier Division was poor. By 29 July, Lieutenant Colonel Porter, the 1st Division G-2, was reporting that the Germans were 'very tired, little ammo, many casualties, morale low'. Two days later II Corps was still advising that 'Indications are Troina lightly held'.[1] Porter found himself encumbered in preparing his estimates by maps that proved wholly inadequate and by fog which had prevented the air force from obtaining current aerial photographs. Despite these limitations all indications still pointed to a German defence of the Cesarò hill mass five miles further east. Colonel Porter was obliged to base his estimates mainly on information from local Sicilians, newly captured POWs and earlier aerial photos which identified a substantial German bivouac area outside Cesarò. Thus, both Porter and Dickson had every reason to believe that the 15th Panzer Grenadier Division would merely continue their delaying tactics at Troina. The Germans, however, had other intentions. Hube was deeply concerned that if Regalbuto fell to the Canadians it would force a premature withdrawal to the Adrano–Randazzo line. To cede Troina without a fight would merely increase the pressure on the Hermann Goering Division. Hube's decision to defend Troina offered some unique benefits. There were few avenues of approach and 15th Panzer Grenadier was able to establish hilltop defences that completely controlled movement along Route 120 and minimized the possibility of encirclement. Excellent gun positions in Troina and the surrounding mountains could deliver effective fire against an attacking force, while the barren terrain provided an attacker with virtually no cover.[2]

The battle for Troina began innocently enough on 31 July when

---

[1] G-2 Journal, 1st Infantry Division, 1215 hours, 29 July 1943, and II Corps G-2 Journal, 31 July 1943, both quoted in *Sicily*, op. cit., p. 325.

[2] *Sicily*, op. cit., p. 325. Hube's strategy also left 29th Panzer Grenadier Division to the north well placed in defence of the San Stefano line.

---

prediction that 'a strong defensive line has been taken up from CATANIA to NICOSIA and the intention is certainly to extend it to the North coast. Some further withdrawal in the centre will probably be inevitable and the likely course of the line is through REGALBUTO and TROINA.' (AFHQ G-2 Weekly Intelligence Summary No. 48, for week ending at noon, 24 July. PRO [WO 204/967].) A week later AFHQ noted that 'the enemy's intention was to halt approximately on the line SAN FRATELLO–TROINA–REGALBUTO–CATENANUOVA and thence to the sea South of Catania'. (G-2 Weekly Intelligence Estimate No. 49, for week ending noon, 31 July.)

Cerami, a town five miles to the west (eight miles by road), was captured by the 1st Division. By that evening the 39th Infantry Regiment* was in possession of Mt dell'Annunziata (Hill 1234)† two miles northeast of Cerami. Meanwhile, the 1st Battalion, 16th Infantry, had also advanced several miles southeast of Cerami and seized Hill 1209 under considerable artillery and mortar fire from German guns on the heights around Troina. Particularly trouble-some was fire from Mt Acuto (Hill 1343), the highest point over-looking Route 120 and Troina.

Both Allen and Bradley had come forward to the 39th CP on the afternoon of 31 July and had expressed confidence that Troina could be taken by the 39th Regiment without assistance. The war diary of the regiment not only recorded their optimism but also that the two generals had repeated reports that Troina contained only a few enemy troops and guns. Encouraged by a false sense of German intentions, Allen had committed only the 39th Regiment to the first attack on Troina, and, despite the heavy enemy artillery fire, the gains made that afternoon apparently reinforced the conviction that its capture would not be a major problem. From positions astride Hill 1209 the 39th commander, Colonel H. A. 'Paddy' Flint,‡ sent two battalions towards Troina, and by noon

---

* The 39th Regiment was a unit of the 9th Infantry Division at that time attached to the 1st Infantry Division. Previously it had been assigned to the Provisional Corps but had been hastily transferred along with the French 4th Tabor of Goums and several artillery units to II Corps. The arrival of the 39th Regiment bolstered the strength of the 1st Division by three infantry battalions and one artillery battalion.

† Denotes height in metres. An accepted custom is to utilize the elevation number on topographical maps to identify terrain during military operations.

‡ Colonel 'Paddy' Flint (USMA 1912) was one of Patton's oldest and dearest friends. A colourful ex-cavalry officer 'Paddy' Flint was an eccentric New Englander who carried the principle of leadership by example to what many considered rash extremes. Bradley had first met him in Tunisia where he pleaded for a chance to command a regiment. When General Eddy later reported he required a new commander to rejuvenate the flagging 39th Regiment, Bradley picked Flint. In Sicily the men of the 39th were still skittish from several severe shellings in North Africa and discipline was poor. Flint quickly made a deep impression on them. Soon after his arrival all helmets and vehicles in the regiment suddenly appeared with a strange new marking which looked like this: AAA-0-. The symbol stood for 'Anything, Anytime, Anywhere – Bar Nothing'. Bradley and Eddy turned a blind eye to this flagrant disregard of a II Corps regulation. When it was brought to his attention Bradley merely grinned and told Eddy he couldn't see any such thing. During the battle for Troina, Flint made himself easily identifiable by walking about the front lines barechested with a helmet, black silk scarf (he called it his lucky necktie), rifle in his hand, often rolling a cigarette as he went. Deliberately exposing himself to German fire, Flint would contemptuously wave his hand towards their positions and say, 'See, there's nothing to be afraid of. The damn Krauts couldn't hit anything in the last war; they can't hit anything in this war. They can't even hit an old buck like me.' Calling himself just a simple country boy, Flint worried Bradley by taking such risks. Patton was delighted. (Bradley Commentaries and A Soldier's Story, op. cit., pp. 152–3.)

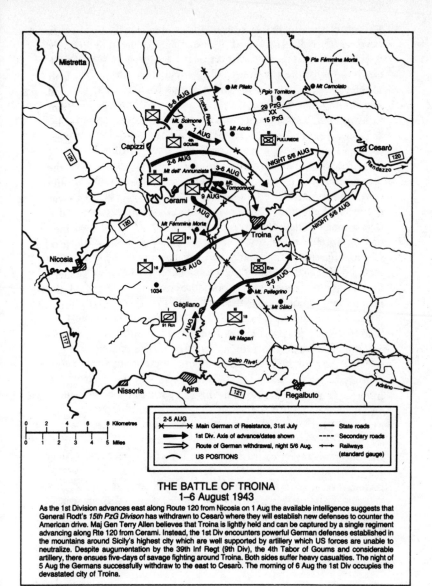

THE BATTLE OF TROINA
1–6 August 1943

As the 1st Division advances east along Route 120 from Nicosia on 1 Aug the available intelligence suggests that General Rodt's *15th PzG Divison* has withdrawn to Cesarò where they will establish new defenses to counter the American drive. Maj Gen Terry Allen believes that Troina is lightly held and can be captured by a single regiment advancing along Rte 120 from Cerami. Instead, the 1st Div encounters powerful German defenses established in the mountains around Sicily's highest city which are well supported by artillery which US forces are unable to neutralize. Despite augmentation by the 39th Inf Regt (9th Div), the 4th Tabor of Goums and considerable artillery, there ensues five-days of savage fighting around Troina. Both sides suffer heavy casualties. The night of 5 Aug the Germans successfully withdraw to the east to Cesarò. The morning of 6 Aug the 1st Div occupies the devastated city of Troina.

THE BATTLE OF TROINA

one battalion had taken possession of the high ground a mile west of the town (Hill 1034).

That afternoon the 15th Panzer Grenadier, now operating as a full division for the first time in the campaign, launched their first counterattack which drove Flint's troops back to their original positions of that morning. To the south a reconnaissance battalion was able to seize Gagliano, a small town five miles southwest of Troina, required as the southern anchor of the division advance. Gagliano fell to the American force only after 'a hell of a scrap to get in'.[1] What Flint's troops had encountered was one of the best-defended German sectors of the entire Sicily campaign. The 15th Panzer Grenadier Division was supported to the north by elements of the 29th Panzer Grenadier Division and the Aosta Division and to the south by units of the Hermann Goering. Rodt had organized his division into two regimental-size task forces; Group Fullreide held Troina and the mountains to the north, including Mt Acuto. Defending Troina's southern approaches was Group Ens, while dispersed around the city was a heavy concentration that included four battalions from the Aosta Division.[2]

The ease with which Hill 1034 had fallen was taken as a signal that the intelligence estimates had correctly identified German intentions not to defend Troina, even though the 3d Battalion had advanced to a point about two miles northwest of the town only to be forced back to its original start line by very heavy fire from the mountains north of Route 120. This same fire had also prevented any further daylight advance by the 4th Tabor of Goums across the open ground to the east of their position. Only later was it learned that the ease with which Major Philip C. Tinley's 1st Battalion had taken Hill 1034 was made possible because Colonel Karl Ens had not yet put his defences in satisfactory order, a problem he was to rectify with a vengeance at nightfall when a savage counterattack 'thumped hell out of A and C Companies'. Badly mauled, the 1st Battalion was forced to withdraw, leaving Group Ens in possession of a vital position.[*]

The events of 1 August forced Allen to reconsider his original decision to permit the 39th Regiment to take Troina. Flint pleaded

---

[1] G-3 Journal, 1st Infantry Division, 1745 hours, 1 August 1943, National Archives.

[2] *Sicily*, op. cit., Chapter XVII.

[*] Hill 1034 was nearly as high as Troina itself and its possession offered an unobstructed view of both the city and the German artillery positions further east.

for a chance to make one further attempt and the 1st Division commander seems to have been strongly influenced by Bradley's earlier admonition that he should commit only those units actually required to complete the capture of Troina prior to the forthcoming relief by the 9th Division. Thus, from Allen's point of view it made sense to allow this 9th Division unit another crack at Troina, especially since his artillery commander, Brigadier General Clift Andrus, had assembled massive supporting fire in the form of approximately sixteen battalions of 105 mm and 155 mm artillery – in all, some 165 guns.[1]

By mid-afternoon Allen had changed his mind. It was a matter of pride to him that the 1st Division finish what it started before handing over to Eddy's 9th Division. More importantly, it would have proved militarily unsound to have attempted to insert a new division into the heart of a hotly contested battle. Allen issued fresh orders that while Flint would still be permitted to make the main attack the following morning, he would be fully supported in the north by Colonel John Bowen's 26th Regiment which was to attack the heights north of Troina, while further to the north the 4th Tabor of Goums was to resume its thrust forward towards Mt Acuto.*

The prevailing sense of optimism was not shared by Colonel Bowen, whose interpretation of the available intelligence led him to warn Allen of 'very strong [German] defences'. 'I think there is a hell of a lot of stuff there . . . We'll be moving right into the teeth of the enemy.'[2] Bowen's scepticism was founded on the belief that he lacked the resources to capture the German mountain positions north of Troina from which heavy fire had made movement along Route 120 impossible.

Allen gave the 26th Regiment nine battalions of direct support artillery fire, but Bowen's fears proved accurate. The attacks by the 26th and 39th Regiments and the Goumiers met with total failure as a devastating hail of German artillery fire prevented any forward progress. Neither the Goumiers nor Flint's troops could advance at all, and Bowen's lead battalion was fortunate to

[1] *Sicily*, op. cit., Chapter XVII.
[2] *Sicily*, op. cit., p. 337.
* In mid-afternoon the 39th Regiment reported 'a steady stream of vehicles and artillery out of Troina, going NE. Looks like a pull-out', which may well have provided further reason to believe the attack on 2 August would succeed. (G-3 Journal, 1st Infantry Division, 1500 hours, 1 August.)

advance a scant half-mile. Whatever confidence there had been about the capture of Troina disappeared on 2 August, leaving Terry Allen in no doubt that to break the German defence of the city would take everything the 1st Division could muster. The statements of POWs revealed that the German troops had been ordered to hold Troina 'at all costs'.[1]

The fourth attempt to capture Troina was a reversion to Allen's forte of the night attack. Before first light the next morning he elected to launch an all-out attack across the entire 1st Division front in the belief that the Germans were not strong enough to resist a simultaneous crushing assault. This time the main effort was assigned to Colonel George Taylor's 16th Regiment which was augmented by the attachment of a rifle battalion of the 18th Infantry. Day 4 (3 August) brought small gains which left the 1st Division tantalizingly close to Troina. But the Germans continued to cling tenaciously to their positions. A counterattack by Group Ens in mid-afternoon forced the suspension of friendly artillery fire because of the close proximity of the combatants. Earlier, only heavy artillery support prevented Taylor's lead battalions from being overrun on the slopes of a ridge west of Troina. An attempt to envelop Troina from the direction of Gagliano stalled and had to be abandoned because of the open, rocky terrain and the exhausted condition of the troops.* Thus, despite gains of one to two miles, the bitter fighting on 3 August was inconclusive.

Day 5 (4 August) saw the most determined American effort to take Troina. It began in the late afternoon with a fifty-minute air and artillery bombardment that left the German defenders dazed and demoralized. While the guns of eight artillery battalions pounded Troina, wave after wave of A-36 fighter-bombers

---

[1] 'A Summary of the Sicily Campaign during World War II (10 July–16 August 1943)', prepared by Terry Allen. Allen Papers, Eisenhower Library.

* The former 1st Division G-2, now (retired) General Robert W. Porter, Jr, believes the key to Troina lay in an envelopment from Gagliano and that the city might have fallen sooner had it not been for faulty maps. An attempt by the 18th Infantry to outflank Troina from the rear by means of a night attack from the southwest failed when they ran into elements of Group Ens. Porter's maps showed only three roads leading into Troina from the south, all but one of which were little more than dirt tracks. Unknown to the 1st Division there was a fourth road that could have brought a successful surprise attack against Troina from the rear. After the attack had jumped off during the night of 3 August, Porter discovered the fourth road when Air Force liaison officers brought him up-to-date maps which depicted a route into Troina from the southeast. Porter believes this track may not have been known to the Germans, but even if it had, there would have been little likelihood of its being defended. (Interview of 15 September 1985, loc. cit.)

(seventy-two in all) attacked and each dropped a single 500 lb bomb.* As battered as the Germans were, when the infantry attacked, the German defences once again held off an American breakthrough.

The arrival of the 60th Regiment (9th Division) signalled an attempt to threaten Troina from the north when Allen sent the regiment, plus supporting artillery and engineers, towards 5,039-foot Mt Camolato (Hill 1536), six miles north of Cesarò. Possession of this terrain would threaten the German artillery and observation posts supporting Troina. Aerial photos had revealed the existence of a previously unknown dirt road running along a portion of the east–west ridgeline that led towards Mt Camolato.

For several days all attempts to advance north of Route 120 had been ferociously rebuffed by the fire from German positions in the rugged mountains north and northeast of Troina. Two of Bowen's battalions were isolated for three days on two mountains and forced to fend off repeated German attacks.† The Goumiers had likewise been pinned down attempting to cross the Troina River and seize Mt Acuto. Until their attachment to the 60th Regiment on 5 August they had made no headway whatever.

By 5 August both Rodt and Hube were aware that Troina could

---

* Close air support of ground operations was rare during the Sicily campaign and of the estimated 1,000 direct-support fighter-bomber sorties recorded, most were against towns and enemy convoys with the object of isolating the battlefield. Provisions for timely response to the requirements of the ground forces were clumsy and inefficient, with the result that response time was far too long against what were often fleeting targets. As the campaign progressed there was some improvement from the use of mobile, radio-controlled air-liaison teams. Nevertheless, throughout Sicily and until the war ended, the problem of air–ground co-ordination and the bombing of friendly troops by Allied aircraft was serious. In Sicily, poor maps, inexperienced pilots and the similarity of the terrain all combined to produce numerous unfortunate incidents. During the battle for Troina, Canadian troops in Regalbuto were bombed several times by US fighter-bombers. Finally, after one particularly close call, Oliver Leese was obliged to ring Bradley to enquire, 'What have we done that your chaps would want to bomb us?' Asked where the bombs had landed, Leese replied, 'Squarely on top of my headquarters; they've really plastered the town.' (*A Soldier's Story*, p. 152.) Bradley understood full well Leese's consternation, for he and Allen had themselves nearly been killed when A-36s had strafed the 1st Division CP for the third time in a single day. On another occasion when American aircraft disregarded prearranged yellow recognition signals and repeatedly strafed a 2nd Armored Division column, the frustrated troops finally fired back in self-defence, despite orders not to fire on friendly aircraft. A P-38 was shot down and the pilot was able to bale out safely, but 'the Air Corps got the message; air attacks against Americans stopped for the duration of the campaign'. Later, when the statistics were compiled it was found that the 2nd Armored lost more men and equipment (fourteen vehicles and seventy-five men killed or wounded) to 'friendly' air attacks than to the Luftwaffe. (Houston, *Hell on Wheels*, op. cit., pp. 175–6; and *A Soldier's Story*, op. cit., pp. 150–1.)

† Private James M. Reese, 26th Infantry Regiment, earned a Medal of Honor for personally fighting off a German attack until killed.

not be held for much longer. Rodt was aware of the attempt to outflank him and threaten Cesarò from the north and could do little about it. The furious stand at Troina had held up the American advance for nearly a week but at an exceptionally high cost: 1,600 killed (nearly forty per cent of the divisional strength).[1] His men were exhausted and fresh reinforcements were non-existent. The frequency of Allied air attacks had disrupted or destroyed most supply dumps and made attempts to use the roads in daylight virtually suicidal. Rodt warned Hube that an American force was threatening to cut off his only escape route to the east. Although his first request on 5 August to abandon Troina was turned down, Hube later that day approved a withdrawal to new positions around Cesarò.

Troina was only one of Hube's many problems. To the south, Eighth Army units had made solid gains and after a series of hard-won battles all across the 30 Corps front, the British were posing a very serious threat to the central anchor of the Etna Line: Adrano. The Canadians had fought their most furious battle of the campaign for the medieval town of Agira (438 casualties)[2] and had gone on to seize Regalbuto. With little left of Italian forces in Sicily, Guzzoni could only offer Comando Supremo the gloomiest of assessments and the hollow claim that every possible resistance would be made to the bitter end. Hube's attempts to convince Guzzoni to relocate his Sixth Army HQ on the mainland were rebuffed even when on 6 August the Italian commander learned to his dismay of Hube's true intentions.[*] Guzzoni was set against an evacuation of Sicily and continued to insist that the remnants of the Italian Army would make a last stand around Messina. Finally, on 9 August Roatta ordered Guzzoni to Calabria along with all Italian units still operational, ending the unhappy saga of his tenure as the Axis C-in-C in Sicily.

After taking Regalbuto the Canadians had advanced to the Troina River (halfway between Regalbuto and Adrano) and, along with the 78th Division which had established a bridgehead

---

[1] *The Mediterranean and Middle East*, Vol. V, op. cit., p. 162.

[2] In a supporting role to the south, Brigadier Urquhart's 231st Brigade took 300 casualties. (Ibid., pp. 154–5.)

[*] Although Hube had been in *de facto* command of the Axis defence of Sicily, formal transfer of this responsibility did not take place until 2 August.

over the Simeto, and the 51st Division which had secured positions north of the River Dittáino, were threatening Adrano from three directions. Not only was the 15th Panzer Grenadier Division threatened with envelopment from Cesarò but the Canadians were now capable of striking north along the Adrano–Troina highway and cutting off the division from the south. Only on the north coast was the situation stable as the 29th Panzer Grenadier Division remained in firm control of the San Fratello Line. Hube, mindful of the strong possibility of amphibious landings in his rear, threatened with an Allied breakthrough of the Etna Line and devoid of reinforcements, elected, over Guzzoni's protests, to shorten his defences along a new line running from Randazzo to Cape Orlando on the north coast.

During the night of 5/6 August the Germans began abandoning their positions all across the Etna/San Fratello Line. In the east, the Hermann Goering had voluntarily begun its withdrawal from Catania on 4 August. The following morning the British entered the city to the welcoming cheers of a populace growing desperately short of food.* Under the cover of darkness, 15th Panzer Grenadier slipped away unseen from Troina. While the German troops took up new positions around Cesarò, their heavy weapons and equipment kept right on moving towards Messina and evacuation to Italy. By the morning of 6 August the rearguard elements had left Troina and its mountain strongpoints and at noon the first of Allen's troops entered the abandoned and destroyed town of Troina. Few of Troina's population of 12,000 had remained. The grisly scene that greeted the Americans is described by an American correspondent:

> . . . a ghostly old woman lying amid crumbling plaster and shattered timber . . . stretched out her hands to us, stared out of sightless eyes, and moaned like the wind whining through pine trees. We went on to the church. Light was shining through a hole in the roof. Below it an unexploded 500-lb bomb lay on the floor. Some American soldier breathed heavily in my ear: 'God, that was a miracle.'. . . In the mayor's office we found a few of the living wounded that our soldiers had pulled out of the wreckage. On a wooden bench lay the thin form of a girl about ten years old. Her black hair was streaked with gray powder

---

* The British arrived to find considerable looting in Catania. The brigadier in charge was formally greeted at police headquarters by a *carabinieri* officer who turned out to be a former landscape gardener from San Francisco. (*Invasion Diary*, op. cit., p. 63.)

plaster. One of her legs was completely wrapped in bandages which our company had placed there. In her two hands she clutched a cracker which a soldier had given her. She didn't move but only stared at the ceiling.

On another bench sat a boy about 13, naked save for a pair of drawers. Over his body were red scars where he'd been burned. Our medics had no salve for burns with them, so the boy sat there, shivering from head to foot; and in great pain. For a long while he remained silent, but finally his lips began to tremble, and his body shook with great sobs . . .

[Lieutenant Colonel Charles P.] Horner was standing by the door with a grim expression on his face. 'I never wanted to capture a town more than this in my life. But now. . . .' He made a helpless gesture.[1]

What had begun under great optimism had taken six days of savage combat against a desperate and skilful enemy who had launched twenty-four counterattacks against 1st Division units. The day after, the exhausted units of the 1st Division were relieved by Manton Eddy's 9th Division. Troina fell the same day that Terry Allen was relieved of his command under circumstances that remain controversial to this day.

The relief of Terry Allen came during the height of the battle for Troina with sudden and traumatic impact. This action was the unhappy culmination of a story that had begun in May when Eisenhower told Patton he was considering recommending Allen for a corps command in the United States. Patton posed no objections except to insist that he keep Allen and the 1st Division for HUSKY, rather than the untested 36th Division. Allen, however, wanted no part of any so-called promotion that would take him away from his beloved 'Big Red One' and submitted a formal written request to Eisenhower to retain command of the 1st Division in preference to a corps command. Patton strongly concurred, stressing the urgent need for his considerable experience as a combat commander.[2]

No more was heard of the matter and it was tacitly understood by Patton that Allen would retain command until a suitably

[1] Jack Belden in *Time*, 23 August 1943.
[2] Letter of 16 May 1943, Allen–Patton–Eisenhower, Patton Papers and Blumenson, *The Patton Papers*, Vol. II, op. cit., p. 251.

appropriate time when a changeover would have no impact on either the division or the outcome of the campaign. No one had even been privately mentioned as a possible replacement until the sudden availability of Huebner, after his dismissal by Alexander on 25 July, led Patton to despatch Lucas to Algiers to deliver by hand a letter to Eisenhower recommending the replacement of both Allen and Roosevelt with Huebner and Colonel Willard G. Wyman. Lucas's diary records a meeting with Eisenhower on 28 July during which he presented the Allied commander with Patton's letter. '. . . Patton wanted Huebner to command the division and, as I told Ike, would take anyone he wanted to send as an assistant. Ike agreed . . . Terry's relief is to be "without prejudice" and I hope he will be given a command at home. The boy is tired.'[1] The same day Eisenhower despatched an 'eyes only' cable to Marshall in which he specified that Allen's removal was 'due to nothing else but weariness, occasioned by long and intensive efforts on the various battlefields of this theater'.[2]

Patton made a point of discussing the matter personally with Eisenhower during the latter's visit to Palermo the next day, 29 July. 'I got Ike's permission to relieve both Allen and Roosevelt . . . on the theory of rotation of command.' Although AFHQ had already replied, 'Allen to be relieved without prejudice and returned to the US for an equivalent command', Patton was troubled that this signal 'made no similar statement with respect to Roosevelt, so left the impression that he was relieved with prejudice. *In my telegram I specifically said that unless they could both be relieved without prejudice I would not ask for their relief.*'[3] (Author's italics.)

Orders were issued for the changeover but no date was specified. It is fair to assume that both Bradley and Patton considered the capture of Troina as a suitable moment. At this point the undertaking became badly bungled. Apparently the order was erroneously placed into administrative channels and routinely sent

[1] Lucas Diary, 28 July 1943.

[2] Cable, # W-5922, AFHQ–War Department, 28 July 1943, copy in Butcher Diary.

[3] Patton Diary, 29 July 1943. To be relieved for 'prejudice' was and still is referred to as 'the kiss of death' to one's military career, and the ultimate transgression. Patton was determined that this fate should not befall Terry Allen. Writing to a friend he said: '. . . as an old cavalryman you know that a horse can be raced too much and the time comes when he has to be turned out to grass, after which he is as good as ever. That is what is happening to Terry now.' (Letter to Lieutenant General J. G. Harbord, 22 October 1943, Patton Papers.)

to the 1st Division in the daily pouch from II Corps, arriving at the CP at the apex of the Troina battle. A clerk handed the order to the shocked and dismayed Chief of Staff, Colonel Stanhope B. Mason, who immediately sought the counsel of Porter. The problem the two officers pondered was whether or not to inform Allen at once when his full attention was required for the capture of Troina or wait until the battle was over. In spite of the appalling timing it was decided Allen must be told at once, for the routine nature of the order's transmission meant that many others who should not have seen it knew of its existence. For Allen to have learned of it from such a source was unthinkable.

Although he had long expected to lose the 1st Division, Allen was nevertheless shocked and turned helplessly to Porter and asked, 'Bob, what do I do with this?' When he telephoned Bradley the II Corps commander lamely replied that he had had the orders for some time and was awaiting a time when the 1st Division was out of the line before making the changeover. There had been a foul-up when the orders were sent via regular Adjutant General channels, he said. Then, 'Carry on, we'll sort this out later.'[1] Years later Allen recalled that Patton had called him and asked if the order had arrived for his relief. When Allen replied, 'Yes', Patton said, 'Well, you're not relieved . . . I say you're not relieved until you've taken Troina and the 1st Division has completed its job in Sicily.'[2]

What was the reason for Terry Allen's relief and who was responsible? Over the years there has been a plethora of theories. Allen himself believed the orders for his relief had come from Washington, while others believe the initiative came from AFHQ, specifically Bedell Smith, who, it is alleged, unduly influenced Eisenhower to get rid of Allen because of the 1st Division incidents in North Africa. Some have singled out Bradley. The case against Bedell Smith, although plausible on the surface, lacks substance even though shortly after the war he uttered some very uncomplimentary remarks to the effect that Allen had 'ruined' the 1st Division. When he heard of them Allen immediately penned an angry letter to both Bedell Smith and Eisenhower. Bedell Smith

---

[1] Porter interview. Given the sequence of events it is doubtful if Bradley had the order for Allen's relief more than a day or two prior to its untimely despatch to the 1st Division.

[2] Profile of Terry Allen, USAMHI.

does not seem to have replied but Eisenhower did and attempted to smooth over the discord by diplomacy.[1]

Shortly after his relief, talk began to circulate among the war correspondents that Allen had been relieved for inefficiency and sent home as a disciplinary measure. In response to an informal War Department query, Eisenhower called these rumours 'a terrible unjustice to General Allen . . . The answer to this one is that I will be glad to have General Allen again as a division commander.'[2] Later, as the Allied Supreme Commander in Northwest Europe, Eisenhower personally approved the hiring and firing of all his (American) division commanders. One who served with distinction in the European Theater of Operations was Terry Allen.

There is no evidence that Allen's relief was instigated either by Bedell Smith or as a result of Eisenhower's displeasure over his personal conduct or that of the 1st Division. Eisenhower's original letter to Patton about replacing Allen was sent about 13 May, when the 1st Division was still in Tunisia, and well before the Oran incidents which occurred later that month.

The decision to replace Allen came from Eisenhower and his initiative came about as a result of his visit to II Corps on 7 May:

> At the First Division headquarters General Terry Allen was roused from a sleep in mid-afternoon to tell his story to the General. Allen had been out most of the night on his duties. Obviously he was very tired. His discussion of the situation was given in monosyllabic monotone. Said some of his companies were reduced to the size of platoons, casualties amongst the combat troops having been high. His men were tired and, without saying so explicitly, his story begged for relief. Ike told him the British had chased Rommel from El Alamein to the Mareth Line and had 'taken it'. Allen had countered that in the World War his division had been proceeding for several weeks, attacking each day. As I heard Allen's story, and knowing of the fine work of the 1st Division I thought how much better it would have been if Allen had been thoroughly cheerful, buoyant and aggressive, as such an attitude would have been more in keeping with the fine performance of his Division and of himself.[3]

[1] Letters, Allen–Eisenhower, 19 August 1947, and Eisenhower–Allen, 23 August 1947, Eisenhower Papers.

[2] Letter, Eisenhower–General Alexander D. Surles, War Department, 14 December 1943, *The Eisenhower Papers*, Vol. III, op. cit., p. 1596.

[3] Butcher Diary, entry of 10 May 1943; and *The Eisenhower Papers*, Vol. V, p. 116, appointment schedule for 7 May 1943. Butcher's Diary entry for 2 August (describing

Terry Allen's relief would have been far less controversial had it not been for Bradley who later muddied the waters by claiming full credit. In his 1951 memoirs he stated emphatically, 'Early in the Sicily campaign I had made up my mind to relieve Terry Allen at its conclusion. This relief was not to be a reprimand for ineptness or for ineffective command. For in Sicily as in Tunisia the 1st Division had set the pace for the ground campaign. Yet I was convinced, as indeed I still am, that Terry's relief had become essential to the long-term welfare of the division.'[1] In Bradley's opinion both the division and its commanders, Allen and Roosevelt, had become too temperamental and disdainful of both discipline and higher command, with the result that the 1st Division 'believed itself to be the only division carrying its fair share of the war'. Bradley considered the retention of Roosevelt would be a disruptive and inhibiting influence to a new commander: 'Roosevelt had to go with Allen for he, too, had sinned by loving the division too much.'[2]

Bradley's version contradicts the evidence, as does his assertion that he personally called Allen and Roosevelt to his CP in Nicosia to break the news of their relief. In his account the two were stopped en route by a II Corps military policeman and ticketed for failing to wear their helmets in violation of uniform regulations.[3] Bradley's official biographer writes that during the battle for Troina, Bradley had made up his mind to relieve both officers, and that at its conclusion 'I relieved both Allen and Roosevelt, one of my most unpleasant duties of the war ... This controversial decision was mine and mine alone. Patton merely concurred.'[4] The diary of his aide, Chester Hanson, has nothing to say about the matter, and in his Commentaries Bradley says only that in Tunisia he had warned Patton that Allen's 'drinking and health were bad ... In Sicily, Patton said I was right about Terry. Mentioned it several times, thereafter asked Ike to relieve him ...'[5]

There is no doubt that Bradley was in favour of replacing Allen

---

[1] A Soldier's Story, op. cit., p. 154.   [2] Ibid., p. 155.   [3] Ibid., pp. 155–6.
[4] A General's Life, op. cit., p. 195. This statement is based on nearly identical remarks in A Soldier's Story, op. cit., p. 156.   [5] Bradley Commentaries.

Eisenhower's visit to Palermo on 29 July) notes that Allen's relief was without discredit for 'war weariness'. 'The First Division has been in more fighting than any other outfit in this operation and there is no doubt General Allen simply became fatigued to such a low level that he was unable to afford the inspiration and leadership, as well as the imagination and discipline that are necessary for a divisional commander.'

but he certainly could not have ordered his relief without Patton's approval. Possibly he believed it was his initiative which resulted in Allen's removal. Certainly his opinion of Allen and the 1st Division had worsened since the invasion. Porter believes one incident in particular prejudiced Bradley in Sicily. During the drive north after the fall of Enna, Porter asked his corps counterpart, Dickson, for permission to use a Seventh Army transportation unit to convey several infantry units that would have otherwise been required to undertake an unnecessary road march. Dickson said it was a good idea and Porter ought to co-ordinate the matter with the II Corps G-3. The G-3 approved and Allen later thanked Bradley who claimed he knew nothing about it. When queried by Bradley, the G-3 feigned ignorance and Allen was (unfairly) censured by an angry Bradley for deliberately evading the chain of command.[1]

Allen later stated that he believed Bradley had initiated the request for his removal, later confirmed by Washington. He certainly bore Patton no ill will. Several letters to Patton and Patton's wife exhibit no traces of resentment. 'I guess I must have been a pain in the neck at times but frankly it was a real pleasure to serve under your command,' he wrote to Patton. To Beatrice Patton went a long letter that ended with his request that she 'Please give George my best and tell the old buzzard that it was a pleasure to have been with him.'[2] Clearly, these are not the words of an embittered man.

The arrival of Major General Clarence R. Huebner came as a considerable shock to the men of the 1st Division. Terry Allen's style of leadership had made him something of a father figure to his men. As one of his officers has observed, 'His biggest strength was instilling in our soldiers that they were the greatest.'[3] While Brigadier General Teddy Roosevelt lacked Allen's tactical genius, he nevertheless had been an inspirational type of leader and was

[1] Porter interview. Porter notes that another point of conflict with II Corps was the inability of the 1st Division staff properly to document recommendations for awards and decorations which the II Corps staff would frequently reject, and which in turn led to complaints by Allen to Bradley. Another sore point was logistics. The division Quartermaster was something of an artist at stockpiling supplies and filling requirements by bartering. The 1st Division's method of doing business irritated Bradley who believed strongly in using, not abusing the Army supply system.

[2] Letters of 13 August and 8 October, Allen–Patton, and letter of 8 October, Allen–Beatrice Patton, Patton Papers.

[3] Letter, Colonel Kenneth P. Lord–author, 6 December 1984. Lord was an assistant G-3 in Sicily.

warmly respected by the troops. Huebner and his new assistant, Wyman, signalled a new direction for the 1st Division.*

Within hours of assuming command Huebner began to make his presence felt. He understood he had inherited a division that had been through two difficult campaigns, was feeling sorry for itself and in the eyes of his superiors lacked discipline. Huebner's methods of restoring the division to a high standard came like cold rain as he began to shake its foundations from top to bottom. The first to feel this stern new broom was the 26th Infantry Regiment which Bradley later singled out as the most undisciplined in the division.[1] The day he took over command, he summoned Porter and told him, 'Porter, I want you to have targets and paste in the 26 Infantry area by 1600 hours for target practice.' Porter protested that the regiment had been in the thick of the battle for Troina and had been out of the line for less than twenty-four hours. Huebner was unimpressed, and that afternoon the 26th Regiment began target practice on a makeshift range which only hours earlier had been a battlefield. Along with the rest of the division they found themselves not only taking target practice but also engaging in such military fundamentals as close order drill. Howls of protest were heard and commanders cursed and openly grumbled, 'Crissake, who is this man who comes in from the States to show us how to march when we've been fighting on these damn hills?'[2]

It took Huebner some months before his men ceased vilifying

---

[1] Bradley Commentaries.   [2] Ibid.

* Major General Clarence Huebner was another maverick and an officer even more outspoken than his predecessor. A career soldier since 1910, he was reared on the plains of Kansas and became an officer through competitive examination in 1916. In his six years of enlisted service he had risen from private to master sergeant, an amazing feat in the small peacetime Army. After a detour to fight on the Mexican border where he barely escaped death from a 37 mm cannon shell that struck him in the armpit, Huebner served in France in 1918 with the 1st Division. During the summer of 1918, First Lieutenant Huebner leapt from command of an infantry company to the grade of lieutenant colonel and command of the 28th Infantry Regiment. Along the way he again escaped death when his helmet saved a bullet between the eyes. By war's end he had been decorated with two DSCs, a Silver Star, two Purple Hearts, the Croix de Guerre and the Distinguished Service Medal, a high decoration normally given only to generals. (Denno, 'Allen and Huebner', op. cit.)

Known throughout the Army as a no-nonsense disciplinarian and a superb teacher, Huebner deeply resented the British and what he viewed as their patronizing attitude towards the US Army. His selection by Eisenhower to serve on Alexander's staff came about because Huebner was the only officer available at the time. His bluntness was typified by his dismissal of Montgomery as a 'really obnoxious bastard'. His attitude to Churchill was equally low: 'I didn't much care for him. He was arrogant, supercilious and seemed to think of Americans as colonials.' (Quoted in *Washington, D.C.*, April 1969.) Diplomacy and tact were never Huebner's strong suit and his sacking by Alexander proved a blessing in disguise which led to his selection to replace Terry Allen.

him and began to realize the changes he had wrought in the 1st Division. What he had done was to whip the division back into shape by imposing tight discipline and enforcing a return to the fundamental elements of training, saluting, uniforms, drill and marksmanship. He said, 'This division is sorry for itself and needs someone to hate – me! They need someone to bring them together. I'm their SOB.' It was, observes Porter, his very effective way of curing their ills.[1] Gradually this tough new commander earned their respect and confidence, a sign of which was his new nickname of 'Coach', for his personal attention to marksmanship training.[*] Ten months later Huebner's leadership passed the sternest test of all when the 'Big Red One' stormed ashore at Omaha Beach on 6 June 1944.

Both officers in their own distinctive ways led the 1st Division through eight major campaigns that began in Algeria in November 1942 and ended in May 1945 in Czechoslovakia. Among veterans of the 'Big Red One', the relief of Terry Allen is still viewed with mixed emotions even though the evidence clearly suggests that it came about as a result of the genuine belief it was time for a change. Eisenhower was not alone in his observation that Allen was a tired man, due in no small part to a serious dental problem that ought to have been taken care of in the United States and which plagued him constantly, necessitating large doses of aspirin and interfering with his ability to rest properly.

While the merits of Terry Allen's relief will likely remain controversial, what is indisputable is that it was handled in an inept manner that did no credit to any of the senior American commanders in Sicily. Equally undeniable was the bitter-sweet irony of the timing of his relief, for the 9 August edition of *Time* featured a portrait of Terry Allen on its cover. Inside, a full-length article entitled 'Allen and His Men' noted that upon Allen and the 1st Division 'there had fallen a special mark of war and history . . . These inseparable reputations – the reputation of the division and that of its commander – are the first of their kind to be made and publicly recognized in the US Army of World War II.'[2]

[1] Porter interview. Huebner had told one of his officers his prescription for successful command: 'When you take over a command, you can start off being an SOB and later become a good guy. But you can never start off being a good guy and later become an SOB.'

[2] *Time*, 9 August 1943.

[*] Huebner soon discovered that one of the division's ills was a tendency to depend too heavily on supporting fire and too little on their own weapons, a problem that was found to be common throughout the Army.

CHAPTER 29

Days of Triumph and Folly

I was a damned fool.
PATTON

The final two weeks of the Sicily campaign were a time of great triumph and adversity for Patton whose impetuous behaviour nearly brought ruin to his military career at the very moment when his star was rising as the conqueror of Sicily. A month earlier he had been playing second fiddle to Montgomery; now his career was about to reach its zenith. Yet in the space of a few moments his unfortunate tendency to self-destruct not only occurred at the very moment when he was on the verge of winning the 'race' against Eighth Army to Messina, but also marked the nadir of his relations with Omar Bradley.

Bradley had never been a great admirer of Patton. On the contrary, by virtue of their temperaments, training and lifestyles it was inevitable that Bradley would eventually be at loggerheads with Patton. Although Bradley seems to have concealed his true feelings masterfully in his official contacts with Patton, privately he had grown increasingly disenchanted with what he considered was meddling in the operations of II Corps. Beneath the school-masterish public façade, Bradley was a stickler for military protocol and was offended when its unwritten rules were violated. Since the invasion Bradley had grown critical of Patton's direction of the American ground effort. He was incensed to learn that Patton had criticized him to Eisenhower for allegedly not being aggressive enough at Gela.* Patton's meek acceptance of Alexander's order to cede Route 124 to Montgomery, and Bradley's belief that the Palermo operation was a monumental waste of time,

* Patton's remarks came as a direct result of Bradley's hostile reaction to Patton's orders to Terry Allen during the Gela counterattack on 11 July. Patton had ordered the 16th Regiment to push inland, countermanding Bradley's earlier order to close a gap between the 1st and 45th Divisions east of Gela.

further strengthened his conviction that Patton was turning out to be a poor commander.[1]

Bradley disliked Patton personally and professionally. Despite the fact that he was to become famous as a result of articles written by correspondent Ernie Pyle,* Bradley was uncomfortable with the outward trappings that accompany senior rank. The carnival atmosphere of Patton's movements bothered Bradley: 'He steamed about with great convoys of cars and great squads of cameramen. Became unpopular with the troops.'[2] Patton's profanity and theatrics irritated Bradley who believed Palermo, and now the fixation with Messina, were thinly disguised ploys for headlines and personal glory at the expense of his troops.

While he has candidly admitted he was just as anxious as Patton to seize Messina ahead of the British, Bradley deeply resented Patton's high-handed interference: 'To George, tactics was simply a process of bulling ahead. He never seemed to think out a campaign. Seldom made a careful estimate of the situation. I thought him a shallow commander.' Bradley had his hands full guiding the difficult drive by II Corps towards Messina and, while he and Patton were in general agreement that II Corps should undertake small amphibious raids behind enemy lines, he was annoyed by the constant reminders that he must gain Messina at all costs. One day the two conferred on the north coastal road and after Bradley explained his strategy for dislodging the Germans, Patton 'in a grandiose fashion said "I want you to get into Messina just as fast as you can. I don't want you to waste time on these maneuvers even if you've got to spend men to do it. I want to beat Monty into Messina." I was very much shocked, and replied, "I will take every step I can to get there as soon as I can." To me the quickest way was through maneuver and that I continued to do.'[3]

Patton made no attempt to interfere in the first amphibious 'end-run' worked out by Bradley and Truscott. Using Navy LSTs based in Palermo, Truscott mounted a reinforced battalion – Task

---

[1] Bradley Commentaries.

[2] Commentaries. Bradley's criticism of Patton was grudgingly moderated by the admission that later (in Northwest Europe) Patton 'had a pretty good feeling of what the enemy could do and could not do. Had this instinct developed to a higher degree than any commander I knew. [But] during the Sicily planning George seldom if ever got into the details of the planning.'

[3] Ibid.

* It was Pyle who coined the nickname by which Bradley became a household name: 'The GI General.'

Force Bernard* – which landed behind the San Fratello Line at
Sant' Agata. Major General Walter Fries had established in the
San Fratello ridgeline a defensive position fully as formidable as
those around Troina, and the 29th Panzer Grenadier Division had
repelled one 3d Division attack after another. Even though the
45th Division had been replaced by the more experienced 3d
Division, Truscott's troops encountered stubborn resistance as the
Germans made such effective use of the terrain and a myriad of
minefields† that even naval gunfire and the use of smoke against
their positions failed to help. In one grim day the 15th Infantry
took 103 casualties without gaining any ground.[1] In terrain that
was virtually impassable to vehicles except along the coastal
highway, the American infantryman faced daily the clever German defences, searing heat and thick dust that quickly sapped the
energy of even the fittest of men. The lasting memory of Lieutenant
Colonel Ben Harrell was 'how damn tired we got just going day
after day'.[2]

Truscott elected an 'end-run' in conjunction with an all-out
attack by all three of his infantry regiments which, after a furious
fight, finally broke the back of the German defences around Mt
San Fratello. Bernard's amphibious task force landed virtually

[1] *Sicily*, op. cit., p. 357. It was during the difficult drive on Messina that the 3d Division
made full use of mule and horse transport. Some had been brought from North Africa and
had been more seasick than their handlers, and the remainder had been acquired in Sicily.
Ex-cavalry officer Truscott formed several Provisional pack-train troops for the coastal
operation. 'All told we were to use more than 400 mules and 100 horses during this advance.
We did not always employ them economically and efficiently, for we lacked trained
personnel and had to improvise much equipment. Nevertheless, without these Provisional
units, the drive for Messina would have been much slower and far more costly.' (*Command
Missions*, p. 230.) On numerous occasions during this drive Patton was heard to deplore the
absence of horse units and pack artillery. When his former cavalry commander, Major
General Kenyon A. Joyce, visited him, Truscott saluted and in his best military manner
reported, 'Sir, I have the honor to report that I have a mounted detachment of 600 in this
infantry division.' (Unpublished manuscript of Major General Kenyon A. Joyce, USAMHI.)

[2] Interview of General Ben Harrell, 17 December 1971, Oral History Collection,
USAMHI. Harrell was G-3 of the 3d Division in Sicily. In his memoirs, Truscott recalls that,
'In ordinary times, the distance to Messina would be a few hours drive of great scenic beauty.
Now it was an area in which a determined enemy had every advantage for defense and
delay.' (*Command Missions*, p. 230.)

* Task Force Bernard was Lieutenant Colonel Lyle W. Bernard's 2d Battalion, 30th
Infantry, supported by two artillery batteries, a tank platoon and a combat engineer
platoon.

† The use of mines continued to be the most devilishly effective German tactic in Sicily.
Seemingly possessed of an inexhaustible supply, the Germans planted mines in defence of
their positions and along the Allied route of march as they retreated across Sicily. As Bradley
notes, not only were mines planted indiscriminately all over Sicily but the iron content of the
lava and rock made detection difficult. Enough mines were left to endanger the population
for many years to come.

unopposed but soon afterwards was obliged to beat off a strong
enemy counterattack that cost the Germans dearly.*

The second amphibious operation took place twenty-five miles
further east at Brolo and was the object of bitter American controversy. After being forced from the San Fratello Line, the 29th
Panzer Grenadier established new defences along the Zappula
River in the Cape Orlando peninsula. By this time Patton was
showing increasing signs of frustration at what he considered was
a sluggish advance by II Corps and kept up constant pressure on
his subordinate commanders to win the race for Messina. The
prospect of another debilitating and costly San Fratello battle led
Patton on 10 August to summon Bradley and order Bernard's task
force to land at Brolo the following morning. The operation was
planned in conjunction with a flank attack against the main German positions around the village of Naso. Originally scheduled for
10 August, the landing was delayed when a Luftwaffe air attack
sank one of the LSTs. 'Now Patton was in no mood for another
postponement, and he left no doubt in Bradley's mind of this
fact.'[1]

Truscott was unable to position the 15th Infantry and his supporting artillery in time to launch the attack on Naso and wanted a
24-hour postponement. He had been told that control of the
operation was entirely his, including the timing, but when General
Keyes visited his CP the night of 10 August, Truscott was warned
that Patton was unlikely to approve any further postponement for
any reason, especially since there would be correspondents
accompanying the task force. According to Keyes, Patton wanted
no criticism resulting from another delay. Both generals spoke on
the telephone with Bradley who emphatically approved a postponement. Keyes then called Patton and the result was explosive.
As Truscott relates:

> An hour later, General Patton came storming into my Command
> Post giving everybody hell from the Military Police at the ent-
> rance right on through until he came to me. He was screamingly
> angry as only he could be. 'Goddammit, Lucian, what's the
> matter with you? Are you afraid to fight?' I bristled right back:
> 'General, you know that's ridiculous and insulting. You have
> ordered the operation and it is now loading. If you don't think I
> can carry out orders, you can give the Division to anyone you

[1] *Sicily*, op. cit., p. 389.
* 250 killed, 100 POWs and numerous tanks and vehicles disabled or destroyed.

please. But I will tell you one thing, you will not find anyone who can carry out orders they do not approve as well as I can.'

General Patton changed instantly, the anger all gone. Throwing his arm about my shoulder he said, 'Dammit Lucian, I know that. Come on, let's have a drink – of your liquor.' We did.[1]

Patton recorded his version of the stormy confrontation with his long-time friend:

> I got to the command post, 3d Division at 2045 ... Truscott was walking up and down holding a map and looking futile. I said, 'General Truscott, if your conscience will not let you conduct this operation I will relieve you and put someone in command who will.' He replied, 'General, it is your privilege to reduce me whenever you want to.' I said, 'I don't want to. I got you your DSM and recommended you for a Major General, but your own ability really gained both honors. You are too old an athlete to believe it is possible to postpone a match.' He said, 'You are an old enough athlete to know that sometimes they are postponed.' I said, 'This one won't be. The ships have already started.' Truscott replied, 'This is a war of defile and there is a bottleneck delaying me in getting my guns up to support the infantry. They – the infantry – will be too far west to help the landing.' I said, 'Remember Frederick the Great: *L'audace, l'audace, toujours l'audace*! I know you will win and if there is a bottleneck you should be there and not here.'[2]

Patton then called Bradley to state the operation would go in as scheduled and he accepted full responsibility for failure. He then strode from Truscott's CP and was not seen again during the battle for Brolo. 'I am not going to the front today,' he wrote, 'as I feel it would show a lack of confidence in Truscott, and it is necessary to maintain the self-respect of generals in order to get the best out of them.'[3] Nor did Patton have more than momentary regrets over the incident with Truscott: 'I may have been bull-headed but I truly feel that I did my exact and full duty.'[4]

The LSTs landed Bernard's 650-man force undetected in the early morning hours of a day that Truscott said 'I will never forget'. As the American force was crossing Route 113 a chance

[1] *Command Missions*, op. cit., p. 235.

[2] Patton Diary, 10 August 1943. The Naval representative of Admiral L. A. Davidson's supporting task force ('General Patton's Navy') also favoured postponement because the operation had begun an hour late. (See also Morison, *Sicily–Salerno–Anzio*, op. cit., Chapter X.)

[3] Diary, 11 August 1943.

[4] Ibid., 10 August 1943.

encounter with a passing German half-track led to the detection of the landing and a swift and violent German reaction to this grave threat to their rear. Bernard's objective was nearby Mt Cipolla which overlooked Brolo and controlled the coastal highway from Cape Orlando to Brolo where it paralleled a four-mile strip of coastal plain. The Americans found no enemy forces on Mt Cipolla but by mid-morning they were beating off the first of many counterattacks. By noon, with the nearest 3d Division unit still some miles away, the situation quickly became extremely grave. As Truscott restlessly prowled the front urging his troops to break through to Bernard, a steady stream of messages arrived pleading for air and naval support. The navy, believing their job done, had returned to Palermo only to be urgently recalled to help break up the German counterattacks. At 1340 came this message: ENEMY COUNTERATTACKING FIERCELY. DO SOMETHING.[1] The naval task force arrived off Brolo at 1400 and delivered welcome supporting fire. The GIs ashore began to cheer. One said, 'The goddam navy. The good old navy. Jesus, there ain't nothin' like navy guns.'[2] Again the navy left, but twice more were recalled to help break up counterattacks. In late afternoon a furious air–sea battle erupted when eight *Focke-Wulf* 190s attacked the fleet and all but one were shot down. Less helpful was the USAAF whose errant bombs knocked out the battalion CP and four artillery pieces.[3] Throughout the afternoon of 11 August there was an air of desperation as the 3d Division fought to relieve their beleaguered comrades. They were unsuccessful on 11 August and all Truscott could do was to employ his attached 155 mm 'Long Toms' which fired at their maximum 26,000-yard range, just barely able to reach Brolo.

The landings had imperilled the 29th Panzer Grenadier's escape route but in spite of heavy American artillery fire, Fries was able to launch one attack after another against Task Force Bernard which lacked the strength to prevent a successful German withdrawal. When contact was finally established early the next morning with their sister 1st Battalion, the 29th Panzer Grenadier Division was long gone. Losses on both sides were heavy. Task Force Bernard

---

[1] *Command Missions*, op. cit., p. 238.

[2] *Time* correspondent Jack Belden in *Still Time To Die*, New York (reprint edition), 1975, p. 281. Belden had been at Troina several days earlier and was one of the correspondents permitted to accompany Task Force Bernard at Brolo.

[3] Morison, *Sicily–Salerno–Anzio*, op. cit., pp. 203–5.

lost 171 men, and most of the supporting tanks and artillery, while German losses were equally severe.* One of the first to greet Bernard when he descended from the mountain was Truscott, 'Thank God, Bernard, for I am certainly glad to see you.' Bernard's reply was a heartfelt 'General, you just don't know how glad I am to see you'.[1]

What did the Brolo operation accomplish? According to the official historians, very little except for compelling Fries to abandon the Naso positions a full day ahead of the German timetable. A larger, regimental combat-team-sized force would undoubtedly have succeeded in trapping 29th Panzer Grenadier at Brolo, thus collapsing the northern anchor of Hube's defences. The effects on other German units would have been equally calamitous, particularly to Rodt's 15th Panzer Grenadier Division, whose escape route into Messina would have been severed and the unsatisfactory ending to the Sicily campaign might have been averted[2]

There was considerable bitterness against Patton in II Corps. Bradley was furious and later wrote that Patton's decision had left him 'more exasperated than I have ever been', but 'as a subordinate commander of Patton's I had no alternative but to comply with his orders'.[3] Equally unimpressed by the Brolo landings was the German naval commander for Italy, Admiral Friedrich Ruge. 'He was unable to understand why the Allies with their overwhelming sea power, had not done this sort of thing earlier, more often, and on a bigger scale.'[4] Despite the heavy losses and the acrimony over Patton's refusal to agree to further delay, the real mistake at Brolo was not his decision but his failure to perceive that a larger, more co-ordinated operation would have garnered a prize worthy of the effort. Nor was Brolo the last American amphibious operation. Several days later Patton had formed another task force, this time utilizing 157th RCT of the 45th Division which was to land on the beaches east of Cape Milazzo. Again, Truscott protested to Keyes, this time for the simple reason that the 3d Division had already advanced *beyond* the landing site. Mindful of the imbroglio over Brolo neither Keyes nor Truscott were willing to arouse Patton again, and the operation took place

---

[1] Quoted in *Command Missions*, op. cit., p. 240.
[2] *Sicily*, op. cit., p. 405.   [3] *A Soldier's Story*, op. cit., p. 158.
[4] *Sicily-Salerno-Anzio*, op. cit., p. 205. Admiral Morison fully agreed with the German assessment which is more fully discussed in the Epilogue.
* American losses were 41 killed, 78 wounded and 58 missing. (See Taggert, p. 71.)

with a predictably ludicrous ending when members of Truscott's staff greeted the first wave on the beach.[1]

The Brolo controversy did not inhibit Patton who continued to prod his subordinate commanders to push on to Messina, much to their outrage and Bradley's contempt. Calling him impetuous and utterly unpredictable, Bradley's embitterment was still palpable after the war: 'I disliked the way he worked, upset tactical plans, interfered in my orders. His stubbornness on amphibious operations, parade plans into Messina sickened me and soured me on Patton. We learned how not to behave from Patton's Seventh Army.'[2] Brolo left a legacy of bitterness among others, including Truscott. Although he was too good a soldier ever publicly to criticize Patton (even after his death), there is little doubt that the confrontation on 10 August severely strained their long friendship.

A week before Brolo there began a chain of events that very nearly undid the great destiny Patton had predicted for himself. August 3 began auspiciously when Patton learned that Eisenhower was to award him the DSC for 'extraordinary heroism' on 11 July at Gela.* That afternoon Patton stopped off en route to II Corps to visit the 15th Evacuation Hospital outside Nicosia. Inside were many newly arrived wounded, most of them 1st Division troops. Scenes of battle-wounded always moved Patton and this occasion

[1] *Command Missions*, op. cit., pp. 242–3, and *Sicily*, op. cit., pp. 413–15. Patton was fully aware that the 157th RCT landing might accomplish little but apparently considered their presence might help the 3d Division capture Messina more quickly. Once again, Bradley's protests had failed to sway Patton.

[2] Bradley Commentaries. Bradley was equally critical of Patton's staff and what Colonel Dickson sarcastically called 'that great silence we call Army'. Lucas was told Seventh Army never maintained telephone lines into II Corps (an established military doctrine) and that no Army staff officer ever visited him during the campaign. (Lucas Diary, 14 August 1943.) Bradley was equally critical of Seventh Army's failure to maintain adequate stocks of ammunition in their rear depots. The problem grew critical before the Troina battle when the artillery was immobilized for twenty-four hours while every available truck was sent clear back to Gela to pick up ammunition. According to Bradley, the ammunition dump at Caltanissetta contained only twenty-five rounds. (Commentaries.) Although Lucas defended him, Bradley was adamant that Patton's known dislike of detail – particularly supply matters – contributed to the breakdown of essential supplies at a critical moment in the campaign. 'We were always short on supply, largely because Seventh Army showed a complete lack of understanding of the fundamentals of supply.' (In British and US military doctrine the corps is strictly a tactical command, responsible for orchestrating the combat operations of a [flexible] number of divisions and other attached units. Supply, transport and communications are an Army responsibility.)

* The initiative for this decoration came from Lucas who prepared and delivered the recommended citation to Eisenhower.

was no exception. Then he encountered Private Charles H. Kuhl of Co L, 26th Infantry Regiment (1st Division) who evinced no visible wounds. Patton asked him why he was being admitted and the soldier replied he was not wounded, 'I guess I can't take it.' This reply brought instant rage to Patton who swore at Kuhl, called him a coward and ordered him out of the tent. When the frightened soldier continued to sit motionless at attention Patton grew even more irate and, according to an eyewitness, 'slapped his face with a glove, raised him to his feet by the collar of his shirt and pushed him out of the tent with a final "kick in the rear" '.[1] That night Patton noted in his diary that he had met 'the only arrant coward I have ever seen in this Army ... Companies should deal with such men, and if they shirk their duty, they should be tried for cowardice and shot.'[2]

The *enfant terrible* surfaced again a week later on 10 August when he arrived unannounced at the 93d Evacuation Hospital. According to his diary he 'saw another alleged nervous patient – really a coward. I told the doctor to return him to his company and he began to cry so I cursed him well and he shut up. I may have saved his soul if he had one.'[3]

First-hand accounts have recorded a far grimmer scene. This is what occurred. In the Receiving Ward, Patton began talking with each soldier about his wounds, offering small talk and words of encouragement. The fourth man he stopped to speak to was Private Paul G. Bennett, an artilleryman assigned to the 13th Field Artillery Brigade who was shivering on a cot. In response to Patton's query as to what his problem was, Bennett replied, 'It's my nerves.' 'What did you say?' bellowed Patton, who believed there was no such thing as 'combat fatigue' and those who claimed to suffer from it were there only to shirk combat duty. 'It's my nerves, I can't stand the shelling any more,' Bennett sobbed. By now Patton was shaking with anger nearly as much as Bennett was

---

[1] Report of Colonel F. Y. Leaver, MC, CO, 15th Evacuation Hospital, 4 August 1943, Eisenhower Papers. Lucas accompanied Patton and recorded a scene of 'brave, hurt, bewildered boys. All but one ... [who] said he was nervous and couldn't take it. Anyone who knows him can realize what it would do to George. The ward sister was really nervous when he got through.' (Lucas Diary, 3 August 1943.) After the war Lucas commented that 'Patton slapped him on the cheek with his folded gloves and ordered him from the tent'. Kuhl was about to undergo treatment for the third time in Sicily for 'exhaustion' and was later diagnosed as 'high strung'. After the slapping incident his medical file indicated Kuhl was suffering from diarrhoea and mild malaria.

[2] Diary, 3 August 1943.   [3] Diary, 10 August 1943.

shaking with fright. 'Your nerves, Hell, you are just a goddamned coward, you yellow son of a bitch. Shut up that goddamned crying. I won't have these brave men here who have been shot seeing a yellow bastard sitting here crying.' He turned to the Receiving Officer, Major Charles B. Etter, and ordered him not to admit this 'yellow bastard'. 'You're a disgrace to the Army and you're going back to the front to fight, although that's too good for you. You ought to be lined up against a wall and shot. In fact, I ought to shoot you myself right now, God damn you!'

Patton then pulled his revolver from its holster and waved it in front of the terrified soldier's face. The tumult brought the hospital commander, Colonel Donald E. Currier, on the run. Patton turned on Currier and ordered, 'I want you to get that man out of here right away. I won't have these brave boys seeing such a bastard babied.' Patton then slapped the quivering Bennett across the face while continuing to curse him. Patton now turned to leave but seeing the distraught soldier crying he hastened back to his cot and hit Bennett a second time with such force that his helmet liner was knocked to the ground. The tumult brought other nurses and doctors to the Receiving Tent in time to witness the second slap.

As he continued his tour of the wards Patton continued to talk about Bennett, once choking back a sob. 'I can't help it, but it makes my blood boil to think of a yellow bastard being babied.' Before departing Patton turned to Colonel Currier and said, 'I meant what I said about getting that coward out of here. I won't have those cowardly bastards hanging around our hospitals. We'll probably have to shoot them some time anyway, or we'll raise a breed of morons.'[1]

The victim of Patton's second outburst was a twenty-one-year-old Regular Army soldier who had served in II Corps since March 1943. According to the official report, Bennett had exhibited extreme nervousness after a fellow soldier was wounded. Although nervous and distraught, Bennett apparently resisted evacuation and begged to stay with his unit, but was ordered to the 93d Evacuation Hospital by his battery surgeon.[2]

---

[1] This account of Patton's actions on 10 August is based on a composite of the official reports of investigation (Eisenhower Papers), Patton's Diary, the account of correspondent Demaree Bess of the *Saturday Evening Post*, *A Soldier's Story*, *A General's Life*, *Crusade in Europe* and *Sicily*, Chapter XXI.

[2] Report of Lieutenant Colonel Perrin H. Long, MC, submitted to the The Surgeon, North African Theater of Operations, US Army (NATOUSA), Eisenhower Papers.

Patton went directly from the 93 d Evacuation Hospital to the II Corps CP where he exuberantly recounted the incident to a horrified Bradley. 'Sorry to be late, Bradley. I stopped off at a hospital on the way up. There were a couple of malingerers there. I slapped one of them to make him mad and put some fight back in him.'[1] According to Bradley:

> He was bragging how he had treated this man to snap him out of being a coward. Thought that if he made the man mad, he would be mad enough to fight. That men were showing a yellow streak. He didn't agree with me that every man has a breaking point. Some are low, some are high. We call the low points cowards. To George anyone who didn't want to fight was a coward. He honestly thought he was putting fight into these men. He was pleased with what he had done. He was bragging about the incident. Next day the surgeon of that hospital handed a written report to [Brigadier General William B.] Kean [II Corps Chief of Staff]. Kean brought it to me ... After reading it, I told Kean to put it in a sealed envelope in the safe – only to be opened by Kean or me. I didn't forward the report to Ike because Patton was my Army commander – I couldn't go over Patton's head.[2]

Whatever his antipathy towards Patton, Bradley never hesitated in deciding that his conscience would not permit him to forward the report. But Bradley's failure to act did not prevent the report from being sent circuitously to Allied Force HQ. When the II Corps Surgeon, Colonel Richard T. Arnest, learned that Bradley would not act he took matters into his own hands and sent it through medical channels (which included Patton's own Seventh Army Surgeon) to the AFHQ Surgeon General, Brigadier General Frederick A. Blessé.

In the meantime, the latest incident quickly became common knowledge among American troops in Sicily. Alexander too soon learned of the incidents but wisely refused to involve himself in what he considered a purely American problem. During one meeting, Alexander said to Patton, 'George, this is a family affair.'[3]

There was considerable outrage at the 93 d Evacuation Hospital over Patton's behaviour. One of the nurses told her boyfriend, a young captain in Public Affairs, who ensured the news was immediately passed to the American correspondents attached to

---

[1] A Soldier's Story, op. cit., p. 160.
[2] Bradley Commentaries.
[3] Quoted in Patton, op. cit., p. 329.

Seventh Army.[1] Four reporters, Demaree Bess of the *Saturday Evening Post*, Merrill Mueller of NBC, Al Newman of *Newsweek* and John Daly of CBS interviewed Major Etter and others, but otherwise made no attempt to file the story. Amongst themselves they decided the matter must be brought to Eisenhower's attention. Three correspondents, Bess, Mueller and Quentin Reynolds of *Colliers*, flew to Algiers and on 19 August a written summary by Bess was presented to Bedell Smith. The Bess report noted that Patton had committed a court-martial offence by striking an enlisted man and ended by stating, 'I am making this report to General Eisenhower in the hope of getting conditions corrected before more damage has been done.'[2]

By this date Eisenhower was already aware that he had a potentially explosive problem on his hands. Two days earlier, on 17 August, General Blessé had presented him with Colonel Arnest's report. While shocked, Eisenhower did not immediately grasp the full implications of Patton's acts and merely remarked that he guessed it would be necessary to give Patton a 'jacking up'. This unwelcome news came the very day Patton had triumphantly entered Messina thus officially ending the Sicily campaign. Eisenhower's spirits were high and without further details he was inclined to believe that the report might be exaggerated. However, the more he reflected on it, the more Eisenhower realized the implications. He ordered Blessé to Sicily at once to investigate the incidents and also to carry a hand-written letter to Patton. 'If this thing ever gets out, they'll be howling for Patton's scalp, and that will be the end of Georgie's service in this war. I simply cannot let that happen. Patton is *indispensable* to the war effort – one of the guarantors of our victory.'[3]

The letter Eisenhower sent to Patton contained the strongest words of censure written to a senior American officer during World War II. In it Eisenhower expressed shock and dismay over the allegations of misconduct. 'I clearly understand that firm and drastic measures were at times necessary in order to secure the desired objectives. But this does not excuse brutality, abuse of the sick, nor exhibition of uncontrollable temper in front of subordinates.' If true, lamented Eisenhower, then 'I must so seriously

[1] Ibid., p. 334.
[2] Bess report, Eisenhower Papers.
[3] Quoted in Ambrose, *The Supreme Commander*, op. cit., p. 229.

question your good judgment and your self-discipline, as to raise
serious doubt in my mind as to your future usefulness.' Contrary
to popular belief, Eisenhower's letter did not require a personal
apology to every soldier and unit in Seventh Army, only that 'you
make in the form of apology or otherwise such personal amends to
the individuals concerned as may be within your power...'[1]

The arrival of the three correspondents reinforced Eisenhower's
awareness that he had a tiger by the tail. What they wanted was a
deal: in return for killing the story they wanted Patton fired.
Correspondent Quentin Reynolds summed up the strong anti-
Patton bias within the press corps when he told Eisenhower that
there were 'at least 50,000 American soldiers on Sicily who would
shoot Patton if they had the chance'. Another, John Daly,
thought Patton had gone temporarily crazy.[2]

Eisenhower had no intention of submitting to what was in
reality a thinly disguised attempt to get rid of Patton. Torn between loyalty to an old friend, the clear necessity that Patton must
be disciplined and the consequences of losing Patton altogether if
the incidents became public, Eisenhower unhesitatingly decided
that 'Patton should be saved for service in the great battles still
facing us in Europe, yet I had to devise ways and means to
minimize the harm that would certainly come from his impulsive
action and to assure myself that it was not repeated.'[3] He summoned the three reporters and made his case for Patton, explaining he had written a sharp letter of reprimand* and had ordered
him to apologize personally for his behaviour. While making it
clear that there would not be censorship if they elected to ignore
him, Eisenhower said he hoped that the correspondents would see
fit to keep the matter quiet in the interest of retaining a commander
whose leadership he considered vital. 'They were flatly told to use
their own judgment.'[4] More out of respect for Eisenhower than of
compassion for Patton, the reporters entered into a gentlemen's
agreement not to publicize the story. This decision has been cited

---

[1] Letter, Eisenhower–Patton, 17 August 1943, *The Eisenhower Papers*, Vol. II, op. cit.,
pp. 1340–1.
[2] *Sicily*, op. cit., p. 427; *Patton*, op. cit., p. 335; and Butcher Diary, 20 August 1943.
[3] *Crusade in Europe*, op. cit., p. 199; *Sicily*, op. cit., p. 431; and *The Supreme Commander*,
op. cit., p. 230.
[4] *Crusade in Europe*, op. cit., p. 200. Bedell Smith successfully implored the press pool in
Algiers to keep mum about the affair.
* The reprimand was unofficial and thus never became a part of Patton's official 201 file.

as the best illustration of what John Steinbeck characterized as 'that huge and gassy thing called the war effort'.[1]

Patton, who had been on top of the world after his victorious march on Messina, was severely jolted by the sudden fury emanating from Algiers. No sooner had General Blessé arrived with Eisenhower's letter of censure than a cable arrived from the Allied C-in-C, ordering him to meet General Lucas at the Palermo airfield on the afternoon of 20 August. Lucas would be carrying a personal message from Eisenhower and he was to listen closely to what Lucas had to tell him.*

Lucas had condoned the first slapping incident as Patton being Patton, believing that his impetuousness was the necessary companion to his intensive drive. But, after meeting Eisenhower the morning of 20 August, Lucas realized Patton was in deep trouble. 'Ike has written him a letter and wants me to go back this afternoon and do what I can. He is in danger this time, I am afraid ... It seems too bad that a really brilliant victory should be marred by such things as this.' Lucas's advice to Patton was 'kindly but firm': apologize to the soldiers he slapped; apologize personally to every division in Seventh Army and promise never to repeat the act.[2] It was on the advice of Lucas rather than Eisenhower's order that Patton made amends to his Army. The first step came on 22 August when several officers and nurses from the two evacuation hospitals were summoned to Palermo to hear Patton explain that during World War I a close friend had committed suicide owing to mental upset, but he believed this officer might have been saved if stringent measures had been taken. Although he had overstepped himself, his actions at each of the hospitals had been guided by a sincere belief that the two soldiers might have been shocked back into reality. One doctor has written 'the General stated that he had always regarded cases of "shell shock" as being most tragic ... He thought that if such men could at once be driven from their own

<hr>

[1] Phillip Knightley, *The First Casualty*, op. cit., p. 304.
[2] Lucas Diary, entries of 20–21 August 1943.
* Lucas enjoyed the full confidence of both generals and was the ideal officer to convey Eisenhower's extreme concern to Patton. He was also ordered to investigate the incidents from the soldiers' points of view. Eisenhower later sent two colonels from the NATOUSA Inspector General's office to investigate the incidents and a theatre medical consultant, Lieutenant Colonel Perrin H. Long, MC, who was ordered to submit an 'eyes only' report directly to Eisenhower. Ironically, Dr Long was from Patton's adopted home town of Hamilton, Massachusetts.

self-concern – for example, by anger directed at someone else – they might be helped toward recovery.'[1]

The doctors and nurses were not impressed by Patton's sudden compassion and the evidence suggests that Patton's real regret was the problem his acts had wrought upon himself. Since World War II a great deal has been learned of the effects of combat on soldiers, but in Patton's time 'shell shock' or 'battle fatigue' was equated by many as a pretext for malingering and cowardice. Patton could never concede that all men are not created with equal tolerance to combat conditions. In the case of Bennett there was neither malingering nor cowardice.[2] Nevertheless, Patton privately insisted that 'my motive was correct because one cannot permit skulking to exist. It is just like a communicable disease. I admit freely that my method was wrong and I shall make what amends I can. I regret the incident as I hate to make Ike mad when it is my earnest study to please him ... I feel very low.'[3]

On 21 August, Bennett was brought in to hear Patton's formal apology which ended with the two shaking hands. The IG report later noted that Bennett's morale was greatly raised and his mental improvement hastened by Patton's action.[4] It did not help that Bennett's brigade commander strengthened Patton's convictions by stating that Bennett had been AWOL and had falsely represented his condition to his battery surgeon. 'It is rather a commentary on justice when an Army commander has to soft-soap a skulker to placate the timidity of those above...'[5]

Patton never understood that throughout the slapping affair Eisenhower had stood firmly behind him and refused to lose the leader who had triumphantly played a key role 'in a campaign which will be a model for study in military schools for decades'.[6] While Patton was complaining that Eisenhower had not congratulated him on his great victory, Eisenhower was agonizing over whether he might yet have to send him home in disgrace. Butcher recorded that 'Ike is deeply concerned and has scarcely slept for several nights, trying to figure out the wisest method of handling

---

[1] Statement of Captain H. A. Carr, MC, 15th Evacuation Hospital, Eisenhower Papers.
[2] NATOUSA IG Report, 18 September 1943, Eisenhower Papers.
[3] Patton Diary, 20 August 1943.
[4] NATOUSA IG Report, loc. cit.
[5] Patton Diary, 21 August 1943. Two days later a similar scene was enacted with Private Kuhl.
[6] Harry C. Butcher, *Three Years With Eisenhower*, op. cit., 1946, p. 338.

this dilemma. The United Nations have not developed another battle leader as successful as Patton, Ike thinks.'[1]

Normally, Eisenhower kept Marshall abreast of everything he did but in the Patton case he did not. In a long letter written on 24 August, Eisenhower withheld details of the slappings, saying only that Patton had conducted:

> a campaign where the brilliant successes must be attributed directly to his energy, determination and unflagging aggressiveness ... in spite of all this – George Patton continues to exhibit some of those unfortunate personal traits of which you and I have always known and which during this campaign caused me some most uncomfortable days. His habit of impulsive bawling out of subordinates, extending even to the personal abuse of individuals, was noted in at least two specific cases. I have had to take the most drastic steps; and if he is not cured now, there is no hope for him. Personally, I believe that he is cured – not only because of his great personal loyalty to you and to me but because fundamentally he is so avid for recognition as a great military commander that he will ruthlessly suppress any habit of his own that will tend to jeopardize it.[2]

Two weeks later Eisenhower reiterated his belief in Patton as 'a truly aggressive commander and, moreover, one with sufficient brains to do his work in splendid fashion'.[3] Had it been up to Bradley, Patton would not have been let off so easily: 'I would have relieved him instantly and would have had nothing more to do with him ... He was colorful but he was impetuous, full of temper, bluster, inclined to treat the troops and subordinates as morons. His whole concept of command was opposite to mine. He was primarily a showman. The show always seemed to come first.'[4]

As Patton made the rounds of every Seventh Army unit his 'apology' generally took the form of an oblique reference of regret 'for any occasions when I may have harshly criticized individuals'.[5] The IG report noted that 'he usually referred to "certain incidents that had better be forgotten". He customarily used "earthy language". The effect of these talks differed with each individual. Many men were inspired to greater effort, others were

[1] Ibid, pp. 338–9.
[2] Eisenhower–Marshall, 24 August 1943, copy in Butcher Diary.
[3] Ibid, 26 September 1943.
[4] Bradley Commentaries.
[5] Blumenson, *The Patton Papers*, Vol. II, op. cit., p. 338.

disgusted. The proportion of the latter is considered large enough to be the cause of serious concern.'[1]

The reaction in most of the combat units was quiet indifference. In Patton's former division, the 2d Armored, there was great enthusiasm and a tendency to discount rumours about Patton as untrue.[2] In the 1st Division the new commander worried that he bore some of the responsibility for the slappings after remarking to Patton that he believed there were some soldiers malingering in the hospital to avoid combat. 'Well, as luck would have it Patton went straight to a hospital.'[3] Patton's speech to the 18,000 men of the 'Big Red One' was greeted with stony silence. Huebner believed this not a renunciation of Patton so much as an acknowledgement that Patton was wrong and the matter should be forgotten as quickly as possible.[4] General Porter recalls that 'the 1st Division had only just arrived in Licata and many of the troops had no idea why Patton was there. Some asked why Patton had to do this. The division was tired, dirty and had been in combat for thirty-eight days. Even I did not know until three hours prior to the speech.'[5]

Patton's appearance before the 60th Regiment, 9th Infantry Division was another matter altogether. Even though the 9th Division had only participated in the final two weeks of the campaign and its troops were not as familiar with Patton as those of the other divisions, the scene described by an infantry major was one of the most extraordinary moments of the war:

> We were assembled in a large ... olive orchard [near Randazzo] ... General Patton arrived in that famous command car of his with two metal flags on either side – three stars and the 'Pyramid of Power,' the Seventh Army emblem – a long trailing cloud of dust, and MPs and so on ... we all stood at attention and put on our helmets and the bugler sounded 'Attention' and General Patton mounted this ... PT platform in front of these 3,000 ... troops ... General Patton had a rather high, squeaky voice, and as he started to address the regiment he said, 'Take seats,' so we sat down on our helmets – it was a practice of those days, to keep us out of the mud or the dust ... and General Patton started to give what we knew was to be his apology. But he never got past the first word, which was 'Men!' And at that point the whole regiment erupted. It sounded like a football game – a touchdown

[1] NATOUSA IG Report, loc. cit.   [2] Ibid.
[3] Quoted in *The Patton Papers*, Vol. II, op. cit., p. 333.
[4] Ibid., p. 340.
[5] Interview with General Robert W. Porter, Jr, loc. cit.

had been scored because the helmets (steel pots) started flying through the air, coming down all over – raining steel helmets and the men just shouted 'Georgie, Georgie,' – a name which he detested. He was saying, we think he was saying – 'At ease, take seats,' and so on. Then he had the bugler sound 'Attention' again, but nothing happened. Just all these cheers. So, finally General Patton was standing there and he was shaking his head and you could see the big tears streaming down his face and he said, or words to this effect, 'The hell with it,' and he walked off the platform. At this point the bugler sounded 'Attention' and again everybody grabbed the nearest available steel helmet, put it on, being sure to button the chin strap (which was a favorite Patton quirk) and as he stepped into his command car and again went down the side of the regiment, dust swirling, everybody stood at attention and saluted to the right and General Patton stood up in his command car and saluted, crying ... He was our hero. We were on his side. We knew the problem. We knew what he had done and why he had done it ... He never came back.[1]

Emotion also ran high when Patton appeared before the entire 3d Division outside Trapani. 'We all loved General Patton regardless of what you hear. Sure, he cussed us out. He called us 'son-of-a-bitch' and 'bastards' ... but there were a hell of a lot of tears shed when Patton had to apologize to my whole division....'[2]

Although *l'affaire* Patton was by the autumn of 1943 common knowledge to thousands, Eisenhower's gentlemen's agreement with the press held until late November when someone told the story to muck-raking columnist Drew Pearson. Pearson, who was called many things in his lifetime but never a gentleman, gleefully sensationalized the story to the American public on his weekly syndicated radio programme.[*] The result was a storm of criticism of Patton and this ground swell might well have forced weaker men than Eisenhower, Marshall and Stimson to sacrifice Patton on the altar of public opinion. Some congressmen and senators called for Patton's dismissal but Marshall and Stimson refused to bow to the pressure, while overseas Eisenhower defended his decision to retain Patton for OVERLORD.

[1] Interview of General Theodore J. Conway, USA Retired, September 1977, Oral history collection, USAMHI. Also published in *Parameters* (The Journal of the US Army War College), December 1980. Conway served in the 60th Regiment in Sicily.

[2] Oral history interview of Lieutenant General John A. Heintges.

[*] Pearson's version of the affair was based on second-hand information and was highly inflammatory. Exaggeration, no matter how vicious, was one of Drew Pearson's trademarks.

Secretary of War Henry L. Stimson was a veteran of the political wars, an old friend of Patton's and, throughout Patton's indiscretions, one of his staunchest backers. Privately, he rebuked Patton, writing of 'his disappointment that so brilliant an officer should so far have offended against his own traditions'.[1] To the Senate went a letter defending Eisenhower's decision to retain Patton on the basis of the pressing need for his 'aggressive, winning leadership in the bitter battles which are to come before final victory'.[2]

Support for Patton came from many sources, including many mothers and fathers of his men. According to his aide-de-camp, Patton's personal mail was about 89% favourable.[3] Considering its sensational nature the storm over Patton abated rather quickly, lending credence to the maxim that the public rarely remembers beyond yesterday's headlines.

What actually went through Patton's mind during the two slapping incidents? Fortunately, a hitherto unpublished record exists in the form of a memoir written by his old friend, Major General Kenyon A. Joyce, who recorded this account of what he called 'as dramatic and soul searing a confession of an inexcusable act as I have ever heard':

> In both instances, the action was inexcusable on my part. I am thoroughly conscious of that. There is no real extenuation but I will tell you what happened in one of the cases.
>
> It was at the peak of the campaign. I was under stress and nervous. I visited a hospital where there were a number of badly wounded and in one ward, there were many cases in desperate condition. [A reference to his visit to the 15th Evacuation Hospital on 3 August.] I went along, visiting with the men and toward the end of the ward, I found a man who was bandaged in many places from head to foot. He had been hit by various fragments from a high explosive shell and was in critical condition. However, in reply to my greeting, he said, 'General, I happened to be in the wrong place at the wrong time but the docs are fixing me up and I'll be O.K. and back with you soon.' That man was great and had the fighting spirit that has made our country. It touched me deeply and I began emoting. You know me. I stammered

---

[1] Henry L. Stimson and McGeorge Bundy, *On Active Service in Peace and War*, New York, 1947, p. 499.

[2] Letter, Stimson–Senator Robert R. Reynolds, Chairman, Senate Military Affairs Committee, reprinted in the *Army-Navy Register*, 4 December 1943.

[3] Codman, op. cit., *Drive*, p. 134. One of the lesser-known results of the slappings was its destruction of the long friendship between Patton and General John J. Pershing. Pershing privately became one of Patton's sternest critics and the two never communicated with one another again.

something about 'You are a fine soldier,' and stepped to the next bunk.

That case was even worse. He was bandaged over one eye. He was in traction for a broken leg and broken arm and was a sight that would move anyone deeply. When I asked what had happened, he said he had stepped on a land mine and was lucky to be alive. I asked how he was getting along and he replied, 'Oh, fine. They are patching me up in style,' and then with a light shining in his unbandaged eye, 'Save a place for me, General. I'll be back.' I stammered something, I don't know what, as I was emoting all over the place by then. You know me when the tears get in the eyes, I'm sunk. I brushed them aside, however and moved to the last bunk in the ward.[1]

At this point the trouble began when Patton found

a man sitting on the side of his bunk, not bandaged or showing any signs of medical care that had been in such tragic evidence all down the ward. I approached him and said, 'What happened to you, my man? Did you get wounded?' He looked like a cowardly rat and whined like one. Coming on top of the wonderful courage and great spirit I had seen displayed by other men in the ward, it caused a consuming revulsion to come over me.

I stepped closer to this supine creature, told him to get up on his feet and try to act like a soldier. I then asked him if the example of those brave men in the ward did not stir up something in him that would make him want to do his part. He said, 'Ah, no, those guys don't mean nothin. I just can't take it.'

With that, something burst in me. I said, 'You rat' and slapped him across the face with my gloves, turned on my heel and walked away. It was inexcusable on my part. I was a damned fool but the contrast between those brave men of valor and this creeping thing did something to me. The other case [on 10 August] was somewhat similar and in that I was equally a damned fool.[2]

The enormous publicity over the slappings ensured that the Germans also heard of Patton's problems. There was genuine perplexity over what the fuss was all about. In the German Army it was not unusual for a soldier accused of malingering or cowardice to be summarily shot without recourse or trial.* Why, they won-

---

[1] Major General Kenyon A. Joyce, unpublished manuscript, Joyce Papers, USAMHI.

[2] Ibid. Patton told Eisenhower's driver, Kay Summersby, that 'I always get in trouble with my gawdamned mouth!' (See Kay Summersby, *Eisenhower Was My Boss*, New York, 1948, p. 81.)

* The warning order issued by the Hermann Goering Division on 2 August for the forthcoming evacuation of Sicily bluntly noted that: 'The *most rigid discipline* is the main

dered, when success in battle was far more important than personal deportment, would the Americans even consider jeopardizing their own effort by punishing their most thrustful leader?

The indignity of an Army commander apologizing to his men might have overwhelmed a lesser man, but Patton managed to retain not only his dignity but even a sense of humour. At his first public appearance in September he was introduced by the chairman of the American Red Cross to a large gathering of GIs. Patton announced that 'I thought I'd stand here and let you fellows see if I am as big a son-of-a-bitch as you think I am'. The assembled troops erupted in cheers.[1]

Had Patton been a lesser general his career most certainly would have ended after Sicily. That his superiors elected to retain him was best summarized by Assistant Secretary of War John J. McCloy who told Eisenhower: 'Lincoln's remark when they got after Grant comes to mind when I think of Patton – "I can't spare this man – he fights." '[2]

---

[1] Quoted in *Patton*, op. cit., p. 338.
[2] Quoted in McCloy memorandum to Eisenhower, 13 December 1943, Eisenhower Papers.

---

condition for the success of all future movements. Anyone not co-operating will be shot. Examples of individuals always work wonders.' (Quoted in Div Order 31/43, 2 August 1943, 'Directive for Future Movements and Battle Actions in Sicily,' Eighth Army War Diary, PRO [WO 169/8519].) Another example was Hube's explicit order that anyone showing signs of panic or indiscipline during the evacuation of Sicily was to be clubbed or shot. (See *The Mediterranean and Middle East*, Vol. V, op. cit., p. 166.)

CHAPTER 30

The Great Escape

> We have not given up a single German soldier,
> weapon or vehicle into enemy hands.
>
> FREGATTENKAPITAEN (BARON) VON LIEBENSTEIN
> Sea Transport Leader, Messina Strait

From the moment Axis forces in Tunisia had surrendered in mid-May, German attention had begun to focus on the lifeline between Sicily and Italy: the Messina Strait. Talks between Kesselring and Grand Admiral Doenitz led to the establishment of an all-German transport service for the Strait under the control of the Navy, who were thought certain to play a leading role in the next phase of the war in the Mediterranean. Doenitz, it will be recalled, had a low opinion of the Italian Navy and was tactless enough to express these views bluntly to the Italians. Even though Doenitz insulted the integrity of the Regia Marina, there was no objection to a German ferry service between Calabria and Sicily.[1] An experienced naval officer, Fregattenkapitaen (Baron) Gustav von Liebenstein,* Senior Officer of the 2nd Landing Flotilla, was appointed Seetransportfuehrer (Sea Transport Leader) Messina Strait.[2]

---

[1] Peter Padfield, *Doenitz: The Last Fuehrer*, London, 1984, p. 294. One reason for the swift Italian acquiescence may have been the fear of the Supermarina becoming too involved in the operational activities of the Germans, whose naval documents later revealed the extent of Italian resentment of Doenitz and his unsolicited counsel. Although the Germans took over a large portion of the transport system between Italy and Sicily, the Italians were accorded twenty-five per cent of the transport space at any time, an offer they never took up.

[2] Vice Admiral Friedrich Ruge, 'The Evacuation of Sicily', Morison Papers, US Navy Historical Center. Ruge was first sent to Italy as the German Naval Attaché and placed in charge of the German staff contingent attached to the Supermarina. Doenitz then sent him to report on the Tunisian supply situation and from mid-March to mid-May Ruge was in operational charge of all German convoys to Tunisia. After the Axis surrender there, he was appointed German Admiral commanding the German Navy in Italy, a misleading title since there was no German Navy for Ruge to command. In mid-August Ruge was dismissed for his criticism of the Naval High Command and his anti-Hitler attitude. Ruge wrote this document in 1948 at the behest of the US Naval Detachment, Bremerhaven.

* Baron von Liebenstein was a naval reserve officer and the son of an army major general. Born in 1891 in Rastatt, von Liebenstein joined the Imperial German Navy in 1909 as an

What von Liebenstein discovered when he assumed command on 28 May was an inefficient and chaotic operation. In peacetime and the early years of the war, traffic across the Strait was efficient and plentiful. Large steam ferries carried the bulk of the traffic and six of these ferries were fitted to carry as many as twenty-five railway wagons each between Messina and Villa San Giovanni and Reggio di Calabria, the two principal termini on the mainland. In war, however, these ferries and their fixed facilities, jetties and sidings were extremely vulnerable to attack and during the Allied bombing offensive before D-Day these lucrative targets on both sides of the Strait were repeatedly attacked.

Sicily had seen little use as a staging area for the desert campaigns until Axis forces retreated into Tunisia and the Sicilian ports began to play a prominent role in their resupply. Allied intelligence soon noted vastly increased road and rail traffic along the southern Italian coast and across the Strait to Messina where resupply runs were then made to northern Tunisian ports under cover of darkness from Palermo, Messina and other Sicilian ports. By early 1943 Messina and Palermo had begun to attract larger and larger air raids. In 1941 a total of 62 tons of bombs were dropped on Messina and in 1942 this figure doubled to 120 tons. During the first six months of 1943 there was a dramatic rise to 2,056 tons – a 1,700 per cent increase over 1942.[1]

Soon after Messina was captured, a British Bombing Survey unit headed by Professor Solly Zuckerman arrived in Sicily to assess the

[1] Bombing Survey Unit, 'Mediterranean Allied Air Forces Report on Air Attacks on Rail and Road Communications', 28 December 1943, Zuckerman Papers. After masterminding the bombing of Pantelleria and Lampedusa, Tedder appointed Zuckerman to head a small *ad hoc* detachment called the Bombing Survey Unit (Sicily) whose task was to compile a detailed appreciation and statistical analysis of the air attacks carried out by the Allied air forces in the Mediterranean Theatre against enemy rail and communications targets. Zuckerman's team conducted an exhaustive examination of Messina. The figures cited above are in short tons (i.e. 2,000 lb) and the main aiming points for the attacking aircraft were the ferry terminals and their associated railway facilities. One of Zuckerman's surveys included an investigation of the effects of a 4,000 lb bomb which had exploded next to a brothel in Syracuse. The Madame and her girls contributed to an animated on-site evaluation! (See Zuckerman's autobiography, *From Apes to Warlords*, op. cit., p. 202.)

---

officer cadet and became a lieutenant in 1912. During World War I he took part in the battle of Dogger Bank and in 1916 served in a torpedo boat during the battle of Jutland. By war's end he was a lieutenant commander and the CO of his own torpedo boat. He received the Iron Cross, 1st Class, and left the Navy for civilian life until 1940 when he was recalled to active duty. After commanding a minesweeping flotilla in the North Sea from May 1942 to February 1943, he was posted to Sicily in April as the commander of the 2nd Landingboat Flotilla based in Marsala.

effects of Allied bombing. The Zuckerman report established that approximately thirty-five per cent of the bombs dropped were in the harbour area. Thus, with the main Allied bombing effort directed against facilities rather than shipping, it is no surprise that during the first half of 1943 a mere eleven vessels were sunk.[1]

By February 1943 it was clear to the Germans that they could not rely on the normal ferry service and they began using a variety of small coastal vessels along three dispersed routes to the north, outside the more vulnerable Messina target area. However slight an improvement, the number of routes remained wholly inadequate and far too susceptible to destruction.* In addition to their shipping problems, rail movements into Sicily were affected by the increased bombing of the rail facilities at Messina, Reggio and San Giovanni, and rail traffic into Calabria was in sharp decline. From December 1942 on, it was increasingly difficult to utilize, and by D-Day was completely paralysed.†

Although the Germans had prudently shifted their movements to new routes, what von Liebenstein found was a chaotic and inefficient use of the sea transport by competing units that included the Luftwaffe, Navy, Army engineers and even the infantry. The Siebel ferries were controlled by the Luftwaffe, while the Army engineer construction battalion that serviced the ports possessed a variety of craft. Each operated independently, usually with total disregard of each other's requirements. Of the 134 vessels in the German inventory‡ in the middle of July, a mere 58 were capable of carrying cargo. To add to the confusion a special envoy from Goering mysteriously appeared one day with vague orders to 'look after things'.

Von Liebenstein immediately made two important changes. The first was to organize his disparate flotillas into an efficient ferry service that quickly increased its daily capacity from 100 tons

---

[1] Ibid.

* The three ferry routes were: Salvatore–Gallico (Siebel ferries); Salvatore–Catona (MFPs); Faro–Cannitello (L-boats). The heart of the German ferry system was the Siebel ferry, which required a jetty or landing stage for loading. With only one landing point on either bank of the Messina Strait, there was considerable danger of a crippling air attack. (See Ruge, 'The Evacuation of Sicily'.)

† Zuckerman attributes this decrease to the success of interdiction raids on the Naples rail network and the small capacity of the eastern railway system which had only one track into Calabria and was unable to take up the slack when the western network came under intense attacks.

‡ This was the total number of German vessels in Sicilian waters or operating between Naples and Messina, also a principal resupply route.

of supplies, 100 vehicles and 100 men to 1,000 tons per day, several
hundred vehicles and several thousand men. The second was to
increase the number of German ferry routes from three to five
principal routes operating from twelve locations on the Messina
side and twelve on the mainland. (See map and Appendix J.) New
jetties were constructed, improvements made at the landing sites
and roads built to move traffic. Before von Liebenstein's arrival,
supplies were transported by truck to landing sites on the mainland, loaded on to a vessel, unloaded on the Messina side, often by
hand, and reloaded on vehicles and sent to a supply depot. Von
Liebenstein instituted what may have been the first roll-on/roll-off
system of moving cargo, a standard method now used in military
and civilian commerce. Using a pool of trucks that rarely exceeded
one hundred, cargoes were loaded on the Reggio side, driven
directly on to a Siebel ferry and directly off on the Messina side to a
depot. So efficient was this system that it averaged only twenty
minutes to load a Siebel ferry with nine to twelve vehicles. When
the Hermann Goering Division arrived in Sicily in late June and
early July, 610 vehicles, 750 tons of supplies and 3,600 men crossed
the Strait in a single day. During the first week of July the Germans
moved 9,500 men, 1,300 vehicles, 40 tanks and 50 guns to Sicily
and, during the month from the invasion to the start of the
German evacuation, 40,000 tons of supplies and ammunition were
successfully ferried into Sicily.[1] Despite enormous damage to the
port facilities of Messina, Reggio and San Giovanni by increasingly frequent Allied air raids, the Germans were able to declare
truthfully that 'losses of men, materiel and time were
insignificant'.[2] Von Liebenstein's ferry service became so efficient
that when the Allies launched two very heavy raids on Messina on
14 and 16 July, which sank three steamers and a large quantity of
ammunition, the ferry service was still reported 'normal'.[3]

Von Liebenstein's 'Navy' consisted of a variety of specialized
vessels, of which the most important and versatile were the Siebel
ferries, a crude but effective makeshift combination of two
engineer pontoons held together by steel girders over which was
laid a platform for vehicles and troops. Originally invented in 1940

---

[1] Ruge, 'The Evacuation of Sicily'.
[2] Ibid.
[3] Ibid. The raid on 14 July was by 139 B-17, B-25 and B-26 bombers, while on 16 July 110
B-17s pounded the ferry terminus at San Giovanni.

by aircraft designer Fritz Siebel for Operation *Seeloewe*, this vessel was usually powered by two aircraft engines (one attached to each pontoon) and steered from a small cabin built in the middle to house the crew. Despite a top speed of approximately eight knots, the Siebel ferry was the workhorse of the Messina Strait. It was of low draught, easily manoeuvrable and could carry forty-five tons on the open sea and nearly sixty tons across the Strait. Some Siebel ferries were converted into deadly, movable flak ships by the installation of either two or three 88 mm or two 105 mm AA guns. Measuring 80 feet by 50 feet, the Siebel ferry could carry an average of ten to twelve vehicles or 250 troops.*

The other workhorse of the German flotilla was the naval ferry barge or *Marine-Fachr-Praehme* (MFP), a smaller, flat-bottomed barge whose bow lowered to form a ramp. The MFP was powered by three 130-horsepower diesel engines that provided a cruising speed of eight knots. Most carried eighty tons of cargo and later models 100 tons, including four to five trucks or three tanks. A variety of other smaller, specialized craft were also used in the Strait: tanker barges for transporting fuel, and several types of freight barges originally built for river and canal work in Europe.† Every vessel was equipped with some form of AA protection which proved surprisingly effective.

While von Liebenstein was performing near-miracles with German sea movement, another officer was performing similar feats on land. On 14 July, Kesselring appointed an Army officer, Colonel Ernst-Guenther Baade, to the new post of German Commandant, Messina Strait.‡ Baade's principal task was to organize the

---

* The Germans mass-produced these remarkable craft in sections so that they could be taken overland to their destination and be easily assembled by their crews. In the 1920s Siebel had befriended a down-and-out World War I air ace by the name of Hermann Goering. This was repaid in 1940 when Siebel was put to work designing barges for *Seeloewe*. (See Ruge and Roskill, *The War at Sea*, Vol. III, Pt I, op. cit., p. 145.)

† Both the MFP and another barge craft called an L-boat could land on open beaches, thus eliminating the necessity for docking facilities.

‡ Colonel Ernst-Guenther Baade was a maverick infantry officer cut from the same cloth as 'Paddy' Flint and Terry Allen. Like von Senger, Baade was of minor Prussian aristocracy and the two shared similar intellectual interests and a love of horses. Baade spoke fluent English and he and his wife were well known in prewar England for their feats as international showjumpers. In 1942 Baade commanded the infantry regiment of the 15th Panzer Division in the western desert where he was a respected and popular commander. His eccentricities included often being seen wearing a Scottish kilt over his uniform and a large bone-handled dagger which replaced his pistol.

In North Africa Baade once forced a British POW to lead him through a minefield and then freed the surprised soldier. His voice became well known to the British because of his practice of informing his enemy on their own radio frequency to 'Stop firing, on my way

diverse AA defences of the Strait which were then fragmented
under various commands. He was also charged with providing the
means to carry out the evacuation of Sicily. Kesselring had bestowed on him the title of Fortress Commander which meant that
he had sweeping powers to carry out his assignment which he did
with stunning efficiency. Insatiable and tireless, he seemed to be
everywhere in the short time given him to prepare for the German
evacuation of the island. Between inspections, conferences and
briefings he somehow found time to write an evacuation guide for
the troops. 'He seems to have overlooked virtually nothing and to
have provided virtually everything, including caches of food,
brandy and cigarettes on the mainland for the troops last to leave
Sicily, whose departure might be particularly hazardous.'[1]

The AA defences of the Messina Strait were reorganized and
strengthened into specific defence sectors on both sides of the
passage and additional German units were added to augment
existing forces. The result was six flak sectors, three on each side,
comprising sixty units. The firepower added up to eighty-two
heavy and sixty light AA guns on the Reggio side from Cannitello
in the north to Cape dell' Armi in the south. On the Sicilian side
were another forty-one heavy and fifty-two light AA guns. Along
the shoreline were ranged additional 3 inch and 4 inch mobile,
dual-purpose guns, estimated to be more than 150 at the height of
the evacuation. To defend the Strait against sea attack were four
batteries of Italian 280 mm (11.2 inch) guns and two batteries of
152 mm (6 inch) guns, later increased by four batteries of German
170 mm (6.8 inch) guns which were commandeered from the 15th
Panzer Grenadier Division and positioned at the northern end of
the Strait between San Giovanni and Pezzo.[2]

Although the Germans totally dominated the defence of the
Strait, the Italian contribution was important, especially their own

[1] *The Mediterranean and Middle East*, Vol. V, op. cit., p. 166.
[2] *The War at Sea*, Vol. III, Pt I, op. cit., pp. 145–6; and War Diary of Fortress Commander, Messina Strait (Baade), US Navy Historical Center. The 170 mm guns were the only two
batteries of heavy German artillery on Sicily and had been providing support to the defence
of Troina until Baade's higher priority caused their removal to protect the Strait.

back. Baade.' Towards the end of 1942 he was assigned to Rome and in May 1943 was sent
to Sicily where he was personally selected by Kesselring to assume the important post of
Commandant, Messina Strait. His eccentricities aside, Baade was an exceptionally able
officer who more than lived up to Kesselring's confidence.

independently run ferry service which by August had achieved a high level of efficiency equal to that of the Germans.*

The German evacuation of Sicily was accomplished in four different phases. The first began almost immediately after the invasion when the Germans ordered all non-essential units from Sicily. These included Luftwaffe communication units, a naval wireless decoding and direction-finding unit, a mobile S-boat base, and naval stores which were moved to new depots in Calabria. Unlike the well-organized final evacuation, these early movements were crude and resulted in chaos along Route 113 between Palermo and the Faro ferry at the tip of the Cape Peloro peninsula. In what must have been one of the most monumental, all-time traffic jams, the congestion took two days for German military police to disentangle and in spite of the emphasis on interdiction of these lucrative targets the Allied air forces failed to detect them, causing Admiral Ruge to observe that the Allies 'lost a good opportunity of destroying a great amount of valuable gear and equipment'.[1]

The second phase was equally hasty and involved the evacuation of western Sicily when Patton began his Palermo offensive. It consisted mostly of the removal of equipment and stores and began a scant four days before the fall of Palermo. Its haste was sufficient to result in near total failure. MFPs were able to evacuate some 100 tons of valuable equipment from Palermo but when these vessels returned for a second try they were attacked by Allied fighter-bombers and four were lost. The apparatus of four radar stations was successfully removed to Italy but little else, and the losses when western Sicily was so quickly overrun were severe, including the crucial loss of an estimated 8,000–10,000 tons of fuel. Goering, whose lust to acquire booty had, by this time, reached maniacal proportions, ordered the sarcophagi of Frederick II† and his family removed from Palermo cathedral, an order which an appalled Admiral Ruge quietly ignored.[2]

---

[1] Ruge, loc. cit.   [2] Ibid.

* The Italians operated four ferry routes: Messina–San Giovanni; Messina–Scilla; Salvatore–Scilla and, from the northern coast, Martelle–Cannitello.

† Frederick II of Hohenstaufen ruled the Holy Roman Empire and was King of Sicily from 1197 to 1250. Known as 'Stupor Mundi' (the Wonder of the World), he was considered one of the true giants of the Middle Ages who brought castles, culture and order to the island. Although Sicily was the tiniest part of his great empire, Frederick is believed to have once said, 'God would not have chosen Palestine for his own if he could have seen my Kingdom of Sicily.'

We now know that the final evacuation of all German combat forces from Sicily was ordained from the earliest days of the campaign when OKW and Kesselring decided that all possible steps must be taken to avoid a repetition of the disastrous losses which befell the Germans in Tunisia. Although von Senger harshly criticized Kesselring's naïveté in believing he could repel the Allied landings, the German C-in-C was nevertheless a pragmatist who never shared Hitler's often-used philosophy of fighting to the death for an impossible object. Hube had received clear instructions from both Kesselring and Jodl to prepare an evacuation and by the end of July he had already begun to finalize a plan, code-named 'Lehrgang Ia'.*

A warning order was issued on 1 August at a time when Guzzoni still believed the German intention was to resist to the end. Hube had yet to be told when 'Lehrgang' was to be implemented but he knew it could not be more than a matter of days before he must start an evacuation or face annihilation. By 4 August the pressure from Bradley's II Corps and Leese's 30 Corps had grown so great that on his own initiative Hube ordered the evacuation of all units that could be spared. This decision was, says his chief of staff, von Bonin, a courageous and risky decision, for Hube had been given specific instructions that the evacuation was *not* to begin without orders from OKW.[1] Hube's decision to defy OKW was a direct result of their warnings that he should expect Allied landings in his rear, and of the threat of an imminent breakthrough at Troina and Adrano. Another proscription that irritated Hube was Hitler's policy of never informing German troops when there was to be a withdrawal. Not only was the intention to evacuate Sicily impossible to conceal from his troops but Hube ensured by indirect means that his men knew they were to be saved.† The reaction,

---

[1] Von Bonin, 'Considerations of the Italian Campaign, 1943–44', loc. cit.

* Literally translated, 'Lehrgang' means 'a course of instruction'. The first official indication an evacuation was being considered occurred on 27 July and was undoubtedly prompted by the fall of Mussolini. The senior operations officers were summoned to Frascati, outside Rome, where a secret meeting was chaired by Kesselring's Chief of Staff, General Siegfried Westphal, who explained the details of 'Lehrgang'. (See Report No. 14, Historical Section (G.S.), Army Headquarters, 6 December 1948, loc. cit.)

† The absurdity of this policy was reflected in the warning order issued on 2 August by the Hermann Goering Division to all units that an evacuation was forthcoming. A surviving annexe to the order discusses specific actions to be taken upon evacuation. Within hours of the order being issued, the entire division knew of the impending action. (See Appendix A to Eighth Army Intelligence Summary No. 534, 11 August 1943, PRO [WO 169/8519].)

recalls von Bonin, was extraordinary. Confidence increased at all levels when German troops learned they would not be needlessly sacrificed in the barren hell-hole of Sicily.[1]

The German evacuation plan was based on the simple premise that first priority went to saving all troops, followed by as much equipment, ammunition and supplies as could be moved to the mainland. Anything immovable was to be destroyed. Prior to 'Lehrgang' there was an understandable mood of pessimism within XIV Panzer Corps. Senior German officers were under no illusions over their odds against success. Few believed they could pull off a miracle and escape.[2] The Army considered severe losses – up to ninety per cent – as unavoidable and were quite prepared to sacrifice most of their equipment to save at least some of their men.[3] One German colonel later wrote that 'In view of Allied superiority we were all fully convinced that only a few of us would get away from the island safe and sound'.[4] The Navy, however, was far more optimistic and never shared this gloomy assessment. Von Liebenstein bluntly told Hube he could evacuate up to 12,500 men per twenty-four hours and planned to take the Army's equipment as well.[5]

Hube's plan called for a phased withdrawal along five defensive lines, each of which grew smaller and smaller across the triangle that made up northeastern Sicily, finally converging on Messina. The first line ran along the San Fratello Line to Mount Etna and Acireale on the east coast. The last line was in the mountains outside Messina itself. As each line of resistance was reached, approximately 8,000–10,000 troops would be released to make their way to the designated ferry sites. According to von Bonin:

> On the fifth line of defence, the last remaining troops were to proceed direct to the boats in the last night before the final evacuation. In the area around MESSINA and in the town itself, the divisions were given clearly defined concentration and embarkation areas. The route for movement to these areas and traffic control on the routes was also rigidly prescribed. Each division had its own ferry route with a number of boats and

---

[1] Ibid. Hitler refused to countenance voluntary retreat and his policy of never informing his troops was based upon the misguided belief that the German Army would fight better if deprived of any suggestion that retreat would ever be permitted.
[2] Ibid.
[3] Ruge.
[4] Ibid.
[5] Ruge and von Liebenstein War Diary, loc. cit.

ferries. Exact orders were also given for landing on the mainland and movement to concentration areas there. . . .[1]

No one involved in planning 'Lehrgang' believed that evacuation by daylight across the Strait was even remotely possible and that six nights would be required to withdraw all German personnel and their weapons. This estimate took no account of vehicles, heavy equipment and armoured vehicles.[2] The days leading up to the evacuation were a time of grave concern and high tension. Speculation centred on what the Allies would do to *prevent* 'Lehrgang' from being carried out. The first of Patton's 'end-runs' had already taken place at Sant' Agata and the German command believed this signalled the start of further operations on an even larger scale which threatened disaster to any evacuation attempt.[3]

All across the front supplies were running dangerously low, leading Hube to establish 10 August as the date when 'Lehrgang' must commence.[4] Practically, this meant that the first quota of troops would board the Messina ferries for evacuation during the night of 11 August. Still lacking was authority to carry out the evacuation, and this point has been the subject of minor controversy. Kesselring later declared that 'I took the decision to evacuate Sicily on my own initiative', an act which made him very unpopular in Berlin for some time.[5] Jodl, who had personally told Hube he was to save the German divisions in Sicily at all costs, stated in a letter dated 16 August that he had ordered Kesselring to begin the evacuation.[6] The issue is irrelevant, but what is significant is that Jodl's order was issued independently of Hitler who continued to postpone the evacuation, in part so as to avoid an Italian pretext for renouncing the Rome–Berlin alliance.[7] What is certain is that, had Kesselring and Hube awaited Hitler's pleas-

[1] Von Bonin.
[2] Ibid.
[3] Ibid.
[4] Ibid.
[5] Kesselring, *A Soldier's Record*, op. cit., p. 198.
[6] *The War at Sea*, Vol. III, Pt I, op. cit., p. 144. According to von Bonin, he personally hand-carried Hube's plan to Kesselring in Rome to obtain his approval and 'for freedom of action for the Commanding General, XIV Panzer Corps, who was to be free to choose for himself the time when withdrawal from the island to the mainland should begin, on the basis of the general situation. Field Marshal Kesselring agreed to the proposal of Hube and promised to obtain from higher Headquarters assent to leaving the decision to the beginning of the withdrawal to the Corps Commander.' Although this portion of von Bonin's account is quite clear, he muddies the waters by remarking that 'in the course of the following days, General Hube received Hitler's consent'.
[7] Warlimont, *Inside Hitler's Headquarters, 1939–45*, op. cit., p. 374.

ure, few if any German troops would have escaped Sicily. In fact, Hitler did not order the evacuation until 16 August, the same day Rommel was ordered to Italy and when the preponderance of Hube's force was already safely on the Italian mainland.[1] The Fuehrer accepted Jodl's and Kesselring's insubordination without histrionics, leading to the conclusion that he too recognized that Sicily had been held for as long as possible.[2]

The third phase of the German withdrawal from Sicily was the preliminary evacuation which took place during the first ten days of August. Significantly, von Liebenstein's ferries managed to transport:

Troops	8,615
Wounded	4,489
Vehicles	3,159 + 3 tanks
Ammunition	446 (tons)
Fuel	527 (tons)
Equipment	5,155 (tons)[3]

In addition to the regular ferry service across the Strait, the Germans employed ferries of the 2nd and 4th Landing Craft Flotillas to transport wounded, fuel, medical supplies, radar equipment and Luftwaffe equipment between Messina and Naples.[4]

All the while the Allies continued round-the-clock bombing of targets in the Messina Strait. According to an RAF account:

While air attacks against battlefield targets were being carried out at full intensity during the first weeks in August, attacks were renewed on a large scale against the harbour marshalling yards, bridges, roads and troops at Messina and towards the end of the

[1] Irving, *Hitler's War, 1942–1945*, op. cit., p. 556. Both Doenitz and Rommel were firmly opposed to any abandonment of Sicily. Doenitz in particular had become one of Hitler's most intimate advisers and was present to influence the German leader at all of the important conferences in August 1943. His biographer writes that 'he was as fanatical about holding the bridgehead in Sicily as he had been for holding Tunisia to the last man... "We are tying up considerable forces in Sicily, which if released to become available for new landings will hang over us like a sword of Damocles. Therefore it is best if we prevent new operations by binding the enemy's forces in Sicily." ' (*Doenitz*, op. cit., p. 314.) Hitler's only concession was to order OB South to prepare plans for a possible evacuation.

[2] Warlimont, op. cit., p. 379. Kesselring duly reported to Berlin on 10 August that 'The evacuation of Sicily has started according to plan'. The decision to withhold this information from Hitler was undoubtedly Jodl's. (See *The Canadians in Italy*, op. cit., pp. 168–9.)

[3] Von Liebenstein War Diary. The British official historians estimate the number of vehicles evacuated between 1 and 10 August as 4,500.

[4] Ibid. Most voyages to Naples were made via Vibo Valentia on the west coast of Calabria.

week against the beaches extending westwards to *Cape Peloro*. The attacks had a dual aim: to prevent last-minute supplies reaching the enemy's hard-pressed forces and to strike at his main evacuation point. From 1st to 7/8th August, inclusive, attacks were delivered by a total of 121 US Fortresses, 269 Wellingtons and 225 RAF and US fighter-bombers ... over 200 US Warhawks and Kittyhawks supplemented our naval operations in the *Messina Straits* by attacks on small craft already described as 'evacuation shipping'; in particular several Siebel ferries and barges were sunk or set on fire and near misses were scored on numerous other small vessels.[1]

The claims of enemy shipping losses were grossly exaggerated; the preliminary evacuation was carried out with no loss of efficiency and with minimal loss. From 31 July to the evening of 10 August the Allied air forces flew 528 bomber sorties against targets in the Messina Strait, dropping 1,217 tons of bombs.[2] While the majority of the attacks were directed against the Messina side of the Strait, port facilities in and around Reggio were also struck.[3] The fighter-bomber effort was primarily directed against evacuation shipping, and in some 759 sorties, 198 tons of bombs were dropped.[4] The Germans reported the destruction of one Siebel ferry, one landing craft, one 'F'-boat and two oil lighters.[5]

What forced Hube to initiate the final German withdrawal from Sicily was the fall of Troina and Adrano. Adrano was the linchpin of the eastern portion of the Etna Line and the intense pressure exerted by 30 Corps finally forced the Hermann Goering Division to abandon Adrano which the 78th Division entered without opposition on the night of 6/7 August. While 13 Corps began its long-delayed offensive up the eastern coast north of Catania, 30 Corps was encountering determined opposition, first at Bronte and then at Maletto. The 78th Division finally took Randazzo on 13 August and found the city virtually destroyed. Randazzo is a medieval city that rises almost without warning in

---

[1] *RAF Middle Eastern and Mediterranean Review*, PRO (AIR 23/6787).
[2] Northwest African Air Forces, 'Analysis of Bombing Operations', 31 July/1 August–14 August 1943, PRO (AIR 23/3553), and Vol. 21 (August–September 1943) 'Air Staff Operational Summaries', Air Ministry War Room. Copies in Air Historical Branch, MoD. With minor exceptions the attacks against the Messina strait were flown by the Northwest African Air Force.
[3] Ibid. and *RAF Middle Eastern and Mediterranean Review*.
[4] Northwest African Air Force, 'Analysis of Bombing Operations'.
[5] Von Liebenstein War Diary, 1–10 August. Allied statistics showed eight craft destroyed and the probable destruction of ten more. While some may have been Italian, the figures appear excessively high.

the barren landscape at the northern base of Mount Etna. The town had become a favourite target of Allied air attacks and more than 1,200 sorties had pounded it to rubble. It was here that US and British forces met at the last lateral road connecting the German flanks. With Randazzo under Allied control the Germans were forced to retire to Messina along one of the two coastal roads.

Montgomery now spurred Dempsey to continue up the eastern coast as quickly as possible, while 30 Corps was halted in place around Randazzo so that the main effort against Messina could be made by Seventh Army. Once again, Montgomery sent a clear signal that Messina had no place in his current priorities.

While the 15th Panzer Grenadier Division was stubbornly delaying the capture of Bronte and Randazzo, the Germans started to put their evacuation plan into operation beginning on the night of 11 August.* For this undertaking von Liebenstein had assembled a flotilla of less than imposing proportions, and way below his minimum requirement for 'Lehrgang': eleven Siebel ferries, five MFPs and ten L-boats. Nine other MFPs were ferrying ammunition from Naples and were unable to return in time; only two eventually returned to participate in the evacuation. Von Liebenstein thus found himself beginning the main evacuation with a bare minimum of ferry craft which were required to transport an estimated 12,500 men per night for the five scheduled nights of the operation.[1]

There was a considerable division of opinion between von Liebenstein and Hube and his planners at XIV Panzer Corps who had mistakenly assumed that evacuation operations could only be carried out effectively during the hours of darkness. They soon found the exact opposite to be true. Although the Allies were continuing their round-the-clock air raids, the Germans soon found their most severe problems occurred during night-time operations. Not only were von Liebenstein's crews unaccustomed to night sailing but no illumination could be used, thus necessitating the use of moonlight. Forced to load and unload in virtual darkness (there was only a partial moon when the evacuation began), operations at night proved far less effective than those in

---

[1] Ibid.

* In order to commence the full-scale evacuation on the night of 11 August it was necessary for the general retirement towards Messina to start on 10 August, which was designated 'X Day'. The order of evacuation called first for the Hermann Goering to evacuate, followed by the 15th and 29th PzG Divisions.

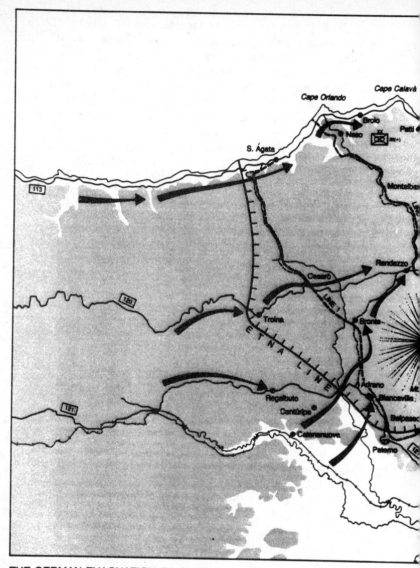

THE GERMAN EVACUATION OF SICILY 1-17 August 1943

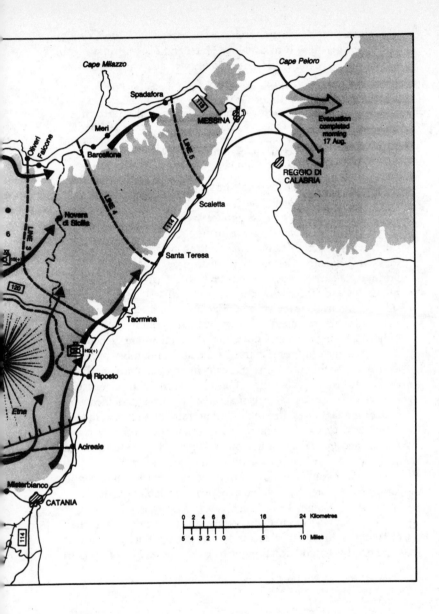

Cape Milazzo

Cape Peloro

Spadafora

MESSINA

Evacuation
completed
morning
17 Aug.

Meri

Oliveri
Falcone

Barcellona

REGGIO DI
CALABRIA

LINE 6

LINE 4

Scaletta

Novara
di Sicilia

6

LINE 3

114

Santa Teresa

120

Taormina

HQ(+)

Riposto

Etna

Acireale

Misterbianco

CATANIA

114

0 2 4 6 8   16   24 Kilometres

5 4 3 2 1 0   5   10 Miles

daylight hours. Von Liebenstein knew better and it took all his powers of persuasion to convince Hube and his staff that night operations were not the solution. In his war diary he noted that:

> For some days the enemy regularly carried out heavy bombing attacks on both sides of the Messina Straits between 2100 (hours) and dawn, with particular attention to the northern jetties at Faro and Cannitello. Frequent interruptions and the loss of indispensable ferry craft were assured . . . In comparison there were few heavy air attacks during the day and these can be fended off with heavy AA fire.[1]

Von Liebenstein made his point the very first night (11/12 August) when exceptionally heavy raids over an eight-hour period hampered loading and destroyed two ferry craft. Along four routes, ferrying could not commence prior to 0200. Dawn found many vehicles still on the Messina side awaiting movement.[2] In spite of these problems the German performance on 11 August was impressive, in part because all movements to Sicily had now been suspended and the ferries could return immediately to the Messina side as soon as their loads were discharged on the mainland.

Operations continued at night but the greatest success was obtained during daylight hours, so much so that von Liebenstein noted that the only restriction was the limited number of ferries available.[3] Night operations gradually improved, in no small part thanks to Allied generosity. On 14 August, von Liebenstein reported the curious absence of air attacks which, combined with better moonlight, resulted in the best performance to date. In fact, the evacuation had become so efficient that operations were suspended at 0100 in the morning on 15 August when no further men or vehicles arrived for evacuation. Von Liebenstein had guaranteed Hube he could move 12,500 men per twenty-four-hour period and was prevented from doing so only by the inability of the Army to deliver that many troops each day.[4]

'Lehrgang' was originally scheduled to last five days, but when operations proved far in excess of expectations, Hube ordered it extended by an additional night to complete the withdrawal of

---

[1] Von Liebenstein War Diary, 10 August.
[2] Ruge, 'The Evacuation of Sicily'.
[3] Von Liebenstein, 13 August.
[4] Von Liebenstein War Diary 14–15 August. Von Liebenstein's promised capability of being able to move 12,500 troops per twenty-four hours across the Strait was valid but inconsistent with Hube's plan for a graduated withdrawal from Sicily by German forces.

German equipment. To the delight of the Army, von Liebenstein had presented them with an opportunity that exceeded their wildest fancy. The enormous success of 'Lehrgang' is evident from these figures:

Date (Aug.)	Troops	Casualties	Vehicles	Tanks	Guns	Ammo/ Fuel (tons)	Equip. (tons)
11	3,631	–	801	–	–	83	1,128
12	3,249	–	950	–	–	204	1,370
13	6,142	440	1,131	7	36	150	1,673
14	7,424	600	1,380	39	42	369	1,728
15	4,810	200	923	1	16	95	956
16[*]	413	–	44[†]	1	34	–	–
Total	25,669	1,240	5,229	48	128	901	6,855[1]

Ferry Routes I and II were operated by an Army unit, Engineer Landing Battalion 771, and during the period 1–15 August this unit evacuated:

Troops	14,282[‡]
Casualties	13,532
Vehicles	4,560[2]
Guns	35
Equipment (tons)	9,936 (tons)

Although it is impossible to arrive at precise figures – as the Germans candidly admitted, 'counting was sometimes inaccurate in the hurry, and under bomb attacks' – the numbers have very likely erred on the conservative side. Taken from all sources, the evacuation figures for the period 1–17 August were:

[1] Ibid., 11–16 August.
[2] Molony, *The Mediterranean and Middle East*, Vol. V, op. cit., p. 180; and von Liebenstein.
[*] Figures for the night of 16/17 August are from Baade's War Diary.
[†] Includes eight tractors and one trailer.
[‡] Includes the 8,615 troops reported evacuated during the period 1–10 August.

Troops	39,951
Casualties	14,772
Vehicles	9,789
Tanks	51
Guns	163
Ammunition/fuel	1,874 (tons)
Equipment	16,791 (tons)[1]

By the morning of 16 August all but the rearguard elements defending the final line outside Messina had safely left Sicily. What was originally thought to have been an undertaking that would likely end in disaster had turned into a stunning success. Von Liebenstein proudly stated that the Army *never* taxed his ferry service to its capacity and that throughout the evacuation *all* requirements for ferry space were met.[2] Although they would later claim differently, the Allied air forces failed to make any semblance of a determined air effort until the final three days of the evacuation. One was a large night raid by seventy Wellington medium bombers which dropped 139 tons of bombs to no effect.[3] Two large daylight raids on 15 and 16 August by ninety-five bombers and 485 fighters and fighter-bombers dropped 154 tons of explosives without sinking a single Axis vessel! Nevertheless, at the end of this daring and exhausting effort von Liebenstein observed that 'there is no Siebel ferry left with two engines in working order'.

The half-hearted Allied attempt to block the evacuation came too late. By then the Germans had already accomplished the impossible. According to von Liebenstein's meticulous war diary, apparently only one German was actually killed by Allied attacks (on 7 August). Otherwise, every single German soldier and casualty able to be moved successfully escaped to Italy.[4]

Nor was this solely a German triumph. Almost unknown is the remarkable performance of the much-maligned Italians. The Italian decision to evacuate Sicily was made independently of Rome as the new head of state, Marshal Badoglio, vacillated over the decision. Despite a combative attitude that suggested a fight to

---

[1] Ibid.
[2] Von Liebenstein.
[3] Northwest African Air Forces, 'Analysis of Bombing Operations', loc. cit.
[4] Von Liebenstein. Every German account reiterates this point. The lone casualty was presumably a naval crewman.

the end, Guzzoni directed Rear Admiral Pietro Barone to begin preparations to evacuate Italian troops beginning on 3 August. The Italians employed two small steamers and one remaining serviceable train ferry, the *Villa*. More than 7,000 men were evacuated in the week before orders came from Rome on 9 August to begin a full-scale evacuation starting on 11 August. The Italians pressed into service another steamer and ten Navy-manned motor rafts when the *Villa* broke down and was undergoing repairs. Although some broke down, the motor rafts 'saved the situation', according to Admiral Barone. More than 20,000 men were moved in this fashion while the *Villa* was laid up. By the time the Italian evacuation ended on 16 August they had withdrawn an estimated 59,000 troops, 3,000 sailors, 227 vehicles, forty-one artillery pieces and twelve mules.[1]

The architects of the Italian evacuation were Admiral Barone, the Italian Naval commander in Sicily, who also doubled as the (Italian) Fortress Commandant of the Messina–Reggio sector (Baade's counterpart), and Brigadier General Ettore Monacci, the land-force commander. Not all of the Italian evacuation was via Messina. Taormina was among the ports used to great advantage to move Italian troops and supplies to Calabria virtually without interference from Royal Navy warships operating in nearby waters. At the end the Italians too were able to claim proudly, 'Not a single man was lost.'[2]

The night of 16/17 August was the culmination of the German evacuation when the last movable equipment and the remaining rearguard troops were brought off the island. The German war diary recorded that 'The last ferries left Messina just before 0600 [hours, 17 August]'.[3] As the Italians completed their evacuation on 16 August they set mines to blow up what remained of the port of Messina. The last to leave was General Monacci.[4] Among the last Germans to leave Sicily was General Hube who, in accordance with German military tradition, stayed until the end. His plan,

[1] Morison papers. Most accounts use higher estimates of 70,000–75,000 troops, 227–500 vehicles and 75–100 artillery pieces; all are in agreement over the twelve mules. This data is based on Bauer MS # R-145, USAMHI. Morison's figures are based on data furnished by Admiral Barone. Most of the Italian heavy guns and many vehicles were either seized by the Germans or destroyed in Sicily, thus accounting for the low numbers evacuated.

[2] Rear Admiral Pietro Barone, quoted in 'Estratto della Relazione sull' Occupazione della Sicilia', 1944 manuscript. Morison papers.

[3] Von Liebenstein War Diary, 17 August 1943.

[4] Bauer, MS # R-145.

'Lehrgang', was so effectively executed that von Bonin could later write without exaggeration that the evacuation had posed no difficulties worthy of mention. 'The time at our disposal was completely sufficient to bring the last man and the last German vehicle to the mainland according to plan.'[1] Von Bonin summed up German feelings with these words:

> We had more than enough retreats [during the war], but through the fault of our higher command, they almost never ended gloriously. Every German soldier on Sicily, however, who after weeks of fighting and tremendous effort, reached the mainland in the middle of August with his weapons, artillery, vehicles and other equipment, could understand what deep truth there is in the term 'glorious retreat' ... After five and a half weeks of battle on an island against an enemy who, in ground forces alone, had four times our numbers, who, in supplies and equipment, was still superior to us; an enemy who had absolute superiority on sea and in the air. The three German divisions, on 17 August, were again on the mainland, ready and equipped to be committed in battle.[2]

Ironically, the last Axis troops to leave Sicily were an eight-man Italian patrol which had stayed behind at Faro and were lifted to safety by a German assault boat at 0830, 17 August.[3]

Captain von Liebenstein had every right to exult: 'We have not given up a single German soldier, weapon or vehicle into enemy hands.'[4] Allied ground forces never succeeded in threatening the Axis evacuation. The terrain continued to favour the defenders right up to the end. Small but powerful rearguard elements were able to delay effectively the advance long enough to permit their comrades to make their way to the ferries. The terrain of north-eastern Sicily is exceedingly rugged with high mountains and virtually no roads. In fact, only the two coastal roads actually lead to Messina and were easily defended. Mines, booby traps and demolitions continued to take their toll. Explosives were used to create road blocks and blow bridges.

Once Catania was abandoned and 13 Corps began to drive up

[1] Von Bonin.
[2] Ibid. Von Bonin also made this observation: '... it was a unique fact that the vehicles essential for motorized divisions had not decreased in number or quality, but had improved ... around MESSINA, the divisions had brought their vehicles up to strength out of the Italian transport which had been blocked there, and which otherwise would have fallen into the enemy's hands or been destroyed'.
[3] Ibid.
[4] Quoted in Pond, Sicily, op. cit., p. 218.

Route 114 towards Messina there was little thought given to the use of amphibious forces to leapfrog ahead and cut off the enemy retreat. Despite the fact that the engineers of the Hermann Goering had so effectively blocked Route 114 that it took a week for the 50th Division to advance some sixteen miles to Riposto from Catania, there is no indication Montgomery ever seriously embraced the amphibious concept even though he was anxious for Dempsey to push on to Messina. Nor is there any indication that Patton's sole reason for employing amphibious operations was anything more than a tactic to ensure Seventh Army got to Messina before the British.

Although constantly harassed by Allied naval gunfire and air attacks the Germans were never seriously bothered during their retirement to Messina.* Both coastal highways ran along steep cliff faces and it was often at such places that the Navy attempted to use gunfire to destroy sections of the roadway. One of the bad habits of the Allies was their predictability. It did not take the Germans long to deduce that the incoming salvoes were always fired at fixed intervals. The retreating German infantry simply timed their movements to these intervals when the engineers were able to clear a single lane for vehicles. The result was few casualties and some inconvenience but as a tactic for impeding the German withdrawal this proved an utter failure.[1]

It was not until 15 August that Montgomery finally decided to employ an amphibious 'end run' in order to speed up British entry into Messina. He ordered the 4th Armoured Brigade commander, Brigadier Currie, to mount a task force consisting of tanks, artillery, engineers and Lieutenant-Colonel J. M. T. F. Churchill's No. 2 Commando which landed near Scaletta, some ten miles below Messina early on the morning of 16 August. By then it was far too late to cut off any portion of the German evacuation. Only a few scattered rearguard German elements remained and these easily eluded Monty's task force.

The thrust by 50th Division up the coastal highway continued to be painfully slow and by the time its advance units reached a point several miles south of the lovely resort city of Taormina there were

[1] Ibid., p. 210.
* The Germans singled out the 3d Division for special praise for its 'exceptional initiative and endurance, an observation which was confirmed later in the battles on the mainland'. (Von Bonin, loc. cit.)

extensive demolitions to overcome. When it became obvious it would take some time to remove these obstacles, Major Harry Llewellyn, Senior Liaison Officer at Eighth Army HQ, went ahead on his own after being told the city was free of enemy forces. Llewellyn's task was to locate suitable accommodations for a new Eighth Army HQ. When he arrived in the city centre Llewellyn was greeted by a senior Italian officer in command of several hundred heavily armed troops. Told Taormina was surrounded by British troops (a considerable exaggeration), the Italians willingly agreed to lay down their arms and formally surrender the following morning. That evening Colonel David Belchem, Monty's Operations Officer, arrived. Llewellyn and Belchem, a noted *bon vivant*, took rooms in Taormina's finest hotel and proceeded to enjoy a gourmet meal in the restaurant, which was full of expressionless Sicilians who twenty-four hours earlier had been dining with German and Italian officers.[1]

The evening of 16 August, while Brigadier Currie's task force was still some miles south of Messina, the 3d Division had emplaced a battery of 155 mm howitzers (Battery B, 9th Field Artillery Battalion) on the heights overlooking the port city and these delivered the first Allied artillery fire across the Strait into the Italian mainland. The first Allied troops to enter the all-but-abandoned and ruined city of Messina at 2200, 16 August, was a reinforced patrol of Company L, 7th Infantry, commanded by First Lieutenant Ralph J. Yates, followed early the next morning by other 7th Infantry units and a platoon of Colonel Ankhorn's 157th RCT.

Meanwhile, Lieutenant-Colonel Churchill, no relation to the Prime Minister, but a man imbued with the Churchill spirit, was determined to beat the Americans to Messina. In the back of his jeep were a large Scottish sword and a set of bagpipes for the occasion.* Churchill told American correspondent Richard Tre-

---

[1] Belchem, *All in the Day's March*, op. cit., p. 169; Llewellyn, *Passport to Life*, op. cit., pp. 150–1; and Llewellyn interview, loc. cit. Kesselring had used Taormina as his HQ when in Sicily and the charm of this lovely resort city lured Montgomery who was given the most luxurious villa in town. With Monty came his menagerie of two canaries, a peacock, twelve chickens and two turkeys, all of whom his ADCs 'thought . . . a "bloody nuisance" and regularly plotted their demise'. (*Monty: Master of the Battlefield, 1942–1944*, op. cit., p. 350.)

* Within the Commandos Lieutenant-Colonel 'Mad Jack' Churchill had an awesome reputation. A one-time second-in-command of No. 3 Commando, Churchill is best remembered for the 1942 raid on the Norwegian port of Vaagso where he led his men ashore by

gaskis that both he and Brigadier Currie were so equipped. At the head of a patrol Churchill set out for Messina, but by the time they had picked their way through numerous mines laid along the highway and around a demolished bridge over a deep ravine four miles south of the city, they found that the last German force of about 500 men had left an hour earlier for the mainland.[1] To their intense dismay they also learned that American forces were already inside Messina.

At 0800, 17 August, an Italian colonel reported to Truscott and offered to surrender. Truscott demurred pending Patton's arrival two hours later. When Patton arrived at 1000 hours to make his triumphant entry he turned to the assemblage and said, 'What in hell are you all standing around for?'[2] and proceeded to lead the American convoy into Messina to the accompaniment of harassing enemy artillery fire from Calabria.* Even this nuisance was not about to deter Patton from his long-sought triumph. Behind Patton and Truscott came a second vehicle containing Keyes and Lucas, who recorded in his diary:

> Doughboys were moving down the road towards the city. They were tired and incredibly dirty. Many could hardly walk but were pushing on. These American boys of ours have remarkable stamina and are terrible in battle. I am glad I am on their side . . . We entered the town about ten thirty amid the wild applause of the people . . . The city was completely and terribly demolished. Worse than Bizerte which was beyond description. From what I

[1] Tregaskis, *Invasion Diary*, op. cit., pp. 86–8.
[2] Quoted in *Sicily*, op. cit., p. 416.
* Later, returning from Messina, Patton's Chief of Staff, General Gay, encountered a staff car parked along the roadside. 'In front of the car stood Lieutenant George Murmane [Gay's aide] – looking utterly disgusted. In the car sat a brigadier general . . . he appeared more disgusted than did Murmane – down the embankment crouched a high-ranking staff officer from General Eisenhower's headquarters – hiding or seeking protection from artillery fire – actually our own, not the enemy's.' When Patton came along a short time later, Gay wrote, 'I have never seen Patton so completely abashed – ashamed of an American.' (Gay Diary, 17 August 1943.) The officer was the AFHQ Chief of Staff, Major General Walter Bedell Smith. Patton was later told that when a battery of 135 mm guns opened up nearby, 'Smith thought it was enemy shells arriving and jumped from the car into the ditch in one leap, and refused to leave it, even when . . . told it was quite safe. When I got back in, he was still pale and shaky.' (Patton Diary, 17 August 1943.) Smith, whom Patton had no great love for and sometimes referred to as an 'S.O.B.', was taken away in Patton's command vehicle.

---

playing the bagpipes to the tune of 'The March of the Cameron Men'. One of the favourite weapons of this unorthodox soldier was a bow and arrow.

could see no house in Messina was without damage and few were habitable.[1]

The 3d Division G-3, Lieutenant Colonel Harrell, had been sent ahead to prepare for Patton's arrival. About the time Patton's command vehicle – its three-star pennants gleaming in the sunlight – rolled into the piazza in the centre of Messina, Brigadier Currie's small force of tanks arrived to join Colonel Churchill.* Correspondent Tregaskis describes the joyful scene:

> Commandos, smiling and shouting, sprawled over the exterior of tanks, and the little parade was made festive with many-colored flowers thrown by Sicilians. Some of the dirty-faced soldiers clutched huge bunches of grapes. Brigadier Currie dismounted from his tank . . . [as] General Patton, dazzling in his smart gabardines, stepped out and shook hands with the tall, lean brigadier. 'We got in about ten,' said Currie. 'It was a jolly good race. I congratulate you.'[2]

Colonel Harrell watched as Patton mounted a pedestal to deliver a brief talk:

> He was very nervous and he had a little Texas Ranger who was his bodyguard, who just adored him. God, he would look at him and old Georgie looked down at him and said, 'You little son-of-a-bitch, you're supposed to guard me, not look at me!'[3]

Harrell was one of the first to encounter Lieutenant-Colonel Churchill's patrol and remembers that they were quite disappointed to find the city already occupied by American troops. 'I think that General Patton should have been pretty darned proud,' he said, 'because we did move along that area [into Messina] and we moved rapidly.'[4]

[1] Lucas Diary, 17 August 1943.

[2] Invasion Diary, op. cit., p. 89. Still chary of Montgomery's motives, Patton believed that Brigadier Currie had been sent deliberately to steal his victory.

[3] Oral history interview of General Ben Harrell, loc. cit. Major Alexander C. Stiller was Patton's junior aide and an ex-sergeant who had served in his tank unit in France in 1918. Stiller, whom Martin Blumenson has described as 'rough and unlettered', was a cowboy from Arizona who had persuaded Patton to take him along on TORCH. He had arrived in Norfolk, Virginia, in October 1942 in his old First World War uniform complete with leggings and had had to be hastily fitted with new gear for his journeys with Patton that lasted until the end of the war. (Patton, Portrait of Patton and The Patton Papers, Vol. II, all contain descriptions of Stiller.)

[4] Ibid.

* In the film Patton, Montgomery is seen to lead a formal British parade down a street in Messina, only to find Patton there before him with a smirk on his face at having beaten his rival for the prize objective in Sicily. The film version is apocryphal fantasy.

Conspicuous that day by his absence was Omar Bradley, whose boycott was meant to send a signal to Patton of his contempt for what he firmly believed was his commander's penchant for pretentiousness. Patton, however, seemed genuinely disappointed at Bradley's failure to rendezvous with him on the hill overlooking Messina: 'Bradley not there – must have failed to get the message. This is a great disappointment to me, as I had telephoned him, and he certainly deserved the pleasure of entering the town.'[1] Like Montgomery, Bradley was not concerned with victory marches, and his anger and disgust with Patton had reached its zenith with Patton's order that no units were to enter Messina 'until he could make triumphal entry. I was furious. I had to hold our troops in the hills instead of pursuing the fleeing Germans in an effort to get as many as we could. British nearly beat him into Messina because of that.' Momentarily, Bradley was tempted to drive into Messina and greet Patton on a street corner when he arrived, which, he admitted, 'would have been playing Georgie's game'.[2]

Although it was a personal triumph for Patton after the dark days of the invasion when it appeared as if Seventh Army's fate was to act as a perpetual shield for Eighth Army, he was quick to laud his Army accomplishments in a stirring Order of the Day.[*] The capture of Messina came as something of a letdown to Patton who, like Lucas, had found his prize 'horribly destroyed – the worst I have seen . . . I do not believe the indiscriminate bombing of towns is worth the ammunition, and it is unnecessarily cruel to civilians.'[3] Having at last won the race, Patton was in a reflective mood: 'I feel let down. The reaction from intense mental and physical activity to a state of inertia is very difficult. I feel that the Lord has been most generous. If I had to fight the campaign over, I would make no change in anything I did. Few generals in history have ever been able to say as much.'[4]

Patton's triumph notwithstanding, the end of the campaign in Sicily was a dismal conclusion to one that had been beset from the start by controversy and indecision. For thirty-eight days the Allies

[1] Patton Diary, 17 August 1943.

[2] Bradley Commentaries. Although Bradley never knew it, it is doubtful Patton's order made the slightest difference in trapping the few rearguard German elements still in Messina.

[3] Patton Diary, 17 August 1943.

[4] Ibid.

[*] The complete text of Patton's message is in Appendix M.

fought some of the bitterest battles of the war in terrain every bit as harsh as they would soon find ahead of them in Italy. Yet their enemy had defied them to the end and had added the final insult by pulling off one of the most dazzling strategic withdrawals in military history. At Dunkirk, British ingenuity and grit had saved the BEF but not their precious equipment. In Sicily, the Germans had saved themselves and virtually everything capable of being ferried to the mainland. Only those captured and the dead were left behind.

Ever defiant to the end, the Germans came away from Sicily feeling they had given as good as they had got. There was an understandable air of pride in having survived and in having fought well against an overwhelmingly superior enemy force. A battalion diarist of the Panzer Regiment Hermann Goering put the German feeling into perspective by writing:

> The campaign in Sicily is over. We were far from fond of the country in which we had been fighting, but for all that we felt strange when the ferry pulled away from Messina, and we had to leave the island to an enemy who was superior to us only in the material sense.[1]

From the time of Alexander's decision to force Seventh Army into a secondary role and Montgomery's errant election to switch his main effort from the plains of Catania to the highlands, the Germans, not the Allies, had been in real control of the timetable for the battle of Sicily. From uncertain beginnings at Gela when the Hermann Goering Division had performed reprehensibly, to Group Schmalz which had delayed the British advance just long enough for the reinforcement of Primosole bridge by the tenacious paratroopers of the 1st Parachute Division who held their ground against nearly impossible odds, and to the defence of Troina and the San Fratello Line, the German Army in Sicily had performed admirably against superior air, sea and ground forces. At the end they added the final insult by their brilliant planning and execution of the great escape.

The Allies should have ended the campaign with a stunning victory; instead, by any objective assessment, they gathered a harvest of bitter fruit.

[1] Quoted in Molony, *The Mediterranean and Middle East*, Vol. V, op. cit., p. 182.

CHAPTER 31

Bitter Victory

By 10 a.m. this morning, August 17, 1943, the last German soldier was flung out of Sicily and the whole island is now in our hands.

ALEXANDER TO CHURCHILL

That Alexander never understood the consequences of the campaign he had so ineptly led typified the unsatisfactory ending to Operation HUSKY. Earlier on 17 August he had signalled Churchill that 'It can be assumed that all Italian forces in [the] island on July 10 have been destroyed, though a few battered units may have escaped to the mainland.'[1] With all the attention focused on the German Army, Alexander may not have been fully aware at this point that an estimated 62,000 Italians had been evacuated to Italy. He was by no means the only offender when it came to extravagant claims that bore little relation to reality. The official US air historians downplayed the German evacuation by enumerating the statistics of sorties flown, targets attacked, hits and near misses in an effort to demonstrate the success of the air effort.

Among the inflated claims was the statement that 'In spite of the efforts of both Tactical and Strategic [Air] the Germans effected a partially successful withdrawal, saving the equivalent of at least one division with equipment.' And, 'The enemy used extensive night traffic which he protected with a good concentration of flak on both sides of the narrow strait – which could be crossed in a matter of minutes. Even so, the air force listed the destruction of 23 craft, direct hits on 43, and near misses on 204.'[2] Despite their considerable contribution to the conquest of Sicily, the tendency of the airmen to overstate their effectiveness is far-fetched in light of what actually transpired. Even more absurd were the postwar

[1] Alexander Papers. Also quoted in Churchill, *Closing the Ring*, Boston, 1951, p. 40.
[2] Craven and Cate (eds), *The Army Air Forces in World War II*, Vol. II, *Europe: Torch to Pointblank, August 1942 to December 1943*, op. cit., p. 473.

claims of enemy shipping losses which, as the official British naval historian has observed, 'bore little relation to the truth'. Roskill cites a 1947 publication by the Royal Institute of International Affairs which asserted that '306 Axis ships evacuating troops were sunk between August 5th and 17th'.[1]

Equally ludicrous are the memoirs of Eisenhower's chief intelligence officer, the AFHQ G-2, Brigadier K. W. D. Strong, who not only failed to heed the growing evidence of the Axis evacuation but later wrote:

> Early in August we deduced that the enemy was contemplating evacuation and by the second week of the month they had indeed started to pull out. We employed our maximum air effort in the hope of preventing a second Dunkirk and in this we were particularly successful. Although sixty thousand men with their equipment escaped to Italy, when Sicily capitulated on 20 August [sic] we were left with over two hundred thousand prisoners, mostly Italians, and masses of aircraft, tanks and guns.[2]

Strong fails to tell us how the escape of the entire German Army force in Sicily, along with their equipment, constitutes a 'particularly successful' interdiction. Small wonder, therefore, that the truth of what actually occurred in Sicily is little known. How then did an estimated 62,000 Italians and the entire German fighting contingent manage to escape from Sicily? The answer to this question lies in the miscalculations with which HUSKY was carried out. To begin with, the original planning never explicitly contemplated a decisive victory or a masterstoke which would strike a crippling blow against the enemy forces defending Sicily. While it is correct to state that the Allied leadership may have deluded themselves in the belief there would be a decisive victory, the conservatism of the HUSKY plan and the failure of the senior Allied commanders to organize a joint command headquarters to administer it, laid the foundation for what ensued.

The key to such a victory in Sicily was always to choke off Axis use of the Messina Strait, and had the Allies been bold enough to launch an operation to seize the southern tip of Calabria, all enemy forces on Sicily would have been trapped on the island. Kesselring has said that a 'secondary attack on Calabria would have enabled

[1] Quoted in Roskill, *The War at Sea*, Vol. III, Part I, op. cit., p. 149.
[2] Major-General Sir Kenneth Strong, *Intelligence at the Top*, op. cit., p. 101.

the Sicily landing to be developed into a devastating victory'.[1] Many reasons have been offered for the eventual outcome, most of them either superfluous or an apologia. Of the senior commanders responsible for HUSKY, only Eisenhower was willing to admit the Allies had blundered.

Before the campaign had even ended Eisenhower acknowledged that the Allies had taken too cautious an approach to Sicily. Butcher records on 14 August Eisenhower's 'pre-breakfast bedroom lecture on the mistakes which history will record as having been made by him; he has mentioned two: the landing at Casablanca and our super-cautious approach to Italy. On the latter, Ike now thinks we should have made simultaneous landings on both sides of the Messina Strait, thus cutting off all Sicily and obtaining wholesale surrender and saving time and equipment, particularly landing craft which would have permitted a rapid rush on the mainland itself.'[2]

Senior German and Italian officers have been universally scornful of Allied conservatism, and point to the invasion landings and their timing as the two most serious mistakes. All felt there was too much precious time lost between the fall of Tunisia and the July landings. They believed the target ought to have been Calabria, not Gela and Syracuse. There were no German Army units anywhere in Italy except for the units on Sicily which were formed into the 15th Panzer Grenadier Division. The principal argument against such a landing had been the lack of tactical air cover and the inability of the Air Force to provide it due to the lengthy distances from Malta and the North African bases. Little has been said of the ability of the Navy to have provided round-the-clock gunfire support to an invasion force that would have encountered only minimal opposition.[*]

The German commanders were appalled at the Allied failure at least to have mounted a secondary operation into Calabria to prevent their escape, at which time full air-cover was available from the captured Sicilian airfields where by early August over

[1] Postwar interrogation of Field Marshal Kesselring, 'German General's Collection' (9/24/117), Liddell Hart Papers, King's College, London.

[2] Butcher Diary, 14 August 1943; also quoted in *Three Years With Eisenhower*, op. cit., p. 330.

[*] The 'toe' of the Italian 'boot' averages twenty-five miles in width, but the distances within and along both ends of the Messina Strait were such that naval gunfire could have protected an invasion force.

fifty-eight RAF and USAAF squadrons were based. One of the most critical was General Heinrich von Vietinghoff,[1] sent by Hitler to command the Tenth Army which was activated shortly after the evacuation of Sicily to defend southern Italy. Von Vietinghoff believed it

> a costly mistake not to have attempted an invasion of Calabria prior to the end of the Sicily campaign. From the German standpoint it is incomprehensible that the Allies did not seize the Straits of Messina, either at the same time as the [invasion] landing or in the course of the initial actions, just as soon as the German troops were contained. On both sides of the Straits – not only in the northeast corner of the island but in southern Calabria as well – this would have been possible without any special difficulty.[2]

Von Bonin wrote that:

> In the following days we could hardly understand that the operation ['Lehrgang'] had been such a complete success. There had been so many chances against us. An indication of the fact that the success could not be understood was the fact that otherwise sane people maintained that the Allies had intentionally allowed the German divisions to escape to the mainland, and they based this nonsense on fantastical political theories. Sober and clear-thinking comrades laughed at this of course, but the fact that such rumours were spread throws remarkable light on the events of the preceding days and week, which seemed like a miracle.[3]

In their postwar assessment both Kesselring and his Chief of Staff, General Siegfried Westphal, stated they expected a secondary Allied landing in Calabria. 'In this case, SICILY would have become a mousetrap to all German and Italian forces fighting down there.'[4] Kesselring was critical of the whole Allied approach to Sicily and later in Italy (Salerno and Anzio notwithstanding) which was a predictable and ponderous advance. Like Bradley, Kesselring never understood the logic behind the Seventh Army

---

[1] Generaloberst Heinrich von Vietinghoff, 'Overall Situation in the Mediterranean up to the Landing on the Italian Mainland', MS # D-116, USAMHI. Colonel General von Vietinghoff was a veteran armoured commander who had commanded 46 Panzer Corps in Russia and the Balkans from 1940 to 1942, followed by the 9th Army from June to December 1942. Since that time he had been in France in command of AOK 15 (15th Army).

[2] Ibid.

[3] Von Bonin, 'Considerations of the Italian Campaign, 1943–44', loc. cit.

[4] Kesselring and Westphal in 'German Strategy during the Italian Campaign,' MS # B-270, USAMHI.

offensive into western Sicily. They 'just marched and captured unimportant terrain, instead of fighting at the [eastern] wing where a major decision had to be reached'.[1]

In his account written for the Canadians, von Bonin asked the puzzling questions the Germans themselves were unable to answer:

> Why was no attempt made to block the Strait of Messina simultaneously with the invasion of Sicily?
>
> Why, in the ensuing fighting, was no such attempt made?
>
> Why did the Allied command in Sicily limit itself to a slow-moving frontal attack?
>
> Why did they not exploit the possibility of landings deep in our flanks and rear?
>
> Did the Allies appreciate the German intention to evacuate Sicily in time to permit an attempt to be made to prevent it?
>
> If so, why was the attempt not made?[2]

By the end of July it was becoming clear by a number of different means that the Germans would eventually attempt to evacuate Sicily. On 31 July, Montgomery noted in his diary, 'On this day we shot an officer who had with him an attaché case containing maps, tracings, and orders giving the whole of the enemy defensive layout and his plans for withdrawal if unable to hold on. This was a most valuable capture, the best we have had.'[3] Alexander spent the night of 3 August at Montgomery's CP where the possibility of a German evacuation was certainly a matter of mutual concern and discussion. Before departing Eighth Army, Alexander sent the following cable to Tedder and Cunningham in which Montgomery's influence is evident:

> Indications suggest that the Germans are making preparations for withdrawal to the mainland when this becomes necessary. It is quite possible he may start pulling out before front collapses. We must be in a position to take immediate advantage of such a situation by using full weight of Naval and Air power. You have no doubt co-ordinated plans to meet this contingency and I for my part will watch situation most carefully so as to let you know the right moment to strike and this may well come upon us sooner than we expect.[4]

[1] Kesselring in MS # T-2/K-1, USAMHI.   [2] Von Bonin.
[3] Montgomery Diary, 31 July 1943.
[4] Eighth Army War Diary, 3 August 1943, PRO (WO 169/8494).

That same day Broadhurst was issuing his own warning to Coningham that a German evacuation was imminent:[1]

> Advanced Headquarters
> Desert Air Force
> 3rd August 1943
> MOST SECRET
>
> Dear Air Marshal,
>
> There were very distinct signs yesterday that the German Army is feeling the strain and that its morale and capacity to withstand further attacks are weakening. If this process continues in the way we hope, it is quite possible that the Hun may attempt an evacuation across the Messina Straits, possibly earlier than was thought possible a few days ago.
>
> If this happens, I suggest that it will need a combined air and naval plan to deal with it, something on the lines of the Tunisian affair but, of course, applied to the particular situation here. I quite realise that we can do a lot with the air forces immediately available, but the exceptional flak on both sides of the Straits of Messina will need, I think, the use of Fortresses if we are to maintain continuous air action to defeat an attempt at evacuation. Presumably the Navy will be able to prevent sea movement at night, but here again they may need some help from us.
>
> It is quite possible that all this has already been planned, but if not I suggest that you might like to give it your attention.
>
> Yours Sincerely,
>
> /s/ Harry
>
> Air Marshal Sir Arthur Coningham,
>   K.C.B., D.S.O., M.C., D.F.C.
> Headquarters, N.A.T.A.F.
> Royal Air Force.

The following day, 4 August, Tedder cabled Portal that 'he expected to be called upon to throw the whole weight of the Allied air resources into preventing German evacuation of the island'.[2] Coningham's great concern was the intense flak concentrated along the Strait and what he was certain was a requirement for the Navy to provide a physical barrier by blockading both ends of the channel. Even so, 'I do not see how we can hope for the same proportion of success as at Cape Bon [i.e., Tunisia]...'[3]

---

[1] PRO (AIR 23/7441).
[2] Quoted in *The Mediterranean and Middle East*, Vol. V, op. cit., p. 167.
[3] Ibid., p. 168.

While there were no direct references to an Axis evacuation, the first week of August saw the Allies intercept clear signs that something was afoot. Among them a 1 August decrypt that specified the location of ferrying points for each of the three German divisions and the elements of the 1st Parachute Division. Brigadier Williams, Monty's astute G-2, had by 5 August begun to question the significance of Siebel ferries arriving in Messina empty at a time when the Germans were noticeably suffering severe supply shortages.[1] The AFHQ G-2, Brigadier Strong, acknowledged the latest intelligence but refused to concede that any evacuation was forthcoming. 'There are at present no adequate intentions that the enemy envisages evacuation of MESSINA bridgehead.'[2] However, by 12 August Strong had more than sufficient evidence to draw the right conclusion, but he would only admit to an evacuation of rear elements and non-essential material.[3] Brigadier Williams had come to the same conclusion five days earlier on 7 August,[4] and on 8 August Eighth Army reported the enemy beginning his evacuation early and 'in the best conditions any evacuation has had in this war ... protected by the heaviest concentration of flak ever encountered by the Royal Air Force in the Mediterranean Theatre'.[5] On 11 August Eighth Army reproduced the captured Hermann Goering warning order issued on 2 August in which specific instructions were issued for the evacuation, including the stern warning that every soldier reporting to the ferries would be in possession of infantry weapons or else! 'These weapons are *tickets* for the ferry. Without those mentioned, soldiers will be ruthlessly prevented from crossing.'[6]

Well before 'Lehrgang' was officially set in motion Eighth Army units were fully aware of German intentions. 30 Corps on 8 August

[1] Hinsley, *British Intelligence in the Second World War*, Vol. III, Pt I, op. cit., p. 96, and Eighth Army Intelligence Summary No. 529, 5 August 1943, PRO (WO 169/8519). That same day the Seventh Army G-2, Colonel Oscar Koch, concluded that 'in all probability evacuation is taking place. The entire operation from the enemy viewpoint, therefore, is to delay advance against time.' (Seventh Army G-2 Periodic Report No. 27, 5 August 1943, quoted in *Sicily*, p. 378.) Two days later Koch reaffirmed his judgment in Report No. 29, 7 August 1943.

[2] AFHQ Weekly Intelligence Summary No. 50, issued 10 August 1943 for week ending 7 August, PRO (WO 204/1967). Also quoted in Hinsley, p. 96.

[3] AFHQ G-2 Report No. 278, 12 August 1943, PRO (WO 204/974).

[4] Eighth Army Intelligence Summary No. 531, 7 August 1943, PRO (WO 169/8519).

[5] Ibid., No. 532, 8 August 1943.

[6] Eighth Army Intelligence Summary No. 534, 11 August 1943, 'Enclosure to [HG] Division Order No. 31/43, 2 August 1943: Directive for Future Movements and Battle Actions in Sicily', PRO (WO 169/8519).

correctly assessed that the Germans were in the first phase of a full-scale evacuation: 'An orderly and unhurried DUNKIRK may well be in progress.'[1] And on 10 August: 'Despite the way in which he has retarded our progress in the last five days, the enemy had none the less decided by 1 August that he would have to evacuate. Further captured orders of the Goering Division dated 1 and 2 August ... make this clear.'[2]

The British official history fails to address the question of the role of intelligence in the Allied failure to halt the Axis evacuation. In the official naval history there is the observation that 'the Intelligence services were late in drawing the correct conclusions; but even when the enemy's intention was plain the action taken suffered from lack of inter-service co-ordination'.[3] This was certainly true at the highest level where it counted, and as the official British intelligence historians have noted, the intelligence summary issued by AFHQ on 17 August 'suggests that its authors may have remained unconvinced until as late as 13 August that a general evacuation was in progress'.[4] In turn, this appears to have influenced 15th Army Group and may well explain why, as late as 12 August, Alexander was telling Brooke that 'the general impression, and only an impression, is that the Germans may withdraw across the Straits shortly'.[5] Had 15th Army Group paid more attention to the Eighth Army warnings it is doubtful that Alexander would have waited until 14 August to cable Tedder that 'it now appears [the] German evacuation has really started'. Undoubtedly AFHQ's wretchedly inaccurate conclusions were those accepted by Alexander's staff.

At the lower levels of command there was no such vacillation about what was occurring in the Strait of Messina. Eighth Army had warned repeatedly and explicitly, starting in the first days of August, that an evacuation was under way and daily photo reconnaissance runs over the Strait confirmed these conclusions.* The

---

[1] 30 Corps Intelligence Summary No. 390, 8 August 1943, PRO (WO 169/8647).
[2] 30 Corps Intelligence Summary No. 392, 10 August 1943, ibid.
[3] Roskill, op. cit., p. 149.
[4] Hinsley, op. cit., p. 98.
[5] Ibid., p. 99. The 15th Army Group, 'G' Operations War Diary reported the noticeable increase in shipping activity in the Messina Strait. (See PRO [WO 169/8457].)
* Photo reconnaissance missions were flown day and night. In their weekly intelligence summary for 31 July–6 August, the NAAF reported that 'It was not unusual during a photographic run to spot as many as 25 "F" boats and 20 Siebel ferries in the vicinity together with a number of smaller craft . . . Frequent photographic coverage indicates a constant

evidence upon which these assessments were issued was based upon incontrovertible evidence: captured official German documents, photographic intelligence, captured German and Italian POWs, the reports of civilians and ULTRA decrypts. Yet AFHQ's indecisive Intelligence Summaries (ISUMs) continued in their refusal to acknowledge the obvious. Incredibly, at the daily operational meeting at AFHQ on 14 August the G-2 report, in contravention of massive evidence to the contrary, insisted that 'there is no evidence of any large-scale withdrawal of troops from Sicily'.[1]

The performance of the Allied ground forces in attempting to halt the evacuation was not exceptional. On 10 August, the same day Patton ordered the Brolo landings, Montgomery cabled Alexander that an American landing in the Funari area* would completely cut off the German retreat.[2] Other than sending the Commandos to Messina on 16 August Montgomery made no other attempt to use an amphibious force to cut the escape route up the eastern coast. By this time Montgomery had replaced 13 Corps with Leese's 30 Corps and was reportedly furious because Captain Geoffrey Keating, the Officer-in-Charge of the Eighth Army Film and Photographic Unit had, like Llewellyn, made it into Taormina unmolested. Montgomery sent for Leese and demanded to know why his infantry couldn't do what Keating obviously could.[3]

The eastern coast of Sicily from Catania to Messina is not ideal for landing amphibious forces but is no worse than the terrain

---

[1] RAF narrative, PRO (AIR 41/52), loc. cit. Even the correspondents were fully aware of the evacuation. On 8 August, correspondent Richard Tregaskis was shown a copy of the Hermann Goering Division evacuation order. The following day he was told by a British intelligence officer that 'From now on it seems to be a question of who can walk back the fastest. The Germans are definitely getting out everything they can. Aerial photographs again confirm the arrival of empty ferries and their departure loaded.' (Quoted in *Invasion Diary*, op. cit., p. 70.)

[2] Cable, Montgomery–Alexander, reproduced in Montgomery Diary, 10 August 1943.

[3] *Monty: Master of the Battlefield, 1942–1944*, op. cit., p. 368. 13 Corps was detached by Montgomery to plan Operation BAYTOWN. Leese was in tactical control of the only Eighth Army formation still engaged: Kirkman's 50th Division.

* Located approximately twenty-five miles further east along Route 113, Funari is situated astride the point where the last interior road joined the coastal highway to Messina. American control of Funari would have cut off the retreat of the 29th Panzer Grenadier Division.

---

shuttling service between the Italian mainland and the beaches of Sicily.' (NAAF Weekly Air Intelligence Summary No. 38, PRO [AIR 23/7452].) Photo reconnaissance averaged a *minimum* of two runs per day by the NAAF Photo Reconnaissance Wing, commanded by the President's eldest son, Colonel Elliott Roosevelt. Copies of the photo intelligence and interpretation reports are in AIR 23/6973.

found on the northern coast of the island. Even though there were few good beaches and exits, the Navy was anxious to land small forces to harass the German withdrawal. Cunningham was later openly critical of Montgomery's failure to make better use of his amphibious capability. 'There were doubtless sound military reasons,' he wrote to the Admiralty, 'for not making use of this … priceless asset of sea power and flexibility of manoeuvre.'[1]

Patton had proposed an airborne/amphibious landing at Barcellona, a few miles east of Funari. A force landing at this point would have effectively severed any German escape along the northern coast to Messina by both the 15th and 29th Panzer Grenadier Divisions. The plan was approved by Alexander but when it was submitted to Tedder on 12 August it called for the 2d Battalion/505th Airborne Infantry (82d Airborne Division) to drop near Barcellona and prevent any German attempt to interfere with the amphibious landing several hours later by the 157th RCT (45th Division). Both the 52d Troop Carrier Wing and the 82d Airborne commanders, Ridgway and Gavin, were sceptical. The drop zones were poor and the Air Force anticipated large losses from a low-level drop and argued the same results could be obtained from fighter-bomber attacks.[2] Patton grumbled but acceded to this advice. It did not really matter, for too much time was lost discussing the matter at the HQs of Tedder and Cunningham and the time lost was crucial. Before the problems could be resolved, the Germans had already retreated east of the target area and the one and only opportunity seriously to interfere with their withdrawal along the northern coast was lost.

There was far too much discussion and too little action. Cunningham and Tedder exchanged signals with each other and 15th Army Group in response to Alexander's cable of 3 August. Cunningham pledged that he already had light craft, MTBs (Motor Torpedo Boats) and MGBs (Motor Gun Boats) operating in the Messina Strait and 'this will be intensified … As the coast batteries are mopped up, it will be possible for surface forces to operate

---

[1] Admiral Andrew Browne Cunningham and Admiral Sir Bertram Ramsay, 'Report of Operations – Sicily', 1 January 1944, PRO (CAB 106/637).

[2] Gavin, *On To Berlin*, op. cit., p. 46; RAF narrative, and *Sicily*, op. cit., Chapter XXI. According to Gavin, he, Ridgway and Brig. Gen. Paul L. Williams (Commander, Northwest African Troop Carrier Command) were summoned to Palermo by Patton who made clear his determination to get to Messina before Montgomery. He was told that drop zones were non-existent and the terrain rugged and forbidding. 'We recommended against it and Patton, although unhappy, went along with us.' (Letter to the author, 11 February 1986.)

further into the straits.'¹ Cunningham also proposed the Air Force operate 'without let or hindrance' in the Messina Strait once the enemy evacuation began.² Tedder's return signal of 4 August accepted Cunningham's suggestion which, he said, ought to be 'put into operation at once'.³

Spaatz's role is less clear but from the total absence of any reference to air operations against the Messina Strait in his diary or papers, it is fair to conclude that the decisions regarding such operations were being made by Coningham and Tedder. Two days earlier an order was issued that Doolittle's strategic bombers were not to be significantly diverted from their current priority targets in Italy and the Rumanian oilfields. The responsibility for the air effort fell to Coningham's Tactical Air Force, even though Tedder's signal of 4 August led to Spaatz's approval of a policy of diverting Doolittle's bombers upon twelve-hour notice from Coningham.⁴

Coningham replied to Broadhurst on 4 August indicating he believed the problem facing the tactical air commanders was how to interfere with the evacuation which would undoubtedly occur only at *night*, and against considerable enemy air opposition – a premise which proved false on both counts.⁵

About the time of the evacuation there was considerable infighting between the senior air commanders over the future role and organization of the Allied air forces. Spaatz tried and failed to separate the USAAF from the RAF, a move firmly blocked by Tedder who remained wedded to the concept of an all-Allied air command. In addition, Spaatz found that Coningham was acting independently with disturbing frequency which included by-passing his headquarters in favour of direct contact with Tedder. Several months earlier, it will be recalled, Coningham had displayed his contempt for Spaatz during the flower incident and now he began to act as if Spaatz did not exist. One American air historian believes Spaatz's loss of influence in the Mediterranean came about because Tedder took over the direction and allocation of the strategic air forces at an inopportune moment. Spaatz played no meaningful role in the decisions and actions taken during the evacuation. 'He certainly would have reacted more

¹ Quoted in Roskill, *The War at Sea*, Vol. III, Part I, op. cit., p. 146.
² Ibid.   ³ Ibid.   ⁴ Ibid., p. 148.
⁵ Ibid., p. 147.

strongly than the British Air Marshals. Shortly before the evacuation, on 4 August, Spaatz stated, in Ike's presence, at a General Officer's meeting, "... it is my belief that it [air] should have been used exclusively in Sicily to expedite the battle there...".[1]

Coningham seemed to have been content to make limited use of the heavy bombers and rely, when the time came, primarily upon his tactical air capability. Until there was evidence of a large-scale evacuation, day and night attacks would continue at approximately the same level as before. Thus, it was not until 11 August that Coningham reported to Tedder that while enemy intentions were plain, there were as yet no signs of substantial evacuation movements by day. Should the withdrawal develop on a larger scale, 'we can handle it with our own resources and naval assistance'.[2] Still, full acknowledgment did not come until the afternoon of 13 August when a message was received stating the evacuation had begun and all tactical air missions were to be directed against enemy shipping and beaches.[3]

At the time Coningham's assessment was correct but within 24 hours the Germans began full daytime movement as von Liebenstein won his argument with Hube. Tedder was advised there no longer existed a requirement to utilize Doolittle's Strategic Air Force to make daylight attacks so long as the Wellingtons of No. 205 Group (RAF) continued their commitment to night operations, which became known as 'The "Milk Run" to Messina'.*

The decision to abandon daylight operations by the strategic

---

[1] See Richard G. Davis, 'Eisenhower's Airman: General Carl A. Spaatz and the United States Army Air Forces in Europe, 1942–1945', doctoral thesis, George Washington University, 1985. Davis believes Spaatz would have proven far more flexible than Coningham in his use of strategic bombers and would not have exhibited the overconfidence in the use of tactical air as an effective substitute. Tedder and Spaatz had parted company over the latter's belief there had been insufficient use of air in Sicily. Tedder later wrote that: 'To use our whole strategic effort to blast a path through the enemy defences in Sicily must seriously decrease our ability to reduce the enemy's air effort before operations in Italy. Our air forces had now been at full stretch for weeks on end, and because of the slow rate at which air crews were replaced their effectiveness must gradually decline. I felt that at this stage our full strength must be reserved for use against the enemy's air forces.' (*With Prejudice*, op. cit., p. 457.) A request by Eisenhower for the temporary loan of four heavy bomber groups from England to employ against Italy was rejected as disastrous to the strategic bombing effort against Germany.

[2] Roskill, op. cit., p. 149. Here, Coningham contradicted an earlier statement to Tedder on 1 August in which he said that he 'considered that the Messina area "flak" was now practically prohibitive for all aircraft except the heavy bombers', which was confirmed by Broadhurst in his letter of 3 August. (See Terraine, *The Right of the Line*, op. cit., p. 579.)

[3] Ibid., p. 148.

* No. 205 Group of the Northwest African Strategic Air Forces flew 691 Wellington

bombers was misleading because there had never been anything even remotely resembling a daytime strategic bomber effort. The total flown by B-17 bombers was a meagre 142 sorties, all of which took place in early August on only three occasions. The decision not to employ these aircraft appears to have been the most serious of the many misjudgments made by the Allies in Sicily. There were approximately 180 heavy (B-17) bombers assigned to Doolittle's Strategic Air Force, and assuming a 15% loss/non-availability rate, their employment against the Messina Strait during the first seventeen days of August was a mere 5.5%.* The only two heavy attacks took place on the mornings of 5 and 6 August when a total of 121 B-17s attacked Messina. Their primary targets, however, were not shipping but the city itself and the crossroads leading into it.[1] During the crucial days of 11–17 August there were only two insignificant attacks: on 13 August by eleven B-25 medium bombers and again on 16 August by twelve B-25s.[2] None of these raids sank any Axis shipping or interfered in any way with evacuation operations. In fact, it was the clear absence of daytime raids by medium and heavy bombers that convinced the German naval command to shift the majority of their operations from night-time to daylight hours.[3]

The truth is that the air forces, despite what appear to have been good intentions, never made anything resembling an all-out effort to interfere with or block the Axis evacuation of Sicily. From dusk on 29 July to dusk on 17 August, Tedder's Mediterranean Air Command flew 9,889 bomber and fighter-bomber sorties. Of this total, 2,514 – a mere 25% – were flown against targets in the Messina Strait.[4] The night attacks by the Wellingtons, mostly

[1] NAAF 'Analysis of Bombing Operations, 31 July–14 August 1943'.
[2] Ibid. Twenty-one B-17s also attacked Messina the morning of 9 August and there were three night attacks: 2/3 August by two B-24 and eleven Halifax (heavy) bombers; 8/9 August by twenty-six Halifaxes and ten B-24s; and 11/12 August by nine Halifaxes and four B-24s.
[3] Von Liebenstein War Diary.
[4] Footnote 1 (p. 169) and Table II (p. 184), Molony, *The Mediterranean and Middle East*, Vol. V; NAAF 'Analysis of Bombing Operations, 31 July–14 August 1943', PRO (AIR 23/3553), and Air Ministry War Room Summaries, Air Historical Branch, RAF, London. Ninety-seven per cent of the missions flown by the Allied air forces during the period of the

medium bomber sorties against targets in the Messina Strait beginning the night of 4/5 August until the night of 14/15 August. This unit also suffered the heaviest losses of any Allied air unit operating in the Strait. The usual practice was to attack during every hour of darkness in groups averaging 8–11 aircraft. The heaviest attacks occurred during the nights of 5/6 August (85), 8/9 August (82), 9/10 August (86), 10/11 August (88), 11/12 August (89), 12/13 August (90) and 13/14 August (70). (Source: Northwest African Air Forces (NAAF) 'Analysis of Bombing Operations, 31 July–14 August 1943', loc. cit.)

against the beaches and Messina, were a considerable nuisance to the German and Italian evacuation commanders but otherwise failed to impede the evacuation. The price paid by No. 205 Group (RAF) was 58% of the total lost over the Strait, the heaviest of any Allied air unit.* Other than the night of 12/13 August when four barges were hit and either damaged or destroyed, no enemy shipping was hit during these raids.[1]

According to the air force after-action reports the average height at which bombs were dropped during the night raids was 5,000 feet, always under intense flak from Baade's AA defences on both sides of the Strait, a concentration generally believed to be one of the heaviest experienced by the airmen any time during the war. Of the 2,514 sorties flown in the Messina Strait, total losses were twelve aircraft, with nineteen more missing,† an overall loss rate of 1.23%.[2] The last two days of the evacuation, the Allies made a last-ditch attempt to halt the evacuation with massive daylight raids on 15 and 16 August during which 39% of the losses were experienced.[3] Thus, while the Messina Strait was undoubtedly one of the most hazardous targets ever attacked by the Allies, the notion that air operations in the Strait were suicidal is a myth unsupported by the evidence. The majority of the missions flown were by fighters and fighter-bombers which suffered the fewest losses – approximately five in 1,464 sorties – 0.34%.[4] Admiral Ruge offers an explanation: 'It became impossible for the heavy AA batteries to deal with the rapier-like thrusts of fighters and fighter-bombers. There was not enough light AA to defend all the landing places.'[5]

[1] PRO (AIR 23/3553). Zuckerman's independent analysis reveals that other than the Italian ferry *Cariddi* destroyed the night of 7/8 June, 'no other ship is recorded as having been struck at night'. ('An Analysis of the Effects of Air Raids on Messina', Zuckerman Papers.)
[2] PRO (AIR 23/3553).
[3] Ibid.   [4] Ibid.
[5] Ruge, 'The Evacuation of Sicily'.
* Eighteen of the thirty-one Allied aircraft lost between 31 July and 17 August were Wellingtons of No. 205 Group. One of the four wings of this group was Canadian, and RCAF aircraft flew 188 of the 691 total Wellington sorties over the Strait.
† The author has been unable to account for the missing aircraft from contemporary records and they are therefore recorded as 'lost'.

Sicily campaign were flown by the NAAF. Of these, 6,591 (67%) were flown against Sicilian targets, including evacuation shipping.
* 180 aircraft × 17 [days]=3,060−[e] 15% non-availability=2,601 available sorties. 142 actually flown=5.5% of the total available.

Von Liebenstein spoke for the other side when he observed in his war diary at the height of the evacuation that 'It is astonishing the enemy has not made stronger attacks in the past days. There frequently has been a pause of 1–2 hours between individual fighter-bomber raids, while high-level attacks have been practically non-existent.'[1]

The reluctance by Tedder and Coningham to employ daylight strategic bomber raids left the burden of attempting to halt the evacuation to the tactical aircraft of Broadhurst's Desert Air Force, and what little success the Allies enjoyed in interdicting targets in the Strait came from this source. Eighty-nine per cent (2,245) of the total sorties flown were by tactical aircraft during daylight hours. These were all low-level attacks of from 1,000 to 4,000 feet.* Despite the barrage balloons and the heavy flak, the lower the altitude of attack the greater the success and the fewer the losses. Prior to the heavy daylight raids on 15 and 16 August the Northwest African Air Forces reported the loss of only three tactical aircraft over the Messina Strait.[2]

The tactical air commitment was likewise a fraction of the aircraft available. Coningham's air force had 137 light bombers and 721 fighters and fighter-bombers, yet only about 18% were committed to Messina operations.† Even more telling is the fact that there was a greater air effort during the pre-evacuation period than during the main withdrawal. There were 1,318 sorties flown between 31 July and 10 August, while only 1,196 took place from 11 to 16 August. Of these latter, fully one-third (399) were flown on 16 August when the Axis evacuation was already a *fait accompli*.[3]

Other than the probable destruction of four barges on the night of 12 August by RAF Wellingtons, the remainder of Axis shipping losses were scored by Allied tactical aircraft during daylight

[1] Von Liebenstein War Diary.
[2] PRO (AIR 23/3553).
[3] NAAF 'Analysis of Bombing Operations, 31 July–14 August 1943' and Air Ministry War Room Summaries, loc. cit.
* Principal aircraft employed were the P-40 Kittyhawk and Warhawk fighter-bomber, each of which tended to attack from low altitude.
† This total may well be exceptionally conservative. The British official history estimates that on 3 September Coningham had available 1,313 fighters and fighter-bombers (Appendix 4, Orders of Battle, RAF and USAAF, *The Mediterranean and Middle East*, Vol. V). Six hundred and seventy-three of these were assigned to the Desert Air Force. Nevertheless, an RAF account states that 'During the last ten days of the campaign the attacks on the enemy's Sicilian evacuation beaches were continued at high intensity'. (*RAF Mediterranean Review*, No. 4, July–September 1943, PRO [AIR 23/6787].)

attacks. Von Liebenstein's war diary provides the most accurate record of German shipping losses:

Damaged	5
Destroyed:	
German	15
Italian	1

The greatest losses occurred not during 'Lehrgang' but between 5 and 12 August. Two vessels each were sunk on 7 and 8 August and on 9 August, the worst day, a total of five.[1]

There were two methods by which the Allies might have stopped the evacuation: by crippling the evacuation fleet, and by sealing off the routes of communication to and from the embarkation points on both sides of the Strait. Although there were frequent attacks against the busy northern jetties at Faro and on the mainland, the Allied failure to employ their strategic bombing capability was undoubtedly the most costly mistake of all. As Admiral Ruge later wrote, 'The chief anxiety was caused by the fact that there was one good road only along either bank which could have been put out of action for a long time by constant plastering. This would have hampered the evacuation of material more than anything else; it was a great relief that Allied Bomber Command never pursued this idea as tenaciously as some others.'[2]

If there was any key to defeat the evacuation even partially it lay in this stratagem. Constant bombardment of the access roads and the landing sites could have seriously crippled the movement of materiel and at least partially impaired the movement of troops. A

---

[1] Von Liebenstein War Diary. Analysis of the after-action reports of the NAAF and the Air Ministry War Room Summaries reflects Allied estimates of Axis shipping losses:

	Probable	Confirmed
1–10 August	11	8
11–16 August	10	5
	21	13

Total	34

It is emphasized that these figures represent the author's analysis of the data available. At the time these reports were compiled they were frequently based on crew observation, other times on photo reconnaissance. Most often they were inconclusive. Weather and flak often made the task of observation less important than a hasty withdrawal from the area. Moreover, it proved impossible to determine which of these possible losses were German and which were Italian, except for the Siebel ferries which were exclusively German. From the above it can be seen that Allied 'confirmed' loss estimates were fairly accurate but the 'probable' losses were well wide of the mark.

[2] Ruge.

total defeat of the evacuation was unrealistic for, as Ruge notes, 'It was next to impossible, even with exceptionally heavy attacks, to knock out enough ferries and landing places to block the traffic effectively.'[1]

One of the most effective defences proved to be the arrival of barrage balloons from Germany in time to be used to protect the Strait in August. These obstacles were attached to the Siebel ferries and MFPs and towed back and forth across the Strait during each passage. The Germans believed this tactic was a significant factor in preventing Allied fighters from flying directly at the ferries and thus spoiling their aim. The results would seem to substantiate this belief fully.[2]

In operating by rote on too many occasions, the Allies failed to help themselves. Night-time raids arrived almost without exception in a pattern the Germans quickly took advantage of, and daylight attacks were almost never made during the hours of dawn, immediately after the noontime dinner hour and in the late afternoon. With justifiable sarcasm, Admiral Ruge observed that by 'taking Anglo-Saxon habits into account' the Germans were able to make excellent use of these predictable respites.[3]

If the Allied air forces proved no more than a nuisance, the Navy was even less of a factor. Royal Navy destroyers were frequently seen at the southern entrance of the Strait but rarely ventured further. About the only Allied vessels to operate in the Strait were British MTBs and MGBs but these small craft were like the veritable needle in the haystack. Operating from Augusta the sailors manning these fragile vessels made valiant efforts to interfere with invasion traffic but were generally thwarted by enemy searchlights and shore batteries. Other than the night of 11 August when three MTBs managed to disrupt ferry service, their impact was minimal.[4] The massive offensive capability of the Navy was never brought into play, yet the secret to defeating the evacuation lay in joint action by both Navy and Air Force. The failure of the Allied naval force even to test the Messina Strait hinged upon two factors: one real, one historical.

There is little doubt that vivid recollections of the disastrous 1915 venture by the Royal Navy into the Dardanelles were still fresh in the minds of the senior British sailors. The Allied Naval

[1] Ibid.
[2] Ruge and von Liebenstein.
[3] Ruge.
[4] Ibid.

C-in-C, Admiral Cunningham, had been a young destroyer captain in 1915 and it was his lack of initiative that shaped the inaction of the Allied fleet. Cunningham's attitude was a complete reversal of Allied determination to seal off any attempt by the Axis to evacuate their forces from Tunisia. Cunningham was not an officer noted for timidity, as evidenced in May when he sent his historic signal to the Allied fleet in anticipation of an Axis Dunkirk operation: 'SINK, BURN, DESTROY, Let Nothing Pass'.

'ABC' had neither forgotten nor forgiven the humiliation of Greece and Crete over which he had presided. His chance came in May 1943. 'We called the operation RETRIBUTION, not in any spirit of revenge or because we intended to slaughter defenceless survivors in the water, as the Luftwaffe had done in 1941, but because we hoped, and most earnestly, that those of the enemy who essayed the perilous passage home by sea should be taught a lesson they would never forget.'[1] The air forces had taken a similarly aggressive stance. As early as 20 March, Spaatz had anticipated the Axis would eventually attempt to evacuate their forces from Tunisia, and he had decreed that, 'The highest priority will be given to preventing organized German units from going into Italy....' Not only was there to be close co-operation between navy and air force, but Spaatz bluntly acknowledged that 'complete annihilation cannot be obtained without acceptance of losses on our part'.[2]

Within the space of three months this aggressive spirit had given way to a state of mind that charitably could only be termed faint-hearted. Neither the Navy nor the Air Force had a plan for attacking the evacuation. Under relentless prodding after the war by American naval historian Samuel Eliot Morison, who refused to accept the notion that nothing more could have been done by the Navy, Cunningham responded with vagueness and forgetfulness.* His biographer has written:

> No attempt was made to produce a co-ordinated plan to subdue the batteries until the first evacuations were well under way. It is certain the matter was raised by Cunningham's staff, but Cunningham himself admits to paying insufficient attention to the

---

[1] Cunningham, *A Sailor's Odyssey*, op. cit., pp. 529–30.
[2] 'Plan of Action to Meet Attempted Evacuation of Tunisia by Axis Forces', Box 11, Spaatz Papers, Manuscript Division, Library of Congress.
* The Morison–Cunningham correspondence took place in late 1953 and early 1954.

matter. His staff were of the opinion he paid attention all right, but could never forget the fate of some of the heavy ships sent in to bombard the gun batteries in the Dardanelles in 1915, and was therefore against the use of ships for this purpose.[1]

A great deal might have been done to neutralize the defences of the Strait. For example, no serious effort was made to attack the source of the problem either from the sea or the air. The Germans throughout remained confident they had little to fear from a surface attack.[2] The Italian heavy batteries were obsolete, the 280 mm mortars and the 150 mm guns were operated by the most primitive form of fire control apparatus. Moreover, these batteries were easily recognizable from the air and it was probable their crews would not have long withstood the fire from heavy capital ships or any form of bombardment from the air. Ammunition had become critically short, and towards the middle of August many AA batteries, particularly the heavies, had only a few rounds left per gun.[*]

According to von Bonin

> The only two batteries of heavy artillery on the island (17 cm guns with a maximum range of 28 km) were detached from under command of the 15 Panzer Grenadier Division, moved over to the mainland, and deployed roughly on both sides of SAN GIOVANNI, to protect the ferry route against enemy vessels. These two batteries, which had only a small supply of ammunition, were, up to the end of the battle on the island, the only (and moreover very questionable) protection we had against action by the enemy navy. There were in Italy no coastal batteries which could be used ... and the effect of 88[mm] AA shells against modern naval vessels had to be considered as nil, even apart from their insufficient range of about 13 km.[3]

A co-ordinated air–naval offensive aimed at interdicting the roads leading to the evacuation points and against the flak most

[1] S. W. C. Pack, *Cunningham*, London, 1974, pp. 258–9.
[2] Ruge.
[3] Von Bonin.
[*] One of the problems plaguing the Germans was the delivery of AA ammunition. Von Liebenstein's ferry crews often never knew what cargo they carried. Boxes were badly marked and there was often considerable confusion over where they were to go, with the result that not only was there delay, but frequently the wrong calibre ammunition was sent to guns which could not utilize it and were incapable of ensuring it was sent to the right batteries. By 12 August, von Liebenstein reported a dwindling supply of flak ammunition for his vessels. One Landing Craft flotilla was at 45% of basic allowance, the others at 15% and 18%. Only the 771 Engineer Battalion had over half its requirement. (Von Liebenstein War Diary, 12 August 1943.)

certainly would have produced positive results. Without the aid of the heavy bombers Broadhurst's tactical aircraft were fighting a losing battle against the flak, but once a portion of these guns were damaged or destroyed there was no time for replacements to arrive.* What was a disadvantage to the effective use of fighter-bombers could have been reversed by the removal of the flak. One who is convinced that not enough was done is Broadhurst, who has written, 'My feeling at the time was that had we applied the same heavy bomber strength to both sides of the Messina Straits that we did to the enemy airfields, although we might not have prevented the escape of a sizeable number of the enemy, we could have turned their success into a disaster.'[1]

Other than the forays by the torpedo and gunboats there is no evidence that the Navy took any further steps to interdict the Strait of Messina. Cunningham's postwar argument was that 'there was no effective method either by sea or air'.[2] In 1953 Admiral Morison began correspondence with Cunningham in an effort to explore the reasons for Allied inaction. Cunningham refused to rise to the bait and repeatedly denied that an all-out naval effort would have been worth the risk. 'Looking back, I don't think it was ever regarded as a feasible operation to stop the German and Italian retreats across 2¼ miles of narrow waterway.'[3]

Cunningham would not accept the premise that attacks by the big guns of his warships from positions off the northern end of the Strait at Cape Peloro against the batteries guarding the northern entrance would have been effective.†

---

[1] Air Chief Marshal Sir Harry Broadhurst, letter to the author, 24 May 1985.

[2] Morison, *Sicily–Salerno–Anzio*, op. cit., p. 216.

[3] Letter, Cunningham–Morison, 12 November 1953. The complete correspondence between Morison and 'ABC' is in the Morison Papers, US Navy Historical Center. Cunningham's letters exhibit none of the aggressiveness that so characterized one of the pre-eminent naval commanders of the Second World War. His replies to Morison's pointed questions lack substance. One of the targets of Cunningham's criticism was Montgomery, with whom he had never been compatible.

* Operating independently the bomb load carried by Allied fighter-bombers was hopelessly inadequate. The Warhawks and Kittyhawks carried only a 500 lb load, whereas a single B-17 averaged 6,000 lb.

† The Chief of Staff, The Mediterranean Station, Commodore (later Rear-Admiral) Royer Dick wrote to Cunningham in 1953 that the water depth off the north coast was deep enough to permit bombardment. While in general agreement with Cunningham that it would have been difficult to halt the evacuation, Admiral Dick noted that 'It does seem that something might have been done in the way of sporadic raids to shoot up the [northern] Straits and everything in them and thus disorganize the passage across.' (Letter of 4 December 1953, copy in Morison Papers.)

Admiral Davidson's TF 88* operating off the northern coast of Sicily was not notified of the evacuation and Lieutenant Commander Stanley M. Barnes's PT Squadron 15, although aware of the Axis withdrawal, was forbidden to operate south of the latitude of Cape Rasocolmo, west of Cape Peloro.[1] Admiral Morison contends that:

> Once these big guns had been silenced, a bold thrust of light cruisers and destroyers up the Strait from the south should have been able to silence most of the 88-mm and 90-mm batteries, and clear the way for MTBs, motor gunboats and even destroyers to operate effectively against the Siebel Ferries and other evacuation craft ... they could not have stopped the bottle completely; but it would have been worth extensive damage to naval vessels to have prevented even one of the German Panzer divisions from leaving Sicily.[2]

Another option was to have launched attacks against the flak batteries from both ends of the Strait in conjunction with similar attacks by strategic bombers, followed by a thrust into the northern end where the majority of the ferry routes were located. There was virtually no enemy air interference to contend with and although it is undeniable there was considerable risk involved, and some of the ships were required for the forthcoming Salerno landings, Morison is justified in observing that their employment 'during the fortnight when the Strait was swarming with evacuation craft seems, in retrospect, to have been little short of frivolous'.[3] He might well have added that had the roles been reversed, the German Navy would have made an all-out effort to prevent the escape of three Allied divisions to Italy.

In his autobiography Cunningham avoids mention of Messina, and his correspondence with Admiral Morison exhibits none of the confidence that made him a personal favourite of Eisenhower who rated him 'at the top of my subordinates in absolute selflessness, energy, devotion to duty, knowledge of his task, and in understanding of the requirements of allied operations.'[4]

One of his biographers cites Messina as one of the few failures of

---

[1] *Sicily-Salerno-Anzio*, op. cit., p. 213.

[2] Ibid., pp. 216-7.

[3] Ibid., p. 217.

[4] Eisenhower, 'Memorandum for Personal File', 11 June 1943, Eisenhower Papers.

* Task Force 88 consisted of the US Navy warships still left in Sicilian waters for the sole purpose of providing support to Seventh Army around Palermo and as it advanced on Messina. Morison calls it 'General Patton's Navy' (op. cit., p. 191).

his illustrious career for which he must bear responsibility.[1] Morison later wrote '... when I was discussing the German evacuation of Sicily with him and somewhat needling him about the failure of the Allied navies to intercept it, he blurted out something like: "I wasn't going to be caught in a trap the way we were in the Dardanelles in the last war!" I realised at once that the Straits of Messina looked on the map very much like the Dardanelles, and that the Admiral naturally hesitated to commit a naval force, as had been done with the Royal Navy in the First World War.'[2]

However deep his reluctance to tackle the Strait, there is no uncertainty that this was a rare lapse in his distinguished career:

> It was never Cunningham's way to be put off by difficulties, which he regarded as a challenge ... considering what Cunningham had been prepared to hazard earlier in the war off Crete, there is no question that, with full air co-operation, he could have repeated 'Retribution' on some scale. He made so few mistakes, allowed so few oversights, that it is with a certain surprise that historians have discovered that even he could, on occasion, misjudge possibilities.[3]

Although the Navy bore an uncharacteristic share in the Allied failure to halt the evacuation of Sicily, we now know that not only did the Air Force use only a fraction of their available air power but they failed to attack the correct targets or use their strategic bomber capability. Far too much emphasis was placed on the ports and port facilities of Messina, Reggio and San Giovanni, none of which was the source of the German evacuation. The official British naval historian believes 'The correct policy was for the strategic bombers to attack terminal ports until they made embarkation impossible, and for the tactical bombers to neutralise the coastal batteries sufficiently to enable our warships to seize control of the narrows; and had a joint plan been made to accomplish those objects, it is difficult not to believe that we could have stopped the evacuation.'[4]

---

[1] Oliver Warner, *Cunningham of Hyndhope*, London, 1967, p. 210.

[2] Quoted in Warner, p. 211.

[3] Ibid., p. 212. Cunningham's offensive capability included 6 battleships, 2 carriers, 15 cruisers and 128 destroyers. See Appendix D. Admiral Hewitt has defended 'ABC' by remarking that 'I think you can be sure that Cunningham would have stopped at *nothing* to prevent the crossing, provided the sacrifice involved would have brought commensurate results.' (Letter of 7 October 1953, Morison Papers.)

[4] Quoted in Pack, *Cunningham*, op. cit., p. 259.

Unfortunately, little had changed since the planning days before HUSKY when all the flaws of inter-service co-ordination and co-operation appeared. The bitter wrangles over the invasion planning may well have contributed to the mistake made by Eisenhower and his three C-in-C's who failed to establish a joint command HQ for HUSKY. Before the end of the Tunisian campaign it had been unanimously agreed that there would be a joint headquarters established at Bizerte, provided the necessary communications were installed in time. For some reason the Naval staff discovered they could not, and Cunningham's operational HQ was moved to Malta which, in turn, compelled Alexander to establish the Land Force HQ on Malta. It was essential for these two commanders to be together to make whatever instant decisions were called for prior to the invasion. With this move the entire concept of a single headquarters collapsed. Tedder elected to remain at his HQ near Tunis and Eisenhower stayed on at AFHQ in Algiers. The first to point out the folly of this split were the British Chiefs of Staff who signalled their collective consternation to Eisenhower in mid-June: 'We cannot disguise our concern that owing to difficulties over communication, Cunningham, Tedder and Alexander will not share same HQ for HUSKY operation. In our view separation of HQs of one commander from that of other two violates one of the most important principles of Combined Operations.'[1] Such liaison as existed between the services was far from adequate. For example, Tedder's deputy, Air Vice-Marshal H. E. P. Wigglesworth complained that 'The Naval Liaison Officer attached to the Air C-in-C's staff was a junior Lieutenant-Commander who was not able to represent the Admiral's views and was not in receipt of specific information from [Cunningham's] naval HQ in Malta.'[2]

Towards the end of the campaign Montgomery anticipated the outcome and lamented the fact that each of the services seemed content to go its own way. Even though Montgomery himself was becoming more and more preoccupied with his responsibility for Operation BAYTOWN, he found time to record his frustration at the lack of initiative and co-ordination among the three commanders-in-chief:

---

[1] Cable, British Chiefs of Staff–Eisenhower, 17 June 1943, (PRO AIR 8/1245).
[2] PRO (AIR 23/5758).

7 August

There has been heavy traffic all day across the Straits of MES-SINA, and the enemy is without doubt starting to get his stuff away.

I have tried hard to find out what the combined Navy-Air plan is in order to stop him getting away; I have been unable to find out.

I fear the truth of the matter is there is NO plan.

The trouble is there is no higher-up grip on this campaign.

CUNNINGHAM is in MALTA; TEDDER is at TUNIS; ALEXANDER is at SYRACUSE. It beats me how anyone thinks you can run a campaign in that way, with each of the three Commanders of the three Services about 600 miles from each other.[1]

Montgomery's dismay had indeed focused on the primary reason for the Allied failure to halt the evacuation, a total absence of inter-service co-ordination. As Monty noted, 'The enemy should never be allowed to get all his equipment out of SICILY, and we should round up the bulk of his fighting troops. It would clearly be impossible to stop him from getting his key personnel away. But the rest we should stop; but we will not do it without a very good combined plan and such a plan does not exist.'[2]

As the official British naval historian has written, the hard facts were these:

It is certain that at no stage did the three Allied Commanders-in-Chief represent to the Supreme Commander that an emergency, such as would justify the diversion of all available air strength, had arisen. The enemy later expressed his astonishment that the Allies had not used their overwhelming air superiority to greater effect.[3]

If there was to have been any hope of stopping the evacuation there needed to be the same careful planning that is required of an offensive operation:

It was in fact, from the Allied point of view, a combined operation in reverse; and if that view be accepted it may reasonably be asked why the Supreme Commander took no steps to bring his service commanders together with the object of quickly producing a joint plan.[4]

[1] Montgomery Diary, 7 August 1943.
[2] Ibid.
[3] Roskill, *The War at Sea*, Vol. III, Part I, op. cit., p. 148.
[4] Ibid., p. 150.

Only Alexander appears to have given the subject attention prior to the invasion. In May he had suggested that, between the time of the invasion and the final conquest of Sicily, an effort should be initiated to 'cross the straits and secure a foothold on the opposite shore ... Securing a bridgehead on the Italian mainland should be considered as part of the plan.'[1] If the subject was ever discussed by the Commanders-in-Chief no record of it has survived in the records of HUSKY. It was a blunder for, as Roskill suggests:

> ... it seems reasonable to suppose that, had the Supreme Commander and the service leaders agreed on such a strategy in the middle of July, by which time the success of the landings in Sicily was assured, the Navies could have assembled the ships and craft needed to carry it out early in August; and that would have been in time to stop the withdrawal of the major part of the Axis armies across the Messina Straits.[2]

The unhappy result was that Eisenhower was only marginally involved with HUSKY operations* and his three principal lieutenants failed individually and collectively to counter not only the evacuation of Sicily but in the first month of the campaign to shut down the constant flow of supplies, ammunition and troops *to* Sicily. During June, July and early August the Germans successfully transported from the mainland:

Troops	59,576
Vehicles	13,689
Supplies	40,000 (tons)[3]

A portion of these ferry runs were in the form of scheduled service from Naples to Messina where the Allies had full control of the sea. Yet, according to the evidence there was insufficient attention paid to the stratagem that blocking resupply was one means of crippling the German defensive effort. Most of the supplies shipped from Naples were badly needed ammunition and as General Rodt later told one British historian, 'This was hardly ever interfered with; by this route we were able to replenish our

---

[1] Quoted in *Alex*, op. cit., p. 245. The Alexander suggestion came at the US–British meetings in Algiers attended by Churchill, Marshall and the other Combined Chiefs of Staff.

[2] *The War at Sea*, Vol. III, Part I, op. cit., p. 152.

[3] Von Liebenstein and Ruge.

* It is reasonable to assume that had the AFHQ intelligence officer warned of the Axis evacuation, as indeed he ought to have, that Eisenhower would have intervened in time to counteract at least a portion of the evacuation.

stocks of mortar ammunition that were about to run out at Troina. The only disadvantage was that supplies had to be brought in by night!'[1]

The intense pressures and preoccupation with planning AVALANCHE and BAYTOWN notwithstanding, much more ought to have been done, a point repeatedly emphasized by the German military leadership. None understood why the Allies failed immediately to follow up their victory in Tunisia. Kesselring thought that 'The defensive capacity of Sicily in May 1943 was, in terms of personnel and material, at its lowest conceivable ebb. An attack following directly upon the capitulation of Tunisia must have had quick and complete success.' The Allies having chosen to land in southern Sicily, Kesselring nevertheless clearly believed Calabria ought to have been a secondary target. 'The operations against Sicily should have had as their aim the destruction or capture of the entire German-Italian force defending the island or by a landing on the south Calabrian coast.' Another factor cited by Kesselring was Montgomery's failure to crack the German defences along the plain of Catania, which ought to have been followed by a hard strike by Allied strategic bombers at the AA covering the Messina road, thus opening Route 114 for a dash to the port city by Eighth Army.[2]

The Germans likened their evacuation to Dunkirk. In terms of morale, this is accurate. In all other respects such a comparison is specious. The Dunkirk rescue operation miraculously saved the BEF, but even this extraordinary effort could not save their equipment all of which had to be left in France. Despite its historical mystique, the men of the BEF returned to England exhausted, disorganized, dispirited and incapable of further fighting without considerable retraining and complete re-equipping. The German evacuation of Sicily was well planned, deliberate and flawlessly executed. The three German divisions plus the elements of the 1st Parachute Division returned to mainland Italy fully equipped and ready to fight, as the Allies would later discover at Salerno, Monte Cassino and Anzio.*

[1] Quoted in Pond, *Sicily*, op. cit., p. 212.
[2] Liddell Hart, 'Notes on talk with Field Marshal Kesselring', German General's Collection (9/24/117), Liddell Hart Papers.
* Although the German Army formations escaped to Italy, most were badly depleted in both mobility and strength. The Hermann Goering, for example, at the end of August was only 50% mobile and at 66% of its authorized troop strength. Appendix I contains an analysis of German strengths and losses in Sicily.

Not only did the Germans (and to some extent the Italians) remove their forces and considerable equipment but their ferry service as well.* In the weeks following the evacuation of Sicily this remarkable 'navy' was once again employed to remove German forces from Sardinia and Corsica. In mid-September when Hitler ordered the evacuation of Corsica, it was the same Baron von Liebenstein who masterminded the sea evacuation.

Other than Eisenhower who grasped immediately the full scope of the Allied failure to win a decisive victory in Sicily and Montgomery who lamented the German escape but who unwittingly contributed to its becoming a reality, there was a complete absence of candour by those who planned and led the campaign. Some, like Tedder[1] and Cunningham, chose to ignore the unsatisfactory ending, while others like Alexander and General Strong lived in a fool's paradise. *The Alexander Memoirs* devote exactly four pages to the Sicily campaign.[2] The hard-headed pragmatists like Montgomery, Bradley and Broadhurst knew full well the truth. Sicily had been a difficult struggle and most preferred to forget that what the Germans justifiably termed a 'glorious retreat' was for the Allies a bitter victory that would return to haunt them time and again. But for the moment there was a lull in the struggle. Another bloody chapter in the history of the Second World War was written. The Sicily campaign had been won and the Italian campaign was about to begin.

[1] Tedder's war memoirs, *With Prejudice*, devote very little discussion to the evacuation. He mentions the legitimate problem of preparing for AVALANCHE (Salerno) and attempting to provide incentive for the Italian armistice, balanced against the needs for Sicily. Nevertheless, what is now clear is that Sicily was on the short end during the critical period in August.

Moreover, Tedder's defence of the Allied air effort is weak. He claims, for example, that 'Our attempt to prevent another "Dunkirk", as I had feared, was by no means so successful as in May' (page 453). Unfortunately, Tedder's statistics are far from accurate. He reports that on 5 August alone, two merchant vessels, a Siebel ferry and twenty-one barges were destroyed, when in fact German losses that day amounted to damage to SF #177 (seven injured). The records of the Northwest African Air Force reflect the sinking of one Siebel ferry and the probable sinking of one other, along with two barges. He also incorrectly states that the Allied air interdiction effort forced the Germans to confine their evacuation to the hours of darkness.

[2] *The Alexander Memoirs, 1940–1945*, edited by John North, New York/London, 1962, is among the least candid and useful of the many memoirs to appear after the war.

* Throughout the daylight hours of 17 August the Sicilian ferries were moored at points along the Calabrian coast near Scilla. Under cover of darkness they set out in groups for Naples. With the exception of two Siebel ferries sunk by fighter-bombers, all of the fleet reached Naples and safety. (Ruge, 'The Evacuation of Sicily'.)

Epilogue

Brute force bereft of wisdom falls to ruin by its own weight.

HORACE

Alexander's plan for Sicily was idiotic.

MONTGOMERY[1]

All the words of praise and self-congratulation that followed the conquest of Sicily never masked the hollowness of the Allied victory. One historian has described Sicily as 'an Allied physical victory, a German moral victory',[2] and undoubtedly this is how the campaign ought to be remembered. Behind the rhetoric there was little joy, and dissatisfaction existed at the highest level where even the War Office after-action report called the campaign 'a strategic and tactical failure' and a 'chaotic and a deplorable example of everything that planning should not be'.[3]

From the outset the Allies had taken the safe, conservative path. The invasion plan was Montgomery's version that opted for safety in numbers and was in no small part the result of the misjudgment of the Allied planners who overestimated the resistance the Italians would offer. The original plan for multiple landings, while bold in conception, was flawed – and Montgomery's compromise plan tried to use only Eighth Army to seize Messina, while relegating Patton's Seventh Army to a minor role. Nevertheless, as the campaign unfolded there were opportunities to have won a decisive victory which were squandered. For the Allied ground forces were left to fight a needless, frontal battle of attrition. The result was that a German Army corps which never exceeded 60,000 men and which was devoid of air and naval support managed to thwart and

---

[1] Interview with Samuel Eliot Morison, circa 1957, Morison Papers.
[2] Hanson Baldwin, *Battles Lost and Won*, op. cit., p. 225.
[3] Quoted in Pond, *Sicily*, p. 220. Combined Operations HQ Bulletin Y/1, published in October 1943, was equally critical of the air role.

then delay the might of two Allied armies whose combined strength exceeded 450,000 troops. What ought to have been a brief, decisive victory lasted thirty-eight days at no small cost. German losses are believed to have totalled nearly 29,000: 4,325 killed, 6,663 captured and an estimated 17,944 wounded,[1] while the Allied armies lost 11,843 British and 8,781 American killed, wounded, missing or captured.[*]

The experience gained in Sicily provided valuable lessons, both positive and negative, not only for the combined operations planners but for the commanders of all services who participated in the long-awaited cross-Channel operation. Sicily ought to have served as a clear warning to the Allied leadership that faint-heartedness and the absence of clearly defined strategic goals were a recipe for future setbacks. Instead, the lessons learned (though later applied to OVERLORD) were ignored in the Italian campaign where the same blunders were repeated time and again. To have needlessly permitted the surviving German force in Sicily to evade destruction was bad enough, but within less than a month the Allies began demonstrating just how little *had* been learned when the Italian campaign opened with the invasion of Salerno and Taranto. Led by Alexander, who continued to exhibit the same lack of imagination and strategic vision he had shown in Sicily, the campaign in Italy was doomed to become the longest, dreariest and most expensive Allied endeavour of the entire war.

That the Sicily campaign lacked strategic purpose was in no small part the result of the concessionary nature of coalition warfare. Britain and the United States never embraced a mutually satisfactory policy for defeating Germany. Casablanca was only one of a series of notable examples of compromises that characterized the Anglo-American alliance. At Casablanca it was never resolved whether Sicily was to be the stepping-stone to a larger objective in Italy or merely an end in itself. The British continued to believe passionately in the necessity for a strong Allied presence in the Mediterranean as a vital ingredient to the defeat of Germany. At the same time the American leadership was left with the impression that neither Churchill nor Brooke was completely sold on the merits of the cross-Channel invasion. In an unpublished

[1] Sources: Nicholson, *The Canadians in Italy, 1943–1945*, op. cit., p. 173; Bauer, MS # R-145; and Morison, *Sicily–Salerno–Anzio*, op. cit., p. 215n.

[*] Complete listings of Allied and Axis losses are in Appendices E and I.

memoir Eisenhower has described how Brooke privately expressed deep misgivings about a cross-Channel venture and spoke
favourably of the advantages of a 'thrust and peck' strategy of
hammering the Axis flanks to the benefit of the Red Army, whose
responsibility should be the destruction of Hitler's land forces.[1]

Some have argued that Eisenhower misunderstood or exaggerated Brooke's views. What is clear is that, both prior to and during
the Quebec Conference in August 1943, the British reaffirmed their
belief in a strong Allied presence in the Mediterranean. Quebec
became another compromise in which Britain traded its full backing for OVERLORD in return for the Italian campaign.* Initially, the
argument put forth by the British Chiefs of Staff was that an
invasion of Italy following Sicily was necessary to knock Italy out
of the war. When a firm commitment to OVERLORD for the late
spring of 1944 was finally hammered out at Quebec, the
justification became one of pinning down valuable German military assets that might otherwise be present in France to help defeat
the inevitable cross-Channel invasion. Marshall feared the consequences of any campaign that left the Allies in a no-win situation,
and his misgivings were more than justified by the campaign in
Italy in which the forces of sixteen nations became mired in a war
of attrition that was utterly without strategic purpose and which
dragged on until May 1945, resulting in the heaviest losses of any
campaign fought by the Western allies in World War II.[2]

The British feared the US would insist on ceasing further active
military operations in the Mediterranean once Sicily was successfully conquered and Allied control of the region in the air and on
the sea was supreme. This fear drew Churchill to North Africa in
May to dissuade the American leadership from such a move in
favour of full attention to OVERLORD. As Eisenhower later related,
'He frankly said that he wanted to do his utmost to see that no such
disaster – as he called it – would occur.'[3] The decision to continue
operations in the Mediterranean after Sicily was, once again, as

---

[1] Eisenhower, unpublished manuscript.
[2] As Hanson Baldwin observes, it is 'difficult to determine who diverted whom'. At its
zenith in the summer of 1944 the American commitment to the Mediterranean theatre was
742,000 men. (*Battles Lost and Won*, op. cit., p. 229.) With the British, French, Canadian,
Polish and other national contingents, the number of troops was in excess of one million.
[3] Eisenhower manuscript.
* The more cynical believe that British opposition to OVERLORD was more imagined
than real, as a ploy to ensure American backing for a continuation of operations in the
Mediterranean.

much of a compromise as HUSKY had been. In return for full British dedication to the cross-Channel operation there would be similar American backing to continued Allied operations in the Mediterranean. That, according to Eisenhower, brought jubilation to Churchill.[1]

The invasion of Sicily had led directly to the fall of Mussolini and the dissolution of Fascism in Italy. Mussolini's removal was hastened as much by Patton and Montgomery as by the bankruptcy of Fascism. Caught in the middle were the reluctant soldiers of the Italian Army, most of whom believed they were fighting the wrong enemy in Sicily. While there were still senior officers and others, who were dedicated to Fascism, the vast majority of the Italian Army were forced to fight for a corrupt regime in the company of an ally they despised, against an enemy who represented their ideal. As a warrior race the Italians of the twentieth century were hardly comparable to the military prowess of the Roman legions of Julius Caesar's time. The modern Italian was far more likely to regard any form of heroism as stupidity. The Italian Army in Sicily was unlike the earlier version in North Africa which, under the forceful and magnetic Rommel, had fought what was essentially a German war. Although Sicily was an alien land to Italian soldiers it nevertheless was seen to be an Italian war in defence of the Italian homeland. The contradiction was that it was a war most Italians preferred not to fight and that any defence of the island was impossible without the support of the Wehrmacht. Most Germans judged the Italians solely by their fighting ability which with minor exceptions was scorned. One of the few senior German officers who grasped the Italian predicament in Sicily was von Senger, who later wrote:

> Our Italian allies did not fight, nor were they able to fight, because their so-called coastal divisions had no modern armament at all and because their four mobile divisions had only such adequate armament as they had received after Italy's entry into the war. These were facts which were bound to demoralize any soldier in any army.[2]

While the generals spoke of military honour, those at the sharp end – and these included some units of the Fascist militia – were concerned with the more fundamental problem of staying alive.

---

[1] Ibid.
[2] Von Senger, 'Liaison Activities with Italian 6th Army', MS # C-095, loc. cit.

Ill-equipped, ill-trained and led by officers and NCOs whose loyalty was to Italy not Fascism, there was little enthusiasm for a confrontation with the Allies. As one Italian journalist has observed:

> The war for them was already finished. Defending meant defending Fascism – and none of them wanted to do that. The 'right' side was the Allied side, not the German one. It was a curious position: men still armed were forced to fire their arms at an enemy that was actually their friend. The enemy was among them: Fascists and Germans. They were only looking for the best opportunity to renounce the struggle. The struggle, in fact, continued only because the Germans (and some of the Fascists) continued to fight. In a situation like this, all of them thought it ridiculous to become a 'hero' – so most of them abandoned their positions and went into hiding.[1]

Led as they were by men of strong military tradition and ability, German soldiers were appalled by the behaviour and performance of their Italian 'ally', as were their British and American counterparts. Few ever understood the dilemma facing the Italian soldier and his commanders.

Sicily effectively marked the end of Italy's ignominious venture into Fascism and Mussolini's fantasy of a modern Roman Empire. As Rommel observed of the Italians, 'Certainly they are no good at war.'

For the men of the Allied armies, Sicily represented two very different campaigns. The men of Eighth Army – with the notable exception of the Canadians who were fighting their first campaign – found Sicily one of the most difficult in an endless chain of battles which had begun many months earlier in North Africa. Many displayed their weariness, and although their famous commander was physically fit and deeply tanned, his own writings testify to his frustration after months spent battling with his own commanders as well as the enemy. The unsuccessful battle for the plain of Catania ranks as one of the most savage fought by his veteran troops, many of whom recall Sicily as far more difficult than

[1] Letter, Romano Giachetti to the author, 12 December 1985. Giachetti, the American correspondent for Rome's *la Repubblica*, grew up under Fascism as a young man in Florence – and, like so many of his countrymen, he has vivid memories of the war, the abysmal failure of Fascism, and of foraging in the countryside for food to help keep his family alive.

anything they had experienced in North Africa. One of the more odious, lesser-known battles of the Sicily campaign was the clash between troops of the 5th Division and the Hermann Goering Division for Sferro, a village on the northeastern edge of the plain which the Hermann Goering had turned into one of the anchors of the Etna Line. A British officer's remembrance of Sferro could well serve as a testament to the entire campaign: '. . . the hot, glaring, parched, dusty, smoky, noisy and deathridden feel of the place, with its aura of putrefaction and cordite, will never leave me'.[1]

Sicily will not rank as one of Montgomery's memorable campaigns. His assertive leadership during the turbulent HUSKY planning had, in the end, infused the Allied planning with a sense of purpose even though the secondary role assigned Seventh Army rankled Patton and his commanders far more deeply than was ever perceived at the time. Once ashore, Montgomery's leadership in Sicily was a curious combination of boldness and an uncharacteristic tendency to react to his enemy's tactics by changes of strategy. By violating his own battle doctrine he made it impossible for his Army to fight a successful campaign on two wide fronts.

Montgomery sought and gained the dominant role in Sicily for Eighth Army and was supported by Alexander, who demonstrated his lack of confidence in the US Army by relegating Patton to an insignificant role. Montgomery's decision to attempt a rapid breakthrough along the eastern edge of the plain of Catania bore an uncanny resemblance to his ill-fated attempts to seize Caen in Normandy in June and July of 1944. Caen was the key to Normandy, and in Sicily Catania was the key to the strategic prize of Messina. The inconsistency lay in his boldness in ordering a night airborne attack to seize Primosole bridge which was only partially successful, followed by an inexplicable conservatism in failing to press his fleeting advantage while there was still time. That advantage was lost by a series of costly, time-consuming and ultimately futile one-dimensional attacks by the Durham Light Infantry. A potentially successful alternative in the form of an amphibious 'end run' by a 5th Division task force to seize Catania was planned too late and cancelled too early. For several days Catania was virtually undefended from a seaborne assault while the Germans

---

[1] Sir David Cole, *Rough Road to Rome*, op. cit., p. 69.

fought to retain their positions around Primosole bridge.* Such an operation in conjunction with a concentrated ground attack fully supported by air and naval gunfire would have doomed the German defenders to a trap from which the only escape was withdrawal into the foothills of Mount Etna.

By shifting his main effort to the west, Montgomery unwittingly presented the Germans with an opportunity to delay the 30 Corps advance long enough to establish the Etna Line and thus deny the British any hope of cutting off Messina. Without 78th Division, 30 Corps lacked the strength to carry out Montgomery's revised strategy across their vast front. To make matters worse the chronic shortage of transport left Eighth Army with a mere thirty per cent of their transport between D+3 and D+14.[1] The failure to capture Catania and Monty's decision to shift his main effort to the 30 Corps front were guarantors of a difficult and ponderous advance to Messina. Montgomery failed to make the best use of his strength and the unwelcome result was a complete loss of the initiative.

Montgomery's decisions were made after only nominal consultation with Alexander, who permitted him a free hand. Alexander's distrust of half his ground force forfeited an enormous advantage. At the very moment when Montgomery decided to usurp Bradley's right boundary at Vizzini, Seventh Army was in a position to end the campaign quickly. Alexander's refusal to entrust the main effort in the west to Seventh Army was the turning point and undoubtedly the most damaging misjudgment of the Sicily campaign. Not only did Alexander's decision bear the stigma of blatant bias but it was made in defiance of evidence that suggested a clear opportunity to trap the German forces in Sicily before they could mount an effective defence in the northeastern corner of the island. Alexander never had a plan for an exploitation and only the vaguest notion of how the campaign would unfold. When presented with a *fait accompli*, Alexander conceded the opportunity on dubious military grounds. His weak explanation was that both his Army commanders had approved of his decision, prior to D-Day, to use Eighth Army for the main effort against Messina.[2]

[1] *The Mediterranean and Middle East*, Vol. V, op. cit., p. 137.
[2] Alexander interview, loc. cit.
* As Christopher Buckley has written, 'improvised attack would have been met with only improvised defence'. (*Road to Rome*, London, 1945, p. 144.)

In contrast to Eighth Army, Seventh Army was not only fully mobile but its commander was eager to take advantage of that mobility in a daring and spectacular manner. By the end of the campaign Patton's use of armour in terrain wholly unsuitable for tank warfare had left Montgomery envious and unable to forget that he 'had saddled himself in the desert with a *Corps de Chasse* that wouldn't chasse'.[1]

After the Gela counterattacks by the Hermann Goering, Seventh Army 'had pushed on strongly, so strongly that its left task force – the reinforced 3d Division – had run out of objectives and was poised to strike inland at the key communication centre of Enna. Highway 124, the important east–west highway, was almost in Seventh Army's grasp. Several huge gaps had been created in the Axis line, gaps that were being held half-heartedly by remnants of the *Livorno* and *Napoli* Divisions.'[2] The 15th Panzer Grenadier Division were still rushing from western Sicily to help close the huge gap and assist the Hermann Goering and were in no position to repel a determined American offensive. The effects of Alexander's failure to seize the initiative were these:

> No *enemy force of any size opposed either the 1st or 45th Divisions. General Bradley, the II Corps commander, was ready and willing to take Highway 124 and Enna, thus encircling the German defenders facing Eighth Army. In North Africa, the remainder of the 82d Airborne and 2d Armored Divisions lay ready to sail for Sicily to reinforce the American effort.* (Author's italics)[3]

When Alexander upheld Montgomery's action to force Seventh Army to remain in the role of flank guard to Eighth Army the campaign was doomed to a dreary ending. '*For all practical purposes, Seventh Army could have stayed on the beaches; its brilliant assault achievements were completely nullified by the new British plan.*'[4] (Author's italics.)

After mixed success in Tunisia, Sicily became the proving ground where the US Army came of age. Despite the tragic outcome of the airborne and glider landings, Ridgway's 82d Airborne and the 1st Airborne Division proved there was future merit in this

---

[1] Sir Edgar Williams, quoted in *Monty: Master of the Battlefield, 1942–1944*, op. cit., p. 360.

[2] *Sicily*, op. cit., p. 422.

[3] Ibid.

[4] Ibid.

new weapon of warfare, provided the newly learned lessons were properly applied. The test was not long in coming when, after the Allied hold on the Salerno beachhead became critical, elements of the 82d Airborne were parachuted at short notice to help stabilize the situation.

American leadership at all levels was generally excellent. The veteran Troy Middleton led an untested National Guard division ably and Lucian Truscott whipped the 3d Division into one of the finest infantry divisions in the Army. The veteran 1st Division upheld their reputation at Gela and survived the change of leadership successfully, if grudgingly. At the higher level, Geoffrey Keyes emerged as a future corps commander of considerable promise and Omar Bradley drew universal praise for his calm, determined leadership that had already made his name known to the public and would shortly carry him to the pinnacle of his profession.

Patton's drive on Palermo was a mixed blessing. Strategically, it was unexceptional and of dubious military value.* The 29th Panzer Grenadier Division was held in Calabria by Hitler until 22 July when permission was finally given for its movement across the Strait and it was not until the following day that the first elements were in a blocking position along the northern coast road.[1] Had the 3d Division and the 2d Armored been directed to thrust to the north coast and then turn east, the back door to Messina would have been wide open for at least twenty-four hours.

The very flamboyance of Patton's offensive brought both Seventh Army and its colourful commander to the attention of the world, and in the final days of the campaign Patton presided over the demise of the notion that American fighting ability was any longer suspect. Patton's use of amphibious 'end runs' was the right idea and would have been far more successful if employed on a larger scale. Despite the objections of Bradley and Truscott, Patton was correct to pursue this tactic rather than continue the slow and costly advance against stubborn German delaying actions. The accomplishments of Truscott's infantry and Gaffey's armour in terrain ill-suited for mobile warfare went largely unrecognized

---

[1] *Sicily, passim.* Hitler authorized the transfer of this division on 19 July but it took until 21 or 22 July for Comando Supremo and OKW to work out the details and decide to fight the campaign in Sicily to the limit of their capability.

* The US official history refers to the dash to Palermo as 'almost a publicity agent's stunt'. (*Sicily*, op. cit., p. 423.)

except by Montgomery and it was not until the following summer in Normandy that Patton and his Third Army removed the last doubts with a stunning demonstration of mobile warfare. The outstanding feature of the US Army in Sicily was how quickly it had overcome the setbacks of Tunisia and absorbed the lessons necessary to become a first-class Army.

Contrary to popular belief, Montgomery greatly admired the accomplishments of the US Army in Sicily. Just as the so-called Patton–Montgomery rivalry for the capture of Messina was a myth, so too was any notion that Monty ever denigrated Patton or the American GI, and as his biographer points out, 'Whatever he might feel about Patton's strategic judgment, Monty had been genuinely impressed by Seventh Army's mobility, speed, and on its eastern flank, rugged determination and professionalism. . . .'[1]

The success of the air effort in Sicily was also mixed, and claims of success often exceeded reality. The greatest achievement was the neutralization of the Axis air forces and their capability to defend the island. With surgical precision Tedder's air offensive battered enemy airfields around the clock and shot his planes from the sky. The pre-D-Day blitz forced over half of the Axis aircraft from Sicily to the Italian mainland and by 17 July the only enemy planes left on the island were an estimated 125 single-engine fighters.[2]

The Luftwaffe lost about 740 aircraft and of the 1,100 planes abandoned or destroyed on the aerodromes of Sicily, an estimated 482–600 were German.[3] Allied losses numbered approximately 375 aircraft.[4] The last Axis aircraft evacuated Sicily on 22 July and thereafter the best the Luftwaffe could mount was an average of sixty sorties a day from bases on the mainland.[5]

[1] *Monty: Master of the Battlefield, 1942–1944*, op. cit., p. 374. Monty refused to permit anything derogatory to Patton to be printed in the newspapers of Eighth Army. An article reporting that Patton was under investigation brought the editor a rare rebuff from Monty, who believed Patton to be a good man and that such criticism reflected badly upon himself.

[2] Craven and Cate, *Europe: Torch to Pointblank*, op. cit., p. 485.

[3] Ibid. The British official history credits the Allies with the destruction of 900 German aircraft and the loss of 482 of 1,100 on the ground in Sicily (*The Mediterranean and Middle East*, Vol. V, op. cit., p. 169), while the official US air history cites the Luftwaffe losses as 600. In *The German Air Force 1939–1945* (London, 1981), British historian Matthew Cooper cites 600 Luftwaffe and 500 Italian aircraft lost on the island. Total Axis air losses from the campaign were an estimated 1,850 (p. 290).

[4] *Europe: Torch to Pointblank*, op. cit., p. 485; Richards and Saunders, *The Fight Avails*, London, 1975, p. 323.

[5] Cooper, *The German Air Force 1939–1945*, op. cit., p. 290.

The defeat of the Luftwaffe fulfilled Tedder's goal of removing Axis airpower as a factor in the defence of Sicily with stunning success. No such claim could be made for air operations in support of the conquest of the island by the ground forces. Tactical air support left much to be desired, particularly Coningham's attempt to isolate the battlefield by crippling the enemy lines of communication leading into it. These targets included not only ports and rail centres such as Milazzo, Acireale, Catania, Palermo and Messina, but also road communications centres inland, among them: Regalbuto, Troina, Adrano and Randazzo. These towns were pounded into rubble. Regalbuto, which was mistakenly bombed on at least one occasion, was hit by 215 American, British and South African fighter-bombers on 26 July alone.* Between 10 July and 7 August Adrano was pounded by 694 aircraft, 'leaving it untenable'.[1] During the first two weeks of August Randazzo received the same treatment from 745 fighter-bombers. The Germans rarely ever established their defensive positions inside a town and the result of these bombings was most often the death of innocent Sicilians and the reduction of the place to ruins. *Daily Telegraph* correspondent Christopher Buckley witnessed many of these bombardments and later wrote that Regalbuto and Randazzo were among those 'blotted out by bombing from the air on a scale unprecedented in the history of war'.[2] The bombing failed on two counts: it rarely killed Germans and it created more problems than it solved. As Buckley observed:

> . . . our objective, which was to block the roads with rubble and render the retreat of the German wheeled vehicles impracticable, was largely frustrated because it was not necessary for the Germans to retreat through the villages. Instead, we found that when our troops entered these places they had to spend hours clearing away the rubble in order to continue the advance. Our own bombing was piling up obstacles in the way of the advance of our ground forces. Nor was occupation of these villages eased by the necessity for coping with the scores of homeless and wounded inhabitants and the hundreds of dead and wounded civilians.[3]

[1] *Europe: Torch to Pointblank*, op. cit., p. 469.
[2] Christopher Buckley, *Road to Rome*, op. cit., p. 107.
[3] Ibid., p. 108.
* Broadhurst's Desert Air Force included a squadron of Kittyhawk fighter-bombers of the South African Air Force (No. 5 Squadron, SAAF).

Troina was another example of the futility of these tactics. Between mid-July and 6 August the town was reduced to smouldering ruins by 374 fighter-bombers even though the Germans avoided exposing themselves to this dreadful experience by establishing their defences elsewhere. 'I could not help feeling,' wrote Buckley, 'that our pursuit tactics resembled the employment of a ponderous sledge-hammer to crush a small but alert reptile which slips away time after time just as the hammer ascends. The Germans lost few men in the process. . . .'[1]

In his study of the Second World War, British historian J. F. C. Fuller called these tactics 'asinine'. Singling out Coningham for his tactics of destroying cities and towns, Fuller scornfully asserted that 'surely it should have occurred to him that low-flying attack with cannon and machine-gun fire would have caused the Germans incomparably more damage than this insensate bombing of villages'![2]

The airmen were not entirely to blame, for these bombings were frequently carried out at the specific request of the Army. One example was Adrano which was flattened at the instigation of 30 Corps. These results disturbed de Guingand, who remarked on the uncertainty of how best to employ this powerful capability, particularly during the 'sticky' period of the battles in the mountains. 'The rather natural and human reaction was "get the air to blow the enemy's positions to pieces". Our air forces as usual loyally accepted and carried out the Army's requests. But there was a feeling not shared by the RAF alone, that the effort employed did not produce commensurate results.'[3]

Sicily clearly demonstrated the need for better co-operation between air and ground forces, and command and control techniques were considerably improved by the time of the Normandy campaign. Another example of the sort of problem encountered in Sicily occurred when Dempsey complained vociferously to Montgomery that his troops had been bombed by Broadhurst's fighter-bombers. Investigation revealed that 13 Corps had established a

---

[1] Ibid., p. 127. So severe was the damage to Troina that it took thirty-six hours to clear the debris to permit single-lane traffic.

[2] Major-General J. F. C. Fuller, *The Second World War 1939–1945*, New York, 1949, p. 266. Fuller called these tactics 'the transference of the psychology of strategic bombing from the enemy's cities to the battlefields. Though the target differed, the idea was the same: to drop an overwhelming weight of metal upon it – it was bulldozing with H.E.!'

[3] *Operation Victory*, op. cit., p. 309.

bombline and then advanced beyond it without informing the air force. Dempsey was summoned by Montgomery and given the severest 'rocket' Broadhurst ever saw a general officer receive.[1]

The key to a successful campaign was not in the air but on the sea. HUSKY was an enormous improvement over TORCH and provided valuable lessons in the development of amphibious warfare that would shortly be used in the preparations for OVERLORD. The newly developed LST, DUKW ('duck') and the LCT/LCI/LCVP proved exceptionally successful as a means of landing men and equipment on a hostile shore. The Navy fully merited Alexander's praise for the 'magnificent' support provided his ground forces.[*]

Completely unknown until after the war was the contribution of the clever deception undertaken by the British with Operation MINCEMEAT and Plan BARCLAY. Through these deceptions the Allies succeeded in introducing the bait needed for the Germans to draw their own false conclusions. Hitler had long since convinced himself that the Allies would invade the Balkans rather than Italy. In the war diary of the German Naval Staff can be seen evidence of the remarkable success of the false documents which purported to reveal Sicily as merely an Allied feint. As intelligence historian Ralph Bennett points out, 'The art of deception is to give your enemy something like what he wants to believe, so that he won't scrutinise the bait too closely.'[2] Although it will never be known for certain how many units were diverted from Italy and Sicily as a result of MINCEMEAT and BARCLAY, the 1st Panzer Division was sent to Greece in June and Sardinia reinforced.[†] Undeniably, the deception operations fabricated in London and Cairo were valuable contributions to the success of the Sicily campaign.

To have defeated the Axis evacuation of Sicily required an integrated, joint air–naval effort which was never forthcoming, thus realizing the worst fears of the British Chiefs of Staff. Sea power was the greatest weapons the Allies possessed and it was never pressed anywhere near its full capability. If an epitaph is to

[1] Interview with Air Chief Marshal Sir Harry Broadhurst, 22 November 1979; and *Monty: Master of the Battlefield, 1942–1944*, op. cit., p. 341.

[2] Letter to the author, 30 November 1985.

[*] Alexander's despatch singled out the Allied Navy for special praise. See *The Conquest of Sicily*, 9 October 1945; reprinted in the second supplement to the *London Gazette*, 10 February 1948.

[†] The official British intelligence historians believe with considerable justification that MINCEMEAT accelerated German reinforcement of the Balkans, Greece and Rhodes. (See Hinsley, Vol. III, Pt I, op. cit., p. 120.)

be applied to the Sicily campaign it would have to be the observation of General Fuller, who wrote:

> The fact remains that the most economical solution was seaborne attack, because in coastal operations he who commands the sea can nearly always find an open flank leading to the enemy's rear – the decisive point in every battle. This was *the* lesson of the Sicilian campaign, and it was not learnt.[1]

[1] Fuller, op. cit., p. 266.

Postscript

This narrative has dealt with the successes and failures of the men who commanded the land, sea and air forces that fought in Sicily during the summer of 1943. Except for Normandy, no campaign ever brought together so many of the top Allied commanders of World War II. After Sicily some remained in the Mediterranean to press the Italian campaign, while others returned to England to prepare for OVERLORD.

During the remainder of 1943 there was considerable speculation over who would be appointed to lead the cross-Channel invasion. Invariably, they all came from the Mediterranean. Both Brooke and Marshall aspired to the command of Allied forces for OVERLORD and both suffered crushing disappointment when Churchill and Roosevelt found they could not spare their most trusted adviser and chief strategist. A measure of the greatness of these two leaders was the gracious acceptance with which they subordinated their pride and ambition to the greater needs of the Anglo-American coalition.

The compromise choice was Eisenhower. Although Brooke and others continued privately to voice suspicion of his ability as a strategist, they were in no doubt of his skill to forge a winning Allied team. Eisenhower's Mediterranean experience was the training ground for Supreme Command in Northwest Europe where he would more than justify his selection. When Eisenhower became the SHAEF commander, Major General Walter Bedell Smith moved to London to serve as his Chief of Staff as a lieutenant general.

The affable Alexander became the Allied ground commander in Italy and, in late 1944, when Field-Marshal Sir Henry Maitland Wilson was sent to Washington, after the death of Sir John Dill, Alexander became Supreme Allied Commander in the Mediterranean where he remained until the German surrender in 1945.

For Lieutenant General George S. Patton, Jr, Sicily had been a roller coaster ride that saw his career rise in dramatic fashion and almost falter in a tide of criticism and bad publicity as a result of the slapping incidents. In the months following the end of the campaign Patton resided in isolated splendour in the palace at Palermo as his Army was gradually stripped away to meet new commitments in Italy and England. Bradley's departure for England and his appointment to command the US invasion army in OVERLORD came as a particularly demoralizing blow. With little to occupy his time, Patton was at the nadir of his career. Having once described himself as 'a passenger floating on a river of destiny', Patton now had to contend with the prospect that he was destined to see the remainder of the war pass him by. 'I have absolutely nothing to do,' he complained, 'and hours of time in which to do it. From commanding 240,000 [men] I now have less than 5,000 ... pretty soon I will hit bottom and bounce.'[1] Privately, Patton continued to criticize Eisenhower, believing he lacked the courage to support him. 'Ike and Beetle [Smith] are not at all interested in me but simply in saving their own faces.'[2]

These feelings were misplaced as Eisenhower continued to reaffirm his backing of Patton. Even after Drew Pearson's revelation of the slapping incidents, Eisenhower would write, 'I still feel my decision sound,' and refused to retract it. But as the official historians point out, the slapping incidents left understandable doubts about the extent of Patton's future potential and shortly after he was appointed the Supreme Commander for OVERLORD, Eisenhower cabled Marshall, 'In no event will I ever advance Patton beyond Army command...'[3]

In a rare tribute to an American officer, Alexander later said of him that 'Patton should have lived during the Napoleonic Wars — he would have been a splendid Marshal under Napoleon'.[4] Patton's own judgment of himself in Sicily was this comment: 'I realize I did my duty in a very tactless way, but so long as my method pleased the God of Battles, I am content.'[5]

After months of near despair Patton was at last summoned to England in late January 1944 and given command of Third Army. During the historic journey across France and Germany his superior was his former subordinate Omar Bradley.

Sicily was the stepping stone to higher command for Bradley

[1] Diary, 17 November 1943.
[2] Ibid., 28 November 1943.
[3] Both quotes in Sicily, op. cit., p. 431.
[4] The Alexander Memoirs, 1940–1945, op. cit., p. 44.
[5] Diary, 21 September 1943.

whose appointment to command First United States Army was announced by Marshall in early September. Bradley was surprised by the news and delighted to leave Sicily, not only because of the promotion but also because it removed him from the control of Patton. He took the principal staff officers of II Corps to England with him to form his new Army staff.

Montgomery soon exchanged the pleasant villa in Taormina for the rain and mud of Italy. Sicily had once again established the great hold this extraordinary commander exerted over the men of the Eighth Army. He soon found the campaign in Italy depressing and even more badly run than Sicily. The guns had barely fallen silent in Sicily when he became embroiled in a fresh controversy over the forthcoming Messina crossing by 13 Corps. For OVER-LORD, Eisenhower wanted Alexander but instead got Montgomery whose appointment to the command of British ground forces was announced at Christmas. As the senior Allied army commander, Montgomery would lead the greatest invasion in history in June 1944. He left behind him in Italy a campaign that he decried as utterly lacking in strategic purpose under Eisenhower and Alexander. Montgomery's reflections of Sicily were equally depressing. To Brooke he wrote, '... I could write a book about the whole HUSKY affair, but it would be quite impossible to publish it!!'[1]

Both of Montgomery's protégés, Leese and Dempsey, went on to Army command. Dempsey became commander of the Second British Army which landed three of its divisions in Normandy on D-Day and fought the battles on the eastern flank of the Allied bridgehead around Caen until joined late July by the 1st Canadian Army. By war's end the quiet, unassuming Dempsey would be as little known as he had been in Sicily in command of 13 Corps. The well-meaning Oliver Leese succeeded Montgomery as Eighth Army commander but he simply lacked the qualities that made Montgomery a respected and charismatic leader.

With the exception of Terry Allen and Hugh Gaffey, the other senior American commanders who fought in Sicily all went on to higher command. Lucas, who served as Eisenhower's 'eyes and ears', was given command of VI Corps for the Anzio invasion on 22 January 1944, and was relieved several weeks later by the Fifth Army commander, General Mark Clark. Many believed Lucas a sacrificial lamb to British criticism and the ineptitude of Clark and

[1] Letter of 29 September 1943, Montgomery Papers.

Alexander. The desperate battle for Anzio led Churchill to comment on more than one occasion that 'I thought we were going to land a tiger cat but all we've got is stranded whale.' Lucas was replaced by Truscott who had led his 3d Division into Anzio before being summoned by Clark to command VI Corps. Truscott led VI Corps into southern France in August 1944 during Operation DRAGOON and soon afterwards was named Fifth Army commander, succeeding Clark who ascended to the command of the Allied armies in Italy. As a four-star general, Truscott succeeded his erstwhile superior in Sicily as the commander of Third Army when Patton was sacked by Eisenhower in October 1945.

Patton's protégé Geoffrey Keyes succeeded Bradley as the commander of II Corps where he fought the entire Italian campaign. Middleton, whose leadership of 45th Division had been so impressive, returned briefly to the United States before being ordered to England by Eisenhower to command VIII Corps in Patton's Third Army. Beginning with the great American breakout in July 1944, Middleton's VIII Corps led the thrust into Brittany. Later, VIII Corps participated in the thick of the fighting during the Battle of the Bulge.

Major General Manton S. Eddy, who commanded the 9th Division in North Africa and whose division took part in the final days of the Sicily campaign, led his division into Normany in June 1944. In August he became commander of XII Corps which spearheaded most of the Third Army advance across France, Luxembourg and Germany.

Clarence Huebner not only led the men of the 'Big Red One' into their most famous battle on Omaha Beach on D-Day but later took command of V Corps in early 1945 in time to participate in the final battles in Germany.

As Patton had predicted, the old racehorse Terry Allen needed only a change of scene to recharge his batteries. After returning to the United States in September 1943 he received the DSM for his service with the 1st Division. In October he took command of the new 104th Infantry (Timberwolf) Division, composed entirely of civilian-soldiers. The general who had been accused by Bradley of running a sloppily disciplined division immediately stamped his personality on the 104th by imposing tough but fair discipline and teaching his men how to fight at night. A year later the Timberwolves relieved the 1st Division in the Rhineland. Until the end of the war the 104th Division repeatedly distinguished itself in a series of bloody battles. When the German surrender came in May 1945 Allen's division had been in action for 195 days and had earned the plaudits of the Allied leadership. Alexander, who rarely praised any American general, called him the finest division commander he had seen in two world wars. Terry Allen became the only American general in World War II to train and lead *two* divisions into combat and a series of brilliant achievements. When asked to explain Allen's extraordinary hold on his men, a fellow division commander and former 1st Division officer replied it was because Allen was so 'damned honest'. His successor, Clarence Huebner said, 'Nobody else could have gotten out of the First what Terry got out of them in North Africa and Sicily.'[1] Allen retired in 1946 and until his death in 1969 at age 81 he remained an outspoken advocate of a militarily strong America.

Brigadier General Teddy Roosevelt spent the remainder of 1943 as an unemployed general at AFHQ. In desperation he finally wrote to Bradley begging for any kind of job in the cross-Channel invasion. 'If you ask me to swim in with a 105 [-mm howitzer] strapped to my back. Anything at all. Just help me get out of this rats' nest down here.'[2] When he received Bradley's summons Roosevelt was hospitalized with pneumonia; and reported to England with a burning fever. On D-Day Teddy Roosevelt led the men of the green 4th Infantry Division ashore on Utah Beach with his usual flagrant disregard for his own safety. Shortly before Operation COBRA both Bradley and Eisenhower decided Roosevelt had earned a division command. However, before he could be informed, Roosevelt died in his sleep of a heart attack the night of 12 July 1944 at age fifty-six. He was later posthumously awarded the Medal of Honor for exceptional gallantry on D-Day. The pall bearers at his funeral were Patton, Bradley, Hodges, Collins and Huebner. Bradley has written of Roosevelt that 'He braved death with an indifference that destroyed its terror for thousands upon thousands of younger men. I have never known a braver man nor a more devoted soldier.'[3] The man who had spent his entire life in the shadow of his famous father had carved his own secure place in the history of the US Army.

[1] Quoted in 'Terry Allen and the 1st Division', loc. cit.
[2] Quoted in *A Soldier's Story*, op. cit., p. 333.
[3] Ibid., p. 334.

Both Ridgway and Gavin went on to become the best-known and respected American airborne commanders of the war. The two officers led the 82d Airborne into Normandy on D-Day near Ste Mère Eglise and both were awarded the Distinguished Service Cross for extraordinary valour. Prior to the great Allied airborne operation at Arnhem/Nijmegen, Ridgway was promoted to command the XVIII Airborne Corps and at age thirty-seven Gavin became the new commander of the 82d Airborne, the youngest American major general of World War II. The names of both men became associated with the great battles of the war: Sicily, Salerno, Normandy, Nijmegen and the Bulge.

Lieutenant Colonel William O. Darby's Rangers participated in the bloodiest battles in Italy: Salerno, Anzio and Cisterna. After two months in the 45th Division as a regimental commander, Darby was sent back to the United States where he found headquarters duty disagreeable. Finally, in 1945 Darby succeeded in returning to combat in Italy. Only weeks before the war ended, Darby became assistant division commander of the 10th Mountain Division and on 30 April, only days before the end of hostilities, he was killed when an 88 mm shell landed outside his CP. Darby was thirty-four and in recognition of his outstanding leadership he was posthumously promoted to brigadier general.

Another colourful commander who did not survive the war was Colonel 'Paddy' Flint who was killed in action while in command of the 39th Regiment near St Lô. As Bradley had predicted, he had exposed himself to enemy fire once too often and died when a single bullet struck him in the head. A deeply saddened Patton attended his funeral the following day.

Major-General 'Hoppy' Hopkinson, the commander of the 1st Airborne Division, was killed early in the Italian campaign near Taranto. His death did not merit even a brief mention in the British official history.

In Montgomery's judgment Major-General Douglas Wimberley was a tired man and badly in need of a rest after commanding the Highlanders from Alamein to Messina. After a very emotional farewell to his beloved division he returned to England to become Commandant of the Staff College, Camberley. In December 1944 Wimberley became Director of Infantry in the War Office. In 1946 he retired to his native Scotland where he died in 1983 at age eighty-seven.

Major-General Sidney Kirkman returned with the 50th Division to England but was soon sent back to the Mediterranean as the commander of 13 Corps in Italy where he took part in the Cassino battles, the advance to Rome and the Gothic Line battles. Near the end of the Italian campaign he fell ill and was invalided home to England. Several years later he was reunited with his old chief, Montgomery, whom he served as Quartermaster General. Kirkman retired in 1950 as a full general and died in 1982.

Major-General Guy Simonds, the young commander of the 1st Canadian Division, participated in Operation BAYTOWN, the Eighth Army assault across the Strait of Messina. In November 1943 he took command of the newly arrived 5th Canadian Armoured Division but his tenure was brief. In 1944 he returned to England to assume command of II Canadian Corps. During the Normandy campaign his corps participated in several major battles in August which contributed to the defeat of Rommel's Army Group B. As a lieutenant-general Simonds remained a corps commander and a favourite of Montgomery until the end of the war.

Major-General Charles Gairdner the former Chief of Staff of Force 141 returned to India and obscurity in the form of a staff position under his former commander, General Sir Claude Auchinleck.

Most of the paratroopers who fought at Primosole bridge remained with the 1st Airborne under its new commander Major-General Robert 'Roy' Urquhart, the erstwhile commander of the 231st Infantry Brigade. Both Brigadier Lathbury and Lieutenant-Colonel John Frost parachuted into Arnhem that fateful Sunday in September 1944. At Arnhem bridge, Frost and his 2nd Parachute Battalion earned a lasting place in the history of the British Army by their valiant stand before finally being forced to surrender to an overwhelmingly superior force. Frost and the survivors of 2nd Para spent the remainder of the war in a German Stalag. Frost continued on active service for another twenty-two years before retiring in 1967 as a major-general. In all, he served in the British Army for thirty-five years. Now retired in Hampshire, General Frost has become a farmer and raises beef cattle.

Colonel George Chatterton and his gallant glidermen continued to risk their lives flying their flimsy gliders into Normandy, Arnhem and across the Rhine. In Salisbury Cathedral there is a memorial window to the 551 Officers and NCOs who were lost flying the 'Wings of Pegasus'.*

Lieutenant-Colonel Alastair Pearson commanded the 8th Parachute Battalion of the 6th Airborne Division on D-Day in Normandy. Despite a painful wound and illness, Pearson and his paratroopers held a critical sector of the tenuous airborne bridgehead. Awarded his fourth DSO, Pearson was described by his division commander, Major-General R. N. Gale, as a leader 'second to none'. 'Men would follow him anywhere and do his bidding with a zest that it was grand to see. Quiet and calm, he possessed immense courage.'[1] After the war Pearson was active in the Territorial Army and from 1956 to 1961 was ADC to the Queen. Since 1979 he has been Lord Lieutenant of Dumbartonshire where he is a farmer.

The powerful air triumvirate of Tedder, Coningham and Spaatz remained in the Mediterranean until the end of 1943 when all returned to England. At Tedder's instigation Coningham was given command of the 2nd Tactical Air Force which supported 21st Army Group throughout the campaign in Northwest Europe. Unfortunately, the blood feud between 'Mary' Coningham and Monty poisoned their relationship beyond all repair.† Tedder was appointed the Deputy Commander, Allied Expeditionary Force (SHAEF) and remained Eisenhower's deputy until the end of the war. Spaatz commanded the 8th Air Force, the US heavy bomber force in England which, along with Bomber Command, carried the strategic bombing effort into Germany for the remainder of the war.

Air Vice-Marshal Broadhurst also returned to England in early 1944 to command No. 83 Group which ably supported Dempsey's Second Army in Normandy and across Northwest Europe. His colourful trademark was the yellow Storch which was frequently seen flying in the skies over Normandy. His postwar career in the RAF included command of the 2nd Tactical Air Force, Bomber Command and as Commander of NATO's Allied Air Forces, Central Europe. After retiring as an Air Chief Marshal, Broadhurst was associated for a number of years with Hawker-Siddeley Aviation. He lives near Chichester.

[1] R. N. Gale, *With the 6th Airborne Division in Normandy*, London, 1948, p. 60.
* The symbol of British airborne forces is Bellerophon mounted upon Pegasus, the great winged horse of mythology.
† See Chapter 8.

'ABC' – Admiral Sir Andrew Cunningham – became the First
Sea Lord in October 1943 upon the death of Admiral Sir Dudley
Pound. He was soon followed to England by Admiral Sir Bertram
Ramsay who became Allied Naval C-in-C and commanded the
invasion fleet on 6 June 1944. Ramsay's departure brought both a
tribute and a lament from Montgomery who wrote from Italy,
'We missed you sadly when you had gone ... You understand us
soldiers and you know more about the land battle than any other
sailor.'[1] His death in an air crash near Paris in January 1945 was
mourned by all who knew this outstanding naval officer.

Even though Italy had surrendered to the Allies, Hitler installed
Benito Mussolini as the head of a German-inspired puppet government in northern Italy where he became little more than a
mouthpiece for Hitler. Mussolini set about avenging his downfall
through a special military tribunal composed of Fascist diehards
whose sole purpose was to convict and summarily execute his
enemies. Five of those who had voted against him in the Grand
Council were executed, including his son-in-law, Count Ciano.
Fascist wrath for the fall of Sicily fell upon the hapless Guzzoni
who was charged with treason. He escaped a firing squad – in no
small part thanks to von Senger who testified to the old general's
loyalty towards the Axis defence of Sicily. Guzzoni's task had been
hopeless from the start and it was to his credit he possessed the
wisdom not to contest the German takeover of the battle of Sicily.

To the end Mussolini continued to justify Fascism and his
leadership of Italy. In April 1945 he was captured by communist
partisans while attempting to flee to Switzerland and executed
along with his blonde mistress, Clara Petacci. The corpses were
taken to a piazza in Milan and publicly hung by their heels. Few
Italians mourned Mussolini's passing and with his death the last
vestiges of Italy's experiment with demagoguery ended inglori-
ously.

Field Marshal Albert Kesselring led the brilliant German
defence of Italy and frustrated the Allies for another twenty
months. After the German surrender Kesselring was imprisoned
and, in 1946, tried by the British for war crimes in connection with

[1] Rear-Admiral W. S. Chalmers, *Full Cycle: The Biography of Admiral Sir Bertram
Home Ramsay*, London, 1959, p. 182.

the execution of 335 Italian civilians by the Gestapo in what became known as the massacre of the Adreatine Caves, and for allegedly ordering the shooting of civilians in reprisal for partisan actions. He was convicted and sentenced to death. Many, however, were appalled by the verdict, among them Churchill and Alexander, then Governor-General of Canada. Churchill was by now long out of power but thought the sentence too harsh, as did Alexander who sent a cable in defence of Kesselring to the new British Prime Minister, Clement Attlee, in which he indicated his distress at the death sentence handed down by the court. 'I hope it will be commuted. Personally, as his old opponent on the battlefield, I have no complaint against him. Kesselring and his soldiers fought hard but clean.'[1] The effect of Alexander's intervention apparently helped, for Kesselring's sentence was commuted to life imprisonment by the Reviewing Authority, General Sir John Harding, Alexander's erstwhile Chief of Staff in Italy. In 1952 Kesselring was released, a rather broken man in declining health. His allegiance to Hitler and his regime were genuine, however misguided. Despite the stamp of 'war criminal' that came with his conviction, history will certainly be a kinder judge of Kesselring as an honourable and able soldier.[*] In postwar Germany he became an immensely popular figure among war veterans. He died on 20 July 1960, the anniversary of the plot against Hitler.

Von Senger was sent to Sardinia and Corsica on another hopeless mission as the senior German commander. Both islands were, like Sicily, successfully evacuated. On Corsica there was considerable fighting between German forces and the Italians and French partisans. The defection of Italy to the Allies led Hitler to order the execution of all captured Italian officers, a directive von Senger refused to carry out. The former Rhodes scholar was finally given a real command in Italy and he made the most of it. In command of XIV Panzer Corps, von Senger became the defender of Cassino

---

[1] *Alex*, p. 344. One of the chief complaints about his trial was that the court seemed not to understand that Kesselring had no authority over the Gestapo and their activities. A member of the tribunal would later admit that he was 'a soldier's soldier, through and through'. (See Raleigh Trevelyan, *Rome '44*, London, 1981, p. 325.)

[*] Kesselring's British biographer, Kenneth Macksey, has written that he was a master of prolonged defensive warfare. 'Of what other general can it be said that, over a period of two and a half years, he fought a virtually incessant delaying action against desperate odds, managed to impose his will upon strong-minded and sceptical subordinates, and yet emerged unscathed by serious rout, leading his men in fighting to the last gasp?' (*Kesselring: The Making of the Luftwaffe*, op. cit., p. 257.)

and the Liri valley where three of the divisions used in the remarkable defence of Cassino were the 15th and 29th Panzer Grenadier Divisions, still commanded by Generals Rodt and Fries, and Heidrich's 1st Parachute Division. Von Senger's attempts to save the Abbey of Monte Cassino came to naught but earned him the respect of the Italians, including the partisans who never attacked him during his many trips through the Italian countryside. Undoubtedly von Senger's military successes were the only reasons he escaped retribution for his repeated defiance of orders he considered illegal and immoral. Imprisoned by the British at the end of the war, he was eventually released and later wrote his memoirs which were published in English.

Another of von Senger's divisional commanders at Cassino was the eccentric Baade, now a major general in command of the 90th Panzer Grenadier Division. Baade and Patton would have understood each other well, for Baade believed in making his presence felt at the front. In addition to providing inspired leadership Baade also left in each of many bunkers throughout the Cassino area a reminder of his presence in the form of a bottle containing a message with the date of the battle just fought, his name and those of his adjutant and his dog![1] In his command bunker he kept a monk's cowl handy, along with a red dress for his youthful adjutant. Baade, who had an almost paranoid obsession with capture and captivity, was determined to escape dressed as a monk. Christmas 1943 saw Baade exchange greetings with the British commanders against whom he had fought in the desert, but there was apparently no substance to the report reaching OKW that he had eaten Christmas dinner with his enemy. He did, however, promptly radio the names of captured American soldiers to their units, calling it 'a great favour for mothers and wives and fiancées'.[2] Baade survived the Italian campaign only to die from injuries received during an Allied air attack near his home on the last day of the war. In a testimonial to his old friend, von Senger wrote of his unique ability to inspire his men. In the German Army, where there had been precious little to smile about in the latter stages of the war, Ernst-Guenther Baade was like a breath of fresh air.

The battle of Monte Cassino considerably enhanced the reputa-

---

[1] Hapgood and Richardson, *Monte Cassino*, op. cit., p. 177.
[2] Ibid.

tions of the two airborne commanders, Heidrich and Heilmann. The 1st Parachute Division was responsible for defending the town of Cassino. One historian recently observed that in the massive bombardments it took approximately three tons of bombs to kill a single paratrooper. The Tenth Army commander, von Vietinghoff, would later tell Kesselring that 'no troops but 1 Parachute Division could have held Cassino'. Further praise came from the Allies, most notably Alexander who was always able to appreciate outstanding soldiering when he observed it. At the height of the battle, as the attacking New Zealand troops were being steadily repulsed, Alexander wrote to Brooke: 'Unfortunately we are fighting the best soldiers in the world – what men! ... I do not think any other troops could have stood up to it perhaps except these para boys.'[1] Geoffrey Keyes who later succeeded Bradley as the II Corps commander in Italy paid the German paratroopers the ultimate compliment by ordering his units to avoid fighting them whenever possible.[2]

After commanding the 1st Parachute Division at Cassino Heidrich was promoted to command the 1 Parachute Corps which surrendered to the Allies in northern Italy in May 1945. In Sicily the Allies had never heard of Heilmann, but at Monte Cassino 'King Ludwig' won immortality in command of the 3rd Parachute Regiment. After it was nearly annihilated in the great battle of the Falaise gap in August 1944, Heilmann was given command of the 5th Parachute Division and won the Knight's Cross with Oak Leaves and Swords during the battle of the Bulge where he was later captured. He was released from a British POW camp in 1947 and until his death in 1959 was a great favourite among German parachute veterans.

Corporal Georg Schmitz was promoted to Feldwebel (sergeant) and took part in the Cassino battles. In 1945 he was promoted to lieutenant and after the surrender spent several months as a POW. He is now a businessman in Stadt/Elbe, an active member of the parachute veterans' organization, and a liberal politician.

Paul Conrath, the commander of the Hermann Goering Division, became only the 276th soldier in the Wehrmacht to win the Oak Leaves to the Knight's Cross for his service in Sicily. He

---

[1] John Ellis, *Cassino: The Hollow Victory*, New York, 1984, Chapter 11, *passim*.
[2] Interview with General Robert W. Porter, Jr, 15 September 1985, loc. cit. After the Sicily campaign Porter became the G-2 of II Corps in Italy.

retained his command in Italy where the division fought at Salerno and Anzio. For the final year of the war he served in Berlin as the commander of Training and Replacement Forces. In January 1945 he was promoted to General of Parachute Troops (General der Fallschirmjaegertruppen). Conrath died in Hamburg in January 1979 at the age of eighty-two.*

Colonel Wilhelm Schmalz, who performed brilliantly in stemming the advance of Eighth Army in the early days of the campaign, was also decorated with the Oak Leaves to the Knight's Cross for Sicily. In May 1944 he succeeded Conrath as commander of the Hermann Goering and ended the war as a lieutenant general. He died in 1983, also at the age of eighty-two.

Colonel General Hans Valentin Hube was one of the few German officers presented a high decoration by the Italians. For his leadership in Sicily, Hube was awarded the Grand Cross of the Military Order of Savoy. He never received the recognition he deserved from the German leadership for masterminding Operation 'Lehrgang', but early in 1944 he was given command of 1st Panzer Army on the Eastern Front where he was killed in a plane crash on 21 April.

After being recalled to Berlin in August 1943, Admiral Friedrich Ruge became the naval adviser to Rommel when he assumed command of Army Group B in November. He became an intimate friend of Rommel and one of the few men whom Rommel trusted. After the war Ruge became the first chief naval inspector of the West German Navy and an internationally known historian. A very popular and respected figure in the international community, Ruge wrote books on marine matters and a memoir of his assignment with Rommel which was published in English. Admiral Ruge died in 1985.

Fregattenkapiten Baron Gustav von Liebenstein was awarded the German Cross in Gold and singled out in the German war communiqué for his outstanding performance in Sicily. In Corsica he duplicated on a smaller scale his success in evacuating German troops and equipment for which he was awarded the Knight's Cross. After his unit was disbanded he spent considerable time in

---

* Data about Conrath and Schmalz furnished by Alfred Otte, a Hermann Goering veteran who is active in the Association of the Armoured Airborne Corps. Conrath was promoted to generalleutnant on 1 July 1943.

hospital, and from January 1944 to the end of the war he served as the chief of staff to the commander of German naval forces in Holland with the rank of Kapitän. In the postwar years he was a member of the board of directors of a large power corporation in Mannheim. Baron von Liebenstein died in 1967 shortly before his seventy-sixth birthday.

Five of the six US divisions that fought in Sicily are still on active service: since the end of the war the 3d Infantry Division has been stationed in West Germany as part of America's commitment to NATO. Its headquarters are at Würzburg. The 2d Armored Division is based at Fort Hood, Texas, and the 82d Division at Fort Bragg, North Carolina, the only remaining airborne unit in an age of the helicopter and air mobility. The 'Big Red One' is now a mechanized infantry division stationed at Fort Riley, Kansas. Doubtless, few of its present-day soldiers are aware of Patton's words to Eisenhower when he demanded the 1st Division for the invasion of Sicily: 'I want those sons of bitches! I won't go on without them!'*

When the combatants moved on to Italy the island of Sicily gradually began to return to some semblance of normality after this latest in the long history of foreign invasions. The destruction of many of Sicily's principal cities was devastating. For years afterwards the mines sowed in their thousands by the retreating Germans were a hazard that claimed more than one life. In recent years the Italian government, perhaps compensating for its long-time neglect, began building an *autostrada* that girds the entire island of Sicily. Where it passes down the eastern coast from Messina and across the Simeto and the plain of Catania the *autostrada* speeds unwary travellers across what was once a bloody battlefield. The same road cuts across the Gela battlefield as does a branch *autostrada* in the area fought over by 30 Corps connecting Catania with the inland city of Enna. The mountain roads traversed by troops of Seventh Army during Patton's Palermo offensive can now be travelled quickly via yet another *autostrada* connecting Enna with the north coast. In 1943 it took Truscott's 3d Division seventeen days to reach Messina; the modern tourist can cover the same distance today in a matter of hours.

---

* The 9th Division was recently reactivated as a motorized infantry division at Fort Lewis, Washington.

More than 500,000 Allied soldiers, sailors and airmen fought in Sicily in some capacity against an estimated 60,000 men of the Wehrmacht.* Most who died there were never taken home, and the few remaining testaments to their presence in 1943 are the several military cemeteries where the combatants are buried. In the shadow of Mount Etna, overlooking the plain of Catania, is an ossuary containing the remains of 4,561 German soldiers.† Nearby, at Catania and Syracuse, are the two British cemeteries containing the fallen of Eighth Army.‡ On a small hill east of the city of Agira is the Canadian War Cemetery of 490 graves. The 2,440 Americans lost in Sicily were buried in four temporary cemeteries at Licata, Gela, Catania and Palermo. In April 1947 these cemeteries were disinterred and their remains transferred to a permanent site in Italy near the ancient Greek city of Paestum, on the Gulf of Salerno.

War correspondent Ernie Pyle, who was killed in the Pacific in April 1945, once wrote about the effect war graves had upon him. His words offer the final commemoration to those who died in Sicily during those thirty-eight days in the summer of 1943:

> There is nothing we can do
> for the ones beneath the
> wooden crosses except to
> pause and murmur, 'Thanks, pal'.

---

* See Appendix I. Of the 500,000+ Allied servicemen, approximately 450,000 served in Seventh and Eighth Armies.

† *Kriegsgraeberfuersorge 3/1976*. The ossuary is at Motta Sant' Anastasia, approximately 8 km west of Catania, near Misterbianco.

‡ The Catania War Cemetery is located 7 km southwest of Catania and contains 2,142 graves; the Syracuse War Cemetery is 3 km west of the city towards Floridia on Route 124 and has 1,066 graves. (Source: Commonwealth War Graves Commission.)

Appendices

Organization of
the Allied Forces in
the Mediterranean*

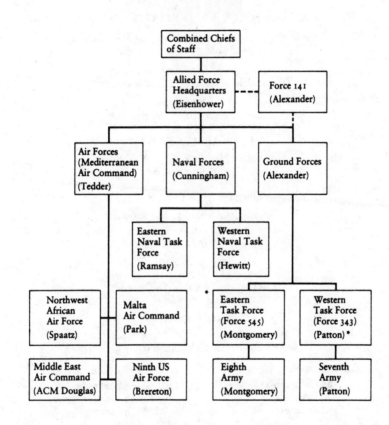

* HUSKY planning was accomplished within each of the Army headquarters. Until D-Day, 10 July 1943, Patton's headquarters was called I Armored Corps.

APPENDIX B

Order of Battle, Allied Ground Forces

ALLIED FORCE HEADQUARTERS (AFHQ)

Commander-in-Chief, Allied Forces in North Africa
General Dwight D. Eisenhower

Deputy Allied Commander-in-Chief
General Sir Harold R. L. G. Alexander

Chief of Staff
Major General Walter Bedell Smith

15th ARMY GROUP

General Sir Harold R. L. G. Alexander
Commander-in-Chief

EIGHTH ARMY (Force 545)

General Sir Bernard L. Montgomery
Major-General Francis W. de Guingand
Chief of Staff

13 CORPS

Lieutenant-General Miles Dempsey
Commander

5th Division
Major-General H. P. M. Berney-Ficklin
Major-General G. C. Bucknall (from 8.3.43)

13th Infantry Brigade	15th Infantry Brigade
2nd Cameronians	1st Green Howards
2nd Inniskillings	1st King's Own Yorkshire
2nd Wiltshire	Light Infantry

17th Infantry Brigade
2nd Royal Scots Fusiliers
2nd Northamptonshire
6th Seaforth Highlanders

Divisional Troops

5th Reconnaissance Regiment
7th Cheshire (MG)
52nd Anti-Tank Regiment
245th, 252nd and 38th Field
Companies

91st, 92nd and 156th Field
Regiments, RA
18th Light AA Regiment, RA
254th Field Park Company, RE

50th Division (Northumbrian)
Major-General Sidney C. Kirkman

69th Infantry Brigade
5th East Yorkshire
6th, 7th Green Howards

151st Infantry Brigade
(The Durham Light Infantry
Brigade)
6th, 8th and 9th DLI

168th Infantry Brigade
1st London Irish
1st London Scottish
10th Royal Berkshire

Divisional Troops

102nd Anti-Tank Regiment, RA
2nd Cheshire (MG)
74th, 124th and 90th Field
Regiments, RA

25th Light AA Regiment, RA
233rd, 501st and 505th Field
Companies, RE

1st Airborne Division
Major-General G. F. Hopkinson

1st Parachute Brigade
1st, 2nd and 3rd Battalions,
The Parachute Regiment

2nd Parachute Brigade
4th, 5th and 6th Battalions,
The Parachute Regiment

1st Airlanding Brigade
1st Battalion, The Border
Regiment
2nd Battalion, The South
Staffordshire Regiment
1st Glider Pilot Regiment (in
support)

4th Parachute Brigade
10th, 11th and 156th
Battalions, The Parachute
Regiment

Divisional Troops

1st Airlanding Reconnaissance Squadron
1st Airlanding Light Regiment, RA
1st and 2nd Airlanding Anti-Tank Batteries, RA
1st Airlanding Light AA Battery, RA
1st, 2nd and 4th Parachute Squadrons, RE

9th Field Company, RE
261st Field Park Company, RE
250th Airborne Light Communications Company, RASC
16th, 127th and 133rd Parachute Field Ambulance, RAMC
181st Airlanding Field Ambulance, RAMC
1st Airborne Division Provost Company
1st Airborne Divisional Signals*

Naval Bombardment Detachment
21st Independent Parachute Company (Pathfinders)

4th Armoured Brigade
Brigadier J. C. Currie

44th Royal Tank Regiment
3rd County of London Yeomanry

30 Corps
Lieutenant-General Sir Oliver Leese

51st (Highland) Division
Major-General Douglas Wimberley

152nd Infantry Brigade	153rd Infantry Brigade
5th Queen's Own Cameron Highlanders	5th Black Watch
2nd and 5th Seaforth Highlanders	5th/7th Gordon Highlanders
	1st Gordon Highlanders

154th Infantry Brigade
1st and 7th Black Watch
7th Argyll and Sutherland
Highlanders

Divisional Troops

126th, 127th and 128th Field Regiments, RA	239th Field Park Company, RE
1st/7th Middlesex (MG)	61st Anti-Tank Regiment, RA
	40th Light AA Regiment, RA

1st Canadian Division
Major-General G. G. Simonds

1st Infantry Brigade	2nd Infantry Brigade
The Royal Canadian Regiment	Princess Patricia's Canadian Light Infantry
The Hastings and Prince Edward Regiment	The Seaforth Highlanders of Canada
48th Highlanders of Canada	The Loyal Edmonton Regiment

* Each British and Canadian division was organized to include a Divisional Signals Section within the Divisional Troops, e.g., 50th Divisional Signals, etc.

3rd Infantry Brigade
Royal 22ᵉ Regiment
The Carleton and York
Regiment
The West Nova Scotia
Regiment

Divisional Troops

4th Princess Louise Dragoon
Guards (4th
Reconnaissance Regiment)
1st Anti-Tank Regiment, RCA
The Saskatoon Light Infantry
(MG)

2nd Field Park Company, RCE
1st Field Regiment, RCHA
2nd and 3rd Regiments, RCA
1st, 3rd and 4th Field Companies,
RCE

231st Infantry Brigade
(attached 51st Division, 10–15 July)
Brigadier R. E. Urquhart

1st Battalion, The Dorsetshire Regiment
1st Battalion, The Hampshire Regiment
2nd Battalion, The Devonshire Regiment
165th Field Regiment, RA
295th Field Company, RE

1st Canadian Army Tank Brigade*
(redesignated 1st Armoured Brigade, 26.8.43)
Brigadier R. A. Wyman

The Ontario Regiment
Three Rivers Regiment
The Calgary Regiment

23rd Armoured Brigade
Brigadier G. W. Richards

40th, 46th and 50th Royal Tank Regiments
11th King's Royal Rifle Corps

RESERVE FORMATIONS

46th Division
Major-General J. L. I. Hawkesworth
(not used in Sicily)

78th Division
Major-General V. Evelegh

11th Infantry Brigade
2nd Battalion, The Lancashire
Fusiliers

1st Battalion, The East
Surrey Regiment

* Attached 1st Canadian Division.

5th Battalion, The
Northamptonshire Regiment

36th Infantry Brigade
6th Battalion, The Royal West
Kent Regiment
5th Battalion, The Buffs

(Royal East Kent
Regiment)
8th Battalion, The Argyll and
Sutherland Highlanders

38th (Irish) Infantry Brigade
6th Battalion, The Royal Inniskilling Fusiliers
1st Battalion, The Royal Irish Fusiliers
2nd Battalion, The London Irish Rifles

Divisional Troops

56th Reconnaissance Regiment,
RAC
64th Anti-Tank Regiment, RA
214th, 237th and 256th Field
Companies, RE

1st Kensingtons (MG)
17th, 132nd and 138th Field
Regiments, RA
49th Light AA Regiment, RA
281st Field Park Company, RE

Miscellaneous Units

1st Special Raiding Squadron
2nd SAS Regiment
No. 3 Commando
No. 40 Royal Marine Commando
No. 41 Royal Marine Commando

SEVENTH UNITED STATES ARMY (Force 343)
Lieutenant General George S. Patton, Jr

Deputy Commander
Major General Geoffrey T. Keyes

Chief of Staff
Brigadier General Hobart R. Gay

II Corps
Lieutenant General Omar N. Bradley

1st Infantry Division
('Big Red One')

Major General Terry de la Mesa Allen
Major General Clarence R. Huebner (from 9.8.43)

16th Infantry Regiment*
18th Infantry Regiment

26th Infantry Regiment

* The infantry regiments of the 1st, 3d and 45th Infantry Divisions were augmented by
the attachment of additional units to form what were called Regimental Combat Teams

Division Artillery
5th, 7th, 32d and 33d Field Artillery Battalions

Special Troops

1st Engineer Combat Battalion
1st Medical Battalion
1st Reconnaissance Troop
1st Quartermaster Company
1st Ordnance Company (LM)
1st Signal Company
Military Police platoon

Attachments
(D-Day landings)

67th Armored Regiment (Medium Tank) (—)
Force X (Darby's Rangers)
    1st and 4th Ranger Battalions
1st Battalion, 39th Combat Engineer Regiment
1 Battalion, 531st Engineer Shore Regiment
3 Coys, 83d Chemical Battalion

45th Infantry Division
Major General Troy H. Middleton

157th Infantry Regiment
179th Infantry Regiment
180th Infantry Regiment

Division Artillery
158th, 160th, 171st and 189th Field
Artillery Battalions

Special Troops

120th Engineer Combat Battalion
120th Medical Battalion
45th Reconnaissance Troop (Mech)
45th Quartermaster Company
45th Signal Company
700th Ordnance Light Maintenance Company
45th CIC Detachment
Military Police Platoon

Attachments

753d Medium Tank Battalion

(RCTs). Conventional World War II infantry organization was basically triangular at the top; each regiment consisted of three numbered rifle battalions. However, each rifle battalion consisted of three rifle companies plus a heavy weapons company and each rifle company was organized into three rifle platoons and a weapons platoon. Battalions and regiments were usually identified by a numeric combination, e.g., 2/16 Infantry designated the 2d Battalion, 16th Infantry Regiment.

JOSS FORCE*

3d Infantry Division (Reinforced)
Major General Lucian K. Truscott

7th Infantry Regiment
15th Infantry Regiment
30th Infantry Regiment

Division Artillery
9th, 10th, 39th and 41st Field
Artillery Battalions

Special Troops

Hq & Hq Co., 3d Infantry Division
10th Engineer Battalion
3d Chemical Battalion (Mortar)
3d Medical Battalion
3d Reconnaissance Troop
3d Quartermaster Company
3d Signal Company
703d Ordnance Company
Administration Center, 3d Inf Division, Rear Echelon

Floating Reserve

Combat Command A, 2d Armored Division
66th Armored Regiment (− 3d Battalion)
41st Armored Infantry Regiment (− 1st Battalion)
Company B, 82d Reconnaissance Squadron
14th Armored Field Artillery Battalion

Attached Units

36th Combat Engineer Regiment
3d Ranger Battalion
4th Tabor Goums
5th Armored Field Artillery Group
77th Field Artillery Regiment
2d Battalion, 36th Field Artillery Regiment
Battery B, 1st Field Artillery Observation Battalion (S & F)
Survey Platoon, Coy B, 66th Engineer Battalion (Topo)
Hq & Hq Battery, 105th AAA AW Group, w/attached units
Naval Shore Fire Control Parties
Air Officer, XII Air Support Command
Far Shore Control
        Force Depot, Beach Group + attached units
Near Shore Control and attached units

---

* Source: *History of the Third Infantry Division in World War II. Sicily and the Surrender of Italy*, Appendix A.

Seventh Army Floating Reserve

2d Armored Division

Combat Command B

67th Armored Regiment (—)
82d Reconnaissance Squadron (—)
17th Armored Engineer Battalion
78th Armored Field Artillery Battalion
92d Armored Field Artillery Battalion
1st Battalion, 41st Armored Infantry Regiment

18th Infantry Regiment (1st Division)

32d Field Artillery Battalion
1 Engineer Company

540th Engineer Shore Regiment

2 Anti-Aircraft Artillery Battalions

82d Airborne Division
Major General Matthew B. Ridgway

504th and 505th Parachute Infantry Regiments
325th Glider Infantry Regiment

9th Infantry Division
Major General Manton S. Eddy

39th, 47th and 60th Infantry Regiments

APPENDIX C

Organization of the Allied Air Forces

MEDITERRANEAN AIR COMMAND

Air Commander-in-Chief
Air Chief Marshal Sir Arthur W. Tedder

Deputy Air Commander-in-Chief
Air Vice-Marshal H. E. P. Wigglesworth

NORTHWEST AFRICAN AIR FORCES

Commanding General
Major General Carl A. Spaatz, USAAF

Deputy Commander
Air Vice-Marshal J. M. Robb, RAF

Chief of Staff
Colonel E. P. Curtis, USAAF

NORTHWEST AFRICAN STRATEGIC AIR FORCE
Major General James H. Doolittle, USAAF

NORTHWEST AFRICAN TACTICAL AIR FORCE
Air Marshal Sir Arthur Coningham, RAF

NORTHWEST AFRICAN COASTAL AIR FORCE
Air Vice-Marshal Sir Hugh Lloyd, RAF

NORTHWEST AFRICAN TROOP CARRIER COMMAND
Brigadier General Ray A. Dunn, USAAF

NORTHWEST AFRICAN AIR SERVICE COMMAND
Major General Delmar H. Dunton, USAAF

**NORTHWEST AFRICAN PHOTOGRAPHIC
RECONNAISSANCE WING**
Colonel Elliott Roosevelt, USAAF

MALTA AIR COMMAND
(RAF)

Air Officer Commanding
Air Vice-Marshal Sir Keith Park, RAF

MIDDLE EAST AIR COMMAND
(RAF)

Air Officer Commanding-in-Chief
Air Chief Marshal Sir William Sholto Douglas

NINTH UNITED STATES AIR FORCE*

Commanding General
Major General Lewis H. Brereton, USAAF

* Under the operational control of Middle East Air Command.

APPENDIX D

Organization of
the Allied Naval Forces

Commander-in-Chief
Admiral of the Fleet Sir Andrew Cunningham
Chief of Staff
Commodore R. M. Dick

Eastern Naval Task Force*
(Royal Navy)

Commander
Admiral Sir Bertram Ramsay
Chief of Staff
Commodore C. E. Douglas-Pennant

FORCE 'A' Rear-Admiral T. H. Troubridge
    13 Corps (5th and 50th Divisions)
    231st Infantry Brigade
    No. 3 Commando; 4th Armoured Brigade

FORCE 'B' Rear-Admiral R. R. McGrigor
    51st (Highland) Division
    23rd Armoured Brigade

FORCE 'V' Rear-Admiral Sir Philip L. Vian
    1st Canadian Division
    1st Canadian Army Tank Brigade
    Nos. 40 and 41 Royal Marine Commandos
    73rd AA Brigade, RA

FORCE 'K' Rear-Admiral C. H. J. Harcourt
    Support Force

---

* Force 'A' sailed from the Middle East; Force 'B' from Tunisian ports; and Force 'V' direct from the United Kingdom. Force 'K' was first composed of four cruisers and six destroyers and responsible for providing additional support for the convoys during their final approaches to Sicily on D−1/D-Day. Later supplemented by monitors and gunboats it was split into bombardment groups supporting each British landing. After the invasion its task was to protect the northern flank of Ramsay's Eastern Task Force.

Western Naval Task Force
(US Navy)

Commander
Vice Admiral H. Kent Hewitt

JOSS FORCE (TF 86 – Licata) Rear Admiral R. L. Conolly
    3d Infantry Division
    3d Ranger Battalion
    CCA, 2d Armored Division (floating reserve)

DIME FORCE (TF 81 – Gela) Rear Admiral J. L. Hall
    1st Infantry Division
    Force X
    2d Armored Division (—) (floating reserve)

CENT FORCE (TF 85 – Scoglitti) Rear Admiral A. G. Kirk
    45th Infantry Division

NAVAL FORCES ENGAGED IN OPERATION 'HUSKY'

Class	Royal Navy	US Navy	Other
Battleships	6	–	–
Fleet Carriers	2	–	–
Cruisers	10	5	–
AA ships	4	–	–
Fighter Direction	2	–	–
Monitors	3	–	–
Gunboats	3	–	2 Dutch
Minelayers	1	3	–
HQ ships	5	4	–
Destroyers	71	48	6 Greek, 3 Polish
Escort vessels	35*	–	1 Greek
Minesweepers	34	8	–
LSI & LST	8†	–	–
Major Landing-Craft	319	190	–
Minor Landing-Craft	715	510	–
Coastal craft	160	83	–
Submarines	23	–	1 Dutch, 2 Polish
Misc. vessels	58	28	–
Merchant ships, troop transports & MT ships	155	66	7 Dutch, 4 Polish / 1 Belgian / 4 Norwegian
TOTALS	1,614	945	31

* inc. 2 Royal Indian Navy.
† Manned by the Royal Navy.
Source: *The War at Sea*, Vol. III, Pt I, p. 121, and *The Mediterranean and Middle East*, Vol. V, p. 30.

APPENDIX E

Allied Casualties
(10 July–17 August 1943)

BATTLE LOSSES

| | UNITED STATES | |
	Seventh Army[1]	US Navy
Killed in action	2,237	546
Wounded in action	5,946	484
Captured	598	–
Missing in action	–	–
	8,781	1,030

| | BRITISH | |
	Eighth Army*	Royal Navy
Killed in action	2,062	314
Wounded in action	7,137	411
Captured	–	4
Missing in action	2,644	–
	11,843	729

NON-BATTLE LOSSES

There were two field and six evacuation hospitals established in Sicily by Seventh Army Medical Corps. During the campaign these processed

[1] Morison, *Sicily–Salerno–Anzio*, p. 223n. Seventh Army figures include USAAF pilot and crew losses since 14 May 1943 but do not include losses from the airborne drops which were 28 killed, 41 wounded and 88 missing.

* Includes Canadian losses: 562 killed in action (including those lost at sea en route from the UK), 1,664 wounded. (*The Canadians in Italy*, pp. 174–5 and *Sicily–Salerno–Anzio*, p. 223n.)

admissions totalling 20,734 of which 7,714 were for wounds or injuries. 13,320 were admitted for diseases of which two-thirds were for malaria and/or diarrhoea. Approximately 50% of the total hospital cases (i.e. 10,000+) were eventually evacuated to other facilities in North Africa.[1] Eighth Army recorded 11,500 cases of malaria,[2] of which 1,200 were Canadian.[3]

[1] *Sicily and the Surrender of Italy*, p. 419.
[2] Molony, *The Mediterranean and Middle East*, Vol. V, p. 145. Casualty and non-battle loss information is completely lacking in this volume. One is forced to consult American and Canadian sources for the relevant data.
[3] *The Canadians in Italy*, p. 176 (period is from 10 July–31 August).

APPENDIX F

Organization of
the Italian Armed Forces
(after 1 February 1943)

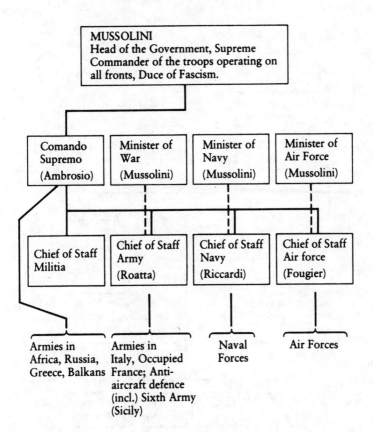

MUSSOLINI
Head of the Government, Supreme Commander of the troops operating on all fronts, Duce of Fascism.

| Comando Supremo (Ambrosio) | Minister of War (Mussolini) | Minister of Navy (Mussolini) | Minister of Air Force (Mussolini) |

| Chief of Staff Militia | Chief of Staff Army (Roatta) | Chief of Staff Navy (Riccardi) | Chief of Staff Air force (Fougier) |

Armies in Africa, Russia, Greece, Balkans

Armies in Italy, Occupied France; Anti-aircraft defence (incl.) Sixth Army (Sicily)

Naval Forces

Air Forces

Source: Howard McGaw Smyth, 'The Command of the Italian Armed Forces in World War II', *Military Affairs*, Spring 1951.

APPENDIX G

Organization of the Axis Forces in Sicily

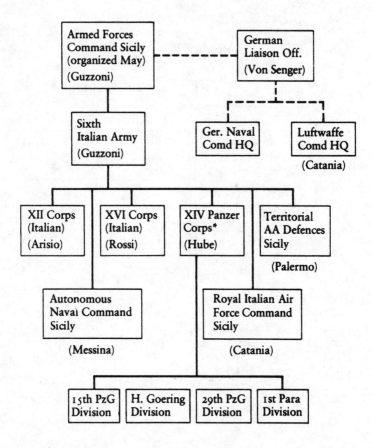

* Tactical control only. Prior to the arrival of XIV Panzer Corps in mid-July the German units in Sicily were under the direct tactical control of Sixth Army.

APPENDIX H

Order of Battle,
Axis Ground Forces*

SIXTH ITALIAN ARMY

Generale d'Armata Alfredo Guzzoni

Chief of Staff

Generale di Brigata Emilio Faldella

Army Reserve

4th (Livorno) Division†

Generale di Divisione Domenico Chirieleison

33rd Infantry Regiment
34th Infantry Regiment
1 Mortar Battalion (81 mm)
XI Commando Battalion
IV Anti-Tank Battalion (47 mm)
28th Artillery Regiment
(4 groups, towed artillery)
3 AA batteries (20 mm)
Engineer Battalion
Service units

15th Panzer Grenadier Division
(Sizilien)

Oberst Ernst-Guenther Baade (to 5 June 1943)

Generalmajor Eberhard Rodt (from 5 June 1943)

Regimental Group (Oberst Ens) (later 104th PzG Regiment) (Reinf)	Regimental Group Fullreide (Oberst Fullreide) (later 129th PzG Regiment)
3 rifle battalions (3 rifle Coys. each)	Same organization as Group Ens – 3rd Infantry Battalion (at Comiso) + 1 artillery battalion. Some tanks probably attached
1 heavy weapons company	
1 engineer platoon	
1 anti-tank platoon	
1 platoon artillery	
Some tanks attached as of 12 June	

* Reconstructed as of D-Day, 10 July 1943. During the campaign there were frequent attachments/detachments as the Axis command attempted to counter Allied pressure.

† The Livorno was the only truly mobile Italian division on Sicily and was far superior to

Regimental Group Koerner
(Oberst Koerner) (later 115th PzG
Regiment
  composition unknown

  1 Armoured Recon. Battalion
    (est.) 30–40 Mk III & IV
    tanks; 1 Tiger company (17
    tanks) (attchd. HG Div.
    prior to 10 July)
  33rd Engineer Battalion
    (3 companies – each attchd.
    to a TF)
  33rd AA Battalion (later 315
    AA Bn.) (deployed in small
    groups on principal
    highways)
  999th Signal Company
  Misc. service units

Artillery Regiment 'Sizilien' (later
33rd Artillery Regiment)
  1st Battalion (med. howitzer)
    (Group Fullreide)
  2nd Battalion (4 btry. 170 mm
    guns)* (Group Ens)
  3rd Battalion (2 med. field
    how. btry.) (1 mortar btry)
    (Group Fullreide)
  4th Battalion (3 med. how.
    btry.) (Group Schmalz)

1 Mortar Regiment (rocket)
  1 Battalion 150 mm mortars
  1 Battalion 210 mm mortars
    (held in Army Reserve until
    approx. 14 July when
    attchd. Group Fullreide)

XII Corps
Generale di corpo d'armata Mario Arisio

  202nd Coastal Division†
  207th Coastal Division
  208th Coastal Division
  136th Coastal Regiment
  Port Defence Group 'N'
  Mobile Groups 'A', 'B' and 'C'‡
  4 tactical groups‡

---

* These guns were moved to the Italian side of the Messina Strait to guard the northern end in early August.

† The coastal formations were static units organized to defend the Sicilian coastline against invasion and consisted of men of older age groups, approximately 75% of whom were locals. These units had a low combat value and numbered approximately 75,000–100,000. Its armament was antiquated and contained no anti-naval guns and what little artillery existed was horse-drawn. Principal weapons were automatic rifles and machine guns. The Italians could muster an average of only thirty-six men for every 1,000 yards and one anti-tank weapon for every five miles of coast. Some battalions had responsibility for sectors nearly thirty miles wide. Their ineffectiveness was clearly demonstrated on D-Day, 10 July 1943.

‡ The mobile and tactical groups assigned to XII and XVI Corps were, along with the Livorno Division and, until approximately 16 July, 15th PzG Division, part of the mobile reserve controlled by the Sixth Italian Army.

---

the other divisions. It had originally been organized for an attack on Malta. Its troops were of high quality and its organic transportation was sufficient to move all of its infantry units simultaneously, including all artillery. The Table of Organization for all Italian 'mobile' divisions was 13,000–14,000 men. (Source: Bauer Manuscript # R-125/126 and Faldella, *Lo sbarco e la difesa della Sicilia*.)

MOBILE FORCES

28th (Aosta) Division
Generale di Divisione Giacomo Romano

5th Infantry Regiment
6th Infantry Regiment
171st 'Blackshirt' Battalion
XXVIII Mortar Battalion
22nd Artillery Regiment
    (4 groups [2 self-propelled])
2 AA batteries (20 mm)
Engineer Battalion
Service units

26th (Assietta) Division
Generale di Divisione Erberto Papini
Generale di Divisione Francesco Scotti
Generale di Divisione Ottorino Schreiber (from 26.7.43)

29th Infantry Regiment
30th Infantry Regiment
17th 'Blackshirt' Battalion
CXXVI Mortar Battalion
25th Artillery Regiment
    (4 groups [all self-propelled])
2 AA Batteries (20 mm)
Engineer Battalion
Service units

XVI Corps
Generale di Corpo d'Armata Carlo Rossi

Static Units

206th Coastal Division
213th Coastal Division
XVIII and XIX Coastal Brigades
Port Defence Group 'E'
Mobile Groups 'D', 'E', 'F', 'G' and 'H'
4 tactical groups

Mobile Forces

54th (Napoli) Division
Generale di Divisione Giulio G. C. Porcinari

75th Infantry Regiment
76th Infantry Regiment
173rd 'Blackshirt' Battalion

54th Artillery Regiment
(4 groups [2 towed; 2 self-propelled])
2 AA Batteries (20 mm)

Hermann Goering Division*
Generalleutnant Paul Conrath

Division HQ
Brigade HQ (for special employment)†
1 Panzer Grenadier Regiment‡
Panzer Regiment HG[1]
Panzer Reconnaissance Battalion[2]
Panzer Pioneer (Engineer) Battalion[2]
Panzer Artillery Regiment HG[3]
Flak Regiment HG (—)[4]
Anti-Tank Company
Supply and Service units

Attached units:
115th PzG Regiment[5] – (Schmalz)
2 infantry battalions[6]
3rd Parachute Regiment (1st Parachute Division) – (Schmalz)
4th Parachute Regiment (1st Parachute Division) – (Schmalz)
remnants Fallschirm Engineer and MG Battalions, Signal coy (1st Parachute Division) – (Schmalz)
Tiger tank coy, 215th Tank Battalion
Fortress Battalion 904 – (Schmalz)
Fortress Battalion 923 – (Schmalz)
Fortress Battalion 'Reggio' – (Schmalz)
Flak Catania[7]

[1] Consisted of 2 tank battalions ([e] 80–90 Mark III and IV medium tanks) and 1 battalion of assault guns (assigned to Schmalz).
[2] Both units were motorized and fought as infantry.
[3] Consisted of 3 battalions: 1 light battalion w/2 batteries; 2 medium battalions (2 medium field howitzer batteries and 1 100 mm battery).
[4] Unit incomplete: 1 mixed battalion of 3 medium and 3 light batteries.
[5] Detached from 15th Panzer Grenadier Division and assigned to Schmalz prior to D-Day.
[6] These two battalions arrived in Sicily on 11 July and were probably part of the 382d Infantry Regiment.
[7] Probably 1 medium artillery battalion and 1 Italian artillery battalion.
* In Sicily the Division was generally employed as combat groups (kampfgruppen) to meet tactical requirements. Kampfgruppe Schmalz consisted mostly of attached formations. Sources for creating an Order of Battle are superficial and often contradictory: Bauer Manuscript # R-125/126; Alfred Otte; 'Report No. 14, Historical Section, (G.S.), Army HQ', Sicily, passim, and The Mediterranean and Middle East, Vol. V, passim.
† Assigned to kampfgruppe Schmalz.
‡ The PzG regiment consisted of the HQ and 1st Battalion, 1st Panzer Grenadier Regiment and the HQ and 1st and 2nd Battalions, 2nd Panzer Grenadier Regiment.

XIV Panzer Corps
General der Panzertruppen Hans Valentin Hube

Chief of Staff
Oberst Bogislaw von Bonin

15th Panzer Grenadier Division
Hermann Goering Division
1st Parachute Division (–)

29th Panzer Grenadier Division*
Generalmajor Walter Fries

15th Pz Grenadier Regiment
  (3 battalions)
71st Pz Grenadier Regiment
  (3 battalions)
129th Armoured Reconnaissance Battalion†
129th Tank Battalion (Assault Gun)
  (1 Coy. only sent to Sicily)
29th Artillery Regiment
  1 light bn. (SP)
  1 light bn.
  1 medium bn.
29th Engineer Battalion
  (1 Coy. only sent to Sicily 18.7.43)
313th AA Battalion
  2 medium batteries
  1 heavy battery
29th Signal Battalion
1 anti-tank company
Division troops†

1st Parachute Division (—)
Generalleutnant Richard Heidrich

3rd Parachute Regiment (FJR 3)
4th Parachute Regiment (FJR 3)
1st Parachute Machine-Gun Battalion
1st Parachute Pioneer (Engineer) Battalion
1st Battalion, 1st Parachute Field Artillery Regiment
elements 1st Parachute Anti-Tank Battalion
1st Parachute Signal Company

---

* Not all of this division were committed to Sicily. Elements of the 382 Infantry Regiment were attached to *Kampfgruppe* Schmalz. Other units began arriving on 15 July but main elements did not cross the Strait of Messina until approximately the third week of July. Operational control was exercised by XIV Panzer Corps.

† Not committed to Sicily.

APPENDIX I

Axis Strengths and Losses

There has been no precise accounting of the exact numbers of Axis forces who fought in Sicily, nor is it likely on the basis of the data available that there will ever be. On D-Day Axis strength was somewhere between 300,000[1] and 365,000.[2] The more conservative Canadian official history estimates the total Axis strength in Sicily on 10 July 1943 as 270,000: 230,000 Italians and 40,000 Germans.[3] The British official history is similar: 200,000 Italians and 62,000 Germans.[4] The discrepancy between the various sources has never been resolved but it may well have been that the higher figures for the Italian forces included Fascist militia and other paramilitary personnel with police and administrative duties.[5]

German strength in the period immediately prior to D-Day was somewhere between 40,000[6] and 62,000.[7] We know that the only major German Army unit there in early June was the 15th Panzer Grenadier Division with a strength of approximately 15,000 men. In the second half of June the Hermann Goering Division began arriving. Its authorized strength was about 18,500 but with a number of units never committed to Sicily (including an entire panzer grenadier regiment) the exact number of Hermann Goering personnel sent to Sicily is unknown. Von Liebenstein's war diary shows the arrival of 17,773 Germans during June, many of whom were undoubtedly troops of the Hermann Goering. The overall strength of the German Army on D-Day was probably about 33,000. The Allied invasion brought about considerable

---

[1] General Siegfried Westphal, *The German Army in the West*, London, 1951, p. 142.
[2] Morison, *Sicily–Salerno–Anzio*, p. 52. Morison's figures of 350,000 are based upon data furnished by the Historical Office of the General Staff of the Italian Army. The highest figure of 365,000 appears in Alexander's despatch (loc. cit.).
[3] Nicholson, *The Canadians in Italy*, p. 55.
[4] Molony, *The Mediterranean and Middle East*, Vol. V, p. 41.
[5] Bauer, Manuscript # R-117.
[6] *The Canadians in Italy*, p. 55.
[7] *The Mediterranean and Middle East*, Vol. V, p. 41.

fluctuations, with the Luftwaffe withdrawing most of its personnel to Italy while ground forces were being reinforced. Admiral Ruge estimates there were approximately 60,000 Germans in Sicily but does not specify the date or dates to which this applied.[1]

The substantial movement of troops back and forth between Italy and Sicily is confirmed by both Ruge and von Liebenstein in their accounts. In July a total of 40,116 arrived;[2] however, during the same period a similar number left Sicily.[3] Throughout the campaign it is doubtful if there were ever more than 65,000 German troops in Sicily at any one time.[*]

Less nebulous were German losses, which were an estimated 5,000 killed[4]† and between 5,523[5] and 6,623[6] captured. There is very little data on the number lost to sickness but what is known suggests that German non-battle losses were, like those of the Allies, considerably higher than their battle losses. For example, the Hermann Goering status report for August 1943 reported battle losses of 1,669 (killed, wounded and missing) versus 2,605 lost to sickness.[7] The 15th and 17th Panzer Grenadier Regiments of the 29th Panzer Grenadier Division reported 1,467 sick on 28 August, which equalled 81% cent of their assigned strength.[8] It is probable that the Germans suffered a malaria rate comparable to that of the two Allied armies.

After the evacuation, few of the German formations were anywhere near full strength and Kesselring's claim of 'complete German formations' which were 'ready for immediate service' was a considerable exaggeration.[9] At the end of August the Hermann Goering reported shortages of 6,139 men (33%) of an authorized strength of 18,466.[10] One of its most battered units was the 115th

---

[1] Ruge, 'The Evacuation of Sicily'.
[2] Von Liebenstein War Diary.   [3] Ibid.
[4] *Sicily–Salerno–Anzio*, p. 215n; and *The Canadians in Italy*, pp. 173–4.
[5] *Sicily–Salerno–Anzio*, p. 215n.
[6] *The Canadians in Italy*, p. 173. Both accounts agree that 3,163 Germans were captured by Eighth Army. The discrepancy is over those captured by Seventh Army.
[7] Report No. 14, [Canadian] Historical Section (GS).
[8] Ibid., based on the War Diary of LXXVI Panzer Corps.
[9] Quoted in *The Canadians in Italy*, p. 173.   [10] Report No. 14, loc. cit.
[*] Admiral Ruge's figures appear to be based upon von Liebenstein's count of those arriving by sea and does not include the estimated 4,700 men of the 1st Parachute Division who saw service in Sicily. German historian Helmut Wilhelmsmeyer estimates there were 3,325 paratroopers defending the Primosole bridgehead in mid-July. The only official historian to estimate the number of German parachute troops was Admiral Morison in *Sicily–Salerno–Anzio*, p. 215n, and his figure of 1,000 is way off the mark.
† The actual number of German dead buried in Sicily is 4,561.

Panzer Grenadier Regiment (formerly *Kampfgruppe* Koerner of 15th PzG Division) which by August was deficient by 375 men (16% of 2,337 authorized) and took losses of 33% (641 men) prior to the evacuation. At the end of the month this unit was reported as 'practically immobile'. At least one other division formation was in far better condition: a 1,138-man AA battalion was at 99.5% strength and 100% mobility. Overall, the Hermann Goering reported only 50% mobility.[1]

Little is known of the condition of 15th Panzer Grenadier Division except that when it reappeared in action against the Allies in early October 1943 it was still short by some 1,600 despite an infusion of reinforcements.[2]

29th Panzer Grenadier Division also reported heavy losses at the end of August: 'Losses of the last two months were high; in the case of 71 PzG Regiment they amounted to 33% . . . Division is fit for employment according to its strength. Fighting power is 50% of normal.'[3]

Despite heavy losses from sickness and combat which left individual German units in varying states of mobility and fighting fitness, the significance of the German escape from Sicily was simply that these veteran formations continued to exist. Rest, reinforcements and the replacement of equipment shortages were sufficient to rejuvenate these forces who repeatedly proved their mettle against the numerically superior Allied forces during the long Italian campaign.

The exact number of German and Italian troops evacuated from Sicily is only approximate owing not only to the incompleteness of the data but the fact that it is impossible to identify the number of German troops on the island on any given date. The total estimated figures are:

13,532	(wounded)	15 July–15 August (L-boats)[4]
8,615	(troops)	1–10 August
4,489	(wounded)	1–10 August
25,669	(troops)	'Lehrgang', 11–16 August
1,240	(wounded)	'Lehrgang', 11–16 August
53,545	Total	

[1] Ibid.   [2] Ibid.   [3] Ibid., based on the War Diary of LXXVI Panzer Corps.
[4] *The Mediterranean and Middle East*, Vol. V, p. 180, shows the dates as 1–15 August, but both Ruge and von Liebenstein clearly specify the period was from 15 July.

This estimated total of German troops evacuated from Sicily is consistent with a peak German strength of 65,000, less the estimated 12,000 killed and captured. An OKW SITREP of 18 August reported the evacuation of 60,000 troops which is undoubtedly high.[1] The problem was, as the British official history notes, that the Sicily figures were 'neither complete nor consistent: characteristic features of the statistics of evacuations'.[2]

German losses in equipment were reported as 78 tanks and armoured cars, 287 guns of various calibres and 3,500 vehicles.[3]

Italian losses were an estimated 2,000 killed, 5,000 wounded and 137,000 captured, most by Seventh Army.[4] Patton claimed his Army had killed or captured 113,350 Axis troops, a figure that proved conservative.[5] Later, the official historians reported that Seventh Army had captured 122,204 Axis troops,[6] of whom about 118,700 were Italian. Of these, 75,000 were sent to POW camps in North Africa and 34,000 Sicilians given parole on the island.[7]

---

[1] *The Canadians in Italy*, p. 173.
[2] *The Mediterranean and Middle East*, Vol. V, p. 180.
[3] *Sicily–Salerno–Anzio*, p. 215n; and *The Canadians in Italy*, p. 174.
[4] *The Canadians in Italy*, p. 174. The US official history (p. 417) reports Italian losses as 147,000 killed, wounded and captured.
[5] *War As I Knew It*, p. 64; see also Appendix M.
[6] *Sicily and the Surrender of Italy*, p. 419.
[7] Ibid.

Principal German Ferry Routes across the Messina Strait[1]

MESSINA SIDE:	USED BY:	REGGIO SIDE:
	Ferry Route I	
Faro–North	MFP	Cannitello–North
Faro–Middle (jetty)	SF	Cannitello–Middle (jetty)
Faro–South	L-boats	Cannitello–South
	Ferry Route II	
Ganzirri–North	MFP and L-boats	Pezzo–North
Ganzirri–South	SF	Pezzo–South (jetty)
(Sea Serpents)*		
	Ferry Route III	
Paradiso		
(Sea Serpents)	SF	Catona–North (jetty)
	MFP	Catona–Middle
		Catona–South
	Ferry Route IV	
San Salvatore + two	MFP	Gallico–North
alternate locations	SF	Gallico–Middle
	Ferry Route V	
Pistunina	MFP	Gallico–South

[1] Source: Vice Admiral Friedrich Ruge, 'The Evacuation of Sicily', US Navy Historical Center.

* The Sea Serpent was a movable landing stage that could be towed to a landing site. Used primarily to load and unload Siebel ferries.

MESSINA SIDE:	USED BY:	REGGIO SIDE:
	Ferry Route VI(alternates)	
Galati	MFP	Occhio
Ponte Schiavo	(not used)	
S. Páolo		

APPENDIX K

The Biscari Incidents

The two incidents near Biscari airfield on 14 July 1943 are examples of one of the most troubling aspects of war: when is killing an enemy with whom one is at war justified? War is the least civilized of man's pursuits; nevertheless, the experience of World War I led to the codification of the so-called Laws of War under the Geneva Convention which prescribed permissible conduct between warring parties. Among its signatories was the United States.

The Geneva Convention accorded certain rights to POWs, among them the right to the protection of their captors. At Biscari, Captain John T. Compton was charged with ordering the execution of thirty-six POWs. Compton's defence was that he had complied with Patton's orders, specifically, that Patton ordered snipers who shot at wounded and medics to be shot if captured. Compton also cited the fact that some of his prisoners were in civilian clothes in violation of the Laws of War. Both the investigating officer and the Judge Advocate who later reviewed the case concluded that Compton had acted unlawfully in ordering his prisoners shot. Nevertheless, the court-martial board disagreed and found Captain Compton 'Not guilty'.

In the West case, another jury decided that the NCO had not only violated orders to escort his POWs to the rear but also that he could not claim temporary insanity as a defence inasmuch as the prisoners were killed several hours after their capture, not in the heat of the moment. West was found 'Guilty' and sentenced to life imprisonment on 3 September 1943. An unusual aspect of Sergeant West's case was that his sentence did not include either forfeitures of pay and allowances or a dishonourable discharge, both of which were virtually automatic in such cases.

The testimony of a 45th Division chaplain at West's trial suggests there may well have been a *third* incident but apparently no action was ever taken to follow up this possibility.

The West case stirred considerable War Department and Congressional interest and raised troubling issues, among them the spectre of unequal justice for an NCO convicted of the same offence for which an officer won acquittal. Within a year West was released from confinement and returned to duty as a private. The records of both courts-martial were handled at the War Department by Under Secretary of War Robert Patterson. As late as 1950 these records were still being held in the Under Secretary's safe, a testament to the sensitivity of both cases.

Captain Compton was transferred to another regiment of the 45th Division and was killed in action in Italy on 8 November 1943.

The Biscari killings were certainly not the only examples of the troublesome problem of distinguishing between what is considered legitimate during war and a war crime. In the latter stages of the Vietnam war the United States Army was obliged to deal with this question after revelation of the My Lai massacre. At Biscari, there is no doubt the 45th Division encountered examples of violations of the Geneva Convention by Axis soldiers and that their men were angry and edgy as a result. The 45th was an excellent fighting division whose commander, Troy Middleton, would never have condoned such acts.

The documentation of the investigation and court-martial of West and Compton is extensive and can be found in the Modern Military Field Branch, National Archives, Suitland, Maryland. The author is indebted to Lieutenant Colonel Joseph A. Whitehorne, USA, the official historian of the Army Inspector General Corps, who kindly furnished these records.

APPENDIX L

Montgomery and
the Canadians

The outbreak of World War II had found Canada even more woefully unprepared for war than Britain. The prewar Army numbered fewer than 5,000 men and in the mid-1930s Canada's Chief of the General Staff, Major-General A. G. L. McNaughton, reported to the Government that there was 'not a single modern anti-aircraft gun of any sort in Canada', that field artillery ammunition stocks were good for only '90 minutes' fire at normal rates', and that the RCAF did not possess a single air bomb or aircraft 'of a type fit to employ in active operations'.[1]

Nevertheless, Canada entered the war united and determined to provide a meaningful contribution. The composition of Canadian forces was on a voluntary basis until the introduction of overseas conscription in late 1944. By the war's end the Canadian armed forces numbered over one million, the vast majority of whom were volunteers. Inevitably, the Canadian commitment took the form of co-operation with Britain, and although Canadian forces were still considered independent, it was agreed that the Army would be employed with, and where appropriate under the control of, British commanders. Where and how they would be committed became a matter for consultation between the two governments.* By 1943, the Army strength was 226,000, and most were based in England. The C-in-C of Canadian forces overseas was the same General McNaughton who had overseen the Army of the 1930s.

The commitment of the 1st Canadian Division to Sicily had not

---

[1] Quoted in C. P. Stacey, *Arms, Men and Governments: The War Policies of Canada, 1939–1945*, Ottawa, 1970, p. 3. Like the USA, Canada during the Depression years of the 1930s placed no priority on funding or modernization of the armed forces. The outlay for 1930–31 amounted to less than $24 million for all services, and in 1932–33 had fallen to $14 million. In the mid-1930s the Navy numbered barely 2,000, the RCAF about 1,100 and the militia 3,500, most of whom were still armed with weapons of 1918 vintage. (See Stacey, Part I, Chapter 1.)

* Canadian sensitivities stemmed from World War I when Haig in 1918 attempted to use Canadian units piecemeal. The Canadians insisted they would fight together or not at all and they were determined there would now be no further repetition of the rancorous arguments of the earlier war in which 425,000 served and 60,000 died.

been without considerable wrangling between McNaughton and the War Office. Brooke attempted to secure an agreement that violated McNaughton's 'fanatic antagonism for employing any portion of the Canadian Forces independently from the whole'. There were many other Canadians who felt that this policy might well result in their having nothing more than a defensive role in England. It proved impossible to employ the entire Canadian overseas force in the Mediterranean and Brooke 'finally got agreement to send out one Canadian Division which would provide an outlet to post officers and men to gain experience. The only Canadian opposed to this scheme seemed to be McNaughton! Another fact that convinced me he was not well suited for his responsible appointment.'[1]

About the time of D-Day a contingent of senior Canadian officers arrived in Malta. Headed by McNaughton, their purpose was to visit the 1st Canadian Division in Sicily. Montgomery and McNaughton had first met in England in 1941 and the chemistry between them had been bad. When Montgomery learned of McNaughton's intended visit he privately sought General Simonds to discourage the visit and later wrote that Simonds replied, 'For God's sake, keep him away.'[2]

Montgomery obliged, and indeed poured gasoline on troubled waters by not only banning McNaughton from visiting Sicily but by threatening to have him arrested if he so much as set foot on the island! It was, says his biographer, 'an act of callous chauvinism' towards a senior officer he had despised since 1941.[3]

One of the curses of modern-day commanders is interference in their exercise of command by officers from higher headquarters and other commands in the form of 'visits', 'liaison visits' and 'inspections'. The reasons for such visitations vary from the perfectly legitimate to the absurd and, however well meaning, invariably result in distracting the field commanders and their staffs from their duties.* This is not to be confused with the necessary

---

[1] Alanbrooke, 'Notes on My Life'.
[2] *Memoirs*, op. cit., p. 184; and C. P. Stacey, *A Date with History: Memoirs of a Canadian Historian*, Ottawa, 1984, p. 234.
[3] *Monty, Master of the Battlefield, 1942–1944*, op. cit., p. 332.
* The Eighth Army staff was dismayed when Churchill's son Randolph turned up in Sicily on some vague pretext. De Guingand said, 'For God's sake, don't let him near the front.' According to Llewellyn, he too was to be placed under arrest if he did so. (Llewellyn interview, loc. cit.)

exercise of command by officers in the chain of command either in person or through personal liaison officers. The practice of visiting units in the field was not uncommon – except in Eighth Army.

Montgomery's long-standing ban on visitors to his field HQ was well known throughout the British Army and, much as he disliked McNaughton, Montgomery did not discriminate against him in the enforcement of this strict policy. For he held the view that commanders busy fighting a war must not be distracted by nosy senior officers whose need to visit the front was usually dubious and whose arrival was invariably harmful to the efficient prosecution of the battle. In short, no matter how well meaning their intentions, any visitor outside his immediate chain of command was sure to incur Monty's wrath. To the dismay of McNaughton and others the rule was ruthlessly enforced. Brigadier Desmond Inglis, who later became Chief Engineer of 21st Army Group in Northwest Europe, was one who attempted to sidestep the embargo but he was found out and informed that if he attempted to land without Montgomery's personal permission he too would be placed under arrest.[1]

De Guingand defended Montgomery with the argument that he was merely protecting the young Canadian commander in his first campaign, and that the Eighth Army commander was deflecting McNaughton's ire on to himself. Opinions were naturally varied but, as de Guingand has written, 'After this the word got around that one could not gatecrash into any of Montgomery's battles.'[2]

An angry and dispirited McNaughton next took his case to Alexander and found even less sympathy. During a swim in the Mediterranean with Alexander, Eisenhower found him 'adamant' in his refusal even to reconsider Monty's refusal.* Alexander's view was that 'McNaughton had no business coming here during an operation and that, while he had treated McNaughton politely, if he had been a junior officer he would have placed him under arrest . . . In view of the critical shortage of transportation and the nuisance to busy staff officers to look after the Canadian

---

[1] De Guingand, *Operation Victory*, op. cit., p. 184.

[2] De Guingand, *Generals at War*, London, 1964, p. 154. The list eventually came to include even Churchill.

* About this time Eisenhower was demonstrating increasing signs of annoyance with Alexander. On 16 July, Butcher recorded that Ike was not 'too happy with Alexander and staff taking a three- or four-hour siesta, good for bathing purposes, leaving only duty officers on watch during the heat of battle'. (Butcher Diary, 16 July 1943.)

Commander-in-Chief, he positively would not grant McNaughton's request.'[1]

Eisenhower was sympathetic and felt Alexander had not given 'sufficient weight to the problem of a democracy conducting a war ... Some means should be worked out for accommodating McNaughton.' Alexander, however, was uncharacteristically outspoken in his vehement opposition to the visit. Eisenhower avoided involving himself further, on grounds that he had no authority to intervene in what was a 'family' quarrel outside the scope of his authority as Allied C-in-C. After the swim, Eisenhower was left to inform a disappointed McNaughton that his intervention had proved fruitless and he was sorry, but the Canadians were out of luck.*

An irate McNaughton returned to England and complained to Brooke. The War Office had never officially sanctioned the Canadian's trip to the Mediterranean and McNaughton found no great sympathy from Brooke, whose diary and papers show a longing to see him replaced. It was an unpleasant afternoon for Brooke, who found the incident both unfortunate and unnecessary:

> Came back to the War Office to meet an infuriated General McNaughton who had gone all the way to Malta to see Canadian troops in Sicily and had not been allowed by Alex (apparently owing to Monty's wishes) to visit Canadians in Sicily!! He had reported the matter to his Government and was livid with rage! I spent 1¼ hours pacifying him! Although I felt inclined to tell him that he and his Government had already made more fuss than the whole of the rest of the Commonwealth concerning the employment of Dominion Forces![2]

Brooke was thoroughly displeased by the manner in which both Montgomery and Alexander had handled McNaughton:

> The McNaughton incident was an excellent example of unnecessary clashes caused by failings in various personalities. In the first place it was typical of Monty to try and stop

[1] Butcher Diary, 18 July 1943; also quoted in *Three Years With Eisenhower*, op. cit., p. 311. Alexander's remarks which were captured by Butcher raise the possibility that it may have been Alexander rather than Montgomery who first inspired this comment, even though a similar comment was made regarding the visit of Brigadier Inglis.

[2] Alanbrooke Diary, 21 July 1943.

* Major-General J. F. M. Whiteley, Eisenhower's [British] Deputy Chief of Staff, sided with Alexander and claimed McNaughton's presence would be 'just a damned nuisance'. 'If McNaughton is the military figure he is supposed to be he will understand the situation and accept the inevitable like a soldier.' (Butcher Diary, 18 July 1943.)

McNaughton for no valid reason, and to fail to realize, from the
Commonwealth point of view, [the] need for McNaughton to
visit the Canadians under his orders the first time they had been
committed to action.

Secondly it was typical of Alex not to have the strength of
character to sit on Monty and stop him being foolish.

Thirdly it was typical of McNaughton's ultra political outlook
to always look for some slight to his position as a servant of the
Canadian Government.[1]

Thus ended the McNaughton affair, which reflected poorly on all
concerned. McNaughton's right to visit Canadian troops was
never at issue, but his timing could not have been worse, especially
in view of the difficult battles being fought by the Canadian 1st
Division. Moreover, McNaughton knew of Monty's aversion to
visitors. General Simonds later recounted that he had been present
before HUSKY when McNaughton had discussed the possibility of
such a visit and heard Brooke warn of Montgomery's well-known
hostility to such visits during combat operations.[2] As the official
Canadian historian points out, despite McNaughton's wretched
timing and stubbornness it might well have blown over if Alexander and Montgomery had consented to a brief, face-saving visit.[3]

Shortly afterwards Montgomery wrote McNaughton a 'Dear
Andy' letter about the progress of the 1st Canadian Division as if
there had never been a problem between the two in the first place.[4]
In the months that followed, Brooke continued to question
McNaughton's fitness for command which ultimately contributed
to his removal at the end of 1943 by his adversary in Ottawa,
Minister of Defence, Colonel J. L. Ralston.* McNaughton was
eventually allowed to visit Sicily at the end of the campaign and
managed to exact a measure of revenge while a guest in Montgomery's requisitioned villa in Taormina. 'Surveying the luxurious
headquarters, he addressed his austere host in terms designed to
reduce him to a condition of speechless rage – "not going soft, are
you, Monty?" '[5]

---

[1] Alanbrooke, 'Notes on My Life'.   [2] *Arms, Men and Governments*, op. cit., p. 227.
[3] Ibid.   [4] Ibid. The letter is quoted on p. 228.
[5] Quoted in Alun Chalfont, *Montgomery of Alamein*, op. cit., p. 210. McNaughton also
paid back his sacking as overseas C-in-C when he replaced Ralston in November 1944 after
the latter had run foul of Prime Minister Mackenzie King and was forced to resign.
* Brooke's biographer later wrote that McNaughton's replacement came as a profound
relief to the CIGS. 'He grieved that MacNaughton [sic] then and in later life appeared to bear
rancour, but he never wavered in his view that the change was essential for the well-being
and performance of the Canadian troops themselves.' (Fraser, *Alanbrooke*, op. cit., p. 422.)

The participation of the 1st Canadian Division in the Sicily campaign occurred when the division was substituted for the 3rd [British] Division which was originally scheduled for HUSKY. Sicily marked the first Canadian venture since the disastrous raid against Dieppe the year before. Montgomery's relations with the Canadians were always controversial, beginning in 1942 when he commanded the South-Eastern Command in England. One Canadian officer remembers well the love–hate relationship between Monty and the Canadians which began before Dieppe: 'In our minds he was an overbearing martinet – a proper bastard. He demanded that we undergo hardships. To toughen us, he broke many in the process. We thought his methods were madness. But his system of training prevailed, and when we eventually went into action we knew he was right.'

During the early days of the Sicily campaign Montgomery managed to spend considerable time with the Canadians and visited every unit. On 13 July he recorded in his diary that they 'had definitely to be rested; the men were not very fit and they suffered severely from the hot sun and many got badly burnt; generally, officers and men are too fat and they want to get some flesh off and to harden themselves. The operational discipline of the Canadians is not very good, and I have spoken about it. Once they get these things right they will be a really first-class division.'[1]

And so they were by the end of the campaign. The division commander, Guy Simonds, was much respected by Monty and later as a corps commander in Northwest Europe came to be regarded by his C-in-C as a first-class combat commander. What enabled Monty to win over the Canadians?

> The most remarkable thing about . . . Montgomery, as we Canadians knew him in our early days together, was his lack of remoteness . . . [Despite] six distinct levels of command . . . [down] to the private soldier, the Army Commander seemed to be his own personal commander, with no one else really in between . . . It was this remarkable ability of Montgomery to project his personality over the heads of all his subordinate formation commanders, right down into the forward slit trench, that made him the soldiers' general . . . When we ended our five weeks of warfare in Sicily successfully, we realized it was because we had been moulded into a hard, disciplined force by the hand of Montgomery, the *bête noire* of our days in Southern

[1] Montgomery Diary, 13 July 1943.

England . . . At the end of the Sicilian campaign Monty arrived one day in an open car to where our whole brigade was formed up awaiting him. He had us break ranks and gather round his vehicle. He then gave us permission to smoke and extolled the fighting virtues of Canadian troops and flattered us by telling us how much we had helped in the conquest of Sicily. He said, 'I regard you now as one of the veteran divisions of my Army, just as good as any if not better. I knew the Canadians on the Western front in the last war and there were no better soldiers anywhere. I wonder what they would say to you now if they could speak to you? I think they would say something like this: "Well done. We have handed you the sword and you have wielded it well and truly." ' We lapped it up.[1]

---

[1] Colonel Strome Galloway, *The General Who Never Was*, op. cit., pp. 180–2.

APPENDIX M

Patton's Message to Seventh Army

Seventh Army, General Orders Number 18

22 August 1943

Soldiers of the Seventh Army: Born at sea, baptized in blood, and crowned in victory, in the course of 38 days of incessant battle and unceasing labor, you have added a glorious chapter to the history of war.

Pitted against the best the Germans and Italians could offer, you have been unfailingly successful. The rapidity of your dash, which culminated in the capture of Palermo, was equalled by the dogged tenacity with which you stormed Troina and captured Messina.

Every man in the Army deserves equal credit. The enduring valor of the Infantry, and the impetuous ferocity of the tanks were matched by the tireless clamor of the destroying guns.

The Engineers performed prodigies in the construction and maintenance of impossible roads over impassable country. The services of Maintenance and Supply performed a miracle. The Signal Corps laid over 10,000 miles of wire, and the Medical Department evacuated and cared for our sick and wounded.

On all occasions the Navy has given generous and gallant support. Throughout the operation, our Air has kept the sky clear and tirelessly supported the operation of the ground troops.

As a result of this combined effort, you have killed or captured 113,350 enemy troops. You have destroyed 265 of his tanks, 2,324 vehicles, and 1,162 large guns, and in addition have collected a mass of military booty running into hundreds of tons.

But your victory has a significance above and beyond its physical aspect – you have destroyed the prestige of the enemy....

Your fame shall never die.

> /s/ GEORGE S. PATTON, Jr.
> Lieutenant General, USA
> Commanding

APPENDIX N

Unholy Alliance:
The Luciano Connection

One day in April 1943 General Sir Alan Brooke penned a cryptic note in his diary that he had met with 'C'* and had been informed there were no British secret agents operating in Sicily.[1] The absence of any semblance of a spy network in Sicily was troubling to the Allied leaders and planners who were hungry for information about Axis activity on the island. Neither the British SIS nor the American OSS had succeeded in penetrating Sicily.[2] Enigma decrypts were able to provide information of varying degrees of usefulness to the Allied planners through ULTRA, but the Italians did not use the Enigma cypher machine and the Allied code-breakers were forced to rely on intercepts of Italian signals through SIGINT; and by the end of May these had become so poor that the most important source of information about Italian preparations in Sicily had become the reading of mail addressed to Italian POWs in North Africa.[3]

The geography and provincialism of Sicily made the employment of spies a nearly suicidal endeavour. In his campaign despatch Alexander would later note that 'so good was the police and counter-espionage system in Sicily that we were unable to

[1] Alanbrooke Diary. The SIS had concluded that 'Sicily must be so closely guarded – also the islands – that it would be wasteful to expend . . . trained agents on such a hot target'. (Quoted in Hinsley, *British Intelligence in the Second World War*, Vol. III, Part I, op. cit., p. 75n.)

[2] Hinsley, p. 75n, citing the official (Office of Strategic Services) 'OSS War Report' (1946).

[3] Ibid. and Hunt, *A Don at War*, op. cit. p. 186. The large volume of mail sent from Italy to POWs in the custody of the British was read by British counter-intelligence agents in Cairo and proved a rich source of intelligence about the location of Italian units in Italy and Sicily. This success also reflected the shocking inefficiency of the Italian censors.

* 'C' is the common identification of the head of Secret Intelligence Service (SIS), more popularly known as MI6, Britain's counter-espionage/counter-intelligence arm. To this day the British intelligence service does not officially exist. As Michael Howard has written, 'In Britain the activities of the intelligence and security services have always been regarded in much the same light as marital sex. Everyone knows that it goes on and is quite content that it should, but to speak, write or ask questions about it is regarded as exceedingly bad form'. (Cf. *The New York Times Book Review*, 16 February 1986, p. 6.) Although completed some years ago, Professor Howard's volume on deception in the multi-volume official intelligence history has only recently been published by the British government.

obtain any information direct from the island'.[1] One of the principal questions the Allied planners wanted answered was how well Italian troops in Sicily would fight. Without first-hand reports and intelligence their conclusions would remain a matter of speculation and continuing deep concern within the Allied high command. One of the most bizarre episodes of the war revolves around one means used to obtain information about Sicily.

In May 1942 Mafia crime boss Charles 'Lucky' Luciano, the forty-four-year old head of the New York City syndicate was quietly transferred from the high security Dannemora Prison in upstate New York to Great Meadow Prison, near Albany. Luciano was considered one of the most vicious and cunning mobsters in America during Prohibition and the early 1930s. But in 1936 he had run foul of a crusading United States Attorney named Thomas E. Dewey who led the most successful investigation and prosecution of organized crime yet seen in the United States. Luciano was convicted on prostitution charges and received a sentence of thirty to fifty years in prison.[2]

Soon after his arrival at Great Meadow Prison Luciano met privately with two New York mobsters, Joseph 'Socks' Lanza, the czar of the lucrative Fulton Fish Market, and the debonair Meyer 'Little Man' Lansky, one of the few non-Italian/Sicilian crime figures of that era. Both men were known close associates of Luciano. Lansky was something of a royal figure within the US underworld and was, like a great many other Mafia figures, intensely patriotic. The American Mafia's connection to the Sicilian Mafia had always existed in the form of blood ties of business and friendship. Despite infrequent contact the Americans had long been sympathetic to their Sicilian brethren under persecution by Mussolini. Most were therefore strongly anti-Fascist and supportive of the Allied cause. Moreover, in spite of their unsavoury profession, these men still thought of themselves as loyal Americans first and criminals second. Lansky was a Jew and had especially good reasons to despise Hitler for his persecution of European Jewry.[3]

The winter of 1941–42 had been grim for Allied shipping. German U-boats operated unhindered virtually within sight of New

[1] Alexander despatch, PRO (CAB 106/594).
[2] Rodney Campbell, *The Luciano Project*, New York, 1977, pp. 1–2.
[3] Ibid, pp. 85–6.

York harbour and had torpedoed nearly a hundred ships in the first three months of 1942. Although no proof was ever established, US intelligence suspected foul play when the erstwhile luxury liner turned troopship, *Normandie*, burned and sank at her Hudson River berth under suspicious circumstances in February 1942.

The United States Navy was responsible for counter-espionage measures and the security of the port of New York and, although the German spy networks in the US had been effectively neutralized, there was a lingering suspicion that perhaps there was a connection between the U-boats and the large Italian community in New York.

The increasingly critical loss of valuable ships and their cargoes came during the height of German U-boat success against Allied shipping in the Atlantic when it was less than certain that the United States could sustain the fragile lifeline to Britain. U-boats were sinking Allied shipping at a rate faster than they could be replaced. Concern on the part of Naval intelligence in New York deepened with each new loss and this led the intelligence officers of the Third Naval District into one of the unholiest alliances ever conceived: the US Navy and the New York Mafia.

The Navy knew the Mafia had a stranglehold on all dock activities in the port of New York and believed they were in a sound position to monitor any subversive activity along the waterfront. Cautious approaches to both Lansky and Lanza in early 1942 met with surprising success. Both mobsters indicated a willingness to help their country in its hour of need. However, it soon became evident that if the Mafia were to assist the Navy in any meaningful way the co-operation of 'Lucky' Luciano was vital. Luciano may have been out of circulation in a top security prison but so powerful was his influence in the New York rackets that his blessing was considered an absolute necessity.*

The moral and ethical aspects of such an arrangement do not appear to have entered into the decision by the Navy to seek Luciano's co-operation; the sole consideration was that it was

---

* The extraordinary tale of Luciano and the Navy–Mafia alliance is documented in Campbell's account which, in turn, is based largely upon a previously suppressed high-level secret investigation conducted in 1954 by the New York Commissioner of Investigations, William B. Herlands. Until Campbell, the editor of the Dewey memoirs, was given access and permission to use the Herlands Report, it had been 'held against the future' at the official request of the US Navy.

sincerely believed such an arrangement would be in the best interests of the United States. Accordingly, steps were taken to move Luciano and to authorize Lansky and Lanza to approach the mob boss and act as go-betweens. The first of several meetings at Great Meadow Prison took place in June 1942 and produced immediate results. Luciano is reported to have said, 'This is a good cause.' He directed Lanza and Lansky to seek the co-operation of two other high-ranking mob figures: Joseph Adonis, the overlord of Brooklyn, and the crafty Frank Costello who acted as the Mafia's politician and fixer. Although understandably less than enthusiastic, the New York authorities agreed to permit the Navy–Mafia alliance for the greater good of national security. Now that Luciano had pronounced the cause worthwhile, it was clear that: 'New York harbor was going to go all the way for the Allies.'[1]

By 1943 this strange union was in full flower and the decision to invade Sicily became a natural source of Navy–Mafia involvement. For some time the Third Naval District had been collecting strategic intelligence about the Mediterranean theatre of operations and it now became a participant in the search for a useful exploitation of the Sicilian connection. One of Adonis' functions was to identify and recruit Italian-Americans with connections in Sicily. 'F' Section was created in May 1943 to collect the mass of raw data being collected by a growing number of naval personnel.

Some time earlier the head of 'F' Section, Commander C. Radcliffe Haffenden, raised the name of 'Lucky' Luciano and according to later testimony told the District Intelligence officer, Captain Roscoe C. McFall, USN, that Luciano was willing to be the Allied point man in Sicily where he would rally Sicilians to back the United States. Of course, this entailed Luciano's release from prison and assistance in getting to Sicily.[2]

Haffenden soon found his scheme to make use of Luciano in Sicily was not supported by the Navy and it quietly died. Any attempt to have Luciano released from prison would have found no sympathy with the New York authorities. Before he would authorize the Navy–Mafia alliance, New York County District Attorney Frank S. Hogan had explicitly affirmed a strict policy of 'no deals for criminals', no matter what their contribution to the

---

[1] *The Luciano Project*, op. cit., p. 100.
[2] Ibid, p. 145.

war effort, as Luciano himself learned in 1943 when he petitioned to have his sentence reduced.[1]

The decision to employ the services of the Mafia had its origins within the Third Naval District, and the official role of the Navy Department in Washington remains deliberately obscure. The only documentary evidence of the alliance is the secret Herlands inquiry in 1954 and the Navy's principal aim at that time was to cover up its wartime collaboration with the Mafia.*

Postwar testimony by Haffenden to the Kefauver Senate Rackets Committee in 1951 bore strong evidence of the Navy's determination to conceal their role in the Luciano affair.[2] Nevertheless, even though higher naval authority was clearly aware of the connection with the New York mob there is no evidence of their involvement in any scheme to release Luciano for a mission in Sicily. Luciano allegedly suggested that the Allies ought to invade west of Palermo along the Gulf of Castellammare.† Virtually nothing is known of Washington's role except that Haffenden fed information he considered pertinent to a spymaster control in the Navy Department.

In May 1943 Admiral Hewitt belatedly discovered that his naval force had no intelligence officers who spoke Italian and urgently cabled Washington to send him six qualified officers at once. Someone in Washington decided this was a superb opportunity to utilize the Mafia connection in order to establish contacts in Sicily itself. Four of the six officers sent to Hewitt came from the Third Naval District. After hasty commando-training in Algeria these officers were given assignments which brought them ashore at Gela and Licata in the first wave on D-Day; their mission – to collect information of value to the Navy about minefields, booby traps and demolitions.[3]

[1] *The Luciano Project*, op. cit., Chapter VIII.
[2] Ibid., Chapter XI, and the *Congressional Record*, 'Investigation of Organized Crime in Interstate Commerce', hearing before the Special Committee of the 81st and 82d Congress, 1951.
[3] *The Luciano Project*, op. cit., Chapter IX.
* Herlands was permitted to take secret sworn testimony from Navy men but only upon condition no classified information be released, thus effectively strangling the entire investigation. Most of Herlands' revelations of Navy involvement came from the testimony of civilians. As expected, the Mafia invoked their traditional silence. (See *The Luciano Project*, op. cit., pp. vii–viii.) There are no known naval records of this affair in US archives.
† One of the original options considered by the HUSKY planners was an invasion in the Gulf of Castellammare. This was long before the Navy in New York would have been aware of Allied intentions. (See *The Luciano Project*, op. cit., p. 146.)

In addition, the four New York officers went ashore with lists of potential contacts furnished courtesy of the New York Mafia. Most of those on the lists were Sicilian underworld figures. One of the officers, Lieutenant Paul A. Alfieri, later testified that:

> One of the most important plans was to contact persons who had been deported for any crime from the United States to their homeland in Sicily, and one of my first successes after landing at Licata was in connection with numerous persons who had been deported. They were extremely co-operative and helpful, because they spoke both the dialect of the region and also some English.

When asked if these contacts belonged to the Mafia, Alfieri replied, 'Well, they would never admit such, but from my investigative experience in New York City, I knew that they were.'[1] An expert in locks and safes, Alfieri's mission at Licata was to penetrate the HQ of the local naval command and obtain information about Axis naval operations. He did so by blowing the safe of the admiral in charge who had fled without destroying its secret contents. Alfieri apparently recovered some useful intelligence in the form of documents showing the disposition of Axis naval forces in the Mediterranean and diagrams of all minefields. This booty was turned over to Admiral Conolly, the JOSS Force naval commander.[2] Later, Alfieri used his experience in observing the operations of Joseph Lanza in New York to organize the fishing fleets in southern Sicily to help acquire food and to report matters of intelligence interest.

The question of the American Mafia's contribution to the liberation of Sicily is clouded with ambiguity and contradiction. According to an account by a long-time Sicilian foe of the Mafia, Michele Pantaleone, Luciano had a hand in paving the way for American intelligence agents to contact certain key members of the Sicilian Mafia. Pantaleone contends that an American agent delivered a Luciano handkerchief to the unofficial head of the Sicilian Mafia, Don Calogero Vizzini, thus establishing a direct link between American and Sicilian Mafia chieftains.[3] Campbell alleges the OSS were deeply involved not only in liberating Mafiosi from Mussolini's jails but also in establishing contact with Mafia ele-

[1] Ibid., p. 176. Lieutenant Alfieri also admitted that his contacts had emanated from the New York mob.
[2] Ibid., pp. 177–8.
[3] Michele Pantaleone, *The Mafia and Politics*, New York, 1966, Chapter 5.

ments on the island through Sicilian-American agents.[1] However, the man who recruited and led these agents was an OSS operative named Max Corvo and he firmly denies there was any connection whatever between the OSS and the Mafia. 'The Lipari Archipelago was liberated near the end of the Sicilian campaign by a joint OSS/Navy force and no criminals were liberated. If there were any Mafiosi on Lipari they could hardly have helped Patton's 7th Army liberate western Sicily from their isolated prison crags.'[2]

Campbell charges that not only was there an American–Sicilian connection tacitly abetted by the OSS and other Allied military sources, including the British, but that the main culprits were Corvo and his Sicilian-American OSS agents.[*] The truth is that the evidence which does exist is far too circumstantial and virtually impossible to corroborate. According to Corvo, the OSS had no interest in either Luciano or the Mafia as a potential source of intelligence and aid to the invasion. 'There was little which men such as Luciano, Adonis, Lanza or some of the others ... could contribute to the conduct of the war since they were [only] famil- iar with their own villages and had left them while still in their teens ...'[3] Some time in late 1942 a Luciano emissary approached the OSS offering to trade the crime boss's freedom for a promise to organize an intelligence operation in Sicily for the benefit of the OSS. The OSS chief, 'Wild Bill' Donovan, who had himself been a crusading prosecutor in upstate New York in the 1920s, wanted no part of a deal with the Mafia which he believed was 'a supra- national conspiracy without any allegiance to the United States'.[4] Thus, despite the fact the OSS had in the past recruited some rather unsavoury characters, including safecrackers and counterfeiters, to help fill their many needs, when it came to godfathers, the answer was a firm 'no'.[5]

The OSS was unsuccessful in placing agents into Sicily prior to D-Day. According to the official postwar report, the OSS had one team ready to be inserted in early June but at the last minute clearance was denied by AFHQ who feared that the team would be

---

[1] Richard Dunlop, *Donovan: America's Master Spy*, Chicago, 1982, p. 398.
[2] Letter, Max Corvo–author, 23 December 1985.
[3] Letter, Corvo–author, loc. cit.
[4] *Donovan*, op. cit., p. 398.
[5] Ibid.
[*] Campbell does not mention Corvo by name but this group were the only Sicilian-American OSS agents operating in Sicily.

detected and the invasion compromised.[1] During the campaign itself the OSS contribution was insignificant and mainly took the form of attempted line-crossings for intelligence and sabotage which were mostly abortive.[2] One agent landed with the first wave of the 3d Division at Licata and was able to pinpoint camouflaged Italian gun emplacements through on-the-spot interrogation of prisoners; otherwise, the OSS effort in Sicily was a disappointment.[3]

The most negative aspect of the Sicily campaign was that the Allied occupation provided the means by which the long-dormant Mafia were able to stage a remarkable return. The liberation of Sicily brought in its wake the bureaucracy of the Allies. Called AMGOT – Allied Military Government of Occupied Territories – its personnel were charged with re-establishing the political, economic and administrative machinery of Sicily and governing the island until the Allies decided to return home rule. Under AMGOT were experts in many areas of civil administration, but these officials comprised only a small cadre and, for it to function, AMGOT had to rely upon local nationals to carry out its directives and policies.

As the combatants moved on and AMGOT struggled with massive problems, the void was quickly filled by men whose purpose was not humane or compassionate. The arrival of AMGOT was like pennies from heaven and signalled a profitable new life for the quiescent Mafia who quickly and successfully penetrated it by placing men into positions where they could gain a complete grip on the most lucrative racket of all: the black market. In war-torn Europe the basic staples of life such as pasta, salt, cooking oil, cereal and flour commanded enormous profits. Luxury goods such as cigarettes and alcohol were literally worth fortunes. As Pantaleone relates, 'The Mafia not only infiltrated into all the offices of the new administration, but also occupied official posts and managed to get into the best positions for controlling the movement

---

[1] Kermit Roosevelt, *War Report of the OSS*, Vol. 2, New York, 1976, p. 62. Roosevelt, the OSS historian, prepared a Top Secret report shortly after the war. In 1975 his report was mostly declassified and later published. An OSS team successfully operated in Corsica beginning in December 1942. An attempt to place a five-man team into Sardinia at the end of June met with failure when the team was captured by the Italians within twenty-four hours and forced to play back their radio under Italian control. A prearranged danger signal was included in their first message and Algiers was alerted to their capture.

[2] Ibid.

[3] Ibid.

and transport of goods.'[1] Sicily's most notorious and influential Mafia godfather, Don Calò Vizzini, was appointed mayor of the tiny town of Villalba, in central Sicily, northwest of Caltanissetta.* Within days the local *carabinieri* chief was found murdered in the middle of the town piazza. Despite being in the middle of nowhere, Villalba became a centre for the movement of truckloads of black market goods to mainland Italy using legal documentation provided by AMGOT who had conveniently (even if unknowingly) furnished the Mafia chief with the trucks necessary to carry out his shipments.[2]

Any doubt about the pervasiveness of the Mafia was unmistakably answered not long after the Allies moved into Italy. Former New York Mafia kingpin Vito Genovese turned up at Nola (near Naples) as an interpreter for US Army intelligence. Genovese had fled to Italy in 1937 to avoid prosecution in New York by Tom Dewey for murder. In Italy he had become deeply involved in drugs trafficking and had managed to curry favour with Mussolini despite the latter's known hatred of the Mafia. One of Genovese's long-time friends was none other than Don Calò of Villalba. As a result of Genovese's 'energetic and diligent efforts, a number of black market operatives were caught in southern Italy. However, the military's pleasure with Genovese's performance vanished when it was discovered that as he unearthed the black marketeers and put them out of business, he simply took over their rackets.'[3]

By the time the US Army caught up with Genovese in 1944 and forcibly returned him to New York to face the long-standing murder charges brought years before, it was too late. Witnesses for his prosecution had long since been silenced and he was free to resume his climb towards the heights of organized crime in New York.†

---

[1] Pantaleone, *The Mafia and Politics*, op. cit., p. 63.   [2] Ibid., p. 62.
[3] Profile of Vito Genovese in Carl Sifakis, *The Encyclopedia of American Crime*, New York, 1982.

* Don Calò was easily the most influential *Mafioso* on the island and the unofficial chief of the Sicilian Mafia. A man of Machiavellian disposition, he too once aided his Fascist enemies because it suited his purposes. So powerful was this portly, bespectacled Sicilian that with a simple telephone call he could speak to a Mayor, Deputy, Prefect, General or Cardinal. For nearly fifty years he cast a larger-than-life shadow across the island of Sicily which 'symbolized the worst aspects of the Mafia's overbearingness, *omertà* and abuses – a man who prevented the state from exercising its powers, a man who administered the "justice of the Mafia", and who managed to get himself and dozens of his followers acquitted for lack of evidence for the crimes they had committed against people or property.' (Pantaleone, op. cit., p. 228.)

† Long considered one of the most ambitious, successful and deadly of the American

The period from the Allied occupation of Sicily until 1946 was one of rebuilding for the Mafia in Sicily. Its resurgence as a major force came from the immense profits made on the black market. Initially, freelance bandits like the famed Giuliano were permitted their share of the spoils but with the departure of AMGOT and a return to civil rule the Mafia began to reimpose tight control over western Sicily. In the years that followed, the Mafia moved into drugs trafficking in a major way.

No evidence has ever surfaced establishing the full extent of the Allied contribution to the re-emergence of the Mafia after the war passed into Italy. Clearly, there would have been an attempt by the Mafia to gain a foothold into the lucrative black market even without AMGOT. Nevertheless, the history of military government in World War II is riddled with instances of graft, corruption and illegal black-market activities. Many ordinary soldiers could not resist the lure of the fortunes to be made by co-operation with the Mafia and criminal organizations in other countries. While AMGOT in Sicily and later in the occupied territories of Europe was a sincere attempt to restore order in countries devastated by war, not all of those who worked for AMGOT were always so inclined. In Sicily AMGOT's policy was to appoint known anti-Fascists to positions of prefect and mayor; all too often these men turned out to be Mafia figures. Pantaleone points out that the irony is: 'These men's criminal records showed that they had indeed opposed Fascism but would have opposed any government which tried to enforce a law which ran counter to their interests.'[1]

The sordid story of postwar years cannot be told in full here except to note that the return of the Mafia as a major force in Sicily was yet another cycle in the cancer that had plagued the island for centuries. Not only was there a rise in the drugs traffic to the United States but within the Mafia itself there was a murderous revolution taking place between the old guard and a new genera-

---

[1] Pantaleone, *The Mafia and Politics*, op. cit., p. 67.

Mafia bosses, Genovese has been credited with establishing the Mafia in the drug trade. Not only did Genovese climb the rungs of the Mafia leadership to become the top figure in *La Cosa Nostra* of the 1950s, but en route he ruthlessly eliminated those who blocked his path. Among his victims was Albert Anastasia, a high mob enforcer who was shot to death in the barber chair of a New York hotel in 1957. Genovese's ultimate downfall came as a result of abortive attempts to kill Frank Costello and Meyer Lansky who proved far smarter than he. These two crafty old dons masterminded a Federal drug bust of Genovese which sent him to prison for fifteen years.

tion of *Mafiosi* who did not subscribe to the traditional ways. Western Sicily, particularly Palermo, became a battleground. The drug wars of the early 1980s saw more than 500 murders in two years of internecine warfare for control of the Sicily heroin traffic. Not only did the Mafia kill each other, but when the Italian government began a major crackdown aimed at again shutting down their operations, the Mafia assassinated judges, police officers – anyone who posed a threat. Palermo became one of the most lethal cities in the world and replaced Marseilles as the drug capital of Europe. In 1984 the code of *omertà* was finally broken by the disclosures of a senior mob figure who took his revenge for the murder of several members of his family in the form of exposure of the 'pizza connection'.[1]

First-hand evidence of Mafia activities is, of course, difficult to come by inasmuch as *Mafiosi* are not noted for their public disclosures. Yet there is the inescapable conclusion that the notorious Navy–Mafia connection had no discernible impact on the Sicily campaign. However, it had a monumental influence upon the future of Charles 'Lucky' Luciano who was paroled in January 1946 and deported to Italy by the same man who had put him in prison: Governor Thomas E. Dewey. Having aided the United States, Luciano applied to the state of New York for payment of the unspoken debt for services rendered. Although there was never any evidence of a 'deal' between the Navy and Luciano or between the State of New York and Luciano, 'Lucky' lived up to his nickname. Whatever the intimations of corruption and a pay-off to Luciano for his services to the US Navy, his release appears to have been granted for other reasons. In fact, as part of its cover-up to avoid public embarrassment for its wartime role the Navy flatly refused to co-operate with New York officials or even to corroborate the fact that they had been involved with Luciano.[2]

In February 1946 Luciano was paroled and immediately deported to his native Italy where he died in 1962, a famed Mafia figure long shorn of his powers. In approving his application for parole, Governor Dewey had noted that 'upon the entry of the

---

[1] See 'The Sicilian Connection' in *Time*, 15 October 1984. In the five years between 1979 and 1984 it was estimated that some 1,650 lb of heroin (worth a staggering $1.65 *billion* on the streets of America) was successfully smuggled from Sicily to a number of small midwestern pizza parlours which served as distribution centres. One of these was located in the tiny town of Paris, Illinois, deep in the farmbelt of midwestern America.

[2] *The Luciano Project*, op. cit., p. 212.

United States into the war, Luciano's aid was sought by the Armed Services concerning possible enemy attack. It appears that he co-operated in such effort, although the actual value of the information procured is not clear.'[1] The same could be said of one of the strangest alliances ever recorded.

[1] Statement by Governor Dewey to the New York legislature in January 1946. Despite the rumours, Governor Dewey's action was based on the recommendation of the New York parole board and was fully vindicated by the Herlands inquiry. Nevertheless, it has been suggested that Dewey's decision may have been based in part on his unspoken gratitude for Luciano having saved his life in 1935. That year Luciano learned that his rival, Dutch Schultz, was planning to assassinate Dewey in violation of the unwritten rule that the Mafia would not draw unnecessary attention by killing policemen or district attorneys. It was Luciano's initiative that led to the slaying of Schultz.

Sources and Bibliography

I. UNPUBLISHED SOURCES:

The archives of the United States, Canada and Britain are rich in published and unpublished material about the Sicily campaign and include official documents, war diaries, personal diaries, oral histories, and private papers and letters. Except for the official histories, very little of this remarkable body of documentation has been taken into account by historians. During the writing of *Bitter Victory* I have, in addition to the collections cited below, relied on interviews and correspondence with surviving participants and the following private collections and unpublished papers which have been kindly made available: the papers of Admiral Sir Bertram Ramsay; 'Scottish Soldier', the unpublished war memoirs of the late Major-General Douglas N. Wimberley's command of the 51st (Highland) Division; 'Operation "Symbol"', Lieutenant-General Sir Ian Jacob's personal diary of the Casablanca Conference; the unpublished manuscript of General of the Army Dwight D. Eisenhower; extracts from the diary of Sir Harry Llewellyn; George Schmitz's 'German Paratroopers and the Primosole Bridge'; Richard G. Davis, unpublished doctoral thesis, 'Eisenhower's Airman: General Carl A. Spaatz and the United States Army Air Force in Europe, 1942–1945'; and J. E. Browne, 'Deception for Operations, Sicily 1943', research paper prepared for the US Army War College.

Principal institutional collections used are:

The Public Record Office, Kew, London:
The Churchill papers (PREM 3); papers, Middle East Forces [including Eighth Army and 15th Army Group] (WO 201); unit war diaries, Middle East Forces (WO 169); military narratives, Cabinet Office Historical Section (CAB 44); AFHQ papers (WO 204); the personal papers of Field-Marshal Lord Alexander (WO 214); Cabinet Office Historical Files (CAB 106); Chief of Air Staff Papers (AIR 8); papers, Mediterranean Allied Air Forces (AIR 19, 23 & 41); and the First Sea Lord papers (ADM 205).

The Imperial War Museum, London:
Department of Printed Books (printed sources); Department of Documents (the papers and diary of General Sir Charles Gairdner, the papers of Captain P. Royle, the papers of Major-General G. H. A. MacMillan, the papers of General Sir William Morgan, various miscellaneous collections); Department of Sound Records; Department of Film and Department of Photographs.

University of East Anglia, Norwich:
The papers of Lord Zuckerman.

Liddell Hart Centre for Military Archives, King's College, London:
The papers of Sir Basil Liddell Hart, including the postwar interrogations, correspondence and notes in the 'German Generals' Collection' (Section 9); the papers and diary of Field-Marshal Lord Alanbrooke; and the papers of General the Lord Ismay.

Air Historical Branch, Ministry of Defence, London:
Air Ministry War Room Summaries; various miscellaneous collections.

Department of Manuscripts, The British Library, London:
The papers of Admiral of the Fleet Viscount Cunningham of Hyndhope.

United States Army Military History Institute, Carlisle Barracks, Pennsylvania:
The papers of General of the Army Omar N. Bradley,* including the papers and diary of Lieutenant Colonel Chester B. Hansen; German Report Series, US Army Europe; OCMH papers and research notes, including the Alexander interviews, the Smyth and Mathews interviews, and the Pogue interviews; the Magna E. Bauer collection; diary and papers of Lieutenant General Hobart R. Gay; diary and papers of Major General John P. Lucas; the papers of: General Mark Clark; General Matthew B. Ridgway; General I. D. White; General Theodore J. Conway; Major General Terry Allen; Major General Kenyon A. Joyce; Brigadier General Oscar Koch; Brigadier General Halley G. Maddox; Guy V. Henry; Eisenhower diaries; WW II miscellaneous collections, Ultra papers; microfilms, 82d Airborne Division G-2 Historical Record and 'Report of Operations of II Corps in Sicily, July–August 1943'. Also, oral histories of General Mark Clark; General Theodore J. Conway; General Ben Harrell; General Matthew B. Ridgway; General I. D. White; General William B. Rosson; General Robert J. Wood; General Lyman L. Lemnitzer; Lieutenant General Ira C. Eaker; Lieutenant General Hobart R. Gay; Lieutenant General John A. Heintges; Lieutenant General Elwood R. Quesada and Lieutenant General William P. Yarborough.

Manuscript Division, Library of Congress:
The papers of General George S. Patton, Jr; the papers of General Carl A. Spaatz and the papers of General James H. Doolittle.

Modern Military Field Branch, National Archives, Suitland, Maryland;
Operational records of Seventh Army; II Corps; 82d Airborne Division and the 1st Infantry Division.

---

* The Bradley collections are deposited at both Carlisle and West Point. As collaborator Clay Blair notes in *A General's Life*, there is some duplication but those at Carlisle deal mainly with the Second World War, while those at West Point are personal.

The S. L. A. Marshall Military History Collection, University of Texas at El Paso:
Extracts from the Hitler transcripts.

The Dwight D. Eisenhower Library, Abilene, Kansas:
The papers of Dwight D. Eisenhower (pre-presidential and presidential); the papers and diary of Captain Harry C. Butcher, USN; the papers of Lieutenant General Walter Bedell Smith; the papers of Lieutenant General Floyd L. Parks; the papers of Major General Terry de la Mesa Allen; the papers of James R. Webb; various official documents and oral histories.

Hoover Institution on War, Revolution and Peace, Stanford University, Palo Alto, California:
German Report Series, US Army Europe; various miscellaneous collections.

George C. Marshall Research Library, Lexington, Virginia:
The papers of General Lucian K. Truscott, Jr.

II. PUBLISHED SOURCES:

Alexander, Field-Marshal Earl of Tunis, *The Alexander Memoirs 1940–1945*, New York, 1962.
Altieri, James J., *Darby's Rangers*, Durham, N.C., 1945
Ambrose, Stephen E., *The Supreme Commander*, London, 1970; and *Eisenhower 1890–1952*, New York, 1983
Ayer, Fred, *Before the Colors Fade*, London, 1964
Baldwin, Hanson, *Battles Lost and Won*, New York, 1966
Barzini, Luigi, *The Italians*, New York, 1964
Belchem, David, *All in the Day's March*, London, 1978
Blair, Clay, *Ridgway's Paratroopers*, New York, 1985
Blumenson, Martin, *Sicily: Whose Victory?*, New York, 1968; *The Patton Papers*, Vol. II, Boston, 1974; *Mark Clark*, New York, 1984; *Patton: The Man Behind the Legend, 1885–1945*, New York, 1985; and Blumenson, Martin, and Stokesbury, James L., *Masters of the Art of Command*, Boston, 1975
Bradley, Omar N., *A Soldier's Story*, New York, 1951; and *A General's Life*, with Clay Blair, New York, 1983
Breuer, William B., *Drop Zone Sicily*, San Rafael, 1983
Brown, John Mason, *To All Hands*, New York, 1943
Bryant, Arthur, *The Turn of the Tide*, London, 1957
Buckley, Christopher, *Road to Rome*, London, 1945
Butcher, Harry C., *Three Years With Eisenhower*, London, 1946
Campbell, Rodney, *The Luciano Project*, New York, 1977
Cave-Brown, Anthony, *Wild Bill Donovan: The Last Hero*, New York, 1982
Chalfont, Alun, *Montgomery of Alamein*, London, 1976
Chalmers, Rear-Admiral W. S., *Full Cycle: The Biography of Admiral Bertram Home Ramsay*, London, 1959

Chandler, Alfred D. (Ed.), *The Papers of Dwight David Eisenhower: The War Years*, 5 vols, Baltimore, 1970

Chatterton, George, *The Wings of Pegasus*, London, 1962

Churchill, Winston S., *The Hinge of Fate*, Boston, 1950; and *Closing the Ring*, 1951

Clay, Ewart W., *The Path of the 50th*, Aldershot, 1950

Codman, Charles R., *Drive*, Boston, 1957

Cole, Sir David, *Rough Road to Rome*, London, 1983

Colville, John, *The Churchillians*, London, 1981; and *The Fringes of Power*, 1985

Cooper, Matthew, *The German Army 1939–1945*, London, 1978; and *The German Air Force 1939–1945*, London, 1981

Copp, DeWitt S., *Forged in Fire*, New York, 1982

Craven, Wesley F., and Cate, James L. (Eds), *Europe: Torch to Pointblank, August 1942 to December 1943*, Chicago, 1949

Cruickshank, Charles, *Deception in World War II*, London, 1979

Cunningham, Admiral of the Fleet Viscount, *A Sailor's Odyssey*, London, 1951

Deakin, F. W., *The Brutal Friendship: Mussolini, Hitler and the Fall of Italian Fascism*, New York, 1962

De Guingand, Francis, *Operation Victory*, London, 1947; and *Generals at War*, London, 1964

Devlin, Gerard M., *Paratrooper!*, New York, 1979

Dover, Major Victor, *The Silken Canopy*, London, 1979

Dunlop, Richard, *Donovan*, Chicago, 1982

Durnford-Slater, John, *Commando*, London, 1953

Edwards, Roger, *German Airborne Troops 1936–45*, New York, 1974

Eisenhower, Dwight D., *Crusade in Europe*, London, 1948; and *At Ease*, London, 1958

Eisenhower, John, *Allies*, New York, 1982

Faldella, General Emilio, *Lo sbarco e la difesa della Sicilia*, Rome, 1956

Farago, Ladislas, *Patton: Ordeal and Triumph*, New York, 1965

Fergusson, Bernard, *The Watery Maze*, New York, 1961

Fermi, Laura, *Mussolini*, Chicago, 1966

Ferrell, Robert H. (Ed.), *The Eisenhower Diaries*, New York, 1981

Fighting Forty-Fifth, The, Nashville (reprint), 1978

Fraser, David, *Alanbrooke*, London, 1982

Frost, Major-General John, *A Drop Too Many* (revised edition), London, 1982

Fuller, Major-General J. F. C., *The Second World War 1939–1945*, New York, 1949

Galloway, Strome, *The General Who Never Was*, Belleville (Ontario), 1981

Garland, Albert N., and Smyth, Howard McGaw, *Sicily and the Surrender of Italy*, Washington, 1965

Gavin, James M., *On to Berlin*, New York, 1978

Greenfield, Kent Roberts (Ed.), *Command Decisions*, London, 1959

Hamilton, Nigel, *Monty: The Making of a General 1887–1942*, London, 1981; and *Monty: Master of the Battlefield 1942–1944*, London, 1983

Hapgood, David, and Richardson, David, *Monte Cassino*, New York, 1984

Harmon, Major General Ernest, *Combat Commander*, Englewood Cliffs, N.J., 1970

Hastings, Max, *Bomber Command*, London, 1979

Hinsley, F. H., *British Intelligence in the Second World War*, Vol. III, Part I, London, 1984

History of the 44th Royal Tank Regiment in the War of 1939–1945, 1965

Hobbs, Joseph P., *Dear General: Eisenhower's Wartime Letters to Marshall*, Baltimore, 1971

Houston, Donald E., *Hell on Wheels*, San Rafael, 1977

Howard, Michael, *Grand Strategy*, Vol. IV, London, 1972

Howe, George F., *Northwest Africa: Seizing the Initiative in the West*, Washington, 1957

Hunt, David, *A Don at War*, London, 1966

Irving, David, *The Trail of the Fox*, London, 1977; and *Hitler's War 1942–1945*, London, 1983

Ismay, Lord, *Memoirs*, London, 1960

Jewell, Lt N. L. A., *Secret Mission Submarine*, London, 1944

Kesselring, Field Marshal Albert, *A Soldier's Record*, Westport, Ct., 1970 (reprint of 1954 edition)

Kimball, Warren F. (Ed.), *Churchill and Roosevelt: The Complete Correspondence*, Vol. II, Princeton, 1984

Knightley, Phillip, *The First Casualty* (revised edition), London, 1982

Kuhn, Volkmar, *German Paratroops in World War II*, London, 1978

Lamb, Richard, *Montgomery in Europe 1943–45*, London, 1983

Lewin, Ronald, *Montgomery as Military Commander*, London, 1968; *Rommel as Military Commander*, New York, 1977; and *Ultra Goes to War*, London, 1978

Liddell Hart, Sir Basil (Ed.), *The Rommel Papers*, London, 1953; and *History of the Second World War*, London, 1970

Linklater, Eric, *The Campaign in Italy*, London, 1951

Llewellyn, Harry, *Passport to Life*, London, 1980

Macksey, Kenneth, *Kesselring*, New York, 1978

Macmillan, Harold, *War Diaries*, London, 1984

Malone, Richard S., *Missing From the Record*, London, 1946

Maugeri, Admiral Franco, *From the Ashes of Disgrace*, New York, 1948

Maund, Rear-Admiral L. E. H., *Assault From the Sea*, London, 1949

Molony, Brigadier C. J. C., *The Mediterranean and Middle East*, Vol. V, London, 1973

Montagu, Ewen, *The Man Who Never Was*, Philadelphia, 1954; and *Beyond Top Secret Ultra*, New York, 1978

Montgomery, Field-Marshal Viscount, *Memoirs*, London, 1958; *The Path to Leadership*, London, 1963; and *El Alamein to the River Sangro and Normandy to the Baltic* (one volume), London, 1973

Morison, Samuel Eliot, *Sicily–Salerno–Anzio*, Boston, 1954

Mosley, Leonard, *Marshall*, New York, 1982

Mowat, Farley, *The Regiment*, Toronto, 1973

Mrazek, James E., *The Glider War*, New York, 1975

Mussolini, Benito, *The Fall of Mussolini: His Own Story*, New York, 1948

Neville, Ralph, *Survey by Starlight*, London, 1949

Nicholson, Lieut-Col. G. W. L., *The Canadians in Italy 1943–1945*, Ottawa 1967

Nicholson, Nigel, *Alex*, London, 1973

Owen, Roderic, *Tedder*, London, 1952

Pack, S. W. C., *Cunningham the Commander*, London, 1974; and *Operation 'Husky'*, London, 1977

Padfield, Peter, *Dönitz*, London, 1984

Pantaleone, Michele, *The Mafia and Politics*, New York, 1966

Patton, George S., *War As I Knew It*, London, 1947

Pawle, Gerald R., *The War and Colonel Warden*, London, 1963

Pogue, Forrest C., *George C. Marshall: Organizer of Victory 1943–1945*, New York, 1973

Pond, Hugh, *Sicily*, London, 1962

Price, Frank James, *Troy H. Middleton*, Baton Rouge, 1974

Public Record Office, *The Second World War: A Guide to Documents in the Public Record Office*, London, 1972

Pyle, Ernie, *Brave Men*, New York, 1944

Richards, Denis, and Saunders, Hilary St George, *The Fight Avails*, London, 1975

Richardson, General Sir Charles, *Flashback*, London, 1985

Ridgway, Matthew B., *Soldier*, New York, 1956

Rissik, David, *The D.L.I. at War*, Durham, 1952

Roosevelt, Kermit, *War Report of the OSS*, Volume 2, New York, 1976

Roskill, Stephen, *The War at Sea 1939–1945*, Vol. III, The Offensive, Part I, London, 1960

Salmond, J. B., *The History of the 51st Highland Division*, Edinburgh, 1953

Saunders, Hilary St George, *The Green Beret*, London, 1949; and *The Red Beret*, London, 1971

Semmes, Harry H., *Portrait of Patton*, New York, 1964

Senger und Etterlin, General Frido von, *Neither Fear Nor Hope*, New York, 1964

Shapiro, L. S. B., *They Left the Back Door Open*, Toronto, 1944

Sheppard, G. A., *The Italian Campaign 1943–1945*, New York, 1968

Slessor, Sir John, *The Central Blue*, London, 1956

Smith, Denis Mack, *Mussolini*, London, 1983

Stacey, C. P., *Arms, Men and Governments: The War Policies of Canada 1939–1945*, Ottawa, 1970; and *A Date With History*, Toronto, 1984

Stainforth, Peter, *Wings of the Wind*, London, 1954

Stimson, Henry L., and Bundy, McGeorge, *On Active Service in Peace and War*, New York, 1948

Strong, Kenneth, *Intelligence at the Top*, London, 1968

Summersby, Kay, *Eisenhower Was My Boss*, New York, 1948

Taggart, Donald G. (Ed.), *History of the Third Infantry Division in World War II*, Washington, 1947

Tedder, Lord, *With Prejudice*, London, 1966

Terraine, John, *The Right of the Line*, London, 1985

Tregaskis, Richard, *Invasion Diary*, New York, 1943

Truscott, Lucian K., *Command Missions*, New York, 1954

Warlimont, Walter, *Inside Hitler's Headquarters 1939–1945*, New York, 1964

Warner, Oliver, *Cunningham of Hyndhope*, London, 1967

Wedemeyer, General Albert C., *Wedemeyer Reports!*, New York, 1958

Westphal, General Siegfried, *The German Army in the West*, 1951

Ziegler, Philip, *Mountbatten*, New York, 1985

Zuckerman, Solly, *From Apes to Warlords*, London, 1978

Index

Following standard practice in the US Army, rank titles are not hyphenated. In the British army they were, and are here.

Hutchins, Colonel Robert B. 264

Inglis, Brigadier Desmond 616, 617n
intelligence *see* SIGINT
Ionian Sea 276
Ireland, Captain Albert 294n
Ironside, Field-Marshal Sir Edmund 37
Irving, David 313
Ismay, General Sir Hastings 36n, 47–8, 143, 181, 340n
Italy: war-weariness 23; British strategy to eliminate from war 41, 49, 142–3; improved fighting spirit in Tunisia 112–13; proposed bombing offensive against 162, 166–7; disbelieves deception plans 190; German disdain for 193; Hitler mistrusts 193, 198–200; military weaknesses 193–4, 204–5; declining relations with Germany 197, 204–5, 437; poor army morale 210–11, 310–11, 436–8; desertions and surrenders as POWs 364–5, 435–40; collapse 428; and downfall of Mussolini 429–30; bombed 434; invasion authorized 455; forces evacuated from Sicily 514–15, 523; mainland shelled 518; Allied campaign in 552, 567; strategic justification for campaign 553; reluctance in fighting Allies 554–5; strength of forces in Sicily 606–9; losses 609
ARMY
  Sixth Army 192, 195; redesignated Armed Forces Command Sicily 195; Kesselring distrusts 198; von Senger as liaison officer with 200, 203; poor condition 204; HQ at Enna 252; and Allied landings 279; evacuation of troops from Sicily 514–15
  Tenth Army 27n, 32
  Corps
  XII 435n
  XIV 194
  XVI 279, 282, 284, 290, 300
  Infantry Divisions
  4th (Livorno) Light Division 208, 282, 288–91, 296, 305, 403n, 435, 454, 558
  26th (Assietta) 437
  28th (Aosta) 437, 454, 462
  54th (Napoli) 208, 279, 300, 310, 315, 403n, 437, 558
  206th Coastal 194, 310, 435n
  207th Coastal 262
  Brigades
  Brigata Mista Pantelleria 213
  Other Units and Formations
  162nd Artillery Battalion 276n
  Mobile Group E 284, 288, 291
  Group Schreiber 437

NAVY
Supermarina 497
submarines 255n

Jacob, Brigadier (*later* Lieutenant-General Sir) Ian 31, 36, 47, 50, 54, 340
Japan 31, 33, 38, 43
Jefferson, USS (cruiser) 304
Jensen, Captain Richard N. 424n
Jewell, Lieutenant N. L. A. 181–2, 256n
Jodl, General Alfred 314n, 430, 504, 506–7
JOHNNY I, II & III (hills) 352, 364, 367, 371, 373 & n, 374–6, 384
Johnson, Lieutenant Colonel Briard P. 299
Joint Intelligence Sub-Committee (of War Cabinet) 162
Joint Planning Staff (British) 36n, 43, 45, 47, 75 & n, 77n, 78–9
Jones, Colonel O. L. 235
JOSS Force 151, 153, 155–6, 167, 174n, 208, 220, 262–3
Joyce, Major General Kenyon A. 131, 132n, 478n, 494

Kasserine Pass 57–60, 62, 67, 137n
Kean, Brigadier General William B. 486
Keating, Captain Geoffrey 531
Keerans, Brigadier General Charles L., Jr. 308
Kefauver, Estes: 1951 Senate Investigation Committee 626
Keitel, Field Marshal Wilhelm 200, 202, 432, 438
Keren, HMS (destroyer) 234
Kesselring, Field Marshal Albert: and Mareth 55; criticizes Allied Sicily strategy 76n, 526–7, 548; and Allied deception plans 190; optimism 192, 196, 202; disagreements with Guzzoni 192, 196–8, 203, 209; qualities 196; and Roatta 198; and von Senger 202–3; and Mussolini 204; forms three new divisions 204; proposes attack on Gibraltar through Spain 206; meets Conrath 207n; controls Axis troops in Italy 210; orders 15th PzG Division to west 284n, 435; orders Hermann Goering Division to counterattack 291; report on Sicily situation 311; Sicilian defence strategy 313–14; sends Heidrich's paratroops to Sicily 353–4; greets Heilmann's escaping troops 377; rebukes Schmalz 378; hears of German cowardice 438; and Hube's complaints of Luftwaffe 455; and German evacuation 497, 504, 506–7; appoints Baade 502; in Taormina 518n; on expected Allied secondary landing in Calabria 524–6; leads defence of Italy